Development Economics and Structuralist Macroeconomics

Frontispiece *Lance Taylor*

Development Economics and Structuralist Macroeconomics

Essays in Honor of Lance Taylor

Edited by

Amitava Krishna Dutt and Jaime Ros

Department of Economics and Kellogg Institute of International Studies, University of Notre Dame, Notre Dame, Indiana, USA

Edward Elgar

Cheltenham, UK • Northampton, MA, USA

Published by
Edward Elgar Publishing Limited
Glensanda House
Montpellier Parade
Cheltenham
Glos GL50 1UA
UK

Edward Elgar Publishing, Inc.
136 West Street
Suite 202
Northampton
Massachusetts 01060
USA

A catalogue record for this book
is available from the British Library

Library of Congress Cataloguing in Publication Data

Development economics and structuralist macroeconomics: essays in honor of Lance Taylor/Amitava Krishna Dutt and Jaime Ros, editors.
p. cm.
Includes bibliographical references and index.
1. Development economics. 2. Finance—Developing countries. 3. Developing countries—Economic policy. 4. Economic stabilization—Developing countries. 5. Globalization—Economic aspects. 6. Macroeconomics. I. Dutt, Amitava Krishna. II. Ros, Jaime.
HD82.D38925 2003
338.9—dc21

2002027145

ISBN 1 84064 939 9

Printed and bound in Great Britain by MPG Books Ltd, Bodmin, Cornwall

Contents

PART IV STABILIZATION, ADJUSTMENT AND GROWTH

PART V BEYOND NEO-LIBERALISM: THE FIRM, INDUSTRIAL POLICY AND COMPETITIVENESS

PART VI THE NORTH, THE SOUTH AND GLOBALIZATION

Figures

Tables

Contributors

Alice H. Amsden	Massachusetts Institute of Technology, Cambridge, MA
Edmar L. Bacha	Banco BBA-Creditanstalt, Sao Paulo
Amit Bhaduri	Jawaharlal Nehru University, New Delhi
Wan-Wen Chu	Academia Sinica, Taipei
William Darity, Jr.	University of North Carolina at Chapel Hill, Chapel Hill, NC
Amitava Krishna Dutt	University of Notre Dame, Notre Dame, IN
John Eatwell	University of Cambridge, Cambridge, UK
José María Fanelli	CEDES, Buenos Aires
Duncan K. Foley	New School University, New York
Roberto Frenkel	CEDES, Buenos Aires
Bill Gibson	University of Vermont, Burlington, VT
Gerry Helleiner	University of Toronto, Toronto
Bobbie L. Horn	University of Tulsa, Tulsa, OK
David A. Kendrick	University of Texas, Austin, TX
Michael Syron Lawlor	Wake Forest University, Winston-Salem, NC
Lihui Lin	University of Texas, Austin, TX
F. Desmond McCarthy	World Bank, Washington, DC
P. Ruben Mercado	Bryn Mawr College, Pennsylvania
Deepak Nayyar	University of Delhi, Delhi
José Antonio Ocampo	ECLAC, Santiago de Chile
Jørn Rattsø	Norwegian University of Science and Technology, Trondheim

Jaime Ros	University of Notre Dame, Notre Dame, IN
Helen Shapiro	University of California, Santa Cruz, CA
Lucio Simpson	CEDES, Buenos Aires
Andrés Solimano	ECLAC, Santiago de Chile
Holger Wolf	George Washington University, Washington, DC

Acknowledgements

We are grateful to the following individuals for serving as referees for the papers in the volume and for their valuable comments on them: Alice Amsden, Edmar Bacha, William Darity, Jr., José María Fanelli, Bill Gibson, Duncan Foley, F. Desmond McCarthy, Kajal Mukhopadhyay, Deepak Nayyar, José Antonio Ocampo, J. Mohan Rao, Jørn Rattsø and Helen Shapiro.

We are grateful to the staff of the Kellogg Institute for International Studies of the University of Notre Dame for their secretarial support that made possible the completion of this project. We would like to express our gratitude for the institutional support of the University of Notre Dame. We would also like to thank Seok-Hyeon Kim for editorial assistance. Finally, we wish to thank the editorial staff at Edward Elgar, especially Caroline Cornish, for seeing the book through to its completion.

PART I

Introduction

1. Development economics and political economy

Amitava Krishna Dutt and Jaime Ros

1 INTRODUCTION

This volume contains chapters written by colleagues, former students, collaborators and, above all, friends of Lance Taylor, presented to him – albeit somewhat belatedly – for his sixtieth birthday. The contributors have dedicated their chapters to him as tributes to his many major and influential contributions to development economics and political economy, and as a token of their warm friendship. The chapters follow the tradition pioneered and charted by Lance Taylor, which is not surprising because many of their authors, especially his former students and collaborators, have been directly influenced by his work.

The purpose of this introductory chapter is to provide brief overviews of the development economics and political economy traditions to which the papers belong, and to situate the contributions in those traditions. Sections 2 and 3 discuss the development economics and political economy traditions, respectively, section 4 provides a brief overview of Lance Taylor's contributions, and section 5 introduces the chapters of this volume.

2 DEVELOPMENT ECONOMICS

The history of development economics is in a sense as old as that of economics itself, with contributions from the mercantilists, physiocrats and Turgot, the classical economists – Smith, Ricardo and Malthus –, Marx, the writers on colonial policy, and nationalist writers in the colonies and elsewhere (see Arndt, 1987, ch. 2). However, the systematic and specialized study of the entire range of problems of less developed countries (henceforth, LDCs) did not begin till just after World War II when there occurred a conjunction of several powerful influences. These included: the rise of Keynesian interventionism, wartime state intervention and planning, the experience of planning in the Soviet Union, the political independence of several LDCs and the consequent desire of – and pressures on – new nationalist governments to prove their capabilities, the creation of international agencies fostering development, and the specter of communism (see Hirschman, 1981, and Meier, 1984).

The history of development economics up to the middle and late 1980s can be divided into three overlapping phases. The first phase, from 1945 to the mid-1950s, emphasized a number of major (and more or less related) themes (see on the subject Ros, 2000 and Dutt, 2002). First, underdevelopment was characterized as a low-level equilibrium caused by factors such as low savings, high rates of population growth, and low investment incentives primarily caused by market failures due to scale economies and external effects, ideas that were explored in classic early works by Rosenstein-Rodan (1943) and Nurkse (1953), among others. Second, the economy was characterized as a dual economy with a backward sector, predominantly agricultural, and a modern industrial sector. The classic formulation was that of Lewis (1954), whose writings resulted in a bias towards seeing the industrial sector as the engine of growth and the agricultural sector as a source of surplus labor, although Lewis himself recognized the importance of balanced growth in order to prevent a deterioration of the industrial terms of trade which could squeeze industrial profits and hence capital accumulation. Third, intersectoral interactions and changes in sectoral composition, related to this agriculture–industry distinction and to different types of industries such as those producing consumption and investment goods, were also emphasized. Arguments were made in favor of both balanced and unbalanced growth, to promote and take advantage of various kinds of linkages between sectors (see Hirschman, 1958, 1977).

A second phase extended from the early 1950s to the late 1960s. The major contributions – from structuralists in the North, such as Chenery, and the South, such as the group of economists working at the UN Economic Commission for Latin America with Raoul Prebisch – maintained the earlier themes but moved further away from neoclassical economics in at least two different ways. First, there was a general recognition that there were many kinds of rigidities present in LDCs which made them very different from the relatively smoothly-functioning advanced economies. For instance, supply rigidities in particular sectors, such as the agricultural sector and the balance of payments due to a rigid import ratio – an idea formalized in the two-gap model (Chenery and Bruno, 1962) – were emphasized, and inflation was seen to be the result of supply rigidities and distributional conflicts in the economy (Noyola, 1956; Sunkel, 1960; Furtado, 1964). Second, there was a general belief that trade could not be relied on as an engine of growth, and that attempts to increase exports were likely to be met with inelastic world demand and hence worsening terms of trade (see Singer, 1950, and Prebisch, 1959). The interaction between rich and poor countries through trade and factor movements, in particular, was argued to give rise to uneven international development (Myrdal, 1957). The recognition of market failures, as in the first phase, together with that of rigidities and 'export pessimism' led to the view that development and growth could not be left to the market. Major reliance was therefore placed on state-led development planning and, in particular, there was general support for protectionist import-substituting trade policies to promote industrialization and to overcome balance of payments problems. This is not to say that there was unanimity on these views. An important dissenting voice was that of Bauer (see Bauer and Yamey, 1957 and Bauer, 1971), who emphasized the corrupting influence of the politicization of economic life as a result of state intervention. Moreover, Marxist writers such as Baran (1952) took a broader view of development by emphasizing political and social factors rather than focusing narrowly on economic factors related to capital accumulation and industrialization, and also drew attention to the inefficiency and corruption of the capitalist state.

The third phase, starting around the mid-1960s, witnessed a reaction from different quarters against several views rife during the first and second phases. The major challenge came from the resurgence of neoclassical economics, which criticized a number of pet themes of development economics of the earlier phases, including surplus labor, export pessimism, the focus on capital accumulation, and the benefits of state-led planned industrialization (see Lal, 1985). This change was partly the result of changes in intellectual currents in economics as a whole reflected in the ascendancy of different forms of monetarism over Keynesianism. It was also due to the actual experiences of LDCs: the blame for development failures in many LDCs was laid at the door of development economics for its focus on *dirigiste* and autarkic industrialization policies, and the emergence and rapid growth of the East Asian economies was perceived by neoclassical economists to be caused by export-oriented and free-market policies (see Little, Scitovsky and Scott, 1970). A second challenge came from those who argued that the focus of development economics on growth and capital accumulation resulted in the neglect of the human dimension of development and of income distribution and poverty (see Little, 1982, chapter 11; Arndt, 1987, chapter 4). This view was bolstered not only by cases of rapid growth and increasing inequality in some LDCs, but also because in the wake of growth failures, it was believed that the urgent priority should be the satisfaction of the basic needs of the poor. To some extent this was a reorientation of the objectives of development – although it can be argued that the early proponents of growth viewed growth as a means to human development and poverty removal – but it also reflected a change in the strategy of development, from a focus on saving, investment and industrialization, to an emphasis on employment creation and direct methods of poverty alleviation. A third challenge came from radical quarters, especially with the rise of the dependency school. This school, although echoing many of the concerns raised in early development economics, saw the root cause of underdevelopment not in the problems of capital accumulation and internal rigidities and market failures, but in the relations of LDCs to rich countries. Marxist and other radical writers focused on the problems created by trade and aid dependence, and most importantly by the activities of transnational corporations (see Little, 1982). These challenges were interpreted by some as reflecting a decline in the discipline of development economics (Hirschman, 1981).

From the middle and late 1980s there has occurred a revival of interest in development economics, which may be interpreted as ushering in a fourth phase in the history of the discipline, which has witnessed the growth of at least four distinct branches. One, new neoclassical approaches have flourished, applying the tools of industrial organization, game theory and information economics, and examining issues such as agrarian relations, income distribution, the causes of poverty, and institutional issues more generally. While applications of microeconomic theory to development economics had existed earlier, the recent flowering in this literature, outlined in recent books such as those by Basu (1998), Ray (1998), Bardhan and Udry (1999), is unprecedented in volume and scope. Two, in the macroeconomic sphere, a theoretical and empirical literature on long-term growth has been rapidly expanding, triggered in the late 1980s by the revival of neoclassical growth economics and the interest in new growth theories. Although these literatures run parallel rather than being closely integrated to development economics, they have recently emphasized some classic themes in development theory such as the role of income inequality, natural resources and increasing returns in the process of economic growth (for a review and evaluation of this literature, see Ros, 2000). Three, also in the macroeconomic sphere, there has been a growth of what can be called the neo-structuralist approach which blends macroeconomic theory drawn from the classical economists, Marx, Keynes and Kalecki, with early structuralist contributions from the second phase described above, to analyse the determinants of growth, income distribution, inflation, and fiscal and balance of payments problems. As discussed later, Lance Taylor's work represents a major contribution to this approach. Fourth, less formal literatures have re-examined the actual experience of developing economies, especially the successful East Asian newly industrialized countries (NICs). Going beyond the boundaries of economics narrowly defined to incorporate and develop ideas from sociology, political science and other disciplines, this revision of the NICs' experiences has shown that the success of these countries cannot be interpreted as an accomplishment of free market economics, and that the state played an active role in the development process (see Amsden, 1991; Wade, 1990). The recent interdisciplinary work suggests that markets and states can play a synergistic role in the development process, and that the nature of markets and of the state are more important than whether the state or the market is allowed a greater role (see Dutt, Kim and Singh, 1994). During this fourth phase there appears to be a move away from extreme views on matters such as state intervention and free market policies with the recognition, as just mentioned, that the state and markets both have a role to play in development.

This brief history suggests that development economics, perhaps more than any other branch of economics, is an area in which a number of different approaches to the subject appear to coexist and flourish. Indeed, many development economists have drawn attention to the existence of different approaches in development economics. Chenery (1975), for instance, distinguishes between neoclassical, Marxist and structuralist approaches, where the first two attempt to adapt systems of thought initially applied to developed economies to less developed ones, and the last 'attempts to identify specific rigidities, lags and other characteristics of the structure of developing economies . . .' (p. 310) which are generally ignored in the neoclassical approach. Bardhan (1988) partitions the subject in a similar manner, distinguishing between neoclassical, Marxist and structuralist–institutionalist approaches, although recognizing that each is a portmanteau category. In Bardhan's view, the neoclassical approach analyses economic behavior in terms of maximizing individuals, the Marxist approach emphasizes structural constraints and the importance of class, and the structuralist approach stresses the structures of particular economies (for instance, the importance of oligopoly and sectoral divisions) and structural differences between economies. There are many ways in which one can divide the discipline, according for instance to differences in method, vision, strategies and objectives (see Dutt, 1992), in addition to those mentioned here, which suffice to show that the existence of alternative approaches is widely acknowledged in the development economics literature.

3 POLITICAL ECONOMY

In the discipline of economics, as in development economics, there exist alternative methodological approaches. However, mainstream economists seldom, certainly less than in development economics, acknowledge the existence of approaches alternative to theirs. What is now mainstream economics, usually called neoclassical economics, emerged around the last quarter of the nineteenth century in the guise of marginalist economics, which involved the use of mathematical optimization models of individual decision-makers (and their interaction) with (usually) given preferences, endowments and technology. Although there were several competing schools initially, by the middle of the twentieth century, neoclassical economics became relatively standardized and established its dominance on the profession (despite the rise of Keynesian economics, which increasingly became 'neoclassicized'). This tendency of neoclassical economics to dominate the economics profession has now reached a point at which most economists (especially in the United States) would define economics as neoclassical economics, and the leading 'mainstream' economics journals publish almost exclusively articles in the neoclassical approach.

Although the term 'political economy' has been used in different senses, we use it to denote the counterfactual subject economics would have been had it not been almost completely dominated by neoclassical economics.[1] Thus, 'political economy' recognizes the coexistence of different approaches to the study of economic behavior, including classical, Marxian, institutionalist and other approaches largely submerged by the neoclassical tidal wave, and the more recent post-Keynesian, structuralist, evolutionary and other approaches, which have not found much breathing space given neoclassical supremacy. No comprehensive surveys of heterodox approaches can be attempted in a few paragraphs, so we confine ourselves to some brief remarks.[2]

Classical political economy follows the traditions of the classical economists, including Smith and Ricardo, and can be subdivided into three branches. First, there is the Sraffian approach to price theory (Sraffa, 1960) which takes output and distribution as given and examines how prices are determined in the long period due to classical competition. Second, there is the approach to growth emphasizing the role of technical change, following Smith's analysis of the division of labor. Major contributors include Young (1928) and Kaldor (1957); mainstream economics has also taken up these issues in what is called new growth theory (Romer, 1986; Lucas, 1988). Third, there is the approach which examines the interaction between accumulation and how income is distributed among different classes in a neo-Ricardian fashion (although excluding the landlord, given the small size of the agricultural sector in developed economies); contributions in this genre include those of Kaldor (1955–56) and Pasinetti (1962).

Marxian and radical political economy builds on the work of Marx. Aside from its broad analysis of historical processes, this approach is concerned primarily with how class struggle determines the distribution of income, how the distribution of income determines the rate of capital accumulation, and how technological change and capital accumulation interact to make the capitalist economy grow. Major themes are the possibility of crisis due to the falling rate of profit caused by technological change, and the cyclical path of the economy due to the interaction of wage squeeze on profits and the role of the reserve army of labor in reversing this (Goodwin, 1967). The labor theory of value has received much emphasis in certain quarters, and has led to much attention on the issue of the transformation of values into prices (see Laibman, 1992). Marxian and radical political economists have also gone far beyond the confines of economics narrowly defined, to examine issues including changes in socioeconomic structures, the state, and the interaction between economic conditions and social and religious factors.[3]

Keynesian and Kaleckian political economy includes contributions which draw on the work of Keynes (1936) and Kalecki (1954, 1971) by stressing the role of aggregate demand in determining output and its rate of growth. A variety of strands are to be found in this literature. In the analysis of the determination of unemployment, post-Keynesian writers have emphasized the importance of uncertainty and money as opposed to the neoclassical–Keynesian preoccupation with wage and price rigidity.[4] While Keynes developed his theory of unemployment with marginalist (Marshallian) microfoundations with pure competition, Kalecki and the post-Keynesians have stressed the role of imperfect competition and mark-up pricing. They have also stressed the role of behavioral differences between classes, following classical and Marxian traditions. Mark-up pricing and the focus on classes has also led to the development of a conflict approach to inflation, as opposed to the monetarist approach of mainstream economics. While Keynes emphasized the role of expectations in the business cycle, and Kalecki's more formal approach emphasized effective demand, capital accumulation and investment lags,[5] subsequent post-Keynesians such as Minsky (1975, 1986), have emphasized the role of banking and finance in causing financial fragility, instability and cycles. While Keynes's interest primarily lay in the short-term determination of output and unemployment, and Kalecki's in the business cycle, subsequent contributors such as Harrod (1939), Robinson (1962) and Kaldor (1957) have drawn on their work to analyse such issues as the role of effective demand in long-run growth, the relation between distribution and accumulation, and the role of technical change.

The structuralist approach in economics can be said to have developed after World War II and is confined to the study of development problems. This approach, in a broad sense, is associated with the main ideas of the first and second phases of development economics, and have been formalized and developed in recent years – most importantly by Taylor (1983, 1991), as discussed in the previous section.

Finally the institutional, evolutionary, behavioral and other approaches can be thought of as a miscellaneous category. The institutionalist approach is rooted mainly in the work of Veblen (1904) and Ayres (1944), who focus on the progressive role of technology and the retarding role of institutions, and in the work of Commons (1934), who was concerned with the creation and modifications of institutions – especially legal ones – and their interaction with technology and production. This approach emphasizes the problem of the organization and control of the economic system, that is, its power structure. Its interest lies, for instance 'in the formation and role of institutions, and the interrelations between economic and legal systems and between power and belief system' (Samuels, 1987). Evolutionary approaches borrow the biological metaphor of competing species and examine how these species interact with each other and how the importance of these different species evolve; the focus is thus on heterogeneity and change, rather than on the optimizing behavior of representative units and their equilibria. One area in which this approach has been used is in examining the generation and diffusion of technological change (see Nelson and Winter, 1982), and follows the work of Schumpeter (1912), who analysed the process of creative destruction, that is, the process in which some entrepreneurs innovated and made temporary profits, to be followed by hordes of imitators, who drove profits down again, heralding a new downturn, which sowed the seeds of a new spurt of innovation. Among other approaches is the behavioral approach, which criticizes the neoclassical notion of optimizing by agents, and suggests alternative rules of behavior involving bounded rationality such as 'satisficing', examines their empirical relevance, and explores their macroeconomic implications (Simon, 1987).

4 LANCE TAYLOR'S CONTRIBUTIONS

Having briefly reviewed the development economics and political economy traditions, we turn to Lance Taylor's contributions to them. Taylor's approach to economics can be expressed in his own words as follows:

> I have convinced myself that economic change (or 'development') is highly constrained by conflicts over income distribution, and proceeds according to what Kaldor and Myrdal called 'cumulative processes' of distributional, institutional and technological change. The outcomes are strongly influenced by public interventions (for instance, to support import-substituting industrialization) and the political background. Putting all this complexity into policy suggestions or

simple models that tell illuminating stories about how observable economies function is no easy task (Taylor, 1992: 579).

For the thirty-odd years that Taylor has devoted to teaching and research, he has been developing insightful and innovative models which tell illuminating stories and he has been providing valuable policy advice in developing countries. He is widely considered to be one of the world's leading development economists, and is one of the leading figures of non-orthodox economics.

When Taylor started his career as a development economist, he was not what can be called a heterodox economist. His dissertation research, written under Hollis Chenery at Harvard, dealt with changes in sectoral production structure in the course of the development process, using econometric and simulation analysis (see Chenery and Taylor, 1968). This work fits right into the traditional focus of early development economics, following earlier contributions by Kuznets and Chenery, and has continued in a large literature on structural change in development (Chenery and Syrquin, 1975). Taylor also made contributions to planning models including work on numerical methods in non-linear programming models with David Kendrick (Kendrick and Taylor, 1970), and on shadow pricing rules for foreign exchange with Edmar Bacha (Bacha and Taylor, 1971). He also wrote a comprehensive and influential review of the theory of planning models (Taylor, 1975).

Although this early work consists of contributions to mainstream development economics, it should be remembered that the work, though written in the third phase of development economics, was mostly in the vein of the first and second phases, which were quite unorthodox in comparison to mainstream neoclassical economics. Taylor (1992: 580) writes that his advisor, Chenery 'displayed a relatively open attitude towards dissent (many of the Harvard graduate students tending toward radicalism in the 1960s received a modicum of intellectual protection from him)', and this may also have had a lasting influence on Taylor. It was while working in Chile that he was exposed to heterodox structuralist ideas of the Economic Commission for Latin America in the late 1960s, and observed first hand how distributional conflict affects the economy, and started leaning toward heterodoxy. Returning from Chile, while teaching at Harvard, he read Kaldor, Kalecki, Robinson and Sraffa (see Taylor, 1992).

Heterodox ideas emerged in some of his early computable general equilibrium models, especially in the work on distributional changes in models for Brazil (Bacha, Cardoso, Lysy and Taylor, 1980). While working on these models Taylor became interested in alternative ways of 'closing' models – such as neoclassical ones with full employment, and other models which were Keynesian. The theoretical ideas behind these alternative model closures for the short run appeared in Taylor and Lysy (1979), which underscored the important role played by how a model was closed for its policy implications. This approach was related to earlier work by Sen (1963) and Marglin (1984), and has continued to play an important role in the development of heterodox macroeconomics (see, for instance, Dutt, 1990). Early theoretical models which deviated from neoclassical full employment assumptions included work on the open economy by Krugman and Taylor (1978) which examined the contractionary effects of devaluation due to a fall in demand in a Keynes–Kalecki model, and a growth model developed by Taylor and Bacha (1976), in which regressive income distribution went hand in hand with higher growth by shifting income towards skilled workers who consumed luxury goods, the growth of which boosted investment in the economy. These and other models are incorporated into Taylor's first major book (Taylor, 1979), which not only includes many heterodox macro models, but also builds models closely related to national income accounting relations – a defining feature of Taylor's structuralist macroeconomics.

The more fully developed structuralist approach to development macroeconomics emerged during what may be called the second phase of his work, incorporated in his second major book (Taylor, 1983). Here the starting point is a basic model of demand-determined output along Keynes–Kalecki lines which is used to analyse the relationships between growth and income distribution. This one-sector economy model with mark-up pricing and excess capacity utilization is one of the earliest contributions that explicitly introduced effective demand issues in less developed countries, the importance of which had been underplayed in the literature. The analysis is then extended to a two-sector economy with a flex-price agricultural market and a fix-price industrial sector with demand-determined output (building on Taylor, 1982),[6] the analysis of wage–price inflation, the stagflationary effects of interest rate increases and stabilization policy issues (building on the analysis of asset market issues developed in Taylor, 1981a). A similar approach was used in Taylor (1981b) to analyse North–South interactions. This is one of the early contributions to the literature on North–South models, which since then has grown remarkably, both in unorthodox and orthodox versions. Alongside these theoretical contributions Taylor also worked on related structuralist computable macroeconomic models, for instance, those on India and Mexico (Taylor, Sarkar and Rattso, 1984; Gibson, Lustig and Taylor, 1986), and on stabilization policy (Taylor, 1981a). He developed, in particular, some of the most rigorous and comprehensive criticisms of IMF-style stabilization policies, based on models of growth, distribution and inflation.

The third phase of his work continues in many different ways to extend his macroeconomics research program. There are a number of dimensions to this work and in all of them the research agenda has been increasingly influenced by international events. First, there are further theoretical structuralist models related to developing country problems. These include three-gap models, which extend earlier two-gap models with saving and foreign exchange constraints to incorporate fiscal constraints on growth, a model of debt crisis in a North–South framework, and contributions to computable models by him and others he has inspired (Taylor, 1990). Some of these contributions are synthesized in Taylor (1991), his third major book. A second aspect is a strengthened attention to macroeconomic policy and institutional issues. Starting from the 1980s, Taylor has organized scholars from many countries and coordinated a number of comparative studies on stabilization, adjustment and reform experiences. The initial focus was on stabilization and balance of payments adjustment problems, following the debt crisis of the early 1980s, in a project sponsored by the World Institute of Development Economics Research (WIDER) at Helsinki. The results of this early project are reviewed in Taylor (1988), and have been widely cited as criticisms of IMF stabilization programs. A second WIDER project turned its attention to medium-term development issues using a three-gap model framework. The papers from this project are edited in Taylor (1993) which also contains a comprehensive analysis by him of the global resource requirements for renewed output growth in the developing world and a critique of the policies of liberalization and structural reform recommended by the 'Washington consensus'. Part of this criticism draws on Shapiro and Taylor (1990) and refers to the view of the State and its role in the economy that is implicit in the orthodox prescriptions. Additional research on medium-term issues and the relations between growth and the environment, also supported by WIDER, was published as a special issue of *World Development* with an introduction by Taylor on gap models and macroeconomic approaches to the environment (Taylor, 1996). Later in the 1990s, collective research and evaluation of economic reforms of trade liberalization, privatization and opening of the capital account of the balance of payments continued to yield fruits that were compiled in Taylor (1999), in a book that focuses on Latin American countries, and in Taylor (2001) in a volume that gives greater emphasis to the social and social policy dimensions of adjustment and reform processes. The third dimension, which characterizes his most recent work,[7] is a shift from a sole focus on development issues to macroeconomic theory more generally, as applied to both developed and developing countries. Taylor (1991) can be thought of as a new and revised edition of Taylor (1983), but even its title represents a shift. While Taylor (1983) was subtitled 'applicable models for the Third World' and is intended to be a contribution to development economics, Taylor (1991) is about structuralist macroeconomic theory which can also be applied to developed countries. His most recent book manuscript, which is yet to be published, makes this transition more fully. This shift is also seen in his attention to post-socialist economies (Amsden, Kochanowicz and Taylor, 1994), and on the global macroeconomy and international financial crises (Eatwell and Taylor, 1998, 2000). This recent work develops the case for international financial regulation in order to address the increased systemic risk and financial instability that has accompanied financial liberalization and globalization in the 1990s.

5 CONTRIBUTIONS TO THE VOLUME

As noted in the previous section, Taylor's work on development started off with contributions to technical orthodox planning models and empirical studies of structural change and then shifted to an emphasis on structuralist macroeconomics in terms of method and to broader aspects of development in terms of emphasis. The first group of chapters in the volume is concerned with these different approaches to development and planning.

David Kendrick, a co-author of Lance Taylor during the early phase of his work (see Kendrick and Taylor, 1970), contributes a chapter written jointly with Ruben Mercado and Lihui Lin. The authors introduce strategies to implement optimal growth models using the GAMS (General Algebraic Modeling System) software program. They first illustrate the use of this program in solving a simple one-sector Ramsey neoclassical growth model with an isoelastic instantaneous utility function and a Cobb–Douglas production function, demonstrating the importance of paying special attention to the specification of the time indexes in the equations and variables of the model. They then turn to the four-sector Kendrick–Taylor model with agriculture and mining, heavy industry, light industry and service sectors and show how this model can now be solved using GAMS on personal computers in contrast to the most powerful computers available at MIT in the late 1960s when Kendrick worked with Taylor.

Bill Gibson, who has co-authored a paper with Lance Taylor which presents a structuralist computable general equilibrium model for Mexico (Gibson, Lustig and Taylor, 1986), and participated with him in several international projects, writes on the methodology of Taylor's brand of structuralism, which he dubs 'late structuralism'. Gibson relates late structuralism to earlier structuralist development economics which emphasized specific rigidities in developing economies that affect economic adjustment and finds it methodologically richer, and to structuralism in the social sciences more generally, with which it shares the focuses on wholeness of the scope of investigation, of the importance of transformations, and self-regulation. He also compares late structuralism to the neoclassical method, and defends it against the charge of ad-hocery. Gibson also discusses the problems of econometric methods, and argues in favor of the use of simulation modeling.

F. Desmond McCarthy has collaborated with Taylor on studying the empirical aspects of structural change using cross-country data, specifically on how the structure of trade changes with development (see McCarthy, Taylor and Talati, 1987). Here he co-authors a chapter with Holger Wolf on the determinants of health, as measured by life expectancy, using cross-country data from Sub-Saharan Africa. They conduct simple decomposition exercises to show that low-income countries in Africa can make significant gains in life expectancy by achieving the level already attained by the most successful low-income country, and then by achieving the level reached by the best performer within their sample (without attaining the level reached by the best performers globally). They then examine the relationship between life expectancy and observable country characteristics of countries, including per capita income, health spending and access to health services and education, using comparative figures and more formal classification tree analysis to show that although life expectancy depends positively on per capita income, appropriate government policies – the most important being policies which increase the share of population with access to health care – can increase it significantly even in low-income countries.

Deepak Nayyar, who has participated with Lance Taylor in international projects, deals with broader aspects of development – inclusion, exclusion and markets – in his contribution to this volume. Influenced by the chaotic transition of Eastern Europe towards markets and democracy and the exclusionary tendencies of globalization, two themes that have been present in Lance Taylor's recent work,[8] Nayyar offers a critique of current ideological trends which 'pair' political democracy and the market economy while at the same time failing to see how economic exclusion (inclusion) interacts with political exclusion (inclusion). On the pairing between democracy and market, Nayyar argues that while political democracy has an intrinsic value, being an end in itself, the market has only an instrumental value: it is a means to an end and its use is justified by its consequences. The chapter also emphasizes and illustrates with examples how, contrary to the 'orthodox dichotomy between economy and polity', economic and social inequalities generated by the functioning of the market economy are reflected in the political process and affect the degree of political equality and the quality of democracy. And vice versa, those whose rights are unprotected in the political sphere become more vulnerable to exploitation in the economic realm. The chapter concludes by commenting on the 'liberal paradox': markets would benefit from inclusion of people, yet it is in their logic to exclude those without entitlements, capabilities and assets; democracy includes people through their right to vote, yet the political process tends to exclude those without a voice.

Financial and other asset markets are a part of the structure of actual economies that Taylor has especially and repeatedly emphasized in his work, and the next part of the book deals with the role that these factors play in the economy.

William Darity, a student of Taylor's at MIT in the late 1970s, who wrote a dissertation under his supervision, contributes a chapter co-authored with Bobbie Horn and Michael Lawlor which argues that financial factors can provide a better understanding of competition. They examine the orthodox approach to competition and find it wanting because perfect competition yields a problematic characterization of competition, is not robust with respect to assumptions about returns to scale, and renders rivalry as an exception or an ephemeral activity. They find the classical notion of competition, as sharpened by Sraffa, which visualizes it as a process leading to the intersectoral equalization of profit rates, as a more useful starting point, but argue that for monetary economies the focus should be on the mobility of financial capital, not of physical capital as in standard formalizations of the classical approach. They argue that in developing the theory of competition which stresses the role of financial capital, it is possible to draw on the work of both Veblen and Keynes, despite their differences with the classical vision. Veblen drew attention not only to the financial manipulations of the business enterprise, but to the role of psychological factors in determining asset values. These themes were taken up by Keynes in his discussion of the effects of radical uncertainty in stock markets, and the connection between them and the classical notion of competition is brought out in his discussion of the process of arbitrage in asset markets that leads to the equalization of the rates of return on assets.

Jørn Rattsø, who has co-authored a paper with Taylor on a computable structuralist model for India (Taylor, Sarkar and Rattsø, 1984), and participated with him in several international projects, develops a theoretical structuralist model to examine the role that a non-produced speculative asset such as land plays in an import-compressed and financially-repressed economy. Specifically, the model is used to understand how speculative booms and stagnation go hand in hand in Sub-Saharan African countries. The model examines the interaction between an asset side with money, real capital and land modeled along the stock equilibrium lines of Tobin, as advocated in some of Taylor's work, and a real side in which output is restricted by the availability of intermediate imported inputs due to a foreign exchange constraint. Expansionary monetary policy leads to an increase in the price level, which reduces exports, the availability of intermediate imports, and hence output, and can encourage speculation by shifting asset demand away from real capital which has a lower rate of return. In the long run the model can imply cycles in which speculation and physical capital accumulation interact to bring about alternative periods of depression and boom accompanied by endogenous changes in the return on the speculative asset.

Duncan Foley, who is currently a colleague of Lance Taylor's at New School University, develops a model of financial instability, building on Taylor's own work on cycles and financial crises based on the work of Hyman Minsky (Taylor and O'Connell, 1985). Foley uses the Taylor–O'Connell model in which output is demand-determined, distribution is exogenously given in a Kaleckian manner, and in which investment depends on the rate of profit, interest rate and a confidence factor. But unlike their model, Foley considers the case of an open economy in which capital inflows respond positively to the interest rate and negatively to the profit rate (since higher profits induce the purchase of foreign assets), which allows him to explicitly analyse financial fragility in a regime with Minskyan speculative finance. Assuming that the monetary authorities adjust the interest rate when the growth rate deviates from its equilibrium level, and that the confidence parameter rises when the growth rate exceeds its equilibrium level and falls when the interest rate exceeds its equilibrium level, he shows that an interest policy which stabilizes the economy may lead it to a Minskyan Ponzi regime in which it becomes vulnerable to a financial crisis. Attempts to stabilize the open economy using restrictive monetary policies can therefore be counterproductive, as has often been argued by Taylor.

Amit Bhaduri, a collaborator with Taylor in international research projects, turns his attention to the foreign exchange market with a model that examines the dynamics of exchange rate changes and capital inflows. In his model, capital movements are driven by exchange rate expectations, and these expectations in turn are affected by the external asset (or reserve) and the liability (or foreign debt) position of the economy. If the response of exchange rate expectations to changes in reserves is large, given other parameter values, the dynamics of capital flows and exchange rates becomes unstable. A higher response of the trade balance to exchange rate changes, and a higher speed of adjustment of the exchange rate to the excess demand for foreign exchange tend to stabilize the system, while a stronger response of capital flows to expected changes in the exchange rate destabilizes the system. Thus, there may be a need for rapid adjustment of exchange rates, but greater intervention in the form of controls on (especially short-run) capital flows are required to stabilize the system. Bhaduri also argues that since marketable public sector assets which can potentially be sold abroad can also be thought of as reserves, their privatization can be destabilizing by increasing the responsiveness of expected changes in exchange rates to reserve changes, which can occur when reserves are at low levels.

The next section deals with the theory and practice of stabilization policy and the macroeconomic aspects of structural reforms, issues which have frequently attracted Taylor's attention. A common theme in the contributions by Bacha, Frenkel and Ros refers to stabilization, capital inflows and growth recovery episodes in Latin America in the 1990s.

Edmar Bacha, a co-author of Taylor since the early stages of his career (see Bacha and Taylor, 1971, 1973; and Taylor and Bacha, 1976), provides an insider's view of the preparation, execution and results of Brazil's 1994 stabilization program known as the *Plano Real.* The economic team that conceived the Plan was a group of academics, including Bacha himself, at the Economics Department of the Catholic University of Rio de Janeiro where Lance Taylor has taught in the past. The Real Plan was successful in sharply reducing inflation from very high levels (in the order of 25 per cent per month and with a tendency to accelerate) and did so without generating an economic recession. A key argument of Bacha's chapter is that by coordinating voluntary price decisions and converting wages by their mean values in the recent past into the new monetary unit (the URV, unit of real value), the program was successful in eliminating the inertia associated with the system of lagged indexation and thus in stabilizing, or at least nearly stabilizing, the price level. At the same time, for several reasons, the program was followed by an economic expansion. A major factor was the fact that by suddenly eliminating an inflation tax of the order of 2 to 3 per cent of GDP, it gave a boost to consumer spending, especially by low-wage earners. The plan, however, was not able to put the Brazilian economy on a path that reconciled high growth, inflation control and a sustainable balance of payments.

Roberto Frenkel, a collaborator of Lance Taylor in several comparative studies projects and a co-author of a critique of the 1991 World Development Report by the World Bank (Fanelli, Frenkel and Taylor, 1994) shares Taylor's concern with unregulated financial systems (a concern that was likely influenced by Frenkel's own writing in the early 1980s on the financial liberalization experiences of the Southern cone of Latin America).[9] In his chapter here with Lucio Simpson, the authors revisit the major episodes of capital market liberalization in Latin America in the 1970s and compare them to those of the 1990s. In both waves of financial liberalization a capital surge combined with a domestic endogenous cycle to produce real exchange rate appreciation, increased external fragility, and financial and real asset bubbles that eventually burst into full blown financial and balance of payments crises. The comparison of country episodes is unfavorable to financial liberalization. In the 1970s, the countries that liberalized most, Argentina and Chile, are those that suffered the deepest recessions and the highest social costs from their financial crises. In the 1990s, Mexico and Argentina were the most severely hit by external and financial crises and suffered deep recessions. They were also the countries that experienced the greatest exchange rate appreciation and most fully deregulated the capital account.

Jaime Ros, another collaborator of Taylor in several international research projects, develops a theoretical model in the structuralist tradition to examine the interactions between growth and inflation in an open economy and applies the model to examine the performance of Latin American economies in the 1990s. Ros emphasizes the effects of inflation on investment and growth and those of growth on capital inflows, which in turn have a feedback effect on inflation through the level of the exchange rate. As a result of these interactions, stabilization (or an autonomous recovery of capital inflows) can trigger a virtuous circle of investment recovery, capital inflows and real currency appreciation which in turn strengthens the stabilization process. Thus, the stabilization and growth recovery of Latin America in the 1990s is seen as a shift from a bad equilibrium with slow growth and high inflation to a high-level equilibrium with low inflation and faster growth. However, because stabilization in most Latin American economies has been achieved at the cost of a process of real appreciation, growth has remained sluggish. Coinciding with Frenkel and Simpson's chapter and Bacha's observations on Brazil, the chapter concludes that economic policy in Latin America has yet to reconcile fast growth with low inflation and a sustainable balance of payments.

The subsequent section deals with neo-liberalism, following Taylor's criticism of orthodox perspectives and the so-called Washington consensus which advocates the liberalization of markets and emphasizes the need to 'get prices right' in markets to achieve microeconomic efficiency.

Helen Shapiro, who co-authored a paper with Taylor on the role of the state in development theory (Shapiro and Taylor, 1990), in her contribution argues against neo-liberal policy analysis for LDCs for not having an adequate theory of the firm. She advocates a departure from the standard assumption of passive, price-taking firms and makes a plea for bringing the firm back into the analysis in a more appropriate manner. Shapiro takes the work of Michael Porter on competitive strategy and its applications to developing countries as her point of departure, and draws on Latin American experiences for most of her empirical analysis. She notes that although the Porter approach gives a central role to the firm, and observes correctly that pursuing comparative advantage on such ephemeral phenomena as cheap labor may have deleterious consequences for countries, it suffers from some serious shortcomings. It often extrapolates illegitimately from the level of the individual firm to the level of a country, and ignores the historical and institutional specificities of LDCs, and ultimately gives policy advice which is neo-liberal in nature. In recommending that firms develop their dynamic comparative advantage in free markets, it ignores the incentives that governments need to create to enable them to develop in this manner. It forgets that in many LDCs industry is dominated by transnational corporations which results in intrafirm trade and import-oriented industrialization with adverse effects on the balance of payments. Moreover, historical factors like sunk investment costs result in low price responses which prevent adjustments in the manner desired by neo-liberal policies.

Alice Amsden, a former colleague of Lance Taylor's at MIT and co-author of a book on economic reforms in post-socialist countries (Amsden, Kochanowicz and Taylor, 1994), turns in her contribution written jointly with Wan-Wen Chu, to her more traditional terrain of East Asia to argue against the neo-liberal policy advice of 'getting the prices right' and to advocate one that would be more in line with Taylor's work: the need to 'get structures right'. Amsden and Chu analyse what kind of structures are important for technological 'upscaling' by latecomers to development, by examining the case of the electronics industry and the modern service sector in Taiwan. Using what they call the second-mover theory, they argue that successful upscaling requires that the size of firms increases rapidly to take advantage of different types of scale economies, and that globalization be selective in nature to ensure the dominance of national, rather than transnational, firms. They argue that this second-mover theory, rather than the theory of latecomer networks according to which a dense network of firms facilitates upscaling, provides a better explanation of Taiwanese experience, although the latter also has some explanatory power.

José María Fanelli, who co-authored with Taylor a critique of the 1991 World Bank Development Report by the World Bank (Fanelli, Frenkel and Taylor, 1992) and has been a collaborator in several international research projects, emphasizes the need for stressing micro–macro interactions that are neglected in the Washington Consensus analysis and policy recommendations. His chapter makes a strong and convincing case that these interactions are essential for understanding the shortcomings of market-oriented reforms in Latin America and makes a contribution to the understanding of such micro–macro interactions in the growth process. For instance, he examines how macroeconomic instability can obstruct productivity growth at the micro level and how trade specialization and financial factors at the micro level may affect macroeconomic stability and aggregate growth through their effects on current account sustainability and productivity growth. One important theme is that in LDCs, characterized by incomplete and fragmented markets as well as weak institutions, macroeconomic disequilibria tend to have permanent effects and even destabilizing consequences that are absent in developed economies with more complete market structures and stronger institutions. Another theme is the role of credit rationing and liquidity constraints in the determination of the aggregate growth rate which Fanelli links to the literature on three-gap models to which Taylor has so notably contributed. The chapter also discusses the links between liquidity and short-run competitiveness and between long-run competitiveness and sustainability as well as the role of trade specialization, productive structure and price and non-price factors in the determination of competitiveness.

The final section turns to the global economy, discussing the economic relations between rich and poor countries (the North and the South), and the implications and challenges of globalization.

Amitava Dutt, a student of Taylor's at MIT in the late 1970s and early 1980s, who wrote his dissertation on models of growth and income distribution in developing countries under his supervision, and who was a collaborator of his in several international research projects, develops a model of North–South trade following Taylor's work to show how uneven development can occur on a global scale. The theoretical model draws on the work of Thirlwall, who showed that if trade between North and South is balanced and if the terms of trade are constant, if the Southern income elasticity to import Northern goods exceeds the Northern income elasticity to import Southern goods, the North will grow faster than the South. The model in this chapter uses Taylor's characterization of a Lewis-type South and a Keynes–Kaleckian North constrained by effective demand to show how growth paths and the evolution of the terms of trade are endogenously determined, and that the model yields a long-run equilibrium with the North growing faster than the South. The chapter also presents empirical results which suggest that the Southern income elasticity of Northern imports exceeds the corresponding Northern elasticity, and may in fact be growing over time, exacerbating the forces of uneven development.

Gerry Helleiner who, with Taylor, has coordinated projects at the World Institute of Development Economics Research, turns to another aspect of North–South relations: foreign aid. He examines a new paradigm in the current literature on official development assistance to LDCs which emphasizes the need for 'partnership' and 'local' partnership, and argues that current realities about aid relations belie this new rhetoric. The effort at evaluating the effectiveness of aid has been primarily driven by the needs of the aid donors, rather than aid recipients, which implies the absence of a true partnership. He recommends a host of reforms which could narrow the gap between rhetoric and reality, including: the timely provision of relevant information by donors to help recipient country governments to utilize the aid more effectively; integration and coordination of aid with national plans and priorities; monitoring of shortfalls from aid promises; provision of compensatory and contingency financing; reducing the ineffective technological cooperation component of aid; and monitoring aid with a long-term perspective by an independent monitoring authority rather than the donor.

Sharing a concern for the increase in systemic risk in the world economy that they saw resulting from international financial liberalization, John Eatwell and Lance Taylor proposed in 1998 the creation of a World Financial Authority (WFA) (Eatwell and Taylor, 1998, 2000). In his contribution here, Eatwell develops the case for international financial regulation by identifying the problems of current regulatory practices and the challenges posed by financial globalization. The chapter stresses the need to address the macro-manifestations of microeconomic risk, the problems arising from the pro-cyclicality of regulation that are compounded by the episodes of contagion induced by risk management techniques, and argues for a new approach to systemic risk in which microeconomic and macroeconomic factors are not treated separately. A central theme of the chapter, as in Eatwell and Taylor (2000), is that 'the domain of the regulator' should be 'the same as the domain of the market that is regulated'. Thus, the major challenge is precisely that while some of the tasks of a WFA, such as information and surveillance, are being performed, they are being performed imperfectly and in an uncoordinated way.

José Antonio Ocampo has collaborated in several international research projects with Lance Taylor and has co-authored a paper with him on trade liberalization (Ocampo and Taylor, 1998). In his chapter here, he also addresses the problems and consequences of financial instability in the world economy, although from a different perspective to that adopted by Eatwell and Taylor. He starts with the observation that financial instability in the world economy generates a strong pro-cyclical performance in what he calls the 'business cycle/policy taking' periphery. As a result, current policies in LDCs are pro-cyclical and accentuate the boom–bust cycles associated with volatile capital flows. During crises, austerity measures are adopted in order to generate credibility in financial markets and this in turn creates economic and political economy pressures for a pro-cyclical policy during the boom. His chapter then provides a comprehensive analysis of the role that domestic policies in developing countries can play in reducing the adverse effects of international financial instability and of the recent experience, in Latin America and elsewhere, with policy innovations in the relevant areas. His approach favors managing booms (and thus preventing crisis) through the following policies: (i) a flexible and managed exchange rate combined with capital account regulations to provide room for anti-cyclical monetary policy; (ii) liability policies aimed at improving private and public sector debt profiles and including capital account and domestic financial regulations as well as public sector debt management; (iii) counter-cyclical management of prudential regulation and supervision of financial systems; and (iv) anti-cyclical fiscal policy through the use of fiscal targets based on structural budgets, stabilization funds for commodities with significant fiscal impact and properly designed social safety nets.

Andrés Solimano, a former student of Taylor at MIT, wrote his dissertation on devaluation, inflation and debt in developing countries under his supervision and has been a collaborator of his in several international research projects. In his contribution to this volume, he addresses the opportunities and risks brought about by increased global interdependence and the corresponding institutional challenges. A major theme of his chapter is that so far the benefits of globalization have been unevenly distributed across and within nations. In addition, global interdependence has brought increased financial volatility and more frequent financial crises. The main challenges are thus the maintenance of global and national financial stability and an increased degree of autonomy of economic policy (fiscal and social policies in particular). Here, Solimano's focus on the reform of the IMF and the World Bank and the role of regional financial institutions in addressing these challenges and the financial needs of globalization complements the chapters by Eatwell and Ocampo. The chapter also reviews orthodox and heterodox views on international trade and finance. While orthodox theorists emphasize the case for free trade (greater economic efficiency and expanded consumption opportunities) – although some are rather skeptical about, or even opposed to, free capital mobility – heterodox views, which Lance Taylor contributed to formalize (see in particular Taylor, 1983), emphasize the asymmetric distribution of the gains from trade between developed and developing countries and the limited capacity of the developing countries to affect global outcomes.

NOTES

1. The definition is similar to that used by Rothschild (1989), and follows the one used by Dutt (1994).
2. The discussion on these heterodox approaches draws on Dutt (1994). It should be noted that the boundaries between the different approaches (and in some cases, with mainstream economics) are not always very clear, and there is often a fair amount of heterogeneity within the approaches. There is no attempt to be exhaustive, but to provide a flavor of some unorthodox approaches.
3. For a sampling of contributions, see Giddens and Held (1982).
4. See Dutt and Amadeo (1990) for an elaboration of this debate, as well as for references to post-Keynesian contributions.
5. See also Kaldor's (1940) cycle model with non-linear investment and saving functions, combining Keynesian and Kaleckian insights.
6. Although the flex-price, fix-price approach was used earlier by Kalecki, Hicks and others, it had scarcely been applied to the macroeconomic problems of developing countries.
7. But not only the recent work, see for example his work on Minsky crises (Taylor and O'Connell, 1985).
8. See in particular Amsden, Kochanowicz and Taylor (1994).
9. See Frenkel (1983). The formal model presented there is restated in Taylor (1991).

REFERENCES

Amsden, Alice (1991), *Asia's Next Giant: South Korea and Late Industrialization*, New York: Oxford University Press.

Amsden, Alice, J. Kochanowicz and Lance Taylor (1994), *The Market Meets its Match: Reindustrializing Eastern Europe*, Cambridge, Mass.: Harvard University Press.

Arndt, H.W. (1987), *Economic Development*, Chicago: University of Chicago Press.

Ayres, Clarence E. (1944), *The Theory of Economic Progress*, Chapel Hill: University of North Carolina Press.

Bacha, Edmar, Eliana A. Cardoso, Frank J. Lysy and Lance Taylor (1980), *Models of Growth and Distribution for Brazil*, New York and London: Oxford University Press.

Bacha, Edmar and Lance Taylor (1971), 'Foreign exchange shadow prices: a critical review of current theories', *Quarterly Journal of Economics*, 85, 197–224.

Bacha, Edmar and Lance Taylor (1973), 'Growth and trade distortions in Chile', in R.S. Eckaus and P.N. Rosenstein-Rodan (eds), *Analysis of Development Problems*, Amsterdam, North-Holland; New York, American Elsevier.

Baran, Paul (1952), 'On the political economy of backwardness', *Manchester School*, 20, January, 66–84.

Bardhan, Pranab K. (1988), 'Alternative approaches to development economics', in Hollis B. Chenery, and T.N. Srinivasan (eds), *Handbook of Development Economics*, Vol. 1, Amsterdam: North Holland.

Bardhan, Pranab (1993), 'Economics of development and the development of economics', *Journal of Economic Perspectives*, **7**(2), Spring, 129–42.

Bardhan, Pranab and Christopher Udry (1999), *Development Microeconomics*, Oxford: Oxford University Press.

Basu, Kaushik (1998), *Analytical Development Economics. The Less Developed Economy Revisited*, Cambridge, Mass.: The MIT Press.

Bauer, P.T. (1971), *Dissent on Development: Studies and Debates in Development Economics*, London: Weidenfeld & Nicholson.

Bauer, P.T. and B.S. Yamey (1957), *The Economics of Under-developed Countries*, Chicago: University of Chicago Press.

Chenery, Hollis B. (1975), 'The structuralist approach to development policy', *American Economic Review*, Papers and Proceedings, **65**(2), May, 310–16.

Chenery, Hollis B. and Michael Bruno (1962), 'Development alternatives in an open economy: the case of Israel', *Economic Journal*, **72**, 79–103.

Chenery, Hollis B. and Moises Syrquin (1975), *Patterns of Development, 1950–1970*, Oxford: Oxford University Press.

Chenery, Hollis and Lance Taylor (1968), 'Development patterns among countries and over time', *Review of Economics and Statistics*, 50, 391–416.

Commons, John R. (1934), *Institutional Economics*, New York: Macmillan.

Dutt, Amitava Krishna (1990), *Growth, Distribution, and Uneven Development*, Cambridge: Cambridge University Press.

Dutt, Amitava Krishna (1992), 'Two issues in the state of development economics', in A.K. Dutt and K.P. Jameson (eds), *New Directions in Development Economics*, Aldershot, UK and Brookfield, US: Edward Elgar.

Dutt, Amitava Krishna (1994), 'Analytical political economy: an introduction' in A.K. Dutt (ed.), *New Directions in Analytical Political Economy*, Aldershot, UK and Brookfield, US: Edward Elgar.

Dutt, Amitava Krishna (2002), 'The political economy of development: an introduction', in A.K. Dutt (ed.), *The Political Economy of Development*, Cheltenham, UK and Northampton, US: Edward Elgar.

Dutt, Amitava Krishna and Edward J. Amadeo (1990), *Keynes's Third Alternative? The Neo-Ricardian Keynesians and the Post Keynesians*, Aldershot, UK and Brookfield, US: Edward Elgar.

Dutt, Amitava Krishna, Kwan S. Kim and Ajit Singh (eds) (1994), *The State, Markets and Development*, Aldershot, UK and Brookfield, US: Edward Elgar.

Eatwell, J. and L. Taylor (1998), 'International capital markets and the future of economic policy', a paper prepared for the Ford Foundation project *International Capital Markets and the Future of Economic Policy*, New York: Center for Economic Policy Analysis; London: IPPR.

Eatwell, J. and L. Taylor (2000), *Global Finance at Risk: the Case for International Regulation*, New York: Policy Press.

Fanelli, José María, Roberto Frenkel and Lance Taylor (1992 [1994]), 'The *World Development Report 1991*: A critical assessment', in United Nations Conference on Trade and Development, *International Monetary and Financial Issues for the 1990s*, Vol. 1, New York: United Nations. Reprinted in Graham Bird and Ann Helwege (eds) (1994), *Latin America's Economic Future*, London and San Diego: Academic Press.

Frenkel, Roberto (1983), 'Mercado financiero, expectativas cambiarias y movimientos de capital', *El Trimestre Económico*, No. 200, Mexico.

Furtardo, Celso (1964), *Development and Underdevelopment*, Berkeley: University of California Press.

Gibson, Bill, Nora Lustig and Lance Taylor (1986), 'Terms of trade and class conflict in a Marxian computable general equilibrium model for Mexico', *Journal of Development Studies*, **23**(1), 40–59.

Giddens, Anthony and David Held (eds) (1982), *Classes, Power, and Conflict*, Berkeley: University of California Press.

Goodwin, Richard M. (1967), 'A growth cycle', in C.H. Feinstein (ed.), *Socialism, Capitalism and Growth*, Cambridge: Cambridge University Press.

Granovetter, Mark (1985), 'Economic action and social structure: The problem of embeddedness', *American Journal of Sociology*, **91**(3), November, 481–510.

Harrod, Roy (1939), 'An essay in dynamic theory', *Economic Journal*, 49, 14–33.

Hirschman, Albert O. (1958), *The Strategy of Economic Development*, New York: Norton.

Hirschman, Albert O. (1977), 'A generalized linkage approach to development, with special reference to staples', *Economic Development and Change*, Vol. 25, Supplement (Essays in Honor of Bert F. Hoselitz), 67–98.

Hirschman, Albert O. (1981), 'The rise and decline of development economics', in A.O Hirschman, *Essays in Trespassing: Economics to Politics and Beyond*, Cambridge: Cambridge University Press.

Kaldor, Nicholas (1940), 'A model of the trade cycle', *Economic Journal*, 50, 78–92.

Kaldor, Nicholas (1955–56), 'Alternative theories of distribution', *Review of Economic Studies*, **23**(2), 83–100.

Kaldor, Nicholas (1957), 'A model of economic growth', *Economic Journal*, 67, 591–624.

Kalecki, Michal (1954), *Theory of Economic Dynamics*, London: Allen and Unwin.

Kalecki, Michal (1971), *Selected Essays on the Dynamics of the Capitalist Economy*, Cambridge: Cambridge University Press.

Kendrick, David A. and Lance Taylor (1970), 'Numerical solution of nonlinear planning models', *Econometrica*, 38, 453–67.

Keynes, John Maynard (1936), *The General Theory of Employment, Interest and Money*, London: Macmillan.

Krugman, Paul and Lance Taylor (1978), 'Contractionary effects of devaluation', *Journal of International Economics*, 8, 445–56.

Laibman, David (1992), *Value, Technical Change and Crisis. Explorations in Marxist Economic Theory*, Armonk, New York: M.E. Sharpe.

Lal, Deepak (1985), *The Poverty of 'Development Economics'*, Cambridge, Mass.: Harvard University Press.

Lal, Deepak (ed.) (1992), *Development Economics*, Aldershot, UK and Brookfield, US: Edward Elgar.

Lewis, W. Arthur (1954), 'Economic development with unlimited supplies of labour', *Manchester School*, **22**(2), 131–91.

Lewis, W. Arthur (1984), 'The state of development theory', *American Economic Review*, **74**(1), March, 1–10.

Little, Ian M.D. (1982), *Economic Development*, New York: Basic Books.

Little, Ian M.D., Tibor Scitovsky and Maurice Scott (1970), *Industry and Trade in some Developing Countries*, Oxford: Oxford University Press.

Lucas, Robert E.B. (1988), 'On the mechanics of economic development', *Journal of Monetary Economics*, 22, 3–42.

Marglin, Stephen A. (1984), *Growth, Distribution and Prices*, Cambridge, Mass.: Harvard University Press.

McCarthy, F. Desmond, Lance Taylor and Cyrus Talati (1987), 'Trade patterns in developing countries: 1964–1982', *Journal of Development Economics*, **27**(1–2), October, 5–39.

Meier, Gerald M. (1984), 'The formative period', in G.M. Meier and D. Seers (eds), *Pioneers in Development*, New York: Oxford University Press.

Minsky, Hyman P. (1975), *John Maynard Keynes*, New York: Columbia University Press.

Minsky, Hyman P. (1986), *Stabilizing an Unstable Economy*, New Haven, Conn.: Yale University Press.

Myrdal, Gunnar (1957), *Rich Lands and Poor Lands*, New York: Harper Brothers.

Nelson, Richard R. and Sidney G. Winter (1982), *An Evolutionary Theory of Economic Change*, Cambridge, Mass.: Harvard University Press.

Noyola, Juan F. (1956), 'El desarrollo económico y la inflación en México y otros países latinoamericanos', *Investigación Económica*, 16: 603–48.

Nurske, Ragnar (1953), *Problems of Capital Formation in Underdeveloped Countries*, Oxford: Basil Blackwell.

Ocampo, José Antonio and Lance Taylor (1998), 'Trade liberalization in developing countries: Modest benefits but problems with productivity growth, macro prices, and income distribution', *Economic Journal*, 108, 1523–46.

Pasinetti, Luigi (1962), 'The rate of profit and income distribution in relation to the rate of economic growth', *Review of Economic Studies*, 29, 267–79.

Prebisch, Raul (1959), 'Commercial Policy in Underdeveloped Countries', *American Economic Review*, **49**(2), May, 251–73.

Ray, Debraj (1998), *Development Economics*, Princeton, New Jersey: Princeton University Press.

Robbins, Lionel (1968), *The Theory of Economic Development in the History of Economic Thought*, London: Macmillan.

Robinson, Joan (1962), *Essays in the Theory of Economic Growth*, London: Macmillan.

Romer, Paul M. (1986), 'Increasing returns and long-run growth', *Journal of Political Economy*, 94, 1002–37.

Ros, Jaime (2000), *Development Theory and the Economics of Growth*, Ann Arbor, MI: University of Michigan Press.

Rosenstein-Rodan, Paul M. (1943), 'Problems of industrialization in Eastern and South-Eastern Europe', *Economic Journal*, **53**, 202–11.

Rothschild, Kurt (1989), 'Political economy or economics? Some terminological and normative considerations', *European Journal of Political Economy*, **5**(1), 1–12.

Samuels, Warren J. (1987), 'Institutional economics', in J. Eatwell, M. Milgate and P. Newman (eds), *The New Palgrave. A Dictionary of Economics*, London: Macmillan.

Schumpeter, Joseph A. (1912), *The Theory of Economic Development*, English trans., Cambridge, Mass.: Harvard University Press (1934).

Sen, Amartya K. (1963), 'Neo-classical and neo-Keynesian theories of distribution', *Economic Record*, 39, 54–64.

Shapiro, Helen and Lance Taylor (1990), 'The state and industrial strategy', *World Development*, **18**(6), 861–78.

Simon, Herbert A. (1987), 'Behavioural economics', in J. Eatwell, M. Milgate and P. Newman (eds), *The New Palgrave. A Dictionary of Economics*, London: Macmillan.

Singer, Hans (1950), 'The distribution of gains between borrowing and investing countries', *American Economic Review*, **40**(2), May, 473–85.

Sraffa, Piero (1960), *Production of Commodities by Means of Commodities*, Cambridge: Cambridge University Press.

Sunkel, Osvaldo (1960), 'Inflation in Chile: An unorthodox perspective', *International Economic Review*, 10, 107–31.

Taylor, Lance (1975), 'Theoretical foundations and technical implications', in Charles R. Blitzer, Peter B. Clark and Lance Taylor (eds), *Economy-wide Models and Development Planning*, Oxford: Oxford University Press.

Taylor, Lance (1979), *Macro Models for Developing Countries*, New York: McGraw Hill.

Taylor, Lance (1981a), 'IS/LM in the tropics: Diagrammatics of the new structuralist macro critique', in William R. Cline and Sidney Weintraub (eds), *Economic stabilization in developing countries*, Washington DC: The Brookings Institution.

Taylor, Lance (1981b), 'South–North trade and Southern growth: Bleak prospects from a structuralist point of view', *Journal of International Economics*, 11, 589–602.

Taylor, Lance (1982), 'Food price inflation, terms of trade and growth', in M. Gersovitz *et al.* (eds), *The Theory and Experience of Economic Development: Essays in Honor of Sir W. Arthur Lewis*, London: Allen and Unwin.

Taylor, Lance (1983), *Structuralist Macroeconomics. Applicable models for the Third World*, New York: Basic Books.

Taylor, Lance (1988), *Varieties of Stabilization Experience. Towards Sensible Macroeconomics in the Third World*, Oxford: Clarendon Press.

Taylor, Lance (1990) (ed.), *Socially relevant policy analysis*, Cambride, Mass.: The MIT Press.

Taylor, Lance (1991), *Income distribution, inflation and growth. Lectures in structuralist macroeconomics*, Cambridge, Mass.: MIT Press.

Taylor, Lance (1992), 'Lance Taylor (born 1940)', in Philip Arestis and Malcolm Sawyer (eds), *A Biographical Dictionary of Dissenting Economists*, Aldershot, UK and Brookfield, US: Edward Elgar.

Taylor, Lance (ed.) (1993), *The Rocky Road to Reform. Adjustment, Income Distribution, and Growth in the Developing World*, Cambridge, Mass.: MIT Press.

Taylor, Lance (1996), 'Sustainable development: an introduction', *World Development*, **24**, 215–25.

Taylor, Lance (ed.) (1999), *After Neoliberalism: What Next for Latin America?*, Ann Arbor, MI: University of Michigan Press.

Taylor, Lance (ed.) (2001), *External Liberalization, Economic Performance and Social Policy*, Oxford and New York: Oxford University Press.

Taylor, Lance and Edmar Bacha (1976), 'The unequalizing spiral: A first growth model for Belindia', *Quarterly Journal of Economics*, 90, 197–218.

Taylor, Lance and Frank J. Lysy (1979), 'Vanishing income distributions: Keynesian clues about model surprises in the short run', *Journal of Development Economics*, 6, 11–29.

Taylor, Lance and O'Connell, Stephen A. (1985), 'A Minsky crisis', *Quarterly Journal of Economics*, 100, Supplement, 871–85.

Taylor, Lance, Hiren Sarkar and Jørn Rattsø (1984), 'Macroeconomic adjustment in a computable general equilibrium model for India', in Moshe Syrquin, Lance Taylor and Larry Westphal (eds), *Economic Structure and Performance*, Orlando, Fl.: Academic Press.

Veblen, Thorstein (1904), *The Theory of Business Enterprise*, New York: Scribner's Sons.

Wade, Robert (1990), *Governing the Market. Economic Theory and the Role of the Government in East Asian Industrialization*, Princeton, NJ: Princeton University Press.

Young, Allyn (1928), 'Increasing returns and economic progress', *Economic Journal*, 38, 527–42.

PART II

Approaches to Development and Planning

2. Modeling economic growth with GAMS

P. Ruben Mercado, Lihui Lin and David A. Kendrick

The theoretical and computational modeling of economic growth has experienced a significant comeback in recent years, particularly in the form of optimal growth models. Qualitative properties of simple one-sector models of optimal growth have been known for a long time, and closed form solutions can be obtained for particular models with simple objective functions and dynamic constraints. However, computational methods become a necessity as soon as we move from simple models to more complex specifications.[1] These methods are very useful not only to obtain solutions and simulations of empirically specified models, but also to explore the behavior of complex theoretical models.[2]

Our goal in this chapter is to introduce some strategies to implement optimal growth models in GAMS (General Algebraic Modeling System).[3] We begin with a simple Ramsey-type model and later present a more complex dynamic multisector model originally developed by David Kendrick and Lance Taylor (Kendrick and Taylor, 1969 and 1970). The last one is particularly interesting since it is a four-sector model with a non-linear objective function, non-linear constant elasticity of substitution (CES) production functions, and non-linear absorptive capacity functions. It was an early effort to show the feasibility of solving multisector non-linear optimization models with the use of computational methods. At that time, its solution required the most powerful computers available at MIT. Today, it can easily be implemented in a personal computer and it provides, among other things, a good training ground in the art of computational growth modeling.

1 A SIMPLE ONE-SECTOR RAMSEY-TYPE MODEL

Consider the following simple one-sector non-linear optimization Ramsey-type model.

$$max \sum_{t=0}^{T-1} (1+\rho)^{-t} \frac{c_t^{1-\tau}}{1-\tau} \tag{2.1}$$

subject to

$$y_t = k_t^{\beta} \tag{2.2}$$

$$k_{t+1} = y_t - c_t \tag{2.3}$$

$$k_0 = \bar{k},\ k_t > 0,\ c_t > 0 \tag{2.4}$$

where: c_t = consumption, k_t = capital stock, y_t = gross income, ρ = rate of time preference, τ = elasticity parameter and β = coefficient on capital.

The general analytical properties of this type of one-sector model are well known.[4] However, to obtain solutions even for simple one-sector models, we usually have to rely on computational methods. Here is how this simple model looks when, given specific values for parameters and initial conditions, it is implemented in GAMS.

```
$TITLE simpler: simple Ramsey growth model

SETS T EXTENDED HORIZON/0*2/

SCALARS
beta exponent on capital/0.75/
rho  welfare discount    /0.03/
eta  elasticity          /0.9/;

PARAMETERS
dis(t) discount factor;
dis(t) = (1 + rho)**(1 - ord(t))/(1 - eta);

VARIABLES
c(t) consumption
y(t) income
k(t) capital stock
j performance index;

EQUATIONS
yd(t) income definition
kb(t) capital stock balance
jd performance index definition;

jd..            j = E = sum(t, dis(t - 1) * c(t - 1)**(1 - eta) );
yd(t)..         y(t) = E = k(t)**beta;
kb(t + 1)..  k(t + 1) = E = y(t) - c(t);
```

```
* lower bounds on variables
c.lo(t)=0.001; k.lo(t)=0.001;

* initial capital stock
k.fx("0")=0.1;

MODEL SIMPLER/ALL/;

SOLVE SIMPLER MAXIMIZING J USING NLP;

PARAMETER REPORT SOLUTION SUMMARY;
report(t, "k")=k.l(t); report(t, "c")=c.l(t); report(t, "y")=y.l(t);

DISPLAY REPORT;
```

This is the usual structure of a GAMS program. We define sets that correspond to indices in the mathematical representation of models, in this case a time index. Also we define scalars and parameters that are single numbers or series of numbers that will remain constant during the solution of the model.[5] Finally, we add variables and equations. Each variable in the program has four associated values: its level (.l), its lower bound (.lo), its upper bound (.up) and its marginal or dual value (.m). For our model, we define lower bounds for consumption and capital stock, and we assign a fixed value (.fx) to the initial capital stock. We then name the model and indicate that all the equations listed above will be a part of it. In other instances, we may decide to list only the specific equations for which the model has to be solved. We continue by asking GAMS to solve the model. Since GAMS uses optimization solvers, we have to specify a variable to be maximized (or minimized), and we also have to specify the solution method we prefer – for our example, non-linear programming (NLP).[6] Finally, to have a condensed expression of the results – though GAMS will automatically generate a generous output containing results and other useful information about the model – we create a report of the results and ask GAMS to display it.

It is particularly important to understand clearly the specification of the equations and of the initial (and eventually terminal) conditions of the model. First notice that all variables and equations, except the performance index, are defined over the set T. However, the capital stock balance equation (kb) is later specified over the set 't+1', while the discount factor and the consumption variable contained in the performance index are specified over the set 't−1'. To understand why we need to proceed in this way, we have to be acquainted with the way in which GAMS builds up the model to be solved.

The procedure in GAMS for generating a dynamic model such as our simple Ramsey-type model is to generate, for each equation, a sequence of as many equations as elements contained in the equation index. For the 'yd(t)' equation, it will generate three equations, since the set 'T' was defined as T = {0, 1, 2}, that is, it contains three elements. For the 'kb(t + 1)' equation, GAMS will generate two equations only, corresponding to the values T = 1 and T = 2. There will not be a T = 3 value, since that value has not been defined as a member of the set T. Finally, for the 'jd' equation, it will generate just one equation containing the sum of two terms only, one containing the values for dis('0') and c('0'), and the other containing the values for dis('1') and c('1'). Notice that there will not be terms such as dis('− 1') and c('− 1'), since the index '− 1' does not belong to the set T previously defined. And when GAMS finds an expression like that, which is a reference to a non-existent element, it will use the default value (zero in this case).[7] In summary, GAMS uses an index like 't + k' to generate all of the elements of the set with k added to each element, where 'k = − 1' if the variable or equation index contains a lag, 'k = 1' when it contains a lead, and so on. It then generates variables or equations for only those values of 't + k' that belong to the set T. After generating all the corresponding equations, GAMS will stack them together and solve them as if they were a unique static model.

Precise information about the exact model generated by GAMS can be obtained from the GAMS output, in the Equation Listing section.[8] For example, our model equation specification:

```
jd..            j =E= sum(t, dis(t − 1) * c(t − 1)**(1 − eta) );
yd(t)..         y(t) =E= k(t)**beta;
kb(t + 1)..  k(t + 1) =E= y(t) − c(t);
```

will generate the following output:[9]

```
---- YD        =E= INCOME DEFINITION
YD(0)..  Y(0) − (1.3337)*K(0) =E= 0 ; (LHS = − 0.1778 ***)
YD(1)..  Y(1) − (4.2176)*K(1) =E= 0 ; (LHS = − 0.0056 ***)
YD(2)..  Y(2) − (4.2176)*K(2) =E= 0 ; (LHS = − 0.0056 ***)
---- KB        =E= CAPITAL STOCK BALANCE
KB(1)..  C(0) − Y(0) + K(1) =E= 0 ; (LHS = 0.002 ***)
KB(2)..  C(1) − Y(1) + K(2) =E= 0 ; (LHS = 0.002 ***)
---- JD        =E= PERFORMANCE INDEX DEFINITION
JD..  − (501.1872)*C(0) − (486.5895)*C(1) + J =E= 0 ; (LHS = − 9.8778 ***)
```

Table 2.1 Variants of the Ramsey model

Case 1	Case 2
jd.. j=E=sum(t, dis(t−1) * c(t−1)**(1−eta)); yd(t).. y(t)=E=k(t)**beta; kb(t).. k(t+1)=E=y(t)−c(t);	jd.. j=E=sum(t, dis(t) * c(t)**(1−eta)); yd(t).. y(t)=E=k(t)**beta; kb(t+1).. k(t+1)=E=y(t)−c(t);
JD.. J=F{ C(0) , C(1) } ; YD(0)..Y(0)=F{K(0)} ; KB(0).. K(1)=F{Y(0) , C(0)}; YD(1)..Y(1)=F{K(1)} ; KB(1).. K(2)=F{Y(1) , C(1)}; YD(2)..Y(2)=F{K(2)} ; KB(2).. K(3)=F{Y(2), C(2)};	JD.. J=F{ C(0) , C(1), C(2) } ; YD(0)..Y(0)=F{K(0)} ; KB(1).. K(1)=F{Y(0) , C(0)}; YD(1)..Y(1)=F{K(1)} ; KB(2).. K(2)=F{Y(1), C(1)}; YD(2)..Y(2)=F{K(2)} ;

Rearranging on a period-by-period basis and keeping the essential information for our purposes, that is, the information associated with each period variable, and where ‘F’ should be read as ‘a function of’, we obtain:

```
JD..    J=F{ C(0) , C(1) } ;
YD(0).. Y(0)=F{K(0)} ;
KB(1).. K(1)=F{Y(0) , C(0)} ;
YD(1).. Y(1)=F{K(1)} ;
KB(2).. K(2)=F{Y(1), C(1)};
YD(2).. Y(2)=F{K(2)} ;
```

Thus, given an initial condition for K(0), GAMS will look for values for C(0) and C(1), and consequently for K(1), K(2), Y(0), Y(1) and Y(2) such that J is maximized. It is interesting to explore what would happen if we tried a different equation specification. For example, consider the following cases, shown in Table 2.1.

- *Case 1:* ‘t’ instead of ‘t+1’ in equation ‘kb’: In this case, GAMS will generate an extra equation for ‘kb’. But notice that the last equation ‘kb(2)’ contains a ‘k(3)’ term for the variable k. Since k is defined over the set T which does not contain the value 3, GAMS will automatically assign the value zero to ‘k(3)’. Implicitly, this means that in our model we are imposing a terminal condition such as ‘c(2)=y(2)’, something we may or may not want to do.
- *Case 2:* ‘t’ instead of ‘t−1’ for c(t) in equation ‘jd’: In this case, GAMS will generate an extra value ‘c(2)’ for the variable ‘c’ in

equation 'j'. Notice that c(2) does not appear in any of the constraints – that is, in YD(.) or KB(.). Thus, its value will be set to an absurd high value when solving the optimization problem in order to maximize the criterion 'j'.

It should now be clear why it is very important to pay special attention to the specification of the time indexes in equations and variables when implementing a dynamic model in GAMS. They crucially determine which model specification we are effectively solving.

As is well known, in some cases it is not very difficult to obtain an explicit expression for the Euler equations corresponding to the optimization problem of interest. For those cases, the system of equations formed by the Euler equations together with the state equations – in our model, the equation for the capital stock evolution – will describe the temporal dynamics of the model. In this way, the optimization problem becomes a problem of solving a system of differential or difference equations. In general, these systems of equations will contain 'pre-determined' and 'jumping' variables and display 'saddle path' type behavior. Thus, they will present a 'two-point boundary-value problem' requiring for its solution the imposition not only of initial conditions but also of specific terminal conditions.[10]

Different constraints can be imposed on our simple Ramsey-type model.[11] Besides the lower bounds on consumption and the capital stock we could, for example, impose pre-specified paths for capital accumulation, or we could impose an upper bound on investment – the difference between income and consumption – as a way of modeling 'absorptive capacity'. These kinds of sophistication of the basic model can be easily accommodated by GAMS, which is particularly powerful in dealing with inequality constraints.

An interesting exercise to explore the dynamics of our model is to impose different terminal conditions for the capital stock. For example, let us assume that we want to bequest to future generations a level of the stock of capital equal to its initial level. Otherwise, given the finite horizon of the simulation, the optimal solution will display a tendency to consume all the capital stock as the end of the simulation period gets closer. To set a terminal capital stock target, we can modify our GAMS program as follows. We first modify the definition of the set T:

```
SETS T EXTENDED HORIZON/0*2/
tf(t) final period;
tf(t)=yes$(ord(t) eq card(t));
```

In this way we define a subset 'tf' of the set T which will contain the last element of the set T (in this case, 'tf(t)=2'). That is, we tell GAMS to set the value of 'tf(t)' as equal to the element of T obtained when the ordinal of the set T equals its cardinality. We then define, at the bottom of the program, a terminal condition 'k.fx(tf) = 0.1'. In so doing, all we have to do when changing the extended horizon is to change its last value, without having to adjust other parts of the program. The graph in Figure 2.1 shows the optimal capital stock path for a 40-period simulation without imposing an explicit terminal condition on the capital stock. As can be seen in the graph, the optimal 40-period capital stock path gets close to the steady-state value that is approximately equal to 0.28.[12] Then at the end of the simulation horizon, the capital stock is consumed, bringing it down to its lower bound equal to 0.001. The graph also shows the results of three other experiments, setting the extended horizon equal to 10, 20 and 30, and with a terminal capital stock equal to 0.1. It can be seen how all the paths nicely display a 'turnpike'-like behavior typical of closed-economy finite-horizon optimization problems.[13] Indeed, in our simple Ramsey-type problem, the optimal path for an infinite horizon would reach the steady-state value and stay there forever. For finite horizons, the optimal paths will arch towards the optimal infinite horizon path.

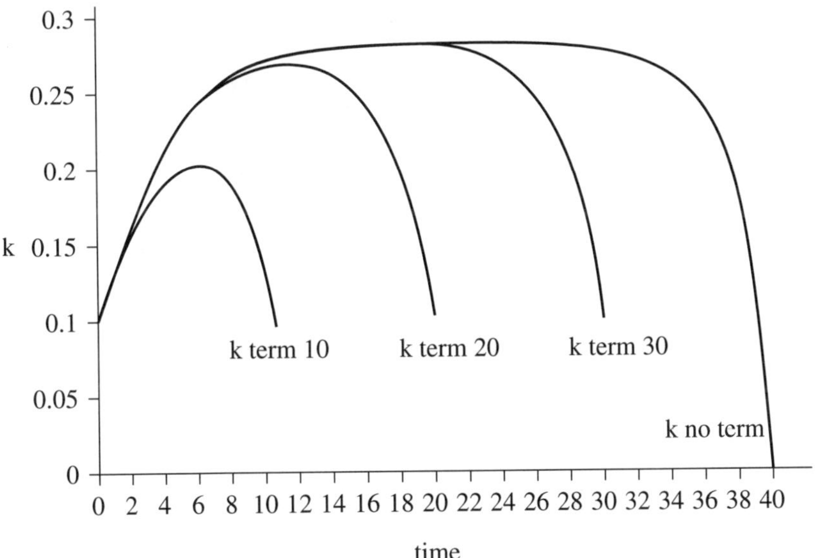

Figure 2.1 Optimal paths for the capital stock

2 THE KENDRICK–TAYLOR'S MULTISECTOR MODEL

This is a four-sector model with agriculture and mining, heavy industry, light industry and services sectors. The basic structure of the model is to maximize a non-linear criterion function subject to constraints in the form of distribution relations, CES production functions, non-linear absorptive capacity functions, foreign exchange constraints, and initial and terminal capital stock and foreign debt constraints. The corresponding groups of equations are presented below.[14]

Criterion Function

The non-linear criterion function is the time-discounted sum of consumption of goods from all sectors.

$$\xi = \sum_{i=1}^{n} (1+z)^{-i} \sum_{j=1}^{4} a_j c_{ji}^{bj} \tag{2.5}$$

where: ξ = criterion value, z = consumption discount rate, c_{ji} = consumption of goods from sector j in period i, and a_j, b_j = consumption shares and income elasticities of demand respectively, with $a_j > 0$ and $0 \leq b_j \leq 1$.

Capital Stock Accumulation

The capital stock accumulation equation is a non-linear difference equation which includes an 'absorptive capacity' term. That is, the effective addition to the capital stock depends not only on the investment input, but on the existing capital stock as well.

$$k_{j,i+1} = k_{ji} + g_j(\delta_{ji}, k_{ji}) \; j \in J, \; i \in I \tag{2.6}$$

where k_{ji} = capital stock in sector j in period i, δ_{ji} = investment level in sector j in period i. The mathematics of the absorptive function g_j are given by

$$g_j(\delta_{ji}, k_{ji}) = \mu_j k_{ji} \left[1 - \left(1 + \frac{\varepsilon_j \delta_{ji}}{\mu_j k_{ji}} \right)^{-1/\varepsilon_j} \right] j \in J \tag{2.7}$$

with ε_j (which affects the curvature of the function) ≥ -1, and μ_j (which affects the asymptotic value) ≥ 0.

Distribution and Production Functions

The equation below insures that the use of each commodity does not exceed its availability. It specifies that production plus imports – those tied and not tied to production levels – must equal the uses of each commodity as intermediate inputs, investment inputs, exports and consumption goods.

$$q_i + Dq_i + m_i = Aq_i + B\delta_i + e_i + c_i \quad i \in I \tag{2.8}$$

where q_i = production vector in period i, D = diagonal matrix of marginal propensities to import for production, m_i = untied imports, A = input–output matrix, B = capital coefficient matrix, e_i = vector of exports in period i, and c_i = consumption vector in period i.

The production functions are specified as constant elasticity of substitution (CES) form.

$$q_{ij} = \tau_j(1+\nu_j)^i[\beta_j k_{ji}^{-\rho_j} + (1-\beta_j) l_{ji}^{-\rho_j}]^{-1/\rho_j} \quad j \in J, i \in I \tag{2.9}$$

where τ_j = efficiency parameter, ν_j = rate of technical progress, β_j = distribution parameter, $\rho_j = (1/\sigma_j) - 1$ = elasticity of substitution parameter, and l_{ji} = labor input in sector j in period i.

Finally, the sum of labor inputs throughout the four sectors is constrained by the available labor force.

$$\sum_{j \in J} l_{ji} = l_i \quad i \in I \tag{2.10}$$

where l_i = labor force in period i.

Foreign Trade Equations

Exports were assumed to be exogenously determined. So the exports in sector j in period i, e_{ji}, are given.

Concerning imports, there are no untied imports in two sectors – agriculture and mining, and in services – while there can be untied imports in the other two – heavy and light industry. This means, $m_{1i} = m_{4i} = 0$ for $i \in I$, where m_{ji} are the imports of sector j goods in period i. There are also tied imports for production and investment which are distinguished by sector of use rather than by sector of origin. Thus, they can include commodities from all sources.

Finally, the foreign debt accumulation equation specifies that foreign debt at any period is a function of the debt in the previous period, the interest rate and the current account deficit.

$$\gamma_{i+1} = (1+\theta)\gamma_i + \sum_{j \in J} (d_{jj} q_{ji} - e_{ji} + \pi_j \delta_{ji} + m_{ji}) \; i \in I \qquad (2.11)$$

where γ_i = foreign debt in period i, θ = interest rate on foreign debt, d_{jj} = diagonal elements of the D matrix, that is marginal propensities to import for production, and π_j = marginal propensity to import for investment.

Initial and Terminal Conditions

Initial conditions and terminal target conditions are specified for the foreign debt and the capital stocks. The initial foreign debt γ_I is given and the terminal foreign debt γ_{N+I} is chosen as a target. The target reflects the desired amount of foreign debt at the end of the time horizon covered by the model. It also represents the negative part of the bequest of one generation to the next.

Similarly, the initial capital stocks in each sector k_{jI} are given and the terminal capital stocks $k_{j,N+I}$ are chosen as targets. The terminal capital stocks reflect the positive part of the bequest.

3 THE KENDRICK–TAYLOR MODEL IN GAMS

The complete GAMS statement of the Kendrick–Taylor model for a time horizon of five periods can be found in the Appendix.[15] Though more complex, its structure is basically the same as the one of the previously presented Ramsey-type model. However, there are some new elements which we will now analyse.

In the sets definitions, notice first that the index 't' rather than the index 'i', as in the mathematics above, is used for time periods, so the set of time periods is the symbol 'T'. Next consider the set of sectors:

```
SETS
      J SECTORS
      /AGRI-MIN AGRICULTURE AND MINING
      HEAVYIND HEAVY INDUSTRY
      LIGHTIND LIGHT INDUSTRY
      SERVICES SERVICES/
      ALIAS(J,I);
```

The 'ALIAS(J,I)' is used to give the additional name 'I' to the set 'J'. This is particularly useful when we need to define and make reference to elements within a table. For example, notice that in the definition of input–output coefficients in the 'PARAMETERS' section we have an expression like:

```
TABLE A(I,J) INPUT-OUTPUT COEFFICIENTS
             AGRI-MIN   HEAVYIND   LIGHTIND   SERVICES
AGRI-MIN       .10        .09        .17        .01
HEAVYIND       .09        .33        .24        .12
LIGHTIND       .04        .02        .12        .05
SERVICES       .03        .09        .09        .08
```

Thus, a reference to any element in the table 'A' will be possible by specifying the appropriate combination of sectors.

The specification of the criterion function and of the inter-period equations such as the capital accumulation equation is similar to what we found in the Ramsey-type model in that the variable C and the time-varying parameter DIS appear with a lag, and the time index of the CAPITALAC equation appears with a lead. However, for the intra-period equations such as the capital addition equation CADDI, we find that the equation and the variables time index appear with a lag. For example, we have:

```
CRITERION.. XI =E= SUM(T, DIS(T-1)*SUM(J,ALPHA(J)*C(J,T-
1)**(PHI(J))));
CAPITALAC(J,T+1).. K(J,T+1) =E= K(J,T) + G(J,T);
...
CADDI(J,T-1).. G(J,T-1) =E= MU(J)*K(J,T-1)*(1-(1+(ETA*DELTA
(J,T-1))/(MU(J)*K(J,T-1)))**(-1/ETA));
```

Notice that all variables and equations were defined over the set T that goes from 1 to 5, unlike the case of our Ramsey-type model in which it started at zero. Thus, for a time horizon of 5 periods, GAMS will generate four inter-period equations with index {2, 3, 4, 5}, since an equation with an index equal to 6, that is, equal to the last element of T plus 1 will not be defined. Also GAMS will generate four intra-period equations with index {1, 2, 3, 4}, since an equation with index equal to zero, that is, the first element of T minus 1, will not be defined. Thus, GAMS will create a consistent specification of the model. The only difference with respect to a specification such as the one of our Ramsey-type model is that here GAMS will generate one less equation for each intra-period equation. That is, if we apply to the GAMS representation of the Ramsey-type model a specification similar to the one used in the GAMS representation of the Kendrick–Taylor model, a 'last equation' such as:

```
YD(2).. Y(2) = F{K(2)} ;
```

in our three-period Ramsey-type model will not exist. This has to be taken into account if we wish to assign terminal values for intra-period variables. In our Ramsey-type model an assignment to Y(2) will be innocuous, since there is no equation containing Y(2) in the model generated by GAMS.

Given the presence of non-linearities in the Kendrick and Taylor model, the GAMS solution method to choose is NLP (non-linear programming). For the representation of the model shown in the Appendix, GAMS will easily converge toward a solution, but that may not be the case for different specifications of the model or for different non-linear models. Several steps can be used to facilitate convergence, such as the provision of initial solution values for important variables; the setting of bounds to avoid undefined operations such as the division by zero or to keep the variables within sensible regions; the re-scaling of variable values; or the reformulation of the objective function so that most non-linearities are contained in it.[16]

The most interesting results from a model like the Kendrick–Taylor model are the investment inputs paths and the foreign debt path shown in Table 2.2, since they convey information on the sectoral allocation of investment and the required foreign financing.

Table 2.2 Results for the Kendrick–Taylor model

Period		**Investment**	**Inputs**		**Foreign Debt**
	Agri-Min	**Heavy ind.**	**Light ind.**	**Services**	
1	0.608	1.259	0.544	0.905	0.250
2	0.657	1.470	0.622	0.827	3.585
3	0.706	1.712	0.711	0.651	7.960
4	0.754	1.989	0.812	0.280	13.352
5					20.000

Of course, these results are based on the assumptions built into the model and on its particular parameterization. For example, concerning exports, in the original model they were assumed to be exogenously determined and growing at 8 per cent per year, and their values were generated with the following GAMS statements:

```
PARAMETER EXPTOT(T) TOTAL EXPORTS;
    EXPTOT('1') = 3.4;
LOOP(T,EXPTOT(T+1) = 1.08 * EXPTOT(T));
DISPLAY EXPTOT;
```

```
TABLE EXPPER(J,T) SECTORAL EXPORT PERCENTAGES
                 1       2       3       4       5
AGRI-MIN      0.20    0.20    0.20    0.20    0.20
HEAVYIND      0.10    0.10    0.10    0.10    0.10
LIGHTIND      0.30    0.30    0.30    0.30    0.30
SERVICES      0.40    0.40    0.40    0.40    0.40

PARAMETER E(J,T) SECTORAL EXPORTS;
E(J,T)=EXPPER(J,T)* EXPTOT(T);
DISPLAY E;
```

A simple way of introducing more flexibility in the determination of exports is to permit unlimited exports – at an implicit fixed world price – and to assume that their level is endogenously determined by the feasibility constraint (2.4). To do so, we only have to delete from the GAMS program the statements just shown above, add the variable E(J,T) to the list of variables, and impose on it a lower bound (e.g. E.LO(J,T) = 0.001).[17] Of course, a more sophisticated modeling of exports could also be implemented, including for example export functions in which exports are a function of foreign income, foreign and domestic prices, and the exchange rate.

Other improvements could be attempted, such as the introduction of commodities and factor prices that would allow, among other things, the analysis of income distribution effects; the introduction of technical change; or the introduction of economies of scale. With the proper conceptual basis, the sophistication of computational growth models along these lines is today feasible thanks to the substantial increase in computers' capacity and speed, the development of new solution methods, and the availability of specialized software such as GAMS.[18]

APPENDIX

```
*A DYNAMIC MULTISECTORAL NONLINEAR PLANNING MODEL
*
*REFERENCE: KENDRICK, DAVID A. AND LANCE J. TAYLOR
*(1969), 'A DYNAMIC NONLINEAR PLANNING MODEL FOR
*KOREA', CH. 8 IN I ADELMAN, PRACTICAL APPROACHES TO
*DEVELOPMENT PLANNING, THE JOHNS HOPKINS
*UNIVERSITY PRESS, BALTIMORE.
*AND
*KENDRICK, DAVID A. AND LANCE J. TAYLOR (1970),
*'NUMERICAL SOLUTION OF NONLINEAR PLANNING MODELS',
*ECONOMETRICA, VOL 38, NO.3, MAY, PP.453–467.
*
*THE GAMS VERSION WAS CREATED BY DAVID KENDRICK AND
*ANANTHA DURAIAPPAH, JULY 1988 AND MODIFIED BY
*LIHUI LIN, FEBRUARY 2000
*

SETS
J SECTORS
/AGRI-MIN AGRICULTURE AND MINING
HEAVYIND HEAVY INDUSTRY
LIGHTIND LIGHT INDUSTRY
SERVICES SERVICES/
ALIAS(J,I);

SETS
T TIME PERIODS/1*5/
TB(T) BASE PERIOD
TT(T) TERMINAL PERIOD;

TB(T)=YES $ (ORD(T) EQ 1);
TT(T)=YES $ (ORD(T) EQ CARD(T));
DISPLAY TB,TT;
* PARAMETERS

SCALAR Z DISCOUNT RATE/0.03/;

PARAMETER DIS(T) DISCOUNT FACTOR;
DIS(T)=(1+Z)**(-ORD(T));
DISPLAY DIS;
```

```
PARAMETER ALPHA(J) COEFFICIENT IN WELFARE FUNCTION
/AGRI-MIN  .48
HEAVYIND   .33
LIGHTIND   .345
SERVICES   .3925/

PARAMETER PHI(J) EXPONENTS IN THE WELFARE FUNCTION
/AGRI-MIN  .85
HEAVYIND   .90
LIGHTIND   .91
SERVICES   .87/

TABLE A(I,J) INPUT-OUTPUT COEFFICIENTS
              AGRI-MIN   HEAVYIND   LIGHTIND   SERVICES
AGRI-MIN         .10        .09        .17        .01
HEAVYIND         .09        .33        .24        .12
LIGHTIND         .04        .02        .12        .05
SERVICES         .03        .09        .09        .08

TABLE B(I,J) CAPITAL COEFFICIENTS
              AGRI-MIN   HEAVYIND   LIGHTIND   SERVICES
HEAVYIND        .6908     1.3109      .1769      .1500
LIGHTIND        .0010      .0199      .0022      .0000

TABLE PRODF(I,*) PRODUCTION FUNCTION PARAMETERS
         ELASTICITY  DISTRIBUT  TECHNICALP  EFFICIENCY  INILAB
AGRI-MIN    1.20        .35        .03          .41       5.10
HEAVYIND     .90        .30        .035        1.26       0.84
LIGHTIND     .90        .25        .025        1.89       0.36
SERVICES     .60        .20        .025         .47       2.30

PARAMETER
  SIGMA(J) ELASTICITY OF SUBSTITUTION
  RHO(J) RHO PARAMETER FOR ELAS OF SUBSTITUTION
  BETA(J) DISTRIBUTION PARAMETER IN CES PRODUCTION
  FUNCTION
  NU(J) TECHNICAL CHANGE PARAMETER IN CES PROD FUNC
  TAU(J) EFFICIENCY PARAMETER IN CES PROD FUNCTION;

SIGMA(J)=PRODF(J,'ELASTICITY');
RHO(J)=(1/SIGMA(J))-1;
BETA(J)=PRODF(J,'DISTRIBUT');
NU(J)=PRODF(J,'TECHNICALP');
TAU(J)=PRODF(J,'EFFICIENCY');
```

```
PARAMETER TECH(J,T) TECHNICAL CHANGE FACTOR;
TECH(J,T) = (1 + NU(J))**(ORD(T));
DISPLAY TECH;

PARAMETER LTOT(T) TOTAL LABOR FORCE;
LTOT('1') = SUM(J,PRODF(J,'INILAB'));
LOOP(T,LTOT(T + 1) = 1.02*LTOT(T));

PARAMETER MU(J) COEFFICIENT IN INVESTMENT FUNCTION
/AGRI-MIN  .275
HEAVYIND   .35
LIGHTIND   .30
SERVICES   .35/

SCALAR ETA COEFFICIENT IN INVESTMENT FUNCTION/0.5/;
TABLE KBAR(J,T) INITIAL AND TERMINAL CAPITAL STOCKS
              1     5
AGRI-MIN    2.02  3.55
HEAVYIND    2.13  5.00
LIGHTIND    1.26  2.55
SERVICES    1.27  2.575

PARAMETER GAMMABAR(T) INITIAL AND TERMINAL FOREIGN
DEBT
/1 .25
5 20.00/

PARAMETER EXPTOT(T) TOTAL EXPORTS;
EXPTOT('1') = 3.4;
LOOP(T,EXPTOT(T + 1) = 1.08 * EXPTOT(T));
DISPLAY EXPTOT;

TABLE EXPPER(J,T) SECTORAL EXPORT PERCENTAGES
              1     2     3     4     5
AGRI-MIN    0.20  0.20  0.20  0.20  0.20
HEAVYIND    0.10  0.10  0.10  0.10  0.10
LIGHTIND    0.30  0.30  0.30  0.30  0.30
SERVICES    0.40  0.40  0.40  0.40  0.40

PARAMETER E(J,T) SECTORAL EXPORTS;
E(J,T) = EXPPER(J,T)* EXPTOT(T);
DISPLAY E;

SCALAR THETA INTEREST RATE ON FOREIGN DEBT/.05/;
```

```
PARAMETERS D(J,J) PROPENSITY TO IMPORT FOR PROD
/AGRI-MIN.AGRI-MIN     .0008
HEAVYIND.HEAVYIND      .0900
LIGHTIND.LIGHTIND      .0300
SERVICES.SERVICES      .0040/

PARAMETERS PI(J) PROPENSITY TO IMPORT FOR INVEST
/AGRI-MIN     .63
HEAVYIND      .98
LIGHTIND      .10
SERVICES      .10/

PARAMETER IDEN(I,J) IDENTITY MATRIX
/AGRI-MIN.AGRI-MIN 1
HEAVYIND.HEAVYIND 1
LIGHTIND.LIGHTIND 1
SERVICES.SERVICES 1/

PARAMETER P(I,J) PRODUCTION COEF IN BALANCE EQ;
P(I,J) = IDEN(I,J) - A(I,J) + D(I,J);
DISPLAY P;

VARIABLES
C(J,T) CONSUMPTION
DELTA(J,T) INVESTMENT
G(J,T) CAPACITY ADDITIONS
GAMMA(T) FOREIGN DEBT
K(J,T) CAPITAL STOCKS
L(J,T) LABOR
M(J,T) IMPORTS
Q(J,T) PRODUCTION
XI CRITERION VALUE

EQUATIONS
CRITERION CRITERION FUNCTION
CAPITALAC(J,T) CAPITAL ACCUMULATION
DEBTALAC(T) FOREIGN DEBT ACCUM
INITCAP(J) INITIAL CAPITAL STOCKS
INITDEBT INITIAL FOREIGN DEBT
TERMCAP(J) TERMINAL CAPITAL STOCKS
TERMDEBT TERMINAL FOREIGN DEBT
CONSUMP(J,T) CONSUMPTION
LABOR(T) LABOR
```

```
PRODUCTION(J,T) PRODUCTION FUNCTIONS
CADDI(J,T) CAPACITY ADDITION
FIXIMPA(T) FIX AGRI-MIN IMPORTS
FIXIMPS(T) FIX SERVICES IMPORTS;

CRITERION.. XI = E = SUM(T, DIS(T - 1)*SUM(J,ALPHA(J)*C(J,T -
1)**(PHI(J))));
CAPITALAC(J,T + 1).. K(J,T + 1) = E = K(J,T) + G(J,T);
DEBTALAC(T + 1).. GAMMA(T + 1) = E = (1 + THETA)* GAMMA(T) +
SUM(J, D(J,J)*Q(J,T) - E(J,T) + PI(J)*DELTA(J,T) + M(J,T));
INITCAP(J).. K(J,'1') = E = KBAR(J,'1');
INITDEBT.. GAMMA('1') = L = GAMMABAR('1');
TERMCAP(J).. K(J,'5') = E = KBAR(J,'5');
TERMDEBT.. GAMMA('5') = L = GAMMABAR('5');

CONSUMP(I,T - 1).. C(I,T - 1) = E = SUM(J,P(I,J)*Q(J,T - 1)) -
SUM(J,B(I,J)*DELTA(J,T - 1)) - E(I,T - 1) + M(I,T - 1);
LABOR(T - 1).. LTOT(T - 1) = E = SUM(J,L(J,T - 1));
PRODUCTION(J,T - 1).. Q(J,T - 1) = E = TAU(J)*TECH(J,T -
1)*(BETA(J)*K(J,T - 1)**(- RHO(J)) + (1 - BETA(J))*L(J,T - 1)**(-
RHO(J)))**(- 1 / RHO(J));

CADDI(J,T - 1).. G(J,T - 1) = E = MU(J)*K(J,T - 1)*(1 - (1 + (ETA*DELTA(J,T
- 1))/(MU(J)*K(J,T - 1)))**(- 1/ETA));
FIXIMPA(T - 1).. M('AGRI - MIN',T - 1) = E = 0;
FIXIMPS(T - 1).. M('SERVICES',T - 1) = E = 0;

* LOWER BOUNDS ON VARIABLES
K.LO(J ,T) = 0.001;
L.LO(J,T - 1) = 0.01;
DELTA.LO(J,T - 1) = 0.001;
G.LO(J,T - 1) = 0.001;
C.LO(J,T - 1) = 0.01;
Q.LO(J,T - 1) = 0.01;
GAMMA.LO(T) = 0.00;
M.LO('HEAVYIND',T - 1) = 0.001;
M.LO('LIGHTIND',T - 1) = 0.001;

* COMPILER SETTINGS

OPTION INTEGER3 = 2;
OPTION REAL1 = 0.2;
OPTION REAL3 = 0.01;
OPTION INTEGER4 = 180;
```

```
OPTION BRATIO = 0;
OPTION LIMROW = 0;
OPTION LIMCOL = 0;
OPTION INTEGER5 = 0;
OPTION ITERLIM = 3000;

* MODEL STATEMENT
MODEL KENTAY / ALL /;

* SOLVE STATEMENT

SOLVE KENTAY USING NLP MAXIMIZING XI;

PARAMETER REPORT SOLUTION SUMMARY;

REPORT(T,'K-AGRIMIN') = K.L('AGRI-MIN',T);
REPORT(T,'K-HEAVYIND') = K.L('HEAVYIND',T);
REPORT(T,'K-LIGHTIND') = K.L('LIGHTIND',T);
REPORT(T,'K-SERVICES') = K.L('SERVICES',T);

REPORT(T,'C-AGRIMIN') = C.L('AGRI-MIN',T);
REPORT(T,'C-HEAVYIND') = C.L('HEAVYIND',T);
REPORT(T,'C-LIGHTIND') = C.L('LIGHTIND',T);
REPORT(T,'C-SERVICES') = C.L('SERVICES',T);
REPORT(T,'FORDEBT') = GAMMA.L(T);
```

NOTES

1. Many mathematical and computational models, earlier developed for growth models, are used today in a wide variety of dynamic macroeconomic models. For a 'state of the art' presentation of solution strategies and computational methods for dynamic macroeconomic models, see Amman *et al.* (1996), Hughes Hallett and McAdam (1999), Judd (1998) and Marimon and Scott (1999).
2. See Judd (1997).
3. For a detailed introduction to GAMS, see Brooke *et al.* (1998).
4. See for example Blanchard and Fischer (1989).
5. In the assignment of value to the discount parameter, the expression 'ord(t)' means the ordinal position in the set T at time t. Thus, at time '0' the ordinal of T will be '1', since zero is its first element; at time 1 the ordinal of T will be '2', since 1 is its second element, and so on.
6. When non-linearities are confined to the criterion function GAMS uses, by default, a reduced-gradient algorithm combined with a quasi-Newton algorithm. For general non-linear problems GAMS uses, by default, a projected Lagrangian algorithm. See Brooke *et al.* (1998).
7. The general GAMS rule is: 'A *reference* to a non-existent element causes the default value to be used, whereas an attempt to *assign* to a non-existent element results in no assignment being made'. See Brooke *et al.* (1998) for examples of this important rule.
8. For this purpose, GAMS provides an option, the 'OPTION LIMROW=..', which is useful to control the number of equations to be displayed in the output. It is convenient to set that option as equal to the number of periods of the solution horizon – in our model, and pay particular attention to the first few and last few equations there listed.
9. The equation listing shows which variables appear in each constraint, and the value of the individual coefficients and right-hand-side values once all the corresponding data manipulations are done. If the multiplier of a variable is between parentheses, then that term is non-linear. For non-linear equations such as YD and JD, the listing shows their corresponding linearization and thus the partial derivative of each variable evaluated at the initial point, which by default is zero unless it has assigned fixed values or lower bounds. For example, the partial derivative of YD w.r.t. the variable k is equal to $(-\beta k_t^{b-1})$. Evaluated at 'k(0)=0.1' it yields 1.3337, while when evaluated at 'k(1)=k(2) =0.001' it yields 4.2176. Finally, 'LHS' is equal to the value of the original equation at the initial point. To learn more about the interpretation of coefficients and LHS values reported in the equation listing, see Brooke *et al.* (1998).
10. For the implementation of these type of problems in GAMS, you are referred to Mercado *et al.* (1998).
11. For examples of more complex one-sector Ramsey-type models containing different kinds of constraints, see the GAMS program CHAKRA that was developed by David Kendrick and based on an earlier work by David Kendrick and Lance Taylor (Kendrick and Taylor, 1971). See also the program RAMSEY that was developed by Alan Manne. Both programs are in the GAMS model library, GAMSLIB.
12. For our simple model example, the corresponding Euler equation can be obtained using dynamic programming, and its expression is:

$$c_t^{-\tau} = \frac{1}{1+\rho} c_{t+1}^{-\tau} a k_{t+1}^{\beta-1}$$

The Euler equation and the dynamic constraint:

$$k_{t+1} = k_t^{\beta} - c_t$$

give us the equations of motion of the model. Solving for the steady-state (that is, setting $c_{t+1} = c_t$ and $k_{t+1} = k_t$) we obtain the steady-state value for the capital stock:

$$k_{ss} = \left(\frac{1+\rho}{\beta}\right)^{\frac{1}{\beta-1}} \cong 0.28$$

13. See Chiang (1992), pp. 126–9, and Kendrick and Taylor (1971).
14. A more detailed description of the model can be found in Kendrick (1990).
15. It can be downloaded from David Kendrick's home page at: http://www.eco.utexas.edu. The GAMS statement of the model does not intend to replicate exactly the original Kendrick and Taylor numerical results. For illustrative and numerical analysis purposes, the model was parameterized by Kendrick and Taylor using data corresponding to the Korean economy at the time of the development of the model.
16. See Brooke *et al.* (1998).
17. If we introduce this modification and run the program, we will see that the export performance becomes worse w.r.t the previous model, while production levels substantially increase in the heavy and light industrial sectors, decrease in the services sector and remain approximately the same in the agriculture and mining sector. The new model – or its parameterization – would seem to contain a bias toward production for domestic use, perhaps due to the fact that the target terminal conditions for the capital stock and the foreign debt remained unchanged.
18. For a more extended treatment of the possible sophistication of growth models, see Kendrick (1990).

REFERENCES

Amman, H., D. Kendrick and J. Rust (eds) (1996), *Handbook of Computational Economics*, Amsterdam: Elsevier.

Blanchard, O. and S. Fischer (1989), *Lectures in Macroeconomics*, Cambridge, MA: MIT Press.

Brooke, A., D. Kendrick, A. Meerhaus and R. Raman (1998), *GAMS: A User's Guide* (http://www.gams.com).

Chiang, A. (1992), *Elements of Dynamic Optimization*, New York: McGraw-Hill.

Hugues Hallett, A. and P. McAdam (eds) (1999), *Analyses in Macroeconomic Modelling*, Boston, Dordrecht and London: Kluwer Academic Publishers.

Judd, K. (1997), 'Computational Economics and Economic Theory: Substitutes or Complements?', *Journal of Economic Dynamics and Control*, **21**(6), pp. 907–42.

Judd, K. (1998), *Numerical Methods in Economics*, Cambridge, MA: MIT Press.

Kendrick, D. (1990), *Models for Analyzing Comparative Advantage*, Boston, Dordrecht and London: Kluwer Academic Publishers.

Kendrick, D. and L. Taylor (1969), 'A dynamic nonlinear planning model for Korea', Ch. 8, pp. 213–37 in I. Adelman (ed.), *Practical Approaches to Development Planning*, Baltimore, MD: Johns Hopkins University Press.

Kendrick D. and L. Taylor (1970), 'Numerical solution of nonlinear planning models', *Econometrica*, **38**(3), May, pp. 453–67.

Kendrick D. and L. Taylor (1971), 'Numerical methods and nonlinear optimizing models for economic planning', in H. Chenery (ed.), *Studies of Development Planning*, Cambridge, MA: Harvard University Press.

Marimon, R. and A. Scott (eds) (1999), *Computational Methods for the Study of Dynamic Economies*, Oxford and New York: Oxford University Press.

Mercado, P.R., D. Kendrick and H. Amman (1998), 'Teaching macroeconomics with GAMS', *Computational Economics*, **12**(2), pp. 125–49.

3. An essay on late structuralism

Bill Gibson*

1 INTRODUCTION

In this chapter I examine the scope and method of the structuralist school in an attempt to identify precisely how it differs from the neoclassical system, in both its mode of analysis and its criteria for validity. There are four conclusions reached: first, the work of Taylor and his followers can be seen as a coherent outgrowth of not only Latin American structuralism, as is often observed (Jameson, 1986), but also the European or early structuralism of Levi-Strauss (2000), Godelier and Piaget (Godelier, 1972), and Piaget (1971). The early work, both Latin American and European, focused on rigidities and frictions in local economies (Chenery, 1975) while in the *late* structuralism of Taylor and his followers, theory not only must account for the 'macrofoundations' of behavior, but also global foundations, that is the constraints the evolution of the global system itself imposes on the players. Third, late structuralism is often criticized as *ad hoc* theory because it is not grounded in optimization models (Agénor and Montiel, 1996). I argue that the *ad hocery* of structuralism is not an accident but a logical consequence of what it defines as its theoretical object and what it considers valid methods by which the theory is codified. The fourth and perhaps most contentious proposition of this chapter is the claim that the nature of structuralist theory naturally leads to numerical simulation modeling as its principal empirical tool. This will not be entirely surprising to some since the simulation approach has gained significant ground in many areas of science in the last decades. Others attack simulation models from the perspective of standard hypothesis testing, upon which the validity of the neoclassical theory is traditionally based. Here it is argued that the structuralist method entails its own internally consistent criterion of validity based on the *scope* as well as the realism of the model.

The chapter is organized as follows: the next section traces the lineage of the structuralist methodology from its earliest roots in the themes of *wholeness, transformation and self-regulation*. Section 3 identifies the main differences in the structuralist approach according to criteria of validity, comparing the role of econometrics in neoclassical theory to realism in structuralist theory. The use of simulation models is then justified in terms of the classical themes. The final section summarizes the conclusions.

2 NEOCLASSICISM AND STRUCTURALISM

At its core the argument of this chapter is simply that *realism* plays a more fundamental role, both in the historical evolution of structuralism and its current mode of validation than in the neoclassical system. Initially the orthodoxy embraced perfect competition in a way that was immediately and permanently rejected by the structuralist school as a fundamental building block of the analysis. But recent neoclassicism is in flux and has shown considerable flexibility and lack of dogmatic attachment to the simple and unrealistic assumptions of its past.[1] Game-theoretic experimental evidence is shaking the foundations of the rational model suggesting that individuals value *fairness* and are often more generous than self-interested models would predict (Henrich *et al.*, 2001). Dutt and Jameson (1992) make the case for some *convergence* of the neoclassical school and structuralism, motivated in part by the blatant lack of realism of the former. There are examples from new trade and growth theory to new-Keynesian orthodoxy that show that neoclassicals can aptly handle imperfect competition and other 'distortions' in their models. Stiglitz goes furthest in rendering a *new neoclassicism* more palatable to non-neoclassicals than the old (Stiglitz, 1988). Taylor himself notes in a recent essay that modern neoclassicism is little more than an effort to co-opt structuralists' correct observations on how the economy works (Taylor, 1992). This usually takes the form of finding a 'first principles' argument that allows the analyst to incorporate the observed behavior in an intertemporal utility maximizing model.

The convergence noted by Dutt is nonetheless one-sided. Structuralists have not, nor, it seems, ever will embrace neoclassical 'first principles' as a way of raising the truth content of their approach. While neoclassicals may ultimately come around to a version of structuralism, it will be a slow and circuitous journey. Even at the end, structuralists and neoclassicals may well differ on what constitutes a valid argument. We shall return to the issue of 'validity' below, but flag here an absence of a dogmatic attachment to *any* theoretical device in structuralism. Rather the approach focuses on the *real*, in both its assumptions and results of its models to the exclusion of privileged theoretical constructs. In my view, this explains structuralists', and indeed Lance Taylor's, early attachment to simulation modeling as opposed to econometrics (Taylor, 1975). This break suggests a research program for the coming decades that will follow the lead of other sciences in which simulation modeling has become an essential tool.

This is a bold claim, of course, and must be established. The argument presented here will unfold in two directions: first, we seek to locate economic structuralism in a broader tradition of structuralist writing in the twentieth century, a tradition that systematically rejected the reductionist, atomistic approach to social theory. Second, the 'early structuralists' validated their work in concrete history and there is a 'thematic unity', to use an early structuralist term (Foucault, 1972), with late structuralism's appeal to global economy-wide simulation models, on one hand, and a deep skepticism about traditional econometric claims for the validity of rational-model based theory on the other.

2.1 Early Structuralism

Structuralism in economics has a distinguished history. In the 1940s and 1950s, it became obvious to the early structuralists, Lewis (1954), Prebisch (1959, 1960), Singer (1950), Nurske (1956), Noyola, and Myrdal (1957), that the nature of the problems facing small, low-income countries were fundamentally different from those of the larger, industrialized countries. As director of ECLA, Raoul Prebisch elaborated the Latin American structuralist approach: the initial condition in the world economy, as seen from the Southern Cone, was that Europe and the US were already industrialized. Trade along the traditional lines of comparative advantage offered little hope for industrialization while the developed economies would block any effort to gain a foothold in the market for manufactured goods. The developing countries were hamstrung by the structure of the world economy (Love, 1980).

The working hypothesis was that the forces that made some countries rich and other countries poor were interlinked and the point was to identify the specific mechanisms at work. Increasing returns to scale in the capital and wage goods sectors of the advanced countries was a key idea. The implications were several: first, the developing economies would not be able to compete even on the basis of low wages in the majority of markets in the world. Second, in the markets in which they could compete, trade barriers would be erected by the advanced countries to protect the jobs of their political constituencies. Third, in the markets that were residually available, the output of developing countries would largely depend on use of *imported* capital equipment. These three structural features acted in concert to slow the industrialization of the Third World in the immediate post-war period (Lewis, 1954; Prebisch, 1959). Initially there was no formal modeling, but eventually dual economy and two-gap models appeared as the formal recognition of different internal structures in the center and periphery.

These observations on the structure of the world economy lay in stark contrast to the neoclassical approach which was based on an extrapolation of the mechanics of perfectly competitive markets in general economic equilibrium, as noted. For orthodox economists, why the advanced countries were rich and the developing economies were poor depended only upon the amount of capital per unit of labor and subsequent labor productivity. Both could increase their income *per capita* by the same means, and relatively independently. The world as a whole would be better off with free trade with both poles pursuing their own comparative advantage.

Even then the realism of the structuralist approach was compelling to many and certainly not all neoclassicals rejected the structuralists' position. In particular, Lance Taylor's Ph.D. advisor, Hollis Chenery, embraced the theory as an alternative to the new-left Marxism of the 1970s. The impact was limited, however, and in orthodox economics, 'structure' came to mean simply 'localized rigidity'. Chenery, writing in the *American Economic Review* in 1975, observed that

> The structuralist approach attempts to identify specific rigidities, lags and other characteristics of the structure of developing economies that affect economic adjustments and the choice of development policy. A common theme in most of this work is the failure of the equilibrating mechanism of the price system to produce steady growth or a desirable distribution of income.

2.2 Links to the Past

Chenery and other structuralist economists at the time made no reference to the structuralist tradition in other fields that pre-existed economics such as Levi-Strauss[2] and Godelier (1972) in anthropology and sociology, Piaget (1971) in psychology and Foucault in philosophy (1972). But it is possible to see structuralist economics, as it emerged in the 1940s, as an outgrowth or extension of earlier work in these and other fields. Jameson suggests the same connection, citing Prebisch who identified the 'deep structure' of the world economy as divided into center and periphery as evidence of the similarity of approaches, but does not develop the argument in any detail (Love, 1980; Jameson, 1986).

European or classical structuralists often spoke of structuralism as defined in opposition to *other* theory, antithetically, by what it is not. In particular, classical structuralists de-emphasized human agency in their critique of existing social theory. 'And in current philosophical discussions,' wrote Piaget (1971) in 1968, 'we find structuralism tackling historicism, functionalism and sometimes even all theories that have recourse to the human subject.' Early structuralism sought truth through detailed empirical work. Levi-Strauss focused on interpretations of myth through the shared structure of language and drew his conclusions from a massive amount of ethnological materials collected by field-workers worldwide (Levi-Strauss, 2000). For insights into the nature of social systems, classical structuralists looked to mathematics such as the Erlanger program of Felix Klein and the N. Bourbaki who used the concept of groups to establish a constructivist approach to foundational mathematics. Structures were not simply enunciated or asserted but rather they had to be constructed. Althusser spoke of the 'production' of knowledge as if it were a function; in effect, a production function with thought as its output and previous thought as the inputs (Althusser, 1971).

Certainly these features are shared in the project of the Latin American and late structuralist school. For Prebisch, the dialectic with neoclassicism was an important and productive force and he came to see the developing world as the inverse image of the developed. Modern structuralists are also comfortable with copious historical detail and, obviously, a mathematical/statistical representation of it. Dutt notes that structuralists begin with 'stylized facts' embedded into a coherent system of national accounting identities (Dutt and Jameson, 1992). In practice, Taylor and his followers rely heavily on the knowledge and expertise of in-country economists as they gather the details of the structure under study. Little attempt is made to generalize the data to a one-size-fits-all model, an often derided approach typical of the multilateral institutions and embedded in the neoclassical theory of the ubiquitous rational agent. Moreover, most, although not all, structuralist theory is rendered in mathematics.[3] Here are two important points to make: first there is little mathematics for mathematics sake. Not that structuralists are immune to the argument about the 'beauty' of mathematical results; it is rather that aesthetics play an insignificant role in the design of necessarily messy theory. Second, since the object of late structuralist discourse is the numerically rendered historical record, some mathematization is required for validation.

From classical structuralism, the modern idiom draws its emphasis on the constraints shaping human choice rather than the choice itself. Jameson (1986) notes several elements of classical structuralism identified by philosophers of science, Keat and Urry (1975), that have reappeared in the modern vernacular.[4] First, interrelated elements are analysed as a whole rather than separately. Second, structures are essential, and often 'deep' rather than surface phenomena. Third, structures change over time.[5] But the classical structuralists were themselves highly self-conscious and wrote of their method from the perspective of their own practice. Piaget, for example, summarizes the major themes of classical structuralism elegantly as *wholeness*, *transformation* and *self-regulation*.

2.2.1 Wholeness

Wholeness relates to the scope of investigation. Structuralists typically ask a broad set of questions about social and political institutions and their dynamics (Lustig, 1992). Feedback effects play an essential role and cannot be ignored. While it is not inconceivable that 'sub-structures' exist, wholeness precludes an analysis of economic phenomena in isolation. Prebisch and the early Latin American structuralists, as Jameson notes, departed from a view of the world as an 'organized set of interrelated elements' the center and periphery (Jameson, 1986). For modern structuralism, *wholeness* is most fully expressed in the analysis of the world systems, center and periphery together, interlocked in a way that renders microeconomic analysis of agents anywhere on the globe entirely secondary. Formally, wholeness came to life in North–South models, pioneered by Taylor (1983), Dutt (1990b), Chichilnisky and Heal (1986), and others. North–South models, unknown to the early structuralists, now specify in a consistent and convincing way the mechanisms by which growth and distribution in one pole of the system affect the other.[6]

Thus, wholeness implies that macroeconomic partial equilibrium arguments are largely absent from structuralism (Jameson, 1986). Most of structuralism's results are obtained from either Keynesian one-sector macromodels, two-sector variants of aggregate models or disaggregated multisectoral computable general equilibrium models. In the immediate short term, demand determines savings (Taylor, 1990). The level of savings, once determined, has feedback only in the next period inasmuch as it, together with capital gains, determines the rate of change of net financial assets. Structuralist models are often criticized as entirely demand-driven; but since net investment accumulates in the form of capital stocks which in turn determine the level of the next period's capacity, technological change, productivity, and other supply-side issues are obviously involved. The point is rather that demand must be balanced to the growth of capacity or the economy will react adversely. Structuralist simulation models focus on capacity utilization as the key measure of the economy-wide balance of forces.

In many if not most of Lance Taylor's models, the financial sector plays a key role. Unlike the neoclassical school, the economy cannot be dichotomized into real and financial magnitudes. Financial shocks in the form of large capital inflows may influence the nominal value of the exchange rate, but it is unlikely that any one player, such as the central bank, will be sufficiently strong to control the real exchange rate. Agents in structuralist models generally control only nominal variables, and only imprecisely; real magnitudes depend on the overall general equilibrium of the system. Inflation may be caused by inordinate growth in the money supply, but that would be an exception rather than the rule. In most developing economies, money is 'endogenous, adjusting to the level of activity and rate of inflation' (Taylor, 1990). Inflation often has roots in conflicting claims or inappropriate indexation or some other localized characteristic of the economy.

Wholeness is ecumenical in structuralist analysis. No behavior is taken as 'given'; there are no privileged, that is, intentionally uninvestigated parts of the social and economic structure. Prices may efficiently allocate scarce resources under some conditions, but price signals may be burdened by the noise of institutional factors or other inherent characteristics of the system. Indeed, signal and noise are often confused and prices can be 'wrong' with little negative impact, and sometimes a positive impact on growth. Queues and rationing can develop for scarce goods or foreign exchange, and capital controls have a positive impact on growth as in South Korea and Chile (Amsden, 2002). Binding constraints are often built into structuralist models in virtual celebration of the *ad hoc*. Above all there are no givens about the role of the public sector; it can be productive or not, depending on circumstances. The relationship between private and public investment, for example, might have both 'crowding in' of private by public sector infrastructure as well as crowding out through the normal interest rate mechanism.

The characteristic of wholeness or completeness identified by Piaget and many others, as fundamental to structuralism, leads to significant differences in how the theories are applied. In neoclassical computable general equilibrium models, agents with the same level of income and wealth behave typically, that is, they save and consume identically. Strictly speaking this implies that the agents share a common preference ordering, but more often any differences which may well exist in the real economy are simply ignored. Lance Taylor, as well as other late structuralists, constructs models that often contain a wide range of social classes that differ in their behavior, even when controlling for wealth and income (Gibson *et al.*, 1986; Taylor, 1990). There is no assumption that economic agents are uniform, small or necessarily price-takers. Some may have swift and powerful reaction functions, while others react with a significant lag or not at all. This range of players must be identified by careful analysis of the existing conditions in the country in question.

At a more basic methodological level there is no attempt in structuralism to maximize the information extracted from a carefully chosen minimum set of parameters. The neoclassical general equilibrium model can be interpreted in this way, and in this regard it is unquestionably one of the major intellectual achievements of the past century. From a minimal parameter set which includes only tastes, technology and initial endowments, early neoclassicals were able to deduce the allocative path of a perfectly competitive economy. In a second wave, the program was extended to include imperfect competition and other distortions, but not with fully rigorous and commonly accepted microfoundations (Rizvi, 1994). But less and less could be said about any specific economy to the point that in 1993 Bliss could observe that 'the near emptiness of general equilibrium theory is a theorem of the theory' (Rizvi, 1998). In his review of the reaction to arbitrariness of the aggregate excess demand function established in the 1970s by Sonnenschein, Mantel and Debreu, Rizvi notes that the absence of microfounded macroeconomics is now widely accepted in the profession. Macroeconomics is increasingly an abandoned field within the orthodoxy as the questions addressed sink into an abyss of partiality and utter lack of wholeness. This is in part due to the nature of the goals which neoclassism set for itself.

Within structuralism, early or late, wholeness precludes the 'max–min' intellectual project as an objective of the theoretical enterprise. Instead, as seen above, structuralists strive to account for a complete audit of the social setting. Historically-specific parameters, temporary constraints and other idiosyncratic features of a given economy are welcomed in structuralist analysis, enhancing rather than detracting from its theoretical prestige. In this, structuralism runs skew to the project of the neoclassicals and in this regard it is difficult even to contemplate any sort of convergence as suggested by Dutt.

2.2.2 Transformation

The early structuralists were sensitive to the criticism that once erected, structures would ossify and have no way of changing over time. Theoretical constructs had to allow for change and thus were necessarily dynamic; *transformation* was embraced by the classical structuralists as fundamental to the program. Transformation is related to the third pillar of structuralist methodology, self-regulation, but it is not the same. To illustrate the difference, consider perhaps the simplest structuralist model, a Markov chain (Berman and Plemmons, 1979). Here the state of the system at any time X_t depends on a transformational matrix M such that:

$$X_t = MX_{t-1}$$

where X_{t-1} is the immediately previous state. The matrix of transitional probabilities, M, generates the change. From a structuralist perspective, this model is inadequate in that matrix M is not time-dependent and second, it is a matrix, but at least it can potentially account for wholeness in a way that a one-dimensional growth model could not.

Markov processes generate steady states if X is an eigenvector of M and thus the transformational system becomes non-transformational. This raises an important problem since it might be argued that modern dynamic models that refer to long-run steady states are also problematic from a structuralist perspective. They ultimately become static in nature and therefore immune to change; the history that these theoretical structures generate, in principle, stops.

It is certainly true that many intelligent and useful dynamic models, which do converge to a steady state, have been elaborated by late structuralists, including Taylor himself. But if, as argued in more detail below, the replication of the numerically rendered historical record is the ultimate test of validity of the structuralists' endeavor, dynamic models that converge to a long-run steady state are ultimately inadequate to the structuralist project.

As one example, consider a simulation model of any real macroeconomy. In practice, there must exist, at a minimum, three distinct forms of capital stock, firm, household and government. Despite the elaborate theories of arbitrage offered by the neoclassicals, there is usually no observable mechanism to bring about an equality of growth rates of these three heterogeneous magnitudes. Indeed, it is even far fetched to argue that a steady state could exist in a two-sector model with heterogenous capital, say industry and agriculture. But it is less plausible still to argue that the housing stock, roads, as well as the capital stock in these two branches of production must all grow at the same rate. Hence, steady-state analysis is irrelevant for the vast majority of, dare we say all, functioning, empirical economies.

Fortunately this is of little practical consequence since steady-state models have found little or no outlet in *applied* structuralist work. While most structuralist models are indeed dynamic, they are typically made up for the medium run, 3–10 years and may or may not converge to a steady state. Note that transformation is implicitly interrelated to the issue of *wholeness*. Longer horizons are likely to run into an inherent contradiction inasmuch as major institutions can and do change and would then be excluded by a supposedly dynamic structuralist analysis. Wholeness with respect to scope is considered in more detail below.

The deeper methodological issue is that if the steady state is not practically relevant, then it follows that long-run stability cannot be part of the *validation* of the theory within the structuralist idiom. This is not true for neoclassicism; explicitly unstable neoclassical models are virtually unheard of and are usually discarded as defective once the instability is discovered. From the structuralist perspective, however, instability can be interesting if there is an evident correspondence to the empirical conditions of the economy under study. As an example, consider speculative runs on currencies defended by central banks. These are often inherently unstable processes. But this does not mean that they are unworthy of serious theoretical consideration. Instability in the structuralist model simply means that some of the 'givens', that is, the structural or institutional parameters of the problem, must undergo change. Financial instability in Mexico in the 1980s ended with the nationalization of the banking system, and Taylor's more recent work has focused on how institutions changed in more or less profound ways as a result of financial crises brought on by globalization.[7]

2.2.3 Self-regulation

In classical structuralism, self-regulation refers to the internal rules of the logical system and how those rules can be used to extend the scope of analysis. In mathematics any *group* is a self-regulating system as is statistical mechanics, or indeed any cybernetic or informational system in which learning takes time. Self-regulating systems incorporate feedback mechanisms in which accumulated values of *state* variables affect current-period *jump* or within-period equilibrium variables. In this regard, the Markov process described above is transformational but ultimately not self-regulating.

As noted, self-regulation was thought to be essential to the classical structuralist program and here late structuralism does not stray from its roots; much of the work of Taylor and his followers concerns self-regulating systems (Taylor, 1983, 1990, 1991). Moreover, static models have only been important as special or transitionary cases, when the real object of interest is a dynamic process. This is in clear contrast to the orthodoxy in which many of the most celebrated theorems are obtainable in static models.

Self-regulation means that there is no *external* force that causes the system to follow a determinate path. Transversality conditions, intertemporal arbitrage or other mechanisms that stand outside the theoretical system are not permissible. To return to the example of the three capital stocks discussed above, if no mechanism for bringing their rates of return into equality can be identified as functioning within the structure of the economy under study, it would not be consistent with the notion of self-regulation to include an equilibrium condition as *deus ex machina*.

For structuralists, self-regulation does not necessarily imply predictability. Take for an example the logistic equation used in population dynamics as well as many other contexts:

$$\frac{dx}{dt} = rx(1 - x/K)$$

where x is the population, t is time, r is the base rate of growth and K is the 'carrying capacity.' In *continuous* time, this differential equation describes a stable path to a steady state with $x = K$ (Clark, 1976). In *discrete* time, however, the analogous difference equation is a simple example of a basic non-linear dynamical system with many of the complexities of higher order systems (Devaney, 1989). The structure is self-regulating but at the same time *chaotic* and unpredictable depending on the underlying nature of the problem.

This is perhaps the simplest and clearest example of a structuralist analysis, a whole, transformational and self-regulating system. The data and in this case even the choice of the units of time can not only make a difference but are indeed capable of fundamentally changing the conclusions of the analysis. While many chaotic neoclassical models exist, few neoclassical models are designed to include critical dependence on the data describing the structure of the economy. Chaotic neoclassical models seek rather to identify regularities, *despite* the possibility of chaos.

In many applied structuralist models, the central variable which conveys self-regulation is capacity utilization. As noted above, it simultaneously registers both demand- and supply-side effects and many of the adjustment processes in the goods and labor markets are keyed to the rate of capacity utilization. Investment is most often related to the accelerator, as is the rate of growth of nominal wages and labor productivity.

2.2.4 Critique

The content of this three-part definition of the methodology of classical structuralism, *wholeness, transformation and self-regulation*, amounts to the following: meaningful economic theory which aims to provide policy advice cannot be based on human behavior alone, especially behavior wrapped in flimsy or non-existent conceptions of time and change. While human agency is not ignored in a structuralist account, the temporal evolution of the social arenas which constrain human behavior is of greater importance. Late structuralist models, as elaborated by Taylor and others, are comprehensive, including real and financial sides, dynamic but not necessarily end-driven, sensitive to initial conditions and responsive to the underlying character of the data to which the model is calibrated. Still they have provoked a good deal of criticism. Agénor and Montiel note that the structuralist models may be 'sensitive to arbitrary assumptions about private sector behavior' (1996). They also note that the Lucas critique, that decision rules should be policy-invariant, is applicable as well as the lack of any explicit welfare accounting (Lucas, 1976). Finally, structuralist models tend to ignore 'transversality' conditions and can lead to conflicts with intertemporal optimization.

The first criticism is by far the most important and leads to the core of the distinction between structuralist and neoclassicals. Assumptions that do not follow the rules of strict optimization are not necessarily arbitrary; they may be historically observed patterns of behavior and if so would take precedence, in the structuralist mode, over rules that were derived from optimizing behavior but that were not grounded in the historical record. Take, for example, mark-up pricing. If there is evidence of regularities in mark-ups available from data or case studies, structuralists will place more faith in these data than the claim that agents 'should' behave otherwise. Structuralists are even more skeptical of extending the rational model to political economy and policymaking: how are rational central bankers supposed to behave, or government officials in charge of important and highly visible national-level investment projects? In trying to describe public officials as rational utility maximizing agents, neoclassicals run the risk of drifting ever farther from a realistic account of the historical process. There is some validity to the first critique of Agénor and Montiel; arbitrary assumptions can do substantial damage to models, and structuralist models are certainly not immune to mistakes, especially when key behavioral parameters must be 'guesstimated'. The method is inherently dependent on the quality of the historical record. But as the record improves, it will strengthen the structuralist position and weaken the neoclassicals.

The Lucas critique falls on deaf structuralist ears. In my structuralist models of the Nicaraguan economy during the Sandinista period, policy was driven by the external shock of the war. Agents in that country were utterly unable to neutralize government policy (Nicaraguan or US) and certainly the Lucas critique was entirely irrelevant to the modeling of that process (Gibson, 1985, 1994). Similarly, the 'Tequila Crisis' of the mid-1990s in Mexico is not easily explained within the confines of the rational model. It is very difficult, in light of only the smallest shreds of evidence that the critique is relevant, for structuralists to accept far fetched reasoning based on unbounded rationality. Ricardian equivalence is perhaps the most extreme example of how, in the view of structuralists, the methodological orientation of neoclassicism leads that framework far off track. There have been few other propositions that have attracted so much theoretical attention while at the same time were so completely lacking in empirical content. This statement could perhaps be challenged by followers of contemporary general equilibrium theory as the quotation of Bliss above suggests, but Ricardian equivalence stands apart inasmuch as it is a theorem about *tax* policy.

The limits of the rational framework apply even more strongly to dynamic optimizing models. The 'transversality' conditions ask to what extent the end state of a dynamic process should condition the path leading to that end state. With structuralists' objections to equilibrium steady-state models, the response to this criticism is already clear: is there any empirical or real world relevance to the absence of transversality conditions in practical models? More generally, structuralists ask: will policymakers be more likely to believe and therefore use models which are consistent with neoclassical first principles or models which have the 'look and feel' of the local economy?

2.2.5 Summing up

Stephen J. Gould notes that had Galileo been a biologist, he would have spent his time at the Leaning Tower categorizing objects according to shape and size, noting that each fell to earth with a unique acceleration (Gould, 1998). But while structuralists are not overt 'lumpers' in the sense of biological taxonomy, neither are they 'splitters'; structuralism is not historicism in that theory has a significant role to play. The structuralist approach is distinguished from the neoclassical in that there is no quest for a 'unified field theory', some general principle that unites the approach. In 'wholeness' structuralists argue that not all problems facing developing economies are facets of one central deficiency, such as lack of savings, distorted markets, or what have you; rather there is an explicit willingness to accept the individuality of each experience. This is a weakness from the neoclassical point of view but a strength from that of the structuralist.

To sum up what this section has achieved and what it has not, I believe it is fair to say that while there is no traceable lineage of citation or direct influence between the early economic structuralists, Prebisch *et al.*, and the classical tradition, there is significant 'thematic unity' of the discursive structures. The same can be said of late structuralists, Taylor and his associates, who by and large have been uninterested in meta-issues of method, especially how ideas might or might not have applied in other disciplines. But whether self-aware or not, it still seems to be true that late structuralism is guided by concerns shared with the classics. When wholeness, transformation and self-regulation are viewed not as three separate criteria that might appear on a checklist, but rather as three aspects of a discursive event, they enjoy some predictive power over which themes tend to recur in structuralism and which do not.

3 VALIDITY

> *The Fundamental Theorem of Econometrics*: There exists a transformation, possibly non-linear, such that any data set can be shown to support any hypothesis. (Conventional Wisdom.)

3.1 Meaningless Regressions

Lance Taylor recently objected to the spate of regression analysis done by the World Bank on the mushrooming data set that has resulted from numerous household surveys financed by the Bank around the world. He claimed that they were 'meaningless regressions.' At face value, this charge may be difficult to understand; on the other hand, structuralists have always had an uneasy relationship with econometrics. In particular, structuralists have not relied on econometrics to validate their theoretical claims about the way the world works. This section of the chapter addresses some of the reasons why.

Arguably, econometrics analyses the real history, that is, the data of actual experience. Because experience, history and the statistical record are held in high regard by structuralists, there would seem to exist a natural affinity to econometrics. But respecting data is not the same as respecting econometric models based on the data. Taylor's comment reported above suggests that structuralists continue to be suspicious of econometric results and Taylor himself argues that the skepticism rises with the degree of sophistication of the technique, as captured in the anonymous quotation at the beginning of this section.

The main reasons are as follows. The first is prosaic: classical statistical theory imposes stringent requirements on data which are not often met in the statistically unclean environment of developing countries. When drawing a sample from an urn of colored balls, one can be confident that all balls of the same color are the same. In a dynamic economy, there is no analogy to the urn of colored balls, especially in time series. If the point of economic development itself is to systematically change the structure of the economy, then the assumption of structural stability required by the classical statistical model is hardly warranted.

Structuralists are also apt to identify a second class of 'meaningless' regressions. These arise when analysts attempt to explain complex economic phenomena using models with one, two or very few variables, in so-called 'reduced forms.' Structuralists hold that the world is a complex place and that there are few single-equation models of much usefulness. Linear combinations of poorly measured or qualitative variables are quite capable of producing spurious correlation with well measured variables on which the former are often indirectly based.[8]

But even if independent variables are properly constructed, structuralists are unlikely to accept simple reduced-form models as convincing evidence of much of anything. They would argue instead that the movers of any given variable are several and may well vary in any direction of influence. Apart from accounting regularities, there is no one variable in economics that determines any other one variable on its own. The theory embedded in the reduced form must be subject to independent verification.

One example is 'crowding in' versus 'crowding out' in the investment function. Whether the impact of government spending on private sector investment is on balance positive or negative depends on the relative strengths of these two forces. The net effect, most usually, must be determined empirically by assessing the relative strengths under the current or appropriate circumstances. Often little can or should be said *a priori*. Structuralists would argue that elevating either, crowding in or crowding out, to the exclusion of the other is wrong even though it is often done.

A second example of misleading, monochromatic modeling is provided by econometric estimates of the accelerator, α. Take, for example, the equation

$$I/K = \beta + \alpha u$$

where I is investment, K is capital stock and u is capacity utilization. For purposes of illustration, let us say that a fictitious estimation procedure produces the following results (t-stats in parentheses).

$$\beta = 10\ (2.2)$$
$$\alpha = 1.6\ (3.5)$$

Thus, with α and β estimated econometrically, we have a calibrated investment function. Now, insert this calibrated equation into a simple Keynesian model:

$$Y = C + I$$
$$C = \bar{c} + cY$$
$$u = Y/Q$$

where Q is capacity income. If autonomous consumption, $\bar{c}$, can be calibrated to a SAM and we have some econometric evidence on the marginal propensity to consume, c, we have a fully specified macromodel. Assume a Keynesian adjustment mechanism:

$$\frac{dY}{dt} = \theta \dot{Y} = \theta\left(\bar{c} + cY + \beta K + \alpha Y \frac{K}{Q} - Y\right)$$

in which output grows if expenditure is greater than income. The adjustment parameter is $\theta > 0$. Capital stock, K and capacity output, Q are given in the short run. Stability of this simple system requires that:

$$d\dot{Y}/dY < 0$$

that is:

$$c + \alpha K/Q - 1 < 0$$

If K/Q is in the range of 2 to 3, and α is estimated at 1.6, it becomes obvious that the marginal propensity to consume must be negative for stability. Because the regression is oversimplified it has become 'meaningless' and certainly not usable outside the context in which it was run. An α borrowed from such a study would cause a model into which it is transplanted to become immediately explosive. This critique of econometrics can be seen as an extension of the concern with *wholeness*. By embedding the theory in a reduced form, the theory itself becomes immune to scrutiny. The validation of theory by econometric tests is then piecemeal and haphazard. There is no comprehensive assessment of all aspects of the model.

But while econometrics is not always trusted, neither can the results be entirely ignored. Still, there are major differences between the way in which structuralists view econometric results and the role they play in neoclassicism. The orthodox model takes rational agency as an *a priori* given and then looks to econometrics for evidence that might falsify that assumption. If the evidence is not found or proves to be controversial, the core assumptions are not effectively challenged, and are retained. Structuralism, however, has few core propositions, and thus it follows that falsification cannot play an important role in the validation processes. Verification, on the other hand, is not logically possible according to the principles of classical statistics and hence, econometrics tends to play a marginal role in the validation of the structuralist enterprise.

If econometrics is not the principal means by which structuralist theory is validated, what might it be? Certainly a range of methods from historical narrative to formal hypothesis testing to numerical simulation have been employed in the past. In the following section we take up the last of these and argue that simulation modeling is uniquely qualified to validate the structuralists' program. It is a method based on verification rather than falsification and, as will be seen below in more detail, provides ways of trapping internal inconsistencies in models that are whole, transformative and self-regulating.

3.2 The Duck Test

> If it looks like a duck, it walks like a duck and quacks like a duck, then we say it is a duck. (Conventional Wisdom.)

As suggested above, it is most likely wrong to think that neoclassical theory is *validated* by econometric models. The ascendancy of game theory, optimal control and stochastic optimization in neoclassical theory in recent decades strongly suggests that other, even less defensible, criteria are in use. To an increasing extent, a result is validated in the neoclassical framework if it is associated with an underlying optimization model.[9] The model is linked to the result and strengthens the result by throwing the additional weight of the optimization model behind it.

Structuralists would argue, however, that an optimization framework cannot increase the exposure of the theoretical framework to independent empirical verification.[10] Adding a utility maximizing model to a general theoretical framework in the neoclassical view does not increase the probability that the entire edifice is *wrong*. The procedure only increases the veracity of theory and only by definition. It is tautologically true that since the rational model is taken to be true *a priori*, the aggregate truth value of the theory is only strengthened, never diminished. In the structuralist mode, it is useless to add unfalsifiable components to the theoretical system. The key point is this: the value of the structuralist theoretical framework can only increase with additional exposure to the historical record. Falsifiability must increase in order for any new components of the theory to be valid. Better theory, for structuralists, is more complete theory in the sense that it has more opportunities to be wrong.[11]

In the neoclassical venue, it is rare that the properties of the underlying optimization model feed back on or affect the overall properties of the model, since it is usually possible to find a maximization model that is compatible with a desired result. The addition of an optimizing model never compromises the overall characteristics of the system and indeed the point is often to find a preference ordering that does not. This problem is not impossible. Debreu has noted that to every allocation in a competitive neoclassical system, there corresponds a preference ordering that establishes that allocation as a competitive general equilibrium. This raises serious questions about the scientific character of the program; in fact Debreu once remarked that it was his 'contribution to radical economics.'[12]

Indeed, it is difficult to think of examples in the neoclassical school in which the inability to generate an underlying optimization framework has caused the demise of the theoretical system. The adaptive expectations approach of the Keynesian model was the most obvious target, but the model has largely been rescued for the neoclassicals by 'New Keynesian' theorists.[13] It is no accident that structuralists have generally been unimpressed by the efforts of the rational choice Keynesians. This is not because structuralists are themselves committed to 'old Keynesianism' but rather that the New Keynesian program fails to increase the 'wholeness' of the theory as we have seen. Structuralist models are validated by how well they represent the complex reality they seek to model. They have gained popularity with policymakers because they pass the 'duck test.' They achieve their prominence by providing a comprehensive and realistic approach to the entire economic system simultaneously.[14]

Complex models that not only track the data well but are also based on algebraic formulations, recognizable as country-specific, can be a powerful tool in an open policymaking arena. As the complexity of the model increases, it might be thought it would become more difficult to portray causal mechanisms adequately. This is true, but it is not the objective of large-scale simulation models to highlight any subset of the mechanism as it might be in a more analytical model. Indeed, it could be argued that the success enjoyed by structuralist models is entirely attributable to the appeal of the mechanisms by which the models are validated. In 1990, Lance Taylor edited a lengthy and influential collection of papers on simulation models written from a structuralist perspective (1990). Several of these models included financial sectors and some were dynamic. Since then, the structuralist models have become increasingly complex, including more of the relevant features of the economies under study and running for longer periods of time.[15]

3.2.1 Wholeness, error and validity

For models to look, walk and quack like a duck, they must evolve into complex entities. Passing the duck test leads structuralism to embrace complex simulation models and methodology. Simulation methodology has enjoyed a good deal of success in the last few decades, in meteorology, geoscience, astrophysics, and molecular dynamics and design, to name but a few areas. In social sciences simulation modeling has made fewer inroads, although as early as the 1960s and 1970s policy models in economics, political science and even sociology were in use. By and large, econometric models have dominated the social sciences. The goal of this interpretation of the structuralist method is to have all the parts of the model function independently and then achieve simultaneous confirmation of the historical record. In this regard, structuralist models take a 'full information' approach which allows cross-checking of one component by way of another. The more complete the model is, the more ways in which it can be wrong and hence, if right, the more confidence it earns.[16] From the user's point of view a complete model is more believable and trustworthy.

In contrast to the decoupling of the unfalsifiable optimizing foundation from its falsifiable results, structuralist models are thus interlinked. This provides an error-trapping facility in structuralist models by-and-large absent in the orthodoxy. An unrealistic characterization in one component of a structuralist model will feed into and produce errors in another. The errors that diffuse through the system are either systematic or random; the latter may well cancel out, but the former multiply (unless one systematic error luckily cancels out another). *Cross-sectional* systematic error grows with the number of equations in the system, imparting content to the notion that wholeness is itself a criterion of validity. This same kind of error propagation is more familiar in time-dependent systems. A time series generated by a chaotical system, as noted above, is fully determined but cannot be predicted because of error propagation, either of measurement of the initial conditions or the model equations themselves. Unstable trajectories fail the same kind of test of realism, but not because the steady state is particularly realistic but because trajectories that lead away from it multiply errors built into the original structure. Hence whether models are ultimately convergent to a steady state is not the relevant issue as noted above; it is rather that they remain transformational and self-regulating over both space and time.

Thus if the notion of wholeness is taken seriously, the structuralist model will not be validated by the methods of classical statistics, but rather in terms of realism and scope relative to its object. The implications of this claim are far-reaching. A fully valid model would be able to pass a suitably modified 'Turing Test' after Alan Turing, in which participants in a blind conversation with an artificially intelligent machine would be unable to tell if it were a human or computer providing the answers to questions (Turing, 1950). In a more relevant context, the policymaker would be unable to tell whether the data provided by the structuralist model were simply computer-generated estimates or the true numbers, no matter how familiar he or she was with the way in which the economy functions.

Structuralist models would then evolve in a direction that would be *less* constrained by individual choice-theoretic formulations and more so by interlocking substructures describing various aspects, real, financial, public, private, formal, informal, social, regional and so on of the economy. One can imagine that a model that was capable of passing a version of the Turing test would be very large, taking into account the diversity of market structures and social classes of which the real economy consists. Just as simulation models of thunderstorms are more accurate as additional observations are employed to characterize local temperature, lapse rates and moisture content of the atmosphere, structuralist models would achieve greater reliability when far more structure than is currently employed is integrated.

In summary, wholeness entails its own criteria of validity. Interlocking systems, whether decomposable or not, propagate errors between their component parts. As larger numbers of subsystems are combined, errors in one part are propagated to other components, often magnifying the effect of the original error. With an arbitrary number of non-decomposable parts, errors in any one subsystem would eventually surface, conflict with the duck test, and presumably be corrected. Bigger, in this framework, becomes better. Just as in robotics, models are more convincing not only when they can perform a task well, but as the number of *different* tasks they perform well, multiplies.

3.2.2 Criticism

Simulation methodology in science generally has been subject to criticism, much of it valid. It is clear, for example, that complete verification and validation is impossible since natural and indeed social systems are *open*. One can never be sure that one will not overlook some crucial feature that causes a turning point or some cross-sectional component that all at once becomes relevant to the model. Cartwright argues that simulations are ultimately *works of fiction* which may resonate with their objects for a time and then arbitrarily (and inconveniently) lose any resemblance to the reality they are supposed to represent (Oreskes *et al.*, 1994). This criticism seems irrefutable but only demonstrates that simulation modeling is an imperfect tool. Moreover, inadequate models are a general problem in science, from robotics to computer graphics animation in motion pictures, and have plagued the development of complex artificial systems since their inception.[17]

Not everyone, even among those sympathetic to structuralism, will be comfortable with the claim that *truth* lies in some expansive numerical rendering of reality. Indeed, Mirowski has already denounced 'machine dreams' as the new foundation of the new *neoclassical* economics. In his view, the program that began with von Neumann, Nash and Weiner, evolved into the information theory of Shannon, Weaver and Simon and ultimately into the artificial life and chaoplexy of Santa Fe, underlies an ultimately distorted vision of economic *agency* as 'cyborgs.'[18] In one passage, Mirowski lines up a number of suspects for summary execution:

> The characteristic moves of the cyborg sciences – capturing feedback motions in metal, framing biological reproduction in equations of automata, reducing thought to the Boolean logic of electrical circuits, leaching the problem of

> meaning out of the definition of information, treating probability as [solving] the problem of induction . . . strategy as dynamic optimality and 'order' out of chaos . . . made their way into economics (1998).

But Mirowski's romantic defense of humanness against machines begs the question of why cyborg methods were so successful in their respective disciplines. Apart from winning World War II, the critique ignores any positive contribution. Indeed, Mirowski does not address the question of validity of simulation at all, content to observe that neoclassicism has abandoned its 'physics envy' and existence proofs in a new urge to *calculate*.[19]

4 CONCLUSIONS

The thread of the argument can now be laid bare. The late structuralists, Taylor, his various students and colleagues have continued the tradition of the early structuralists, adding a significant body of theory. The structuralist project has, as a result, moved into closer conformity with the mandate of the early European writers. For the classical structuralists more detail is better than less, and we observe this same proclivity in late structuralism. The structuralist method is *ad hoc* and happily so, and would look askance at attempts to validate theory via theoretical purity, as the neoclassicals have. Structuralists must ultimately validate their theories by reference to the structure itself, called here the duck test.

As the theoretical object of structuralism becomes more complex, simulation modeling presents itself as a natural alternative. Simulation models avoid the need for unrealistic assumptions, such as perfectly competitive markets, steady states, terminal and transversality conditions and perfect foresight. Just as in many other areas of science, simulation models in structuralist economics are becoming increasingly realistic, taking on the look and feel of the real economy as recorded in the data base. The classical themes of structuralism, wholeness, transformation and self-regulation can be interpreted as guidelines for the future evolution of structuralism.

NOTES

* I gratefully acknowledge the inspiring comments of Amitava Dutt, Jaime Ros and an anonymous reviewer of this volume. Many thanks are due also to James Farrell, Abu Rizvi and Diane Flaherty, who carefully read and critiqued earlier drafts.

1. This chapter does not intend to paint the neoclassicals *couleur de rose* and I hope that readers are not unhappy about how they are characterized here. Indeed neoclassicism is

only 'characterized' rather than defined because of the inherent difficulties in nailing down precisely what is and is not neoclassical.

2. Levi-Strauss's work focused on interpretations of myth through the shared structure of language (Levi-Strauss, 2000).
3. See Dutt (1990a) for a spirited defense of the method. Lance Taylor's undergraduate degree is in mathematics (from Cal Tech).
4. These ideas are treated in depth by Lane (1975).
5. Jameson also mentions *semiology* and *binary opposition* as critical elements retained by modern structuralists. As crucial as the notion of cultural interpretation of signs might be to anthropology its use is somewhat forced in its application to late structuralist economics. Similarly, binary conceptual frameworks, master–slave, industry and agriculture, center–periphery, and so on, appear now as dated signatures of classical structuralism rather than important methodological precepts.
6. As the Latin American structuralists began to break away from the neoclassicals, a structuralist analysis of the economic relations between the North and South came into being, but in an immature state. There seemed to be no connection between the work of Sunkel, Prebisch, Singer, Lewis and Levi-Strauss, Godelier and Piaget. Only in Emmanuel (1972) was there a suggestion that the structuralists' observations on unequal development could be grounded in a more profound, radically anti-neoclassical theoretical framework. Unfortunately, it was too radical, suffering in particular from the inherent limitations of classical Marxism. The late structuralists were unencumbered by any such theoretical attachments and developed a far more sophisticated vision of unequal development by way of North–South models.
7. When dynamics are taken into account in the neoclassical system, it necessarily becomes more structuralist in nature. Take, for example, a rise in the real wage. Will this cause firms to substitute capital for labor? The answer is clearly 'yes' in traditional neoclassical analysis, for any time and place. To say that agents will use more of the expensive factor of production violates the basic premise of rationality that underlies the model. In the structuralist school, it is common to use fixed coefficients technology for any one period of time. As the economy moves through time, the coefficients can change, but relative factor cost is only one reason why they might; technological change is also an important factor. The typical way in which structuralists model technological change is to link it to capacity utilization. The 'stylized fact' is that technological change is labor-saving, not capital-saving or neutral even though these are often presented in the neoclassical treatments as equally likely alternatives.
8. Measures of 'economic freedom' are often derived from proxies for the very growth they are correlated with.
9. For interesting history of these methods see Sent (1998).
10. Dutt has argued that the optimizing framework of the neoclassical school is part of its core principles and therefore not meant to be realistic or subject to verification. He refers to optimization as an 'organizing principle,' that is, a way in which explanations are structured and which 'make no statement about the real world' (Dutt and Jameson, 1992). But he then begs the question of what the organizing principle for structuralists is and it becomes simply what structuralists *do*. Realists, who argue that organizing principles are not even necessary, are dismissed by Dutt. I am, in effect, arguing that the organizing principle of the late structuralists in terms of the characterization of what they *do* is the joint application of the same three principles enunciated by the classical structuralists as discussed above.
11. Obviously, the process of verification may be subject to Kuhnian problems of paradigmatic focus. But as Sokal and Bricmont point out in their sympathetic assessment of the excesses of Kuhn and Feyerabend, relativism cannot be sustained over time in the observational evidence that supports scientific progress; better is simply better and comes to be recognized as such (1998).
12. From private conversation. See Debreu (1974) and Rizvi (1994) for an interpretation.
13. The same cannot be claimed for Marxism. When analytical Marxism insisted that some

microfoundations be adduced, some elements of Marxist theory died away, for example, the capital logic school from which little has been heard recently.

14. For an introduction to simulation models, see Pindyck and Rubinfeld (1991), Chapter 12. Simulation models differ from econometric models, although they are closely related. As noted above, individually fitted regression equations can track historical data well, but when combined in a simultaneous equations model, may not pass the 'duck test'. Simulation models use regressions results, parameter guesstimations and other formal and informal techniques to represent their theoretical object adequately. There is nothing 'pure' about them, and their reputations hinge on how well they reproduce the 'look and feel' of the real economy as portrayed in the historical record.
15. Certainly there is a large number of neoclassically based simulation models in the literature. But often these models reflect little about the economies they study and are often unconvincing to policymakers. In recently published joint work, we provide a concrete example of a head-to-head comparison of two models, one structuralist and the other neoclassical, that were applied to the transition from apartheid in South Africa. In that comparison the neoclassical model does not appear at all realistic. What is surprising is that the neoclassical model has enjoyed far more influence than its credibility would suggest. See Gibson and van Seventer (2000) and Gibson (2000).
16. Structuralists do not claim, as Milton Friedman (1955) once ignominiously did, that the method imposes no constraints on the components of the theory or that a theory is only as good as its overall predictive value. Structuralists attempt to get each component of a model to form an image of the reality they have in mind and ultimately to work together with all other parts of the model. No block of equations is immune to scrutiny and all must faithfully represent its object.
17. See, for example, the 'crazy hair' outtake in the DVD version of Dreamwork's *Shrek*.
18. See Mirowski (1998) for an extensive set of references to the literature.
19. The critique will probably meet some stiff resistance. Most thorough-going neoclassicals, Lucas, Sargent *et al.* explicitly reject *ad hoc* models and even optimal control models on the grounds that agents' expectations are represented in an overly mechanistic way (Sent, 1998). They apparently do not recognize that the bodies of their rational actors are about to be snatched by Mirowski's cyborgs.

REFERENCES

Agénor, P. and P. Montiel (1996), *Development Macroeconomics*, Princeton: Princeton University Press.

Althusser, L. (1971), *For Marx*, London: New Left Books.

Amsden, A. (2002), *The Rise of the Rest: Challenges to the West from Late-Industrializing Economies*, Oxford: Oxford University Press.

Berman, A. and R. Plemmons (1979), *Nonnegative Matrices in the Mathematical Sciences*, New York: Academic Press.

Chenery, H. (1975), 'The structuralist approach to development policy', *American Economic Review* (*Proceedings*), **65**(2), 310–16.

Chichilnisky, G. and G. Heal (1986), *The Evolving International Economy*, Cambridge: Cambridge University Press.

Clark, C. (1976), *Mathematical Bioeconomics: The Optimal Management of Renewable Resources*, New York: John Wiley and Sons.

Debreu, G. (1974), 'Excess demand functions', *Journal of Mathematical Economics*, **11**, 15–23.

Devaney, Robert L. (1989), *An Introduction to Chaotic Dynamical Systems*, Redwood City, CA: Addison-Wesley.

Dutt, A. (1984), 'Stagnation, income distribution and monopoly power', *Cambridge Journal of Economics*, **8**(1), 25–40.

Dutt, A. (1990a), 'Analytical political economy', Introduction to A. Dutt (ed.) *New Directions in Analytical Political Economy*, Aldershot, UK and Brookfield, US: Edward Elgar.

Dutt, A. (1990b), *Growth, distribution and uneven development*, Cambridge: Cambridge University Press.

Dutt, A., and K. Jameson (eds) (1992), *New Directions in Development Economics*, Aldershot, UK and Brookfield, US: Edward Elgar.

Emmanuel, A. (1972), *Unequal Exchange*, New York: Monthly Review Press.

Foucault, M. (1972), *The Archaeology of Knowledge*, New York: Harper.

Friedman, M. (1955), *Essays in Positive Economics*, Chicago: University of Chicago Press.

Gibson, B. (1985), 'A structuralist macromodel for post-revolutionary Nicaragua', *Cambridge Journal of Economics*, **9**(4) pp. 347–69.

Gibson, B. (1994), 'The break-up of the mixed economy in Nicaragua', in A. Dutt (ed.) *New Directions in Analytical Political Economy*, Aldershot, UK and Brookfield, US: Edward Elgar.

Gibson, B. (2000), 'The transition to a globalized economy: poverty, human capital and the informal sector in a structuralist CGE model', University of Vermont, Burlington, VT (available at www.uvm.edu/˜wgibson).

Gibson, B. and D. van Seventer (2000), 'A tale of two models', *International Review of Applied Economics*, **14**(2) (May).

Gibson, B., N. Lustig and L. Taylor (1986), 'Terms of trade and class conflict in a Marxian computable general equilibrium model for Mexico,' *Journal of Development Studies*, **23**(1), 40–59.

Godelier, M. (1972), *Rationality and Irrationality in Economics*, New York: Monthly Review Press.

Gould, S. (1998), 'Showdown on the Burgess Shale', *Natural History*, **107**(10): 48–55.

Henrich, J., R. Boyd, S. Bowles, C. Camerer, E. Fehr, H. Gintis and R. McElreath (2001), 'In search of homo economicus: behavioral experiments in 15 small scale societies', *American Economics Review*, **91**(2) (May), 73–8.

Jameson, K. (1986), 'Latin American structuralism: a methodological perspective', *World Development*, **14**(2), 223–32.

Keat, R. and J. Urry (1975), *Social Theory as Science*, London: Routledge & Kegan Paul.

Lane, M. (1975), *Introduction to Structuralism*, New York: Harper.

Levi-Strauss (2000), *Structural Anthropology*, New York: Basic Books Classics.

Lewis, W.A. (1954), 'Economic development with unlimited supplies of labour', *Manchester School*, **22**(4), 131–91.

Love, J. (1980), 'Raoul Prebisch and the origins of the doctrine of unequal exchange', *Latin American Resource Review*, **15**(3), 45–72.

Lucas, R. (1976), 'Econometric policy evaluation: a critique', in K. Brunner and A. Meltzer (eds), *The Phillips Curve and Labor Markets*, Amsterdam: North-Holland.

Lustig, N. (1992), 'From structuralism to neostructuralism: the search for a heterodox paradigm,' in Patricio Meller (ed.), *The Latin American Development Debate*, Boulder, CO: Westview Press.

Mirowski, P. (1998), 'Machine dreams: economic agents as Cyborgs', *History of*

Political Economy (1998; Annual supplement: *New Economics and its History*) **29**, 13–40.
Myrdal, G. (1957), *Rich Lands and Poor*, New York: Harper.
Nurske, R. (1956), *Problems of Capital Formation in Underdeveloped Countries*, Oxford: Basil Blackwell.
Oreskes, N., K. Belitz and K. Frechette (1994), 'Verification, validation, and confirmation of numerical models in earth sciences', *Science* (Feb 4), 641–6.
Piaget, J. (1971), *Structuralism*, New York: Harper and Row.
Pindyck, R. and D. Rubinfeld (1991), *Econometric Models and Economic Forecasts*, 3rd edn, New York: McGraw-Hill.
Prebisch, R. (1959), 'Commercial policy in underdeveloped countries', *American Economics Review (Proc.)*, **49**(2), 251–73.
Prebisch, R. (1960), *The Economic Development of Latin America and its Principal Problems*, United Nations: Economic Commission for Latin America.
Rizvi, S. (1994), 'The microfoundations project in general equilibrium theory,' *Cambridge Journal of Economics*, **18**, 357–77.
Rizvi, S. (1998), 'Responses to arbitrariness in contemporary economics', *History of Political Economy*, (1998; Annual supplement: *New Economics and its History*) **29**, 273–88.
Sent, E. (1998), 'Engineering dynamic economics, *History of Political Economy* (1998; Annual supplement: *New Economics and its History*) **29**, 41–62.
Singer, H. (1950), 'The distribution of gains between investing and borrowing countries', *American Economics Review (Proc.)*, **40**, 473–85.
Sokal, A. and J. Bricmont (1998), *Fashionable Nonsense*, New York: Picador Press.
Stiglitz, J.E. (1988), 'Economic organization, information and development', in H. Chenery and T. Srinivasan (eds), *Handbook of Development Economics*, **1**, Amsterdam: North-Holland.
Taylor, L. (1975), 'Theoretical foundations and technical implications', in C. Blitzer, P. Clark and L. Taylor (eds), *Economy-Wide Models and Development Planning*, Oxford: Oxford University Press for the World Bank.
Taylor, L. (1983), *Structuralist Macroeconomics*, New York: Basic Books.
Taylor, L. (1990), *Socially Relevant Policy Analysis: Structuralist Computable General Equilibrium Models for the Developing World*, Cambridge, Massachusetts: MIT Press.
Taylor, L. (1991), *Growth, Income Distribution and Inflation: Lectures on Structuralist Macroeconomic Theory*, Cambridge, Massachusetts: MIT Press.
Taylor, L. (1992), 'Structuralist and competing approaches to development economics', in A. Dutt and K. Jameson (1992).
Turing, A. (1950), 'Computing machinery and intelligence', *Mind*, **59**(236), 433–60.

4. Poverty is not destiny: comparative life expectancy in Africa

F. Desmond McCarthy and Holger Wolf

1 INTRODUCTION

Rising incomes and improving medical technology have lifted health standards in most countries, alongside other indicators of the quality of life (Easterly, 1999). Policies fostering growth are thus accompanied by indirect health benefits. Yet, income per capita is only part of the story. Health indicators differ dramatically between countries with similar income levels located in close proximity: within the group of low-income countries (under $1000 GNP per capita) in Sub-Saharan Africa, life expectancy ranges from 38 in Guinea-Bissau to 58 in Kenya (World Health Report, 1999).

These observations provide prima facie evidence that potentially major health improvements can be obtained at unchanged income levels by adopting best practices within the peer group of countries on similar development levels. In this chapter, we explore the size of these potential gains in terms of life expectancy for a sample of African countries.[1] We focus on documenting existing disparities and inquiring whether these are related to observable country characteristics. While causality may at times be intuitive (such as for a positive link between life expectancy and access to safe water), it is not our focus, and indeed would be more convincingly tested in a time series/panel framework.

2 A SIMPLE DECOMPOSITION

We begin with a simple decomposition aiming to differentiate the various life expectancies within low-income African countries, all African countries, and all countries worldwide. Our empirical analysis is straightforward. The measure of interest is the difference between the highest life expectancy among all sample countries and the life expectancy within a particular low-income country in Africa. We then decompose this health

Table 4.1 Life expectancy in Niger

Life expectancy in Niger	47
Gain from catching up to highest life expectancy in peer group	+11
Additional gain from catching up to highest life expectancy in Africa	+13
Additional gain from catching up to highest life expectancy globally	+9

gap into three parts. The first part is the intra-group difference between the country in question and the low-income African country with the highest life expectancy. The second part is the difference between this reference country and the African country (at any income level) with the highest life expectancy. The third part is the difference between the African country with the highest life expectancy and the highest life expectancy worldwide.

For illustration, Table 4.1 reports the decomposition for Niger, with a life expectancy of 47 years, compared to 58 years in Kenya (the low-income country with the highest life expectancy), 71 years in Mauritius (the African country with the highest life expectancy) and 80 years in Japan (the country with the longest life expectancy globally).

The division allows a direct comparison of the gains of moving to the level of the best local health performer within the same income group with the gains from moving up to regional and global best performers. The latter two comparison countries typically have substantially higher income levels, the second and third gain component are thus likely to partly capture the indirect gains along the development path alluded to above.

Table 4.2 reports the three gaps for all countries in the low-income group. The differences in life expectancy within the low-income group are marked; there is no uniform link between income per capita and life expectancy. The gap between the highest life expectancy within the group of low-income countries and the highest life expectancy in all of Africa is commensurate with the within-group gap for about half of the low-income countries, providing prima facie evidence for substantial potential health gains obtainable at unchanged income levels for many low-income countries.

The second difference can be interpreted as the potential medium-term gain from best economic and health policies within a broader spatially defined peer group, while the third difference captures the more distant potential gains from long-term development, assuming convergence. The table suggests that the sum of the first two gaps accounts for the lion's share of the overall gap, and thus that very substantial health benefits can be reached with the resources obtainable from regional rather than global convergence.

A look at the country with the highest life expectancy, Mauritius, gives

Table 4.2 Life expectancy gaps

	GNP in 1999 US$ PPP	Life expectancy at birth	Gap to highest life expectancy in the low-income group	Gap to highest life expectancy in Africa	Gap to highest life expectancy globally
Zaire	384	52.0	6.4	13.0	9.0
Sierra Leone	414	39.8	18.6	13.0	9.0
Tanzania	478	50.9	7.5	13.0	9.0
Burundi	553	49.5	8.9	13.0	9.0
Rwanda	576	39.2	19.2	13.0	9.0
Malawi	581	43.2	15.2	13.0	9.0
Guinea-Bissau	595	38.4	20.0	13.0	9.0
Ethiopia	599	49.0	9.4	13.0	9.0
Angola	632	47.3	11.1	13.0	9.0
Zambia	686	45.6	12.8	13.0	9.0
Mali	693	49.6	8.8	13.0	9.0
Niger	727	46.6	11.8	13.0	9.0
Nigeria	744	52.8	5.6	13.0	9.0
Madagascar	766	52.0	6.4	13.0	9.0
Mozambique	797	46.5	11.9	13.0	9.0
Chad	816	48.1	10.3	13.0	9.0
Benin	886	50.2	8.2	13.0	9.0
Congo	897	51.0	7.4	13.0	9.0
Burkina Faso	898	48.7	9.7	13.0	9.0
Kenya	975	58.4	0.0	13.0	9.0

an indication of the factors that may be associated with sustained gains in life expectancy: stable growth, absence of civil conflicts, military expenditures that are among the lowest in Africa, and nearly universal access to clean water and sanitation; perhaps even more notable is that 99 per cent of the population has access to health facilities. Of course, the comparability of Mauritius to continental African countries is limited by geography: as an island located quite far from the continent, it is less subject to some insect-borne diseases, nor does it suffer from cross-border river pollution. Small geographic and population size also arguably ease the challenge of providing access to water and health care.[2] The special role of size should probably not be overestimated in this instance, however: the life expectancy in Mauritius is only marginally higher than that of three larger continental countries, Algeria, Tunisia and Botswana, clustered at around half the income-per-capita level of Mauritius.

3 WHY DO HEALTH OUTCOMES DIFFER AMONG POOR AFRICAN ECONOMIES?

The table provided above illustrated that poverty is not destiny as far as health outcomes are concerned: countries with very low per capita incomes, such as Tanzania, boast life expectancy comparable with those in much richer economies. It is of evident interest to ascertain whether such intra-group differences are random or whether they are robustly associated with observable country characteristics, including some amenable to policy.

To answer this question, we divide the sample countries in Africa into three groups; depending on income per capita in 1999 PPP based US$. The first group (LOW) includes countries with per capita incomes below $1000;[3] the second group (MIDDLE) comprises countries with per capita incomes between $1000 and $2000;[4] the third group (HIGH) includes countries with per capita incomes above $2000.[5]

Table 4.3 reports the minimum, maximum and median of a set of health outcome indicators for these three groups. The last three columns report the medians. The results are unsurprising: higher income per capita is associated with better health outcomes. Life expectancy rises from 48.8 years in the low-income group to 64.2 years in the high-income group, with one exception (low birth weight children in middle-income countries); all other outcome medians improve with income. The result is well known, reflecting the positive feedback loop between improved health, improved productivity and income, and improved capacity to provide health services (Pritchett and Summers, 1996).[6]

The first six columns report the maximum and minimum within each

Table 4.3 Health outcomes by income groups

	Low income min.	Low income max.	Middle income min.	Middle income max.	High income min.	High income max.	Low income median	Middle income median	High income median
Female life expectancy	37.8	60.2	43.6	60.8	53.3	66.3	49.1	51.6	66.3
Male life expectancy	34.8	56.7	43.9	56.7	50.3	68.1	45.3	48.9	61.4
Total life expectancy	38.4	58.4	41.7	58.7	54.7	70.6	48.8	50.0	64.2
Infant mortality rate	58.0	179.4	55.7	131.3	16.1	88.6	111.8	96.6	55.3
Mortality rate age <5	90	236	86	220	20	145	184	159	75
Maternal mortality rate	490	939	430	1100	50	400	590	580	200
Low birth weight	10.0	18.0	5.0	35.0	7.0	15.0	13.0	14.5	9.7
Malnutrition in children	22.3	50.0	13.6	44.0	9.0	26.0	30.1	23.5	10.6

country group. The overall positive link between outcomes and income is preserved. However, a comparison of low-income and middle-income countries reveals that the best performers in the low-income countries (Kenya and Madagascar) achieved better outcomes than the worst performers in the middle-income group (Uganda and Guinea). More surprisingly, the same result holds for a comparison of low- and high-income countries: the best performers in the low-income per capita group have achieved comparable if not better health outcomes than the worst performers in the high-income group (Gabon, Lesotho). The results again suggest that poverty is not destiny as far as health outcomes are concerned.

Table 4.4 provides background information on one potential cause of the differences, health spending and access to health services. Again, the first six columns report the maximum and minimum values for the three groups, while the last three columns report the medians. The results match the findings of Table 4.3. Overall, the provision of health services increases with income per capita. In comparable PPP adjusted US$, the median low-income country spends $22 per inhabitant, while the median middle- and high-income countries spend $50 and $310. Across most other indicators, the median values display the same positive relationship with income. Overall, higher spending is thus, not surprisingly, associated with improved health service outputs.

Comparing the first six columns, it is however again striking that the best performing low-income country commits more resources compared not only to the worst performing middle-income country, but also to the worst performing high-income country. In Tanzania, with a per capita income of $478, an estimated 93 per cent of the population has access to health care even though public expenditure on health care is only about $6 per capita. On the other hand in Morocco, with public health spending of $42 per capita (total health spending per capita is $140) only 62 per cent of the population has access to health care. The results are indicative of sharp differences in the mapping between financial resources spent on health care and health services ultimately delivered to the population.[7]

A substantial body of work suggests that declines in the mortality rates (in particular for children) are to a large extent driven by improved prevention in addition to improved treatment, consequently, the extent to which the population has access to clean water and sanitation is likely to influence health outcomes (Savedoff and Schultz, 2000) even for a given health service infrastructure. As Table 4.4 reveals, relative access rates differ dramatically across countries, with the best access rates among the poorest countries again exceeding the lowest access rates among the high-income group.

Table 4.5 reports matching statistics on two other variables widely

Table 4.4 Health system resources and outputs by income groups

	Low income min.	Low income max.	Middle income min.	Middle income max.	High income min.	High income max.	Low income median	Middle income median	High income median
Health spending									
– as % of GDP total	0.7	7.9	2.2	5.2	3.5	7.4	3.3	3.8	5.3
– as % of GDP public	0.2	4.0	1.0	2.9	0.6	3.8	1.7	1.8	3.0
– per capita in PPP US$	6	62	15	83	124	571	22.5	50	310
Access (% of population)									
– to health care	24	93	45	76	55	99	55	70	90
– to essential medicines	10	65	15	100	30	95	50	70	80
– to safe water (total)	24	70	7	82	57	100	42	50	67
– to safe water (rural)	8	63	24	86	17	66	42	62	42
– to safe water (urban)	18	97	48.5	97	80	100	75	77	99
– to essential sanitation (total)	9	86	6	60	11	100	22	37	56
– to essential sanitation (urban)	11	97	12	85	20	100	63	59	90
Immunization rates									
– DPT	18	98	40	93	48	96	57	67	78
– Measles	24	99	31	88	50	94	54	66	78
Contraceptive use	4	39	2	24	16	75	7.7	14.0	49.0
Doctors per 1000 pop.	0.0	0.3	0.0	0.2	0.1	2.1	0.1	0.1	0.5
Hospital beds per 1000 pop.	0.1	3.4	0.4	2.6	0.5	3.2	1.1	0.9	1.9

Table 4.5 Other health determinants by income groups

	Low income min.	Low income max.	Middle income min.	Middle income max.	High income min.	High income max.	Low income median	Middle income median	High income median
Illiteracy	21.8	86.4	19.0	66.9	14.9	56.3	45.1	51.0	29.5
Illiteracy female	28.0	93.4	31.9	78.1	18.0	69.0	58.2	64.2	38.9
Education spending/GDP	0.7	6.5	0.9	5.1	2.9	9.1	2.3	3.2	5.1
Primary enrollment	25	97	36	107	69	136	70	60.5	114
– Female	19	92	24	86	56	139	59	50	111
Secondary enrollment	4	28	11	36	8	75	10	16.5	50.5
– Female	2	25	5	28	29	77	6	12	54
Gini	28.9	62.9	32.7	61.3	28.9	60.9	47.1	39.8	48.1
Income share bottom 20%	1.1	9.7	2.0	8.4	2.7	9.8	5.1	6.4	5.0

thought to affect health outcomes: broad access to education, in particular for women who provide the majority of in-family health services; and the ability of poorer families to pay for health services. Both of the patterns evident in the previous two tables are again present: most indicators improve with median income across the three groups (though there is a suggestion of a U-curve relationship for some variables); while the best performing poor countries again display better education statistics than the worst performing high-income countries.

Table 4.6 reports the ranking of health service indicators by life expectancy.[8] The sample countries are again divided into three groups. The first group[9] (LOW) comprises countries with life expectancies below 50 years, the second group[10] (MIDDLE) includes countries with life expectancies between 50 and 60 years, and the last group[11] (HIGH) comprises countries with life expectancies above 60 years.

Based on the medians, the table reveals a positive association between resources devoted to the health care sector and health sector outputs, measured by access rates and immunization rates. More resources devoted to health care and greater output of health care services are also associated with higher life expectancy. Comfortingly, the table is thus consistent with the view that an increase in resources devoted to health care will (in most instances) improve public health.

As before, the ranges reported in the first six columns suggest that these linkages are far from uniform, in two senses. First, the link between spending measures and outputs of health services is quite unstable. Several countries with per capita health expenditures below $50 report immunization and access rates above those of countries spending several times more on health care per capita. While not the main theme of our chapter, the finding suggests that a substantial improvement in health service provision may be obtained at moderate financial cost in some countries.

Second, several countries with life expectancies below 50 years report immunization rates and rates of access to clean water, sanitation and health care that are significantly above those reported by countries with life expectancies above 60 years. The link between resources devoted to health care, the output of medical services generated by these resources, and the effect of these services on at least some measures of public health thus appears to be far from linear.[12]

Finally, Table 4.7 reports statistics for a number of other variables that might be thought to be associated with life expectancy. Commencing with the median, education variables uniformly improve with life expectancy, as does the income share of the bottom 20 per cent of population. In both cases, causality presumably is two-sided. No clear unconditional linkage emerges for military expenditures, the debt-to-GDP ratio or government

Table 4.6 Health system resources and outputs by life expectancy

	Low min.	Low max.	Middle min.	Middle max.	High min.	High max.	Low median	Middle median	High median
Health spending									
– as % of GDP total	1.3	7.9	0.7	7.4	3.5	7.1	3.7	4.2	4.5
– as % of GDP public	0.6	4.0	0.2	3.8	1.3	3.7	1.9	1.6	2.9
– per capita in PPP US$	7	50	6	399	124	571	31	66	310
Access (% of population)									
– to health care	24	80	42	93	62	99	37	67	94
– to essential medicines	20	93	10	100	51	95	58	65	80
– to safe water (total)	7	61	25	82	57	100	38	56	70
– to safe water (rural)	17	86	8	85	17	67	45	44	53
– to safe water (urban)	18	97	48	99	100	100	78	80	100
– to essential sanitation (total)	6	63	9	86	11	100	33	36	55
– to essential sanitation (urban)	12	82	11	98	20	100	58	69	91
Immunization rates									
– DPT	18	98	35	96	56	93	57	69	78
– Measles	24	99	31	94	66	92	58	62	82
Contraceptive use	2	21	6	48	16	75	8	17	50
Doctors per 1000 pop.	0.0	0.2	0.0	0.3	0.1	2.1	0.0	0.1	0.6
Hospital beds per 1000 pop.	0.1	1.7	0.2	3.4	1.0	3.1	0.9	1.3	1.9

Table 4.7 Other health determinants by life expectancy

	Low min.	Low max.	Middle min.	Middle max.	High min.	High max.	Low median	Middle median	High median
Illiteracy	19	86	15	67	17	56	53	37	30
Illiteracy female	29	93	18	77	18	69	67	47	43
Education spending/GDP	1.5	5.4	0.7	9.1	3.1	8.6	2.3	4.0	5.1
Primary enrollment	25	97	52	136	69	118	63	77	107
– Female	19	92	26	139	56	122	41	70	110
Secondary enrollment	4	16	5	52	8	75	10	23	52
– Female	2	13	4	54	29	77	5	16	55
Gini	28.9	62.9	32.7	60.9	28.9	59.3	48.0	42.9	39.9
Income share bottom 20%	1.1	9.7	2.7	8.4	2.8	9.8	5.0	5.7	6.2
Military expenditure/GDP	1	20	1	5	0.35	5	2.8	2.0	2.65
Debt/GDP	28	340	16	325	13	64	63	89	52
Government consump./GDP	7.5	47	6.6	31	12.3	32	12.8	11.2	16.4

consumption. Considering the distribution statistics, very substantial variation is again apparent: several countries with low life expectancies boast education levels above those of countries with much higher life expectancies, similar variation is observed for the other variables.

4 CLASSIFICATION TREE ANALYSIS

The stylized facts reported above suggest a positive unconditional association between life expectancy and income per capita, as well as a positive association between health service outputs and income per capita. One interpretation of the results is that the primary determinant of life expectation is income per capita. Yet, the substantial variation documented in the preceding section suggests that while an important determinant, poverty is not destiny as far as life expectancy is concerned. We now examine the linkages between health spending, health service outputs, other determinants and life expectancy in a cross-section framework. We use a classification tree methodology to allow for the likely presence of nonlinearity.

As the methodology is relatively seldom used in economics, Box 4.1 provides a brief summary. In essence, a classification tree provides a useful way of characterizing a binary variable with respect to a set of potential associated factors. The dependent variable is high (1) and low (0) life expectancy. High life expectancy is defined as the top third of observations in the sample (life expectancies above 55.7 years). Low life expectancy is defined as the bottom third of observations (life expectancies below 49 years). Both groups have 16 observations. The middle third is dropped to provide contrast.

The resulting classification rule is presented in Figure 4.1. The figure in brackets provides the probability (relative to the overall sample). The figures on each node provide the number of observations. The single best predictor of high versus low mortality is the percentage of population with access to health care, with a threshold of 50 per cent. For those countries falling below the threshold, a high female secondary enrolment ratio lifts the chance of belonging to the HIGH group to one third, while countries with low access rates and low female secondary enrolment rates have a less than 10 per cent chance of being in the high life expectancy group.

The methodology also provides a ranking of the relative importance of all variables, which takes into account the relative quality of each variable at all thresholds. Thus, a variable that never is the single best discriminant at any node (and thus does not appear in the tree) might be ranked second at several nodes, and thus have high discriminatory power between

BOX 4.1 CLASSIFICATION TREE METHODOLOGY

Classification trees consist of a sequence of rules for predicting the value of a binary dependent variable based on a vector of independent variables. For the present purpose, the binary variable is defined as high (1) and low (0) life expectancy.

The objective of classification tree analysis is to determine the set of rules (consisting of a discriminant variable and a threshold), which permits the best sorting of the dependent variable into its two constituent groups. At each branch of the tree, the sample is split into two sub-branches based upon a threshold value of one of the explanatory variables. The splitting is repeated until a terminal node is reached. Suppose, for example, that in all countries falling into the 'high' group, health spending is above 4% of GDP, while in all countries falling into the 'low' group, health spending is below 4% of GDP. In this case, the rule *if health spending is above 4% then classify the observation as HIGH* perfectly discriminates between the two groups, and the resulting decision tree would have a single branching with two nodes. In practice, perfectly discriminating rules are rare, and rules have associated type I and type II errors. In this case the algorithm selects the rule (consisting of the variable and the associated threshold) which minimizes a weighted sum of type I and type II errors. For the present purpose, equal weights are used. By construction, any additional sub-branch reduces the overall error rate of the classification scheme. Akin to an adjusted R^2 criterion, the algorithm terminates at a node if the reduction in the overall error rate falls short of a penalty on the number of branches.

Binary classification trees possess a number of advantages for the problem at hand. First, the algorithm establishes a priority ordering among the potential discriminants, discarding secondary variables and thus reducing the need for subjective preparsing. Second, the procedure permits subsamples to be described by different rules, thus allowing for context dependence. Third, because the procedure will typically split on an interior threshold, it is quite robust to outliers.

Importantly, the classification tree should be viewed as a way to characterize complex data, rather than as a set of formal statistical hypothesis. In particular, it does not imply causality.

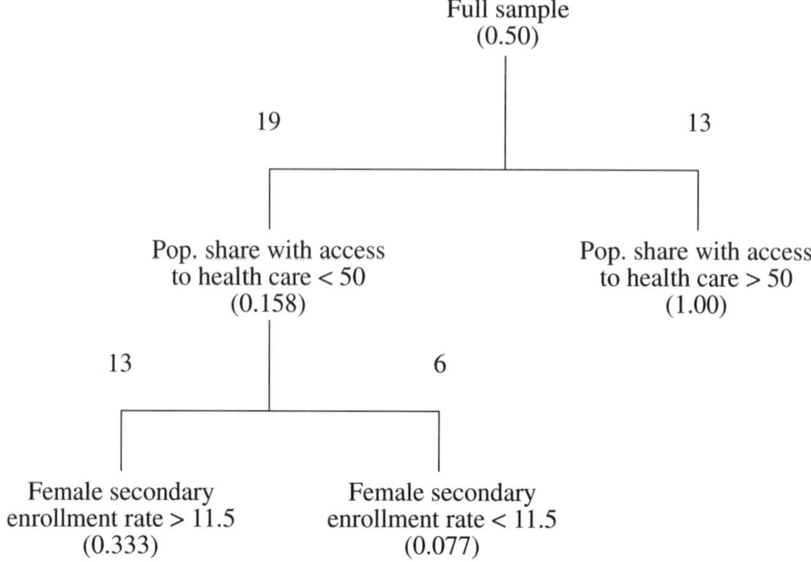

Figure 4.1 Classification tree: incidence of high versus low life expectancy

the two groups. Table 4.8 reports the relative importance, with the score for the first variable set equal to 100.

The share of population with access to health care is the best overall discriminant, followed by GNP per capita, the fertility rate and the share of population with access to safe water. Income is thus an important determinant of life expectancy (and vice versa), but it is not destiny, as above-average provision of access to health care and safe water – themselves not exclusively determined by income, as revealed in Table 4.3 – can sharply affect life expectancy.

5 CONCLUSION

Is poverty destiny, as far as health outcomes are concerned? We addressed this question by assessing life expectancy in Africa. While health outcomes are positively correlated with income, the link is far from uniform. Indeed, several of the poorest African countries boast better health outcomes compared to countries with much higher income levels. Nor does health expenditure, either as percentage of GNP or per capita, appear to be a particularly good predictor of health outcomes (leaving aside the endogeneity issue).

Table 4.8 Relative power as discriminants

Variable	Importance
Share of population with access to health care	100
GNP per capita (US$ PPP adjusted)	68
Fertility rate	66
Share of population with access to safe water	49
Institutional investor risk rating	33
Female secondary enrollment ratio	17
Public spending on health care	11
Total illiteracy ratio	11
Male illiteracy ratio	11
Primary enrollment ratio	10

The key variable associated with good health outcomes[13] (controlling for health expenditures) are access rates – to health services, to clean water and sanitation, and last but not least to education, particularly for women. While we do not examine formally, the findings suggest that, for given expenditure rates, the benefits of allocating greater shares to improving access warrant further study[14] (Hammer, 2000).

To be sure, modesty is required in drawing any policy implications from as aggregate a dataset as the one explored here. Apart from data problems, we are looking at a single year, and thus cannot easily account for the complex dynamic linkages between health system inputs, outputs, development and health outcomes; nor can we establish causality patterns. That said, the absence of a link between health expenditures, health service outputs and health outcomes however appears to be quite sturdy, suggesting marked differences in the mapping from spending to services, and from services to outcomes. The relative payoffs to raising health expenditures versus improving the productivity of service provision and the linkages between service provision and outcomes would thus seem to warrant careful study. Among the pertinent questions here are the best division of health care spending between public sources, NGOs and households; the appropriate shares of public expenditures devoted to preventive relative to curative measures; and the relative importance attached to sanitation infrastructure versus traditional health care.

NOTES

1. The focus on a single continent is motivated by the desire to keep the *ceteris paribus* assumption reasonably applicable. The prevalence of many common diseases in poorer

economies is significantly influenced by a myriad of environmental factors including prevalence of transmitting insects, temperature and humidity, and so on, and by focusing on a regional cluster, it is hoped that differences in these factors will be less important.

2. Effective access may also differ by season, depending on the quality and density of the road/transportation network.
3. Congo, Sierra Leone, Tanzania, Burundi, Rwanda, Malawi, Guinea Bissau, Ethiopia, Angola, Zambia, Mali, Niger, Nigeria, Madagascar, Mozambique, Chad, Benin, Democratic Republic of Congo, Burkina Faso, Kenya.
4. Eritrea, Central African Republic, Uganda, Equatorial Guinea, Djibouti, Sudan, Senegal, Togo, Cameroon, The Gambia, Mauritania, Cote d'Ivoire, Guinea, Ghana.
5. Lesotho, Zimbabwe, Morocco, Egypt, Cape Verde, Swaziland, Algeria, Gabon, Namibia, Tunisia, Botswana, South Africa, Mauritius.
6. Their results suggest there is a structural relationship between income and health with causation running from income to health. They also find that differences in income over the last three decades explain roughly 40 per cent of the cross-country differences in mortality improvements.
7. Some caution regarding the precision and cross-country comparability of data, in particular for non-budget measures such as the access variables, is warranted.
8. Gwatkin *et al.* (2000) provide a broader picture on many of the other factors that can affect health status.
9. Guinea-Bissau, Rwanda, Sierra Leone, Uganda, Malawi, Guinea, Zambia, The Gambia, Mozambique, Niger, Angola, Eritrea, Chad, Central African Republic, Burkina Faso, Equatorial Guinea, Ethiopia, Burundi, Mali, Djibouti.
10. Senegal, Benin, Tanzania, Congo, Mauritania, Madagascar, Congo Democratic Republic, Nigeria, Sudan, Gabon, Cote d'Ivoire, Togo, Cameroon, Zimbabwe, Swaziland, Kenya, Ghana, Namibia.
11. Lesotho, Egypt, South Africa, Cape Verde, Morocco, Botswana, Tunisia, Algeria, Mauritius.
12. See Hammer (2000) for a case study of Zambia.
13. Our study was focused on the national level. We thus do not take account of cross-national aspects of disease transmission (river pollution) or disease prevention and treatment. There have been a number of success stories in coordinated health measures, including sharp reductions in smallpox, river blindness and polio. A cross-national perspective on improving health is thus increasingly seen as an essential component of a global health strategy (Sachs, 2000) and may yield benefits on top of those obtainable by the national measures discussed here.
14. Hammer (2000) provides a revealing case study of Zambia. Morocco provides an illustration of a high-income country with a low population share with access to clean water, while Tanzania provides an example of the opposite case: perhaps not accidentally, the relative health outcomes for Morocco and Tanzania are at the bottom and at the top of their respective peer groups.

REFERENCES

Easterly, William (1999), 'Life during growth', Journal of Economic Growth, **4**(3), September: 239–75.

Garenne Michel and Gakusi Eneas (2000), *Health Effects of Structural Adjustment Programs in Sub-Saharan Africa*, CEPED, Paris.

Gwatkin, Davidson R., Shea Rustein, Kiersten Johnson, Rohini Pande and Adam Wagstaff (2000), *Socio-Economic Differences in Health, Nutrition, and Population*, World Bank.

Hammer, Jeffrey (2000), *Zambia, Public Expenditure Review*, Washington, DC: World Bank (draft).

Huttly, S.R.A., S.S. Morris and V. Pisani (1997), 'Prevention of diarrhoea in young children in developing countries', *Bulletin of the World Health Organisation*, **75**(2); 163–74.

Jack, William (1999), *Principles of Health Economics for Developing Countries*, Washington, DC: World Bank.

Pritchett, Lant and Lawrence H. Summers (1996), 'Wealthier is healthier', *Journal of Human Resources*, **31**(4): 842–68.

Sachs J. (2000), Chairman of the Commission on Macroeconomics and Health of the WHO, Various progress reports, Paris, France.

Savedoff William and Paul Schultz (2000), *Earnings and the Elusive Dividends of Health*, Washington, DC: Inter American Development Bank.

Wang, Jia *et al.* (1998), *Measuring Country Performance on Health*, Washington: World Bank.

World Bank (2001), *World Development Report*, 2000–2001, Oxford and New York: Oxford University Press.

World Health Organization (1999), The World Health Report 1999, Statistical Annex.

5. The political economy of exclusion and inclusion: democracy, markets and people

Deepak Nayyar*

I INTRODUCTION

As we enter the twenty-first century, *market economy* and *political democracy* are buzzwords: not only in turbulent Eastern Europe attempting a transition to capitalism, but also across a wide spectrum of countries in the developing world from Latin America through Africa to Asia. This is partly a consequence of the collapse of planned economies and excessive or inappropriate state intervention in market economies. And it is partly attributable to a concern about authoritarian regimes, particularly in countries where there has been no improvement in living conditions of the common people, but even in countries where economic development has been impressive despite which there is no movement towards a democratic polity. Consequently, the mood of the moment is such that markets and democracy are perceived as both virtue and necessity. In this process, some countries are in search of new models of development, while others are attempting to adapt their erstwhile models of development.

The theme of this chapter is that, contrary to the ideology of our times, markets and democracy may not ensure prosperity for everyone but may, in fact, exclude a significant proportion of people, particularly the poor, from the process of development. Section II explains why markets and democracy provide no magic wand. It stresses that market economy and political democracy are not separate worlds but are closely interconnected. Section III analyses how markets exclude people. It shows that exclusion and inclusion are in the logic of markets. Section IV explores the interaction of economics and politics to question orthodoxy. It argues that there is no equality among economic agents or political citizens in terms of their economic or political freedom to choose.

II DEMOCRACY AND MARKETS

The virtues of a market economy, articulated more than two centuries ago by Adam Smith, are spelt out at length in orthodox economic theory.[1] It is efficient as it optimizes production (in terms of resource allocation) and consumption (in terms of utility maximization). It is democratic insofar as it offers an equal opportunity to all. It is libertarian insofar as it gives every person the right of self-determination. For the contemporary enthusiasts, as much as for Adam Smith, private initiative is the means and economic prosperity is the end. Similarly, the virtues of a political democracy can be traced to Anglo-Saxon and European thinking about liberalism. Its basic tenets are freedom for individuals, pluralism of values, importance of rights and equality among people. In such political thought, these tenets are sacrosanct and the limits, if any, are enshrined in a *social contract* where individuals can be coerced by collective decisions only if they have consented to being subjected to the system.[2]

These virtues of market economy and political democracy, stressed by orthodoxy, have come to occupy centre-stage in the context of reforms in the contemporary world, particularly in the erstwhile socialist countries but also elsewhere. It is striking that democracy and markets are often considered together as if they are indivisible and are of equal importance. There are two limitations of this worldview.

First, there is an underlying presumption that democracy and markets are inseparable and almost ensure each other. This is wrong. The existence of a political democracy is neither a necessary nor a sufficient condition for the functioning of a market economy. The East Asian examples, of market economy without political democracy, provide ample support for this proposition. In terms of logic, it implies that the existence of a market economy is neither a necessary nor a sufficient condition for sustaining a political democracy.

Second, the pairing suggests that democracy and markets are at par. This is questionable. The introduction of democracy in a polity is a fundamental issue, whereas the use of markets in an economy is an institutional matter. For its intrinsic value, democracy is an end in itself. Markets, on the other hand, are means, the use (non-use) of which has to be justified by consequences. For some, economic freedom is an end in itself, so that markets can also have some intrinstic virtues, embedded in free or greater choice. In any event, both cannot be posited as fundamental requirements, for if there is a democracy it is up to the people to decide whether or not, or how much, to use markets.[3]

It is, therefore, reasonable to suggest that democracy and markets are distinct from each other. It is also plausible to argue that, even if both are institutions evolved by humankind, democracy and markets are simply not at the same level. Yet, orthodoxy believes that, insofar as democracy is about political freedom for individuals and markets are about economic freedom for individuals, the two together must serve the interests of the people. However, there is little basis for this inference either in theory or in practice.

For one, democracies function on the principle of majority rule or some variant thereof. This is clearly preferable to monarchies or oligarchies associated with the rule of an individual or of a few. But democracy can lead to the *tyranny of majorities*.[4] What is more, in countries characterized by social and economic inequalities that run deep, it is not clear how universal adult franchise alone can create political equality. We must not also forget that universal suffrage is a twentieth century phenomenon even in Europe. Indeed, we would do well to remember that it was property rights, rather than equality, which were at the foundation of liberalism. And, for a long time, it was property that endowed people with a right to vote so that access to political democracy was the privilege of a few, and not the right of everyone.

For another, the proposition that markets create equal opportunities for all depends on the critical assumption that the initial distribution of property rights is equal. Thus, any defence of the market on the premise that it is good in terms of actual outcomes must rest on a defence of the initial distribution of property rights. The argument that markets protect the interests of individuals or groups (ethnic, religious or political),[5] which even democracies cannot, is limited, for such individuals or groups are not guaranteed access to the market as buyers if they have no incomes, or as sellers if they have nothing to sell. It is important to recognize that while democracy may be about the *tyranny of majorities*, markets may be about the *tyranny of minorities*.

In practice, we know that the combination of democracy and markets is neither necessary nor sufficient to bring about an improvement in the living conditions of the majority of the people in a society. Consider egalitarian development, which brings about material well-being of people together with some equality of economic opportunities. We have seen such egalitarian development in planned economies without political democracy, as in the erstwhile socialist countries of Eastern Europe, and in market economies without political democracy, as in some East Asian and South-East Asian countries. In sharp contrast, markets and democracy together, where these institutions are not sufficiently developed and have not evolved over a long period of time, as in countries of Eastern Europe, have only produced chaos.[6] The outcome is prosperity for a few and misery for the many. Clearly, there are no magic wands. Democracy and markets are both institutions. The outcome depends on how they are used.

The orthodox belief system about market economy and political democracy is obviously open to question. It is clear enough that the democracy and markets, together, do not necessarily serve the interests of people. The fundamental problem with orthodoxy is that it treats the two spheres of market economy and political democracy as separate from each other. For, in isolation, each provides freedom to choose. This is a convenient abstraction. But it is not a correct presumption. The reality is very different as the two are simply not separable. In fact, the two are closely interconnected. It is the interaction between market economy and political democracy that shapes outcomes for people. This interaction of economics and politics, which is critical, is explored later in the chapter.

III EXCLUSION AND INCLUSION

Joan Robinson once said: 'There is only one thing that is worse than being exploited by capitalists. And that is not being exploited by capitalists.' The same goes for participation in markets. For there is an exclusion in the process.[7]

The term *exclusion* has become a part of the lexicon of economists recently, although it has been in the jargon of sociology and the vocabulary of politics in Europe for somewhat longer. The phrase *social exclusion* is used to describe a situation, as also to focus on a process, which excludes individuals or groups from livelihoods and rights, thus depriving them of sources of well-being that have been assumed, if not taken for granted, in industrial countries.[8] The essential point is that economic stratification is inevitable in market economies and societies that systematically integrate some and marginalize others to distribute the benefits of economic growth in ways that include some and exclude others.

The literature on developing countries has, in contrast, sought to study marginalization or deprivation of majorities through a focus on poverty and inequality. The concept of exclusion may be useful in the context of developing countries if it helps us understand how the spread of markets affects the common people. Exclusion is inherent in the logic of markets. Markets may exclude people as consumers or producers or both.

Markets exclude people as consumers or buyers if they do not have any incomes, or sufficient incomes, which can be translated into purchasing power. In Amartya Sen's terminology, this exclusion is attributable to a lack of *entitlements*.[9] Such people are obviously excluded from the consumption of goods and services which are sold in the market. But they may also be excluded from non-market allocations such as the public provision of goods and services if they live in clusters such as urban slums, or rural settlements, where drinking water, sanitation facilities, roads, electricity or even street lights are not provided. It is, then, the location of the poor (and not their income) which deprives them of access to public services which may be (almost) free elsewhere.

Markets exclude people as producers or sellers if they have neither *assets* nor *capabilities.* People experience such exclusion if they do not have assets, physical or financial, which can be used (or sold) to yield an income in the form of rent, interest or profits.[10] Even those without assets could enter the market as producers or sellers, using their labour, if they have some capabilities.[11] Such capabilities which are acquired through education, training or experience are different from abilities which are endowed. But the distribution of capabilities may be just as unequal if not more so. It is these capabilities which can, in turn, yield an income in the form of wages. Hence, people without capabilities, the poor who cannot find employment, are excluded. In fact, even people with capabilities may be excluded from employment if there is no demand for their capabilities in the (labour) market.[12] And, in the ultimate analysis, such capabilities must find acceptance, or use, in the market. That is the problem.

In addition, markets exclude people both as consumers and producers or as buyers and sellers if they do not accept, or conform to, the *values* of a market system. The most obvious example of such exclusion is tribal populations or forest communities in market economies. The same can be said, perhaps, for pockets of pre-capitalist formations in what are essentially capitalist systems. Such exclusion may also take other forms. There may be people who are unable or unwilling to sell their assets: for instance, a person may be unable or unwilling to sell an ancestral house in the market. Or, there may be people who are unable or unwilling to sell their capabilities: for instance, a person may be unable or unwilling to charge fees as an astrologer or a musician because of a belief system that such talents cannot and should not be sold. In other words, people who are excluded because of their set of norms can find some kind of inclusion in the market once they accept a different set of norms. In general, the terms of such inclusion are such that it intensifies insecurity and exploitation at least for some time.

As a concept, exclusion may describe a situation or characterize a process.[13] In describing a situation, whether it refers to a point in time or to a permanent state, the concept of exclusion is much the same as the concept of poverty. The object is to identify the excluded and the poor respectively. In characterizing a process, the concept of exclusion goes further to focus on how the operation of economic and social forces recreates or accentuates exclusion over time. This may be attributable to the logic of markets, which give to those who have and take away from those who have not, as the process of cumulative causation leads to market-driven virtuous circles and vicious circles.[14] This may be the outcome of patterns of development where economic growth is uneven between regions and the distribution of its benefits is unequal between people, so that there is growing affluence for some combined with persistent poverty for many. This may be the consequence of strategies of development, as a similar economic performance in the aggregate could lead to egalitarian development in one situation, and growth which bypasses the majority of the people in another situation. It is clear that institutional arrangements which mediate between economic development on the one hand and social development on the other are critical. For these institutional mechanisms may accentuate exclusion or foster inclusion, just as they may limit the gains to an affluent minority or spread the gains to the poor majority. The initial distribution of assets and the subsequent distribution of incomes are important determinants of whether the vulnerable sections of the population are marginalized and excluded or are uplifted and included.

It must be recognized that the impact of exclusion from markets is at different levels: individuals, social groups, regional and national.[15] Individuals are excluded from access to markets if they do not have the requisite entitlements, assets, capabilities or values. Groups in society such as the landless, the illiterate, the handicapped, the lower castes (as in India), women (in some occupations), migrant workers or ethnic groups are sometimes excluded from participation in the economy.[16] This could mean that identifiable social groups are at a disadvantage in their access to markets and may even be subjected to systematic exclusion from livelihood. Regions within countries, particularly those without natural resources, those with a difficult terrain, those at a distance, or those without skilled labour, may be excluded from development. This may take the form of exclusion from infrastructure, from public goods and services, or from economic and social opportunities. Some of these exclusions from the market also exist at the national level. There are many examples of this in poor countries such as exclusions from land, from employment, from social protection, from health care, from education and even from basic human needs such as food, clothing and shelter.

The analysis so far may suggest that exclusion is bad and inclusion is good. But it is not meant to. It must be said that the nature of inclusion or exclusion matters. Inclusion is not always good. Coercive inclusion by markets, whether child labour, tribal populations or immigrant workers can be exploitative. The employment of women as wage labour on terms inferior to those of men, or the employment of migrants from rural areas in the unorganized urban sector at wages lower than those of workers in the organized sector, provide other examples. The basic point is that inclusion which is coercive or on inferior terms is not desirable. And the terms of inclusion matter. For similar reasons, exclusion is not always bad. To those who do not accept the values of the market system, any voluntary exclusion from markets, on the part of individuals or groups, should be perfectly acceptable.

IV ECONOMICS AND POLITICS

It has been suggested earlier that market economy and political democracy cannot and should not be separated from each other as if they constitute two different worlds. The reason is simple enough. In every society, economy and polity are closely intertwined. It is, therefore, essential to explore the interaction of economics and politics, in this context, which shapes outcomes for people.

The essence of the tension between the economics of markets and the politics of democracy must be recognized. In a market economy, people vote with their money in the marketplace. But a political democracy works on the basis of one-person-one-vote. The distribution of votes, unlike the distribution of incomes or assets, is equal. One adult has one vote in politics, even though a rich man has more votes than a poor man, in terms of purchasing power, in the market. This tension may be compounded by a related asymmetry between economy and polity. The people who are excluded by the economics of markets are included by the politics of democracy. Hence, exclusion and inclusion are asymmetrical in economics and politics. The distribution of capabilities is also uneven in the economic and political spheres. The rich dominate a market economy in terms of purchasing power. But the poor have a strong voice in a political democracy in terms of votes. And there is a mismatch. It is clear that, in reconciling market economy and political democracy, a sensible compromise must be reached between the economic directions which the market sets on the basis of purchasing power and the priorities which a political system sets on the basis of one-person-one-vote.[17] In this context, it is not surprising that successive generations of economic thinkers and social philosophers have stressed the role of the state in this process of mediation. The reason is important even if it is not obvious. Governments are accountable to their people, whereas markets are not. In a democracy, of course, governments are elected by the people. But even where they are not, the state needs legitimation from the people, most of whom are not rich or are poor. The task of reconciliation and mediation is obviously difficult but clearly necessary.

Markets are responsive to the demands of rich people and not to the needs of the poor people. This is inherent in the logic of markets where decisions about what is produced are based on demand and not on need. Thus, markets produce goods for which there is enough purchasing power.

The output-mix depends upon the composition of expenditure and the size of the market. Since the rich have more purchasing power, markets, left to themselves, are likely to produce more cellular phones and not improved ploughs or more soft drinks and not safer drinking water.[18] In this manner, markets include people with entitlements but exclude people without entitlements. In theory, every economic agent has the freedom to choose. In practice, there is a choice for some but not for others. And there is more choice for some than for others.

Democracies are more responsive to people with a voice than to people at large. People without a political voice are often simply neglected. There are, of course, problems associated with majority rule which might lead some democracies to exclude minorities. Even if we abstract from such problems, however, the principle of one-person-one-vote does not make every citizen equal in a political democracy. For, in the real world, social and economic inequalities are inevitably reflected in the political process. In theory, democracy provides every citizen with political freedom in the form of civil rights and political liberties. In practice, there is freedom for some but not for others. And there is more freedom for some than for others.

The orthodox dichotomy between economy and polity simply does not conform to any reality. It is only to be expected that there is an interaction between exclusion from the market in the economic sphere and exclusion from democracy in the political sphere. An economic exclusion from livelihood often creates or accentuates a political exclusion from rights. Thus, for the poor in a democracy the right to vote may exist in principle, but in practice it may be taken away by coercion or coaxed away by material incentives at the time of elections. Similarly, the very poor are vulnerable to exploitation or oppression because their civil rights or equality before the law exist in principle, but they are difficult to protect or preserve in practice. The reason is simple. They do not have the resources to claim or the power to assert their rights.

Exclusion extends beyond the economic and the political to the social and cultural spheres. The social manifestations of exclusion can be powerful. This is best illustrated with an example from India where the underprivileged in society, such as the lower castes, are poor because they have little in the form of entitlements, assets or capabilities, but even where they are better endowed in terms of these attributes, their exclusion from markets, particularly from the market for land and labour in rural India, persists for social rather than economic reasons. At the same time, economic exclusion accentuates social exclusion, while social exclusion accentuates political exclusion. Similarly, cultural exclusion such as that of immigrant groups, minority communities or ethnic groups interacts with economic exclusion from the market and political exclusion from democracy.

Clearly, there is an overlap between those excluded by market economy and those excluded by political democracy, just as there is an overlap between those included by market economy and those included by political democracy. The poor who are marginalized in the economy also do not have a voice in the polity, just as the rich who are dominant in the economy also have a strong political voice. Economic deprivation and political marginalization go hand-in-hand in much the same way as economic strength and political power go hand-in-hand. Thus, the real world around us does not conform to the characterization in the orthodox belief system. There are two divergences which yield two propositions. For one, the economy and the polity are connected and interdependent. For another, there is no equality among economic agents or political citizens in terms of their economic or political freedom to choose. There is, in fact, a hierarchy of freedoms, with more for some and less for others, where there is a significant overlap in the economic and political sphere. These two propositions, which emerge from the analysis in this chapter, add to our understanding of markets and democracy.

In conclusion, it needs to be said that the liberal paradox is much deeper. On the one hand, markets exclude people without entitlements, assets or capabilities. It is in the logic of markets. Yet, markets would like to include as many people as possible. For, in the words of Adam Smith: 'the division of labour is limited by the size of the market'. On the other hand, democracy includes people by a constitutional right to vote. It is the foundation of democracy. Yet, political processes seek to exclude or to marginalize those without a voice. That is what the pursuit and exercise of political power is about. The irony of this paradoxical situation is striking.

NOTES

* I would like to thank Amit Bhaduri and Satish Jain for helpful discussion which clarified my ideas on the subject. I would also like to thank Jean Dreze for useful suggestions.

1. This literature began life in the era of classical political economy. The most important contributions were those of Smith (1776) and Mill (1848). See also Hayek (1960).
2. The classic statements of liberalism are to be found in the writings of Adam Smith, Jean Jacques Rousseau and, in particular, John Stuart Mill. More recent contributions, representing different views, are Berlin (1969), Sen (1970), Rawls (1971) and Sugden (1981).
3. For a discussion on the importance of democracy, in the context of market economies, see Sen (2000). Democracy, Sen argues, has three distinct virtues: (i) its intrinsic importance, (ii) its instrumental contributions, and (iii) its constructive role, in the creation of values and norms. Sen recognizes that markets have obvious instrumental virtues. But he also goes on to argue that, if an extension of the choice set is good, a market economy may have intrinsic virtues.
4. The principle that the will of the majority should always prevail in a democracy has been a matter of debate for a long time. John Stuart Mill, for example, argued that 'the government of the whole by a mere majority of the people', the principle of majority rule, is

undemocratic. This was, then, developed into an argument for proportional representation (Mill, 1946).

5. The argument is that even when a minority group is treated with hostility by the majority (say a group of people with extremist political views who wish to produce a newspaper), the market system offers the minority significant protection (say buying newsprint and employing journalists). See Sugden (1981). Similarly, Friedman (1962) points out that Jewish people were able to survive the hostile environment in medieval Europe largely because they were engaged in commerce and trade. And the economic (self) interest of the population prevailed over religious discrimination. Becker argues that markets protect minorities through the force of competition. Firms that discriminate against certain minority groups will be driven out of business by those that do not. This argument is much more limited. It may also be wrong because, under certain circumstances, discrimination can maximize profits.
6. Cf. Amsden *et al.* (1994). See also, Taylor (1993).
7. Much the same, I have argued elsewhere, is true of globalization. For a detailed discussion, see Nayyar (2000).
8. See Commission of the European Communities (1993). For an extensive discussion on social exclusion, ranging from conceptual issues through country studies to policy issues, see Rodgers *et al.* (1995).
9. This term was first used by Sen (1981) in his work on poverty and famines.
10. The rural poor in the developing world, who are landless, experience such exclusion. The landless are deprived not only of a source of livelihood but also of a status in society. Exclusion, then, is both economic and social.
11. In this chapter, I use the word *capabilities* to characterize the mix of natural talents, skills acquired through training, learning from experience and abilities or expertise based on education, embodied in a person, that enable him or her to use these (capabilities as a producer or a worker) for which there is not only a price but also a demand in the market. It follows that even persons with capabilities may be excluded from employment if there is no demand for their capabilities in the (labour) market. It is essential to note that the same word, *capabilities*, has been used in a very different sense by Amartya Sen, who argues that the well-being of a person depends on what the person succeeds in *doing* with the commodities (and their characteristics) at his command. For example: food can provide nutrition to a healthy person but not to a person with a parasitic disease; or, a bicycle can provide transportation to an able-bodied person but not to a disabled person. Thus, for Sen (1985), *capabilities* characterize the combination of functionings a person can achieve, given his personal features (conversion of characteristics into functionings) and his command over commodities (entitlements).
12. Open unemployment means simply exclusion from the labour market. But there is also exclusion within the labour market experienced by those who are under-employed in the agricultural sector and by those who are self-employed or in casual employment in the urban informal sector. The segmented labour market means that access to good jobs which are secure and well-paid is exceedingly difficult whereas access to bad jobs which are insecure and poorly paid is easier.
13. Cf. Rodgers *et al.* (1995).
14. For an analysis of cumulative causation in the process of development, in particular spread effects and backwash effects, see Myrdal (1968).
15. For a detailed discussion, see Rodgers *et al.* (1995), pp. 269–75.
16. Some, like Becker, would argue that women and minorities would be helped by markets which reduce discrimination. But this is not possible if such groups do not have the requisite entitlements, assets or capabilities. What is more, discrimination persists for social and political reasons.
17. For a discussion of this problem, in the Indian context, see Bhaduri and Nayyar (1996).
18. Similarly, R&D which is market-driven is more likely to focus on tomatoes with longer shelf-lives or maize used as poultry-feed and not on drought-resistant crops for dry lands. It is not surprising, then, that only 0.2 per cent of worldwide R&D on health care is devoted to tuberculosis, gastric diseases and pneumonia, even though these account

for almost 20 per cent of the disease burden in the world. Vaccines are the most cost-effective technologies known in health care, for they prevent illness with one dose. But the proportion of private R&D expenditure in the pharmaceutical sector on vaccines is negligible because they cannot produce profits year after year.

REFERENCES

Amsden, A., J. Kochanowicz and L. Taylor (1994), *The Market Meets its Match,* Cambridge: Harvard University Press.

Berlin, I. (1969), *Four Essays on Liberty*, Oxford: Clarendon Press.

Bhaduri, A. and D. Nayyar (1996), *The Intelligent Person's Guide to Liberalization*, New Delhi: Penguin Books.

Commission of the European Communities (1993), *Towards a Europe of Solidarity: Intensifying the Fight against Social Exclusion and Fostering Integration*, Brussels: EC.

Friedman, M. (1962), *Capitalism and Freedom*, Chicago: Chicago University Press.

Hayek, F.A. (1960), *Constitution of Liberty*, London: Routledge and Kegan Paul.

Mill, J.S. (1848), *Principles of Political Economy*, with an introduction by W.J. Ashley London: Longmans.

Mill, J.S. (1946), *On Liberty (1859)* and *Considerations on Representative Government (1861)*, with an introduction by R.D. Mc Callum, Oxford: Oxford University Press.

Myrdal, G. (1968), *Asian Drama: An Inquiry into the Poverty of Nations*, London: Allen Lane.

Nayyar, D. (2000), 'Globalization and Development Strategies', in J. Toye (ed.), *Trade and Development: Directions for the Twenty-first Century*, Cheltenham, UK and Northampton, US: Edward Elgar, forthcoming.

Rawls, J. (1971), *A Theory of Justice*, Oxford: Clarendon Press.

Rodgers, G., C. Gore and J.B. Figueiredo (eds) (1995), *Social Exclusion:Rhetoric Reality Responses*, Geneva: International Labour Organisation.

Sen, A.K. (1970), *Collective Choice and Social Welfare*, Amsterdam: North-Holland.

Sen, A.K. (1981), *Poverty and Famines: An Essay on Entitlement and Deprivation*, Oxford: Clarendon Press.

Sen, A.K. (1985), *Commodities and Capabilities*, Amsterdam: North-Holland.

Sen, A.K. (2000), *Development as Freedom*, New Delhi: Oxford University Press.

Smith, A. (1776), *The Wealth of Nations*, with an introduction by Andrew Skinner (1970), Harmondsworth: Pelican Books.

Sugden, R. (1981), *The Political Economy of Public Choice: An Introduction to Welfare Economics*, Oxford: Martin Robertson.

Taylor, L. (1993), *The Rocky Road to Reform: Adjustment, Income Distribution and Growth in the Developing World,* Cambridge: The MIT Press.

PART III

Finance and Asset Markets

6. Finance and competition

William Darity, Jr., Bobbie L. Horn and Michael Syron Lawlor*

The motive of business is pecuniary gain, the method is essentially purchase and sale. The aim and usual outcome is an accumulation of wealth.

(T. Veblen, 1904, p. 20.)

I INTRODUCTION

When Sraffa surveyed the field of value theory in the prefatory comments of his influential 1926 article on the Marshallian theory of competitive price, what he found most remarkable was the relative lack of contention concerning questions of value theory: 'A *striking* feature of the present position of economic science is the almost unanimous agreement at which economists have arrived regarding the theory of competitive value.' (1926 p. 535). One might be tempted to say that Sraffa spent the rest of his career in an attempt to upset this tranquility – and, that he was substantially successful in that effort.

As theoretical controversies go, taking a broad view of Sraffa's almost invisible influence, the dispute raised by Sraffa over the fundamental approach of economic theory to the question of relative price formation has proved to be a protracted and enduring one, at least since the 1960s. Elements of the debate have ranged across all levels of economic discussion, from interpretation of the history of the discipline to the central theoretical framework of contemporary economics to ideology.[1] At bottom, these disputes concern a challenge, premised on an interpretation of the classical economists, to the orthodox[2] conception of the process by which a modern capitalist economy produces, prices and distributes the social output.[3]

In terms of the critique of the orthodox paradigm that was mounted in this challenge, a history of the controversy would have to include (but not be limited to) the following points:

1a. The internal consistency of the Marshallian theory of the firm in a long-run setting and the external correspondence of the 'laws of return' with observable industrial developments (Sraffa, 1926; Sylos-Labini, 1985).
1b. The confessed inability to construct any general 'laws' concerning distribution based on the marginalist principles underlying orthodox factor market analysis (Harcourt, 1972; Harcourt and Laing, 1971).
1c. The question of the compatibility, and/or generality of one over the other, between the orthodox and classical visions when expressed as a general equilibrium system (Hahn, 1982; Walsh and Gram, 1980).

Furthermore, within the classical revivalist camp itself, there are now disputes over the precise nature of the classical system supposedly resurrected by Sraffa in 1960 and claimed by his followers as an alternative framework for value theory to the orthodox conception. Among the issues these debates have addressed are:

2a. The question of the interpretation of Sraffa's 'prices of production' and in particular whether or not they represent some meaningful element in the complex operation of the economic system to which the observed prices can be said to gravitate' (Garegnani, 1984; Roncaglia, 1978; Harcourt, 1981);
2b. The extent to which the Sraffian system illuminates the aims of the classical and/or Marxian traditions of political economy (Steedman, 1977; Rowthorn, 1974; Harcourt, 1986; Hollander, 1985).
2c. The possibility of using Sraffa's 'classical' approach to value theory as the basis for a price-theoretic underpinning to the Post-Keynesian goals of reformulating macroeconomics (Eatwell and Milgate, 1983; Milgate, 1982; Casarosa, 1985; Harcourt, 1981).
2d. The precise nature of the forces which are appropriate to the analysis of the distribution issue within the Sraffian approach, given the relative openness of that system to these questions (Garegani, 1984; Hamouda and Harcourt, 1988), and
2e. The question of whether the whole basis of the 'Classical' – Sraffian price system, equating value theory with the specification of states exhibiting equality of rates of return, can be justified on the basis of an analysis of the dynamic properties of the system when it is out of such an equilibrium state. (Duménil and Lévy, 1987; Nikaido, 1983; Morishima, 1973; Steedman, 1984; Flaschel and Semmler 1987).

When this large range of controversy is considered, and especially when it is combined with ongoing developments within the orthodox camp itself concerning internal questions of the more dominant paradigm in value theory (such as non-linear dynamic modeling and path-dependent equilibria most recently), it seems clear that value theory, far from exhibiting tranquility (outside of textbooks), is in a very considerable state of upheaval.

Our purpose here is to attempt to outline a possible path toward reconciliation of some of the above-mentioned disputes through an analysis of the underlying concepts of competition implicit in the orthodox and classical conceptions of value theory, and in the scope each of these conceptions offers for the role of the financial usages of modern capitalist economies. It will be our contention that the developments cited in (1a) and (1b), above, necessitate admitting the obvious faults that the theoretical critique unleashed by Sraffa has revealed in the dominant theory, and require us to examine what elements might be salvageable from that wreckage. This will be the subject of section II.

In section III we will briefly outline the extent to which an alternative classical conception of competition so revealingly illuminated by Sraffa's 'prelude to a critique', but which also has continually underpinned at least the theoretical *aspirations* of the post-marginal revolution tradition, offers a way out of some of the impasses thrown up by the orthodox conception.

Yet in light of the points cited above, we will also have to note some obvious problems that recent research has revealed with the classical framework. Thus in section IV we offer what we see as a possible line of development of the classical conception via an explicit role for financial markets for which we find support in the work of Veblen and Keynes. We attempt to show that not only does this conception provide a possible answer to some of the questions concerning the classical competitive processes, but that it may also provide both clues to some of the questions whose traditional answers were negated in the critique of neoclassical theory in section II, and a possible role for the still vibrant flotsam of the wreckage of the dominant conception that the classical critique has identified.

II THE ORTHODOX COMPETITIVE STATE

In an ironic reflection of Sraffa's comments in his original assault on the Marshallian view of competition that still dominates economic theory, what perhaps most aptly characterizes that view itself is its air of tranquility. Organized around the static conditions associated with price-taking behavior by a discrete organizational unit of production, in a discrete 'industry', Marshallian competition proceeds by the orderly behavior of these passive firms in the short and the long run.

In the short run, the firms passively adjust output until the profit-maximizing marginal conditions are met. In the long-run, passive entry and exit into already existing industries brings industry output in line with firm average costs, given by the various 'laws of return'. And, importantly, for this is the link between the modern and the older classical view of competition, this same long-run equilibrium state is characterized by equal profit-rates or rates of return over cost in each industry (usually defined as zero). The final detail is the allowance for differential productivity and organizational efficiency across firms accruing as rent to explain interindustry differentials from the equal (zero) rate of return. It is appropriate to describe this conception of competitive behavior as a *state of affairs view of competition*. Competition is identified by the initial assumptions used to describe the condition that renders the firms paralyzed at the start, price-taking behavior. Furthermore, it is on the basis of the standard use of this state as a benchmark against which states of lesser degrees of competitiveness are defined. Industries are classified as competitive or non-competitive accordingly. Thus, it also is proper to identify this concept further as a *market structure view of competition*.

Although it continues to display remarkable resilience in modern economics, the market structure concept of competition has long attracted substantive expressions of dissatisfaction from diverse quarters. The terms of the dissatisfaction include complaints of an intractable nature that strike at the core of the theory of the firm, the evolution of industrial structure, the theory of capital, and the characterization of equilibrium. It is worthwhile to review some of these critiques briefly.

As early as the mid-1920s, Piero Sraffa (1926) launched a withering attack on the inapplicability of Marshallian long-period perfect competition analysis to all conditions of costs and returns to scale. Sraffa's conclusion was that the only logically consistent method by which the Marshallians could retain the assumption of price-taking behavior by individual firms was by assuming that any economies of scale were external to the firm although internal to the industry group. Under this assumption, the individual firms could still be treated as satisfying the standard convexity conditions (that is, U-shaped average cost curves and all that). They could still be passive price takers and earn a 'normal' profit.

But for Sraffa (1926) there was nothing, or at most very little, in the space thus carved out to reconcile increasing returns with perfect competition – those economies of scale external to the firm but internal to the industry. Even for Frank Knight (1925, p. 333) in his reaction to a paper by Frank Graham, 'the category of decreasing cost under stable competition remains an "empty economic box"'.

Knight, like Sraffa in 1926, argued that to introduce increasing returns required the monopoly element. Sraffa (1960) later adopted instead a non-market structure view of competition, as we shall see below, rooted in Classical rather than Marshallian economics.

More recently, Helpman and Krugman have expressed reservations about external economies models in the international trade field where such models are extremely popular. External economies models permit the analyst to maintain the perfectly competitive imputation and to duck the problem of surpluses above and beyond rewards that take the form of direct factor payments.

Some 40 years after Sraffa's missive, Paul McNulty (1968, p. 641) expressed discomfiture with the extreme orthodox cases of industry structure – perfect competition and monopoly – pointing out that both of them rule out the more customary notion of competition as *rivalry*. The monopolist is faced with no contestants, and the price-taking perfect competitor is oblivious to all other participants in their industry. It is only in the intermediate cases where 'every act of competition on the part of a businessman' (McNulty, 1968, p. 641) occurs that rivalry is apparent. Those cases fall under the heading of *imperfect* competition in the standard typology.

It is in the region between perfect competition and pure monopoly that varieties of industrial strategy and struggle appear on the horizon – product differentiation, conflict over market shares, predatory pricing, and so on. But all of these activities by definition are taken by orthodoxy indicators of something other than perfect competition. In a discussion of the Marxist concept of competition, John Weeks (1981, p. 160) has observed:

> . . . bourgeois (i.e., neoclassical) theory initiates the discussion of competition at a relatively low level of abstraction and, as a result, treats it in an extremely complex form, at a level where one must at the outset account for price competition, product differentiation, capital movements, barriers to those movements, and the process of centralization. As a consequence, the analysis proceeds eclectically, and the forms the competitive struggle take under capitalism do not derive from the concept itself but as exception to it.

In a sense, Weeks is too polite. The analysis proceeds not merely 'eclectically' but more accurately in an *ad hoc* fashion, since the region between perfect competition and pure monopoly is an ill-defined and non-systematic continuum.[4]

Intra-industry rivalry thus is relegated to the status of an imperfection in the characterization of competition in the orthodox scheme. Intra-industry rivalry remains a relatively undeveloped arena, including the emergent contestable markets hypothesis. The latter requires a condition of potential entry to prevail; in fact potential entry becomes the essence of competition once the contestable markets hypothesis is embraced.

However, it must eliminate the case of pure monopoly or some variants of oligopoly theory premised from the outset on immutable entry barriers. The source of the immutability is rarely explained and when explained is not generally explained satisfactorily.

Even the intermediate case of monopolistic competition can be converted into a special case of perfect competition. In a clever paper Michael Murphy (1978) has demonstrated that a world of product differentiated firms can look like the world of perfect competitors, if the output of the former is converted into quality adjusted units. The only substantial element of rivalry in this case, rivalry over variation in the product, would be suppressed for analytical purposes.

Robin Marris (1964, p. 187), as did Kurt Rothschild (1947) even earlier, argued for the predominance of oligopoly as the most typical industry structure. 'Competition', now variously defined, can then be treated as a special case of oligopoly, and oligopoly is clearly a setting for strategy, forecasting of the actions of other businessmen, and conflict. And, as Rothschild (1947, p. 305) so presciently anticipated, oligopoly theory is the playground for game theorists:

> . . . the influence of analogies drawn from mechanics and biology – so fruitful in the fields of perfect and monopolistic competition respectively – must be discarded when we deal with powerful active agents like duopolists and oligopolists. If analogies have to be used . . . then they will have to be drawn from those spheres where writers deal with moves and counter-moves, with struggles for power and position – in short, from books dealing with the general aspects of politics, and military strategy and tactics.

An environment dominated by oligopolistic industries, where each participant is necessarily charting a strategy premised on the actions of other enterprises' outcomes, depends upon the characterization of the reaction–response behavior of each participant – a characterization that can vary from model to model and paper to paper at the discretion of the theorist. Moreover, barring relatively simple assumptions about what each participant believes about the actions of rivals, outcomes are frequently indeterminate on *a priori* grounds.

Rather than seeking a set of conditions at the firm or industry level consistent with stable output decisions, the equilibrium condition associated with a world of oligopolistic industries could be economy-wide. Such an approach was suggested by one of the foremost advocates of a monopoly power approach to the determination of prices, Michal Kalecki, in his response to a critic. Kalecki (1942, pp. 122–3) felt that the only reasonable way to depict the equilibrium position of an economy where firms engaged in mark-up pricing, was one where all firms earn a uniform rate of profit.

Equilibrium then goes beyond the indeterminate closing of the game to a circumstance where there is no opportunity to earn a higher rate of profit in any one single activity than in any other. This, however, is precisely the Classical notion of competitive equilibrium, independent of particular assumptions about industry structure, rather than the neoclassical idea linked to marginal conditions for profit maxima at the firm or industry level. More recently, Dutt (1987, 1995) has argued that the Classical view of competition – the tendency of an economy to achieve a uniform rate of profit – is the view most consistent with the Kalecki–Keynes traditions.

We come next to the problematic characterization of equilibrium associated with the orthodox theory of the firm. Under perfect competition there are a set of (ideal?) marginal conditions that apply at the firm level (price = marginal cost = marginal revenue = average cost = average revenue). These conditions, divorced from an assessment of enterprise profitability particularly since this type of firm is earning zero pure profit under constant returns to scale, pose the question of whether this really is a theory of the firm/business enterprise or merely a theory of optimal production for a plant within a firm.

The inattention to overall enterprise profitability implies a certain 'temporary' nature of equilibrium even when all markets clear, because there could be substantial rates of return or profit rate differentials across firms in different industries. The presumption of the orthodox approach is simply that the conditions of perfect competition will lead these returns to equalize. Greater atomism leads to a greater propensity toward uniformity of rewards; greater concentration leads to a reduced propensity toward uniformity of rewards (for a useful discussion see Clifton, 1977, especially pp. 142–3).

It is at this stage that the orthodox development of the concept of competition conflates its own industry structure-based notion of competition with the Classical conception which emphasizes equalization of rates of profit. The latter concept slips in by the back door, pushing the characterization of competitive conditions away from the individual firm and/or individual industry to the properties possessed by the economy as a whole.

It is neither obvious nor necessarily true that an economy with perfectly competitive firms – firms whose operations are predicated on the belief that whatever actions they take will not affect anyone else and vice versa – will be more conducive to equalization of profit rates. Unless, of course, one views the relevant profit rate as zero and the world of perfectly competitive firms as a world of zero profits; then, and only then, in a tautological sense does perfect competition automatically mean a zero profit rate.

Finance, as we argue below, could afford an escape route from these conundrums, but finance fits uneasily within the neoclassical typology of competitive conditions. Instead of permitting the financial sector to take sway over the characterization of competition, the tendency among modern economists has usually been to subordinate finance to the industry structure concept of competition.

For example, theoretical inquiries often take perfectly competitive financial markets as their starting point. Fama and Miller (1972, p. 21) opened a text by adopting what they described as a '. . . particularly fruitful, special set of attributes . . .':

1. All traders have equal and costless access to information about the ruling price and all other relevant properties of the securities traded.
2. Buyers and sellers, or issuers of securities take the prices as given; that is, they do, and can justifiably, act as if their activities in the market had no detectable effect on the ruling prices.
3. There are no brokerage fees, transfer taxes, or other transactions costs incurred when securities are bought, sold, or issued.

Then Fama and Miller (1972, pp. 21–2) immediately add the following disclaimer about the real world irrelevance of such a construct, compelling them, for logical consistency, to push financial markets into the imperfectionist intermediate region of industry structures: 'Needless to say, no such market exists, in the real world, nor could it. Rather, what is an idealization of the same kind and function as that of a perfect gas or a perfect vacuum in the physical sciences.'

Such idealizations impel us to focus on the 'exceptions' to the competitive ideal embodied in perfect competition. In the context of finance theory, the securities market becomes just another market that fails to meet the conditions of perfect competition for Fama and Miller, that is, another market characterized by one of the near infinite varieties of imperfect competition.

With respect to lending institutions a similar problem crops up. The perfectly competitive imputation is taken to mean that such institutions would make an unlimited supply of credit available to borrowers at a fixed interest rate.

There would be no price discrimination with respect to borrowers, no rationing of credit. The volume of credit absorbed would be dictated by the demand of the borrowers, although this must presume some substantial absence of overlap between lenders and borrowers. There have been some brilliant intellectual gymnastics performed to lend greater 'realism' to the analysis of the lending industry. Information asymmetries are especially popular, one version of which is the theory of adverse selection which has been used to explain the upward stickiness of the loan rate in an environment where there is not an unlimited supply of credit. In summary, the orthodox concept of perfect competition is (1) not robust with respect to assumptions about returns to scale, (2) renders rivalry an exception or a transitory activity rather than the norm in the assessment of the competitiveness of business activity, (3) yields a problematic characterization of competition.

Having said this, let us pause for a moment and consider the problems of the orthodox theory in historical perspective. It was clearly the professed intention of all of the great theorists of the so-called 'second marginal revolution' (that is, Wicksell, Marshall and Clark) to use the marginalist tools introduced by their immediate predecessors (that is, Menger, Jevons and Walras) to construct a *complete* theoretical system – where 'complete' meant that in addition to a set of relative prices, the marginalist analytic machine would provide answers to the traditional preoccupations of the classical economists, in particular distribution (see Kompas, 1992, and Milgate, 1982).

Yet we can now see that it is principally the marginalist answers to these *long-period* problems that were severely called into question by the theoretical debates of the last decades, which emanated from the classical critique launched by Sraffa. As a result, it now seems that the only logically consistent use of marginalism is limited to *short-period* problems of a 'temporary equilibrium' nature. Among these are the set of Walrasian prices consistent with the allocation of a fixed amount of resources among alternative uses; the short-run output of a *plant* (not a *firm*), given the prices of outputs and inputs; and the laws governing short-run changes in *market* prices, given temporary conditions of supply and demand.

Interestingly, to the old classical economists such conclusions would have seemed eminently sensible, given their almost complete lack of interest in the intricate workings-out of the 'laws of supply and demand' (see, for example, chapters 4 and 30 of Ricardo's *Principles* (1951), or for a modern statement of the same outlook, Garegnani, 1983). Thus, in historical perspective, the outcome of the debates over the classical challenge to orthodoxy has revealed that the traditional marginalist underpinning to short-run supply and demand problems appears to fall to pieces at each point that they are pushed into the long-run setting that was the domain of classical theorizing, just as the classical analysis itself had always implied.

From a logical standpoint, this situation reveals a theoretical dilemma for the further development of 'economic science'. On the one hand, we could follow the lead of the general equilibrium theorists in abandoning the traditional conception of competition as a process of equalizing rates of return in the long-run, in favor of a generalized and logically watertight specification of simultaneous supply and demand equilibrium. Here all that is required of equilibrium is that all markets clear, and the whole idea of rates of return becomes subsumed under the extended construct of an intertemporal price system.

From our standpoint, what is most noteworthy about this line of development is the fact that given the ancillary role accorded rates of return (they merely fall out as 'own-rates' based on the equilibrium price vector), there is a complete *abandonment* of the whole issue of the long-period competitive process as conceived by both the classical and earlier marginalist traditions.[5] In essence this view amounts to accepting the proposition that if the process of competition of the capitals for equal profits cannot be captured by orthodox methods, then it does not exist. What we want to suggest is that for those who see this process of competition as integral to the workings of the economic system, a method of incorporating it into economic theory is offered by that alternative concept of competition inherent in the classical vision.

III THE CLASSICAL COMPETITIVE PROCESS

As noted above, the alternative concept of competition finds its origins in Classical political economy and is not plagued by the same limitations as the orthodox industry structure approach. The various writers in this tradition, from Smith to Ricardo to Marx, are all united in *defining competition by the existence of a tendency toward the equalization of rates of profit.* Equilibrium, or more generally the abstract object of theoretical discussion, then becomes defined as a state where this tendency is realized fully.

This position taken by the Classical tradition thus stands apart from much of modern economics. The latter constrains competition to be treated in terms of industrial structure – number of firms, homogeneity of products, negligible or significant influence over price by individual firms, and so on. Finance, from the orthodox perspective, is secondary to this prior industry structure characterization of competition, an impulse broadly consonant with the tendency to treat finance as a veil over 'real' activity. In classical theory in contrast there is a role for finance to play in a fundamental sense. But the recognition of that role was a long process of development.

In Adam Smith's hands, the classical object of theoretical discussion, the definition of a condition where profits are equalized, was characterized by his theory of 'free competition' (1776, p. 111) via 'perfect liberty' (p. 60). Smith's theory of natural prices for final products and for factors of production was premised on factor mobility. Factors would always seek to move to the activity offering them the rate of return that exceeded the norm set by their natural price and would leave the activity offering them a return less than their natural price. It was this factor flow in response to differential returns that set up the tendency toward factor price equalization in Smith's analysis (see Smith, 1976, especially pp. 62–5).

In a putative equilibrium, remaining differentials for a particular factor could only be due to compensating variations in the Smithian theory. Smith (1976, p. 70) even used the term 'competition' to describe an environment in which there was perfect liberty for prices to be bid up and down to bring market price into conformity with natural price, subject to the freedom of factors to change activities at will.

Dennis O'Brien (1975, pp. 53–4) has described Smithian competition as 'dynamic' and certainly not to be confused with 'perfect competition'. This is not to imply that it should be confused with imperfect competition either. It is a concept independent of the specific assumptions made about industry structure, similar to the position taken by Kalecki (1942) in a much later debate, as long as those structural features do not inhibit the free movement of factors of production. Smith (1976, p. 132) was explicit in his claim that competition is limited if restraints are placed on 'the free circulation of labour and stock'.

In Ricardo's hands, Classical theory moves the focus away from Smith's emphasis on general factor mobility to the mobility of capital alone – and capital in a financial rather than a physical sense at that. The hallmark of the Classical theory is the assumption that short-term deviations (Ricardo, 1951, p. 88) from long-period positions of the system of relative prices would be internally self-corrected by a dynamic adjustment of investment flows. For Ricardo, the assumption of intersectoral capital mobility is driven by the 'restless desire on the part of all the employers of stock to quit a less profitable for a more advantageous business'. In his analysis the operation of this mechanism ensures the validity of treating 'natural' prices as proportional to cost of production and provides a rationale for ignoring temporary 'market', that is, supply and demand prices, altogether – a rationale that comes to fruition in Sraffa's (1960) *Production of Commodities by Means of Commodities*.

Yet in Ricardo there is very little discussion of *exactly* how this competitive process operates or how the natural rate of profit reaches any particular value (although the time path of profits for an 'improving' economy is clearly discussed). What we get by way of explanation is a short discussion in chapter 4 of his *Principles* where Ricardo mentions the role of the class of 'monied' men and bankers who facilitate the transfer of resources from low- to high-profit industries by borrowing and lending 'floating capital'. Ricardo (1951, p. 92) seems to take this process as self-evident and limits his comments to the claim that it is 'more active than is generally supposed'. At this stage the cost of finance must become an element in the determination of the general rate of profit and in the dynamic of adjustment to Classical (uniform profitability) equilibrium.

As the last of the great nineteenth century classical economists (Walsh and Gram, 1980), Karl Marx elaborated on the classical conception of competition as much as he did on the classical notion of value. For Marx the process of competition between firms within and between industries was the predominant characteristic of the capitalist mode of production. In a historical sense, Marx describes competition as developing along with the development of capitalism. Markets expand and more of production is organized along capitalistic lines by the competition of capital to expand into pre-capitalistic spheres and to break down 'barriers' posed by existing legal and institutional structures.

> While free competition has dissolved the barriers of earlier relations and modes of production, it is necessary to observe first of all that the things which were a barrier to it were the inherent limits of earlier modes of production. . . . The limits which it tore down were barriers to its motion, its development and realization. It is by no means the case that it thereby suspended all limits nor all barriers, but rather only the limits not corresponding to it (Marx, 1973, pp. 649–50).

Thus in an interesting comparison to modern market structure theories of competition, the role of 'barriers' to competition, (by definition 'entry' in the orthodox conception), was integral to Marx's concept of competition as well. But these barriers are not disembodied limits that define the states of competitiveness for passive firms; they are created and destroyed by the very process of competition itself. Thus, for Marx, firms are seen as powerful economic agents, not paralyzed price takers, endowed with price-setting abilities; their goal is to expand and capture transient surplus profits through the weapons of reorganization of the firm and technical change (Semmler, 1987, p. 540).

From this view follows the characteristic Marxist view of the violence and fierce rivalry involved in competition that marks it off so distinctly from the orthodox conception. Yet if Marx's view of capitalism allows such a wide ambit for rivalrous erection of barriers in what sense is it 'competitive'? It is here that we see the re-emergence of the great classical theme of competitiveness.

Although firms participating in the competitive process continually attempt to create barriers to defeat rivals, other firms are also continually in the process of overcoming existing ones and so establish a tendency toward the equalization of rates of return. Donald Harris (1988, p. 140, emphasis added) has put it as follows:

> Thus, beneath the surface of this turbulence there exists an underlying systemic imperative. That imperative has the remarkable feature that it manages to subordinate the expansionary drive of capitals to a *process of convergence in their profit rates* and hence to homogeneity of their objective performance despite the heterogeneity and diversity among them in all other relevant dimensions of their existence as identifiable units of capital. *This convergence constitutes a law of motion of the economic system analogous to the law of gravitation of the natural order*.

Thus, although Marx (1967, p. 778) sees the process of competition as one that leads to concentration and centralization, it can simultaneously account for the formation of a single market price gravitating towards his prices of production 'within spheres' and the equalization of rates of profit in the 'different spheres' (see Marx, 1894, ch. 10, esp. p. 180). This conjunction of self-erected barriers for the creation of what modern economists would term monopoly-power, with pricing behavior and a tendency toward profit equality which are associated in modern discussions with 'competitive' behavior is another clear example of the divergence of the classical from orthodox conceptions of competition.

The classical conception of competition is centered around the description of systems which tend toward equalization of rates of profit. Market activity drives prices toward values defined by a theoretical analysis of otherwise independent market phenomena, variously denominated 'natural', 'costs of production' or 'labor values'. No restrictions are placed upon the behavior and tactics firms may use to compete, yet there is little fear on the part of the classicists that 'monopoly' will inhibit the competitive process.

Such complacency was due to the consistent view that competition depended upon free mobility of factors and, especially, the mobility of capital. Finally, starting with Adam Smith's view of the personal nature of capital accumulation as centering on the activities of the parsimonious capitalist who both financed and organized production, the emphasis of Classical theory increasingly shifted toward the view that capital mobility was a specialized province of organized financial markets.

As noted earlier, after the rise to dominance of supply and demand analysis in the 1870s (see Bharadwaj, 1978), the basis of Classical value theory was altered, but the role of intersectoral capital mobility in the analysis of long-period positions remained intact (Milgate, 1982). As an example of this shift, we see Marshall replacing Smith's natural prices with 'normal' prices. The exact reasons for this shift are in dispute, but it is clear that the attempt to reformulate value theory on the marginal principles coincided with the concept of competition becoming the subject of intense study (Stigler, 1987, p. 532).

It was in this context that the view of competition associated with a *state* description of *industry structure* rose to dominance as well. As attention was shifted to the allocational efficiency properties of a process of *exchange*, all of the familiar elements of 'perfect competition' come to the fore – most notably the inordinate attention to the 'negligibility' of each individual agent (see Aumann, 1964 and Khan, 1987).[6] The role of capital mobility then falls into the background, hemmed in by the restrictions placed upon agents' behavior and is reduced to the anonymous entry and exit phenomenon. Yet, for a century attempts were also made to construct marginalist-based accounts of the definition of long-period positions as well. It is most significant for our theme that it is in the attempt to define these long-period positions in marginalist terms that many of the principal impasses of modern theory arose. The definition and measurement of 'capital', the meaning of the long-period supply schedule, and the determination of the general rate of profit are all examples – and dead-ends – encountered in various attempts to use supply and demand theory to answer Classical questions concerning the nature of equilibrium. Significantly each of these problems involves some reliance on capital mobility from the Classical approach to competition. And in these various attempts no more illumination was forthcoming than in Ricardo's time.

It is only at a higher stage of marginalist abstraction, in the work of the modern general equilibrium theorists, that the reliance on capital mobility to ensure a tendency toward an equal rate of return has been abandoned completely as the means of describing economic equilibrium (Milgate, 1982). Of course, along with such a rejection had to come a willingness to abandon the operation of this tendency as a significant economic phenomenon.

IV TOWARDS A FINANCIAL VIEW OF THE CLASSICAL COMPETITIVE PROCESS

If the orthodox conception of competition is so flawed and limiting, and if its use in defining theories of the long-period has resulted so consistently in theoretical dead-ends there are grounds for attempting a fuller development of the old classical conception of the operation of competitive forces. In fact, various recent authors appear to be doing just that. This was at least part of the message of Sraffa's (1960) return to classical modes of thought. Furthermore, an underground literature exists that elaborates the Classical view in the work of Veblen and Keynes.

The literature devoted to the alleged phenomenon of 'financial repression' in developing countries has emphasized the distortion-lifting effects of deregulation of interest rates and commercial banking in LDCs. This could be understood as making the financial sector in developing countries more like the ideal of perfect competition. But in Ronald McKinnon's (1973, p. 9) treatment, lifting 'repression' increases competitiveness in a quite different sense.

McKinnon wants to overcome what he perceived to be a high degree of 'fragmentation' in the financial sector in LDCs that results in 'great discrepancies in rates of return'. If those discrepancies could be bridged, a larger volume of finance would be available, more efficiently allocated, and would lead to higher rates of economic growth according to McKinnon (1973, p. 9):

> . . . let us define 'economic development' as the reduction of the great dispersion in social rates of return to existing and new investments under domestic entrepreneurial control. The capital market in a 'developed' economy successfully monitors the efficiency with which the capital stock is deployed by pushing returns on physical and financial assets toward equality, thereby significantly increasing the average return.

Whether reduced 'fragmentation' will raise the average rate of return rather than lower it or leave it unchanged is not clear, but what is evident is the basis for an alternative concept of competition to the neoclassical industry structure approach. Here is the idea that competition can be linked to the degree to which there is a tendency for returns to become uniform across all categories of investment, presumably in a prospective sense.

Contemporary Marxists also embrace a notion of competition that centers on the existence of a tendency toward equalization of rates of profit (see, for example, Semmler, 1984). Drawing again from the Classical rather than the neoclassical tradition, Semmler (1984, p. 35) has noted '. . . free competition is based on mobility of capital' – mobility of capital being the condition that ostensibly facilitates the establishment of the uniform rate of profit. This view of competition has led to a major controversy among Marxist theorists over whether to view changes in industry structure as processes that enhance or reduce the tendency toward equalization of returns.

In an important paper, Donald Harris (1988, p. 144) argued that virtually all the conditions that obtain for neoclassical perfect competition – with the exception of price-taking behavior – must hold for adequate capital mobility to exist to bring about the uniform rate of profit. But a former student of Harris argued a decade earlier that increasing concentration and centralization of industry could improve the tendency toward equalization of returns in all activities if capital is understood in its financial rather than its physical form (see Clifton, 1977, p. 146).

Clifton (1977, p. 146) stresses that orthodox theory sets up 'the conditions of free capital mobility . . . by confusing durable capital goods with financial capital. Not even the buying and selling of firms is required for competition to exist throughout the system.' Clifton recommends breaking through that confusion. Indeed it is physical capital mobility that leads to the Steedman conundrum for the Classical concept of competition also discussed cogently by Harris (1988, p. 145). The interdependent structure of an economy where produced commodities serve as means of production can mean that the movement of physical capital to a sector offering a higher than general rate of return will not necessarily lower the rate of return in that industry toward the general rate. Similarly, movement of physical capital away from a sector offering a lower than general rate of return will not necessarily raise that sector's rate of return toward the general level.

But this is a conundrum specific to physical capital flows as the mechanism for equalization. *It is not a problem associated with an interpretation of the Classical theory that sees the uniform rate of profits established via the mobility of finance*. In fact, Clifton (1977, pp. 145–50) has argued persuasively that when capital is taken to have financial form, the modern corporation, though highly concentrated, increases the tendency toward uniformity in rates of return. Veblen, as we will demonstrate below, offers us deeper insight into this issue.

If Classical theory is to go forward, if it is to be useful in addressing the theoretical structure of capitalist economies, financial activity should be seen as the grinding stone of competition. It is this tradition of thought – where competition is defined by the existence of a tendency toward equalization of rates of profit, and equilibrium is a condition where the tendency is realized fully – that finds recent echoes in McKinnon's unusual definition of 'economic development' and in the Marxist debate over the consequences of the rise of the modern corporation for the relative mobility of capital. But in the matter of clues toward fuller development of the Classical concept, the history of economics offers us further assistance. Two major deviations from the main line of orthodox theoretical development point toward promising avenues for extension of the Classical approach to competition (and equilibrium) – the work of Veblen (1904) and Keynes (1936).

To fit Thorstein Veblen's work into the classical terrain we have covered so far presents some peculiar difficulties and some surprising insights. The difficulties lie in the fact that Veblen's unique viewpoint carries with it such a tremendous amount of baggage that a full account of his ideas would necessarily involve long side excursions into method, philosophy and history. The surprise, given the traditional view of Veblen as a complete outsider to orthodox economic discussions, is that he had much to say about the competitive process, a topic that we have seen has been of longstanding concern to what Veblen would call 'the guild of economists'.

Thus, to avoid confusion and to keep to our theme it will be useful, at the acknowledged risk of violence to Veblen's whole message, to force parts of his *Theory of Business Enterprise* into the Classical competitive framework already outlined. It is hoped that this will illuminate our main theme and provide some fresh insight into Veblen as an economist. But the reader should be alerted that even treading along well-worn paths such as this, Veblen's irrepressible iconoclasm and realism forces to the surface deep issues that disfigure the Classical competitive state to such an extent that it is left a barely recognizable ancestor of its Smithian and Ricardian forbearers. This is, of course, most fitting and paves the way to link Keynes with this attenuated version of an economy whose motive force is an equalization of rates of return, financially considered.

To begin, Veblen offers a historical analysis of the classical competitive state. His notion of the rise of 'business enterprise' gives concrete form to our textual interpretation of the increasingly impersonal and financial characterization of the competitive process at the hands of the Classicals.

For Veblen the characterization of competition and the role of finance in this process evolves historically with western capitalism. The crucial divide is between the early modern period, featuring handicraft forms of production and *commercial* enterprise in banking and trade and the latter period evolving over the nineteenth century of industrial production, carried forth on the basis of scientfically founded machine processes and organized by large *business* enterprise. Veblen sometimes calls the former the period of commercial enterprise or the money economy, while the latter is dubbed the period of industrial enterprise or the credit economy.

For Veblen it is in the early modern period of commercial enterprise, when the institutional basis of the rights of ownership is worked out by the natural law philosophers, that 'business principles' of freedom of disposability of property and the inviolable nature of contract come to dominate culture. Yet production continues to be organized largely on a small-scale handicraft basis and the competitive process operates on the principle of 'unsophisticated productive efficiency'. Significantly, for our theme, this is also the period in which the outlook of the Classical economists was formed:

> So long as the machine processes were but slightly developed, scattered and, relatively isolated, and independent of one another industrially, and so long as they were carried on on a small scale for a relatively narrow market, so long the management of them was conditioned by circumstances in many respects similar to those which conditioned the English domestic industry of the eighteenth century. It was under the conditions of this inchoate phase of the machine age

> that the earlier generation of economists worked out their theory of the business man's part in industry. It was then still true, in great measure, that the undertaker was the owner of industrial equipment, and that he kept an immediate oversight of the mechanical processes as well as the pecuniary transactions in which the enterprise was engaged; and it was also true, with relatively infrequent exceptions, that an unsophisticated productive efficiency was the prime element of business success. A further feature of that precapitalist business situation is that business, whether handicraft or trade, was customarily managed with a view to earning a livelihood rather than with a view to profits on investments. (Veblen, 1904, p. 23.)

Note that Veblen has situated the historical origin of the classical view of competition in the *personal* nature of early modern commercial enterprise. What is so different about this from modern economies (so different that Veblen goes so far as to identify the early modern state as 'precapitalist') in his eyes is the limited scope for purely pecuniary interests, that is those not directly related to production of actual goods and services, to guide the economic process. As Veblen sees it, the growth and transformation of the system from one founded on commercial enterprise to one founded on industrial enterprise is driven by technology, but results in a new, dominant role for financial interests.

'In proportion as the machine industry gained ground, . . . the conjunctures of business grew more varied and of larger scope at the same time that they became more amenable to shrewd manipulation' (Veblen, 1904, p. 24). Now the pecuniary side of business enterprises comes to require more attention and the opportunities for business gain and loss grow from financial activity alone. These circumstances create a 'spirit of business enterprise' whose aim is the accumulation of monetary claims and whose method is buying and selling on financial markets. For Veblen, this regime of *business* enterprise replaces the old 'unsophisticated efficiency' grounds of the Classical competitive state with competition focused in financial terms:

> With a fuller development of the modern closeknit and comprehensive industrial system, the point of chief attention for the business man has shifted from the old survelliance and regulation of a given industrial process, with which his livelihood was once bound up, to an alert redistribution of investments from less to more gainful ventures, and to the strategic control of the conjunctures of business through shrewd investments and coalitions with other business men. (Veblen, 1904, pp. 24–5.)

What is most important is Veblen's point that the historical evolution of technology and institutions required a modification of the view of competition given by the 'rationalistic, normalizing speculations of the eighteenth-century philosophers' (Veblen, 1904, p. 83n)[7] if we are to extend their framework to deal with the modern situation. Veblen's 'theory of business enterprise' provides a catalogue of the theoretical medications needed. A brief account of some of the points related to our theme that Veblen touches upon follows:

1. In the context of a vast machine technology in the control of business interests competing on financial terms, there is no longer any necessary coincidence between productive efficiency and competitive success. Bearing witness to the Trusts, Robber Barons and plutocracies of his day, Veblen characterizes the net result of these financial manipulations of ownership as on the whole inimical to the serviceable functioning of the industrial system. He then makes a clear distinction between activities directed at making money and making goods, or between business enterprise and the machine industry. Business men seek to make 'money' and the making of goods is only of interest as it serves this end. Thus competition should be recognized as a process defined in *money* terms, not material terms.

   As a result of this bifurcation he notes that the old classical notion of uniformity rate of profits becomes somewhat blurred in the modern context, as it loses its analogy to the return to workmanlike efficiency of the owner of an industrial concern. Although it is still a 'normal', commonplace notion to the businessman (as Marshall would have it), it has come to take on an increasingly pecuniary and prospective character:

   > The phenomenon of a uniform rate of profits determined by competition has fallen into the background and lost something of its matter-of-fact character since competition in the large industry has begun to shift from the position of a stable and continuous equilibration to that of an intermittent, convulsive strain in the service of the larger business men's strategy. The interest of the business community centers upon profits and the shifting fortunes of the profit maker, rather than upon accumulated and capitalized goods. Therefore the ultimate conditioning force in the conduct and aims of business is coming to be the prospective profit yielding capacity of any given business move, rather than the aggregate holdings or the recorded output of the product. (Veblen, 1904, p. 90.)

2. But even as financial reckoning of business success assumes this impersonal and subjective tendency toward uniformity, the characterization of competition, unlike the tranquil neoclassical view, becomes ever more strategic and tactical. This is where the antisocial tendency of competition arises for Veblen:

> It is commonly a struggle between rival business men, and more often than not the outcome of the struggle depends on which side can inflict or endure the greater pecuniary damage. And pecuniary damage in such a case not uncommonly involves a set-back to the industrial plants concerned and a derangement, more or less extensive, of the industrial system at large. The work of the greater modern business men, in so far as they have to do with the ordering of the scheme of industrial life, is of this strategic character. (Veblen, 1904, p. 32.)

3. This type of business climate fosters the growth of monopoly power (just as Sraffa's more scholastic analysis later suggested to Joan Robinson), as only those businesses large enough to wage financial warfare with each other will survive. The industrial organization counterpart of Veblen's theory reflects this in the place it finds for modern realities that the orthodox notion can only address uneasily as disturbing causes. Businesses grow large and interconnected where they can summon enough 'goodwill' to gain access to financial capital on organized markets. This need not be for any industrial reason as the modern conglomerates make clear. Instead, various plays on the vertical and horizontal integration of industry serve strategic pecuniary ends in certain conjunctures of events. Two new forms of competitively necessary costs grow in magnitude and importance for the modern enterprise, which is now seen explicitly as publicly traded corporation. Advertising becomes essential for firms who need to manage the goodwill their monopoly power represents. And firms now use what Veblen calls 'loan credit', or access to finance broadly conceived, to increase the speed and magnitude of their turnover of money capital (Veblen, 1904, pp. 35–65 and 92–104).
4. This competitive necessity of loan credit financing to leverage the firm and speed up its turnover means that all business enterprise is conditioned by the state of financial markets. It is no longer possible to earn the 'normal rate' without resort to a highly leveraged position. This is the source of Veblen's precocious and much neglected theory of recurrent business crises. As the extension of credit fuels a business expansion, the price of the underlying capital goods is bid up faster than production can keep pace. This process goes on until the representative value of the firm based on 'prospective earning capacity', discounted at the normal rate, becomes so out of touch with the now overvalued equity capital that a crisis occurs (Veblen, 1904, pp. 104–35).
5. Lastly, Veblen brings us back to the issue which in a sense started off the whole modern debate over value theory and the characterization of competition, 'capital'. For Veblen, all of the foregoing combines into an argument that modern business capital in a credit economy is 'a

fund of money values' and is no longer necessarily related in a strict and fast manner to material items at all. Here is a clear divergence from the usual conceptions of capital in both the orthodox productivity sense, and the classical materialist sense so acutely perfected by Sraffa. The problems of the productivity view are now manifest. The classical notion, at the heart of the recent classical revival, has so far in current discussions only been questioned on the grounds of consistency with the process presumed to define it in the classical scheme (by Steedman, 1984, and others, cited above). To Veblen, the classical notion of capital as the value of a stock of material means of production, while perhaps appropriate to an early modern economy like that witnessed by Adam Smith, is irrelevant to a situation in which 'the substantial foundation of the industrial corporation is its immaterial assets'.

For Veblen the significant institutional fact is that the valuation of the fund of money values commonly called 'capital' in modern business enterprises is done by trading on financial markets and that the basis of this evaluation is wholly one of prospective earning capacity of the firm, or as he is wont to call it, the firm's 'goodwill'. Historically this development is due, of course, to the advent of organized markets where ownership claims can be bought and sold: the stock market. This is the source of the evolution from the early modern commercial enterprise to the modern business enterprise with its separation of ownership and management. Under this regime of financial capital – note the Keynesian vision emerging – the valuation of capital takes on an immaterial and psychological character:

> The market fluctuations in the amount of capital proceed on variations of confidence on the part of the investors, on current beliefs as to the probable policy or tactics of the business men in control, on forecasts as to the seasons and the tactics of the guild of politicians, and on the indeterminable, largely instinctive, shifting movements of public sentiment and apprehension. So that under modern conditions the magnitude of the business capital and its mutations from day to day are in great measure a question of folk psychology rather than of material fact. (Veblen, 1904, pp. 148–9.)

The reader will sense that many themes usually associated with Keynes were developed quite extensively by Veblen 30 years before the *General Theory* was written. It is also the case that Veblen took his view of what Keynes would later call a 'monetary economy'[8] into areas Keynes did not, such as the theory of the firm and industrial organization. But of course, due to history and the sociology of the profession, Veblen's message fell mostly on deaf ears, while Keynes' reinvention of these themes has had widespread influence. Thus, rather than repeat in any detail Keynes' well known views, we wish to end by focusing on that part of Keynes' thought which relates directly to the discussion of competition and finance, his views on the fundamental properties of a monetary economy. It is in chapter 17 of the *General Theory* that Keynes most forcefully and originally addressed these issues. There he sets up a generalized view of asset market equilibrium that merits more attention than it has been given (see Cottrell and Lawlor, 1991). But first it is useful to stop for a moment, and to consider how Veblen's analysis leaves us on the question of equilibrating tendencies in a financial economy.

The argument throughout this chapter has been that the Classical framework draws strength from the fact that it is founded upon equilibrium states, but equilibria defined in a manner which frees the analysis from the defects associated with orthodox conceptions of competition. Veblen, as an evolutionary theorist, as arch critic of the marginalist writers of his day, as the author of the biting 'lightning calculator' satire of the individual equilibrium associated with marginal utility analysis, is mostly concerned with describing social *processes*, not equilibrium states.

But what does he make of the classical concept of a tendency toward the equalization of rate of return? It must be said that Veblen's suspicion concerning mechanistic analogy to social phenomenon carries over to some extent to this concept as well, at least in its original form. He does address the issue seriously, but when he is done with it, we want to argue, the way is open for a type of equilibrium like that provided by Keynes in chapter 17.

As noted above, Veblen clearly felt that such tendency toward equalization of material profits as had existed under the regime of commercial enterprise had been wholly transformed under the regime of business enterprise into a more elusive concept, one dependent on immaterial estimates of prospective profit and largely determined by folk psychology. It is just at this point that Veblen claims that 'competition in the large industry has begun to shift from the position of a stable and continuous equilibration to that of an intermittent, convulsive strain in the service of the larger business men's strategy'.

At a metaphysical level, one could say that Veblen has introduced *financial* strategy as a competitive force to disrupt the formerly smooth functioning of the classical competitive process. This becomes particularly clear in his later discussion of the operations of 'trust making' by market 'insiders' (Veblen, 1904, pp. 119–32 and 160–74). In this activity the gains are so tactical, so much a matter of *cours majeure* in the interest of the establishment of a new strategic position for the large players involved (just think of Ivan Boesky, Michael Milkin, T. Boone Pickens or, more recently, Warren Buffet), and the returns typically so immediate and large, that any reference to a 'normal' rate falls away completely:

> In this higher development of corporation finance, in the manipulations of vendible capital, the interval of the turnover spoken of above becomes an indeterminate factor. The gains of the business come to have but an uncertain and shifty relation to the lapse of time and cannot well be calculated per cent per time-unit. There is, therefore, on these higher levels of business management, properly speaking no ascertainable ordinary rate of earnings. (Veblen, 1904, p. 162.)

But this higher business enterprise, Veblen makes clear, depends upon the existence of an underlying market process that includes participation of outsiders who the insiders can prey upon effectively. It is this ordinary asset market equilibration – fragile, expectational, psychological and open to abuse – that is the last ground upon which Veblen leaves the classical competitive state. And it is upon this ground that Veblen meets Keynes.

In Keynes' vision the crucial role for differential rates of return in determining the pace and direction of investment flows is grounded in the nature of organized financial markets. For Keynes, a monetary economy is one where the financial system provides an outlet for the expectations of investors, borrowers and speculators to affect productive activity today.

Starting from his recognition of the radical uncertainty faced by economic actors, Keynes analyses the operation of asset markets in general. Since in this situation expected, money-denominated rates of return (own rates of interest) can be calculated for any asset, he offers a basis for uniting financial and investment activity under one theoretical framework. Furthermore, since these expected own rates will be intricately connected with expected future prices (compared with prevailing spot prices) there is a direct link between the system of relative prices and the structure of own rates (Keynes, 1937b).

In chapter 17's framework, Keynes deals explicitly with the process by which equalization of rates of returns is achieved. In any market period the structure of spot and future prices of assets – whether physical or financial – move until the expected money rates measured in money are brought into equality by trade in the existing stock of assets. The existence of securities markets makes it possible for business enterprises as a whole to be bought and sold as assets as well. This leads, again, to an arbitrageur's equilibrium in a direct sense. The equilibrium (uniform) rate of return is compared with expected rates of return on newly produced assets to determine the direction and volume of new investment.

Note that many of the older themes of the Classical economists are still present here, such as the tendency toward equality of rates of profit and the capital mobility inducing effects of differential rates. Yet the setting of the analysis is radically different from Smith's since we are now on the terrain of a monetary economy in Keynes' (and Veblen's) sense. Here the role of expectations, uncertainty and speculation can play a decisive role through the competitive process. Keynes (1937a, pp. 242–3, n. 2) undoubtedly was conscious of this implication, observing a bit later, '. . . I find, looking back, that it was Prof. Irving Fisher who was the great-grandfather who first influenced me strongly towards regarding money as a "real" factor'. For Keynes in chapter 17 – a chapter at a stage of *The General Theory* that his most astute contemporary interpreter Hugh Townshend (1937a, p. 324) described as revealing Keynes' vision released from the 'debris' of orthodoxy – it is the own rate of interest on money that all others, standardized in terms of money, must gravitate towards (see Cottrell and Lawlor, 1991). Keynes has the money rate of interest ruling the roost, in contrast to the relationship postulated by Marx who had the rate of return on interest-bearing capital adapting to the production rate of profit (see Panico, 1980).

Accompanying Keynes' switch to an authentic monetary theory – rather than a 'real exchange economics' *à la* Marshall – is a subtle change in Classical characterization of the short- versus long-period equilibrium. Since in Keynes' analysis the own rates equilibrium is virtually continuously achieved by arbitrage, it is a very short-period affair, a fragile circumstance based as it is on the psychology and beliefs of market participants. But in a sense it provides a conceptually robust characterization of short-period equilibrium again divorced from industry structure considerations. It engenders a theory of relative prices that is dependent upon the state of financial markets as well as the typical cost and demand considerations. It is indeed Keynes' value theory, as Townshend (1937a, p. 324) deftly suggested, that dictates a 'direct *causal* influence of expectations on *all* prices'.

Necessarily, the long-period equilibrium for Keynes must be cast in expectational terms as well. Thus, we can follow Keynes' (1936, p. 48) own discussion of long-period equilibrium:

> If we suppose a state of expectation to continue for a sufficient length of time for the effect on employment to have worked itself out so completely that there is, broadly speaking, no piece of employment going on which would not have taken place if the new state of expectation had always existed, the steady level of employment thus attained may be called the long-period employment corresponding to that state of expectation.

Keynes is direct in saying that we never get into his long period, but it is a useful reference point for analytical purposes. For practical purposes as well as analytical purposes, however, the own rates equilibrium has far greater potential relevance. The own rates equilibrium remains a fairly undeveloped portion of Keynes' analysis both from a theoretical and empirical standpoint, but it points the way toward a rich research agenda and a logically consistent characterization of Classical competitive equilibrium.

As Walsh and Gram (1980, p. 296) have observed, in Classical theory 'competition among capitalists is taken to mean that, in equilibrium, the rate of profit is equalized in all sectors of production'. The centrality of this idea of competition has been lost in much of modern economics, but it lives a furtive life in occasional passages in works of economists whose instincts lead them to dip off the edges of the mainstream in the field. In the works of Veblen, Sraffa and Keynes the concept lives an explicit existence and may provide a basis for overcoming the analytical limitations produced by the orthodox concept of competition.

Adoption of the alternative concept would also call for a revolution in the subfield of industrial organization. To the extent that industry structure is a matter of concern it would be of interest from the standpoint of the dynamic development of the economy as a whole and from the standpoint of determining the extent to which changes in industry structure facilitate or inhibit the tendency toward equalization of rates of profit. And now the equalization must be understood in the context of the mobility of finance capital.

NOTES

* Thanks are due to Allin Cottrell, Geoff Harcourt, T.K. Rhymes and the Duke University History of Thought Workshop for helpful comments and suggestions.

1. At the root of this dispute is the question of whether relative prices and distribution should be approached from the standpoint of the production and allocation of a social *surplus*; or whether the point of value theory should be an investigation of the properties of a system whereby given resources are allocated among competing ends. For an illuminating discussion of the analytical issues these alternative views raise for the construction of general equilibrium models see Walsh and Gram (1980). For a historical account see Bharadwaj (1978). Cohen (1989) provides an interesting analytical comparison. And, for a scholarly view of this distinction as it pertains to growth theory, rather than value theory, see Eltis (1976).
2. We consciously choose the more neutral term 'orthodox' to label the ruling paradigms of value theory in deference to our firmly held opinion that the more common term 'neoclassical' now has little if any useful meaning, due to overuse. Thus in various guises, a 'neoclassical' has appeared as everything from a Wicksellian concerned with the long-run analysis of distribution based on equalized, physically determined, marginal productivity returns to factors, to a modern temporary equilibrium theorist whose concern is to utilize the efficiency properties of dynamic programming to characterize a state in which prices for all 'time' are simultaneously determined and no tendency toward equal rates of return is even recognized. The recent work by Aspromourgos (1987) showing the Veblenian origins of the term 'neoclassical' should be enough to convince anyone that it is a term hand-crafted for use in producing mischief and confusion. In the interest of stylistic variety, we also reserve the right to describe the more general viewpoint of orthodoxy as 'dominant'. But for the most part we will try to treat specific theories specifically.
3. See Caravale (1985) and the references contained therein for a view of the debate over Ricardo. Also see Walsh and Gram (1980) and Hahn (1982) on the implications for general equilibrium theory, and see any issue of the *Cambridge Journal of Economics*,

Political Economy: The Surplus Approach, Contributions to Political Economy for representative examples of applied classical economics.

4. But for an heroic mathematical attempt to be precise about the power to be assigned individual agents and the exact meaning of 'negligibility' of individual traders in terms of the traditional view of perfect competition as many agents, see Aumann (1964).
5. For a penetrating discussion and a clear statement of the general equilibrium view of these matters see Bliss (1975), who has this to say about the essential incongruity between the intertemporal equilibrium framework and the notion of equalized rates of return:

   > Notice the special assumptions that are necessary for an intertemporal equilibrium to have associated with it a single constant rate of interest. In general, all that is known is that in any week there is a uniquely defined own-rate of interest for any good, but this may differ from the own-rates of interest for other goods in that week or from the own-rates of interest from that good in a different week (Bliss, 1975, p. 55).

6. Reinforcement of this view can be found in the entry on 'perfect competition' by M. Ali Khan in *The New Palgrave Dictionary of Economics*:

   > A formalization of perfect competition hinges on how the intuitive notions of 'negligibility' and 'many agents' are made precise. . . . Since the essence of these ideas can be fully communicated in the context of an economy without producers, that is an 'exchange economy', we shall confine ourselves to this case and develop some notation and terminology regarding it. Khan, 1987, p. 831).

7. It is worth noting that Veblen sees this eighteenth century viewpoint as non-evolutionary and hopelessly outdated in its preconceptions. Thus he follows the sentence quoted with 'and such is, in substance, the view spoken for by those who still consistently remain at the standpoint of the eighteenth century'. It goes without saying who he had in mind here. But note that a complete 'return to classical modes of thought', such as the Sraffa revival is sometimes characterized as, with no recognition of the social evolution that has occurred since then, would equally well earn Veblen's scorn on this head.
8. Veblen claims (1904, p. 133) to have worked out his distinction between the era of commercial enterprise and business enterprise in terms of the 'teminological precedents set by German writers' according to whom 'the late modern scheme of economic life is a "credit economy", as contrasted with the "money economy" that characterizes early-modern times'. Keynes is known to have worked with similar categories in his early attempts to work out the *General Theory.* Thus his contribution to the Spietoff Fetschrift in 1933 was termed a 'Monetary Theory of Production' which he distinguished from Marshall's 'real exchange economy'. Also his early drafts of the *General Theory* and his lecture notes (see Rhymes, 1990) from this period bear evidence of having worked along these same lines. Nevertheless he abandoned this *language* in the final form of the *General Theory.* Dudley Dillard (1984) has noted how closely this brings Keynes into line with Veblen's vision.

REFERENCES

Aspromourgos, T. (1987), 'Neoclassical', in John Eatwell, Murray Milgate and Peter Newman (eds) *The New Palgrave: A Dictionary of Economics*, London: Macmillan.

Aumann, R. (1964), 'Markets with a continuum of traders', *Econometrica*, **32**, 39–50.

Bharadwaj, K. (1978), *Classical Political Economy and Rise to Dominance of the Supply and Demand Theories*, Calcutta: Longman.

Bliss, C.J. (1975), *Capital Theory and the Distribution of Income*, Amsterdam: North Holland.

Caravale, G. (1985), *The Legacy of Ricardo*, Oxford: Blackwell.

Casarosa, C. (1985), 'The "new view" of the Ricardian theory of distribution and economic growth', in G.A. Caravale (ed.), *The Legacy of Ricardo*, Oxford and New York: Blackwell, pp. 45–58.

Chick, Victoria (1986), 'Speculation, the rate of interest and the rate of profit', Paper Presented at the Meetings of the American Economic Association, 27–30 December.

Clifton, J. (1977), 'Competition and the evolution of the capitalist mode of production', *Cambridge Journal of Economics*, **1**(2), 137–51.

Cohen, A.J. (1989), 'Prices, capital, and the one-commodity model in neoclassical and classical theories', *History of Political Economy*, **21**, Summer: 231–51.

Cottrell, A.F. and M.S. Lawlor (1991), 'Natural rate mutations: Keynes, Leijonhufvud and Wicksell on the "natural" rate of interest', *History of Political Economy*, Winter.

Dillard, D. (1984), 'Keynes and Marx: a centennial appraisal', *Journal of Post Keynesian Economics*, **6**(3), Spring, 1984, 421–32.

Duménil, G. and D. Lévy (1987), 'The dynamics of competition: a restoration of the classical analysis', *Cambridge Journal of Economics*, **11**(2), June, 133–64.

Dutt, A.K. (1987), 'Competition, monopoly power and the uniform rate of profit', *Review of Radical Political Economics*, **19**(4), Winter 1987, 55–72.

Dutt, A.K. (1995), 'Monopoly power and uniform rates of profit: a reply to Glick–Campbell and Duménil–Lévy', *Review of Radical Political Economics*, **27**(2), June, 142–53.

Eatwell, J. (1982), 'Competition', in I. Bradley and M. Brown (eds), *Classical and Marxian Political Economy*, London: The Macmillan Press, pp. 203–28.

Eatwell, J. (1987), 'Competition: classical conceptions', in J. Eatwell, M. Milgate and P. Newman (eds), *The New Palgrave Dictionary of Economics*, London: Macmillan.

Eatwell, J. and M. Milgate (eds) (1983), *Keynes's Economics and the Theory of Value and Distribution*, New York: Oxford University Press.

Eltis, W. (1976), *The Classical Theory of Economic Growth*, Oxford: Basil Blackwell.

Fama, E.F.. and M.H. Miller (1972), *The Theory of Finance*, New York: Holt, Rinehart and Winston.

Farjoun, E. and M. Machover (1983), *Laws of Chaos: A Probabalistic Approach to Political Economy*, London: Verso.

Flaschel, P. and Semmler, W. (1987), 'Classical and neoclassical competitive adjustment processes', *The Manchester School of Economic and Social Studies*, March.

Garegnani, P. (1978–79), 'Notes on consumption, investment and effective demand', *Cambridge Journal of Economics*, Vols II and III, December 1978 and March 1979.

Garegnani, P. (1983), 'The classical theory of wages and the role of demand schedules in the determination of relative prices', *American Economic Review*, **73**, May.

Garegnani, P. (1984), 'Value and distribution in the classical economists and Marx', *Oxford Economic Papers*, **36**.

Hahn, F. (1982), 'The neo-Ricardians', *Cambridge Journal of Economics*, **6**(4) December.

Hamouda, O. and G.C. Harcourt (1988), 'Post Keynesianism: From criticism to coherence?' *Bulletin of Economic Research*, **40**(1), 1–33.

Harcourt, G.C. (1972), *Some Cambridge Controversies in the Theory of Capital*, London: Cambridge University Press.

Harcourt, G.C. (1981), 'Marshall, Sraffa and Keynes: incompatible bedfellows?', *Eastern Economic Journal*, **7**, January.

Harcourt, G.C. (1986), 'On Piero Sraffa's contributions to economics', in O.F. Hamouda (ed.), *Controversies in Political Economy: Selected Essays of G.C. Harcourt*, New York: New York University Press, pp. 75–89.

Harcourt, G.C. and N. Laing (eds) (1971), *Capital and Growth*, Harmondsworth, Middlesex: Penguin.

Harris, D.J. (1988), 'On the classical theory of competition', *Cambridge Journal of Economics*, **12**, 139–67.

Hollander, S. (1985), 'On the substantive identity of the Ricardian and neoclassical conceptions of economic organization: the French connection in British classicism', in G.A. Caravale, *The Legacy of Ricardo*, Oxford: Blackwell.

Kalecki, M. (1942), 'Mr Whitman on the concept of "degree of monopoly" – a comment', *The Economic Journal* **52**, April 121–7.

Keynes, J.M. (1933 [1973]), 'A monetary theory of production', in *Der Stand und die nächste Zukunft der Konjunkturforschung: Festschrift für Arthur Spietoff*. Reprinted in *The Collected Writings of John Maynard Keynes*, Vol. 13, London: Macmillan, pp. 408–11.

Keynes, J.M. (1936), *The General Theory of Employment, Interest, and Money*, London: Macmillan.

Keynes, J.M. (1937a), 'Alternative theories of the rate of interest', *The Economic Journal*, **37**(186), June.

Keynes, J.M. (1937b), 'The theory of the rate of interest', reprinted in *Readings in the Theory of Income Distribution*, Philadelphia: Blakiston Company (1946). Originally published in the Irving Fisher *festschrift* (1937).

Khan, M. (1987), 'Perfect Competition' in J. Eatwell, M. Milgate, and P. Newman (eds) *The New Palgrave Dictionary of Economics*, London: Macmillan Press.

Knight, F (1925), 'On decreasing cost and comparative advantage', *Quarterly Journal of Economics*, **39**(2), February, 331–3.

Kompas, T. (1992), *Studies in the History of Long-Run Equilibrium Theory*, Manchester: Manchester University Press.

Marris, R. (1964), *The Economic Theory of 'Managerial' Capitalism*, New York: Basic Books.

Marx, K. (1867 [1976]), *Capital*, Vol. I, Harmondsworth: Penguin.

Marx, K. (1894 [1967]), *Capital*, Vol. III, New York: International Publishers.

Marx, K. (1973), *Grundrisse*, Harmondsworth: Penguin.

McKinnon, R. (1973), *Money and Capital in Economic Development*, Washington: Brookings.

McNulty, P.J. (1968), 'Economic theory and the meaning of competition', *Quarterly Journal of Economics*, **82**(4), November.

Milgate, M. (1982), *Capital and Employment* New York: Academic Press.

Morishima, M. (1973), *Marx's Economics. A Dual Theory of Value and Growth*, Cambridge: Cambridge University Press.

Murphy, M. (1978), 'The consistency of perfect and monopolistic competition', *Economic Inquiry*, **16**(1), January, 108–12.

Nikaido, H. (1983), 'Marx on competition', *Zeitschrift für Nationalökonomie*, **43**(4), 337–62.

O'Brien, D.P. (1975), *The Classical Economists*, Oxford: Clarendon Press.

Panico, C. (1980), 'Marx's analysis of the relationship between the rate of interest and the rate of profits', *Cambridge Journal of Economics*, **4**, 363–78.

Rhymes, T.K. (1990), *Keynes's Lectures, 1932–1935, Notes of a Representative Student*, Transcribed, edited and constructed by T.K. Rhymes, Ann Arbor, MI: University of Michigan Press.

Ricardo, D. (1951), *Principles of Political Economy and Taxation*, Cambridge: Cambridge University Press.

Roncaglia, A. (1978), *Sraffa and The Theory of Prices*, New York: John Wiley and Sons.

Rothschild, K.W. (1947), 'Price theory and oligopoly', *The Economic Journal*, **57**(227), September, 299–320.

Rowthorn, B. (1974), 'Neo-Classicism, neo-Ricardianism and Marxism', *New Left Review*, **86** (July–August), 63–87.

Semmler, W. (1984), *Competition, Monopoly and Differential Profit Rates*, New York: Columbia University Press.

Semmler, W. (1987), 'Competition: Marxian conceptions' in J. Eatwell, M. Milgate and P. Newman (eds), *The New Palgrave Dictionary of Economics*, London: Macmillan.

Smith, A. (1776 [1976]), *The Wealth of Nations*, Chicago: University of Chicago Press.

Sraffa, P. (1926), 'Laws of returns under competitive conditions', *The Economic Journal* **36**(144), 535–50.

Sraffa, P. (1960), *Production of Commodities by Means of Commodities*, Cambridge: Cambridge University Press.

Steedman, Ian, (1977), *Marx after Sraffa*, London: New Left Books.

Steedman, Ian, (1984), 'Natural prices, differential profit rates and the classical competitive mechanism', *The Manchester School*, June, 123–40.

Stigler, G. (1957), 'Perfect competition, historically contemplated', *Journal of Political Economy*, **65**(1), February, 1–17.

Stigler, G. (1987), 'Competition', in J. Eatwell, M. Milgate, and P. Newman, (eds), *The New Palgrave Dictionary of Economics*, pp. 531–5.

Sylos-Labini, Paolo, (1985), 'Sraffa's critique of the Marshallian theory of prices, *Political Economy: Studies in the Surplus Approach*, **1**(2), 51–72.

Townshend, H. (1937a), 'Review of Hawtrey's *Capital and Employment*', *The Economic Journal*, **37**(186), June.

Townshend, H. (1937b), 'Liquidity-premium and the theory of value', *The Economic Journal*, 157–69.

Veblen, Thorstein (1904 [1975]), *The Theory of Business Enterprise*, New York: Augustus M. Kelley.

Walsh, V. and H. Gram (1980), *Classical and Neoclassical Theories of General Equilibrium*, New York: Oxford University Press.

Weeks, J. (1981), *Capital and Exploitation*, Princeton: Princeton University Press.

7. The macroeconomic role of speculative assets under import compression and financial repression

Jørn Rattsø*

1 INTRODUCTION

Taylor (1991, ch. 6) discusses four historical episodes when output stagnation has been combined with expanding speculative finance. He offers a framework to understand them as a result of regressive income redistribution. Income concentration tends to squeeze output through demand. My interest in this issue relates to observations in Sub-Saharan Africa during 'socialism' in the 1980s, notably in Zimbabwe. Stagnation coincided with booming domestic markets for housing and land, and both seemed to be linked to the foreign exchange constraint. The African socialism looks like history now. But it is still of interest to understand how regulations work. And stagnation and speculative finance have not disappeared with liberalization anyway.

The paradox of combined stagnation and boom is addressed in a model including portfolio adjustment and import rationing. The study can be seen as integrating Taylor's understanding of speculation into a model of import rationing and supply constraint.

The economic performance of the region in this period is associated with a foreign exchange constraint, the result of foreign debt accumulation, import dependency and export stagnation. A comprehensive empirical literature documents the role of these factors in explaining the economic stagnation. Wheeler (1984) and Helleiner (1990) show how the foreign exchange situation has influenced the performance of the whole region. Country studies emphasizing the import constraint include Chhibber *et al.* (1989), Green and Kadhani (1983) and Davies and Rattsø (1993) on Zimbabwe, and Bevan *et al.* (1990) and Ndulu (1986, 1993) on Tanzania. The economies are characterized by import dependency related to both investment and intermediate goods. To handle the foreign exchange constraint, governments typically introduce quantitative import rationing. The rationing, combined with limited substitution possibilities for imports, produces a tradeoff between capacity utilization and growth. The government allocation of foreign exchange between imported intermediates and investment goods influences the determination of output and investment. Typically the short-run capacity utilization is held back by the limited access to imported intermediates. Moran (1989) confirms that many less-developed countries share the above characteristics.

In the theoretical literature, various attempts at integrating the foreign exchange constraint into macroeconomic models can be identified since the two-gap model. The present approach is based on the general open economy macromodel of Buffie (1986), as modified by Rattsø (1994a) to take into account the importance of intermediate imports for foreign exchange spending and domestic capacity utilization. The model is reformulated to allow for portfolio adjustment mechanisms including a speculative asset.

The portfolio adjustments at work with speculative assets have been investigated by several authors. Dutt (1986) allows for the holding of food stocks for speculative gain. Lizondo (1987) introduces a black market for foreign exchange and the holding of foreign money in the portfolio. Both types of speculation are relevant in Sub-Saharan Africa, but the analysis here is limited to a speculative asset in fixed supply, such as land. A general portfolio set-up including the role of inflation hedges and unproductive tangible assets is proposed by Montiel (1991). In practice the population of even the most underdeveloped economy may choose between a wide variety of productive and unproductive assets for their wealth accumulation. The most visible speculative booms observed in Africa concern land prices and housing for the rich. Macroeconomic imbalances and political factors motivate the rich to store their wealth in this way. The speculation can have real economic consequences when investment (construction) is directed towards less productive activities.

The economic stagnation and speculation should be understood on the background of the prevailing policy regimes of the region. Expanding monetary base and overvalued currency are two key characteristics. The analysis is focused on the macroeconomic policy context of speculation.

2 THE PORTFOLIO ALLOCATION

The portfolio side of the economy is formulated to represent an economy with repressed financial markets. It is assumed that restrictions prevent the private sector from holding foreign assets and that no domestic bond markets exist. Wealth accumulation is limited to money, real capital and a speculative asset.

Buffie (1986) provides the benchmark without the speculative alternative. A static portfolio allocation decision determining the demand price of capital is assumed. The demand price feeds into a Tobin q-type investment function. A dynamic investment model including anticipated capital gains is suggested by Gavin (1992). Since this study concentrates on the dynamics of speculation, anticipated capital gains for real capital are ignored.

The model concentrates on portfolio adjustment and foreign exchange constraint. We have left out labor market adjustment and income distribution effects, and some comments about their likely effects are given in the final section. Since the portfolio allocation depends on the marginal productivity of capital, the structure of production is important for the motivation to speculate. The output Q is assumed to be produced by combining intermediate imports B and productive capital K, and the production function can be written $Q = Q(K,B)$. The capital stock is fixed in the short run. The production function has the conventional properties, and important in this context, the rationed imported intermediates have a positive effect on the marginal productivity of capital, $Q_{12} > 0$.

Wealth is divided between the speculative asset Z, productive capital K and high powered money M as stated in (7.1). The demand prices of the speculative asset P_z and the real capital P_k are determined to satisfy the portfolio equilibrium in (7.2) and (7.3). The asset demand functions G and H depend on the real rates of return to the two assets, the return to capital $P\,Q_1/P_k$ (P is the price level and Q_1 is the marginal productivity of real capital) and the expected capital gain of the speculative asset Π_z. The expected return Π_z is exogenous in the static version.

$$A = P_z\,Z + P_k\,K + M \tag{7.1}$$

$$P_z\,Z = G(P\,Q_1/P_k, \Pi_z)\,A \tag{7.2}$$

$$P_k\,K = H(P\,Q_1/P_k, \Pi_z)\,A \tag{7.3}$$

The rates of return of the two assets are fundamentally different. The return to buying productive capital is the nominal value of the marginal productivity measured against the demand price for capital. When the demand price of capital goes up, the rate of return is reduced. The return to the speculative asset is the expected capital gain, here assumed to be independent of the actual price of the speculative asset. The nominal wealth A is endogenously determined by the allocation decision, since the asset prices respond to market conditions.

The calculation of the reduced form portfolio equilibrium solution is shown in Appendix 1, and some assumptions are made to reach the signs of the partial derivatives shown above the right-hand side variables:

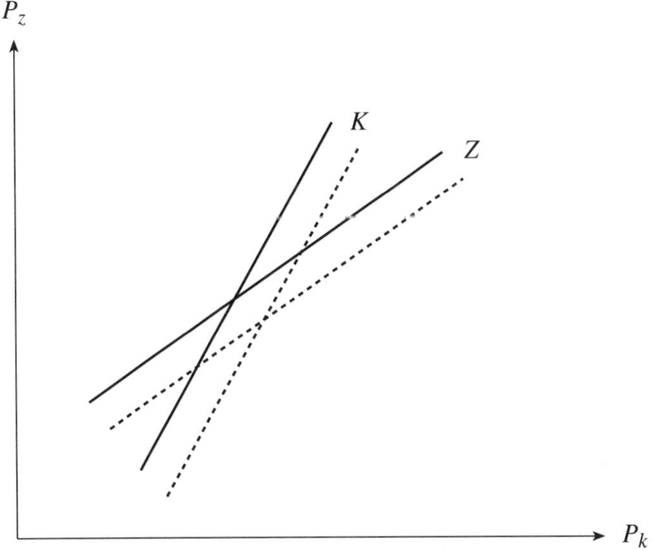

Figure 7.1 Portfolio equilibrium

$$P_z = \overset{-\;\;-\;\;+\;\;+}{L(P, B, M, \Pi_z)} \tag{7.4}$$

$$P_k = \overset{+\;\;+\;\;+\;\;-}{J(P, B, M, \Pi_z)} \tag{7.5}$$

A full description of the portfolio adjustments is given in Figure 7.1. The equilibrium conditions of the two asset markets are drawn linearly, and both are upward sloping. An increase in the demand price of productive capital stimulates the demand for speculative capital both through a wealth and a substitution effect, and the price P_z is driven up. The equilibrium condition at the market for productive capital is upward sloping since an increase in the speculative price creates excess demand by increasing the nominal wealth. When the loci cross as in Figure 7.1, the local stability condition holds. Portfolio instability will result if the indirect effects are too strong.

The portfolio adjustment is influenced by the import rationing system. The rationed availability of intermediate imports B, is a determinant of the marginal productivity of capital. More imported intermediates increase the marginal productivity of capital and generate a shift in the equilibrium portfolio prices as shown. The relative asset prices definitely go in favor of the productive capital, and the speculative price will fall when the direct effects at each market dominate, $L_2<0$ and $J_2>0$. The other way around, tighter import compression will increase the price of the speculative asset. Contraction and speculative boom go hand in hand, as analysed in more detail below.

A rise in the price level (exogenous in the portfolio model), typically the result of demand expansion, influences the portfolio allocation through the rate of return to capital. The return goes up and is followed by substitution from the speculative asset to productive capital. The shifts go as in Figure 7.1, and the speculative price is likely to fall. The rate of return to capital rises with the price level and is assumed to reduce the demand price of the speculative asset and increase the demand price of productive capital, that is $L_1<0$ and $J_1>0$.

The portfolio allocation is influenced by monetary policy. Expansionary monetary policy, increased stock of money M, will definitely lead to increased demand prices of both assets since the nominal wealth goes up, $L_3>0$ and $J_3>0$. The higher asset prices imply that the new money is held voluntarily in the private sector.

The dynamics of the portfolio allocation are driven by changes in the state variables, the expected return to speculative capital and the productive capital stock. When the expected return to speculative capital shifts up, speculation is more attractive, and the price of the speculative asset increases. Speculation is easily self-propelling, since the nominal wealth expands along with the speculative price. The mechanism is emphasized by Minsky (1986) and modeled in a similar way by Taylor (1991, chapter 6). The dynamic aspects are analysed in section 5.

3 THE MACROECONOMIC MODEL

The adjustment of the asset demand prices will feed into the investment function of the real side of the economy, implying complicated and important interactions between the real and the financial side. The formulation highlights the role of import dependence and import rationing. Compared to the original model of Buffie (1986), the supply side is reformulated by introducing rationed intermediate imports. As in Rattsø (1994a), the import dependency of the region is reflected by the assumption that the short-run output varies with the availability of intermediate imports and that the import share of the investment goods composite is fixed. As explained below, the private savings decisions are also linked up to the import rationing.

The foreign exchange transactions are described by the current account balance (7.6):

$$S_f^* = (1-\theta)\, I(P_k/P_c) + B + C^m - X(e/P) \tag{7.6}$$

The foreign savings S_f^* are defined as the sum of the imports of investment, intermediate and consumption goods C^m less exports X. The nominal exchange rate is e, and all foreign prices are set to 1. To simplify the algebra, we exclude foreign interest rates and foreign aid. Investment I is a composite good, and a fixed share $(1-\theta)$ is imported. The investment demand function depends on the ratio between the demand price P_k and the supply price P_c of capital, with $I(1)=0$ and the partial derivative $I_1>0$. Exports X are assumed to be supply constrained and sold at given world market price dependent on the real exchange rate e/P. The supply price of capital is defined by (7.7), a weighted sum of the domestic price level and the foreign price in own currency:

$$P_c = \theta\, P + (1-\theta)\, e \tag{7.7}$$

Endogenous import compression is represented by a specific policy rule for the government import rationing: consumer and intermediate imports have been compressed, while investment imports have had priority. The rule is based on the import rationing systems described by Davies (1991) for Zimbabwe, and Ndulu (1986) for Tanzania, and it reflects the common understanding that the stagnation of the region is related to lack of imports of intermediate goods, the main conclusion of Wheeler (1984). The rationing of consumer and intermediate goods is dependent on the import capacity, a system called endogenous trade policy by Bevan *et al.* (1990). A similar formulation of the rationing system is used by Rattsø (1994b) in a study of the dynamics of sectoral balances. The trade balance is exogenous and defines the foreign exchange scarcity, the result of government interventions, rationing in international credit markets, or both.

Fixed shares of the residual import capacity are divided between intermediates and consumer goods. To simplify the formulation, foreign savings are assumed to finance imported investment goods. The consequences of the simplification are commented on when it is of importance. The formulation implies that imported intermediates and consumer goods can be written as shares of export revenues:

$$B = \beta\, X(e/P) \tag{7.8}$$

$$C^m = (1-\beta)\, X(e/P) \tag{7.9}$$

Implicitly it is assumed that there is always an excess demand for imported intermediates and consumer goods at the existing prices.

In an import-compressed economy, external disturbances tend to have strong output effects. Changes in foreign exchange revenues influence the capacity utilization from the supply side when imported intermediates are rationed. The supply function is derived from the production function and the foreign exchange rationing (7.8), setting P and e initially equal to 1:

$$dQ = Q_2\, dB = Q_2\, \beta\, X_1\, (de - dP) \tag{7.10}$$

The supply curve AS may be written in terms of the relationship between the price level and the imported intermediates, as in Figure 7.2, because of the production function linkage between the imported intermediates B and the output Q. The supply curve is downward sloping, as drawn in Figures 7.2 and 7.3, since a higher domestic price level crowds out exports, and fewer imported intermediates are available. Devaluation is supply-side expansionary.

The demand side described by equations (7.11) to (7.14) is more conventional, except for a relationship between savings and import compression. The domestic output is used for consumption of home goods C^h, investment $\theta\, I$ (domestic share θ of total), and exports X (measured in foreign prices) in (7.11). Private consumption is equal to the national income less savings S in (7.12). Nominal savings are motivated by the gap between desired A^d and actual A nominal wealth as in (7.13). The speed of adjust-

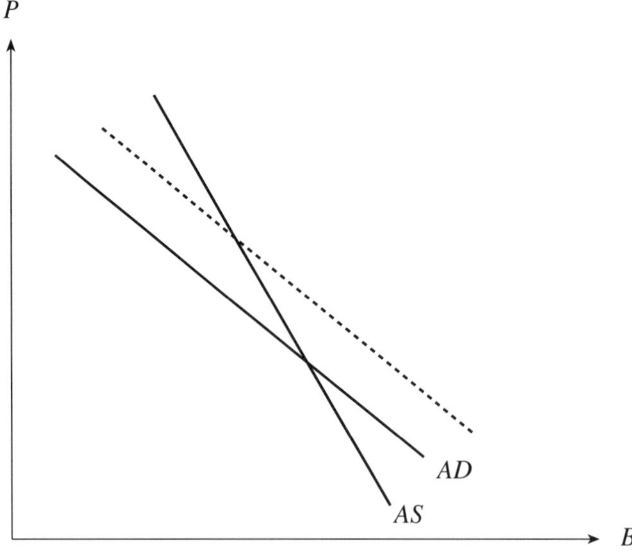

Figure 7.2 Macroeconomic equilibrium

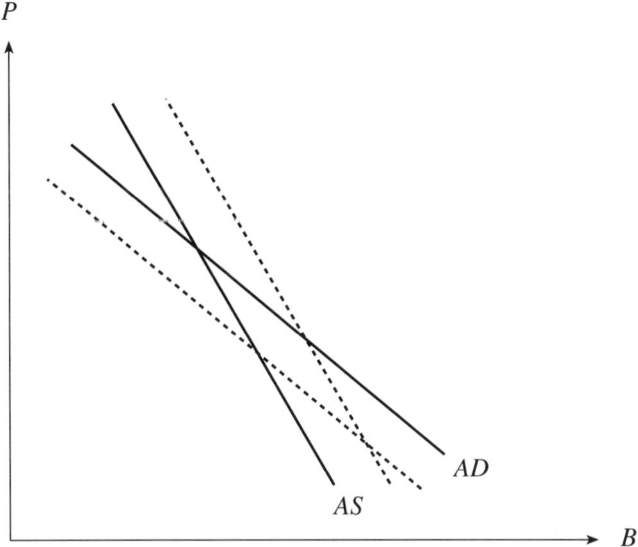

Figure 7.3 Macroeconomic effect of devaluation

ment to the desired wealth is determined by ψ. Desired wealth is related to gross nominal income in (7.14). Compared to an assumption where value-added motivates wealth-holding, our formulation simplifies the calculations with no consequences for the results.

To capture the stylized fact that the import rationing stimulates private savings, the desired wealth–income ratio g is made dependent on the availability of consumer imports. When consumer imports are restricted, households must allocate their consumption over time in a non-optimal way. When they expect the restrictions to be lifted in the future, they will hold back on consumption when rationed. A stock formulation of this relationship implies that the g-function has a negative partial derivative with respect to rationed consumer imports C^m. Theoretical justification is offered by Torvik (1997). Econometric evidence of the negative relationship between private savings and import allocations in Zimbabwe is provided by Chhibber *et al.* (1989) and Morande and Schmidt-Hebbel (1991).

$$Q(K,B) = C^h + \theta\, I(P_k / P_c) + e/P\, X(e/P) \tag{7.11}$$

$$P\, C^h + e\, C^m = P\, Q(K,B) - e\, B - S \tag{7.12}$$

$$S = \psi\, (A^d - A) \tag{7.13}$$

$$A^d = g(C^m)\, P\, Q(K,B) \tag{7.14}$$

The demand side of the economy is described by the savings–investment balance derived from equations (7.11) to (7.14), using (7.1), (7.4), (7.5) and (7.7):

$$\psi\,(g(C^m)\;P\;Q(K,B) - L(P,B,M,\Pi_z)\;Z - J(P,B,M,\Pi_z)\;K - M) \tag{7.15}$$
$$-\,P\,\theta\;I(J(P,B,M,\Pi_z)/(\theta P + (1-\theta)e)) = 0$$

The price level interacts with the excess savings when portfolio adjustments are taken into account, as worked out in Appendix equation (A7.3). The standard stability condition of reduced excess investment demand with increased price level is assumed. Since a higher price level reduces the import capacity, the rationing of consumer imports contributes to stability. When the price level goes up, reduced access to imported consumer goods increases the desired wealth, represented by the *g*-function, and the higher savings reduce the excess demand at the goods market.

The slope of the aggregate demand curve *AD* is determined by the influence of intermediate imports rationing on savings and investment. It is downward sloping when the savings effect dominates; higher output stimulates savings by raising desired wealth. To have local stability, aggregate demand must be more sensitive to price adjustments than aggregate supply, as drawn in Figures 7.2 and 7.3. It should be noticed that the *AD* curve may be upward sloping when the effect of intermediate imports on investment dominates. More imported intermediates increase the demand price of capital by increasing the productivity of capital, and investment demand goes up.

Two perverse effects are built in compared to the standard aggregate demand–aggregate supply model. The supply curve is downward sloping due to the import rationing and export price response. The demand curve reflects the endogenous rationing of consumer imports influencing private savings. Since the excess demand is reduced by a higher price level through this channel, the slope of the demand curve is made less steep. The demand curve can be upward sloping when the investment response to Tobin's q is strong and the demand price of capital reacts significantly to the productivity of capital.

4 MONETARY AND EXCHANGE RATE POLICY

The machinery developed can throw some light on the relationship between macroeconomic policies, macroeconomic performance and the role of speculation. Two stylized facts of the macroeconomic policies of the region are evaluated, monetary expansion and overvaluation of the currency. Monetary expansion is related to public sector deficits and thin financial markets. Overvaluation typically results from the inconsistency between the fiscal policy and the exchange rate arrangement.

Monetary policy affects the economy through several channels. The demand side effects are described by Appendix equation (A7.3). Expansionary monetary policy drives up the price level through the wealth effect on savings. The rise in nominal wealth follows both from the higher money stock itself and the indirect influence on the two asset prices. The higher private wealth reduces the incentive for savings and the asset price response stimulates investment demand. The aggregate demand curve of Figure 7.2 shifts up.

Conventional analyses of monetary policy can be turned around when our policy rule of import rationing is allowed to operate. Expansionary monetary policy has a contractionary effect. The mechanism is explained by the endogenous rationing of import intermediates. The demand side effects of more money bring the price level upward by reducing savings and increasing investment demand in standard fashion. The price effect tends to depress exports, thereby reducing the import capacity. Expansionary demand policies are contractionary in the short run. If the model is realistic, the economic stagnation of the region cannot be a result of low demand. The result is valid also when the aggregate demand curve is upward sloping (and local stability conditions are satisfied).

As shown in Rattsø (1994a), the contractionary effect is strengthened if the imports of investment goods are allowed to influence the residual import capacity. When more money stimulates the investment demand and the imports of investment goods, there is even less room for intermediate imports, and the supply curve shifts to the left.

As mentioned in the introduction, expansionary monetary policy and economic stagnation are observed together with booming speculative markets. The reduced form expression for the price of the speculative asset, equation (7.4), helps explain the stylized fact. More money and fewer intermediate imports both help the speculative price to increase. The first is a wealth effect. The import factor reduces the marginal productivity of capital, thereby inducing an asset shift from productive capital to speculation. A higher price level will increase the rate of return to capital, thereby counteracting the increased speculative price.

Overvaluation of the currency is the other striking aspect of the policy regimes of the region. The economic consequences of overvaluation can be understood by studying the effects of devaluation. When the import capacity is binding, as assumed here, devaluation has favorable supply-side effects by expanding exports. More room for intermediate imports is created, and the *AS* curve shifts out as in Figure 7.3.

The net demand effect of devaluation depends on the strength of two opposing forces. The higher costs of imported investment goods reduce investment demand. The channel of effect between exports and savings is explained by the rationing of consumer imports. More exports allowing for more consumer imports discourage savings when consumption has been held back by import rationing.

The case of dominating investment effect and a downward shift in the *AD* curve is drawn in Figure 7.3. The positive supply-side response contributes to an expansionary devaluation and a fall in the price level. Reduced demand brings further price reduction and output expansion. Only a strong fall in savings can turn the result around. Overvaluation of the currency is a likely source of stagnation under the assumptions discussed. The result is the opposite of the contractionary devaluation model of Krugman and Taylor (1978) and different from models with intermediate imports summarized by Lizondo and Montiel (1989). The foreign exchange constraint on output explains the result. The expansionary devaluation is a short-run effect at the cost of reduced investment. There is a conflict between short-run capacity utilization and long-run growth. Overvaluation of the currency and the consequent compression of imports contributes to high savings and a high price of the speculative asset. The policy can explain speculative boom with output contraction.

Optimism with respect to speculation may be short-run expansionary, and again the import compression mechanism is the key feature. When the expected return to speculation goes up, portfolios shift away from productive capital. The demand price of capital is reduced, and productive investment is discouraged. Speculation is not helpful to long-term growth. However, the short-run effect is expansionary since reduced domestic demand allows for higher export revenues and gives room for imports of intermediates.

5 DYNAMICS

We have shown above that the speculative price tends to be driven up by expansionary monetary policy and appreciating currency. The immediate response is carried over to the medium run via the expected return to speculation and capital accumulation. To investigate the dynamics, some assumption must be made about the formation of expectations. Since not much that is new is brought into play by assuming adaptive expectations, we will look at a rational expectations version, or perfect foresight in our non-stochastic set-up. We will look at two types of dynamics. In the first conventional saddle-point equilibrium, P_z is treated as a jump variable, while the expected return Π_z adjusts. In the other alternative, possibly interpreted as a predator–prey relationship between the capital stock and the speculative price, we assume that the speculative price is determined in the temporary model. In the first saddle path, capital accumulation and speculative booms are shown to go hand in hand. In the second we will look at possible cyclical fluctuations where speculative booms can be associated with contractions.

The long-run stationary equilibrium is defined by the model when actual wealth is equal to the desired wealth, $A = A^d$, investment is zero, $S = I = 0$, and the expected return to speculation is zero, $\Pi_z = 0$. The conditions determine stationary values of the asset price P_z^* and the capital stock K^*. The dynamic adjustments of the speculative price and the capital stock are determined by the asset equilibrium condition for the speculative asset and the investment function, taking into account the macro interactions.

The dynamics of the equilibrium condition at the speculative market follows from the Appendix equation (A7.1), and is written on reduced form:

$$dP_z / dt = Z(P_z, K, M) \tag{7.16}$$

Assuming that the direct effects at the speculative market dominate, as we will assume below, one important result follows immediately. The speculative price drives its own growth rate, a mechanism typical to financial instability. The higher price P_z leads to excess supply of the speculative asset and the expected return must go up to attract investors. A higher capital stock K makes the speculative asset more attractive, and the expected return must go down to equilibrate the market. When the stock of money goes up, the excess demand also must be eliminated by a fall in the speculative price.

The accumulation of capital is determined by the investment function, and the dynamics is related to the adjustment over time of the demand and the supply prices of capital:

$$dI = I_1 \, (dP_k - P_k \, \theta \, dP) \tag{7.17}$$

The relationships between the state variables and the two prices involved are derived in Appendix 3, and the assumptions needed to reach the dynamic rules below are explained. In the dynamic analysis, we will allow the capital stock to decumulate. Such a reduction in the capital stock reflects depreciation, not explicitly introduced, and implies an additional restriction to the time path.

The dynamics in the neighborhood of the stationary equilibrium can be written as[1]

$$dP_z / dt = \pi(P_z - P_z^*, K - K^*), \ \pi_1 > 0, \ \pi_2 < 0 \tag{7.18}$$

$$dK / dt = \upsilon(P_z - P_z^*, K - K^*), \ \upsilon_1 > 0, \ \upsilon_2 < 0 \tag{7.19}$$

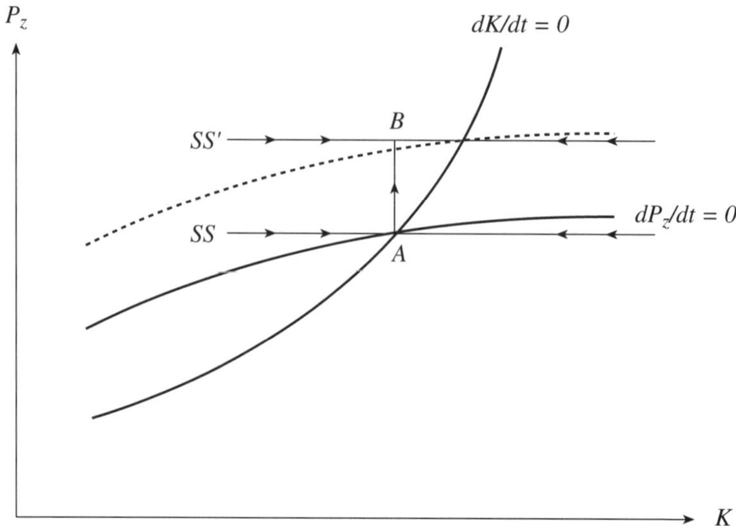

Figure 7.4 Dynamics of unanticipated monetary expansion

The system involves the saddle point property when the determinant of the Jacobian is negative:

$$\pi_1 \upsilon_2 - \pi_2 \upsilon_1 < 0$$

The saddle point equilibrium is described in Figures 7.4 and 7.5. The phase line representing a constant speculative price is upward sloping. A higher capital stock K switches portfolio allocations towards the speculative asset and the excess demand requires a higher price P_z. The concave shape of the phase line in Figure 7.4 reflects the standard assumption in production theory that the fall in the marginal productivity of capital (Q_{11}) is decreasing with increasing capital stock. The higher the capital stock, the smaller the decline in the marginal productivity. Consequently, a given increase in the capital stock requires a smaller adjustment of the speculative price to counterbalance the reduced attractiveness of capital.

The phase line describing a constant capital stock is also upward sloping. It is assumed that the positive effect of a higher speculative price on the investment demand (via P_k) dominates. The effect of a higher capital stock on its own dynamic path is ambiguous and involves non-linearities related to the shape of the production function. The stable case with a negative effect of higher capital stock on investment is drawn in the figures.

The saddle path SS leading to the stationary equilibrium A implies that the speculative price and the capital stock move together. The economy is

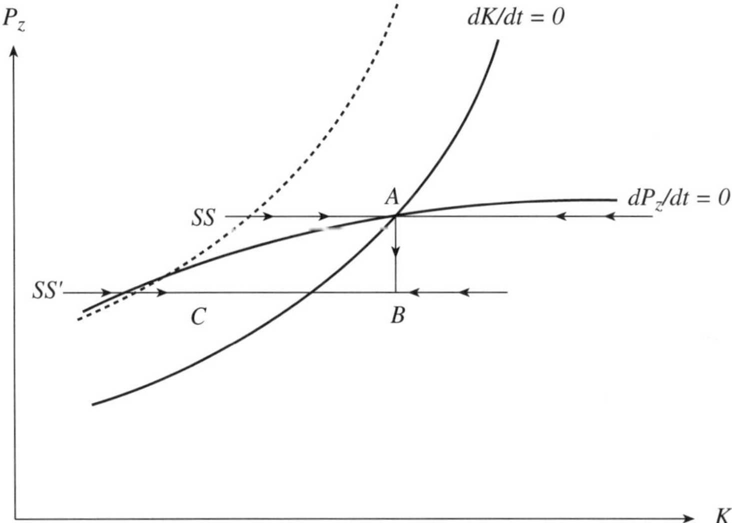

Figure 7.5 Dynamics of devaluation

assumed always to choose an instantaneous equilibrium on the saddle path. The saddle path equilibrium cannot explain a development where the speculative price moves in the opposite direction to the accumulation of capital.

The dynamics of a permanent unanticipated positive shift in the money stock is shown in Figure 7.4. The phase line representing $dP_z/dt=0$ shifts up, since the new portfolio equilibrium requires a higher speculative price. The isocline representing zero investment is assumed to stay, as the positive effect on the demand price of capital can be counterbalanced by the higher price level resulting from lower savings. The excess demand at the speculative market induces a jump in the speculative price from the initial equilibrium *A* to position *B* on the new saddle path *SS′*. The higher speculative price drives the demand price of capital further up, and a period of positive investment is started up. Along the saddle path, the speculative price and the capital stock move together towards the new stationary equilibrium *C*.

The medium-run effects of an unanticipated devaluation are outlined in Figure 7.5. Devaluation increases the supply price of capital, and a stationary equilibrium requires a lower capital stock. The isocline representing $dK/dt=0$ shifts to the left. The stationary condition at the speculative market is basically unaffected by the devaluation. The immediate effect involves a negative shift in the speculative price from the initial *A* to point *B* on the new saddle path *SS′*. The reduced speculative price, and the fall in the demand price of capital that goes with it, implies a decumulation of capital along the saddle path towards C. Once again, the dynamics means that speculative price response and capital accumulation move together. The short-run story explained in section 4 does not carry over to the medium run under saddle point equilibrium.

In the second interpretation of the model, the price of the speculative asset is taken as given in the temporary equilibrium. The dynamic rules (7.18) and (7.19) can generate cyclical fluctuations. A possible cyclical path is described in Figure 7.6. Let us first establish the intuition of this case and then the technicalities. The damped oscillations towards equilibrium can be interpreted as a predator–prey relationship on the way to a stable coexistence. In this model, the capital stock serves as predator and the speculative price as prey.

Starting out in the beginning of a depression (as in Figure 7.6), a fall in the price of the speculative asset brings with it a fall in investment, and eventually the decline of the capital stock. When the prey is reduced, the predator goes with it. When the capital stock is reduced, the price of the speculative asset eventually goes up. The reduced capital stock motivates a portfolio shift towards the productive capital, and the expected (and actual) return of the speculative asset must go up to make it more attractive. The reduced number of predators opens up for new growth of the prey. The speculative price rise drives up the nominal wealth and thereby the demand price of capital. The speculative boom and the capital accumulation go

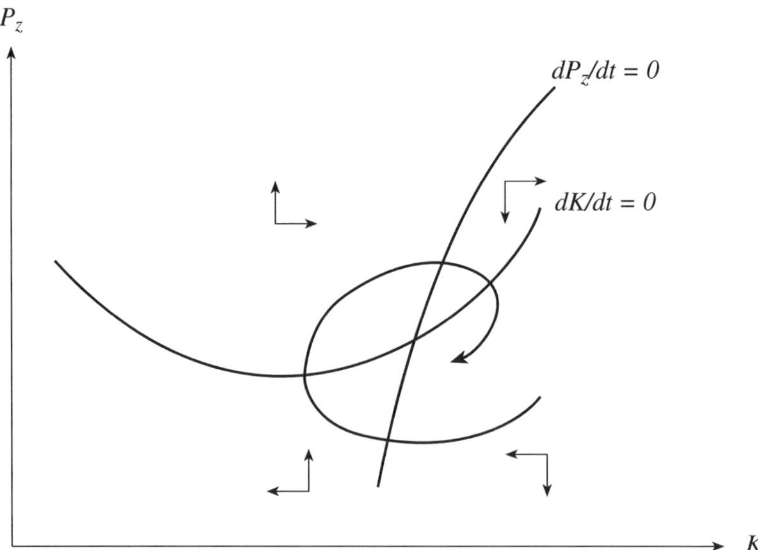

Figure 7.6 Predator–prey dynamics

hand in hand. More prey makes room for more predators. The capital accumulation itself contributes to the culmination of the speculative boom. The higher capital stock shifts portfolio allocations towards the speculative asset. To reduce the attractiveness of speculation, the expected return must go down. Under favorable conditions described below, the process reaches a stable equilibrium.

The analytics of the possibly stable fluctuations are guided by the two dynamic equations (7.18) and (7.19). To have damped oscillations towards a stable equilibrium, the trace of the Jacobian must be negative and the determinant positive :

$$\pi_1 + \upsilon_2 < 0 \text{ and } \pi_1 \upsilon_2 - \pi_2 \upsilon_1 > 0$$

Since the speculative price feeds its own growth, speculation is a source of instability. The investment dynamics may counterbalance the instability in the region where the capital accumulation itself is stable, that is when K is sufficiently large and the wealth effect dominates.

6 CONCLUDING REMARKS

A theoretical framework has been developed to analyse the role of key characteristics of the Sub-Saharan Africa region during 'socialism', import compression and financial repression. The approach has produced explanations of the combined economic stagnation and booming speculation that have been observed.

The macroeconomic policies of the region during this period can be described as monetary expansion and overvalued exchange rate. They follow from public deficits and fixed exchange rate regimes. Both monetary expansion and overvaluation of the currency seem to contribute to prolonged stagnation and booming prices of speculative assets under import rationing. The model predicts a long-run cost of policy reorientation, however, since investment will be reduced by monetary contraction and devaluation. Experiences of structural adjustment programs summarized by World Bank (1990) tend to confirm this negative investment effect. There is a tradeoff between productive investment and capacity utilization under foreign exchange shortage.

When perfect foresight is assumed for the expected return to speculation, various dynamic adjustment paths are derived. In the case of saddle point equilibrium, the speculative price and the capital accumulation are shown to move together along the saddle path. The model also includes the possibility of cyclical fluctuations with speculative boom and investment depression.

APPENDIX 1: THE PORTFOLIO MODEL

The determination of the two equilibrium asset demand prices, P_z and P_k, are associated with the excess demand functions :

$$G(P\,Q_1/P_k, \Pi_z)\,(P_z\,Z+P_k\,K+M)-P_z\,Z=0 \qquad \text{(A7.1)}$$

$$H(P\,Q_1/P_k, \Pi_z)\,(P_z\,Z+P_k\,K+M)-P_k\,K=0 \qquad \text{(A7.2)}$$

Differentiation of the two excess demand functions with respect to P_z, P_k, P, B, M, and Π_z, setting the prices $P=e=1$ initially, implies:

$$a_1\,dP_z+a_2\,dP_{\mathrm{k}}=a_3\,dP+a_4\,dB+a_5\,dM+a_6\,d\Pi_z$$
$$b_1\,dP_z+b_2\,dP_{\mathrm{k}}=b_3\,dP+b_4\,dB+b_5\,dM+b_6\,d\Pi_z$$

$$a_1=-(1-G)\,Z<0$$
$$a_2=(G\,K-(A\,G_1\,Q_1)/P_k^2)>0$$
$$a_3=-(A\,G_1\,Q_1)/P_k>0$$
$$a_4=-(A\,G_1\,Q_{12})/P_k>0$$
$$a_5=-G<0$$
$$a_6=-A\,G_2<0$$
$$b_1=H\,Z>0$$
$$b_2=-((1-H)\,K+(A\,H_1\,Q_1)/P_k^2)<0$$
$$b_3=-(A\,H_1\,Q_1)/P_k<0$$
$$b_4=-(A\,H_1\,Q_{12})/P_k<0$$
$$b_5=-H<0$$
$$b_6=-A\,H_2>0$$

The determinant of the excess demand functions, $D=(a_1\,b_2-a_2\,b_1)$, is assumed to be positive to have local stability. As usual, the indirect effects between the two markets are not allowed to dominate. The trace condition holds.

The following partial derivatives can be calculated:

$$dP_z/dP=(1/D)\,(a_3\,b_2-a_2\,b_3)=(A\,Q_1\,K/P_k\,D)\,(G_1(1-H)+H_1\,G)\,?$$
$$dP_z/dB=(1/D)\,(a_4\,b_2-a_2\,b_4)=(A\,Q_{12}\,K/P_k\,D)\,(G_1(1-H)+H_1\,G)\,?$$
$$dP_z/dM=(1/D)\,(a_5\,b_2-a_2\,b_5)=(1/D)\,(G\,K+(A\,Q_1/P_k^2)\,(H_1\,G-G_1\,H))>0$$
$$dP_z/d\Pi_z=(1/D)\,(a_6\,b_2-a_2\,b_6)=(A/D)\,(K(G_2(1-H)+H_2\,G)+((A\,Q_1/P_{\mathrm{k}2})(G_2\,H_1-G_1\,H_2)))\,?$$
$$dP_k/d\mathrm{P}=(1/D)\,(a_1\,b_3-a_3\,b_1)=(A\,Q_1\,Z/P_k\,D)\,(H_1(1-G)+G_1\,H)\,?$$
$$dP_k/dB=(1/D)\,(a_1\,b_4-a_4\,b_1)=(A\,Q_{12}\,Z/P_k^2\,D)\,(H_1(1-G)+G_1\,H)\,?$$

$dP_k / dM = (1/D)\,(a_1\, b_5 - a_5\, b_1) = (1/D)\, H\, Z > 0$

$dP_k / d\Pi_z = (1/D)\,(a_1\, b_6 - a_6\, b_1) = (A\, Z/D)\,(H_2(1-G) + G_2\, H)$?

The partial derivatives are summarized by the asset demand price functions (7.4) and (7.5) in the text under specific assumptions. In general, the direct effects at each portfolio market are assumed to dominate: P and B influence the return to K, and the direct effects imply dP_k/dP and $dP_k/dB > 0$, dP_z/dP and $dP_z/dB < 0$. Π_z influences the return to Z, $dP_z/d\Pi_z > 0$ and $dP_k/d\Pi_z < 0$.

APPENDIX 2: THE MODEL SOLUTION

The differentiation of the savings–investment balance (7.15) produces a demand-side relationship between P and B:

$$c_1\, dP = c_2\, dB + c_3\, dM + c_4\, de + c_5\, d\Pi_z \qquad \text{(A7.3)}$$

$$c_1 = \psi\, Q\,(g - g_1\, X_1\,(1-\beta)) - \psi(Z\, L_1 + K\, J_1) - \theta\, I - \theta\, I_1(J_1 - P_k\, \theta)$$

$$c_2 = -\,\psi\, g\, Q_2 + \psi(Z\, L_2 + K\, J_2) + \theta\, I_1\, J_2$$

$$c_3 = \psi\,(1 + K\, J_3 + Z\, L_3) + \theta\, I_1\, J_3 > 0$$

$$c_4 = -\,\psi\, Q\, g_1\, X_1\,(1-\beta) - \theta\, I_1\, P_k\,(1-\theta)$$

$$c_5 = (\psi\, K + \theta\, I_1) J_4 + \psi\, Z\, L_4$$

$c_1 > 0$ implies that the excess demand is reduced by a higher price level and is the standard condition for local stability. A downward sloping demand curve follows when the savings effect of intermediate imports dominate and $c_2 < 0$. As discussed in the text, $c_2 > 0$ when the investment response via P_k dominates. Monetary expansion is demand-side expansionary. Devaluation discourages savings through the rationing of consumer imports and investment through the supply price, and the sign of c_4 is a priori undecided. The demand effect of a change in the expected return to speculation is ambiguous, but c_5 will be negative when the investment demand effect through P_k dominates.

APPENDIX 3: THE DYNAMICS

The dynamic model with endogenous expected return to speculation includes equations (A7.1), (A7.2), (7.15) and the investment function, taking into account the rationing in (7.8) and (7.9), determining the dynamic paths of P_z and K. The dynamics of the speculative price is described by equation (7.16). To solve out the path of capital accumulation from equation (7.17), the dependence of P_k and P on the state variables in the stationary equilibrium must be identified. The direct effects at the two markets are assumed to dominate. From the portfolio equilibrium condition (A7.2) for capital, we get

$$((1-H)K+(A\ H_1\ Q_1)/P_k^2)\ dP_k \\ =H\ Z\ dP_z-(P_k(1-H)+(A\ H_1\ Q_{11})/P_k)\ dK \tag{A7.4}$$

with

$$P_k=P_k(\overset{+}{P_z},\overset{-}{K}) \tag{A7.5}$$

The stationary equilibrium differentiation of the savings investment balance (7.15), taking into account (7.8) and (7.9), implies

$$(\psi\,(g_1\ Q\ X\,(1-\beta)(1-\varepsilon_x)+g\ Q+g\ Q_2\ \beta\ X\,(1-\varepsilon_x))+\theta\ I_1\ P_k\ \theta)\ dP \\ =\psi\ Z\ dP_z+\psi\,(1-g\ Q_1)\ dK \tag{A7.6}$$

with

$$P=P(\overset{+}{P_z},\overset{?}{K}) \tag{A7.7}$$

A higher capital stock has two conflicting effects on the price level. On the one hand, the wealth effect tends to reduce savings and stimulate demand. On the other, the output effect increases desired wealth and savings, thereby reducing demand. If higher capital stock reduces the price level in stationary equilibrium, this effect is not allowed to dominate in (7.19). Since the marginal productivity of capital is declining with a higher capital stock, the output effect may dominate when the capital stock is small. When the stock is larger, the wealth effect is likely to dominate, as assumed here.

NOTES

* I appreciate discussions with Rob Davies, Halvor Mehlum, Lance Taylor, Ragnar Torvik and Michael Walton, comments from Amitava Dutt and an anonymous referee, and at seminars in Oslo and Trondheim. The funding is provided by the Norwegian Research Council and the Ministry of Foreign Affairs, Norway.

1. Different types of dynamic behavior are built into the equations, as can be seen from the characteristic roots:

$$\lambda_1, \lambda_2 = \tfrac{1}{2}\{(\pi_1 + \upsilon_2) \pm \sqrt{[(\pi_1 + \upsilon_2)^2 - 4\,\pi_1\,\upsilon_2 + 4\,\pi_2\,\upsilon_1]}\}$$

REFERENCES

Bevan, B., P. Collier and J. Gunning (1990), *Controlled Open Economies: A Neoclassical Alternative to Structuralism*, Oxford: Clarendon Press.

Buffie, E. (1986), 'Devaluation, investment and growth in LDCs', *Journal of Development Economics*, 20: 361–79.

Chhibber, A., J. Cottani, R. Firuzabadi and M. Walton (1989), 'Inflation, price control and fiscal adjustment in Zimbabwe', PPR Working Paper No. 192, Country Economics Department, The World Bank.

Davies, R. (1991), 'Trade, trade management and development in Zimbabwe', in J. Frimpong-Ansah, S.M. Ravi Kanbur and P. Svedberg (eds), *Trade and Development in Sub-Saharan Africa*, Manchester: Manchester University Press.

Davies, R. and J. Rattsø (1993), 'Zimbabwe', in Lance Taylor (ed.), *The Rocky Road to Reform: Income Distribution, Politics and Adjustment in the Developing World*, Cambridge: MIT Press.

Dutt, A. (1986), 'Stock equilibrium in flexprice markets in macromodels for less developed economies: the case of food speculation', *Journal of Development Economics*, 21: 89–110.

Gavin, M. (1992), 'Monetary policy, exchange rates, and investment in a Keynesian economy', *Journal of International Money and Finance*, 11: 145–61.

Green, R. and X. Kadhani (1983), 'Zimbabwe: Transition to economic crises, 1981–83: retrospects and prospects', *World Development*, 14: 1059–83.

Helleiner, G. (1990), 'Structural adjustment and long-term development in Sub-Saharan Africa', Development Studies Working Papers No. 18, Centro Studi Luca d'Agliano – Queen Elizabeth House, Torino and Oxford.

Krugman, P. and L. Taylor (1978), 'Contractionary effects of devaluation', *Journal of International Economics*, 8: 445–56.

Lizondo, J. Saul (1987), 'Exchange rate differential and balance of payments under dual exchange markets', *Journal of Development Economics*, 26: 37–53.

Lizondo, J. Saul and P.J. Montiel (1989), 'Contractionary devaluation in developing countries: an analytical overview', *IMF Staff Papers*, 36: 182–227.

Minsky, H. (1986), *Stabilizing an Unstable Economy*, New Haven: Yale University Press.

Montiel, P. (1991), 'The transmission mechanism for monetary policy in developing countries', *IMF Staff Papers*, **38**(1), 83–108.

Moran, C. (1989), 'Imports under a foreign exchange constraint', *World Bank Economic Review*, 3: 279–95.

Morande, F. and K. Schmidt-Hebbel (1991), 'Macroeconomics of public sector deficits: the case of Zimbabwe', PPR Working Paper No. 688, Country Economics Department, The World Bank.

Ndulu, B. (1986), 'Investment, output growth and capacity utilization in an African economy: the case of manufacturing sector in Tanzania', *East Africa Economic Review*, 2: 14–30.

Ndulu, B. (1993), 'Tanzania', in Lance Taylor (ed.), *The Rocky Road to Reform: Income Distribution, Politics and Adjustment in the Developing World*, Cambridge: MIT Press.

Rattsø, J. (1994a), 'Devaluation and monetary policy under import compression', *Open Economies Review*, 5: 159–75.

Rattsø, J. (1994b), 'Medium run adjustment under import compression: Macroeonomic analysis relevant for Sub-Saharan Africa', *Journal of Development Economics*, **45**(1), 35–54.

Taylor, L. (1991), *Income Distribution, Inflation and Growth*, Cambridge, MA: MIT Press.

Torvik, R. (1997), 'Real exchange rate dynamics and trade liberalization: the case of multiple tariffs and unemployment', *Journal of International Trade and Economic Development*, **6**(3), 329–44.

Wheeler, D. (1984), 'Sources of stagnation in Sub-Saharan Africa', *World Development*, 12: 1–23.

World Bank (1990), *Report on Adjustment Lending II: Policies for the Recovery of Growth*, Washington DC: IBRD.

8. Financial fragility in developing economies

Duncan K. Foley

1 INTRODUCTION

The epidemic of financial crises in developing and newly industrializing countries that accompanied the liberalization of domestic and international capital markets in the 1990s has underlined the relevance of Hyman Minsky's (1975, 1982) conception of financial fragility to the contemporary world economy. Minsky's own work focused on financial fragility in fully industrialized capitalist economies with highly developed financial institutions and markets. Minsky saw a tendency for financial positions to become increasingly indebted in periods of prosperity, and hence increasingly vulnerable to debt-deflation crisis, as both borrowers and lenders become tolerant of higher ratios of debt to equity finance. In Minsky's view a financially fragile economy posed a difficult problem for a central bank; in attempting to control financial fragility by tightening monetary policy and raising interest rates, the central bank could trigger the financial crisis it sought to avert.

The drama of financial crisis in the international economy in the 1990s played out in a rather different context. Industrializing economies with high structural profit rates and good opportunities for profitable investment but relatively undeveloped financial institutions faced large inflows of short-term debt capital in the context of the 'Washington consensus'-inspired liberalization of international capital flows. Positive shocks to investment and profitability in these economies triggered unstable capital inflows which led in turn to external and internal financial crisis as the resulting current account deficits became unmanageable. In this repeated pattern of events, however, we can see the outlines of Minskian crisis based on increasing financial fragility.

The purpose of this chapter is to modify the model of Minskian crisis put forward by Lance Taylor and Stephen O'Connell (1985) to analyse the crises of the 1990s. Taylor and O'Connell study a Kaleckian economy in which capacity utilization and the profit rate vary to bring about a short-run equilibrium of aggregate demand and supply. They introduce an investment demand function into this economy which has a variable 'exuberance' factor to represent a potentially destabilizing tendency for firms to increase their investment plans during booms. One curious aspect of the Taylor–O'Connell model is that it maintains the closed economy Kaleckian relation between the growth rate and the savings out of profits, $g = sr$, which, assuming $s < 1$, imposes a regime of Minskian hedge finance in which $r > g$.

Opening the economy to capital inflows from abroad is a natural way to allow domestic growth rates to exceed domestic profit rates, and thereby to allow the economy to reach Minsky's speculative regime where $g > r$. The modified model, however, remains true to the basic insight of Taylor–O'Connell that the growth rate and profit rate are highly positively correlated in a Kaleckian economy, which may make it very difficult to reduce financial fragility by lowering the growth rate. Indeed, the modified model exhibits paths, even around stable equilibria, which force the economy into the financially fragile regime of Ponzi finance as growth rates and profit rates fall in the course of a stabilizing correction.

While there are undoubtedly relevant 'supply-side' factors constraining growth in industrializing economies, particularly the challenge of improving infrastructure to complement capital accumulation and the stress of rapid growth on entrepreneurial capabilities, the modified model suggests that higher target growth rates are likely to be more robust financially. Central bankers and their advisers from international agencies would do well to ponder the interaction of Kaleckian aggregate demand dynamics and Minskian financial constraints in the short-run dynamics of structural adjustment in industrializing economies.

2 THE ANALYTICS OF FINANCIAL FRAGILITY

Financial fragility arises from the widespread practice of firms using debt contracts to finance production. In a debt contract the borrowing firm receives finance from a lender in exchange for promising a contractually fixed stream of interest and principal payments (*debt service*) over the duration of the loan. The failure of the borrowing firm to make one of these contractual payments triggers its *bankruptcy*, which interrupts the firm's normal operation, and puts its other creditors at risk of not receiving the payment of their contracted debt service. An economy is financially fragile, in Minsky's terms, if the bankruptcy of one firm can set off a chain reaction of bankruptcies of other firms.

Minsky analyses financial fragility in terms of a firm's cash flow accounting categories. In a highly aggegated form, the cash flow identity equates the firm's sources of funds from net operating revenues, R, and new borrowing, D, to its uses of funds for investment, I, and debt service, V. (For simplicity I abstract from the payment of dividends.)

$$R + D \equiv I + V \tag{8.1}$$

This organization of the cash flow identity in terms of sources and uses of funds is somewhat arbitrary, since it is possible for R to be negative, if the firm is operating at a loss, for D to be negative if the firm is repaying debt, for I to be negative if the firm is selling assets, or for V to be negative if the firm is a net creditor.

The net worth of the firm, W, is equal to the difference between the value of its assets, A, and the value of its debts, B. Net worth is increased by investment, which is the change in assets, $\dot{A} = I$, and reduced by borrowing, which is the change in debt, $\dot{B} = D$.

$$W = A - B \tag{8.2}$$

$$\dot{W} = \dot{A} - \dot{B} = I - D \tag{8.3}$$

If a bankrupt firm turns out to be insolvent, $W \leq 0$, then its creditors will be unable to recover the principal value of their loans.

Minsky identifies three possible firm financial states.

A *hedged* firm has $R \geq V + I$, so that $D \leq 0$. The firm's net revenues cover its debt service and investment, so that it is in a position to reduce its net indebtedness. A hedged firm may still get into financial trouble, of course, if its net revenues decline (as might happen in a business downturn) or its debt service rises (as might happen in a credit crunch). Hedged firms are financially relatively secure, but this may be due to their lack of attractive investment opportunities. The net worth of a hedged firm is increasing, and as long as it stays hedged it will never become bankrupt.

A *speculative* firm has $R \geq V$, but $R < V + I$, so that $D \geq 0$, but $D < I$. The speculative firm can cover its current debt service out of its net revenues, but it is borrowing in order to finance some part of its investment. The speculative firm's creditworthiness depends on the prospective profitability of its investments. In the event of a rise in its debt service costs it has some margin of financial security in restricting investment, as long as its net revenues remain strong. Almost all successful capitalist firms go through a speculative phase in their development, since successful firms generate investment opportunities that exceed their capacity for self-finance. The net worth of a speculative firm is increasing. As long as its investments remain profitable, it will not go bankrupt.

A *Ponzi* firm has $R<V$, so that $D>I$. The Ponzi firm is borrowing to pay part of its debt service. The Ponzi firm's creditworthiness depends on its ability to convince potential lenders that its net revenues will rise in the near future, since it has no margin of financial security. A rise in debt service makes it harder for a Ponzi firm to find willing borrowers. Many successful capitalist firms have gone through Ponzi phases as the result of unanticipated but short-lived shocks to their net revenues or debt service. But a Ponzi firm is living on borrowed time, since it will become insolvent in a finite time on its current financial path. If its creditors lose faith in the firm's revenue prospects, they will refuse new loans to pay its debt service, and bankrupt the firm immediately.

3 THE DYNAMICS OF FIRM FINANCE

The path of firm finance is easiest to work out in terms of rates of change and return on assets and debt. Let $g=I/A$ be the growth rate of the firm's assets, $r=R/A$ be its profit rate, and $i=V/B$ be its interest rate (the ratio of debt service to the stock of debt). Then the cash flow identity can be written:

$$\dot{B}=D=I+V-R=(g-r)A+iB \tag{8.4}$$

If we look at paths on which g is constant, so that $A(t)=A_0e^{gt}$, this differential equation has the general solution:

$$B(t)=\left(B_0-\frac{g-r}{g-i}A_0\right)e^{it}+\frac{g-r}{g-i}A_0e^{gt} \tag{8.5}$$

It is more convenient to write this solution in terms of the ratio of debt to assets, $\phi=B/A$. The firm is solvent as long as $\phi<1$. The path of ϕ is, writing $\phi^*=(g-r)/(g-i)$:

$$\phi(t)=\phi^*+(\phi_0-\phi^*)e^{(i-g)t} \tag{8.6}$$

If $g>i$, the second term vanishes asymptotically, and $\lim_{t\to\infty}\phi(t)=\phi^*$. If $i>g$, then the second term dominates and $\lim_{t\to\infty}\phi(t)=\pm\infty$ as $\phi_0><\phi^*$. There are thus two types of paths on which the firm becomes bankrupt in finite time: those on which $g>i$ and $\phi^*>1$, and those on which $i>g$ and $\phi_0>\phi^*$.

On paths where $r>i$, the firm will not go bankrupt. When $r>g>i$, $\phi(t)\to\phi^*<0$ and the firm is an asymptotic creditor. When $r>i>g$,

$\phi^* > 1 > \phi_0$, $\phi(t) \rightarrow -\infty$ and the firm is an asymptotically unbounded creditor. On both these paths the firm is always hedged.

But a firm for which $r > i$ has a strong incentive to increase its investment by raising g. If $g > r > i$, $\phi(t) \rightarrow \phi^* < 1$. This is the case of speculative finance. The firm is never hedged, since it is always borrowing to carry out its investment, but its debt grows asymptotically at the same rate as its assets.

If the firm expects $i > r$ indefinitely, it is better off putting its net worth into financial assets and becoming a bank. The policy that achieves this is to lower g, making it negative if necessary.

On paths where $g > i > r$, $\phi(t) \rightarrow \phi^* > 1$, and the firm must go bankrupt in finite time. This is the classic case of Ponzi finance. While it is unlikely that a reputable firm would choose a Ponzi path voluntarily, a firm might be trapped into a Ponzi posture at least temporarily by events beyond its control. A rise in the interest rate, as a result of policy or market developments beyond the firm's control, for example, will transform a speculative financial strategy into a Ponzi strategy. In this situation the firm either has to hope that the interest rate falls below its profit rate before it becomes insolvent, and that its lenders are willing to see it through the crisis, or it has to try to save itself by lowering g.

How successfully can a Ponzi firm manage to stabilize itself financially by restricting investment? With $g < i$, $\phi(t) \rightarrow (\phi_0 - \phi^*)\infty$, so the firm must aim for $\phi^* = (r-g)/(i-g) > \phi_0$, or $g < (r - \phi_0 i)/(1 - \phi_0)$. The lower is r, the higher i, and the higher ϕ_0, the more must the firm lower g to reach safety. If a large number of firms try to stabilize themselves by cutting back investment expenditures, they may reduce aggregate demand and wind up reducing their profit rates as well, setting off a decline in output and national income, and making it that much harder to reach stability.

4 FINANCIAL FRAGILITY OF NATIONAL ECONOMIES

The equations describing the financial dynamics of a firm apply equally well to a national economy, viewed as a collection of firms. In reality, the ensemble of firms making up a national economy will be distributed statistically among different financial states – some proportion of the firms at any moment will be hedged, some proportion speculative, and some proportion Ponzi. But, following Lance Taylor and Stephen O'Connell (1985), we can get some insight into the economy-wide dynamics by studying a model where the firms of a nation are averaged into one representative firm.

Consider a small, open Kaleckian economy in which real output X is distributed as wages, $W = (1 - \pi)X$, all of which are spent immediately, and profits, $P = \pi X$, a fraction s of which are saved, so that consumption $C = W + (1 - s)P = (1 - s\pi)X$. We take the profit share, π, as an unvarying exogenous parameter. All quantities are measured in real terms (or equivalently at world prices.) For simplicity we will abstract from government taxation and spending. Investment is I. D, the current account deficit, or, equivalently, capital account surplus, is the difference between expenditure and output, $D = C + I - X = I - s\pi X$. This D for the whole economy is analogous to the D defined above for an individual firm, since it represents net new borrowing. Writing $d = D/K$, $g = I/K$, and $r = \pi\ X/K$ where K is the capital stock, we have:

$$d = g - s\,r \tag{8.7}$$

Given d and g, the actual output–capital ration, X/K, must adjust to determine a realized profit rate r that satisfies equation (8.7). Taylor and O'Connell's closed economy has $d = 0$, which implies that $g < r$, on the assumption that $s < 1$. As a result, their economy cannot actually get into the speculative regime where $g > r > i$. The open economy of the present model, however, can import capital to finance investment, so that it can reach the speculative regime.

Assume that the capital account surplus, d, depends on the real interest rate i, controlled by the monetary authority,[1] and the profit rate r:

$$d = d_0 + \eta i - \psi s r \tag{8.8}$$

The parameters η and ψ are positive, on the assumptions that a rise in the real interest rate will increase capital inflows, and that capitalists use some proportion of their saved profits to buy foreign assets.

Following Taylor and O'Connell, assume that the growth rate of capital depends on the profit rate r, the real interest rate, i, and a confidence factor ρ, representing the exuberance of the investing capitalists:

$$g = g_0 + h(r + \rho - i) \tag{8.9}$$

The parameter h is positive. We see that:

$$r = \frac{g - d}{s} = \frac{g_0 - d_0 + (h + \psi)r + h\rho - (h + \eta)i}{s}$$

Solving for r:

$$r = \frac{g_0 - d_0 + h\rho - (h + \eta)i}{s(1 - \psi) - h} \tag{8.10}$$

A rise in the interest rate leads to an increase in capital inflows and imports, and a fall in domestic investment, both reducing domestic output, the output–capital ratio, and the profit rate. An increase in exuberance raises domestic investment, the output–capital ratio, and the profit rate.

In the same fashion we can solve for g:

$$g - \frac{s(1-\psi)g_0 - hd_0 + hs(1-\psi)\rho - h(s(1-\psi)+\eta)i}{s(1-\psi) - h} \tag{8.11}$$

Thus we can view the equations (8.7), (8.8) and (8.9) as determining r, g, and d, given ρ, i and the structural parameters. In this way of approaching the model, ρ and i are the state variables. Since g and ρ are related monotonically, we can alternatively take g and i as state variables, understanding that ρ is being determined implicitly. This approach to the dynamics has the advantage of allowing us to visualize the dynamics of the economy in (g,i) space, where the relationships defining financial fragility are more transparent. In this way of approaching the model, we can write r (and the current account deficit, d) in terms of g and i:

$$r = \frac{g - d_0 - \eta i}{s(1-\psi)} \tag{8.12}$$

$$d = \frac{\psi g - d_0 - \eta i}{s(1-\psi)} \tag{8.13}$$

Figure 8.1 shows the regions in (g,i) space corresponding to the different regimes of finance. The dashed 45-degree line on which $i=g$ is the boundary between the $g>i$ regime below and the $i>g$ regime above. Each combination of g and i determines a particular profit rate r in short-run equilibrium through equation (8.12). The bold line in Figure 8.1 is the locus of (g,i) pairs on which $r=i$. Above this line $i>r$, which, as we have seen signals the unsustainable state of Ponzi finance. An economy which crosses this boundary is vulnerable to a financial crisis. The undashed line is the locus of (g,i) pairs on which $r=g$, and marks the boundary (where $i \leq r$) between the regime of hedged and speculative finance. Figure 8.1 emphasizes the linkage between the growth rate and the profit rate in the open Kaleckian economy. In this economy a *rise* in the growth rate *diminishes* financial fragility because it raises the profit rate.

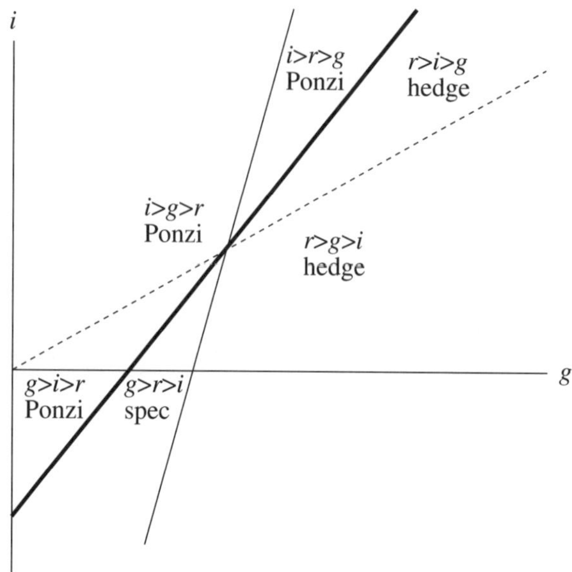

Note: On the dashed 45° line $i = g$. The bold line is the locus of points on which $r = i$, and is the lower boundary of the Ponzi region. The undashed line is the locus of points on which $r = g$ and is the upper boundary of the hedge finance region.

Figure 8.1 Different regimes of finance

5 MINSKIAN DYNAMICS

In order to study the dynamic paths of the model, we need to specify laws of motion for the state variables, ρ and *i*. We suppose that exuberance, ρ, increases as the growth rate rises above its equilibrium level, $\bar{g}$, and falls as the interest rate rises above its equilibrium level, $\bar{\imath}$:

$$\dot{\rho} = \beta(g - \bar{g}) - \delta(\dot{i} - \bar{\imath}) \tag{8.14}$$

While Taylor and O'Connell analyse monetary policy in the context of a full asset equilibrium model, we can follow the simpler route of taking the real interest rate as the monetary policy instrument. The target is equally simple: the authorities raise the interest rate as the growth rate rises above its equilibrium level:

$$\dot{i} = \gamma\,(g - \bar{g}) \tag{8.15}$$

Differentiating equation (8.11) with respect to time we see that:

$$\dot{g}=h\left(\frac{s+h}{s}\right)\dot{\rho}-h\left(\frac{s+h+\eta}{s}\right)\dot{i}$$

or

$$\dot{g}=\left(\frac{h}{s(1-\psi)-h}\right)(\beta(s(1-\psi))-\gamma(s(1-\psi)+\eta))(g-\bar{g})$$

$$-\left(\frac{h}{s-h-\psi}\right)\delta(s(1-\psi))(i-\bar{\imath}) \qquad (8.16)$$

Equations (8.16) and (8.15) define the dynamical system representing the economy. The monetary authority determines the equilibrium by choosing its target $\bar{g}$. At equilibrium $\rho=0$ and $i=\bar{\imath}$, where, from equations (8.7) to (8.9) we have:

$$\bar{\imath}=\frac{s(1-\psi)g_0-(s(1-\psi)-h)\bar{g}+hd_0}{h(s(1-\psi)+\eta)} \qquad (8.17)$$

The Jacobian of the system is:

$$\begin{bmatrix} (\frac{h}{s(1-\psi)-h})(\beta(s(1-\psi))-\gamma(s(1-\psi)+\eta)) & -(\frac{h}{s-h-\psi})\delta(s(1-\psi)) \\ \gamma & 0 \end{bmatrix} \qquad (8.18)$$

We have $\mathrm{tr}J=(\frac{h}{s(1-\psi)-h})(\beta(s(1-\psi))-\gamma(s(1-\psi)+\eta))$ and $\det J=\gamma(\frac{h}{s-h-\psi})\delta(s(1-\psi))>0$. The system has either two real roots of the same sign or a pair of complex roots. In either case the stability depends on the trace. We will assume that the monetary authority is sufficiently vigorous, that is, chooses a high enough γ to stabilize the economy, so that the trace is negative.

But an interest rate policy that stabilizes the economy may also expose it to financial crisis. A central bank attempting to cool off an economy by raising the interest rate may transform a large number of speculative firms into Ponzi firms, and force a drastic non-linear contraction of investment plans.

Figure 8.2 shows the phase diagram of the system for a stable equilibrium in the speculative regime, $\bar{g}>\bar{r}>\bar{\imath}$, where a small, open economy with good investment prospects seems likely to find itself. The $\dot{i}=0$ locus is the vertical dashed line at $\bar{g}$. At higher growth rates, $g>\bar{g}$, the monetary authorities raise the interest rate. At a stable equilibrium the $\dot{g}=0$ locus is downward-sloping. To the right of this locus the growth rate is decreasing, and to the left it is increasing. The phase arrows show the general motion

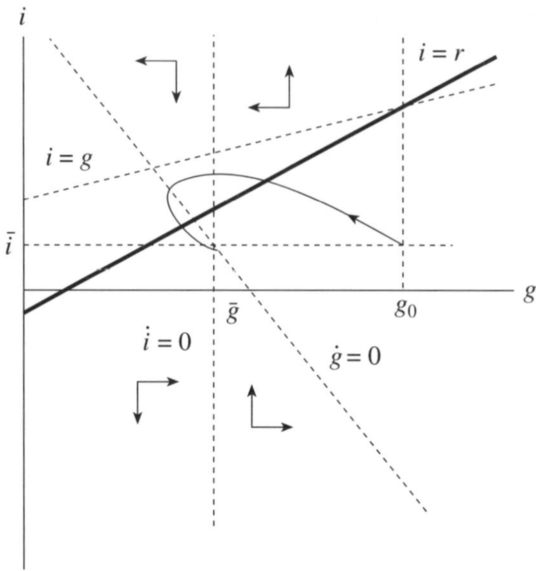

Note: An economy at a stable equilibrium in the speculative finance regime may respond to a positive shock to the growth rate by following a path that crosses into the Ponzi finance regime.

Figure 8.2 Phase diagram for a stable equilibrium in speculative finance regime

of the system in the four regions. It is clear that, whether there are two negative real roots or a pair of complex roots with negative real parts, a positive shock to the growth rate sets off a dynamic path on which the growth rate falls and the interest rate rises, such as the one drawn. For reference the $r=i$ locus which is the boundary of the Ponzi financial region is drawn as well. But this is precisely the sequence of events that forces the economy from speculative into Ponzi finance and makes it vulnerable to a financial crisis. The positive shock to the growth rate increases exuberance, which is more than offset by the rising interest rate, but sets the stage for overshooting the equilibrium. On its way back to equilibrium the economy crosses the line into the Ponzi region as the interest rate overtakes the profit rate, and becomes financially fragile.

In more conventional political economic terms, the positive shock to the growth rate leads the central bank to raise the real interest rate in one way or another in order to bring growth back to its target level by reducing the rate of investment. The lower rate of investment, however, depresses aggregate demand and the profit rate and lowers the economy's capacity utilization. This decline in capacity utilization will often be accompanied by a rise in unemployment, the familiar side-effects of a policy of monetary austerity. But as the interest rate rises and the profit rate falls, the economy, which started at a speculative equilibrium, slides into the Ponzi regime. Everyone understands that this is a 'temporary' situation resulting from the attempt to adjust to the positive shock in the growth rate, but this does not alter the fact that the economy has to pay its debt service with new borrowing during this period. If the country can convince private or public lenders to tide it over, it can pass through this phase without a financial crisis. As the trajectory of the figure indicates, eventually growth falls below the target rate and the real interest rate will be allowed to decline, easing the financial pressure on the economy. Growth and profit rates continue to fall, however, until a turning point is reached where growth starts to rise again. Sometime after this the growth rate and profit rate will rise and the interest rate fall sufficiently to get the economy back into the speculative regime.

But during the Ponzi-finance period the economy remains vulnerable to a financial crisis precipitated by the unavailability of new borrowing in sufficient magnitude. Such a crisis may interrupt the smooth adjustment back to equilibrium sketched in Figure 8.2, driving real interest rates sharply higher, and growth and profit rates sharply lower, forcing many firms or financial intermediaries into bankruptcy.

6 CONCLUSIONS

The small, open, Kaleckian economy has two important lessons for policy makers. Both stem from the fact that in the short run the growth rate and profit rate of this type of economy are strongly positively correlated. The small, open, Kaleckian economy becomes financially fragile when its growth rate falls and drags down the profit rate. This insight is in sharp contrast to the conventional wisdom that the way to avoid financial crisis is to reduce the growth rate through austerity policies based on restrictive monetary policy.

The first lesson is that the central bank should not target too low a growth rate as its equilibrium. At low growth rates, profit rates are low, and the economy is closer to the Ponzi regime. The economy may face other constraints that limit its growth rate, such as the provision of complementary infrastructure and the supply of competent entrepreneurship, but within these constraints it is more likely to avoid financial crisis at higher rather than lower targeted growth rates.

The second lesson is that in trying to stabilize the economy against a positive shock by raising interest rates, the central bank should take into account the impact of the relation of interest rates and profit rates on the financial viability of firm balance sheets. An overly vigorous interest rate policy may inadvertently trigger financial fragility and financial crisis.

In a small, open, developing economy it is likely that the state will come under pressure to absorb the debts of firms in periods of financial fragility in one way or another. Thus the financial fragility of the private sector is converted into financial vulnerability of the public sector, and the financial crisis that occurs can appear in the form of a crisis of public finance and foreign exchange reserves.

NOTE

1. The exact mechanisms through which the monetary authority controls the real interest rate will depend on institutional details such as the foreign exchange regime (floating or fixed), and the structure of the domestic financial markets, but do not need to be specified to carry out the analysis of financial fragility. The ways in which a crisis of financial fragility manifests itself will also depend on these institutional details, but the underlying cause will be the long-run unviability of the country's financial path.

REFERENCES

Minsky, Hyman P. (1975), *John Maynard Keynes*, New York: Columbia University Press.

Minsky, Hyman P. (1982), *Can 'It' Happen Again? Essays on Instability and Finance*, Armonk, NY: M. E. Sharpe.

Taylor, Lance and Stephen A. O'Connell (1985), 'A Minsky Crisis', *Quarterly Journal of Economics*, **100**, Issue Supplement, 871–85.

9. Selling the family silver or privatization for capital inflows: the dual dynamics of the balance of payments and the exchange rate

Amit Bhaduri*

I INTRODUCTION

The ideology of market-driven economic development is gaining ground at a time when the 'globalization of capital' is also proceeding at a dizzying pace. Multinational corporations, banks and other financial institutions like mutual funds are major players in this process characterized by overwhelmingly large private capital flows. The daily volume of foreign exchange transactions is estimated currently (*circa* 2001) at nearly 2 trillion dollars in spot and future markets together including various 'options'- and 'derivatives'-related financial transactions (Felix, 1996). This daily flow is enough to wipe out the entire stock of reserves of all the Central Banks put together and less than 2 per cent of this flow is related to trade, while an even smaller percentage is accounted for by direct foreign investment. The overwhelmingly large proportion of this transaction is in the form of 'foot-loose' portfolio capital, often of a short-term nature (cf. Neal, 1990).

The process of globalization of capital dominated by private players seems to present unprecedented opportunities and dangers at the same time to the developing economies. Privatization of the public sector is often considered a window of opportunity in this context. The programme of privatization proves to be a convenient way of attracting private foreign capital. While this provides opportunities for faster growth through relaxing the constraint of foreign exchange, it is intertwined with the danger that such capital inflow may, for example, lead to an artificial appreciation of the home currency. This means not only a decline in the price competitiveness in international trade, requiring more capital inflow to cover the current account deficit. It might also stimulate speculative bubbles of further capital inflow encouraged by the expected or actual appreciation of the home currency which is unlikely to be a stable economic configuration. Because, as the international indebtedness grows through such capital inflows, the confidence in the currency gets eroded through expectations of a future devaluation. This leads ultimately to outflow of capital, and the 'mania' of lending to a particular country turns into a 'panic' of sudden withdrawal from lending, leaving the country in the grip of a financial 'crash' (Kindleberger, 1978). With some variations, this story line has repeated itself frequently enough in the recent past in Latin America and South-East Asia. It may repeat itself once more in some of the countries of East Europe, where the public sector is often viewed as an unfortunate historical legacy in need of being privatized.

The interrelation between short-term foreign capital flow, driven especially by privatization and the consequent exchange rate expectations, and the nature of the economic instability it might generate is the subject matter of this chapter. In a different context, a similar range of problems have been studied widely both analytically and empirically (for example, Dornbush, 1976; Krugman, 1979; Diaz-Alejandro, 1985; Flood and Garber, 1984). Section II of this chapter outlines an analytical model to facilitate such an enquiry by examining the dynamic interactions between capital flow, the current account and the exchange rate over time. To keep the focus sharp, we abstract deliberately from interest rate differentials as an inducement to capital flows, except for its consequence in terms of holding reserve by the central bank in a developing economy (see later equation 9.4). Section III shows that the dynamics of the balance of payments and of the exchange rate are so closely interrelated through capital flows that the stability/instability property of one implies that of the other. The final section concludes with some further observations.

II THE ANALYTICAL FRAMEWORK: CAPITAL FLOW–CURRENT ACCOUNT DYNAMICS

We follow the usual practice in developing countries of using the US dollar as the international accounting unit. Therefore, r = the exchange rate, that is, the amount of domestic currency per unit of dollar, so that a higher r implies a 'weaker' or cheaper domestic currency in terms of US dollars. Moreover, measuring all the relevant magnitudes like foreign debt (D) and reserve (R) in dollar units, we avoid some unnecessary accounting complications that might arise in the present context, due to the revaluation of these stocks in domestic currency.

Let, M = import
E = export

Z = net factor payment, so that the current account deficit (B) is given definitionally as

$$B = (M - E) + Z = T(r) + Z \tag{9.1}$$

where $T(r)$ = net import, which would be a decreasing function of r, that is, trade balance improves through depreciation, if the usual Marshall–Lerner condition on trade elasticities is satisfied, giving (for simplicity in the linear case),

$$dT/dr = T'(r) = -\ b, \tag{9.2}$$

The net factor payment, especially when privatization with foreign ownership is a significant component, becomes the result of a complex set of factors. Due to the on-going privatization programme, payment of dividends is increasingly an important item for foreign-held equity capital. In addition, the servicing cost of debt through interest payment is an important item. The interest earned on reserves needs to be deducted from debt servicing, especially when holding large reserves from accumulated capital inflows turns out to be quantitatively significant.[1] A more elaborate accounting along these lines would be,

$$Z = (1 - \lambda)\ \rho K_f + i_b\ (D - K_f) - i_1 R \tag{9.3}$$

where K_f = equity capital held abroad, $(1 - \lambda)$ = fraction of profit distributed, ρ = rate of profit, i_b = borrowing rate of interest and i_1 = lending rate of interest.[2]

Thus,

$$dZ/dt = (I - \lambda)\ \rho\ I_f + i_b\ dD/dt - i_1\ dR/dt \tag{9.4}$$

where I_f = foreign direct investment (FDI)
$dD/dt = F$ = gross capital inflow
dR/dt = change in reserve,
which definitionally equals,

$$dR/dt = F - B \tag{9.5}$$

Hence (9.4) reduces to,

$$dZ/dt = [(I - \lambda)\rho - i_b]\ I_f + (i_b - i_1)F + i_1\ B \tag{9.6}$$

or,

$$dZ/dt = c.dD/dt = cF \tag{9.7}$$

where,

$$c = (i_b - i_1) + [(I - \lambda)\rho - i_b]\,(I_f / F) + i_1\,(B / F) \tag{9.8}$$

that is, c = time weighted average cost of foreign borrowing given by (9.8), which changes over time due to changing composition of capital inflow.

The movements in the exchange rate may be assumed to be governed by the usual demand–supply relation in the foreign exchange market, that is

$$dr / dt = \theta\,[B - F] \tag{9.9}$$

where θ = speed of adjustment in the foreign exchange market, reflecting both the degree of deregulation and intervention by the central bank.

Differentiating (9.1) with respect to time, and using (9.2), (9.7) and (9.9), we obtain the movements over time in the current account of the balance of payments as,

$$dB / dt = -b\,\theta\,B + (c + b\,\theta)\,F \tag{9.10}$$

Note from (9.8) that c changes over time if the weights change due to change in the composition of interest-based debt-creating (F) and profit-based non-debt-creating (I_f) borrowing. For expositional simplicity, we assume temporarily that c is given.

We focus on the influence of exchange rate on capital flows by abstracting from other factors like cross-border interest or tax differentials. Thus, capital flow is represented as consisting of two parts: a long-term flow L, not influenced by exchange rate expectations and short-term flow driven entirely by exchange rate expectations,

$$F = L + a(r - \hat{r}),\ a > 0 \tag{9.11}$$

where $\hat{r}$ = the expected exchange rate. Thus, $(r - \hat{r}) > 0$ implies expected appreciation of the domestic currency which stimulates capital inflow in anticipation of capital gains on foreign exchange transactions; obversely, $(r - \hat{r}) < 0$ retards capital inflow due to fear of capital loss on foreign exchange transactions.

The expected exchange rate depends primarily on the external asset (R) and liability (D) position of the economy. Thus, other things being equal, a larger external debt strengthens market sentiments about depreciation of the currency in future, while a larger reserve encourages sentiments about future appreciation. Formally,

$$\hat{r} = H\,(D, R)$$

or

$$dr/dt = (\partial H/\partial D).dD/dt + (\partial H/\partial R).dR/dt \quad (9.12)$$

Using (9.5) in (9.12),

$$dr/dt = (m-n)\,F + n\,B \quad (9.13)$$

where,

$$\partial H/\partial D = m > 0 \text{ and } \partial H/\partial R = -n,\ n > 0.$$

For algebraic simplicity, m and n are assumed constant for the time being over the relevant range.

Differentiating (9.11) with respect to time, and using (9.9) and (9.13) we obtain the time movement in capital inflow as,

$$dF/dt = a(\theta - n)\,B - a\,[\theta + (m-n)]\,F \quad (9.14)$$

Equations (9.10) and (9.14) together define the basic dynamical system, depicting the interaction over time between the current account (B) and capital inflow (F).

The system has its equilibrium at the origin ($B=0$, $F=0$) with no current account deficit or interest-based debt-creating capital inflow (F). The equilibrium at the origin is asymptotically stable provided the trace (τ) is negative and the determinant (Δ) is positive, that is,

$$\tau < 0, \text{ implying } \theta\,[\,I + (b/a)\,] + m > n \quad (9.15)$$

$$\Delta > 0 \text{ implying } a\,[\,\theta(bm - c) + cn\,] > 0 \quad (9.16)$$

Together, (9.15) and (9.16) restrict the value of n for stability in the open interval,

$$P = \{\theta\,[\,I - (bm/c]\} < n < \{\,\theta\,[\,I + (b/a)\,] + m\,\} = Q \quad (9.17)$$

Given the value of n, the range of the open interval, ($Q-P$) in (9.17) increases with b, m or θ, but decreases as a or c increases. This means that a greater improvement in trade balance in response to depreciation (that is, higher b), a stronger depressing effect of higher debt on the expected exchange rate depreciation, for example due to a more cautious attitude of the lenders (that is, higher m) as well as a greater adjustment in the spot foreign exchange rate to demand–supply disequilibrium met through a change in reserve (that is, larger θ), would all tend to increase the probability of the system being stable. On the other hand, however, not only a higher servicing cost of external debt (that is, larger c), but a stronger response of capital flows to an expected change in the exchange rate (that is, larger a) would reduce the probability of the system being stable. Interestingly, the model suggests that, while raising the extent of exchange rate response (θ) to demand–supply disequilibrium reflected in the change in the reserve position through greater deregulation and less intervention may help in stabilizing the interactive current account and capital flow dynamics, it might need to be combined with greater regulation on short-term capital flows (that is, lowering the value of a). This also suggests that the debate should not be about regulation versus deregulation, but rather that it should be about the correct mixture of regulation and deregulation needed in stabilizing the current account in a regime of short-term capital flows (see section IV).

On the other hand, if we treat all other parameter values (a, b, c, θ, m) as constant except n, it will be noted from (9.15), (9.16) and (9.17) that the system, while stable for some values of n (satisfying 9.17), is unstable for higher values of n. Thus, as n becomes larger, the system tends to be unstable. A larger value of n economically means that a small change, such as a decrease in reserve, leads to expectation of a relatively large future depreciation of the exchange rate. Thus, when reserves are already at a 'dangerously' low level, a further depletion of reserve sets up expectations of large devaluation and discourages strongly capital inflows. As a result, the currency depreciates, but this does not improve trade balance sufficiently (violating condition 9.15), and reserve is depleted even further in an unstable downward spiral. This is how the model captures the phenomenon of the 'mania' of lending and capital inflow in a phase which remains insensitive to the level of reserve, that is, relatively low n turning into a 'panic' of withdrawals from lending and capital outflow in a phase when n is relatively high because lenders become sensitive to the level of reserve. In our model, this is governed by the sensitivity of the lenders to variations in the reserves, as the parameter n undergoes a change at different levels of reserves. However, this requires n to be a function of R, and introduces an essential non-linearity into the system, which our local linear analysis of stability can at best provide a glimpse of.

As a final point, it may be noted from (9.15) that as n increases, the trace τ turns from negative to positive, while the determinant Δ remains positive at that critical value of n for which $\tau = 0$. By the negative criterion of Bendixson, the existence of a 'limit cycle' cannot be ruled out. Although it remains only a conjecture without further specification of the non-linear system, if such a limit cycle exists, it would mean that both capital flow and the current account may also undergo sustained fluctuations over time with the 'mania' of capital inflow and the 'panic' of capital outflow alternating at intervals over time.

III THE ACCOMPANYING DYNAMICS OF THE EXCHANGE RATE

Although we have so far examined only the interactive dynamics of the current account and capital flow, together they also imply the accompanying dynamics of the exchange rate. The exchange rate would exhibit qualitatively the same type of stability and instability properties that we have elaborated formally in the previous section. In order to establish this formally, we use the explicit linear form of the current account in (9.2), that is:[3]

$$B = G - br, \text{ and } G = \bar{B} + cD \tag{9.18}$$

Using (9.9), (9.11) and (9.14), this permits us to write the dynamical system of actual and expected exchange rate as

$$dx / dt = \theta[(G - L) - (a + b)r + a\hat{r}] \tag{9.19}$$

$$dx / dt = (m - n)L + nK + [a(m - n) - nb]r - a(m - n)\hat{r} \tag{9.20}$$

The equilibrium attained at $dx/dt = 0$, yields equilibrium value.

Note that the actual (r^*) and the expected ($\hat{r}^*$) exchange rates are not equal, if $L \neq 0$ in equilibrium. From (9.11), this means that in equilibrium, the short-term capital flow induced by expectations of change in the exchange rate offsets exactly the long-term capital flow (L) so that the overall capital flow remains zero ($F = 0$), and the current account is also exactly balanced ($B = 0$). This again characterizes the origin ($B = 0$, $F = 0$) as equilibrium, as in section II.

Since (9.19) and (9.20) entail a non-homogeneous system, we make the comparison easier by transforming it into a homogeneous system and considering deviations from the equilibrium values given by (9.21).
Let,

$$\begin{aligned} x &= (r - r^*) = r - (K/b) \\ y &= \hat{r} - \hat{r}^* = \hat{r}\,(L/a) - (K/b) \end{aligned} \tag{9.21}$$

so that on recomputation, (9.19) and (9.20) yield the homogeneous system:

$$dx/dt = -[\theta\,(a + b) + (ca/b)]\,x + [\theta\,a + (ca/b)]\,y \tag{9.22}$$

$$dy/dt = [a\,(m - n) - bn - (ca/b)]\,x + [(ca/b) - a(m - n)]\,y \tag{9.23}$$

It is easy to check that the trace and the determinant of (9.22) and (9.23) are exactly the same as those of the earlier dynamical system (9.10) and (9.14), that is from (9.22) and (9.23), trace $\tau = -\theta\ (a+b) - am + an$, which is the same as in condition (9.15); and determinant $\Delta = a[\theta(bm-c)+cn]$, which is the same as in condition (9.16).

It follows that the characteristic roots of (9.22) and (9.23) are the same as those of (9.10) and (9.14) and therefore the two systems are equivalent in all their qualitative dynamic properties. Economically, therefore, the time behaviour of the exchange rate will be characterized by the same stability/ instability regimes discussed in Section II along with the same interpretations of the role played by the economic parameters (a, b, c, m, n and θ) characterizing the system.

IV CONCLUSIONS: SOME IMPLICATIONS OF THE ANALYSIS

1. The question of deregulating the foreign exchange (spot) market should not be viewed in isolation. While a larger measure of adjustment (θ) of the exchange rate to changes in reserves caused by demand and supply disequilibrium in the foreign exchange market exerts a stabilizing influence in isolation, it can become destabilizing when short-term capital flows also respond strongly (that is, a relatively large value of parameter a) to expectations of variations in the exchange rate, especially through a change in reserves. Thus, some regulation of short-term capital flows together with greater deregulation of the (spot) market for foreign exchange might provide the correct perspective on the policy mix to be followed rather than a simplistic debate about regulation versus deregulation.
2. An interesting upshot of our analysis is to point out that the responsibility for avoiding instability in the foreign exchange market lies as much with the borrowers as with the lenders. Thus, a greater sensitivity on the part of the lenders of the consequence of an increase in debt on the expected depreciation of the currency, that is a higher value of the parameter m even before the instability becomes apparent, would tend to act as a stabilizer by lengthening the interval (Q − P) in (9.17). While it requires greater transparency and stricter rules of disclosure in reporting debt by the borrowers as is often emphasized, it also requires international (for example border- or Tobin-tax) or national regulations (such as fixed term deposit with the central bank of a part of the foreign capital inflow) to induce lenders to follow a more cautious attitude, especially against short-term lending.

3. In our analysis (for example, inequalities 9.17), the lenders' reaction to changes in reserve, that is the parameter n, is identified as a critical variable. It must lie within an open interval to make the system stable. Thus, when reserves are large, and n is small, – because, lenders may not worry too much about depletion of reserves – short-term capital inflow may continue for some time to push the system away from equilibrium, despite a deteriorating current account with rising debt and falling reserve. On the other hand, at a 'dangerously' low level of reserve, lenders might react strongly to further depletion of reserves with a large value of the parameter n. Thus, reserve depletion due to a current account deficit, threatens to plunge the economy into a financial crash, when reserves are perceived to be low and the current account is in deficit. Note further from the extreme left-hand inequality in (9.17) that a sufficiently low, serving cost of borrowing in terms of parameter c, for example through direct foreign purchase encouraged by privatization, may stabilize the system. However, this will only be temporary, until large repatriation of profits becomes an unavoidable reality.
4. It is not always realized that, so long as public sector assets exist on a large enough scale and the policy to privatize those assets continues by selling them to foreign buyers, these public sector assets might act as a proxy for reserves. With adequate reserves in the form of 'marketable' public sector assets, the response of foreign lenders to a small depletion in liquid reserves may not be strong (that is n is small in the model), and the regime of exchange rate and current account appears reasonably stable. However, when little remains to be privatized, the picture and the lenders' response may change rather sharply – a further small depletion in reserves may trigger off serious instability characterized by a continuously depreciating currency and widening current account deficit, resulting ultimately in an economic crash. Note moreover that net factor payments especially in the form of repatriation of profits also increase if the privatized (former public) enterprises are mostly held by foreign equity holders. This accentuates the problem of instability insofar as a larger capital inflow is needed to cover the larger current account deficit and to stabilize expectations about the exchange rate. Such larger capital inflows, however, might become all the more difficult to attract, when little remains to be privatized in an economy, and the family silver has already been sold.

NOTES

* I am grateful to J. Lopez and an anonymous referee for comments, while I record my special debt to K. Laski and M. Riese for saving me from errors in an earlier draft. The paper grew out of my contribution to a research project coordinated by Professor K. Laski at the Vienna Institute for Comparative Economic Studies (WIIW) on the external payments problem in some former socialist countries of Eastern Europe, and some parallel work I was also doing on the management of the exchange rate in developing countries.

1. To take only one example, in 1998, the reserve held by the Bank of Poland grew by 6 billion US dollars, of which 80 per cent was held as short-term liquidity (Slawinski, 1999, p. 2).
2. Hunya and Richter (1999, p. 2) report that in 1998, after large-scale privatization, more than one third of the increase in Hungary's current account deficit (of 4.8 per cent of GDP) was accounted for by repatriation of profits on foreign direct investment.
3. We get $B = G - br$ by integrating (9.2) where G is the maximal current deficit with $\bar{B}$ at $r = 0$ (implying an extreme appreciation of currency) at given net factor payment, cD.

REFERENCES

Diaz-Alejandro, Carlos (1985), 'Good-bye financial repression, hello financial crash', *Journal of Development Economics*, vol. 19, pp. 1–24.

Dornbush, R. (1976), 'Expectations and exchange rate dynamics', *Journal of Political Economy*, vol. 84 (December), pp. 1161–76.

Felix, D. (1996), 'Financial globalization versus free trade', *UNCTAD Review*, pp. 63–104, Geneva.

Flood, R.R. and P.M. Garber (1984), 'Collapsing exchange rate regimes: some linear examples', *Journal of International Economics*, vol. 17 (August), pp. 1–13.

Hunya, G. and S. Richter (1999), Hungary: FDI, profit repatriation and the current account', *The Vienna Institute Monthly Report*, WIIW, no. 3.

Kindleberger, C.P. (1978), *Mania, Panics and Crashes*, New York: Basic Books.

Krugman, P.R. (1979), 'A model of balance of payments crisis', *Journal of Money, Credit and Banking*, vol. 11 (August).

Neal, L. (1990), *The Rise of Financial Capitalism*, Cambridge: Cambridge University Press.

Slawinski, A.S. (1999), 'Capital inflows and current account deficit: the case of Poland', *The Vienna Institute Monthly Report*, WIIW, no. 8/9.

PART IV

Stabilization, Adjustment and Growth

10. Brazil's *Plano Real*: a view from the inside

Edmar L. Bacha[1]

1 INTRODUCTION

Launched under peculiar political conditions, in the last year of a weak and divided government, and without the support of the International Monetary Fund, the 1994 Real Plan succeeded in doing away with Brazil's chronically high inflation, with a homegrown monetary reform program.

Brazilian academics associated with the Department of Economics of the Catholic University of Rio de Janeiro, where Lance Taylor taught in the early 1980s, conceived and implemented the Real Plan. Taylor's neo-structuralist macroeconomics was a permanent source of inspiration for this group of academics.

This chapter contains an analytical description of the Real Plan in the 1993–96 period. It starts in the next section with the economic and political context under which it was developed. There follows in section 3 an explanation of the three stages of the plan. Section 4 details the main features of the monetary reform: a pre-announced sudden stabilization, preceded by a full indexation phase, introduced without a price freeze, a capital levy on financial assets, or an economic recession, and followed by flexible exchange rate and monetary policies.

The initial success of the plan was so complete that its political mastermind, Fernando Henrique Cardoso, became Brazil's president. As described in section 5, this was just in time to cope with the impact of the Mexican balance of payment crisis and the growing macroeconomic disequilibria that resulted from the Plan's introduction. During 1995, the government introduced harsh monetary measures and fuller de-indexation mechanisms. At the cost of a temporary recession and increased financial fragility, such measures succeeded in maintaining inflation on a declining path, as summarized in section 6. Section 7 concludes.

2 ECONOMIC AND POLITICAL CONTEXTS: 1993

When the Senator and Foreign Relations Minister, Fernando Henrique Cardoso, became Minister of Finance in May 1993, Brazil's inflation was running at 25 per cent per month, in a trajectory of slow but persistent acceleration of 1 to 2 percentage points per month. Cardoso's nomination was extremely well received, in view of his eminence both as a politician and an intellectual, but the mood of Brazil's economic elite was one of total incredulity that an effective anti-inflation policy could be implemented during President Itamar Franco's half-term. This was particularly on account of the fact that Cardoso was already the fourth Finance Minister in the eight months of Franco's presidency.

Cardoso and his small initial economic team (of which the author was a member) thus decided to adopt a very conservative economic policy course, and presented a Program for Immediate Action, with total emphasis on the adjustment of the public sector accounts, the disequilibria of which were identified as a fundamental component of Brazil's chronic inflationary condition. A previous paper spells out the analytical underpinnings of that program.[2] The basic argument was that in Brazil there occurred a reverse Olivera–Tanzi effect, that is, inflation helps to balance the budget, because taxes are protected against inflation, whereas spending is fixed in nominal terms. The Olivera–Tanzi effect asserts, on the contrary, that the budget deficit increases when inflation goes up, on the presumption that government spending is fixed in real terms, whereas tax revenues are ill-protected against inflation.

Inflation thus served the traditional purpose of generating an inflation tax, but perhaps more importantly it reduced real spending. The conclusion was that controlling inflation presupposed that the government balanced its *ex ante* budget, that is, that it showed the political determination to cut from the budget the excess spending claims that were previously eroded by inflation or financed by the inflation tax.

Considerable progress was achieved in the first months of Cardoso's administration in terms of the targets of the initial program, which included deep cuts in the federal budget for 1993, renegotiation of the debts of local state and municipalities with the federal government, clearing up the Central Bank accounts with the national Treasury, and renegotiation of the external debt. Inflation, however, continued to accelerate.

Personal and political disputes led in late August and early September 1993 to the resignation of the presidents of the Central Bank and of the National Development Bank. These two worrisome developments, however, turned out to be extremely positive, as they provided an occasion for a substantial strengthening of Cardoso's initial economic team. A common characteristic of most members of Cardoso's enlarged economic team was that they had been colleagues at the Department of Economics of the Catholic University of Rio de Janeiro, where, since the early 1980s, they had been doing research on Brazil's inflationary process. A number of them (including the author) were also active members of Senator Cardoso's Brazilian Social Democratic Party.

Cardoso and his now enlarged team knew quite clearly that, to control inflation, they needed to go beyond the fiscal targets of their initial economic program, which aimed at controlling the *ex ante* operational budget deficit, but did not act on the nominal budget deficit. The difference between the nominal and the operational deficit is that the former includes the nominal interest payments on the public debt. The latter only includes the real (that is, inflation corrected) interest payments. Since nominal interest payments depend on the inflation rate, under high inflation the nominal deficit can be very large even when the operational budget deficit is in equilibrium. Thus, in 1993, when the consumer price inflation was 2490 per cent, the operational balance displayed a surplus of 0.25 per cent of GDP, and the nominal balance a deficit of 58.4 per cent of GDP.

The operational budget could be under balance, but as long as inflation kept the nominal budget deficit at a high level, the broad money supply would continue to expand fast, thus feeding back on the inflation rate. Controlling the nominal budget deficit was a monetary, not a fiscal problem, in the sense that if inflation ceased, the nominal deficit would be equal to the operational deficit; hence, if the latter was balanced, the broad money supply would stop growing, thus validating the cessation of inflation. To deal with this vicious circle of interaction between inflation and broad money supply growth, three strategies could be contemplated. First, to declare a wage and price freeze, similar to the failed 1986 Cruzado plan.[3] Second, to set the dollar exchange rate, the public sector prices, and the oligopolistic private sector prices according to a slowly declining path, as in the failed 1980 stabilization program of Mr. Delfim Netto.[4] Third, to adopt a major monetary reform program.

After considerable soul searching, in September 1993 the economic team chose the third alternative, in spite of the extremely high risks involved. Repeating the Cruzado plan was anathema to several members of the team (including the author), who had participated in that major failed attempt to cope with Brazilian inflation. To use a technique of prefixing the path of critical prices to bring inflation slowly down was also against the deep-seated conviction of the team that gradualist techniques were impotent in dealing with Brazil's chronic inflation.

The members of the economic team had already debated at length the general course of the monetary reform program. It involved a two-stage procedure of substitution of the old inflated currency by a new stable one, first as a unit of value, and then as a means of payment. Persio Arida and Andre Lara Resende co-authored the original proposal to fight chronic inflation through a monetary reform preceded by full indexation.[5] In a 1984 seminar at the Institute of International Economics, in which their paper was first presented, Rudiger Dornbusch baptized it as 'the Larida proposal'.

Briefly, the idea was to institute a domestic unit of account, the URV (the initials of 'unit of real value'), with a virtual exchange rate value of 1URV = US$1.00. Furthermore, the domestic currency value of this unit (as well as that of the US dollar) would be raised daily by the Central Bank *in tandem* with the ongoing rate of inflation. Then, according to a set of pre-specified rules, all price and wage contracts would be converted into multiples of this unit of value, thus replacing all previous existing contracts, which were set according to different price indexes, overlapping periods, and time frames. Once all contracts had thus been converted into multiples of URVs, this unit of account would start being issued, under the name of Real, as the new currency of the country, with an initial parity value of R$1.00 = US$1.00. This new currency would entirely replace the old currency, the cruzeiro real.

The first reaction of foreign macroeconomists unfamiliar with the Brazilian economy when presented with this program is inevitably to ask: why not simply adopt a dollar anchor right away, rather than going through such a complex conversion mechanism? The main reason why a dollar anchor would not solve the problem of contract conversion is that existing contracts, written in domestic currency with varying indexation clauses, did not have invariant dollar values. Thanks to generalized indexation and the existence of domestic currency substitutes protected against inflation, the Brazilian economy did not dollarize, in spite of a chronically high inflation. With foreign currency-based contracts being forbidden, contracts were written in domestic currency terms, with periodic readjustment clauses according to the evolution of domestic price indexes. The Real plan thus opted to find a path towards price stability by perfecting this homemade mechanism of contractual indexation.

The novelties of the proposed program *vis-à-vis* the original Larida proposal were that the two-stage monetary reform should be preceded by the approval by Congress of a constitutional amendment to equilibrate the *ex ante* federal budget, and that it should be entirely pre-announced. It was only under such conditions that the economic team felt it possible to build the public confidence necessary to succeed in such an ambitious endeavor, in the last year of a weak and divided government. President Itamar Franco had hoped for a program with quicker results and fewer preconditions, but gave his consent for Cardoso and his team to proceed as they saw fit. The program was also submitted in a closed-door meeting to the leadership of the Brazilian Social Democratic Party. After a night-long discussion, the then Senator Mario Covas synthesized the politicians' reaction more or less in the following terms: 'you economists are as important to the party as we are; if this is the only way you think possible to proceed, ok, we will follow you . . . to the precipice!'

In spite of such political half-endorsements, Cardoso's team knew quite well that the policy course that they were advising had never been tried before, in Brazil or elsewhere, and its success was far from guaranteed. The fact that the IMF, after a long negotiation, failed to give its blessing to the program did little to help improve the expectation of its success. The Fund staff wanted much deeper budget cuts than was politically feasible, and a much tighter monetary stance than the team felt advisable. They also felt very uncomfortable with the proposed two-stage monetary reform program. For they failed to see how inflation could fall abruptly with the introduction of the new currency, if the fiscal and monetary stance were not very different from that observed in the old currency – the fiscal stance being measured by the operational budget deficit, and the monetary stance by the level of real interest rates.

The authors of the plan failed to convince the IMF staff that the reason why the monetary reform 'magic' could work was that Brazil operated in a regime of widespread wage and price indexation, with a totally passive monetary and exchange rate regime. This was the reason why the inflation rate did not respond either to the operational budget deficit (which was zero, and, in this sense, did not require the inflation tax as a financing mechanism), or to the real interest rate (which was in line with the Brazil risk, as indicated by the positive net inflows of foreign capital).[6]

The point of the economic team was that, once contractual prices and wages were de-indexed with the introduction of the new currency, active monetary and exchange rate policies could be implemented – but that was to happen in the days after the stabilization, not before it. Perhaps the Fund staff felt intellectually attracted to these propositions. However, they had tarnished their reputation with their support of repeated failed stabilization attempts in Brazil in the recent past, and felt obviously uncomfortable with the uncertain political context under which the plan would have to be implemented. Thus, they chose to sit aside rather than get involved with such a novel scheme.

At year-end, the level of tension in the economic team increased to boiling point with the decision of a couple of its members to quit, before the launching of the program.

3 THE LAUNCHING OF THE REAL PLAN: 1994

The Real Plan was a three-stage pre-announced stabilization program, the sequential nature of which was presented to the country by Cardoso, on 7 December, 1993.[7] The first stage was a budget-balancing mechanism. The second was the introduction of a stable unit of account to align the most important relative prices in the economy. The third was the conversion of this account unit into the new currency of the country, at a semi-fixed par rate with the US dollar.

The first stage of the program consisted of balancing the *ex ante* operational federal budget, through deep cuts in the budget proposal for 1994. The implementation of these cuts required the Congress to approve a constitutional amendment (which became known as the Social Emergency Fund), allowing the sterilization, for the 1994 and 1995 fiscal years, of 20 per cent of previously earmarked expenses.

The purpose of the first stage was to demonstrate that the federal government could put into practice its budgeted expenses without the need of inflation-generated revenue.

Upon Congressional approval of this amendment – which occurred in February 1994 – the government introduced, on 1 March 1994, a stable unit of account (which was denominated as the Unit of Real Value, or URV), at a par with the US dollar. With few exceptions, existing contracts were required to be re-denominated in this new unit of account. Except for wages, housing rents, school bills, and public sector prices and tariffs, the contracting parties could freely agree on the terms of these conversions, provided that indexation clauses of less than one year were abolished.

The main purpose of this stage of the plan was to align the most important relative prices in the economy. The existence of overlapping indexed contracts with varying lags implied that at any moment of time there was a significant dispersion of relative prices in the economy, with some prices having been recently readjusted and others lagging far behind. Under such circumstances, a sudden stop to the inflationary process would catch some prices at their peak values and others at their trough. Such price misalignments would inevitably tend to impose additional inflationary pressures, as previously existing indexation clauses would continue to force up the prices lagging behind. This lagged indexation mechanism provided the so-called inertial component of Brazilian inflation, as distinct from the structural component associated with the *ex ante* operational federal budget deficit.

On 1 July 1994, after a four-month period of contract conversion, the Central Bank started issuing the URV, then re-denominated as the Real, as the new currency of the country, the parity value of which was set at no more that one US dollar to one Real. The Central Bank was committed to sell US dollars every time its market value reached one Real, but it was not obliged to intervene in cases where the value of the US dollar stood at less than one Real. This became known as the asymmetric band exchange rate policy, with an upper limit of one US dollar per Real and an undeclared lower limit, which in practice proved to be about US$0.83 per Real.

In conformity with the initial program statement, a 30-day advance notice was given of the monetary conversion date. The government also set a conversion rate of one Real to 2750 cruzeiros reais (this was the value of one URV in cruzeiros reais on 30 June 1994) as the rate for the replacement of the money stock, and more generally for the re-denomination into Reais of contracts and prices not yet converted from cruzeiros reais into URVs. This essentially completed the three-stage monetary reform that comprised the Real Plan. With the substitution of the Real for the cruzeiro real as the legal tender of the country, all contracts whose value had been previously set in *real* terms (that is, in URV units) became fixed in *nominal* terms (that is, in Reais).

4 SALIENT FEATURES OF THE MONETARY REFORM

The Real Plan had some very peculiar characteristics when compared with previous monetary reform programs in Brazil or abroad. First, wage and price de-indexation was preceded by a phase of full indexation. Second, the monetary reform was pre-announced, openly negotiated with Congress, and introduced without the adoption of wage or price freezes. Third, stabilization was achieved without the imposition of a capital levy on financial assets. Fourth, post-reform monetary and exchange rate policies followed a flexible course, rather than complying with strict monetary targets or fixed exchange rate rules. Fifth, price stabilization was achieved in the context of an expanding economy.

4.1 De-indexation Preceded by Full Indexation

The most interesting and controversial aspect of the program was its second phase, that is, the introduction of a stable unit of account to align relative prices in the economy through a full-indexation procedure. This would seem at first sight to be a contradiction in terms, given the widely accepted diagnosis that the difficulty of fighting Brazilian inflation resided specifically in the high degree of indexation of the economy. How could an accentuation of this indexation mechanism possibly help to fight inflation?

The critical point to clear up this apparent paradox is the procedure of conversion by the mean values. Let us specifically consider wage contracts, although the reasoning applies to any income stream subject to backward indexation. A speeding up of indexation (say, a reduction of the wage revision period from four to two months) tends to lead to inflation acceleration if the starting point is the peak value of contractual wages. In this case – with output being maintained constant by a passive monetary policy – faster inflation is required to depress the wage to its previous average real value along the wage cycle. However, when wages are first converted at their mean values, and only then is fuller indexation applied, inflation acceleration is no longer required to reduce the real wage back to its previous equilibrium value.

A more subtle point is that, with the URV, the length of the wage indexation period was not only shortened, but reduced to approximately zero. The length was not exactly equal to zero because the URV was corrected not by the contemporaneous rate of inflation but by the rate of change of price indexes that reflected current inflation with approximately a one-month lag. In any case, in this new context, wages would respond one-to-one and very rapidly to any change in the rate of inflation. As a consequence, the rate of inflation required to bring wages down became very high indeed. The saving grace was that, since wages were already converted by their mean values, no further inflation-induced real wage erosion was required. The problem, however, is that the same mechanism of nearly full indexation applied to the exchange rate, which was readjusted daily *pari passu* with the URV, and, partially, also to the money supply.

Money in the (quantitatively unimportant, at the time, in Brazil) narrow sense of currency and demand deposits was not converted into URVs – for this was the final step of the monetary reform. However, money substitutes in general, such as overnight funds, were revalued daily either according to the URV or the short-term interest rate, set by the Central Bank according to the current inflation rate. A system of automatic rediscounting guaranteed that commercial bank reserves were made available as required to cover the banking system's liquidity needs in the overnight market. In this sense, the growth rate of the monetary base was totally demand-determined. The conclusion is that the monetary system became virtually anchorless, and extremely susceptible to inflation acceleration caused by adverse expectations or supply shocks. Hence, the dilemma of the policy maker. On one hand, perfecting the indexation system was necessary to free the economy from price and wage inertia, thus guaranteeing that no inflationary memory remained in force, once the trick was performed of transforming the URV, from universal indexer to the new non-indexed currency, the Real. On the other hand, the better the indexation, the more susceptible the economy became to entering a hyperinflation spiral provoked by adverse expectations or supply shocks.

A compromise had to be reached, and it took various forms. First, the URV was made to move according to lagged inflation rather than current inflation. This was in part also required by the fact that the production of price indexes required a minimum of one week for a representative sample to be collected and another week to process the price information. The economic team wanted to use these indexes to calculate the URV, demonstrating that it was an objective measure of inflation in cruzeiros reais, not subject to manipulation or optimistic guesswork.

Second, it was at first forbidden for financial contracts to be converted into URVs, and then a step-by-step procedure was introduced to allow successive layers of such instruments to be issued in URVs, such as trade bills, banks' CDs, Treasury bills, overnight funds, and so on. The precaution in the conversion of financial instruments reflected a desire to maintain intact the demand for cruzeiros reais, that is, to avoid a flight from domestic money, which could cause a sudden acceleration of inflation.

Third, it was at first forbidden for the prices of goods and services for immediate payment to be denominated in URVs, with the purpose of not reducing the menu costs of daily price changes, which were thought to put some rein on inflation acceleration. Towards the third month of the URV period, this restriction was lifted, with the purpose of accustoming the population to the experience of invariant prices in URV units. Fourth, public sector prices and tariffs were converted into URVs according to a step-by-step procedure, with a progressive shortening of the readjustment period of prices in cruzeiros reais, while maintaining real average prices approximately constant.

The final compromise was on the duration of the period of life of the URV. Some influential economists argued that, once wages had been converted into URVs by their mean values, most of the necessary work was already done, and the life of the URV should be shortened to two months at most. This argument also had a political overtone, in the following sense: at first wage earners would be contented to see their four-monthly wage indexation period replaced by monthly readjustments. But then their annoyance would grow with the fact that, once their monthly wages were earned in cruzeiros reais, they would be melted down by the daily inflation which continued to occur. Thus, to maximize the goodwill of wage earners, while avoiding the risks of hyperinflation, the phase of the URV should be shortened rather than lengthened.

Other economists, however, thought that political conditions were not ripe for stabilization, and that the URV should have its life extended until a new government took over. The apprehension was that the capacity of the economic team to control fiscal and monetary policy would decline abruptly as soon as the monetary reform brought inflation to a sudden halt.

The argument was also made that an extended duration of the URV would favor voluntary conversions, while a shorter period would require more government intervention.

Within the economic team, the idea was proposed, but eventually rejected, to introduce an intermediate dual currency phase to the monetary reform program, during which the Real would be issued only in large denominations, while the cruzeiro real would continue to circulate freely. In this case, the monetary reform would be completed only after a new president took over.

The four-month period finally adopted proved too short for the conversion of rents, school bills and health plans, which left some inflation-overhang for the period of the Real. However, in these three cases, the problem was not of an economic nature, but was mostly derived from pressures within the government against the conversion rules proposed by the economic team for these contracts. A compromise solution came only at the end of the URV period, which provoked an inflation in Reais that should ideally have been absorbed, in cruzeiros reais, during the lifetime of the URV.

Another element in the choice of the period of duration of the URV was political. General elections, including that for the country's presidency, were scheduled for 3 October 1994. Cardoso resigned from the Ministry of Finance in early April 1994, to become the presidential candidate of a centrist party coalition, with the support of President Itamar Franco. Ambassador Rubens Ricupero replaced him, but he maintained in their respective posts all the members of Cardoso's economic team. If Fernando Henrique Cardoso had a good chance of being elected, the markets would naturally anticipate that the program would continue in the next government, and this would help stabilize expectations and avoid speculative attacks. Alternatively, the electoral perspectives of the leading opposition candidate, Lula da Silva, of the left-wing Workers' Party, might continue to improve, partly based on his speech against the government failure to deal with escalating inflation. In this case, the financial markets might anticipate a discontinuation of the program, and a speculative attack could succeed, provoking a sharp acceleration of inflation, with negative social effects which could endanger the electoral process.

Maintenance of democratic stability, thus, suggested that the new stable currency should be introduced before the presidential elections. With initial inflation control attained, all candidates would need to align their electoral speeches to the new monetary reality, committing themselves to maintain the Plan intact if they were elected. This in fact occurred, but naturally, the main beneficiary of the success of the Plan was its author, Cardoso. When he resigned from the Ministry of Finance in early April 1994, opinion polls showed Cardoso to have less than half of the votes of the leading candidate, Lula da Silva. Soon after the introduction of the Real, Cardoso took the lead in the opinion polls, and was elected President with a 54 per cent majority in the first round of the elections, on 3 October.

4.2 Sudden Stabilization without a Price Freeze

The negotiations between the private parties on the terms of the conversion of their contracts to URVs proved to be frequently acrimonious, because of the difficulty of dividing between the parties the gains and losses of the inflation float implicit in previous contracts. An interesting case was the conversion of municipal bus prices, controlled by their respective municipalities. These prices were typically readjusted monthly according to measured inflation. In spite of federal government efforts, during the period of the URV the municipal governments resisted the idea of progressively shortening this readjustment period while maintaining the same real average value of the bus tickets. In general, these prices were converted from cruzeiros reais into Reais on 1 July, immediately after a full-month price hike, which implied a considerable increase in the average real price during a 30-day period, as such prices then ceased to be eroded by the inflation occurring between successive monthly readjustments. Subsequent negotiations between the federal government and the municipalities resulted in some reversion of these decisions, but not in most cases.

The argument used against a downward revision shows the complexities of income redistribution caused by inflation. The argument of the municipalities was that the monthly bus price increases, which took effect immediately, corresponded to the monthly wage increases of the bus companies' employees, which were due only after a 30-day period. Thus, while the real value of bus tickets declined during the month (*vis-à-vis* the overall price level), they did not decline in relation to wage costs, which were also depreciated by the ongoing inflation. When inflation stopped, the erosion of wages during the month also stopped; hence, in terms of wage costs, bus prices continued to be the same, even though in terms of the general price index they were higher than before.

The main purpose of the URV period was to allow substantial wage and price alignment, and the elimination of backward-looking indexation, without the need of a subsequent wage and price freeze to stop inflation, as in previous stabilization plans. Backward indexation was eliminated because the URV itself was a price index. Even if it did not reflect the instantaneous rate of inflation, it changed the wage rule from a four-month cycle to a daily indexation regime, thus helping to convince the labor unions to accept the conversion of wages by their mean values (instead of by their peaks), without the promise of a subsequent price freeze.

The trickiest part of the deal was the widely anticipated inflation acceleration during the URV period and the lack of a protective mechanism for wages. To insure the approval by Congress of the URV (which was introduced by a government decree with the status of law for renewable one-month periods), two wage-protection mechanisms were introduced in the original government bill. The first permitted a wage increase, at the date of the subsequent yearly wage readjustment of each trade union, in case, over the four-month period of duration of the URV, the sum of the URV-converted wages proved to be less than would have been the case under the previous wage law. For most cases, the difference was in fact positive in favor of the URV, thus this mechanism did not affect the course of wages under the Real, and answered the criticism of supposed wage losses in the URV-conversion procedure.

The second mechanism introduced an official price index to measure inflation under the Real, constructed in such a way as to incorporate the inflation acceleration in the last days of the URV. Because of the lag in price index measurement, this acceleration was not computed in the last value of the URV set on 30 June. The concession was that, during the first year of the Real, at the date of the yearly wage settlement of each trade union, wages would be fully readjusted according to the evolution of that price index. Thus, a softened mechanism of wage indexation remained valid for the first 12 months of the Real.

Unfortunately, partly because of sharp increases in residential rents and certain other services, this official price index accumulated an inflation rate of nearly 12 per cent in the first two months of the Real, thus generating a wage-push mechanism that led to a significant real appreciation of the new currency. One favorable counterpart to the political concessions was that they helped convince the labor courts to cooperate with the government in accepting to apply the strict terms of the new wage law, without attempting to restore the previous wage peak at each yearly wage negotiation, as they would normally tend to do. Despite the price hike in the last days of the URV, the subsequent success of the Real in keeping inflation low proved correct the highly disputed point that inflation could be instantaneously reduced to nearly zero without the use of wage and price freezes. Foreign experts had unanimously advised the economic team to adopt a temporary price freeze at the inception of the Real. The same experts considered it a 'madness' to pre-announce the date of the introduction of the Real, for fear of a widespread movement of defensive price hikes accompanied by a run on the currency.

Sure enough, public sector prices and tariffs were frozen and the exchange rate could not devalue beyond its parity value. Wages in principle could be freely negotiated (beyond the terms of the wage law) if the resulting wage hikes were not passed on to prices. This last restriction was not in fact in the law (mainly because the economic team understood that if this were the case, the labor courts would feel more at ease to endorse wage hikes, while leaving to the government the impossible task of preventing subsequent price rises). It was introduced in the government speech as a type of moral imperative which businessmen were expected to observe.

Through informally negotiated price conversion rules, moral suasion agreements were reached between the government and the most important business groups in the country to maintain constant their prices in Reais. However, this is very different from the use of formal price controls, as it involved a consulting mechanism, through which cooperation was ensured rather than imposed. Critical business sectors were invited to become partners of the stabilization effort, rather than operating as their opponents. It is also important to note that no formal social pacts were attempted, because these were deemed to be impossible to negotiate in the context of Brazil's heterogeneous society and atomistic polity, particularly on account of the fiercely disputed electoral campaign for the country's presidency which was under way.[8]

4.3 Stabilization without a Financial Asset Levy

At the time of the introduction of the Real, Brazil's monetary base stood at only 0.6 per cent of GDP, and M1 was an equally meager 1.1 per cent of Brazil's GDP. The money that mattered was held in the form of overnight funds, on which checks could be written, because commercial banks provided automatic free-of-charge conversion of such funds into checking deposits. The backing of such funds was typically provided by one-month Central Bank bills, which could be automatically rediscounted with the Central Bank at the daily overnight interest rate. In principle, the Central Bank stood ready to provide immediate and costless liquidity to the whole of the federal public debt (Treasury plus Central Bank bills in the hands of the public), which was mostly carried within the banking system itself, not by final non-financial holders. This debt amounted to some 6.8 per cent of GDP and served as a domestic money substitute. This allowed Brazil, in spite of very high inflation rates, to avoid the dollarization of its domestic monetary system.[9]

Affluent Brazilians continued to hold domestic money deposits, because they were protected against inflation, and the banks were willing to provide such protection because the Central Bank guaranteed interest and liquidity. This was the case for medium to large checking deposits; currency and small checking deposits did not enjoy such protection, which meant that the inflation tax was mostly paid by the poorest members of the society.

Brazil thus operated with a monetary system in which broad money paid interest, with its yield held roughly constant in real terms by the Central Bank. As a result, an increase in the domestic price level immediately translated itself into a similar rise in the nominal amount of the broad-money stock held by the public. If, at the higher price level, additional narrow money was also demanded, this would automatically be provided in the form of additional commercial bank reserves, through the automatic rediscounting mechanism of the Central Bank.

This characteristic of the monetary system led several authors to believe that Brazil had a money overhang problem to deal with in order to perform a stabilization program. In view of several previous stabilization effort failures, the argument was made that a sudden stop to the inflationary process would not be credible, even if the operational government budget was under temporary balance. Thus, domestic money would continue to be held only if nominal interest rates continued to be sky high, which meant that the nominal public sector deficit (which fed the broad-money supply) would continue to be large even if the operational deficit was under balance. In these circumstances, the drop in inflation, as induced for example by a wage and price freeze, could only be temporary, because the broad-money supply would continue to rise. To attempt to solve this problem by bringing nominal interest rates suddenly down was widely believed to cause a flight from domestic money, generating substantial pressure on the foreign exchange market, and thus putting the stabilization program at peril.

This reasoning led to the conclusion that a suppression of the moneyness of the overnight funds was a necessary ingredient of a successful stabilization program in Brazil. The Collor Plan I epitomized such reasoning when it decreed on 16 March 1990, that 75 per cent of all bank accounts would be frozen for an 18-month period, and only the remaining 25 per cent would be available as immediate liquidity.

The architects of the Real Plan opted for a different line of attack to the problem. They first tried to build a national consensus on the need for a zero *ex ante* operational budget deficit as a precondition for stabilization, and then obtained from Congress the constitutional amendment required to make such equilibrium possible in the 1994–95 periods. They then committed themselves to a step-by-step monetary conversion procedure, respectful of existing contracts, in a strategy of gradual and pre-announced introduction of the new currency. The idea was to build public confidence in the promise of 'no shocks, no freezes, no confiscations' repeated *ad nauseam* by the Minister of Finance and his economic team: to do only what was announced, to announce only what would be done.

This public relations effort was carried out with conviction because the economic team were trusted with having a unique opportunity to perform a monetary reform without the traumas provoked by a capital levy on financial assets. This confidence was provided by the large build-up of foreign reserves that had occurred since 1992. At the moment of the monetary conversion, on 30 July 1994, foreign reserves on a cash basis amounted to US$40.1 billion, equal to 12.5 times the monetary base, and 62 per cent of broad money (federal, state, and municipal debt in the hands of the public plus currency and checking deposits). Sure enough, it was only 30 per cent of the broadest money supply concept (including saving deposits and banks' CDs), but it still seemed sufficiently high to provide a strong line of defense for the new currency, particularly because existing restrictions on capital outflows remained untouched.

A critical decision, however, related to the overnight interest rate that the Central Bank would set for the first day of the Real. The overnight interest rate had been pegged at 50 per cent per month on the last day of the cruzeiro real, and it opened at 8 per cent per month on the first day of the Real. A very large drop indeed, but one that still left substantial scope for international interest rate arbitrage in view of the fixed upper limit of one-to-one on the US dollar exchange rate. The 8 per cent rate was also very high in real terms, since most of the residual inflation reflected in the price indexes of July was almost entirely determined by the float left over from the June price indexes. Correctly measured from 1 July, the core inflation rate in the first month of the Real was near zero. This, however, was not known beforehand and took a while to appear in the price indexes.

In August, the Central Bank let the overnight rate drop to 5 per cent per month, and the downward movement continued until October. Interest rates in the first months of the Real were sufficiently high to maintain saving deposits in place, and did not induce a flight to consumption. In the end, the money overhang problem proved to be non-existent. On the contrary, Brazilians took a fancy to their new stable currency and rapidly built up the stock of non-interest paying narrow money. Additionally propelled by a 100 per cent marginal reserve requirement on bank deposits, the monetary base rose 300 per cent from late June to late September, making it difficult for the economic team to comply with the monetary targets that they had set for this variable. The counterpart to this re-monetization was a reduction in the holdings of overnight funds, thus helping to diminish the quasi-fiscal deficit of the federal government. On the other hand, the high differential between domestic and interest rates attracted foreign funds, forcing the government to raise the barriers against short-term capital inflows, while allowing the Real to appreciate by some 15 per cent against the US dollar.

The strategy of allowing a voluntary conversion of government domestic debt at market interest rates was more costly in budgetary terms than the alternative of forcing a compulsory lengthening of this debt at fixed interest rates. However, this relates to the flow fiscal problem, not the stock monetary problem emphasized in the money overhang literature. In view of the primary budget surplus that they felt capable of producing, the economic team considered the fiscal cost worth accepting, in order to strengthen public confidence in the program, for they had promised to stabilize prices 'with no shocks, no surprises, no confiscations, no freezes'. They also believed that if the stabilization program was successful, a voluntary lengthening of domestic debt at lower interest rates could take place in due time, favored by the evidence of the government's determination to respect existing contracts.

4.4 Stabilization with Flexible Monetary and Exchange Rate Policies

In macro textbooks, two polar cases for the monetary regime of an open economy are presented. One is the fixed exchange rate regime with a passive domestic monetary policy. The other is the floating exchange rate regime with an active domestic monetary policy. The initial stages of the Real Plan fall somewhere between the two. On one hand, the economic authorities were legally committed to a fixed upper bound of one-to-one on the exchange rate of the Real to the US dollar. On the other hand, high domestic interest rates caused an appreciation of the Real with respect to the US dollar. Moreover, impediments were created to limit the inflows of short-term foreign capital, avoiding a further appreciation of the Real. In practice, initially the Real operated in a wide exchange rate band regime, with the authorities pegging the US dollar rate close to the band's lower end, and using inward capital controls as an instrument to maintain some freedom to pursue an independent monetary policy.

More complex is the answer to the question of what exactly were the operational targets of this monetary policy. Initially, for confidence-building purposes, the authorities committed themselves to strict targets for the monetary base, which proved futile in the face of the much higher than expected acceptance of the new currency.

Monetary policy was still exerted, as before the Real, by targeting the overnight interest rate at levels judged adequate to maintain private demand under control. The problem was, however, that interest rate changes seemed to have a limited impact. On one hand, the substitution effect exerted a contractionary effect on private demand; on the other, the 'income' effect exerted an expansionary effect. The latter occurred because the private sector as a whole was a net creditor, while the public sector was a net debtor, with most public debt held in the form of short-term floating interest rate notes, and hence not declining in value when the interest rate increased.[10]

For this reason, monetary policy under the Real started by focusing on measures designed to restrict the capacity for credit creation of the banking system. Initially, a 100 per cent reserve requirement at the margin was set for checking deposits. As banks managed to continue expanding their loans with the use of CDs and other liabilities, in December 1994 the authorities decided to set a 15 per cent reserve requirement directly on the volume of such loans, while also limiting the number of instalments on consumer loans.

4.5 Stabilization without Recession

While the progressive control of moderate inflation is normally accompanied by a reduction of economic activity, the sudden end of very high inflation tends to bring about a revival of economic activity. The Real Plan was no exception to this rule: a significant acceleration of economic activity took place following 1 July 1994, in spite of the federal budget being in balance and the observance of high real domestic interest rates. Several factors contribute to explain this phenomenon.

First, the Real Plan brought to an abrupt end the collection of an inflation tax of some 2 to 3 per cent of GDP. This was previously paid by low-income earners without access to the interest-paying bank accounts that protected the financial wealth of rich Brazilians. It meant that, under high inflation, the actual purchasing power of monthly wages tended to be some 10 to 15 per cent lower than their nominal take-home value, because of the deteriorating effect of inflation on money holdings during the wage-spending period. Wage earners tried to defend themselves from this deterioration by concentrating their purchases at the beginning of each month, but this was of little avail, because shopkeepers concentrated their price rises at the end of each month, in anticipation of the beginning-of-the-month surge in wage earners' demand. For they knew that the search procedures of wage earners for better deals would be obliterated by the anguish of observing the daily melting of their earnings by inflation. To illustrate this point with a topical story, in early 1994 the rural workers in a large São Paulo farm asked their boss to keep secret their payment day, so that they could reach the shops in the neighboring town before the shopkeepers learned that their wages had been paid out.

A second reason for the demand surge was that, with low inflation, financial savings protected by indexation clauses became less attractive as a hedge against the relative price variations of real assets, as this variability was brought down by the end of high inflation. Under low inflation, real asset values became less volatile than before, thus causing an increase in the desired level of both inventories and real investment. Third, the income uncertainty brought about by high inflation tended to induce a measure of prudential savings as a hedge against future real income variation. This also became less necessary in view of the relative real income stability observed after the introduction of the Real. Thus, consumption out of current income was also favored by the reduction of real income uncertainty. Fourth, the uncertainty about the sustainability of price and exchange rate stability may have induced an anticipation of consumption and investment spending. Finally, real income stability made both consumers and firms much more creditworthy than before, thus inducing an abrupt rupture of existing credit constraints previously limiting both banks' and shopkeepers' loan supply.

The government reacted to the surge of private demand by tightening credit and lowering import barriers. The exchange rate appreciation that occurred because of capital inflows acted in the same way. At the end of 1994, the risk of excessive overheating still presented a major challenge to the Real Plan, as indicated by a rapidly increasing industrial capacity utilization rate, and an equally rapid reversal from positive to negative of the foreign trade accounts.

5 ECONOMIC DISEQUILIBRIA: THE PLAN IN EARLY 1995

On Senator Fernando Henrique Cardoso's inauguration as President of the Republic, on 1 January 1995, the initial success of the Real Plan was incontestable. Inflation had fallen abruptly from some 45 per cent per month in the first half of 1994, to 1 to 2 per cent per month at year-end. The strength of the Real Plan was tested by the resignation of two finance ministers. First was in April 1994, when Cardoso became a presidential candidate. He was replaced by Rubens Ricupero, an experienced diplomat. However, because of political indiscretions inadvertently transmitted on TV, Ricupero had to be hurriedly replaced in early September by Ciro Gomes, a young governor of the north-eastern state of Ceara.

Although both Ricupero and Gomes kept untouched the economic team put together by Cardoso, neither of them enjoyed his capacity to maintain full control over the economic policy making process. Thus, in late June, Ricupero had to threaten to resign when the Minister of Justice proposed to introduce several modifications, including price control measures, to the decree prepared by the economic team launching the Real. Ricupero was also unable to convince President Franco not to raise civil servant salaries in early September.

In the second half of 1994, the plan also survived a major frost, one of the longest droughts in Brazilian history, and a surge of commodity prices in international markets.

The initial success of the Real Plan demonstrated in practice the correctness of the theoretical propositions it relied on. First, that it was necessary to muster the political will to balance the government accounts without the help of the inflationary erosion of budgeted spending. Second, that the conversion of wages and other contracts from cruzeiros reais to a unit of account with daily indexation (the URV) would not necessarily lead to a sudden acceleration of inflation in cruzeiros reais, provided that conversions were made according to mean real values. Third, that, through a monetary reform, inflation could be brought to a halt, in a pre-announced way, without confiscation of financial assets, or price and wage freezes.

In spite of the first months of the Real having been auspicious, it was clear that a cumulative disequilibrium was occurring. This, if the government did not take action, could provoke problems similar to those that had condemned to failure the previous attempts at price stabilization in Brazil.

One of the main problems was the discrepancy between the nominal wage increases determined by the rules of wage policy, and the exchange rate appreciation, determined by the course of monetary and exchange rate policies. Wages were converted into URVs, in March 1994, according to the mean real values of the previous four months. These mean values, however, were calculated in payment days, not in average days of spending. This implied a gain in the purchasing power of wages, equivalent to the inflation tax that previously eroded wages, between payday and the average day of spending.

Furthermore, wages began to be paid month after month in a currency with a relatively constant purchasing power. Before this they had suffered a major deterioration between the peaks that followed the four-month readjustment and the valleys that preceded such readjustments. Although the average values might be the same, an additional gain of real income was obtained because of the elimination of the real wage uncertainty associated with the strong oscillation of real values, previously observed within the four-month period of wage readjustment.

Such gain was made explicit in the market by the increased ease with which wage earners began to have access to consumer credit. Such credit expanded considerably in the period, in spite of the Central Bank, in the beginning of the Plan, having imposed a compulsory deposit of 100 per cent at the margin on demand deposits in commercial banks. Between June and December 1994, loans from the financial system to individuals expanded by nothing less than 150 per cent.[11]

Even more importantly, the annual indexation of wages was maintained for 12 months, based on a new price index, the IPCr (restricted consumer price index), which in the first six months of the Plan accumulated a variation of 23 per cent. This variation was determined mostly by a combination of a carry-over of the inflation in cruzeiros reais of June 1994, with seasonal problems in food supply and substantial increases in residential rents. It was not thus a measure of the core inflation in Reais (which fell to close to zero, as indicated by the behavior of the industrial WPI (wholesale price index). Thus, when incorporated to wages, this variation implied an increase in the real costs of production, signaling the difficulty of maintaining the freeze imposed on public sector prices and tariffs, as well as of the informal controls imposed on the prices of the oligopolistic sectors in commerce and industry.

Meanwhile, the combination of high domestic interest rates produced by a tight monetary policy with the asymmetric band exchange rate policy, resulted in an appreciation of the Real with respect to the dollar. From a unitary parity at the beginning of the Plan, the Real appreciated to R$0.846 per US$1.00 on 31 December 1994. This represented a nominal appreciation of 15 per cent, which further contributed to a decline in the ratio of the exchange rate to wages. A decision adopted by the economic team in September 1994 to accelerate the rhythm of import liberalization, as a means of avoiding the pass-through to prices of cost and demand pressures, amplified the impact of the exchange rate appreciation on the external accounts.

The demand pressures which originated from the increase in the purchasing power of wages as previously described, added to a movement of anticipation of purchases, both of durable goods and equipment, in the expectation that stabilization would be only temporary, as suggested by previous failed stabilization experiments. An expansion of 37 per cent in the loans of the financial system to the private sector between June and December 1994[12] validated such increase in demand.

Demand pressures from the public sector came on top of those exerted by the private sector. In the first place, in September and December 1994, in spite of opposition from the economic team, President Franco increased the salaries of the armed forces and those of the lower earning groups in the federal executive branch, with the justification of providing isonomy with the salaries of the functionaries of the legislative and the judiciary. In January 1995, all public sector employees benefited from the wage indexation law, not only with an integral readjustment according to the IPCr, but also with the replacement, by the higher 12-month mean, of the lower 4-month mean which had been adopted in March 1994 for the conversion of wages into URVs. The original version sent to Congress of the government decree instituting the URV did not have a provision for the monetary correction of wages either in the public or the private sectors, but only the replacement of the 4-month average by the 12-month average in the first annual wage settlement after the introduction of the Real. However, the economic team had to negotiate a one-year indexation of wages by the IPCr in Congress, in order to guarantee the legislative approval of the URV decree, before launching the Real.

In March 1995, President Cardoso decreed a significant increase in the salary supplements of the top brass of the federal executive. Finally, in May 1995, the minimum wage was readjusted to R$100, 10 per cent more than the variation of the IPCr, in a movement that also benefited the social security pensioners.

Altogether, these decisions led to a strong increase in the wage bill and social security payments of the public sector as a whole, since similar decisions, if not more generous ones, were adopted in the states and municipalities.

The expansion of domestic demand, part of which was channeled towards imported products, had two major consequences at the end of 1994: a high degree of capacity utilization in industry and a rapid deterioration of the trade balance. The behavior of the Vargas Foundation's industrial WPI (excluding from it food products, due to their seasonal behavior, and petroleum derivatives, the prices of which were controlled by the government) indicates that the combination of domestic cost pressures with the increase in domestic demand was sufficiently strong to provoke an upward movement in core inflation. This occurred in spite of the increase in external competition propitiated by the exchange rate appreciation and the speeding-up of import liberalization.

It was in this context of strong change of relative prices and in the relation between demand and production, that Brazil was hit by the Tequila effect of the Mexican balance of payment crisis. This led to a reflux of foreign capital flows, putting more pressure on the international reserves of the country, coming on top of those present since September 1994 as a consequence of the trade balance deterioration. Consequently, Brazil's international reserves experienced a pronounced fall following the end of 1994.

6 THE SECOND PHASE OF THE PLAN: 1995–96

Between March and June 1995, the new government of President Cardoso adopted a sequence of drastic economic policy measures to deal with the previously identified disequilibria which threatened the sustainability of the Real Plan.

In the first place, the decision was taken to increase substantially the basic interest rate and to impose additional restrictions to credit expansion.

These restrictive measures came on top of those already adopted in December 1994, which imposed compulsory deposits of 30 per cent on certificates of deposit and of 15 per cent on bank credits.

Simultaneously with the monetary crunch, in March 1995 the government promoted a 5 per cent devaluation of the Real with respect to the US dollar, replaced the asymmetric band by a sliding exchange rate band, and decreed a sharp increase from 20 to 70 per cent of the import tariffs on automobiles and household appliances.

In June 1995, the government issued a de-indexation decree abolishing the IPCr, and instituted a system of free wage bargaining from July 1995. More precisely, in the annual wage settlements starting from this later date, only the residual of the IPCr accumulated from July 1994 to June 1995 not granted in previous annual settlements would be legally enforceable. Thus, for example, a labor union with an annual settlement in October 1995 would have the right to the IPCr of October 1994 to June 1995, but would freely negotiate any eventual compensation for the inflation occurring between June and September 1995. This decision established a historical rupture with the regime of wage indexation, introduced by the military government in 1964, with the technocratic intent of replacing social conflict by the arithmetic computation of past inflation. The only result of this was the institutionalization of inflation as a means of accommodating income disputes between workers and employers.[13]

The adjustment measures succeeded in reverting, from April 1995, the inflation trend manifest in the industrial WPI. The measures adopted in March 1995 (added to the lagged effects of the compulsory deposits created in December 1994) also succeeded in temporarily reversing the external deficit: from July 1995, the trade balance started presenting small surpluses, in a situation that was kept under control until the first half of 1996. From this point onwards, however, as the economy began recovering from the credit crunch of mid-1995, the trade deficits began to increase again.

From the second half of 1995, there was also a reversal of the adverse movements in the capital account. As a consequence, international reserves, which had declined by some US$10 billion in the first half of 1995, more than recovered their losses and increased continuously until the 1997 Asian crisis.

The negative consequences of the credit crunch appeared in at least three areas: economic activity, financial fragility and the public sector deficit.

GDP grew at an accelerated pace after the launching of the Real Plan until the first quarter of 1995. The credit crunch not only stopped this growth, but also led to a decline in the level of economic activity in the second and third quarters of that year. Starting from then, the economy began to recover, slowly at first, and more strongly following the second half of 1996.

The slowdown of economic activity in the second half of 1995, associated with continuously high interest rates and the previous boost to wage rates, aggravated the financial situation of firms which had gone into debt in the economic boom of the previous 12 months. Agriculture and agricultural machinery production were particularly affected, as food prices found themselves under pressure because of a super-crop in 1995. Furthermore, the appreciation of the Real and the deepening of the process of trade liberalization brought additional difficulties to the more fragile firms in sectors more directly affected by foreign competition, such as capital goods, car parts, toys, leather and footwear, and textiles. Consequently, the volume of overdue credits as well as bankruptcies grew significantly. The share in the total loans of the financial system to the private sector that were overdue or in liquidation rose from 7.5 per cent in December 1994 to 15.4 per cent in December 1995. It kept increasing to 19.8 per cent in August 1996.[14]

For the commercial banks, the losses with such credits came on top of the end of the gains from the inflation tax, which they had previously obtained, fully on demand deposits and transfer funds, and partly on time deposits.

The fragility of part of the financial system became clear when the Central Bank, to stop a run on agencies, found itself forced to close Banco Economico (the seventh largest private bank in the country) in August 1995. It was then that the belated decision was taken to institute an expanded system of protection for demand deposits, and to create a program of private sector bank restructuring (PROER).

A third impact of the policy of high interest rates was on the public sector deficit. The public sector is defined as the sum of the federal government (including Social Security and the Central Bank), state and municipal governments, and their respective non-financial state enterprises. In the operational concept, the consolidated balance of the public sector shifted from a surplus of 1.3 per cent of GDP in 1994 to a deficit of 4.8 per cent of GDP in 1995, a deterioration of 6.1 percentage points of GDP. Three quarters of this deterioration was due to the previously mentioned increase in wages and pensions, as the primary balance shifted from a surplus of 5.1 per cent in 1994 to only 0.4 per cent of GDP in 1995. Also significant was the impact of the real interest account, which increased from 3.8 per cent to 5.1 per cent of GDP between 1994 and 1995.

The increase of the operational deficit in 1995 implied an interruption to a process of progressive decline of the net debt of the public sector as a ratio to GDP, which had been happening since the beginning of the decade. Between December 1994 and December 1995, the public sector net debt increased from 28.1 per cent to 29.9 per cent of GDP, and then to 34.2 per cent of GDP in December 1996.

7 CONCLUSIONS

Although the Real Plan was extraordinarily successful in its first six months of life, it seems clear that the Brazilian economy found itself on an unsustainable path when the Mexican crisis erupted, in terms of a growing disequilibrium between both demand and output, and wages and prices. The causes of these trends were multiple: wage indexation, public sector deficit, appreciation of the exchange rate, and credit expansion to the private sector.

The contractionary measures adopted in the first half of 1995 succeeded in overcoming the initial problems of the Plan, and maintained inflation on a downward course. The resumption of large trade deficits from September 1996 indicated, however, that the adopted economic policy mix was sustainable only under abundant international liquidity.

The conclusion is that the Real Plan succeeded not only in bringing inflation rates down, but also in keeping them down – by 1998 Brazil would reach inflation rates comparable to those of its trading partners. The Real Plan, however, failed to generate an economic path along which such inflation control was made compatible with sustained economic growth and reasonable external equilibrium.

NOTES

1. This chapter uses material from a previous paper: 'O Plano Real: uma avaliação', in A. Mercadante (ed.), *O Brasil Pós-Real*, Campinas, SP: Unicamp/IE, 1997: pp. 11–70.
2. See E. Bacha, 'O fisco e a inflação: uma interpretação do caso brasileiro', *Revista de Economia Política*/53, **14**(1), Jan/March 1994: 5–17.
3. For an evaluation, see E. Modiano, 'A ópera dos três cruzados', in M. Abreu (ed.), *A Ordem do Progresso: Cem Anos de Política Econômica Republicana, 1889–1989*. Rio de Janeiro: Editora Campus, 1990, pp. 347–86.
4. For an evaluation, see D.D. Carneiro, 'Ajuste externo e desequilíbrio interno', in M. Abreu (ed.), *A Ordem do Progresso*, (op. cit), pp. 323–46.
5. See P. Arida and A. Lara-Resende, 'Inertial inflation and monetary reform', in J. Williamson (ed.), *Inflation and Indexation: Argentina, Brazil and Israel*, Washington, DC: Institute for International Economics, 1985.
6. For a modeling of the Brazilian type of inflation with a zero operational public sector deficit and interest earning money, see appendix B to E. Bacha, 'O fisco e a inflação', op. cit.
7. See 'Plano FHC', *Revista de Economia Política*/54, **14**(2), Apr/June 1994: 114–31.
8. On the complex interactions between economic policy and modern Brazilian society and politics, see B. Lamounier and E. Bacha, 'Democracy and economic reform in Brazil', in *A Precarious Balance. Vol. 2. Democracy and Economic Reforms in Latin America*, San Francisco, CA: ICS Press, Institute for Contemporary Studies, 1994: 143–86.
9. For a technical analysis, see M. Garcia, 'Avoiding some costs of inflation and crawling toward hyperinflation: the case of the Brazilian domestic currency substitute', *Journal of Development Economics,* **51**(1), October 1996: 139–59.

10. For a further analysis, see F. Lopes, 'The monetary transmission mechanism in Brazil', mimeo, 1997.
11. Source: *Boletim do Banco Central do Brasil*, **32**(4), April 1996, p. 98.
12. Source: same as in note 11.
13. For an early critique of Brazil's indexation system, cf. A. Fishlow, 'Indexing Brazilian style: inflation without tears?', *Brookings Papers on Economic Activity*, 1, 1974.
14. Source: *Boletim do Banco Central do Brasil*, **32**(12), December 1996, pp. 106 and 110.

11. The two waves of financial liberalization in Latin America

Roberto Frenkel and Lucio Simpson*

I INTRODUCTION

The economic history of Latin America in the past three decades suggests that the most sensible approach to evaluating the regional processes of financial liberalization, is not to see them as policy initiatives that can be isolated from their context, but rather as a set of experiences that share a set of common features. However, there are still enough noteworthy contrasts in policies and performance between the different LA countries to be able to draw important lessons about the relative merit or lack of it of specific measures.

The long-term trend towards financial liberalization in LA has not been a continuous process but one with a marked break during the 1980s as a result of the crises brought about by the failure of the 'first wave' of liberalization attempts. These were labeled the 'Southern Cone liberalization experiments', and we especially analyse the cases of Argentina and Chile. Though they were short-lived, these experiences are for our purposes closed episodes with well-defined beginnings and ends.[1]

With respect to the 1990s our view is particularly influenced by five national cases: Argentina, Brazil, Colombia, Chile and Mexico. These are the biggest economies in the region. Together they represent more than three-quarters of the regional product and were the main recipients of the capital inflows. They also provide good examples of a variety of policies and economic performances. However, even though chronologically in the past, evaluating the liberalization processes in the 1990s is complicated by the fact that some are not closed cases in a strict sense. Fortunately, it is possible to draw stronger conclusions, particularly regarding the issue of sustainability, by considering the experiences of Mexico and Argentina in the first half of the decade. This period, whose end was marked by the December 1994 Mexican devaluation, was long enough for the endogenous dynamic processes we analyse to fully work their way into a crisis.

The chapter is organized as follows: in the next section we review Latin

America's experience with capital market liberalization and comment on those features of the process shared by most economies in the region. In section III we analyse the liberalization experiences in the 1970s. In section IV we examine the experiences of the 1990s, focusing on the problem of sustainability.

II SOME SPECIFIC FEATURES OF CAPITAL MARKET LIBERALIZATION IN LATIN AMERICA

It is never simple to explain observed economic performance exclusively as the consequence of the implementation of a certain policy. Contexts change and the specific measures we attempt to evaluate are often part of a wider set of initiatives whose effects most often overlap. These considerations are particularly relevant in the case of capital market reforms in Latin America (or LA).

In the first place, with respect to the overlapping of effects, financial liberalization and opening have not been isolated policy initiatives but have always been implemented in LA as components of wide-ranging structural reforms and stabilization programs. Packages of this kind were practiced in the region in the second half of the 1970s and their implementation became generalized in the 1990s. For this reason, the outcomes of financial reforms have always emerged in combination with the effects of trade opening and public-sector reforms, as well as with the measures and results of macroeconomic stabilization policies. Both in the cases of the 1970s and in the more important ones of the 1990s, a fixed exchange rate was a first-order ingredient in stabilization packages.

In the second place, regarding the external context of the policies, financial reforms coincided with boom periods in international financial movements. They were always accompanied by massive capital inflows with their own significant effects on the working of the economy.[2] Because of this correlation, the effects of liberalization in LA are not easily distinguishable from those of drastic changes in the size and composition of capital flows.

In the first boom of capital flows into developing economies – the period that followed the 1973 oil shock – the region pioneered drastic financial reforms. (The Argentine and Chilean cases are the most notable experiences.) This phase came to an abrupt end with deep financial and external debt crises. They were followed by the nationalization of private external debts and the establishment of an institutional arrangement in which external financing had to be intermediated by negotiation with the international banks and the IMF, because LA was segmented from international markets. Apart from this link of permanent negotiation, the region remained practically isolated from international capital markets for the rest of the decade. If we were to date that period more precisely, we could say that it lasted between the 1982 Mexican moratorium and the signing of the first Brady Plan to restructure external debt (Mexico's plan in 1990). During that time the region operated under a regime characterized by two stylized facts: external financing was rationed and negotiations with creditors and multilateral financial organizations generally imposed macroeconomically significant transfers abroad.

The constraints set by external financial rationing and these transfers dominated policy design and economic performance during the 1980s. In the initial years, control over the external and financial crises was absolute policy priority and the institutional setting of financial markets was subordinated to this target. For instance, private external debt was nationalized through massive interventions such as the nationalization of the banking system in Mexico, the generalized refinancing of private debts in Argentina, and a total bailout of the banking system in Chile. In this phase the priority given to external adjustment and the need to regain control over as many policy instruments as possible led to the reversal of previously adopted liberalization and opening policies. As policymakers sought to stabilize their economies, they implemented emergency measures, such as the reintroduction of exchange controls to block capital flight, and interest rates regulations to ease the management of the financial crisis.

Although the urgency of the early 1980s removed financial liberalization from the immediate policy debate, it reappeared on the agenda of conditionality that accompanied the external debt negotiations. This link became clear in the mid-1980s with the appearance of the adjustment-cum-growth Baker Plan. Since then, coordination between the IMF, the World Bank, and other agencies has increased and the Washington Consensus has become more clearly defined. Even so, capital market liberalization was of secondary relevance in the 1980s. The history of the economic performance during that period – especially in Argentina, Brazil and Mexio, the largest economies in the region – is basically about a sequence of attempts and failures of comprehensive macroeconomic stabilization programs. Inflation and the balance of payments were stabilized for some time before new destabilizing trends required further adjustments and stabilization measures. There were huge real fluctuations around a stagnant trend. Variations in the institutional framework of the financial sector were of secondary importance compared to these cycles.

The 1980s' stabilization programs attempted to reconcile the external financial constraint with the achievement of three conflicting goals: debt service, inflation reduction and recovery of a positive rate of growth. While some countries – Chile and Colombia, for example – could resolve this conflict in the second half of the period and stabilize the performance of their economies,[3] the biggest were unable to do so until the end of the decade. In Argentina, Brazil and Mexico stabilization was only achieved in the 1990s, when transfers abroad reversed abruptly and the region became the recipient of massive capital inflows. Financial liberalization gained new relevance under these conditions. The external constraint ceased to be binding.

The market segmentation of the 1980s, the instability that lasted until the end of the decade, and the joint effects of both circumstances on the domestic financial markets determined other specific features of the experiences of the 1990s. Similar circumstances characterize the Chilean and Argentine liberalization experiments of the 1970s.

Among the 'initial conditions' of the Southern Cone experiments during that period was the particular situation of domestic financial markets. They had recently undergone deep crises and restructuring (Chile 1971–76, Argentina 1974–77), were emerging from a long period of segmentation from international markets, and had adapted to a high inflation environment. The financial markets of the biggest economies in the region found themselves in similar conditions at the end of the 1980s. Especially in the three largest countries, the 'second wave' of financial liberalization and capital inflows, like the first, generally took the form of a shock in economies that until then had shown low levels of monetization and financial deepening, weakly developed banking systems, a poor menu of financial assets, and scarce credit for the private sector.[4]

The enthusiasm with which liberalization was adopted in the absence of necessary institutional underpinnings left financial systems facing largely unchartered territory. Not surprisingly, they were unable to allocate the strong injection of funds efficiently. The small size and poor diversification of financial markets gave rise to a natural tendency for capital flows to induce major disturbances. Their magnitude was large compared to the existing stocks of money, credit and domestic financial assets. Such high flow/stock ratios implied strong appreciation pressures in the exchange market and/or high credit and liquidity expansion rates according to the degree of intervention of the monetary authority. They also generated a swift appreciation of financial and real assets, such as land and real estate. Those tendencies were enhanced under the fixed exchange-rate regimes found in the majority of experiences. More generally, the shock implied the emergence of important expansionary financial effects in domestic demand. That is why the initial phase of a real and financial boom and the propensity to generate speculative bubbles – widely observed in developing countries associated with financial liberalization and massive capital inflows – were closely linked to these 'initial conditions' in the LA cases.

Lastly, the region's passage from the 1980s to the 1990s signified the transition from a situation of external financial rationing and transfers abroad to one of abundant financing. This change, in itself, could only have had beneficial effects on macroeconomic performance. The stabilization programs could succeed; there was a generalized drop in inflation; GDP and domestic absorption grew – the latter more than the former. However, the fact that macroeconomic performance improved does not support the view that accepting globalization in the terms of the Washington Consensus was an optimal policy.

In the first place, as already mentioned, the impact of the surge in capital inflows is difficult to distinguish from the effects of liberalization policies. The fact that these policies were undertaken may have played a 'signalling' role that encouraged capital inflows, but there is strong evidence that most capital (perhaps with the exception of FDI) flowed to LA in response to decreases in the expected rates of return in the main international markets. In the second place, the performance of LA economies during the 1980s is not a relevant basis on which to evaluate the experience in the 1990s, since it represented, to a large extent, the unsuccessful attempts by LA countries to overcome the constraints posed by their high debt burden and credit rationing. Thus, though in this chapter we are emphasizing the negative aspects of globalization, we are not arguing that the 'lost decade' was preferable to the 1990s. Rather, one of the lessons of the painful experience of the 1980s is that policy makers should strive to preserve fluid access to the international financial markets. The experience in the 1990s, in turn, shows that, to minimize the risks it poses, integration in the global economy must be carefully implemented, both in terms of speed and depth.

III THE LIBERALIZATION EXPERIENCES IN THE 1970s

In the mid-1970s Argentina and Chile were undergoing similar political and economic processes. The Peronist and *Unidad Popular* governments had been overthrown by military dictatorships in the midst of deep economic crises. The first phase of the macroeconomic policy of the military administrations did not deviate significantly from the traditional stabilization recipes that both countries had repeatedly put into practice since the 1950s. Price controls were lifted, wage increments were repressed, and the exchange rate was devalued. After that, a crawling-peg regime was adopted. Fiscal adjustment was mainly based on the contraction of wage expenditures. Real wages fell dramatically in both countries and employment dropped sharply in Chile. The fiscal adjustment was deep and permanent in the Chilean case and less significant and lasting in the Argentine. An innovation in economic policy was domestic financial reform: the interest rate was freed and most regulations on financial intermediaries were relaxed or removed.

Both economies had been isolated from international financial markets in the first half of the 1970s. The eurodollar bank market was already booming in that period, particularly after the 1973 oil shock. (Brazil, for instance, was utilizing this source of external financing intensively.) In the mid-1970s the Argentine and Chilean economies did not have sizable external debts. Their balance of payments had already been equilibrated by the stabilization packages. The orthodoxy of the military administrations gained credibility with the IMF and international banks despite the fact that both economies were experiencing high rates of inflation. High domestic financial yields attracted capital inflows even before the capital account had been opened. Confronted with these pressures the authorities initially gave priority to the control of the domestic money supply and attempted to curb inflows by imposing regulations.

In the second half of the 1970s, first Chile and shortly after Argentina implemented new and similar policy packages. Liberalization of the exchange market and deregulation of capital flows were added to the domestic financial reform that had previously been implemented. Trade liberalization programs were launched simultaneously. Tariff reductions were scheduled to converge in a few years to a flat and low tariff.[5] Exchange rate policy was the anti-inflation component of the package. Exchange rates were fixed by announcing predetermined paths for monthly devaluation rates, converging to a nominal constant exchange rate (the 'tablitas'). This macroeconomic stabilization package was inspired by the 'monetary approach to the balance of payments'.

The following features characterize the external and real performances after the packages were launched. There were massive capital inflows and a first phase of reserve accumulation and high rates of growth in money and credit. There was a strong expansion in domestic demand, led by consumption (and, to a lesser degree, by investment), as well as the emergence of bubbles in financial and real assets. The real exchange rate appreciated continuously because domestic inflation was systematically higher than the rate of devaluation plus the international inflation rate. Current account deficits rose fast and persistently and the external debt soared. When US monetary policy drove up the international interest rate in late 1979, both economies were already showing huge current account deficits and external debt. From then, the increased international rate contributed its own effect to their external fragility. The crisis broke soon afterward. The exchange rate regime collapsed in Argentina in early 1981 and in Chile in 1982. External market financing closed for both economies in 1982 and massive bailouts were implemented to confront the resulting financial crises. Both economies fell into deep recessions.

How can we evaluate economic performance in these cases? The depth and duration of the real consequences is well known. The key question is about the sustainability of growth during and after the crises. The negative external shock played a fundamental role in the genesis of the LA debt crisis. The rise in the international interest rate not only had a direct financial impact, but also other indirect negative effects caused by the ensuing world recession and the fall in the terms of trade. (In the case of Brazil, a highly dependent oil importer at the time, higher import prices added to the effects of the 1979 second oil shock.)

Secondly, the crisis encompassed the entire region. In the highly liquid and low interest rate context of the 1970s, many economies had major current account deficits and accumulated important debts. At one end of the spectrum of institutional and policy regimes were the Argentine and Chilean liberalization and opening packages. At the other was the indebtedness policy of Brazil's plan for deepening import-substituting industrialization (or ISI) whereby capital flows were mediated and administrated by the government. Mexico combined elements of both, with increases in public expenditures, as in Brazil, and some market deregulation, as in Argentina. The crisis affected all of the highly indebted economies, and others by contagion, such as Colombia. In the 1970s this country had explicitly refused to join the newly developed international financial market by changing its policy regime and had reduced its External Debt/GDP ratio by a half.

Taking into account this diversity, one way of evaluating Argentina's and Chile's liberalization policies is to compare their performances with those of the countries that reached the crisis with other policy settings. Were the real effects less important in the Southern Cone? Did market cushioning mechanisms operate as had been foreseen to limit the extent of the crisis and to reduce its social cost?

With regard to the real effects, Chile experienced the deepest recession in the region and Argentina's contraction can be counted among the largest. In the first half of the 1980s GDP in both countries contracted more than Mexico's and Brazil's and also more than the regional average. In Chile the adjustment led to a drastic cut in labor demand and unemployment rates reached 30 per cent. In Argentina the adjustment took place principally through a drastic fall in real wages and a sustained three-digit inflation ensued. The extension, depth and social costs of the Southern Cone's financial crises also surpassed the relative importance they attained in the other countries facing a negative external shock.[6] Market stabilizing mechanisms – that is, price and interest rate flexibility and real resource allocation and portfolio flexibility – either did not work as had been foreseen or gave rise to perverse effects such as the deepening of the crisis due to a rise in domestic interest rates. Be it for the greater relative importance of capital flight (Argentina), for worse previous external debt indicators (Chile), for higher financial fragility (both countries), or for fewer available policy instruments (both countries), the Chilean and Argentine policy regimes showed low ability to defend themselves against the volatility of international financial markets. An inter-country comparison does not favor financial liberalization.

An alternative way to evaluate the policy packages is to analyse the macroeconomic dynamics they generated while attempting to weigh the significance of the jump in the international interest rate. Was growth on a sustainable path prior to the external shock or did local macroeconomic dynamics already show signs of instability? One important fact is that both countries' domestic financial crises preceded their external crises and devaluations by over one year. In Argentina, the collapse of the exchange rate regime occurred one-and-a-half years before the Mexican crisis.

In fact, both countries show strong evidence of an endogenous cycle with a turning point and contraction phase which emerged independently of the evolution of the international interest rate. It was jointly driven by domestic financial developments and the evolution of the balance of payments. Cross effects were positive in the first phase and negative in the second. The cycle affected the real economy mainly through financial linkages: the evolution of credit, asset holders' portfolio decisions, and the financial situation of firms, though a key factor aggravating the dynamics and magnitude of the disequilibria was also the strong tendency for the increase in the relative price of non-tradable goods, to levels that implied a severe deviation of the real exchange rate from its long-term equilibrium level. The cycle's phases can be clearly discerned in the trajectories of the current account, the level of international reserves, and the domestic interest rate. The stylized facts are as follows.[7]

The opening of both the trade and capital accounts was accompanied by the predetermination of the nominal exchange rate. From that moment on there was persistent exchange rate appreciation. The inflation rate tended to fall but was systematically higher than the sum of the programmed rate of devaluation plus the international rate of inflation.

The launching of the package was followed by an injection of funds from abroad. The monetary base, bank deposits and credit grew swiftly, as did the number of financial intermediaries. There was rapid appreciation of domestic financial and real asset prices. Domestic demand, production and imports tended to expand. The increment in imports caused by trade opening, exchange rate appreciation, and expansion in domestic demand steadily widened the trade deficit. Likewise, the current account deficit showed an increase, which was only gradual because the external debt was initially small. Initially, capital flows were higher than the current account deficit and reserves accumulated. Its increment led to the domestic money expansion mentioned above.

The evolution of the external accounts and reserves marked one aspect of the cycle. There was a continuous but gradual increase in the current account deficit, while capital inflows could shift abruptly. At a certain moment the deficit surpassed the level of inflows. Reserves reached a maximum and then contracted, inducing monetary contraction overall. However, the cycle was not exclusively determined by this mechanical element: the size of capital flows was not an exogenous datum. Portfolio decisions regarding assets denominated in domestic currency and dollars were not independent of the evolution of the balance of payments and finance. Both played a crucial role in the process.[8]

The domestic interest rate was a clear indicator about financial aspects of the cycle. It fell in the first phase and then turned upward after a certain point. Because the exchange-rate rule initially enjoyed high credibility, arbitrage between domestic and external financial assets and credit led at the beginning to reductions in the domestic interest rate and the expected cost of external credit. The latter became negative in both countries. The real domestic bank lending rate became negative in Argentina and fell dramatically in Chile (to a quarter of its previous value). Lower interest rates helped spur real and financial expansion. However, financial fragility in the sense of Hyman Minsky (1986) increased significantly, due to both the rise in leverage and the increasing currency mismatch between assets and liabilities, two factors that would become crucial once interest rates started to rise.

In the second phase, rising domestic interest rates and episodes of illiquidity and insolvency appeared, first as isolated cases and then as a systemic crisis. What explained the increase in nominal and real interest rates? The nominal domestic interest rate can be expressed as the sum of the international interest rate, the programmed exchange-rate devaluation rate, and a residual accounting for exchange and financial risks. This was the main variable explaining the increase in the interest rate. On the one hand, financial risk rose in conjunction with financial fragility. But, more importantly, the risk premium increased with the evolution of the external sector. The persistent increment in the current account deficit – and at some point the fall in reserves – reduced the credibility of the exchange rate rule. Higher interest rates were needed to equilibrate portfolios and attract foreign capital. In turn, illiquidity and insolvency spread *à la* Minsky, threatening a systemic crisis. Episodes of bankruptcies in banks and firms further contributed to reducing the credibility of the exchange rule. This dynamics proved to be explosive in both Argentina and Chile. At the end of the process no interest rate was high enough to sustain the demand for domestic assets. There were runs on Central Bank reserves, leading finally to the collapse of the exchange rate regime. The resulting devaluations further deepened the financial crisis.

This analysis highlights the relatively minor (direct) role of the international interest rate in domestic financial developments. Its increase in the late 1970s overlapped with the endogenous cycle and surely contributed to a more rapid deterioration of the current account, but this seems to have been its principal impact on the domestic cycle. As pointed out earlier, the exchange rate and financial risk premia were the main contributors to the upward trend in domestic interest rates in the second phase.

We should also mention that neither the fiscal deficit nor the existence of public guarantees on bank deposits played significant roles, but merely exacerbated the dynamics driven by the mechanisms we are emphasizing. Argentina had both, and before Chile's program unravelled, the conventional wisdom[9] attributed its troubles to these 'sins'. In the end, however, Chile suffered the same fate as Argentina, despite the fact that it was recording a fiscal surplus and that it had eliminated deposit guarantees with the explicit purpose of making the working of the financial system more efficient and less risky. In this regard, though it certainly contributed to the crises, the importance of moral hazard in the 'Southern Cone' experiences has been greatly exaggerated in some literature. Though the weaknesses of the financial system played a very important role as destabilizing factors, they should be mostly attributed to the deregulation of banking in a context of very lax supervision and enforcement by the Central Bank.

Those are the generic features of liberalization and opening processes in Latin America. If having a robust, diversified and well-supervised banking system had been considered a prerequisite for implementing financial opening packages, then none of them would have been put into effect, either in the 1970s or the 1990s.[10]

IV THE EXPERIENCES OF THE 1990S

In this section we do not enjoy 100 per cent hindsight. LA experiences in the 1990s are not far-off closed cases, but rather current or recent history. However, enough time has passed for some features to be discerned. With respect to sustainability in particular, the Mexican and Argentine 1994–95 crises mark a watershed and delimit a period – the early 1990s – which can be analysed as a *fait accompli*. In the first part of this section, we examine macroeconomic performance early in the decade, contrasting Mexico's and Argentina's stylized facts with those of other economies in the region whose dynamics proved to be more stable.

IV.1 Sustainability Problems[11]

IV.1.1 The region's macroeconomic performance in the early 1990s

Stabilization efforts in the 1980s confronted the extremely difficult task of reconciling external debt service obligations with the preservation of basic macroeconomic balances, both external and fiscal. This was made more difficult by the fact that the deterioration in the external accounts was closely related to that in the fiscal accounts, via the rise in interest payments on the foreign debt.

As a consequence, LA countries overburdened with debts and facing credit rationing were extremely vulnerable to any unfavorable developments on its external or fiscal fronts, even to shocks that, in other circumstances, would not have been so destabilizing. On the other hand, occasional positive shocks were not enough to drag the countries out of the mud. This asymmetric response of LA economies showed that their fate was mostly determined by their debt overhang and lack of access to foreign financing.

This situation reversed in the 1990s. Almost every country closed its fiscal and external gaps. This important difference made possible the lower inflation rates and higher rates of growth observed across the region. Changing international financial conditions and their impact on the evolution of the external sector are the main causes of the improvement.

With the relaxation of the external constraint, macroeconomic performance improved because most of the destabilizing negative-feedback mechanisms could be deactivated. Firstly, the availability of external resources allowed domestic absorption and activity to expand. Capital inflows were of such a magnitude that many countries experienced an excess supply of foreign currency despite rapid growth of imports. There was generalized reserve accumulation and exchange rate appreciation.

Higher economic activity and exchange rate appreciation favored stability. The latter contributed significantly to the reduction in inflation and improvement in the fiscal accounts by diminishing the real value of interest payments on the external debt. At the same time, tax receipts improved with the rise of activity and sales. Lower inflation rates also helped raise tax collection, directly by increasing the real value of taxes and indirectly by easing the implementation of tax and administrative reforms. Additionally, fiscal equilibrium was facilitated in some countries through the implementation of massive privatization schemes, mostly financed with foreign capital.

IV.1.2 The Mexican crisis and its repercussions

Until mid-1994 Brazil was the main and important exception to these regional trends. The Real Plan stabilization program, launched in July 1994, then put the economy in line with the rest of the large LA countries, with respect to inflation, the balance of payments and appreciation of the exchange rate.

Paradoxically, only a few months after the Brazilian economy was synchronized with its neighbors, Mexico and Argentina were hit by external and financial crises and confronted another round of adjustments. Official and multilateral support to both countries in 1995 prevented a default on external payments and the reemergence of a scenario like that in 1982. In contrast to that experience, financial markets rapidly reopened for Latin America.

Mexico had been at the forefront of the region's stabilization and structural reform processes. It led international investors' expectations about Latin America as a whole. Its evolution in the early 1990s was assessed as a stable development process with increasing international trade and financial integration, particularly with the United States. Mexico was seen as the vanguard for similar changes elsewhere in LA. The Mexican crisis abruptly changed perceptions by showing that the good performance of the 1990s was not immune to a resurgence of instability. In this sense, the crisis marked a watershed for the region as a whole. It ended a period whose beginning can be situated in 1990, when Mexico signed the first Brady agreement.

Both the Mexican and the Argentine crises, triggered by the Tequila effect, suggest we explore the region's sustainability problems in the early 1990s by comparing these two cases – with proven difficulties – with other countries which demonstrated more robust performances.

IV.1.3 Capital flows, the exchange rate appreciation and the external fragility

In 1991–93 net inflows of financial resources into the region amounted to about US$166 billion, while current account deficits added up to $98 billion. In every country net capital inflows were higher than the current account gaps, giving rise to the accumulation of reserves. Of total inflows, $75 billion went to Mexico, $29 billion to Argentina, $20 billion to Brazil and $8 billion to Chile. These four countries received 80 per cent of the total regional inflow in 1991–93, and Mexico alone absorbed about 45 per cent. Outside these countries, capital inflows were also significant in Peru and Venezuela.

Exchange rate appreciation was universal, but its magnitude differed across countries. Mexico and Argentina experienced the greatest appreciation in comparison with the real exchange rate prevailing in the second half of the 1980s. In 1994 Chile and Colombia were at the other end of the spectrum. The degree of relative appreciation was determined by the level of the exchange rate at the beginning of the 1990s and its subsequent dynamics. In Mexico, where the stabilization program dated from late 1987, a significant appreciation had taken place in 1988. The process persisted at a slower pace until 1990 and accelerated from 1991. In Argentina, the exchange rate experienced an important appreciation in 1990 and was nominally fixed at the already appreciated real level in 1991. Further appreciation continued into the early 1990s. In contrast, Chile and Colombia entered the 1990s with relatively depreciated exchange rates. Chile's subsequent rate of appreciation was lower than in the rest of the countries. In Colombia, the process accelerated in 1994. Brazil maintained a depreciated exchange rate until 1993. The exchange rate appreciated strongly after the Real Plan was launched, particularly in its first year, and it kept rising, though at a slower pace, reaching a maximum in early 1996. Despite a minor devaluation, at the end of 1998 the real exchange rate was still as high as it was at the beginning of 1996. In the end, and despite an IMF support package, Brazil was forced to abandon its exchange rate regime and adopted a system of dirty floating as from the January 1999 devaluation.

The different evolution of exchange rates was associated with the macroeconomic policies each country followed. Mexico and Argentina implemented stabilization policies in which a fixed nominal exchange rate was a crucial ingredient, fully deregulated their capital accounts, and adopted a passive attitude *vis-à-vis* capital inflows. On the other hand, Colombia, Chile and Brazil (until 1994) included real exchange rate targets in their exchange, fiscal and monetary policies.[12] Chile and Colombia adopted crawling-band exchange rate regimes, regulated capital inflows by imposing differential taxes according to the types of flows – which required the maintenance of some control over the foreign exchange market – and implemented sterilization policies. These strategies did not always completely fulfill their objectives, but they did lead to better overall performances.[13]

The region's trade deficit showed an increasing trend, reaching $15 billion in 1993. However, this total is biased by Brazil. During 1991–94 Brazil accumulated a $50 billion trade surplus despite the jump in imports induced by the Real Plan in 1994. By contrast, Mexico's trade deficit was $63 billion in 1991–93. The Argentine deficit was $8 billion. In both cases the deficit resulted from a rapid growth of imports. This trend persisted in 1994 when the deficit of the two countries totaled $29 billion. Imports also grew fast in Colombia, where the trade balance passed from a $2.3 billion surplus in 1991 to a $2.1 billion deficit in 1994. In Chile the trade account was in surplus in the early 1990s, except for 1993.

The region's annual growth rate in imports went from 10.3 per cent in the second half of the 1980s to 16.1 per cent in the 1990s, while the rate of growth of exports declined (except in Brazil). In Mexico, growth of imports had already tripled that of exports in the second half of the 1980s and this ratio persisted into the 1990s. In Argentina, exports increased by 5.5 per cent per year in 1991–94, while imports grew by 55.6 per cent per year in the same period.

Overall, the Current Account Deficit/Exports ratio (CAD/X) for Latin America was 27.5 per cent in 1993 and slightly lower in 1994. This regional average is biased by the more favorable results of Brazil's external sector, where the current account was practically in equilibrium. With this in mind, the regional average for the indicator of external fragility can be used as a standard for the comparison of the national cases.

It is interesting to underline the situation in 1993 because it constitutes the most immediate antecedent to the changes that took place in 1994 and which we describe below. In 1993 the ranking of countries by different external fragility indicators showed a clear pattern. Regarding the CAD/X ratio, Chile and Colombia had lower levels than the regional average while Mexico and Argentina doubled it. Moreover, the ranking remains unaltered if account is taken of the proportion of the current account deficit financed by FDI,[14] with Argentina and Mexico appearing at the bottom of the list. The External Debt/Exports ratio exhibited a similar pattern, although Brazil's high relative external indebtedness pushed its level close to that of Mexico and Argentina. In 1994 Colombia's CAD/X ratio rose slightly – but remained lower than the regional average – and the ratio fell in Chile. Meanwhile, the ratios worsened in Mexico and Argentina, increasing by 20 per cent with respect to 1993.

IV.1.4 The turning point in 1994

At the end of 1993 Mexico and Argentina were the economies with the most unfavorable indicators of external fragility in the region. Difficulties in sustaining the macroeconomic performance of the early 1990s were foreseen, to the extent that the dynamics resembled the initial phases of the Southern Cone experiences analysed in the previous section. Thus, a turning point with a subsequent contraction was to be expected. In fact, some evidence of a turning point was visible in 1994, well before Mexico's December devaluation. One indicator of such a change was a shift in the trend of international reserves in both Mexico and Argentina.

However, the precise timing of the contractionary phase can be anticipated or delayed by events that are external to the endogenous cycle. It was precisely one of these events, the strong rise in interest rates engineered by the Federal Reserve from February 1994, which created the background for the attack against Mexico late in the same year. Following the Fed's decision there was an upward shift in the yield curve in the US, but there was a more than proportional impact on LA bond prices. Consequently, along with the increment in interest rates, there was an increase in the region's country-risk premia. They rose significantly more for Mexico and Argentina than for other countries, in line with their higher levels of external fragility. The relative performance of financial assets is symptomatic: important drops were observed in the cases of Argentina and Mexico early in 1994; a slightly smaller decline occurred for Brazil; and prices stabilized for Chilean assets.

The rise in the risk premia of LA assets in reaction to the increase in US interest rates represented the first wave of herd behavior against emerging markets, a behavior which would later reappear[15] in the Asian and Russian crises and would also manifest itself in the 'strange' positive correlations between the Nasdaq Index and emerging-market asset prices.[16]

How can this rise in the country-risk premia in response to the change in the Fed's policy be explained? A plausible hypothesis is that international investors perceived an increase in external fragility as a result of the impact of the higher interest rate that the debtors had to confront. But, by reducing their exposure to higher risk – that is, demanding higher compensation for the risk – financial-market players accentuated the original unfavorable impact of the higher international interest rate. This movement, in turn, increased the probability that the economy might be pushed towards a 'bad equilibrium'. This set the stage for the sudden shift in market sentiment that would later coordinate the negative expectations that precipitated the Mexican devaluation. In turn, Argentina's perceived weaknesses immediately led to contagion. In this sense, the Mexican and Argentine crises did not erupt suddenly in a quiet landscape, but were the last episodes in a period of increasing financial tension ignited by the changes in monetary policy in the US.

Together with the increase in country-risk premia came a decline in capital flows to Argentina and Mexico which significantly modified the trend in the regional aggregate. In 1994 total inflows amounted to $47 billion, compared to an annual average of $55 billion in 1991–93 and a maximum of $70 billion in 1993. The reduction was fully explained by the two countries, and particularly by Mexico, whose capital inflows dropped from $30 billion in 1993 to $10 billion in 1994. In contrast, Brazil's and Colombia's capital inflows augmented in 1994 and the rest of the region's were similar to their levels in the preceding year.

The fall in capital inflows in Mexico and Argentina was concomitant with an increase in the current account deficit in both cases. In 1993 the deficits had amounted to $23.5 billion in Mexico and $7.5 billion in

Argentina. They grew to $30.6 billion and $11.1 billion in 1994, respectively. As the joint outcome of lower capital inflows and higher current account deficits both countries recorded reductions in their reserves in 1994 for the first time in the 1990s. In Argentina, because of its currency board regime, falling reserves induced contractionary monetary effects even before the Tequila effect triggered the crisis.

IV.1.5 The Tequila effect

The initial turbulence generated by the Mexican devaluation affected Latin America and other more distant markets for some time. But after a relatively brief period, the economies of Chile and Colombia did not register further perturbations. In the case of Brazil, the abrupt balance-of-payments effects of the Real Plan had already placed the economy in a fragile external position and in the first half of 1995 the country had capital outflows. Nevertheless, Brazil had abundant reserves and the turbulence only brought about a deceleration in growth.[17]

In contrast, the Tequila crisis hit Argentina with full force. The contagion effect in this episode appears to be a continuation of the common trends mentioned above and was associated with the similarities of the Mexican and Argentine macroeconomic situations. In Argentina, the Mexican crisis triggered a financial crisis and a strong outflow of private capital in the first half of 1995 – partially compensated for, as in Mexico, by the increase in the public external debt. Both economies experienced deep recessions. In 1995 GDP contracted by 6.6 per cent in Mexico and by 2.8 per cent in Argentina. Both countries' 1995 unemployment rates doubled those of 1993.

V SYNTHESIS AND CONCLUSIONS

Latin American macroeconomic experience in the 1990s was similar in some key aspects to that of the 1970s. The combined effects of liberalization and opening of financial markets, massive capital inflows, trade opening, and exchange-rate appreciation generated growing external and financial fragility. Economies became prone to perverse financial cycles and vulnerable to changes in international conditions. The similarity with the experience of the 1970s is closest in the cases of Mexico and Argentina. They showed strong parallels between the real, financial and external developments of the 1991–94 period and the initial expansionary phase of the Southern Cone experiments. This parallelism was specifically related to the role exchange rate policy and capital inflows were intended to play in the two countries' macroeconomic programs and with respect to the goal of achieving full integration with international financial markets. Capital inflows were encouraged through various means (including complete deregulation) but policy was predominantly passive with respect to their domestic monetary and financial effects.

There were, however, some differences compared to the 1970s, particularly the fact that fiscal policy was less expansionary and benefited from the proceeds generated by the privatization of public enterprises. Moreover, in the case of Argentina the financial system's regulatory framework was much better than in the 1970s and required banks to maintain levels of reserves well above the international average. The better health of its banks contributed to save Argentina from a final debacle *à la* Mexico but it did not spare it from having to ask for a multilateral rescue package to stop a capital outflow that was depleting deposits and international reserves. In the end, smaller fiscal deficits as compared to the 1980s seem only to have influenced the timing of the crisis, but not its eventual outbreak.

In effect, in the Southern Cone experiences the turning point was reached in a shorter time via domestic financial developments. For this reason, the real dimension of the cycle was mainly a reflection of the financial cycle. The expansionary phase of the financial cycle lasted longer in the Mexican and Argentine experiences in the 1990s, giving rise to deeper and longer-lasting real effects of the combination of trade opening and exchange rate appreciation.[18]

The analysis we presented above highlights the 1994 increase in the international interest rate as the external factor which triggered the change of trends in capital inflows and reserves observed that year in Mexico and Argentina. Obviously, this increase is not comparable in magnitude and duration to the 1979 increase. Besides, its incidence on external fragility took a different form because of the distinct external financing mechanisms that predominated in the 1970s and the 1990s. Floating-rate bank credit predominated in the 1970s, so that the increase in the international interest rate affected external fragility mainly by raising the current account deficit. Bond debt predominated in the 1990s but also, because of the implementation of the Brady debt-restructurings, there was a drop in the percentage of debt paying market interest rates both in Mexico and in Argentina. In this context, the increase in the international interest rate affected external fragility mainly by reducing capital inflows and augmenting the country-risk premium, and not so much by increasing the average interest rate paid. Thus, whereas in the 1970s the current account was more sensitive to variations in the international interest rate, in the 1990s it was less sensitive (until late in the decade) but capital flows were more volatile.

Lastly, let us consider the comparison between Mexico and Argentina and the countries showing more robust paths. It is clear that the different performances could not be exclusively explained by the elements examined in this chapter. With this caveat in mind, the above analysis suggests two types of factors differentiating the countries' performances.

First, differences in macroeconomic policy stand out, particularly regarding the exchange rate. Greater fragility is associated with more exchange rate appreciation whose degree, in turn, is related to the nature of the exchange rate regimes and monetary policies adopted by the different countries. The other important difference lies in the conception that ruled the interaction between the domestic financial system and the international capital markets. Both aspects appear to be associated, so that policies relating to the capital account are congruent with a country's macroeconomic orientation. Mexico and Argentina implemented an unrestricted opening of the capital account. In contrast, the countries that attempted to preserve some monetary and financial autonomy (like Chile and Colombia) implemented regulatory norms aimed at cushioning the capital flows and influencing their composition.[19] These policies seem to have reduced the volatility generated by short-term flows, even if they were not able to filter all 'speculative' capital movements.

NOTES

* This chapter draws on Roberto Frenkel (1998), 'Capital market liberalization and economic performance in Latin America', *Working Paper Series III, Working Paper No. 1*, CEPA, New School University. The authors are grateful to two anonymous referees for their helpful comments.

1. There is surely no cause for objection in the case of Argentina, although there could be in the case of Chile. The most commonly told story about the path of reforms there sees the process as a somewhat continuous sequence in which the first steps were completed in the 1970s. In this narrative the external and financial crisis of the 1980s and its real consequences have secondary significance and do not represent a discontinuity. Chile was certainly the country in Latin America that most preserved the reforms implemented in the 1970s during and after the crisis. Therefore, the point is debatable. However, there is no room in this chapter for a detailed analysis of Chile's history. For our purposes, the Chilean crisis in the 1980s closes a period whose performance can be evaluated by itself. With this, we do nothing more than recover the perspective from which the Southern Cone experiments were observed in the years following the debt crisis. The story mentioned above was constructed later on in the late 1980s, when Chile was deemed the prime LA example of the Washington Consensus's success. See Williamson (1990), Fanelli *et al.* (1992a), World Bank (1991) and Fanelli *et al.* (1992b).
2. Cases in which liberalization has not been followed by massive capital inflows are rare but do exist. Bolivia, in the second half of the 1980s, did not receive private inflows despite having deregulated and fully opened its financial markets in 1985. There are cases in both the 1970s and the 1990s of significant capital inflows without major liberalization measures. Brazil is the most important example in both periods.
3. Chile and Colombia, for different reasons, were cases of minimal transfers abroad. In Colombia, this was because its external debt was relatively small. Chile showed the highest regional debt/GDP ratio but its transfers were minimal because it received a relatively greater proportion of multilateral support. See Damill *et al.* (1994).

4. The relatively deeper development of Chile's financial system in the late 1980s makes it a relevant exception to this observation. Chile did not undergo inflation rates of the order registered in the biggest economies and its macroeconomic performance was stable in the second half of the 1980s. Colombia's macroeconomic performance was also stable, but its financial system was small and poorly diversified.
5. The tariff reduction schedules were considered rapid at the time. They would be perceived as gradualist under the current conventional criteria.
6. In Argentina the fiscal direct cost of the post-crisis bailout is estimated at $5 billion (at that time the private external debt was $14 billion.) In Chile the issue of public domestic debt to finance the bailout amounted to one third of GDP. See Damill *et al.* (1994).
7. We presented a formal model in Frenkel (1983). It is sketched in Williamson (1983) and restated by Taylor (1991).
8. Neoclassical models based on different 'adjustment speeds' of the trade and capital accounts following a simultaneous trade and financial opening were constructed to interpret the cycle. These models replicated the initial expansionary phase but neither the contractionary one nor the crisis. See Edwards (1984). The symmetry of neoclassical models suggested a second phase in which downward price flexibility could correct exchange rate appreciation and the current acount deficit, leading the economy to a new equilibrium. There was no such deflation in the cases we are considering here. In addition to the complete implausibility of a deflation of the size and velocity that would be necessary to re-equilibrate the current account, these models ignored financial relations. In the financial system, there is no symmetry between the expansionary and contractionary phases. In any case, the supposed deflation would aggravate the liquidity and insolvency problems that characterize the contractionary phase.
9. See McKinnon (1982).
10. Liberalizing and opening capital markets only after the economy is stabilized, open to trade and financially robust is precisely the recommendation of the 'sequencing' literature, developed in the 1980s after the evaluation of the Southern Cone experiments, among other cases. These orthodox prescriptions were lost along the roads to the Washington Consensus as actually applied. See Edwards (1984) and McKinnon (1991).
11. The following discussion draws on Frenkel (1995).
12. Some capital flow regulations were implemented in Brazil after the launching of the Real Plan according to the changing circumstances of capital flows. However, the set of exchange, monetary and capital account policies resembles those of Argentina and Mexico more than those of Chile and Colombia.
13. Mexico and Argentina, on the one hand, and Chile and Colombia, on the other, entered the 1990s with different economic realities and varying degrees of freedom to define their policies. Chile and Colombia had stabilized their economies in the mid-1980s and were growing at relatively high rates in the second half of the decade. It is understandable that their macroeconomic policies were oriented in the direction of preserving stability in the face of capital inflows. In contrast, Mexico had only recently implemented its stabilization program while Argentina began in 1991. Both programs used a fixed exchange rate as the main 'anchor' for inflation. Their sustainability depended fundamentally on continuing capital inflows.
14. Even though financing a current account deficit with FDI is clearly preferable to other more volatile sources, the long-term contribution of FDI flows to the balance of payments should not be overestimated. First, the growing presence of multinational firms is usually associated with a permanent increase in the level of imports. Second, the rate of reinvestment of profits can fall drastically after a first period of rapid expansion, particularly during a recession which depresses 'animal spirits', leading to an increase in profit remittances, even in the context of a recession. In essence, insofar as FDI requires a risk premium with respect to the rate of return on external debt, its servicing should likely be more expensive, even if it is more desirable because of its lower volatility.
15. In some countries with even less basis in terms of 'fundamentals'.
16. In some cases the correlations are indeed paradoxical. Thus, the rise in oil prices, which should have improved expectations about the Mexican economy, was associated with a

decrease in that country's asset prices. What convoluted argument can justify such behavior?

17. Though, as mentioned before, Brazil was finally forced to give up its exchange-rate regime in January 1999, after a period of very strong pressures against the Real following the Russian crisis in August.
18. Emerging out of a very deep recession in 1990, Argentina's GDP grew swiftly in the early 1990s. Instead, Mexico's slow growth suggests that depressing real effects were important from the beginning of the 1990s. We have already mentioned that trade opening and exchange rate appreciation had been operating in this case for some years beforehand. See Fanelli and Frenkel (1999) on Argentina and Dornbusch and Werner (1994) and Ros (1995) on Mexico.
19. Brazil is an intermediate case. It turned restrictions on and off applying selective taxes to limit short-term capital inflows.

REFERENCES

Amadeo, Edward (1996), 'The knife-edge of exchange-rate-based stabilization: impact on growth, employment and wages', *UNCTAD Review*, Geneva.

Balassa, Bela, G.M. Bueno, P.P. Kuczynsky and M. Simonsen (1986), *Toward Renewed Economic Growth in Latin America*, Washington DC: Institute for International Economics.

Damill, Mario, José María Fanelli and Roberto Frenkel (1994), *Shock Externo y Desequilibrio Fiscal: La Macroeconomía de América Latina en los Ochenta*, Santiago de Chile: CEPAL.

Damill, Mario, José María Fanelli and Roberto Frenkel (1996), 'De México a México: el desempeño de América Latina en los noventa', *Desarrollo Económico*, special issue, vol. 36, Buenos Aires.

Dornbusch, Rudiger and Alejandro Werner (1994), 'Mexico: stabilization, reform and no growth', *Brookings Papers on Economic Activity*, vol. I.

Edwards, Sebastián (1984), 'The order of liberalization of the balance of payments', *World Bank Staff Working Papers*, No. 710.

Fanelli, José María, Roberto Frenkel and Guillermo Rozenwurcel (1992a), 'Growth and structural reform in Latin America. Where do we stand?', in A. A. Zini Jr. (ed.), *The Market and the State in Economic Development in the 90s*, New York: North Holland.

Fanelli, José María, Roberto Frenkel and Lance Taylor (1992b), 'The world development report 1991: a critical assessment', in *International Monetary and Financial Issues for the 1990s*, UNCTAD, New York: United Nations.

Fanelli, José María, and Roberto Frenkel (1993), 'On gradualism, shock treatment and sequencing', in *International and Financial Issues for the 90s*, vol II, United Nations.

Fanelli, José María, and Roberto Frenkel (1999), 'The Argentine experience with stabilization and structural reform', in Lance Taylor (ed.), *After Neoliberalism: What Next for Latin America*, Ann Arbor, MI: University of Michigan Press.

Frenkel, Roberto (1983), 'Mercado financiero, expectativas cambiarias y movimientos de capital', *El Trimestre Económico*, No. 200, Mexico.

Frenkel, Roberto (1995), 'Macroeconomic sustainability and development prospects: Latin American performance in the 1990s', *UNCTAD Discussion Papers*, No. 100, Geneva.

Frenkel, Roberto (1997), 'New Prospects for Latin American development', in Roy Culpeper *et al.*, *Global Development Fifty Years After Bretton Woods: Essays in Honour of Gerald K. Helleiner*, Basingstoke, UK: Macmillan.

Frenkel, Roberto and Martín González Rozada (1999), 'Apertura comercial, productividad y empleo en Argentina', in Víctor E. Tokman and Daniel Martínez (eds) *Productividad y Empleo en la Apertura Económica*, Lima, Peru: OIT Oficina Internacional del Trabajo.

Krueger, Anne O. (1986), 'Problems of liberalization', in M. Armeani, A.M. Choksi and D. Papageorgiou (eds), *Economic Liberalization In Developing Countries*, London: Basil Blackwell.

McKinnon, Ronald (1982), 'The order of economic liberalization: lessons from Chile and Argentina', *Carnegie-Rochester Conference Series on Public Policy, 17.*

McKinnon, Ronald (1991), *The Order of Economic Liberalization. Financial Control in the Transition to a Market Economy*, London: Johns Hopkins University Press.

Minsky, Hyman P. (1986), *Stabilizing an Unstable Economy*, New Haven CT: Yale University Press.

Ros, Jaime (1995), 'Trade liberalization with real appreciation and slow growth: sustainability issues in Mexico's trade policy reform', in G.K. Helleiner (ed.), *Trade Policy and Industrialization in Turbulent Times*, London and New York: Routledge.

Taylor, Lance (1991), *Income Distribution, Inflation and Growth*, Cambridge, Massachusetts: MIT Press.

Tokman, Víctor and Daniel Martínez (1997), 'Costo laboral y competitividad en el sector manufacturero de América Latina', in Edward Amadeo *et al.*, *Costos laborales y competitividad industrial en América Latina*, Peru: OIT.

Williamson, John (1983), *The Open Economy and the World Economy*, New York: Basic Books.

Williamson, John (1990), 'What Washington means by policy reform', in John Williamson (ed.) *Latin American Adjustment: How Much has Happened?*, Washington DC: Institute for International Economics.

World Bank (1991), *The World Development Report 1991: The Challenge of Development*, Washington DC: World Bank.

12. Inflation, stabilization and growth: multiple equilibria in a structuralist model

Jaime Ros*

A major feature of Latin America's economic performance in the 1990s has been the resumption of economic growth, at an overall modest pace and with a variety of performances across countries. A growing literature addresses the role that macroeconomic stabilization has had in this growth recovery and by now a wide consensus exists that stabilization has been an important factor, if not the major factor in some cases, behind economic recovery.[1] A gap in this literature, however, is that the reverse causation going from growth to macroeconomic stability has been largely absent from the analysis. This chapter presents a growth model in the tradition of Taylor's structuralist macroeconomics in which inflation stabilization results in a shift from a bad equilibrium with slow growth and high inflation to a high level equilibrium with low inflation and faster growth. The basic point of the model is that stabilization can trigger a virtuous circle of investment recovery, capital inflows and real currency appreciation which in turn strengthens the stabilization process. The triggering factor may be a heterodox price and wage freeze, a fiscal adjustment, a revival of animal spirits and private capital inflows or the resumption of international lending to the public sector. Usually more than one factor had a role; for example, fiscal adjustment followed by a recovery of international lending as in Chile in the mid-1980s, heterodox stabilization accompanied by debt relief as in Mexico in the late 1980s, or heterodox stabilization based on monetary reform together with fiscal adjustment as in Brazil in mid-1994 (see Chapter 10 by Bacha in this volume).

The chapter contains four sections. The first shows the stylized facts on stabilization and growth in the 1990s. The second and third present the analytical framework. The final section applies this framework to examine the effects of stabilization.

Table 12.1 *Growth and inflation performance in Latin America and the Caribbean*

	GDP growth (% per year)			Inflation (% per year)			
Group	1981–90	1991–99	change	1985–90	Average 1991–99	1999	Countries
1	−0.8	4.1	4.9	3301.7	9.4*	3.3	Arg, Bol, Nic, Per
2	1.8	4.1	2.3	35.5	9.5	5.4	Chi, Dom, Sal, Gua, Mex, Par
3	0.7	2.5	1.8	8.3	10.3	5.9	Bar, CRica, Haiti, Hon, Pan, Tri
4	1.2	2.4	1.2	209.2	141.4	19.0	Bra, Col, Ecu, Uru, Ven
Mean	0.8	3.3	2.4	691.2	41.6	8.4	

Note: * 1992–99 for Argentina and Nicaragua; 1993–99 for Peru (see Appendix).

Source: See Appendix.

1 INFLATION AND GROWTH PERFORMANCE

Table 12.1 summarizes the experience of inflation and growth in the 1980s and 1990s in four groups of Latin American and Caribbean countries. The first group is characterized by dramatic stabilizations as these countries successfully brought inflation under control in the 1990s starting from very high levels (three digits or more) in the second half of the 1980s. In fact, each of the four countries included in this group experienced a hyperinflation at some stage. Group 2 includes countries with more gradual stabilizations or, more precisely, that successfully stabilized starting from medium levels of inflation (above 20 per cent and below three-digit levels). Group 3 includes a significant number of countries where inflation was on average below 20 per cent in both the latter half of the 1980s and the 1990s; that is, this is a group of stable countries where inflation did not get out of control in the 1980s. Finally, group 4 includes countries that failed to stabilize (until late in the 1990s), that is, countries that continued to feature high or medium levels of inflation during most of the 1990s and/or recorded a worsening of inflation performance from the latter half of the 1980s to the

1990s. By the end of the 1990s, however, inflation in this group had also been brought under control.

As shown in the table, the main improvements in growth performance in the 1990s are largely concentrated in the first two country groups. The difference in inflation performance in the 1980s, much worse in the first group than in the second, probably explains the very significant difference in growth performance during that period – with group 2 having a growth rate 2.6 percentage points higher than group 1. As both groups of countries successfully stabilized in the 1990s, their growth rates tended to converge, at 4.1 per cent per year. But since the initial conditions were much worse in the first group, the change in growth performance was much larger in this group (4.9 versus 2.3 percentage points in group 2).

This comparison between groups 1 and 2 points to the adverse effects of high inflation on growth during the 1980s and the positive role of stabilization in the resumption of growth in the 1990s. This role is also clearly revealed in the comparison between groups 2 and 4. While in the 1980s these two groups of economies grew at not too dissimilar rates (1.8 per cent vs. 1.2 per cent per year), their performances clearly diverged in the 1990s when a difference of 1.7 percentage points (4.1 versus 2.4) emerged in their growth rates. This difference is even greater if one includes Haiti, a borderline case between groups 3 and 4, in group 4.[2]

Certainly, not all of the increase in the growth rate can be explained by the reduction of inflation. There was a clear improvement in the GDP growth rate across *all* groups of countries, including group 3 of countries where inflation never went out of control in the 1980s and, as already mentioned, group 4 of failed stabilizations. Yet this improvement is rather modest: the average increase in the growth rate, excluding groups 1 and 2, is 1.5 percentage points.

2 THE ANALYTICAL FRAMEWORK

The analytical framework, in the tradition of structuralist macroeconomics, is a streamlined version of Ros (1994) which in turn draws on and extends the gap model presented in Taylor (1991). An important difference with Ros (1994) refers to the model closure. Instead of having public investment endogenously adjusting to preserve balance of payments equilibrium, the model presented here has a variable real exchange rate. The motivation for this change is that we want to capture the real appreciation of the domestic currency that has been so fundamental to the stabilization process in the Latin American region.

Savings and Investment

The economy considered has three sectors: private, government and foreign, indicated in what follows by subscripts P, G and F respectively. Consider first the savings–investment identity:

$$i = i_G + i_P = s_G + s_P + s_F \tag{12.1}$$

where i refers to investment and s to savings and all variables are expressed as a fraction of potential output (Q). Private and public savings as a fraction of potential output are:

$$s_P = s(1-t)\,u \tag{12.2}$$

$$s_G = tu - c_G \tag{12.3}$$

where u is capacity utilization (GDP/Q), s is the propensity to save out of private disposable income, t represents tax revenues as a fraction of GDP, and c_G is public consumption (as a fraction of potential output). We neglect, for simplicity, interest payments on public debt as part of government expenditure and private or foreign sector income.[3]

Private investment (i_P, expressed as a fraction of potential output) is assumed to be a function of expected profitability – determined by profit margins and capacity utilization[4] – as well as of the inflation rate:

$$i_P = i_0 + \alpha u - \beta p, \qquad \alpha,\ \beta > 0 \tag{12.4}$$

where the constant term i_0 captures the effects of interest rates and profit margins on investment. The justification for including capacity utilization in the investment function is as follows. We can think of the economy as a continuum of sectors some of which, at a given point in time, will have a higher than desired utilization of capacity, and a positive marginal profit rate, while others have a lower than desired capacity utilization, and a zero marginal profit rate. As average capacity utilization increases, the fraction of sectors with higher than desired utilization increases, with a favorable effect on the overall marginal profit rate and investment. Differences across sectors in the short-run income elasticity of demand are a sufficient condition for aggregate demand to have differential effects on sectoral capacity utilization.

There is considerable empirical evidence supporting the hypothesis that inflation has adverse effects on investment and growth.[5] Possible reasons for these negative effects include the following. First, high inflation tends to make long-term financial contracts disappear and has resource misallocation effects associated to the greater price variability and uncertainty about future returns. Second, in the absence of full financial indexation, inflation leads to the premature amortization of business sector liabilities which is a consequence of higher nominal interest rates and results in an increase in effective financial costs. Finally, the greater uncertainty on expected real interest rates and exchange rates, especially in the absence of indexation, stimulates capital flight and, to the extent that foreign assets and domestic investment are substitutes, has a negative effect on private investment. This effect can operate either through the higher interest rate necessary to retain capital in the home economy, or at parity of interest rates, through increased private capital flight.

There are also good reasons and some empirical evidence for the view that the relationship between inflation and investment is non-linear (see, in particular, Bruno and Easterly, 1998). On the one hand, the negative effects of inflation on investment operate only after a certain threshold level of inflation has been reached: low inflation may not be a serious obstacle to investment and growth while medium and high inflation can have more than proportionate adverse effects. On the other hand, at very high inflation rates, when investment has already collapsed and/or the economy has developed mechanisms of protection against the effects of inflation, further increases in the inflation rate are unlikely to have large effects on investment. This implies that in equation (12.4), coefficient β changes with the level of inflation, being small at both low and high inflation rates and large at intermediate levels of inflation.

The Foreign Exchange Market

Consider now the balance of payments identity. Setting the change in international reserves equal to zero, it becomes the equilibrium condition in the foreign exchange market stating the equality between the current account deficit (or foreign savings, s_F) and the capital account surplus:

$$s_F = d_P + d_G \tag{12.5}$$

where d_P and d_G are respectively the inflows of foreign capital to the private and public sectors. Again, all variables are expressed as a fraction of potential output.

The current account deficit increases with capacity utilization (as higher utilization rates reduce exports and increase imports) and decreases with the real exchange rate (e, which stimulates net exports):

$$s_F = mu - fe \qquad m, f > 0 \tag{12.6}$$

where, for simplicity, we neglect factor services in the current account. External public borrowing (d_G) is exogenous. Yet, below a maximum level (d_P^*), private net capital inflows are endogenous, since the private sector budget constraint links private savings, asset demands and private investment. Neglecting the net acquisition of domestic financial assets, usually a small fraction of output, the change in net foreign assets held by the private sector must add up to its financial surplus ($s_P - i_P$). Private capital inflows are thus determined as:

$$d_P = i_P - s_P \qquad \text{for } d_P < d_P^* \tag{12.7}$$

Thus, while the government is rationed in foreign credit markets and public external indebtedness is exogenous, private capital inflows are endogenous. This treatment seems more appropriate for developing countries with substantial capital flight and capital repatriation in the recent past than the assumption of fully exogenous capital inflows, present in two-gap and most three-gap models where credit rationing applies to both the government and private sectors.[6]

Inflation

The inflation equation is derived from the price–cost identity, assuming a constant mark-up over labor and import costs, a wage inflation Phillips curve and given indexation mechanisms for wages and the exchange rate:

$$p = \pi_0 + \pi_1 u + \pi_2 e \qquad \pi_0, \pi_1, \pi_2 > 0 \tag{12.8}$$

The current inflation rate can then be seen as determined by an inertial component (π_0, the inflation rate in some base period) plus the effects of demand shocks (reflected in u) and real exchange rate shocks. Coefficients π_1 and π_2 in the equation reflect the labor and imports shares in domestic production (and the response of wages to capacity utilization), as well as the wage and exchange rate indexation mechanisms. The greater and faster their adjustment to current inflation, the higher these coefficients and, thus, the higher current inflation itself relative to its base period value.

Growth Rate of Potential Output

The model is completed with the definition of the growth rate of potential output which in the medium-term equilibrium path, characterized by a constant utilization rate, must be equal to the GDP growth rate (g). Thus:

$$g = v\,i, \tag{12.9}$$

where v is the incremental output–capital ratio and $i = i_G + i_P$.

Model Closure

To close the model, either the real exchange rate or public investment has to be taken as given. Ros (1994) adopted the first closure; public investment is then endogenously determined so as to achieve external balance. Here, we shall take public investment as given, as one of the key features of the process of inflation stabilization we are interested in is precisely the real appreciation of the domestic currency. Here then, the real exchange rate is endogenous and moves to clear the foreign exchange market.

The model can be simplified into a four-equation system. Substituting from the domestic savings functions (equations 12.2 and 12.3) and the current account deficit (equation 12.6) into the savings–investment identity and solving for u, we obtain the level of capacity utilization that clears the goods market. This is an increasing function of private investment and the real exchange rate (which increases net exports) as well as of the exogenous level of public spending ($c_G + i_G$):

$$u = z\,(c_G + i_G + i_P + fe) \qquad z = 1/[s(1-t) + t + m] \tag{12.10}$$

Substituting from the current account equation (12.6) into equation (12.5) yields a balance of payments equilibrium equation with u, e and d_P as endogenous variables:

$$mu - fe = d_G + d_P \tag{12.11}$$

Substituting from the private savings function into equation (12.7) shows private capital inflows as an increasing function of private investment and a negative function of capacity utilization:

$$d_P = i_P - s\,(1-t)\,u \tag{12.12}$$

Finally, substituting from the inflation equation into the private investment function yields:

$$i_P = i_0 - \beta\pi_0 + (\alpha - \beta\pi_1)\,u - \beta\pi_2 e \tag{12.13}$$

Equation (12.13) shows that capacity utilization has two opposite effects on private investment: an accelerator effect operating through parameter α, and a negative indirect effect arising from the fact that a higher degree of capacity utilization raises the inflation rate (parameter $\beta\pi_1$), which in turn has a negative effect on private investment. On the other hand, a higher real exchange rate has a contractionary effect on private investment (given u) due to its positive effect on the inflation rate.

The model can be simplified further by noting that equations (12.10), (12.11) and (12.12) imply together the budget constraint of the government sector:

$$c_G + i_G = tu + d_G \tag{12.14}$$

Thus in the model, capacity utilization adjusts to meet the government budget constraint given the values of public spending and government's external indebtedness. These variables, together with the tax rate, fully determine the equilibrium value of capacity utilization regardless of the values of other exogenous variables and parameters (including the private investment and net exports function).[7] Let u^* in what follows be this equilibrium value of capacity utilization. From (12.14):

$$u^* = (c_G + i_G - d_G)/t \tag{12.14'}$$

Equations (12.10) to (12.14) determine four unknowns: u, e, i_P and d_P. These variables determine the equilibrium growth path of the economy consistent with external balance and a constant level of capacity utilization. The key adjustment mechanisms in the model are the degree of capacity utilization which changes in the face of disequilibrium in the goods market and the real exchange rate which adjusts to preserve equilibrium in the foreign exchange market.

3 DEMAND CONSTRAINTS ON THE RATE OF GROWTH

The model is subject to two inequalities. Current output cannot be persistently above productive capacity (u must be less than or equal to one) and private capital inflows cannot be larger than the level d_P^*. We shall assume here that capacity utilization never reaches its maximum level and focus on the medium-term paths in which growth is demand-constrained. When $d_P = d_P^*$, the economy is said to be under a foreign exchange constraint; when $d_P < d_P^*$, the economy operates under an investment constraint.

The Foreign Exchange Constraint

When private capital inflows reach their maximum value, investment will be constrained by the level of domestic savings forthcoming at the less than full capacity level of output and by the (now exogenous) level of foreign savings. This model closure amounts to dropping the private investment function and introducing a foreign credit constraint on private investment. Substituting from (12.14) into (12.12) and setting $d_P = d_P^*$ yields the corresponding rate of private investment:

$$i_P = s(1-t)u^* + d_P^* \tag{12.15}$$

Substituting from (12.14) into (12.11) and setting $d_P = d_P^*$, yields the equilibrium real exchange rate:

$$e = (mu^* - d_G - d_P^*)/f \tag{12.16}$$

The resulting growth rate is here constrained by foreign exchange, with resource utilization and domestic savings being below their potential values due to the inelasticity of capital inflows. In this sense, the model resembles a conventional two-gap model with a binding foreign exchange constraint, except for the fact that the real exchange rate is here an endogenous variable.

The properties of this model closure can be illustrated by some simple comparative static exercises (see equation 12.14′). An increase in public investment has the effect of increasing the equilibrium level of capacity utilization. This stimulates private investment as the domestic savings constraint on investment is relaxed and causes a real depreciation (see equation 12.16) as the current account deficit deteriorates at the initial level of the real exchange rate.[8]

An increase in public external indebtedness causes a downward adjustment in u^* (see equation 12.14′). The reason is that the larger capital inflows do not lead the government to increase spending while, at the same time, they cause a currency appreciation that has adverse effects on net exports and output. The real exchange rate falls to the extent necessary to preserve the government's budget constraint. The effect on private investment is negative as private savings fall following the lower equilibrium level of capacity utilization.

Larger private capital inflows also cause a real appreciation (see equation 12.16): the real exchange rate must fall to generate a larger current account deficit that matches the larger capital inflows (note that since equilibrium capacity utilization remains constant, this is the only way in which the current account deficit can increase). Unlike the previous case, the effect on private investment is now positive as the larger capital inflows relax the credit constraints on private investment.

Finally an increase in public investment financed by larger public external indebtedness (an increase in i_G and d_G by the same amount) leaves equilibrium capacity utilization unaffected. Private investment remains constant and the real exchange rate falls, as balance of payments equilibrium requires a larger current account deficit in the face of a larger capital account surplus.

The Investment Constraint

When capital inflows remain below their maximum value, the model, as shown in section 1, yields equilibrium values for private investment and the growth rate. The equilibrium values of private investment and the real exchange rate are derived as follows. Substituting from (12.14) into (12.13) we obtain an IS locus of (i_P, e) combinations along which the goods market clears. The locus slopes downwards due to the effects of the real exchange rate on inflation and the adverse effects of inflation on private investment:

$$i_P = i_0 - \beta\pi_0 + (\alpha - \beta\pi_1)\, u^* - \beta\pi_2 e \tag{12.17}$$

Substituting from (12.14) and (12.12) into (12.11) we obtain a BP locus along which the balance of payments is in equilibrium. The BP line also slopes downwards: an increase in private investment improves the capital account in the balance of payments, and a fall in the real exchange rate, which raises the current account deficit, is required to maintain external balance:

$$i_P = [s(1-t) + m]u^* - d_G - fe \tag{12.18}$$

The determination of the equilibrium levels of private investment and the real exchange rate is illustrated in Figure 12.1. The resulting growth rate can be said to be investment-constrained as both domestic savings, due to the underutilization of resources, and private capital inflows are below their maximum or potential levels. In contrast to two-gap models, the origin of resource underutilization is not the lack of foreign exchange but rather a too-low level of investment which may arise, in particular, from a low level of public investment or from a high inflation rate exerting depressive effects on private investment.

Stability in the foreign exchange market requires $f > \beta\pi_2$ and thus an IS which is flatter than the BP line.[9] Assuming this condition to be fulfilled, together with the absence of strong accelerator effects of capacity utilization on private investment ($\alpha < s(1-t) + m + \beta\pi_1$), consider the effects of a change in public investment and public external indebtedness. The effects on the real exchange rate are similar to those in the economy with a foreign exchange constraint and for the same reasons: an increase in public investment leads to a real depreciation (as equilibrium capacity utilization

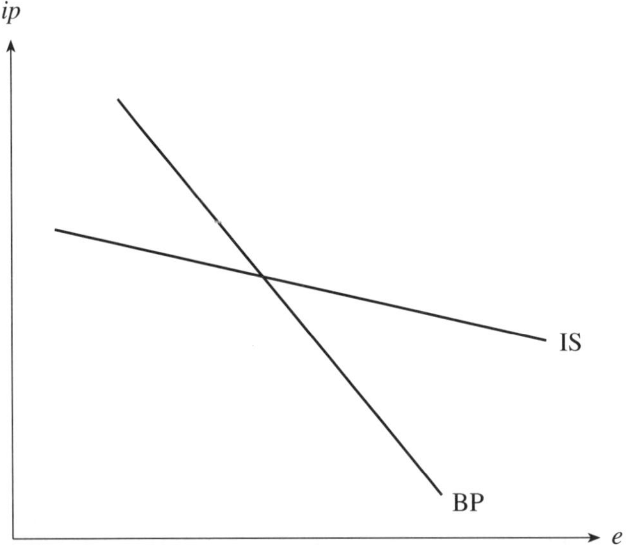

Figure 12.1 The investment constraint on growth

increases and the current account deteriorates) and an increase in external public indebtedness leads to real appreciation as the capital account surplus improves. However, the effects on private investment are now ambiguous. A higher level of public investment raises capacity utilization and inflation (because equilibrium utilization and the real exchange rate both increase). The effect on capacity utilization tends to increase private investment while the effect on inflation tends to reduce it. Depending on the strength of these two effects, the overall effect may be to increase or reduce the level of private investment. Analogously, a higher level of external public indebtedness reduces capacity utilization and inflation as it causes real appreciation. The overall effect on private investment may be positive or negative.

4 STABILIZATION AND GROWTH

As mentioned in the introduction, within the recent literature that examines the effects of economic reform on growth performance in Latin America, there seems to be a consensus that successful macroeconomic stabilization has been a major factor behind the resumption of growth in the 1990s. This is why, as discussed in the first section, among the 'success stories' of the 1990s we find countries such as Argentina and Peru, that, starting from hyperinflation at the end of the 1980s, managed to stabilize and bring inflation under control. We turn now to an analysis of the interactions between stabilization and growth using the framework presented in the previous section.

The upper section of Figure 12.2 shows the investment constraint closure of the model with the current account deficit (s_F) and the capital account surplus ($d = d_P + d_G$) of the balance of payments in the vertical axis and rate of inflation in the horizontal axis. The equation relating the current account deficit and inflation (the $s_F - p$ line) is obtained by substituting from equation (12.14) into (12.6) and using equation (12.8) to eliminate e from (12.6). This yields:

$$s_F = f\,\pi_0/\pi_2 + (m + \pi_1/\pi_2)\,u^* - (f/\pi_2)\,p \qquad (12.19)$$

The explanation for the negative slope of this line is straightforward: a lower current account deficit requires a higher real exchange rate which in turn generates higher inflation.

The equation relating the capital account surplus and inflation ($d-p$ curve) is derived using (12.14) and substituting from equation (12.4) into (12.12). This yields:

$$d = i_0 - [s(1-t) - \alpha]\,u^* + d_G - \beta p \qquad d = d_P + d_G \qquad (12.20)$$

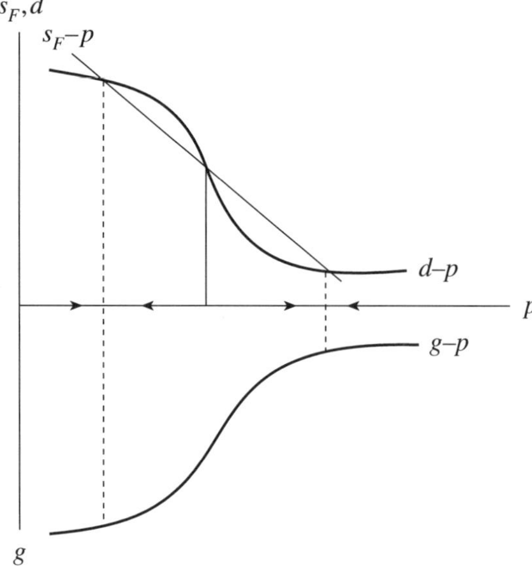

Figure 12.2 Growth, inflation and the balance of payments

The schedule slopes downwards: a higher inflation rate inhibits private investment and stimulates capital flight thus reducing the capital account surplus. Given the non-linear relationship between inflation and investment, the d−p curve is relatively flat at low and very high inflation levels and rather steep in between. These non-linearities make the growth–inflation curve ($g-p$ curve) in the lower part of Figure 12.2 also to be non-linear. The equation of the $g-p$ curve is obtained from substitution from (12.14) into the private investment function and then using the definition of the growth rate:

$$g = v(i_0 + i_G + \alpha u^* - \beta p) \qquad (12.21)$$

The non-linearities of the $d-p$ curve generate the possibility of multiple equilibria, as shown in Figure 12.2. Assuming that the real exchange rate (and thus the rate of inflation) increases when the overall balance of payments is in deficit (and thus $s_F > d$) and falls when it is in surplus ($d > s_F$), two of the three equilibria – with respectively high growth and low inflation and low growth and high inflation – are stable, while the equilibrium with intermediate inflation and growth is unstable. Of the two stable equilibria, the one with high growth features a large current account deficit while the one with low growth features a small current account deficit.[10] Inflation and investment interact with each other in the stable equilibria. In the bad equilibrium, for example, a low level of investment implies a small capital account surplus which, for balance of payments equilibrium, requires a small current account deficit and thus a relatively high real exchange rate. This generates a high inflation rate which contributes to keep investment low.

In this framework the period of low growth, high inflation and large current account surpluses following the debt crisis of the 1980s can be interpreted as a result of the move from a high-level to a low-level equilibrium. The contraction of public external indebtedness after 1982 shifted the $d-p$ curve inwards and the s_F-p line outwards, leading to sharp real devaluations, an acceleration of inflation and a growth slowdown. In this view, high inflation and low growth were both the outcome of a negative shock to foreign capital flows and interacted with each other, keeping the economy in a low-level equilibrium.

Consider now an economy suffering from high inflation and low growth, the situation at the end of the 1980s in many Latin American economies. An economy in this bad equilibrium can move to a high-level equilibrium with high growth and low inflation in four different ways (and combinations thereof). A contraction of public spending and an increase in public external indebtedness both reduce equilibrium capacity utilization (u^*) and thus shift the $s_F - p$ line inwards and the $d - p$ curve outwards. This tends to reduce the hold of the low-level trap and can make the bad equilibrium disappear. The mechanism is the fall in the current account deficit (plus the increase in the capital account surplus in the case of an increase in d_G) which appreciates the domestic currency with favorable stabilization and growth effects that mutually reinforce each other.

A fall in the constant term in the inflation equation (π_0) resulting from, for example, a coordinated wage and price freeze shifts the $s_F - p$ line inwards and can also make the bad equilibrium disappear. Here the fall in inflation does not *initially* involve a real appreciation and the positive effects on private investment follow thus directly from the lower inflation rate. Afterwards, the higher growth rate finances itself, so to speak: the higher private investment generates capital inflows which further reduce the inflation rate (through real appreciation) with positive effects on investment. Similar effects follow from a revival of animal spirits (an increase in the constant term i_0 in the investment function) which shifts the $d - p$ curve outwards. The increase in i_0 raises private capital inflows, appreciating the domestic currency, reducing inflation and raising private investment.

In all these cases, the economy moves towards a high growth-cum-low inflation path through self reinforcing processes between stabilization, which stimulates private investment and growth, and higher private investment which promotes capital inflows, real appreciation and lower inflation. The final effects on growth depend, however, on the particular course of action. A revival of animal spirits (an increase in i_0) not only tends to move the economy away from the low-level equilibrium but it also increases the rate of growth in the high-level equilibrium by shifting the $g - p$ curve outwards (see equation 12.21). An exogenous reduction of inflation (a fall in π_0) is neutral in its effects on the $g - p$ line. In contrast, a contraction of public investment and an increase in public external indebtedness both shift the $g - p$ line inwards with adverse effects on growth in the high-level equilibrium. The negative effects on growth are larger in the case of a contraction of public investment since in addition to the fall in the equilibrium level of resource utilization there is a direct negative effect on the rate of growth.

The previous analysis suggests that the scope for growth resumption is greater, the worse the initial conditions are. As discussed in section 1, this seems to have been the case: growth recoveries were faster, the larger the reduction in inflation. On the other hand, the move to a high-growth equilibrium with low inflation does not guarantee the sustainability of this growth path. The size of the current account deficit in relation to the rate of economic growth may make the high-level equilibrium fragile in the sense of implying an unsustainable accumulation of external liabilities. If this is the case, the private sector will eventually hit an external borrowing constraint moving the economy towards a path with a foreign exchange constraint, slower growth and a smaller current account deficit. Moreover, stabilization has been achieved at the cost of real exchange rate appreciation, so that, even when external constraints are not binding, growth has remained sluggish. Economic policy in many Latin American countries has yet to reconcile fast growth with inflation control and a sustainable balance of payments.

APPENDIX

Growth and inflation performance in Latin America and the Caribbean

Country	GDP growth (% per year)			Inflation (% per year)		
	1981–90	1991–99	change	1985–90	Average 1991–99	1999
Group 1						
Argentina	−0.7	4.7	5.4	1216.2	3.8[1]	−1.7
Bolivia	0.2	3.9	3.7	1383.9	8.5	2.4
Nicaragua	−1.5	3.2	4.7	8526.0	11.8[2]	7.7
Peru	−1.2	4.7	5.9	2080.5	13.4[3]	4.8
Group 2						
Chile	3.0	6.0	3.0	21.1	9.0	2.6
Dominican Rep.	2.4	5.0	2.6	43.2	7.3	6.6
El Salvador	−0.4	4.4	4.8	23.8	8.3	−0.6
Guatemala	0.9	4.2	3.3	25.2	9.7	5.2
Mexico	1.8	3.1	1.3	71.7	19.3	13.9
Paraguay	3.0	2.1	−0.9	28.1	12.5	4.6
Group 3						
Barbados	1.1	1.4	0.3	3.8	2.6	2.0
Costa Rica	2.2	4.1	1.9	17.6	15.6	9.4
Haiti	−0.5	−1.2	−0.7	7.9	19.1	10.1
Honduras	2.4	3.1	0.7	10.6	17.9	10.6
Panama	1.4	4.7	3.3	0.5	1.1	0.8
Trinidad and Tob.	−2.6	3.0	5.6	9.3	5.5	2.6
Group 4						
Brazil	1.3	2.5	1.2	855.8	565.5	8.0
Colombia	3.7	2.5	−1.2	25.7	20.3	9.7
Ecuador	1.7	1.9	0.2	45.6	37.9	53.5
Uruguay	0.0	3.2	3.2	83.1	36.0	3.4
Venezuela	−0.7	1.9	2.6	35.6	47.5	20.2

Notes:
[1] Excludes 1991 with an inflation rate of 84%.
[2] Excludes 1991 with an inflation rate of 865.6%.
[3] Excludes 1991 and 1992 with inflation rates of 139.2% and 56.7% respectively.

Sources: CEPAL, *Balance preliminar de las economías de América Latina y el Caribe*, 1993 and 1999.

NOTES

* I am grateful to Amitava Dutt for valuable comments.

1. See Easterly *et al.* (1997), Fernandez-Arias and Montiel (1998), Lora and Barrera (1998), and Stallings and Peres (2000).
2. Haiti recorded a significant worsening of inflation performance (from 7.9 per cent to 19.1 per cent from the second half of the 1980s to the 1990s) but inflation remained below 20 per cent.
3. In fact, as we shall see later, we shall neglect the domestic acquisition of financial assets by the private sector and thus implicitly assume away domestic public debt.
4. See, for similar specifications, Rowthorn (1981), Dutt (1984), Taylor (1985), Bhaduri and Marglin (1990) and, for an earlier discussion, Steindl (1952).
5. See, among others, Kormendi and Meguire (1985), Barro (1997), Bruno and Easterly (1998) and, specifically on Latin America, Cardoso and Fishlow (1989) and De Gregorio (1992).
6. The present model also differs from standard open economy models where there is no credit rationing, and capital inflows, both public and private, are fully endogenous. Moreover, the treatment of private capital inflows is different from the more conventional one which specifies an explicit function for net capital inflows, the demand for domestic bonds being then implicitly determined by the private sector budget constraint. Our treatment also reflects a difference in approach. Foreign assets and domestic investment are here close substitutes: a fall in private investment will lead to a reduction of net capital inflows even when interest rate differentials remain unchanged. For many developing countries, this seems more appropriate than the conventional approach for at least one reason: foreign direct investment – which is just as pro-cyclical as overall private investment – is an important component of net private capital inflows.
7. This result is a consequence of the assumption that the net acquisition of domestic financial assets by the private sector is nil. For a related formulation, see Cripps and Godley (1983).
8. This is unlike the Mundell–Fleming model in which a fiscal expansion causes a real appreciation and no output increase. The difference is due to the fact that in the present closure of the model there is no international capital mobility.
9. In the face of a small increase in the exchange rate, $di_P = -f de$ is the change in private investment that is required to keep the balance of payments in equilibrium while $di_P = -\beta\pi_2 de$ is the actual change in private investment. If the actual fall in private investment is less than the required one ($\beta\pi_2 < f$), capital inflows are larger than required and the overall balance of payments surplus increases with a stabilizing effect on the exchange rate.
10. Of course, multiple equilibria are only a possibility: with a $d-p$ curve sufficiently to the right of that in Figure 12.2 the model would feature a single equilibrium with high growth and low inflation; while an s_F-p line sufficiently to the right would generate a single equilibrium with high inflation and low growth.

REFERENCES

Barro, R. (1997), *Determinants of Economic Growth*, Cambridge, Mass.: MIT Press.

Bhaduri, A. and S. Marglin (1990), 'Unemployment and the real wage: the economic basis for contesting political ideologies', *Cambridge Journal of Economics*, 14: 375–93.

Bruno, M. and W. Easterly (1998), 'Inflation crisis and long run growth', *Journal of Monetary Economics*, **41** (February): 3–26.

Cardoso, E. and A. Fishlow (1989), 'Latin American Economic Development: 1950–1980', NBER Working Paper no. 3161.

Cripps, F. and W. Godley (1983), *Macroeconomics*, Oxford: Oxford University Press.

De Gregorio, J. (1992), 'Economic growth in Latin America', *Journal of Development Economics*, **39** (July): 59–84.

Dutt, Amitava K. (1984), 'Stagnation, income distribution, and monopoly power', *Cambridge Journal of Economics*, **8**.

Easterly, W., N. Loayza and P. Montiel (1997), 'Has Latin America's post-reform growth been disappointing?', *Journal of International Economics*, **43**, (3/4), November.

Fernandez-Arias, E. and P. Montiel (1998), 'Reforma económica y crecimiento en América latina durante la década de 1990', *Pensamiento Iberoamericano*, special edition.

Kormendi, R. and P. Meguire (1985), 'Macroeconomic determinants of growth: cross country evidence', *Journal of Monetary Economics*, **16**: 141–63.

Lora, E. and F. Barrera (1998), 'El crecimiento económico en América Latina después de una década de reformas estructurales', *Pensamiento Iberoamericano*, special edition.

Ros, Jaime (1994), 'Fiscal and foreign exchange constraints on growth', in A. Dutt (ed.), *New Directions in Analytical Political Economy*, Aldershot, UK and Brookfield, US: Edward Elgar.

Rowthorn, Robert (1981), 'Demand, real wages, and economic growth', *Thames Papers in Political Economy*,' Autumn.

Stallings, B. and W. Peres (2000), *Growth, Employment, and Equity: The Impact of the Economic Reforms in Latin America and the Caribbean*, Brookings Institution /ECLAC.

Steindl, Josef (1952), *Maturity and Stagnation in American Capitalism*, Oxford: Basil Blackwell.

Taylor, Lance (1985), 'A stagnationist model of economic growth', *Cambridge Journal of Economics*, **9**: 383–403.

Taylor, Lance (1991), *Income Distribution, Inflation and Growth: Lectures on Structuralist Macroeconomic Theory*, MIT Press.

PART V

Beyond Neo-liberalism: The Firm, Industrial Policy and Competitiveness

13. Bringing the firm back in

Helen Shapiro[1]

INTRODUCTION

For five years at the Harvard Business School, I taught a required MBA course on international political economy. When discussing policy alternatives for less-developed countries, many students gave unqualified support to an approach in which market forces, rather than government intervention, determined the allocation of resources. They were typically critical of import substitution strategies and thought that a country's productive structure should be determined by its comparative advantages, that is, low wages, natural resources, and so on. Even if they acknowledged that industrial policies may have had a positive role in the East Asian NICs, they were generally skeptical about the government's capacity to intervene fairly and efficiently, and thought that state-owned enterprises should be privatized. In short, they were very much in sync with the neo-liberal approach or the so-called Washington consensus, assuming that once prices were correctly aligned and trade was liberalized, the private sector would invest enthusiastically and efficiently.

I found this ironic, because at the same time that they were taking my class, they were also taking a course entitled 'Competition and Strategy' based on the work of Michael Porter.[2] In that course, while wearing the hat of CEO rather than that of a public policymaker, they focused on how firms must create and exploit 'competitive' advantages. They emphasized how a firm's strategy should be based not on ephemeral, 'non-sustainable' cost advantages such as low wages or depreciating exchange rates, but on non-price factors such as brand identification, product quality and service delivery. It became clear that in each class, the students were implicitly operating with different underlying notions of industrial structure and firm behavior. Essentially, the business strategy world was one of oligopolized industries in which firms created and exploited competitive advantages. In contrast, implicit in the orthodox macroeconomic policy recommendations is a world of competitive industries in which firms are price-takers and relative prices are the main determinants of private sector behavior.

Unfortunately, this conceptual schizophrenia continues and is not unique to business school curricula.[3] Many of the same LDC government and corporate leaders who have embraced neo-liberal reforms have also embraced Porter and his notion of competitive advantage. Though based on empirical studies of developed economies, his books have circulated widely and US-based consulting firms working with similar frameworks have been commissioned by private sector associations and governments alike. The compatibility of these two frameworks remains an implicit, if not explicit, assumption.

Although the term 'competitiveness' has spread throughout both popular and economic discourse, economics and business strategy literatures remain largely distinct. In particular, economists working on macroeconomic and trade policy in developing countries have paid little attention to the firm.[4] While in policy circles it is now less often assumed that 'getting the prices right' is sufficient to sustain economic growth in LDCs, work has focused on the need for complementary meso-level institutional reforms in the areas of financial markets, regulatory agencies, and so on. Other work has focused on the state itself or on social actors within civil society. The lack of analytical attention to the firm is a particularly glaring omission given that the engine of development is now seen to reside in the private sector rather than the state.[5]

This chapter will argue that it is incumbent upon economists to 'bring the firm back in' to their analysis and policy prescriptions.[6] Ten years ago, Shapiro and Taylor (1990) noted that even though early development theorists relied on the state as an agent of change, they had no explicit theory of the state, so that its superior capacity to allocate resources remained an article of faith. Likewise, failure to incorporate an appropriate theory of the firm in the LDC context leads to an inability to account for anomalous results and increases the potential for policy mistakes.

Moreover, this oversight abandons the policy terrain to those working from the conceptual vantage point of business strategy. While the international reputation and influence of these scholars and consultants have helped convince policymakers that macro-reforms alone cannot create an environment in which firms can become more competitive,[7] their approach has serious shortcomings. As will be discussed below, it often reduces national development to the micro-level of the firm and ignores the historical and institutional specificities of LDCs, both with respect to firms and governments. In particular, Porter and others focus almost exclusively on nationally based firms while industries in many LDCs are dominated by transnational corporations. Finally, the chapter will suggest that one reason this approach has generated interest in LDC policymaking circles is its support for only a limited government role in creating competitive advantage. Unlike many experts on LDC industries who have supported more targeted industrial policies or who have questioned the implementation of structural reforms, this approach does not explicitly challenge the prevailing macroeconomic orthodoxy. Indeed, it is generally supportive of neo-liberal reforms, despite its inherent contradictions with the underlying assumptions behind them.

The chapter will review the work of Michael Porter and those working within his framework in the LDC context. Porter's work has been chosen not only because of its influence but also because it explicitly addresses the implications of firm competitiveness for government policy. Most LDC examples will come from the Latin American experience.

THE COMPETITIVE ADVANTAGE OF LESS-DEVELOPED NATIONS

In his 1980 book, *Competitive Strategy*, Porter assessed the implications of industrial organizations' theories of imperfect competition for firm strategy. He argued that firms need to analyse the nature of competition in their industry based on 'five forces' and to strategize accordingly. Those forces included the power of a firm's consumers, the degree and nature of rivalry among competitors, the threat of new entrants, the threat of substitutes, and the power of a firm's suppliers. Thus, firms in oligopolistic industries faced different pressures than those in more competitive ones. They could not be passive price-takers but had to anticipate the future moves of their competitors and create 'competitive' advantages that did not rely on ephemeral phenomena such as cheap labor.

In his 1990 book, *The Competitive Advantage of Nations*, Porter extends his framework to explain the economic performance of entire countries. He argues that rising productivity is key to national well-being and that firms, rather than governments, are the prime agents of productivity growth. The book provides extensive documentation of 50 successful export industries in mostly advanced industrial countries. Based on these case studies, he concludes that countries in which 1) consumers are sophisticated and demanding, 2) firms face a high degree of domestic competition, 3) supplier industries are strong, and 4) skilled labor and infrastructure are plentiful, produce internationally competitive firms. He argues that governments have an important but only indirect role to play by strengthening these four points of the 'diamond'.

This work has become enormously popular and widely cited, though also subject to debate.[8] Though based primarily on firms from developed countries, it has also been widely read by policymakers and business people in less-developed countries seeking relevant lessons. Porter himself has supported and participated in the extension of these ideas to poor countries, arguing '. . . that we had to understand how the rich countries got rich before we could understand how the poor countries could get richer.'[9] Several country studies, as well as a large, high-level project in Central America led by US-based researchers and consultants, have been undertaken.[10] One such book, *Plowing the Sea: Nurturing the Hidden Sources of Growth in the Developing World,* by Michael Fairbanks and Stace Lindsay, consultants at Porter's consulting firm, received a glowing book jacket endorsement from James Wolfensohn, the president of the World Bank (Fairbanks and Lindsay, 1997).

In general, while these studies acknowledge that poor countries must rely on their comparative advantage in cheap labor and natural resources at the start of the development process, they argue that in the absence of effective policies, factor endowments alone are not sufficient to ensure competitive advantage.[11] Moreover, to really see productivity, and thereby income, growth, countries' competitive advantage must ultimately be driven by innovation. The government's role is to improve upon factors of production such as skilled labor, infrastructure, and supporting industries, and to promote domestic competition among firms.

The weak performance of firms in these countries is attributed to both government and firm failure. Governments are criticized for price-distortions ('getting prices wrong'),[12] protectionism, and paternalism. Fairbanks and Lindsay conclude that poor interfirm cooperation, that is, supporting industry relations, poor understanding of customers, poor knowledge of relative competitive position, failure to forward integrate, and government paternalism explain why firms in the Andean countries failed to become internationally competitive. They also go so far as to condemn the over-reliance on sources of traditional comparative advantage and blame it for the lack of economic growth in the region. They point out that low-cost strategies based on cheap labor and natural resources rather than on innovation are not sustainable. Someone, somewhere, will always be able to produce more cheaply, forcing firms (and countries) to cut wages even further. Thus, 'The tremendous advantages developing nations have in natural resources, in expensive labor, and fertile soil have ultimately sustained their poverty rather than created economic growth' (1997, p. 16).

These studies contain many useful insights for Latin America. Their particular contribution has been the close examination of firms and what lies behind their success or failure. Nevertheless, several points are problematic.

HISTORICAL LESSONS AND GOVERNMENT POLICY

While the studies detail the negative impacts of past government policies on firm performance, they don't analyse the historical context in which these policies emerged and their own recommendations are presented as if for the first time. For example, Fairbanks and Lindsay criticize Latin American countries for relying on raw material rather than manufactured exports. 'When the structure of an economy is geared toward exporting natural resources, there is very little corresponding investment in the competitive environment that might yield more success in complex industries' (1997, p. 244). They go on to blame import substitution policies for this outcome: 'The predominant paradigm governing Latin American economies has been a vision of wealth creation through *comparative* advantages such as natural resource endowments. It is clear that the import-substitution policies . . . stemming from that paradigm are no longer effective.' (1997, p. 253).

This portrays an ignorance of Latin American history since the intent of ISI policies was precisely to shift production away from raw materials to manufactured goods. Indeed, many of the authors' suggestions were anticipated by Prebisch and others almost 50 years ago. The issue is important not just for the sake of historical accuracy but because of the implications for government policy.

The authors all seem to agree with the intent of ISI policies, but criticize the means, that is price distortions created by protectionism and subsidies. Firms are not to rely on government protection or subsidized inputs or depreciated currencies because they are out of their control and are not sustainable advantages. Therefore, they argue that market forces should determine relative prices since 'government steering mechanisms tend to distort real market signals, and limit the ability of firms to position themselves strategically (Fairbanks and Lindsay, 1997, p. 177).

But in contrast to the Washington consensus which assumes that 'getting the prices right' will encourage firms to make investment and production decisions in accordance with a country's underlying comparative advantage, these authors advise firms to *ignore* short-run price incentives, which will undoubtedly favor the exploitation of 'comparative advantage'. They recommend exporting more sophisticated (that is, high end) products, which are 'macroeconomic-proof', in that a firm can pass on the cost increases from inflation, wage rates, or exchange rates more easily.

More critically, it is precisely those firms which presumably are most in need of their advice, that is, national firms that are passive price-takers in competitive market segments, that can ill-afford to ignore these short-run relative costs. As others have pointed out, this framework offers a reasonable *ex post* explanation for how firms should and do operate – once they have attained some kind of sustainable competitive advantage and enjoy higher profit margins.[13] It is more difficult to apply to firms like the Colombian leather producers, for example, that have yet to achieve the quality, brand recognition, or reputation of their Italian counterparts.

The question remains how to shift investment and production patterns without, to use Amsden's phrase, 'getting the prices wrong' or subsidizing/protecting these firms in the short run. Or, as Shapiro and Taylor argued, 'At issue is Gerschenkron's long-forgotten point about backwardness and inertia: more than a market signal is required to displace the previous 'equilibrium' in order to make nontraditional export markets and investment projects attractive' (1990, p. 856). While Porter discounts the importance of early government assistance and protection to the leading global competitors of his survey, others have emphasized the importance of government support even in industrialized countries. Likewise in Latin America, the export capacity of firms – which is generally taken as the indicator of competitiveness – was predicated upon a pre-existing industrial base created under ISI. The investment and trade patterns of these firms are profoundly influenced by path dependence and continue to be the outcome of complex interactions with governments.[14] The dichotomy presented by Fairbanks and Lindsay between 'taking the Minister to lunch' (to ensure the continuation of government support) or 'reshaping the industry' is a false one.

THE ROLE OF TRANSNATIONAL CORPORATIONS AND TRADE

With respect to the Porter 'diamond', import-substitution policy regimes created an environment of undemanding consumers, little domestic rivalry among firms, weak links with suppliers, and poor infrastructure. In the face of small, protected domestic markets, firms grew via product diversification and vertical integration. Vertical integration was also a response to poor supplier networks. Markets were concentrated, and there was little competitive pressure to innovate.

Throughout Latin America, import-substitution policy regimes have been dismantled and free trade and structural reforms have been implemented. These authors support such policies to change these conditions. Consumers could be more demanding of domestic firms when allowed the alternative of imports; imports would also generate more rivalry among firms and force improved efficiency and cost reduction; firms could follow an alternative growth strategy by pursuing market niches and exports based on a country's factor and demand advantages; firms could also attain inputs from the best suppliers regardless of location and force local firms to meet international standards.

Recent studies in Latin America have shown that firms have demonstrated heterogeneous responses to structural adjustment, depending on their history and capacities.[15] The changes have often come quickly and many firms have had difficulty adjusting to the sea change in their environments. But as predicted, many firms have become less vertically integrated. Some have specialized in particular product lines or components for the domestic market and/or for export and have imported inputs and/or additional product lines. Some have become assemblers of imported components or have stopped production altogether and have become distributors of imported goods.

But the adjustment process has not produced a sort of level playing field for all firms in the absence of government intervention. Foreign firms have been in a privileged position, particularly in the context of very quick trade opening and overvalued exchange rates which have characterized most countries of the region. Porter's *The Competitive Advantage of Nations*, based primarily on firms in advanced, industrialized countries, deals almost exclusively with national firms. However, there is virtually no discussion of the role of foreign firms in the works cited on Latin America. This is astonishing, since a large and growing percentage of manufacturing in the region is controlled by foreign firms. They have dominated the most dynamic sectors since their inception, and are important as consumers and suppliers of inputs.

According to Garrido and Peres, sales by the biggest 100 industrial firms in Latin America broke down as follows for 1996: 40.2 per cent by private, national firms; 57.3 per cent by private, foreign firms; and 2.5 per cent by state-owned firms.[16] The share held by private national firms had fallen from 45.9 per cent in 1990. In Argentina, TNCs' share of the sales of the 500 largest industrial firms rose from 33 per cent in the early 1990s to over 50 per cent in 1995.[17] In the Latin American context, one cannot talk about competitiveness without discussing the role of these firms.

Even large national conglomerates which have held dominant positions in their local markets have found themselves poorly positioned to confront trade liberalization. As mentioned, under ISI, these firms grew via diversification and vertical integration. Many of the products they produced are not tradable, limiting export markets and their ability to compete with imports. In country after country, 'national champions' that had existed alongside transnationals in concentrated industries from auto parts to toothpaste to beer are selling out to foreign firms or forming joint-ventures.

Transnational firms buy them to gain new or increased access to local markets that have resumed growth after years of stagnation.[18]

Rather than having to search the globe for world class suppliers, these firms are simply integrating their subsidiaries into their global production strategies. Or, they can limit national production to particular product lines and can then complement them with imports. They also provide export markets within their corporate framework. Numerous studies have shown transnational firms are leading an 'import-intensive' or 'deficit-prone' industrialization process in the region.[19] In regard to Argentina, Kosacoff writes:

> In short, the data show that the manufacturing sector has itself utilized trade openness and economic deregulation to increase its imports not only of parts and components but of finished products, too. This is indicative of a trend towards the vertical de-integration of activities that affects both manufacturing activities (as revealed by the levels of parts and components purchases from abroad) *and* commercialization activities (as revealed by the way that product lines for sales purposes are rounded out with imported products). (2000, p. 188)

In addition,

> . . . the importance of the role played by imports of final goods for subsequent sale (which represented nearly 40% of total imports in both 1991 and 1992) points up one of the characteristics of the transnationals' new position within Argentine industry, in which the marketing of products imported from other units of the corresponding corporations is just as important as the local production of manufactures, and in some cases more so. (2000, p. 78)

For many firms in Argentina, intra-firm trade is even higher within Mercosur than with the rest of the world. 'In that regard a study of a representative group of main subsidiaries of transnational corporations in Argentina reveals that 60% of their exports and 78% of their imports are intra-corporate transactions . . . Of the imports, 56.6% correspond to inputs and 40.4% to final goods.' (2000, p. 188)

This literature on competitiveness in LDCs does not consider the ramifications of transnational firms' global strategies on national industrial development or balance of payments. Nor does it give enough attention to how the combination of these firms' history under ISI, their access to resources, and the speed of opening have put these firms in a privileged position relative to national firms. Still, these are firms that have in fact adopted 'competitive strategies'. While the firm strategy literature is less useful, as pointed out above, in advising about how firms can become global competitors, it does say a lot about how firms operate once they have become global players. And in that world, they are not passive price-takers but exert some market power and attempt to anticipate and overcome market forces. To the extent that a firm can become 'macroeconomic proof' by exporting more sophisticated products that can be more easily sheltered from cost increases resulting from inflation, wages, or exchange rates, as Fairbanks and Lindsay recommend, they are the firms that have done so.

It is this insight into firm strategy that can help explain some of the anomalous results with respect to economic growth and trade performance in countries that have instituted market reforms. To the extent that growth has been slower than anticipated or trade patterns have been perverse (in the sense that they haven't reflected a country's underlying comparative advantage), for example, many macroeconomists have blamed governments for incomplete trade liberalization or structural reform. In contrast, this literature on firm strategy suggests an alternative explanation – that firms are not likely to behave as comparative statics might predict. Even if governments 'get the prices right', path dependence, global production and trade strategies, in addition to government interventions, rather than comparative advantage as revealed by current relative prices, influence investment, production, and trade decisions.

For example, research on Latin America during the 1980s showed that exports did not always respond predictably to relative prices. In Brazil, Bonelli found that total manufactured exports continued to climb in the second half of the 1980s despite a loss of relative competitiveness, as indicated by the effective real exchange rate, relative export prices, and unit labor costs. He postulated that a lagged response to changes in relative prices helps explain Brazilian firms' behavior. In this case, firms continued to export in the face of an appreciating exchange rate due to the sunk costs incurred in penetrating export markets.[20] Studies on Colombian and Mexican exports have documented this type of influence of sunk costs on exports and concluded that the firms already engaged in exporting respond to exchange rate variation differently than firms that are new to exporting.[21] (These results suggest that 'correct' prices may not be sufficient to get firms to export even in the face of trade liberalization due to the costs associated with entering export markets; additional incentives may be required.)

Another explanation for anomalous export performance is that firms in Latin America used export markets as a vent for surplus when the domestic market was recessed, a phenomenon observed elsewhere.[22] In Brazil, econometric analyses indicate that low capacity utilization rates, used as a proxy for weak domestic demand, had the most explanatory power for export performance in the 1980s.[23] In Argentina, Kosacoff found that even after trade liberalization of the 1990s, some firms still use exports as a vent for surplus. Those firms, often TNC subsidiaries, which developed under import substitution, continue to produce for the domestic market, albeit with greater import content and/or specialization; their exports are still countercyclic to domestic economic activity.

Finally, another explanation for the Brazilian experience of the late 1980s is the growing importance of intra-industry and intrafirm trade. In Brazil, TNCs were responsible for 38 per cent of manufactured exports in 1980 and 44 per cent in 1990. Fritsch and Franco (1991) suggest that as much as three-quarters of TNC exports in 1985 was intrafirm trade. This hypothesis suggests that price elasticity is likely to be lower in the short to medium run for intrafirm, as compared to interfirm, trade.

As TNC presence in Brazil and elsewhere increases, this tendency towards intrafirm trade is likely to intensify. Likewise, these firms are moving to regional investment and trade strategies. This pattern has been encouraged by trade agreements like NAFTA and Mercosur, but it also reflects firms' attempts to rationalize production across borders after years of market closure. These regional investments are not simply based on current comparative advantage indicators, but reflect both past investments based on ISI policies and/or government-imposed export targets, as well as anticipated future growth. To the extent that trade liberalization in the region encourages specialization, inter-subsidiary trade should increase and is likely to be less responsive to variations in the exchange rate or other determinants of relative cost.[24]

Prior to import liberalization in some Latin American countries, many exports did not show a sensitivity to price in the short run, due to the reasons listed above for Brazil: excess domestic capacity, sunk costs associated with entering export markets, export targets negotiated with the government, or specialized export production capacity for use within a firm's global network. Indeed, the logic behind import substitution policies in part was to force foreign and domestic firms to make large investments that were not easily reversible. An auto complex does not pick up and move locations easily, for example. These types of investments constrained a firm's options; they were subsequently forced to consider the need to protect access to these markets and their past investments, which they did not treat as sunk costs. Exporting excess capacity was one option; in other cases, firms took on new export projects in exchange for greater access to imports for domestic production.[25]

With trade liberalization, firms have new options. While path dependence still influences investment decisions, they can now integrate their subsidiaries into global sourcing networks. The motivation is quality and product standardization, not only price. As a result, some supplier industries are drastically shrinking. The number of Argentine auto parts firms, for example, was less than half in 1994 as compared to that of the 1970s.[26] A similar shake-out process has occurred in Brazil.[27] In Argentina, steel and petrochemical firms are being squeezed by imports. These industries are difficult to replace. Even should relative comparative advantage indicators change, in some sectors there may be no domestic substitutes remaining to replace imports.

The firm strategy literature emphasizes the importance of strong supplier industries and criticizes import substitution and trade protection for creating weak supplier networks. Enright *et al.* (1994) suggest that import liberalization will both provide firms with access to the highest quality inputs and generate competitive pressure on domestic supplier industries. Yet here again, the speed of liberalization, in combination with foreign firms' access to global sourcing, puts enormous strain on domestic suppliers. Once these transnational links are established and domestic producers have disappeared, re-establishing domestic suppliers will be extremely difficult.

Kosacoff argues that in Argentina, vertical de-integration and the increased dependence on imports explains why the costs of adjustment have been higher, and growth in output, slower, than anticipated. Recent work on Mexico by Moreno Brid raises similar issues. Using a balance-of-payments-constrained growth model, he shows how Mexico's income elasticity of import demand has doubled over the last 15–20 years. Export growth, although impressive, has not been dynamic enough to compensate. As a result, there has been a tighter balance of payments constraint on growth. Moreno Brid suggests that this is mostly due to a one-time effect from trade liberalization.[28] Further empirical work is needed on how different firms respond to changes in prices and exchange rates, but to the extent that local subsidiaries are incorporated into a firm's global networks, and local supplier industries are weakened or destroyed, a change in relative prices is unlikely to cause TNCs to import-substitute with local production.

In fact, LDCs like Mexico have seen enormous export success in maquiladora industries, which by definition have virtually no backward linkages to the national economy. Countries compete for these industries on the basis of government incentives and low wages – in accordance perhaps with traditional comparative advantage indicators but at odds with competitive strategy recommendations. Relying on an 'import-oriented industrialization'[29] strategy has thus far demonstrated little success in either generating adequate employment and export growth (to compensate for imports) or in creating 'competitive' firms as characterized by Porter.

CONCLUSION

The recent attention paid to the state by development policy experts and institutions just when its economic role has diminished is paradoxical. It is particularly jarring to see such attention paid to the independent nation state as if it was operating in a world of arm's-length market transactions in an era of so-called globalization. At the same time, the firm, a key institution in the reform process, is still virtually ignored in these policy debates. Economists' basic assumption is still that governments are more prone to fail and that markets – albeit with some regulations – get things right. Increasingly, 'markets' are referred to as actors, rather than the firms (as in 'how will the markets react'). The Washington consensus is still deemed correct as long as macro policies are complemented by state reform.

Despite the contradictions inherent in its support for the Washington consensus and its description and prescription for actual firm behavior, the firm strategy literature, for all its shortcomings, offers important insights into how firms operate. By shedding light on firms as actors, it can help get the macro right.

Nevertheless, even firms that have a great deal of market power and higher profit margins can never be completely 'macro-proof', as Fairbanks and Lindsay suggest they become.[30] Just as many macro-oriented economists ignore the firm, this approach dismisses the importance of the larger political economy and also fails to bridge the micro–macro gap. One cannot extrapolate a national development strategy from a focus on successful firms and industries.

More importantly, theories of the firm and the actual restructuring processes underway in Latin America raise the question of whether what is good for the 'competitive firm' is good for national development more broadly. As Moreno Brid's work shows, what works for an important subset of firms may make the national economy more prone to balance of payments crises and slower growth in the short to medium run. Likewise, it may make sense for firms to avoid competing in price-sensitive, competitive markets and a dependence on low wages beyond their control, but this may not generate much employment.

NOTES

1. The author would like to thank Wilson Peres and Lou Wells for their helpful comments on an earlier version of this paper which was presented at the Latin American Studies Association Congress, Chicago, 24–27 September 1998.
2. Based in particular on *Competitive Strategy* (1980).
3. In economics, while the literatures on endogenous growth, investment under uncertainty, irreversibilities and path dependence have paid increased attention to the firm and microfoundations, they have had little influence on macroeconomic stabilization and restructuring policies in developing countries. In part, this reflects both the intellectual division of labor within the economics profession and the difficulties in translating theory into policy. Neither is a new issue. A similar intradisciplinary dissonance resulted from indus-

trial organizations' work on imperfect competition and oligopolistic behavior – the economic foundation for much of Porter's work – and the standard assumptions and policy implications of trade theory. When the two areas were subsequently integrated by Paul Krugman and others under the rubric of strategic trade theory, the discussion remained largely in the realm of theory. To the extent that it had a direct impact on policy, it was within the advanced industrial countries and partly in the East Asian NICs, policy applications which were subsequently disavowed by Krugman. It has not influenced macroeconomic or trade policy in most LDCs.

4. Lance Taylor has clearly been an exception to this generalization. He has been one of the few macroeconomists working on developing countries to incorporate firm heterogeneity and industrial structure into his models. See in particular Amsden *et al.* (1994), and Berg and Taylor (eds) (forthcoming).
5. Celso Garrido and Wilson Peres (1998) make a similar point.
6. This is an obvious play on *Bringing the State Back In* (1985), the influential book by Evans, Reuschemeyer, and Skocpol, and more recently, on Amsden's 'Bringing production back in,' in *World Development* (1997). For examples of work on industrial structure and firm strategy by economists who have long-argued this point and who have provided comprehensive studies in the Latin American context, see Katz (1996), Kosacoff (2000), and Peres (1998).
7. Thanks to Wilson Peres for pointing this out.
8. Some critics have argued it is an *ex post* analysis of successful firms, and offers little by way of how to create the attributes necessary for growth (see, for example Thurow, 1990). Others, while not addressing Porter's work directly, voice concern about the concept of competitiveness and argue that the requirements and conceptual framework related to running a firm are different from those needed to manage a national economy (see Krugman, 1994).
9. 'HBS Study Assesses India's Competitiveness', *Harvard Business School Bulletin*, February 1995.
10. Examples include Enright *et al.* (1994) and Fairbanks and Lindsay (1997).
11. See Enright *et al.* (1994) on the Venezuelan pulp and paper and oil-related industries.
12. Enright and Scott Saavedra, (1994) p. 14.
13. See Thurow (1990).
14. See Yoffie (1994).
15. Kosacoff (2000) shows how in the case of Argentina, firms have not responded in the undifferentiated and instantaneous manner assumed by most macro-models.
16. Garrido and Peres (1998), p. 37.
17. Kosacoff (2000), p. 75.
18. See Peres (1998) and Kosacoff (2000).
19. For Mexico, see Dussel Peter (1996), Lustig and Ros (1999), and Moreno Brid, chapter 4 (2000).
20. Bonelli (1992). For more on Brazilian exports and export policies, see Shapiro (1997).
21. For Colombia, see Roberts and Tybout (1995); for Mexico, see Maloney and Azevedo (1995).
22. For studies showing capacity utilization as a significant determinant of exports in LDCs, see Faini (1994), Moran (1988), and Sachs (1989).
23. In the Brazilian case, exports were concentrated in long-term, capital-intensive intermediate goods whose supply is relatively inelastic in the short run (see Batista, 1993). A similar trend was observed in Mexico over the 1980s, when the chemical, auto, and metal-mechanical industries successfully shifted 10–15 per cent of production to exports (Casar, 1994).
24. In some cases, government policies are in fact accentuating this tendency towards intra-industry and intrafirm. For example, auto companies already producing within Mercosur are allowed to import parts and components and models not locally produced, more easily than those firms not producing locally. See Kosacoff (2000), pp. 60–61. Based on revealed comparative advantage, some have argued that Mercosur has encouraged perverse trade patterns, whereby low-cost imports from non-Mercosur countries were

being replaced by high-cost imports from member countries. While policies have influenced these trade decisions, they also reflect firms' regional strategies which may not be based on comparative advantage indicators. Ford-US, for example, exports little to Europe, a decision that is not based only on comparative costs. Moreover, the US share of world auto trade obscures the role of US firms in world production and trade; country-based indicators of revealed comparative advantage obscure this point. See Yeats (1997) and Devlin (1996) for this debate on Mercosur.

25. See Shapiro (1994) for how this applied to the Brazilian and Mexican auto industries.
26. Kosacoff (2000), p. 61.
27. See Posthuma (1997).
28. See Moreno Brid (2000), chapter 4.
29. The term is used by Dussel Peter (1996) to refer to Mexico since 1988.
30. Fairbanks and Lindsay (1997), p. 41. They use the term in the context of encouraging firms to export more high-end products which would allow firms to pass on cost increases from inflation, wage increases, or exchange rate appreciation more easily. Enright *et al.*(1994) argue that in the absence of a sound macroeconomic environment, all other government policies will fail.

REFERENCES

Amsden, Alice (1997), 'Editorial: bringing production back in by understanding Government's economic role in late industrialization', *World Development*, **25**, (14), pp. 469–80.

Amdsen, Alice, Jacek Kochanowicz and Lance Taylor (1994), *The Market Meets its Match: Restructuring the Economies of Eastern Europe*, Cambridge: Harvard University Press.

Batista, Jorge Chami (1993), 'A insercao das exportacoes brasileiras no comercio internacional de Mercadorias: uma analise setorial', 23 Estudos BNDES, Rio de Janeiro, September.

Berg, Janine and Lance Taylor (forthcoming), *External Liberalization, Economic Performance and Social Policy*, New York: Oxford University Press.

Bonelli, Regis (1992), 'Fontes de crescimento e competitividade das exportacoes Brasileiras na decade de 80', *Revista Brasileira de comercio Exterior*, April–June.

Casar, Jose I. (1994), 'Un balance de la transformation industrial en Mexico', mimeo for Programa CEPAL/IDRC de Estudios sobre Organizacion Industrial, Sistema Innovativo y Competitividad Internacional, Santiago, May.

Devlin, Robert (1996), 'In Defense of Mercosur', *The IDB*, December.

Dunning, John H. (1992), 'The competitive advantage of countries and the activities of transnational corporations', *Transnational Corporations*, **1**(1), February.

Dussel Peter, Enrique (1996), 'From export-oriented to import-oriented industrialization: changes in Mexico's manufacturing sector, 1998–1994', in Gerardo Otero (ed.), *Neoliberalism Revisited*, Boulder, Co: Westview Press.

The Economist (1997), 'Murky Mercosur', July 26.

Enright, Michael and Edith Scott Saavedra (1994), 'Executive summary of *Venezuela: The Challenge of Competitiveness*', Harvard Business School Working Paper, 95–040, November.

Enright, Michael, Antonio Frances and Edith Scott Saavedra (1994), *Venezuela: el reto de la competitividad*, Caracas: Editiones IESA.

Evans, Peter, D. Rueschemeyer, and T. Skocpol (eds) (1985), *Bringing the State Back In*, Cambridge: Cambridge University Press.

Faini, Riccardo (1994), 'Export supply, capacity and relative prices', *Journal of Development Economics*, **45**(1).

Fairbanks, Michael and Stace Lindsay (1997), *Plowing the Sea: Nurturing the Hidden Sources of Growth in the Developing World*, Boston: Harvard Business School Press.

Fishlow, Albert (1991), 'Liberalization in Latin America', in T. Banuri (ed.), *Economic Liberalization: No Panacea*, Oxford: Oxford University Press.

Fritsch, Winston and Gustavo H.B. Franco (1991), 'Politica comercial, de competicao e de investimento estrangeiro: analise da experiencia recente e proposta de reforma', Discussion paper no.63, FUNCEX, October.

Garrido, Celso and Wilson Peres (1998), 'Las grandes empresas y grupos industrialies Latinoamericanos en los anos noventa', in W. Peres. (ed.), *Grandes empresas y grupos industriales latinoamericanos*, Mexico: Siglo ventiuno editores and CEPAL.

Hikino, Takashi and Alice Amsden (1994), 'Staying behind, stumbling back, sneaking up, soaring ahead: late industrialization in historical perspective', in W.J. Baumol, R.R. Nelson and E.N. Wolff, (eds), *Convergence of Productivity: Cross-National Studies and Historical Evidence*, New York: Oxford University Press.

Katz, Jorge M. (ed.) (1996), *Establizacion macroeconomica, reforma estructural y comportamiento industrial*, Santiago de Chile and Buenos Aires: CEPAL and Alianza Editorial S.A.

Kosacoff, Bernardo (ed.) (2000), *Corporate Strategies under Structural Adjustment in Argentina*, New York: St. Martin's Press.

Krueger, Anne O. (1992), 'Conditions for maximizing the gains from a western hemisphere free trade agreement', IDB-ECLAC Working Papers on Trade in the Western Hemisphere, WP-TWH-6, July.

Krugman, Paul (1994), 'Competitiveness: a dangerous obsession', *Foreign Affairs*, March–April, pp. 28–44.

Krugman, Paul (1996), 'A country is not a company', *Harvard Business Review*, Jan.–Feb.

Lustig, Nora Claudia and Jaime Ros (1999), 'Economic reforms, stabilization policies, and the "Mexican Disease"', in Lance Taylor (ed.), *After Neoliberalism: What Next for Latin America*, Ann Arbor: University of Michigan Press.

Maloney, William F. and Rodrigo Azevedo (1995), 'Trade reform, uncertainty and export promotion: Mexico 1982–1988', *Journal of Development Economics*, 48.

Moran, C. (1988), 'Manufactured exports for developing countries: a structural model', *World Bank Economic Review*, **2**(3).

Moreno Brid, Juan Carlos (2000), 'Essays on the balance of payments constraint with special reference to Mexico,' Ph.D. dissertation, Faculty of Economics and Politics, Cambridge University, October.

Peres, Wilson (ed.), (1998) *Grandes empresas y grupos industriales latinoamericanos*, Mexico: Siglo ventiuno editores and CEPAL.

Porter, Michael (1980), *Competitive Strategy*, New York: Free Press.

Porter, Michael (1990), *The Competitive Advantage of Nations*, New York: Free Press.

Posthuma, Anne Caroline (1997), 'Autopecas na encruzilhada: modernizacao desarticulada e desnacionalizacao', in Glauco Arbix and Marco Zilbovicius (eds), *De JK a FHC: A Reinvencao dos Carros*, Sao Paulo: Scritta.

Roberts, Mark J. and James R. Tybout (1995), 'An empirical model of sunk costs and the decision to export', Policy Research Working Paper 1436, World Bank,

International Economics Department, International Trade Division, March 1995.

Roberts, Mark J., Theresa A. Sullivan, and James R. Tybout (1995), 'What makes exports boom? Evidence from plant-level panel data', paper prepared for World Bank research project 'Micro Foundations of Successful Exports Promotion' (RPO 679–20), preliminary draft, December 18.

Rodrik, Dani (1996), 'Understanding economic policy reform', *Journal of Economic Literature*, **34**(1), 9–41.

Sachs, Jeffrey (1989), 'Introduction', in J. Sachs (ed), *Developing Countries Debt and Economic Performance*, Chicago: University of Chicago Press.

Sachs, Jeffrey D. and Andrew M. Warner (1995), 'Natural resource abundance and economic growth', NBER, Cambridge, Mass, December, working paper 5398.

Shapiro, Helen (1994), *The Engines of Growth: The State and Transnational Auto Companies in Brazil*, Cambridge: Cambridge University Press.

Shapiro, Helen (1997), 'Review of export promotion policies in Brazil', *Integration and Trade*, **1**(3), Sept.–Dec. pp. 69–91.

Shapiro, Helen and Lance Taylor (1990), 'The state and industrial strategy', *World Development*, **18**(6).

Thurow, Lester (1990), 'Global trade: the secrets of success', *New York Times Book Review*.

World Bank (1991), *World Development Report 1991*, Oxford and New York: Oxford University Press.

World Bank (1997), *World Development Report 1997*, Oxford and New York: Oxford University Press.

Yeats, Alexander (1997), 'Does Mercosur's trade performance raise concerns about the effects of regional trade agreements?', Research Policy Paper, 1729, February, World Bank.

Yoffie, David (ed.) (1994), *Beyond Free Trade*, Boston: Harvard Business School.

14. 'Getting the structure "right"': upscaling in a prime latecomer

Alice H. Amsden and Wan-Wen Chu

Lance Taylor's work, unlike that of most economists, has been oriented towards 'getting the structure "right"' as opposed to 'getting the prices "right"' or even 'getting the institutions "right"'. The structure of an economy comprises both sets of prices and institutions, but involves more. It encompasses interactive sub-systems at the micro and macro levels that influence the rate of growth, such as the sectoral composition of production, who saves and who invests, patterns of productivity change and trends in employment. The 'right' macro prices (of the real wage, interest rate and exchange rate) are not absolute, but must conform with the specificities of any given economy's structure. Thus, the 'right' exchange rate from the typical economist's viewpoint may be 'wrong' in an economy with a large raw material export sector that is suffering from Dutch Disease. The 'right' institution (clear and well-defined property rights, for instance) may be 'wrong' in an economy that is undergoing radical structural adjustment, with firms inventing the most useful organizational forms as they go along (as in the town and village enterprises of post-reform China). 'Getting the structure "right"' is thus a lifetime intellectual, technical and participatory venture involving theory and practice, at which Lance Taylor has excelled.

In honor of Taylor's work, this chapter addresses the question of how latecomers upscale into more technologically complex industries and commercially demanding services at the stage in their economic development at which they already have basic industry but neither operate at the world technological frontier nor still profit from low, unskilled wages.[1]

Upscaling becomes more of a challenge as latecomers become more integrated into the world economy, which exposes them directly to its ups and downs. Latecomers that successfuly upscale are not immune to business or product cycles, but, we would argue, they are better positioned to enjoy fewer, shorter and shallower downswings. This is because at the heart of upscaling is an ability to adjust quickly to global demand changes and to manufacture 'new' products.

Success at upscaling is viewed differently by rival theories of the firm:

some emphasize the importance for quickness of networks (which encourages flexibility among small-scale enterprises); others, the market (which allows resources to flow rapidly across borders); and still others, big business (whose deep pockets and hub of knowledge put them at the head of the queue). We argue that all institutional theories of firm behavior need to be modified to understand countries whose firms lack cutting-edge skills, but the theory closest to reality is the one that emphasizes the importance of big business and the advantage of the 'first mover'.[2] In its modified form, this theory predicts that for latecomers to upscale into higher-tech industries, their national business organizations must also scale up to mass-produce, investing more in managerial and technological capabilities and expanding their production scale and scope. The most enterprising latecomer firms will gain '*second mover advantage*' in global markets, and the more numerous a latecomer's second movers, the better its national economic performance is likely to be.

By definition, latecomers do not have technology that is state-of-the-art. Therefore, even in 'high-tech' industries, and even with the support of returning expatriates ('reverse brain drain'), they manufacture products that are new to them but mature globally. From these two defining characteristics of lateness – relative technological backwardness and the maturity of high-tech products – we derive the economic patterns that govern their upscaling. Mature products typically earn declining and eventually paper-thin margins. To survive, a latecomer must exploit unique types of scale economies and manufacture in large volume. Even if a firm starts small, it must ramp up very rapidly to achieve a high output level, a process that requires building assets related to project execution, production engineering and integrative design (in the case of electronics). Unless such knowledge-based assets are accumulated by nationally owned firms, the development of high-tech industry will be slower and there will be no 'globalization' in the form of outward foreign direct investment. National ownership is a precondition for aggressive entrepreneurship in high-tech as well as outward FDI (without a new set of nationally owned firms, the total number of countries with multinational enterprises will remain unchanged).

Empirical evidence comes from two sectors in Taiwan: electronics and newly-liberalized services.[3] The evidence derives from heretofore unpublished data and firm-level interviews. Given Taiwan's stellar performance economically and politically until at least 2001, at which time global depression struck, other latecomers should find the nature of its upscaled firms and revamped industrial policies of general interest. In the 1980s and 1990s, Taiwan's GNP grew at an average annual rate of 8.3 and 6.3 per cent respectively (see Table 14.1). Its electronics industry and modern service sector grew much faster, while its political system democratized.

Table 14.1 Leading economic indicators, 1971–2000

	National economy: average annual growth (%)					Electronics industry: average annual growth (%)	
Years	Population	GNP	Per capita income	Exports	Wages	Production	Exports
1971–80	2.0	9.8	7.0	29.5	–	–	–
1981–90	1.4	8.3	7.0	10.0	7.4	14.0	14.8
1991–2000	0.9	6.3	5.0	10.0	2.9	13.0	17.4
1971–2000	1.4	8.1	6.4	16.5	5.0	13.5	16.2

Sources: Taiwan (Council for Economic Planning and Development) (various) and Taiwan (Ministry of Finance) (various). Real wage rate growth: DGBAS website, http://www.dgbas.gov.tw/. A revised series on electronics production was provided by the Department of Statistics, Ministry of Economic Affairs.

Economic development in Taiwan has been attributed to networks of small-scale enterprises (whose transactions are personally rather than anonymously mediated), and Chinese Americans returning to Taiwan from California's Silicon Valley.[4] We argue, however, that even in Taiwan reality is otherwise. Instead of buying from each other in tightly woven networks, latecomer firms buy their critical inputs from foreign vendors. Small-scale firms (with 100 or fewer workers) are not notably innovative. They have predominated in the *non*-electrical machinery sector, but this sector's share in GNP has stagnated. In electronics – the chief example offered as evidence in favor of network theory – and in newly liberalized modern services – which tend to be neglected altogether in such theory – the relatively big business has grown from small to large in a very short time period and has acted as the most progressive and developmental force. Local geographical clusters of small-scale firms support national assemblers, but such clusters have been agglomerations whose transactions are arm's-length.

High-tech industries in latecomers begin by importing their key peripherals, parts and components. Latecomer governments like Taiwan's, therefore, selectively and systematically promote import-substitution to insure timely access to such inputs and to create domestic high-wage industries. This process is comparable to their import substitution of mid-tech industries in the past. What differs are the policy tools used at the two stages of development. Instead of state-owned enterprises, spin-offs from government R&D laboratories and science parks are the catalyst in high-tech sectors. Instead of tariff protection, the government promotes the research and development that is necessary for the private sector to climb the ladder of technological complexity and to compete in world markets. Despite a global ethos of liberalization, the Taiwan government has systematically planned and promoted the growth poles around which networks and high-paid jobs have emerged. Thus, local networks have been 'state-led' rather than autonomously driven.

SECOND MOVER ADVANTAGE

The theory of 'second mover advantage' may be stated as follows.

1. Product Maturity and Scale Economies

High-tech products and services are already technologically 'mature' by world standards when a latecomer economy begins to supply them. The first latecomer entrant into such an industry earns a higher rate of profit than normal, or than later entrants earn insofar as the profit rate of mature products is still high when production overseas begins, but tends to decline steeply once production achieves a large volume. Declining profit margins and standardization are incentives to exploit *economies of scale*. Three types of scale economies may be distinguished. *Type I* concerns the usual production-related economies with respect to learning-by-doing from longer production runs, cost savings from fuller capacity utilization and bulk purchases of inputs, and so forth. *Type II* also concerns fixed costs but with respect to design. This generic scale economy is not unique to latecomers although latecomers in electronics mastered a unique design skill – the integration of the many parts and components that comprise mass-produced devices such as hand-held calculators, notebooks and cell phones. Given fixed costs of design and prototyping, and design modularities for different customers, unit design costs tend to be lower the greater the output. *Type III* scale economies concern *information, signaling and transactions costs*, and are unique to latecomers. To become a subcontractor for a big foreign firm, a latecomer enterprise must itself be large. First movers in advanced countries use size to identify potential foreign subcontractors (or joint venture partners in the case of services) in order to reduce their own risk and monitoring costs. In the personal computer industry, for instance, a subcontractor in Taiwan must typically meet a minimum percentage of a first mover's total volume of business, and a maximum percentage of its own business for any single foreign buyer. These conditions entail annual production runs in the millions. Thus, scale signals a potential subcontractor's eligibility for an OEM or ODM contract.[5] The larger the contract, the lower the average costs. Similarly in the case of foreign vendors, the bigger a buyer, the better a vendor's service. When global demand for a high-tech product surges, key parts and components may be in short supply, and bigger buyers are served first. In normal times, bigger buyers are given greater technical assistance by vendors, who typically act as the agent to provide a road map for where an industry's technology is moving. Access to leading foreign vendors is critical for latecomers given their high initial dependence on imported inputs and the technology transfers inherent in vendor relations.

As first movers around the year 2000 began to demand more products and after-sales service from a single subcontractor ('one-stop shopping'), and as the supply chain became more rationalized (fewer transactions in the sequential supply of parts and components to an ultimate final buyer), the scale and scope demanded of international subcontractors further increased. By the same token, consolidation among service providers in the advanced economies raised the minimum acceptable scale for foreign joint venture partners. The larger firms became, and the more concentrated markets became in advanced economies, the larger and more concentrated they became in latecomer economies. In this respect, global tendencies converged.

2. Skills

Two types of skills are required for latecomers to become second movers in mature, high-tech industries. First, they need technological knowledge about a new product such that it can be produced commercially once it matures. Second, they need project execution and production capabilities in order to be first-to-market at the lowest cost. In Taiwan, the second skill was privatized and the first was 'statized'. To insure the efficient operation of large-scale facilities and thus enjoy second mover advantage, nationally owned firms invested heavily in professional management and engineering talent. For its part, the government largely took the initiative in creating the institutions (including second movers) and investing proactively in the R&D necessary for the private sector to enter promising high-tech sectors.

3. Ramping Up

The growth path of a second mover may start with either a large or small investment. In the latter case, ramp-up in the face of potential scale economies must be extremely fast. Aside from project execution skills, the rapidity of ramp-up will depend on the availability of capital, human resources and de-bugged technology (a function of government-sponsored research and product maturity). If these resources are available, then a firm can grow from small to large quickly (even ignoring mergers and acquisitions).

It follows that rather than a new organic entrant, an existing firm (or one of its spin-offs) will tend to be the agent of diversification in a latecomer country, including diversification into new market segments within the same industry. In advanced countries, by contrast, a path-breaking innovation is typically the origin of a new company (the assembly line in the case of Ford Motor Company, the telephone in the case of Ericsson, and so on). Without a commercial innovation, an inexperienced small firm in a latecomer country is disadvantaged relative to larger existing firms in access to capital and experienced personnel.

As existing firms diversify, more competition may be expected among them in new product markets, but aggregate concentration at the economy-wide level will tend to increase. Even at the industry-wide level, a shake-out among firms competing for market share and lower costs may be expected after a period of intense competition. The form national competition may then be expected to take is a struggle among established second movers for supremacy in still 'newer', mature product markets.

4. Globalization and 'De-Globalization'

'Globalization' may be predicted to differ systematically between advanced and latecomer economies (in terms of both a country's inward and outward foreign direct investment as well as its international subcontracting). The ratio of inward foreign direct investment to outward foreign direct investment, FDI_{Ii}/FDI_{Oi}, defined for the *i*th industry, is also likely to differ. The greater the fall in the ratio over time, the greater the operating scale of a national firm and the lower its unit costs of production, design and distribution.[6]

Given an advanced economy's frontier technology, its leading enterprises exploit the advantages they derive from innovative products in the richest countries. Thus, it is a stylized fact that the most popular venue for US outward FDI has been Canada and Europe, and vice versa. Upscaled latecomers, by contrast, exploit their competitive advantage in manufacturing efficiency, by shifting production to lower wage countries in order to cut their manufacturing costs. In services as well, the outward FDI of a latecomer tends to be concentrated in a 'soft' market (one with geographical proximity, cultural affinity, and so on). On both counts, the locus of outward FDI by leading enterprises from latecomer countries may be expected to occur mainly in those neighboring countries with relatively low per capita incomes. Advanced economies also seek to cut their labor costs by relocating production to lower-wage countries, but on net, their outward FDI will be dominated by new product development and concentrated in countries with high incomes per head. Given different stages of economic development, the locus of outward foreign direct investment may thus be expected to differ.

Taiwan's first outward FDI was in Southeast Asia. Once government loosened investment restrictions on the Chinese mainland, the floodgates opened and outward FDI (in both manufacturing and services) flowed to China. The electronics industry was responsible for Taiwan's largest share of outward FDI (as well as for the largest share of its domestic manufacturing output). Only as electronics firms began to compete on the basis of technology did an increasing share of their outward FDI go to the US, in the form of both listening posts and distribution outlets for their products.

The ratio of inward to outward FDI depends on the share in GNP of nationally owned firms and on country size (measured by population). The greater national ownership of productive entities, the smaller FDI will be in terms of inflow and the greater it will be in terms of outflow (the outflow may be expected to be zero in the case of nil national ownership).[7] National ownership will crowd out inward FDI and will act as a necessary condition for outward FDI. If, therefore, foreign ownership of productive entities is greater in a latecomer compared with an advanced economy, then the ratio FDI_I/FDI_O will be higher in the latecomer.[8] Overall, its chances for exploiting global economies of scale will be less.

Holding ownership constant, the ratio of inward and outward FDI may be expected to depend on a country's size. The larger the country, the more likely it will be to attract inward FDI and to eschew outward FDI. If a large population entails 'unlimited' labor supplies (Lewis, 1954 p. 187), there is also no need for a firm to invest abroad in search of lower wages, as in India and China.

From 1952 to 2000, *Taiwan's total accumulated amount of approved inward and outward FDI were both estimated to be around US$44 billion* (see Table 14.2). This ratio is almost certain to be overstated given the understatement in official statistics of approved outward FDI to China.[9] As in Taiwan itself, outward investments depended for their profitability on large volume and high capacity utilization. Parts suppliers only followed national assemblers to China when the volume was large enough to warrant it. Taiwan companies operated their China plants 24 hours a day, 7 days a week, making use of young Chinese female labor that earned extremely low wages and welcomed overtime work.

As for inward FDI, in Taiwan's electronics industry its share in total output started high and then fell over time until it reached insignificant

Table 14.2 Globalization, 1952–2000

	Inward			Outward		
Year	No. cases	US$ mil invest.	Average value per case, $mil.	No. cases	US$ mil invest.	Average value per case, $mil.
1952–1983				–	134	–
1984	175	558.7	3.2	22	39	1.8
1985	174	702.5	4.0	23	41	1.8
1986	286	770.4	2.7	32	57	1.8
1987	480	1,418.8	3.0	45	103	2.3
1988	527	1,182.5	2.2	110	219	2.0
1989	547	2,418.3	4.4	153	931	6.1
1990	461	2,301.8	5.0	315	1,552	4.9
1991	389	1,778.4	4.6	601	1,830	3.0
1992	411	1,461.4	3.6	564	1,134	2.0
1993	324	1,213.5	3.8	9655	4,829	0.5
1994	389	1,630.7	4.2	1258	2,579	2.1
1995	414	2,925.3	7.1	829	2,450	3.0
1996	500	2,460.8	4.9	853	3,395	4.0
1997	683	4,266.6	6.3	9484	7,228	0.8
1998	1140	3,738.8	3.3	2181	5,331	2.4
1999	1089	4,231.4	3.9	1262	4,522	3.6
2000	1410	7,607.8	5.4	2231	7,684	3.4
1952–2000	12,521	**44,566**	3.6	29618	**44,059**	1.5
1989–95	2,935	13,729	4.7	13375	15,306	1.1
1996–2000	4,822	22,305	4.6	16011	28,160	1.8

Source: Adapted from Taiwan (Ministry of Economic Affairs) (various).

proportions (less than 6 per cent of total exports). By contrast, its share in services started low and then began to rise with liberalization, although to less than 20 per cent of total output.

Foreign production may assume different *modes*: foreign *direct* investment, foreign *indirect* investment, or subcontracting. The predominant one may be predicted to depend on the *product immaturity* and *asset specificity* of the foreign investor, and on the *production and project execution skills* of the host country.

When product immaturity and asset specificity of a foreign investor are at their highest, production may be expected to remain at home (as analysed by Hymer, 1976). As immaturity and specificity start to fall, but the skills of a host country remain low, globalization may be expected to take the form of an outward foreign *direct* investment (*equity ownership*). This was the case when American television manufacturers began to invest in Taiwan in the 1950s and 1960s, and when Taiwan electronic calculator manufacturers and later computer manufacturers began to invest in South-East Asia and China in the 1990s and 2000s. Initially, almost all Taiwan's investments in China exhibited the FDI mode. By contrast, when a foreign investor's product immaturity and asset specificity are low (a product is relatively mature and knowledge about its design and manufacture are general, as presumed in the later stages of the 'product cycle' theory or 'flying geese' model[10]), and when the skills of a host country are high, globalization tends to take the form either of a foreign *indirect* investment, involving *debt* (for example, a US company lends money to a Taiwan company to undertake production), or of international subcontracting (the US company exploits its original technology and brand-name and contracts its production to a Taiwan firm).

The mode of outward globalization is thus *not* likely to differ substantively over time between first and second movers. At any given moment in time, however, their behavior may be expected to differ because their development stage differs. The US may be subcontracting to a latecomer (Taiwan) when a latecomer is making a foreign direct investment in a still lower-wage country (China). The international division of labor, therefore, will assume different forms simultaneously. So, too, will ownership patterns of production facilities. As a foreign investor (the US) shifts its mode of operation in a latecomer (Taiwan) from foreign direct investment to indirect foreign investment or international subconcontracting, the ownership of production facilities in the latecomer changes, from foreign to national. 'De-globalization' may thus be occurring in Taiwan at the same time as Taiwan is extending its field of ownership by 'globalizing' in China. There is a fall in the ratio FDI_{Ii}/FDI_{Oi}, and lower unit costs (assuming global scale economies).

In general, as first movers in advanced economies get leaner through international subcontracting or foreign indirect investment, second movers in latecomer economies get fatter through integration. *The international division of labor is not necessarily reproduced domestically.*

In traditional models of economic development, the foreign investor from an advanced economy is the agent of transformation and growth. The skills it brings to an underdeveloped country supposedly diffuse through various means (usually employment of top managers and engineers), and through diffusion and the local procurement of parts and components, nationally owned enterprises evolve.[11] These nationally owned enterprises then mature and invest in other countries, and so economic development is predicted to spread globally.

In the case of Taiwan, the progression from the arrival of foreign investment to the emergence of nationally owned firms did not occur spontaneously, by dint of market forces alone, as the market model suggests. It was mediated by the government and by other non-market institutions. Even the first instance of a major inward foreign investment in the electronics industry, televisions, did not approximate *laissez-faire*. Technology transfer was most intense, not from American companies operating in export enclaves but from Japanese joint ventures that were subject to tariff protection and local content requirements, and primarily served the domestic market. The transition in Taiwan from inward foreign investment, to national ownership, to outward foreign investment by nationally owned firms was systematically planned and institutionally driven.

SERVICES

In the newly liberalized service sector of a latecomer, comprising such specializations as telecommunications, finance, retailing and fast foods, most of the assumptions and hypotheses apply that also apply in the electronics sector. There is a general absence of cutting-edge skills in national enterprises, technology is mature and hence subject to standardization, and economies of scale are important (especially regarding brand name). The major difference between a mature high-tech industry and a modern service is that there is no international (or intra-national) subcontracting. Foreign firms cannot outsource the provision of services in the same way that they outsource the manufacture of certain products. Therefore, national firms tend to compete head-on in services with foreign firms, which exploit their long-standing advantages with respect to technology, scale, and global logistical experience and brand-name recognition. The survival of nationally owned firms in newly liberalized services, therefore, partly depends on a government's regulatory policies. *In Taiwan, the government restricted foreign entry in the immediate period following market opening, of services ranging from banking and insurance to telecommunications and transportation.*

For a latecomer firm to enter a modern service industry typically requires a large capital outlay and advanced project execution skills. Therefore, newly-liberalized services, like new high-tech industries, are likely to be dominated by extant enterprises rather than new start-ups. In the case of nationally owned firms, a diversified group tends to have the most expertise in diversifying, and thus may be expected to dominate among national firms in liberalized services, as they have done in Taiwan.

Given entry into newly liberalized services by multiple groups, the immediate result is over-capacity. Then follows consolidation and rising concentration at the industry level coupled with rising aggregate economic concentration. As Taiwan's old business groups diversified into services, and as new business groups emerged in electronics, the share in GNP of its top 100 groups jumped from less than 30 per cent in 1986, when liberalization began in earnest, to 54 per cent in little over a decade.

COMPARING FIRST MOVERS AND SECOND MOVERS

We are now in a position to contrast first and second movers. Both exploit the same generic advantage – they are first in their respective domains to invest in optimal-size plants and managerial and technological resources. Their actions in both cases contribute to consolidation and rising industry-level concentration. But they differ in several respects.

One, the basis of their competitiveness differs. The first mover earns technological rents by exploiting its advanced knowledge-based assets: its corporate R&D determines what new products it will produce; its vendors and alliance partners are the best worldwide; its employees are premier and well-motivated because entrepreneurial rents can support high salaries; and its accumulated reserves allow it to weather cyclical storms (Chandler Jr. and Hikino, 1997). The second mover, by contrast, is not at the center of *world* knowledge and must contend with low margins from producing mature products. *It competes on the basis of relatively low wages for its engineers, who accumulate skills in project execution, production engineering and detailed design.* These skills enable the second mover to ramp up fast, exploit scale economies and thus chase global demand for the hottest products, which are determined exogenously.

Two, the structure of leading enterprises differs. The first mover tends to limit its diversification to markets broadly defined by its own R&D. The second mover, due to its absence of cutting-edge skills, tends to extend its diversification to whatever global demand dictates. The second mover follows rather than leads the product cycle. Thus, *within the electronics sector*, the first mover is likely to be less diversified than the second mover. Or the second mover's diversification pattern is likely to be altogether technologically unrelated, as in the business groups of Taiwan, Korea, India, China, Malaysia, Indonesia, Thailand, Turkey, Argentina, Brazil, Mexico, and Chile, the most industrialized latecomer countries (Amsden, 2001).

Three, sources of knowledge differ. Even ignoring discrepancies in R&D, and acknowledging that the first and second mover both rely on the vendor of parts and components for up-to-date technology, the reliance of the second mover on *foreign* vendors is intense. This is because the second mover tends to 'source' its critical inputs from overseas, at least initially. Dealing with foreign vendors at the world technological frontier is a major source of learning. The reliance of second movers on government for knowledge is also deeper. Governments everywhere promote science and technology, but in the upscaling stage of a latecomer such as Taiwan, they incubate start-ups, import substitute high-tech components and parts as well as take the risk for long-term R&D into 'new' industries.

Four, marketing activity is likely to differ. If a latecomer firm produces for world markets under subcontract to a foreign firm, then its investments in its own-brand marketing will be deferred, or restricted to peripheral products. The 'three-pronged' investment of first movers – in manufacturing, management (including technology) and marketing[12] – will become two-pronged, excluding marketing. A dependence on foreign brand names and distribution is likely in the absence of the knowledge-based assets that are necessary to create a cutting-edge product, one that commands consumer loyalty and brand-name recognition worldwide. The accumulation of knowledge-based assets, however, is 'limited by the size of the market' the latecomer can penetrate.

Five, globalization is likely to differ. Initially, the lion's share of a latecomer's outward direct foreign investments will occur where production costs are lower (a poorer country) whereas those of an advanced economy will occur where demand for new products is greatest (the richest countries). At a given movement in time, an advanced economy may access the lower wages of another country through subcontracting whereas a latecomer may access them through direct foreign investment. Finally, if the share of national ownership in total output differs in the two cases, then the ratio of inward to outward FDI, FDI_I/FDI_O, will differ as well. The greater national ownership and the lower the national firm's inward to outward ratio, the greater its potential to exploit economies of scale and to reduce average unit costs of production, development and distribution.

STATE-LED NETWORKING

A network is a locus of transactions among firms that are mediated *personally* rather than *anonymously*, as they supposedly are in market theory. A network's strength may be measured conceptually by its number of transactions, their value, and the degree to which they are mediated personally (that is, based on 'trust'). By these criteria (number, value and degree of personal interface), networking is likely to vary by industry – it is supposedly strong in the electronics sector. Even in the electronics sector, however, networking is likely to be relatively weak *within* a latecomer, even if it is strong between a latecomer and an advanced economy in the form of international subcontracting.

In terms of value of transactions, an electronics network tends to be weak within a latecomer due to a heavy reliance on imports for 'active' components and parts (active in terms of relatively advanced technology and customization).

In terms of personal interface, network activity may be divided into four overlapping types, all of which involve some personal element: the *subcontracting* of parts or components; the *customization* of inputs that require close interfirm cooperation (such as tools and prototypes); '*in-processing*', or the processing of materials supplied by one firm to another firm that specializes in such a process (for example, paper for printing or fabrics for dyeing); and the *local procurement* of peripherals (equipment), parts or components from known suppliers. Local procurement is the weakest form of networking because the personal element may be superficial; parties to a transaction may know one another personally but may act strictly opportunistically, at arm's-length and in response only to existing market signals. Subcontracting is the strongest form of networking because it is premised on a contract, implicit or explicit. It may not necessarily involve a long-term commitment; contracts between computer companies in low-wage and high-wage countries – say, DELL and QUANTA – are typically negotiated on a yearly basis. Still, subcontracting is the most personal form of networking, yet the least likely to exist within a latecomer. Within the electronics sector of Taiwan, subcontracting is virtually nil.

Subcontracting is weak in a latecomer because the incentives for it are weak. Additionally, foreign buyers may impose an outright ban on a subcontractor's own freedom to outsource. In terms of incentives, whereas international subcontracting is premised on a large wage differential between countries, the wage differential among firms within a latecomer is not necessarily large. Whereas the co-generation of technology in advanced economies is premised on risk-sharing, long-term planning and a large element of trust, the incentive for firms in latecomer countries to co-generate technology is weak because no firm is at the world technological frontier (the defining characteristic of lateness), a prerequisite for the development of genuinely new technology. Electronics assemblers in latecomer countries tend to buy 'passive', standardized parts and components locally, but the procurement of such inputs can be handled at arm's-length.

Given high import dependence and the absence of cutting-edge skills, the role of the government in promoting the growth poles around which networks flourish is likely to be greater in a latecomer than in an advanced economy. The government becomes the leading actor in promoting the import substitution of high-tech components and parts. It leads in the development of advanced technologies to the point where their commercialization is possible once they mature. In Taiwan, the government targeted key sectors and directly intervened in them. The model in electronics was to create spin-offs from a government-owned research institute (ITRI).[13]

Whereas import substitution of basic industries largely relied on the policy tools of tariff protection, financial subsidies and local content rules, the import substitution of high-tech industries relied on the policy tools of government-sponsored or government-subsidized R&D, as well as regulatory policies that limited foreign entry in services (however briefly).

In general, the government was a leading actor in Taiwan's economic development. Starting in the 1950s and continuing through the 1990s, the government accounted for roughly *half* of all gross fixed capital formation, a share that was unsurpassed by any other latecomer (Amsden, 2001). The government deliberately limited firm size and thereby contributed to the growth of small, specialized firms by means of its policies related to industrial licensing, bank lending, debt-to-equity ratio requirements, and constraints on mergers and acquisitions. As for discipline, when the government wielded power over the purse, discipline operated through the imposition of performance standards on subsidy recipients *and subsidy providers* – bureaucrats in state-owned banks, for example, were held personally responsible, in terms of their salaries and promotion, for the health of their loans (Wade, 1990). Later, globalization played the role of disciplinarian. The threat of a 'hollowing out', meaning the relocation by firms of their production and other business functions overseas (especially in China), dominated government thinking. Its strategy to invest heavily in education, R&D, import substitution and science parks was aimed deliberately at upscaling in order to keep industry in Taiwan.

Thus, the networks of early and late industrializers may be expected to vary in three critical respects: the unit value of their transactions; the degree to which their transactions take the form of subcontracting and are based on 'trust'; and the degree to which 'new' industries and 'new' technologies evolve autonomously or are a function of systematic government intervention and planning.

GEOGRAPHICAL AGGLOMERATIONS

Taiwan's elecronics assemblers benefited from a dense network of passive parts and components suppliers. Personal intermediation was insignificant, and the value of each transaction was relatively small, but the *number of total transactions* was large and highly beneficial to the electronics industry at large. In the case of personal computers, by the late 1990s assemblers of notebooks were still sourcing 60 or 70 per cent of the *value* of a notebook from abroad, but were sourcing 97 per cent of the *number* of its parts locally. Taiwan's electronics network thus took the form of a geographical agglomeration of firms whose transactions were arm's length (for the general case of spatial clusters, see Fujita, Krugman *et al.* (1999) and Neary (2001).

The emergence in latecomers of dense networks based on a large number of transactions depends on several variables. First, a network tends to arise in a latecomer with a certain composition of manufacturing output, one that comprises industries with a large number of discrete parts, each of which must be designed, prototyped and produced (such as garments, transportation equipment and machinery) rather than continuous process industries (such as steel, chemicals and cement). The larger the share of manufacturing in a country's GNP, and the larger the share of such sectors in its total manufacturing (both of which are partially a function of government policy), the more likely the emergence of a network.

Second, in the case of networks in the 'new economy', the greater the size of an educated elite, and the greater the engineering orientation of such an elite (both partial functions of government policy), the greater the likelihood of a network comprising commercially-minded, learning-based firms.

Third, networking is encouraged by geographical proximity. The greater such proximity among firms, the more cohesive a network is predicted to be.

Fourth, networks operate best where governments operate best. The more systematic and disciplined government policy with respect to skill formation and import substitution, the greater the success of a network is likely to be.

Among latecomers, Taiwan excelled on all four counts. The share of its manufacturing sector in GNP and the share of its machinery sector (electrical and non-electrical) in manufacturing output were both outstanding by latecomer standards. Moreover, Taiwan's educational attainments and engineering training were especially high (Amsden, 2001). Its relatively small total population and concentration of manufacturing activity in a small, densely populated geographical area facilitated personal communication among a small educated elite. Finally, the quality of its state intervention was high because of discipline.

The origin of Taiwan's network began with its pre-war and immediate post-war manufacturing history. This history is rich in foreign connections. An influx of entrepreneurs from the mainland after China's 1948 revolution created the foundation for a dense agglomeration of machinery manufacturers, including manufacturers of bicycles and machine tools (Chu, 1997 and Amsden, 1977 respectively). Later, when the electronics industry began to boom, machinery makers shifted to manufacturing electronic devices. A supply of small- and medium-size firms thus already existed when opportunities to export and win foreign subcontracting jobs presented themselves. Government policies that strongly promoted exports beginning in the late 1950s encouraged exporting further (see, for example, Wade, 1990). Japanese colonialism ended with World War II and decolonization, which had the virtue of clearing the decks for the emergence of nationally owned firms and government-controlled banks. But business connections with Japan were instrumental in winning international subcontracts. Many Taiwanese and Korean firms were known personally by leading Japanese manufacturers through pre-war supplier relations (examples being TATUNG and TECO in the case of Taiwan, and SAMSUNG and LG in the case of Korea). Japan itself began much of its globalization in Taiwan and Korea before investing in other South-East Asian countries (Ozawa, 1979). Japan had been the original locus for subcontracting by American multinationals in the bicycle, radio, TV and calculator industries. But as Japan's wages began to rise in the 1960s, both American and Japanese multinationals looked to Japan's neighbors for cheaper labor. Wages in Korea and Taiwan were low even by Latin American standards.[14] Thanks to foreign aid, both countries had good infrastructure. Under repressed political conditions, organized labor was weak.

CONCLUSION

By way of conclusion, the theory of second movers and the theory of latecomer networks are not necessarily incompatible. To a degree, both networks and second movers may exist and nurture one another, as they have done in different ways in advanced economies. Nevertheless, we would argue that the dynamics behind Taiwan's upscaling, and hence the explanation behind its rapid growth in the late 1980s and 1990s, was the exploitation of *second mover advantage*. Competition among second movers for foreign contracts led to the exploitation of scale economies, domestically and globally. This resulted in the emergence of large-scale firms that survived by investing internally in their own proprietary knowledge-based assets, especially in the areas of automation and product design. High levels of concentration were a further consequence, and one that generated the entrepreneurial rents necessary to invest still more internally, in the capacity and especially knowledge needed to expand into still newer product lines and geographical markets.

All this conforms with the way Lance Taylor has examined latecomer economies. Nevertheless, we do not presume that he would agree with our conclusions. Nor do we pretend to attain anywhere near his level of insight, technical proficiency and sprightly prose.

NOTES

1. By upscaling we mean (1) exploiting a different set of competitive assets from previously, (2) using altered organizational and institutional structures to do so, and (3) subjecting these structures to new mechanisms of discipline and control.
2. For 'first mover' advantage, see Chandler Jr. (1990) and Chandler Jr. and Hikino (1997).
3. This chapter is based on our forthcoming book, *'Second Mover Advantage': Latecomer Upscaling in Taiwan*, MIT Press.
4. See, among many others, Borrus (1997), Chou and Kirby (1998), Hamilton (1991), Numazaki (1997) and Saxenian and Hsu (2001).
5. OEM refers to original equipment manufacturer and ODM refers to original design manufacturer.
6. Assume first that the scale of a latecomer's production in a given industry depends initially only on domestic production. If a foreign firm acquires some of that production capacity, then the production scale of nationally owned firms in that industry will fall, and their unit costs will rise. Then assume that the scale of production of a national firm also depends on its outward foreign direct investment. If its total capacity rises due to that outward investment, then its overall scale will increase. If its foreign capacity substitutes for its domestic capacity, but unit costs are lower due to lower wages overseas, then the firm's profits will be higher and it can invest more in capacity, thereby lowering its unit costs further, or it can lower its prices, thereby increasing potential demand and the prospects for investing overseas in additional capacity.
7. Without nationally-owned and nationally-controlled enterprises to shift selective operations abroad, a country itself cannot globalize. At most the foreign-owned enterprises operating in one country can globalize further, to still other countries, but the total number of countries with their own multinational enterprises (one measure of which is the locus of their corporate headquarters) will remain the same.
8. The ratio may be expected to vary among latecomers because their mix of national and foreign ownership varies substantially (Amsden, 2001).
9. The ratio may be biased if exchange rates are biased because inward FDI is usually measured in undeflated US dollars, whereas outward FDI is measured in a local undeflated currency converted into dollars.
10. See Vernon (1966) and Akamatsu 1961 [1938]).
11. For the literature on 'spillovers', see among many others, Aitken, Hanson *et al.* (1997), Blomstrom and Kokko (1998) and Okada (1999). For historical cases of foreign investment spurring economic development, see Calderon, Mortimore *et al.* (1995) for Mexico, Hill (1989) for Indonesia, Schive (1978) for Taiwan, and Hou (1965) for China. For critical assessments of the role of foreign investment in economic development, see Cairncross (1962) and Amsden (2001), who argue, *inter alia*, that foreign investment usually arrives after a growth momentum has started; it does not initiate industrial transformation although it may accelerate it.
12. See Chandler Jr. (1990).
13. Industrial Technology Research Institute.
14. American TV manufacturers in the early 1960s initially invested in both Taiwan and Mexico, but wages in Taiwan were roughly half of those in Mexico (Levy, 1981).

REFERENCES

Aitken, B., G. Hanson *et al.* (1997), 'Spillovers, foreign investment and export Behavior', *Journal of International Economics*, **43**: 103–32.

Akamatsu, K. (1961 [1938]), 'A theory of unbalanced growth in the world economy', *Weltwirtschalftliches Archiv*, **2**.

Amsden, A.H. (1977), 'The division of labor is limited by the "Type" of market: the Taiwanese machine tool industry', *World Development*, 5: 217–34.

Amsden, A.H. (2001), *The Rise of 'the Rest': Challenges to the West from Late-Industrializing Economies*, New York: Oxford University Press.

Blomstrom, M. and A. Kokko (1998), 'Foreign investment as a vehicle for international technology transfer', in G. Barba Navaretti, P. Dasgupta, K.-G. Maler and D. Siniscalco (eds) *Creation and Transfer of Knowledge: Institutions and Incentives*, Berlin: Springer, pp. 279–311.

Borrus, M. (1997). Left for dead: Asian production networks and the revival of US electronics', in B. Naughton (ed.) *The China Circle: Economics and Electronics in the PRC, Hong Kong and Taiwan*, Washington, DC: Brookings.

Cairncross, A.K. (1962), *Factors in Economic Development*, New York: Frederick a. Praeger.

Calderon, A., M. Mortimore *et al.* (1995), *Mexico's Incorporation into the New Industrial Order: Foreign Investment as a Source of International Competitiveness*, Santiago, Chile: Economic Commission for Latin America and the Caribbean.

Chandler Jr., A.D. (1990), *Scale and Scope. The Dynamics of Industrial Capitalism*, Cambridge: Harvard University Press.

Chandler Jr., A.D. and T. Hikino (1997), The large industrial enterprise and the dynamics of modern economic growth', in A.D.J. Chandler, F. Amatori and T. Hikino (eds) *Big Business and the Wealth of Nations*, Cambridge, UK: Cambridge University Press: 24–62.

Chou, T.L. and R.J.R. Kirby (1998), 'Taiwan's electronics sector: restructuring of form and space', *Competition and Change*, **2**(3): 331–58.

Chu, W.-w. (1997), 'Causes of growth: a study of Taiwan's bicycle industry', *Cambridge Journal of Economics*, **21**(1): 55–72.

Fujita, M., P. Krugman *et al.* (1999), *The Spatial Economy: Cities, Regions, and International Trade*, Cambridge, MA: MIT Press.

Hamilton, G.G., (ed.) (1991), *Business Networks and Economic Development in East and Southeast Asia*, Hong Kong: University of Hong Kong, Centre for Asian Studies.

Hill, H. (1989), *Foreign Investment and Industrialization in Indonesia*, Singapore: Oxford University Press.

Hou, C.-m. (1965), *Foreign Investment and Economic Development in China*, Cambridge, MA: Harvard University Press.

Hymer, S. (1976), *The International Operations of National Firms: A Study of Direct Foreign Investment*, Cambridge, MA: MIT Press.

Levy, J.D. (1981), 'Diffusion of technology and patterns of international trade: the case of television receivers', *Economics*, New Haven, CT: Yale.

Lewis, W.A. (1954), 'Economic development with unlimited supplies of labour', *The Manchester School*, **22**(2): 139–91.

Neary, J.P. (2001), 'Of Hype and Hyperbolas: Introducing the New Economic Geography', *Journal of Economic Literature*, **XXXIX**(2): 536–61.

Numazaki, I. (1997), 'The Laoban-led development of business enterprises in

Taiwan: an analysis of the Chinese entrepreneurship', *Developing Economies*, **XXXV**(4): 485–508.
Okada, A. (1999), 'Skill formation and foreign investment in India's automobile industry', *Urban Study and Planning*, Cambridge, MA: Massachusetts Institute of Technology.
Ozawa, T. (1979), *Multinationalism Japanese Style: the Political Economy of Outward Dependency*, Princeton, NJ: Princeton University Press.
Saxenian, A. and J.-Y. Hsu (2001), 'The Silicon Valley–Hsinchu connection: technical communities and industrial upgrading', *Industrial and Corporate Change* **10**: 893–920.
Schive, C. (1978), Direct foreign investment, technology transfer and linkage effects: a case study of Taiwan', *Economics*, Cleveland, Case Western Reserve.
Taiwan (Council for Economic Planning and Development) (various), *Taiwan Statistical Data Book*, Taipei: Council for Economic Planning and Development.
Taiwan (Ministry of Economic Affairs) (various), *Statistics on Overseas Chinese and Foreign Investment, Outward Investment, Outward Technical Cooperation, Indirect Mainland Investment, Guide of Mainland Industry Technology*, Taipei: Investment Commission.
Taiwan (Ministry of Finance) (various), *Monthly Statistics of Exports and Imports*, Taipei: Ministry of Finance.
Vernon, R. (1966). 'International investment and international trade in the product life cycle', *Quarterly Journal of Economics*, **LXXX**(May): 190-207.
Wade, R. (1990), *Governing the Market: Economic Theory and the Role of the Government in East Asian Industrialization*, Princeton, NJ: Princeton University Press.

15. Micro–macro interactions, competitiveness and sustainability

José María Fanelli[1]

INTRODUCTION

The continuous implementation of market-oriented reforms and the increasing influence of globalization have been two salient characteristics of the 1990s in Latin America (LA). As a consequence, today, the structure of the LA economies presents substantial changes. They are considerably more open to international trade and capital flows, and domestic markets are much freer than in the post-war period. In this new scenario, key macroeconomic indicators such as the inflation rate showed an encouraging evolution while the growth prospects improved as compared to the debt-crisis period. In spite of this, however, the old challenge of achieving a sustained growth rate that could gradually close the income gap with developed countries appears to be no less difficult than in recent decades. There are two relevant obstacles that the market-oriented reforms have encountered. The first is that markets are underdeveloped in LA. There exist important failures in the factor, services and goods markets that tend to affect significantly the optimality of the market outcome. The second is that institutional development is weak and, thus, government interventions and regulations tend to be inefficient. The combination of these two factors represents a serious obstacle to the development of a denser market structure capable of exploiting the potential benefits of market liberalization. In a context of market failures and weak institutions, policymakers have a limited capacity to manage the complex interactions between productivity growth, macroeconomic stability and integration in the global economy that arise in the process of growth. They cannot rely, without uncertainty, on either free markets or government institutions.

A major difficulty for understanding the development process and improving policy design is the absence of an analytical framework within which productivity, macroeconomic stability, integration in the world economy, and institutional problems can be integrated. The Washington Consensus (WC) attempted to deliver such a framework in the 1980s

(Williamson, 1990). The WC put together the lessons drawn from the analysis of concrete development experiences and the theoretical contributions of the 'liberalization' approach to development theory. It was extremely effective at revealing the inefficiencies and inconsistencies of the older development paradigm based on import substitution and state intervention and at establishing new guidelines for policies oriented at liberalizing repressed markets and reducing the size and functions of the state. In fact, part of its popularity was due to its ability to present an integrated framework for policy design in a wide range of areas which embraced both economic and institutional factors. A good number of developing countries put into practice the policy recommendations of the WC and succeeded in eliminating many of the inefficiencies of the old development model such as high and widely dispersed protection rates, excessive involvement of the state in production and elevated inflation rates.

Today, however, the WC approach and globalization are under scrutiny. After ten years of reforms the outcomes in terms of growth, productivity and macroeconomic stability are falling short of expectations. The process of catching up with the developed world is far from secure and social equity is by no means improving. In fact, an important weakness in the WC approach was that the sources of a sustained increase in productivity were not clear enough. This is apparent in the WC's policy recommendations. It is generally explicitly assumed that market deregulation and outward orientation (that is, 'undistorted' integration in the world economy) should be sufficient conditions to ensure an upward trend in productivity.[2] But the recent LA experience suggests, nonetheless, that market deregulation alone may not suffice to take full advantage of the creativity of the private sector and to enhance productivity growth. In this regard, a central flaw of this vision is that it downplays the role of market failures and real adjustment costs. The assumption that product and factor markets will function well following liberalization may be unwarranted in the case of developing countries, where imperfections are pervasive in the markets for knowledge, labor, infrastructure services and finance. These markets have a determinant influence on the evolution of productivity. Likewise, the WC also tends to downplay the permanent effects that the sizeable macroeconomic disequilibria that usually follow liberalization can have at the microeconomic level, such as the loss of accumulated skills and lengthy periods of unemployment.

But, beyond the question of the 'long-run' evolution of productivity, in the second half of the 1990s, the Tequila, Asian and Russian crises gave rise to new questions about the precise way in which developing countries could take advantage of globalization and the market economy while avoiding their perils. One of the most important sources of uncertainty in this regard was the fact that, somewhat unexpectedly, some of the highly successful outward-oriented countries, like Korea and other 'tigers', experienced steep macroeconomic disequilibria which matched some of the characteristics of Latin American instability, such as currency attacks, financial fragility and deep falls in the activity level. These facts made it evident that imperfections exist in the functioning of international capital markets which can jeopardize even the most successful countries and that, under such circumstances, outward orientation *per se* is not enough to protect a given country from exposure to capital flow volatility. Likewise, on the domestic side, the crises show that macroeconomic instability, financial fragility and the capital structure of the firms are closely associated.

The uncertainties about recent developments in LA are no less important. A few examples extracted from the recent experience of LA countries will suffice to show the character of such uncertainties. Argentina followed an audacious WC strategy and grew much faster than in the 1980s. But its economy was severely hit by both the Tequila and the Asian/Russian crises. The reforms were unable radically to eliminate the tendency to generate 'excessive' current account deficits which had been a structural characteristic of the Argentine economy during the import substitution period. Today the question is not only whether the economy will be able to sustain the average growth path of the 1990s, but also whether it will be able to meet its external financial obligations. Chile, which also consistently followed a WC strategy, has shown an outstanding growth record for more than a decade and was practically unaffected by the Mexican devaluation. The Chilean authorities, however, were unable to isolate the economy from the turbulence in emerging markets in 1998–99 and it was clear that the Chilean economy's low degree of export diversification leaves the country too exposed to terms-of-trade shocks. In fact, neither Argentina nor Chile had been able to break their traditional dependence on the surplus of natural resources to finance their net imports of sophisticated industrial products (Fanelli, 2000). Openness was basically beneficial to the development of non-traditional exports in natural resource-intensive sectors. Finally, Mexico and Brazil's experience in the 1990s, the two major economies in the region, was much less encouraging. Their rates of growth were lower than those of Chile and Argentina and they underwent periods of serious macroeconomic disequilibria.

Beyond the diversity of these national experiences, there are a number of stylized facts, which can be identified in the LA experience with stabilization and structural reforms.[3] For the purpose of this chapter, it will be useful to highlight three sets of facts, which are related to the macroeconomy, the integration in the world economy and financial intermediation:

- *The macroeconomy*
  The monetary and exchange rate regimes are not neutral for the microstructure and, hence, for growth.
  Nominal factors affect competitiveness via its effects on the expected value and the volatility of relative prices and, particularly, the real exchange rate.
  Although macroeconomic instability may hinder productivity growth, macroeconomic stability is neither a sufficient condition nor the fuel of sustained growth.
- *Integration in the world economy*
  Access to international capital markets is imperfect and it has two important consequences. First, it creates liquidity constraints, makes 'competitiveness' critical to short-run macroeconomic equilibrium, and is a source of permanent concern of policymakers. Second, imperfect access to foreign credit markets has significant effects on productivity growth because it makes it difficult to manage risk and puts severe constraints on the intertemporal allocation of resources.
  The trade specialization pattern at the micro level influences macroeconomic stability and growth via its effects on the current account and the 'sustainability' of the process.
- *Financial imperfections*
  The lack of financial deepening matters at the macro level (that is, the cycle and overall evolution of productivity) via their influence on the firms' capital structure and investment behavior, and the government's capacity to implement counter-cyclical policies. Under such circumstances, there frequently occur 'twin crises' which usually have long-lasting negative consequences on financial deepening and macroeconomic dynamics.
  Financial factors matter to productivity and competitiveness to the extent that there may be an anti-innovation or anti-trade bias in the allocation of financial resources.

In sum, in today's LA, the problems of lagging productivity, financial fragility and balance-of-payments disequilibria are at the core of economic policy discussions. In such discussions, the concepts of competitiveness and sustainability of the growth process play a prime role. But the meaning of these two concepts is far from clear in common usage. The key purpose of this chapter is to elaborate on the meaning of competitiveness and sustainability.

One important obstacle to understanding the meaning of competitiveness and sustainability in the context of 'emerging countries' is that, beyond important exceptions, there is no systematic analysis of the interactions between competitiveness and sustainability, on the one hand, and productivity, macroeconomic equilibrium and international integration on the other. Such interactions are implicit in most of the stylized facts that we have mentioned earlier. A second important purpose of the chapter is to explore the hypothesis that the consideration of micro–macro interactions may be of relevance to understanding the issues at stake. I use the notion of micro–macro interactions as defined in a previous work on the issue (Fanelli and Frenkel, 1995). Basically, five main hypotheses will be explored:

I. Macroeconomic disequilibria may have permanent effects on the microeconomic structure.
II. The interactions between nominal and real magnitudes have real effects.
III. When markets are incomplete, finance matters for the real side.
IV. Market failures generate coordination failures at the macroeconomic level.
V. Institutional underdevelopment is an obstacle to market creation and to the government supply of coordination instruments to make up for market failures.

The chapter has three sections. Section I analyses hypotheses I and II. To that purpose it develops a framework for understanding micro–macro interactions. It emphasizes the role of price rigidities, liquidity constraints and international financial market failures. Section II analyses hypotheses III and IV and briefly comments on hypothesis V. Section III applies the framework to the analysis of the concepts of competitiveness and sustainability. There is a systematic examination of the linkages with macroeconomic factors, productivity and financial stability.

I MICRO/MACRO LINKAGES AND NOMINAL VARIABLES

Trend and Cycle

Hypothesis I assumes that macroeconomic disequilibrium may have permanent effects on the microeconomic structure and on growth potential. In the discussion about economic policy, this hypothesis is taken for granted. However, at the analytical level, there is a certain scarcity of studies offering a rationale for it. Perhaps, the reason for the scarcity of analyses of micro–macro linkages is that until recently economic theory made a sharp distinction between the economy's growth trend and cycles. Traditionally, business cycle theorists have analysed detrended data and considered the trend as exogenous to the cycle, and growth theorists have focused on characterizing a long-run growth path. One important weakness of this approach is that it cannot account for the existence of stochastic trends (Aghion and Howitt, 1997). The view that, under certain circumstances, macroeconomic disequilibrium can have permanent effects on the microeconomic structure (Fanelli and Frenkel, 1995) implies that temporary shocks may be embedded in long-run paths and hence this view is consistent with the approach of some endogenous growth models. It is interesting to note, in this regard, that although there is a consensus on the fact that excessive macroeconomic instability and sluggish growth in developing countries (particularly in Latin America) have not been independent phenomena, there have been no systematic attempts until recently to analyse the effects of either volatility or prolonged/deep disequilibrium periods on the growth trend.[4]

It must be stressed, nonetheless, that temporary shocks can either hamper or benefit growth. For example, if the real exchange rate is artificially maintained at a low level for an extended period, it may hamper the productive capacity of the tradable sector permanently. But we can also easily think of situations in which a temporary boom can have permanent positive effects. Suppose there is a surge in capital inflows which reduces the interest rate and, as a consequence, credit-constrained firms experience a long period of excess liquidity. It is possible for the higher investment rate which will result from a softer liquidity constraint to have permanent favorable effects on productivity, if learning and skill accumulation are complementary to physical capital accumulation. Mechanisms of this kind have been present in the experiences of countries like Argentina and Peru in the 1990s. In conclusion, when trends are assumed to be stochastic, not only the temporary shocks that hit the economy but also the characteristics of the short-run macroeconomic adjustment path may have long-lasting effects. This fact is a primary source of concern to policymakers.

An obvious necessary condition for the micro–macro interactions to be empirically relevant is that macroeconomic disequilibrium exists. This makes our approach inconsistent with several dichotomies which are usually explicitly assumed in economic theory and are often implicit in policy discussions. This is the reason why hypothesis II states that the dichotomy between real and nominal magnitudes is not valid, while hypothesis III affirms the inconvenience of separating financial from real decisions. We will discuss these issues briefly.

The Dichotomy between Nominal and Real Magnitudes

The discussions about the interactions between nominal and real variables have a long tradition in macroeconomics. Indeed, one fundamental reason for the existence of macroeconomics is that the data disconfirm the predictions of traditional microeconomics which say that the absolute value of variables such as the overall price level or the quantity of money do not have a bearing on the real side. In this sense, hypothesis II is not stating anything new. There is, however, a difference between the conventional macroeconomic literature and the issues we discuss under the heading of micro–macro interactions. In macroeconomics it is normally assumed that whatever the influence of nominal variables on real values, they are only felt in the short run. In the long run the influence of nominal variables must fade away because the equilibrium values of real variables are independent of nominal magnitudes. In contrast with this view, I assume explicitly that the long-run equilibrium values can be affected by short-run disequilibria and that it is precisely because of this that the trend and the cycle may not be independent.

I will present hypothesis II in a way that will be useful for the later discussion of the choice of the exchange rate and monetary regime. I will use a simple model to exemplify the nominal/real dichotomy and how short-run disequilibria may induce permanent real changes. In a small open economy, if we assume perfect arbitrage in the markets for goods, services and financial assets and perfect foresight, in equilibrium it must be true that:

$$\varepsilon = \pi - \pi^*, \tag{15.1}$$

$$\pi = \theta - g, \tag{15.2}$$

$$r = r^* + \varepsilon. \tag{15.3}$$

Equation (15.1) states that the relative PPP condition holds and, so, the rate of depreciation of the domestic currency (ε) exactly equals the difference between the domestic (π) and the international (π^*) inflation rates. Likewise, if prices are flexible and financial markets are functioning properly, money will be neutral and the inflation rate will equal the difference between the rate of growth of the nominal supply of money (θ) and the economy's growth rate (g). Under perfect capital mobility, the uncovered interest rate parity condition must hold and, hence, the nominal interest rate in domestic financial markets (r) must equal the sum of the international nominal interest rate (r^*) and the rate of currency depreciation.

If we assume that the representative agent lives in a Modigliani–Miller world in which Fischer's Separation theorem holds, it is very easy to characterize the microeconomic structure on the basis of the 'reduced form' expression for the growth rate:

$$g = g\,(r^* - \pi^*) \tag{15.4}$$

Given the technology, the rate of growth of the economy depends on the international real interest rate. In this world, the work of the entrepreneur is not that difficult. She should undertake all projects which are profitable at rate r^*, without bothering about how to finance them or what the temporal preferences of the owners of the firm are. Perfect capital markets will make the plans of principal and agents and consumers and investors consistent.

For a small economy open to capital and trade flows, r^* and π^* are given and, hence, it is possible to determine the equilibrium rate of growth of the economy using equation (15.4) exclusively and without reference to the others. Notice the strict dichotomy between the 'micro' structure represented by equation (15.4) and the 'macro' structure represented by (15.1), (15.2) and (15.3).

In the literature, it is common to assume either price rigidities, which preclude conditions (15.1) and/or (15.2) from holding, or capital market imperfections which will affect, at least, the parity in equation (15.3).[5] The two hypotheses, however, are not completely independent under normal circumstances. Suppose, for the sake of the argument, that prices are sluggish because of imperfect competition. Under such circumstances, π becomes exogenous while the rate of variation of the real exchange rate (δ) is now an endogenous variable because relative PPP ceases to hold. We need to rewrite equation (15.1) as:

$$\varepsilon = \delta + \pi - \pi^*. \tag{15.1'}$$

However, if the real exchange rate varies and we accept temporal deviations from the equilibrium relative PPP rule,[6] it will affect the current account. Specifically, a lagging real exchange rate will induce an increasing current account imbalance and, thus, there will be a tendency for the country's 'leverage' (for example, the debt–GDP or debt–exports ratios) to increase. Under these circumstances, creditors will take account of the fact that relative price disequilibria may be long-lasting and, hence, that there may be transactions at 'false' prices. Rational investors will take into consideration that they live in a world in which disequilibrium and unfulfilled expectations exist, a world of uncertainty in which contracts may be violated. It would be very artificial to maintain the assumption that investors and creditors do not care about macroeconomic imbalances. They will perceive that a lower real exchange rate means less competitiveness, a higher current account deficit, greater leverage and, hence, an increased risk of default. As soon as we leave the perfect market world, the problems of competitiveness and growth sustainability appear. In this new world it would be more realistic to replace equation (15.3) with:

$$r = r^{*} + \varepsilon + \gamma, \qquad (15.3')$$

where γ is the 'country risk' premium. On the bases of our previous arguments, it seems reasonable to write that γ depends on the leverage observed in the previous period (d_{t-1}) and δ, thus:

$$\gamma = \gamma\,(\delta;\, d_{t-1}) \qquad (15.5)$$

Risk must be taken into account in investment decisions insofar as it affects the cost of capital. Therefore, the equation for the growth rate becomes:

$$g = g\,(r^{*} - \pi^{*} + \gamma), \qquad (15.4')$$

Imperfect price flexibility and a positive country risk rate completely change the role of macroeconomic factors. In the first place, it is not possible to determine the growth rate using only equation (15.4′) and, in this way, the dichotomy between the micro structure and the macroeconomy is broken. In this new scenario, the policy choices of the authorities regarding nominal values are no longer irrelevant to the real side. If the authorities opt for a fixed exchange rate regime, equation (15.1′), alone, defines the value of the real exchange rate and the direction of causality completely changes. Now, it runs from macro to micro. If, on the other hand, the authorities choose a flexible exchange rate regime, there will not be a precise direction of causality and the value of all variables will be determined simultaneously. There will be a two-way interaction between micro and macro factors. It is precisely under these conditions that the choice of the exchange rate regime becomes a source of concern and creates dilemmas.

I believe that the policy dilemmas associated with the choice between alternative exchange rate regimes are deemed critical because policymakers know that the adjustment paths under alternative exchange rate regimes are different. If the effects of the adjustment path on the long-run equilibrium are non-neutral, the adoption of a particular exchange rate regime matters to the evolution of competitiveness. Let us take the example of the recent crises in Asia and Latin America. The balance of payments disequilibria typically arose in the context of (approximately) fixed exchange rate regimes. Under such circumstances, there were two basic policy reactions. The most usual option was the devaluation of the currency and the change in the exchange rate regime. Other economies (notably Argentina and Hong Kong), on the contrary, did not resort to devaluation and privileged the maintenance of the regime over the need to correct the exchange rate parity to preserve competitiveness. Devaluation proved to be very effective at correcting external imbalances in the short run. Why, then, have there been countries which did not devalue? The case of Argentina is very interesting in this regard. The diagnosis behind the decision to maintain convertibility was that changing the regime would be too costly. That is, it would induce undesired mutations at the microeconomic level. The most important costs were considered to be the higher volatility of key relative prices and the increase in the fragility of the financial system. These costs would more than offset the benefits of correcting the misalignment of the exchange rate in the short run. Independently of whether or not the Argentine authorities were right in their assessment of the costs and benefits of a regime change, the Argentine case clearly shows that relative prices are not the only channel through which macroeconomic factors influence microeconomic decisions and competitiveness. Volatility and instability also matter to them. The Argentine case suggests that under certain circumstances there is a kind of trade-off between the mean and the variance of the real exchange rate. To be sure, we do not mean that the level of the real exchange rate does not matter. We suggest that the way in which a certain correction is achieved is non-neutral to the real side and, hence, micro–macro interactions should be carefully evaluated when designing economic policy.

One important conclusion that our analysis of micro–macro interactions suggests is that competitiveness means more than just getting the relative prices (and, particularly the exchange rate) right. The presence of fragmented or missing markets and weak institutions in developing countries determines that externalities, spillover effects, financial constraints and strategic interactions between economic actors are pervasive. Under these circumstances, when a negative macroeconomic shock occurs, the market forces (that is, relative price changes driven by excess demand) which should automatically restore equilibrium are too weak. As a consequence, there will be a tendency for the disequilibrium to set in motion destabilizing forces such as deep recessions and increased volatility accompanied by high and persistent inflation and/or unemployment. I think this is an important reason why macro disequilibria in developing countries are deeper and more unstable than the disequilibria observed in economies with a more complete market structure.

In sum, I think that to give a rationale for many practical concerns in developing countries, it is necessary to break the dichotomy between real and nominal variables and to account for the fact that macroeconomic disequilibrium may induce permanent changes in the micro structure.

II FINANCIAL INTERMEDIATION AND DISEQUILIBRIUM

The Dichotomy between the Real and the Financial Side

If we assume that it is possible to explain the competitive performance of a firm without making any explicit reference to financial issues, we are implicitly assuming that Modigliani–Miller's theorem and Tobin's and Fisher's separation theorems hold. The company's funding decisions are irrelevant to the choice of projects. The present value of each project is independent of the way in which it is financed. This assumption is too strong in the context of most developing countries because there are highly significant failures in factor and capital markets. Accordingly, hypothesis III states that in developing countries, it is a priori misleading to assume that the firms seeking to exploit a competitive advantage can always finance their productive projects. In strong contrast with the world of perfect capital markets, in the developing world a firm which is potentially competitive may be forced to forgo investment opportunities either because of liquidity constraints created by credit rationing, or because interest rates are abnormally high as a consequence of market imperfections or an excessively volatile macroeconomic setting. In such a world, 'real' decisions should not be isolated from financial ones (Fazzari *et al.*, 1988).

In the developing world, market segmentation is the rule rather than the exception. It is very easy to find two firms with the same potential levels of competitiveness but very different performances. One might be able to finance projects very easily while the other might not because of extremely high interest rates or credit rationing. Often in developing countries, suppliers of raw materials and intermediate goods provide their buyers with credit, especially small- and medium-sized ones who do not have access to credit from financial institutions (Petersen and Rajan, 1996). Market segmentation may be very harmful. It may be a serious obstacle to the development of strong and competitive firms and financial intermediaries which, in turn, contribute to generating and perpetuating the dual economic structures we observe in developing countries. This issue can be analysed from both a static and a dynamic perspective.

From the static point of view, in a context of segmented capital markets it is not natural to assume that marginal productivity conditions hold and all factors of production are used with the same profitability. Financial institutions are supposed to screen for the best projects and monitor their development. Consequently, if key segments of the capital markets are missing it implies that there will be less screening and monitoring and, hence, a worse allocation of resources. A company that has no bank monitoring may suffer an inefficient allocation of real resources and have suboptimal risk management. In a modern capitalist economy the financial institutions have the important task of equalizing the profitability in the use of the resources in all sectors. The weaker the financial institutions, the weaker are the forces pushing to equalize the productivity with which a given factor is used in different sectors and regions and, thus, the higher is the probability that a dual economic structure results.

From a more dynamic point of view, financial intermediaries have another critical task: 'picking the winners' in a decentralized way. In this regard, finance matters to growth because financial institutions contribute to fostering productivity and hence absolute advantage. Financial intermediaries can spur technological innovation by identifying and funding those entrepreneurs with the best chances of successfully implementing innovative products and production processes. In this way, the development of financial institutions and markets is a critical and inextricable part of the growth process (Levine, 1997). Following the thinking of Schumpeter and the more recent literature on finance and endogenous growth, Rajan and Zingales (1998) state that capital markets make a contribution to growth by reallocating capital to the highest value use while limiting risks of loss through moral hazard, adverse selection or transaction costs.

One weakness in the literature on growth and financial deepening, however, is that it is not completely clear why financial deepening is low in developing countries. From the micro–macro perspective we adopt here, it is necessary to introduce the role of macroeconomic factors. In particular, we have seen the negative effects of the higher volatility of prices and quantities and of changes in the foreign investors' sentiment. In this perspective, it is also important to consider the effects in the opposite direction: the lack of financial deepening is an important source of macroeconomic disequilibria. The difficulties in managing liquidity, risk and the intertemporal allocation of resources, increase the probability that transactions are carried out at false prices. Likewise, the lack of financial deepening represents a tight constraint on policymaking. A good example is the difficulties that many LA countries encountered when trying to sterilize capital inflows in the 1990s. So large were these flows compared to the existing stock of domestic bonds that the sterilization attempts quickly led to unsustainable increases in domestic interest rates.

Market Failures and Macroeconomic Disequilibrium

In a world of perfect markets, there are virtually no restrictions on the range of contracts that can be signed. In the real world of developing economies, however, uncertainty, informational asymmetries and difficulties in enforcing contracts *ex post* limit the contracts which are feasible *ex ante*. We have analysed how imperfections may generate micro–macro interactions that may hinder the quality of the domestic market structure. The restrictions posed by imperfections in the international setting are also severe (Obstfeld and Rogoff, 1996). There are two especially negative characteristics. The first is market segmentation. Some developing countries face upward-sloping supply curves while others are rationed out. The second is volatility. The stochastic processes governing the evolution of prices and quantities show periods of instability and, consequently, the market conditions can change abruptly. Even countries with a reasonable access under normal conditions may experience periods of credit rationing. These characteristics make the hypothesis that developing countries are price-takers in capital markets particularly inadequate.

One important consequence of the failures in international capital markets is that they create liquidity constraints. Hypothesis IV highlights this fact as a source of coordination failures and, hence, of macroeconomic disequilibrium. I stress the link between market failures and liquidity constraints because the theoretical literature emphasizes other aspects. The literature usually privileges the study of the consequences of imperfections on risk management and the intertemporal allocation of resources and demonstrates that a country is better off when it can use the international markets to take advantage of the differences between the 'autarky' and the international price of risk and of future consumption. These results are very important because they clarify the way in which missing markets may erode an economy's growth capacity. In addition to this, I believe it is necessary to highlight that in a world of incomplete markets true uncertainty exists and, hence, liquidity constraints matter. The tightness of the liquidity constraint a country faces is a function of the conditions under which it can obtain financing to manage unexpected short-run financial squeezes. And such conditions, in turn, are not independent of the degree of market completeness. This point is critical in the LA context, as the region's recurrent problems with balance of payments testify.

We can use equations (15.1)–(15.4) to exemplify the way in which failures in the microeconomic structure can generate liquidity constraints and micro–macro interactions. For the sake of simplicity we will illustrate this with the case of credit rationing. Under credit rationing, the country is condemned, at least temporarily, to a situation resembling autarky. This has two immediate consequences. First, the country will face an external liquidity constraint and Fisher's separation will not hold any more. It ceases to be true that all profitable projects will be undertaken. One can easily imagine, for example, that there will be a maximum current account deficit (or capital account surplus) that the country can run. If there are projects that are profitable at the rate r^* and the liquidity constraint becomes binding, such opportunities will simply be lost. Second, the interest rate will be domestically determined. Under these circumstances, we must replace equation (15.3) with an equation for the equilibrium in domestic capital markets:

$$D(r, \pi) = K + S(r, \pi) \tag{15.3''}$$

Where D is the fiscal deficit, S is the surplus of the private sector and K is the maximum amount of foreign credit under rationing. We are also obliged to change equation (15.4) accordingly:

$$g = g(r, \pi) \tag{15.4''}$$

It can easily be seen that the external liquidity constraint (K) breaks the dichotomy between nominal and real variables because equation (15.4″) alone does not allow us to solve the equilibrium value of g. As we have already seen, this gives rise to micro–macro interactions. Notice, on the other hand, that under rationing, the economy's rate of growth now depends on the amount of net credit available to the country. In this way a country can show low growth rates not because of a lack of potentially profitable projects but because profitable investment opportunities are missed due to the shortage of finance. This link between growth and liquidity may clarify the reason why ECLAC takes the trouble to calculate the level of the external transfer from abroad received yearly by LA countries. Notice, also, that when countries face an upward supply curve, the changes in γ in equation (15.4′) have the same effect of creating a link between the growth rate and fluctuations in the investor's market sentiment.

Given the simple structure of our model, the main real effects of changes in K are felt on the growth rate. The appearance of the liquidity constraint has the effect of introducing a wedge between the 'effective' and the 'notional' growth rate. That is, the observed growth rate will be lower than the 'notional' rate that would be observed if international markets were perfect. In this sense, our approach naturally calls for the application of the disequilibrium notion used in macroeconomics (Leijonhufvud, 1981; Benassy, 1993) to a growth setting. In macroeconomics, disequilibrium pertains to the realm of the short run. It is assumed that the imperfections that give rise to disequilibrium (that is, price or interest rate rigidities) will disappear in the long run. In the micro–macro approach, on the contrary, short-run disequilibria may have long-lasting consequences. They can permanently hinder the market structure and, hence, the microeconomy. It is only a question of logic to conclude that this could induce a permanent reduction in the 'effective' growth rate. For example, we have stressed above that when financial markets are segmented, it cannot be assumed that equilibrium marginal productivity conditions hold. The equality between the marginal productivity of capital and the market interest rate will cease to hold. And, if the markets in general are not functioning properly, it is natural to expect that a given factor of production can either be utilized with different productivity/price combinations in different sectors and regions or go unemployed. From my point of view, this kind of 'long-run disequilibrium' is one important reason for the 'dual' economic structures which are commonly observed in developing countries. The pervasive failures in the market structure preclude the 'traditional' sector from catching up with the 'modern' one, thereby creating the observed intrasectoral productivity differences.

Obviously, we could easily complicate the model to allow for short-run effects of changes in K or γ and generate the more usual difference between the short-run notional and effective values. For example, in a context of sluggish price adjustments, a shortage of foreign exchange would affect the activity level and, hence, unemployment. In fact, this is the kind of adjustment highlighted by the three-gap models developed to explain macroeconomic dynamics under the extreme rationing which existed during the debt crisis. Although gap models would be somewhat rudimentary under the present setting of free capital movement and deregulated markets, the basic idea that there exists a linkage between financial market imperfections, growth and macroeconomic coordination failures is still valid, as the notion of long-lasting disequilibria is implicit in the gap notion.

In our rationale of hypotheses III and IV, the lack of market development plays a salient role. One important policy lesson that follows is that the most important task in developing capitalist economies is not market liberalization but market creation. In this way, insofar as a critical input of market creation is institution-building, it makes sense to include hypothesis V as an essential part of the framework to analyse micro–macro interactions. Besides, when market failures exist, there are institutional tools that could help the market achieve a better allocation of resources. For example, governments usually develop institutions that allocate credit to small businesses or establish funds to fuel the regional catching-up process. However, as hypothesis V states, in developing countries organizational problems are as pervasive as market failures and, hence, non-market solutions are often useless. Rent seeking and corruption are usually not the exception when institutions are poorly monitored. In this way, the dual economy is the consequence of neither the market nor the institutions doing the job.

I believe that the incomplete market setting plagued with liquidity constraints and insufficient price flexibility creates the conditions for the 'mistaken' obsession with competitiveness and sustainability to appear recurrently. In the next section we will further analyse the relationship between competitiveness and sustainability and use the LA experience of the 1990s as a way to test its utility.

III COMPETITIVENESS AND SUSTAINABILITY

Krugman (1996) argues that competitiveness is a rather irrelevant concept and that the increase in national productivity is what matters to the improvement of the standard of living, independently of the productivity of the rest of the world. There are two strong arguments against the idea that a country can be permanently more competitive than all the others. The first is the very well-known principle of comparative advantage. Every country is competitive in something. The second is Hume's antimercantilist idea that the attempt to be more competitive in everything is self-defeating. A country cannot show a continuous surplus in its current account without harming its overall competitiveness; the monetary side of the economy would induce the appropriate relative price changes. Neither does the concept of sustainability seem to be strictly necessary from an analytical point of view. The intertemporal approach to the balance of payments only needs the concept of solvency, that is, that a country does not play a Ponzi game.

Why, then, are the concepts of competitiveness and sustainability so popular in the economic policy discussions in developing countries? I think there are three reasons, which are closely related to the points stressed in the previous sections. The first is the existence of liquidity constraints in a world of imperfect markets and uncertainty. The second is the necessity for policymakers to signal their willingness and ability to pay in an uncertain environment, especially when their behavior is under scrutiny because of a worsening in the country's future prospects. And the third reason is that competitiveness, growth potential and ability to pay are not independent phenomena in developing countries. This section discusses these three points in more detail.

Liquidity Constraints and Uncertainty

Two conclusions follow from our discussion in the previous section. First, the failures in the world's capital markets give rise to liquidity constraints which make short-run competitiveness relevant for both macroeconomic equilibrium and financial stability. Second, the incompleteness of capital markets is a source of uncertainty. The problems of enforcement and asymmetric information make the solvency of a country very difficult to evaluate.

It is precisely in this kind of situation where the issues of competitiveness and sustainability arise in the discussions about economic policy. And, typically, the concept of competitiveness is used with two different meanings. According to one, the concept refers to short-run macroeconomic imbalances. The other use alludes to long-run problems of stagnant growth which makes it difficult to meet external obligations. These two uses of the word are not necessarily contradictory but it is advisable to examine their relationship further to avoid confusion and, also, to establish their linkages with growth sustainability.

Reputation and short-run adjustment

When the concept of competitiveness is used in reference to the short run, it is usually in the context of mounting current-account disequilibria and upward moving country risk premia. It is assumed that if a country surpasses a given current account deficit–GDP ratio (for example, the so-called Summer's rule), it has a 'competitiveness problem' and should introduce changes to increase the traded sector's supply and improve the external balance. This could occur, for instance, after an unexpectedly large worsening in the terms of trade or a rise in the international interest rates. Under these circumstances, fiscal and monetary adjustment-cum-devaluation will frequently be recommended. In a disequilibrium context in which creditors express concern over a country's solvency and the latter faces a tight liquidity constraint, the authorities may find it worthwhile to increase its competitiveness in the short run in order to signal both its willingness and its ability to honor the debt services.

In a world of imperfect contract enforcement and limited information, reputation has a positive value. Consequently, the authorities will have a strong incentive to meet the country's obligations. If interest rates are momentarily unusually high or the country is rationed out in credit markets, it will pay off to generate liquidity by other means. Specifically, a temporary increase in the real exchange rate might do the job. Given price sluggishness, an expeditious way to do it would be via nominal depreciation. By means of inducing a short-run deviation of the real exchange rate from its long-run equilibrium path, the country could suddenly become 'highly competitive' and get some extra cash. To meet obligations with the country's own money is a sensible way to show that the country is experiencing liquidity rather than solvency problems. Devaluation, in this sense, may be assimilated to the behavior of an individual firm which decides to liquidate stocks at a price below the cost just to honor bank debt and thereby preserve the value of its reputational capital. In sum, short-run macroeconomic disequilibrium becomes functional to preserve reputation and send the signal that the external sector is sustainable.

Sustainability, the trade pattern, and solvency

The second meaning of competitiveness makes reference to long-run problems. In developing countries, 'development' means, in the first place, approaching the per capita GDP of industrialized countries and, hence, developmental success means reducing the income gap between the country under consideration and the wealthier ones. In this way, achieving a rate of growth in overall productivity which is higher than the average rate observed in the developed world becomes a key target for economic policy. A country whose productivity increase surpasses the rest of the world's is a competitive country. In this context, however, appealing to the concept of competitiveness does not seem to be too compelling. It would be, at most, a fancy way of labeling productivity differences between countries. The picture changes, however, if we take into account two issues. First, the 'endogenous growth' approach to the linkages between the trade specialization pattern and growth and, second, the relationship between growth prospects and the ability to pay in an uncertain world.

The specific features of the trade specialization pattern may affect productivity growth and, hence, have a bearing on growth sustainability. There are three points which are highly relevant to our discussion. First, a natural-resource-exporting country may show a lagging productivity pattern. According to Sachs and Warner (1997), Dutch-Disease effects may render the 'static' equilibrium inefficient if it impedes the economy from developing backward and forward linkages, learning, and taking advantage of externalities. The second is that a country specializing in natural resources may show higher variance in net foreign exchange cash flows. In an incomplete market setting in which developing countries face serious obstacles to risk diversification, higher variance means higher risk. For example, a country which depends on the surplus generated by a small set of products with high price volatility to close the external gap, can be more unstable than another with a more diversified surplus structure (Fanelli, 2000). In this way, the trade specialization pattern might be a source of macroeconomic instability *per se*. The third is that a country which depends on a volatile surplus of primary products to finance capital imports may experience a volatile accumulation of physical capital that may hinder growth.

When we take into account the micro dimension of the problem, it is clear that if a country specializes in the least dynamic industries (with flat learning curves, low returns to scale, small scope for innovation) it will enjoy little productivity growth and will lose competitiveness (Aghion and Howitt, 1997). If this is the case, it is plausible to think that changing relative prices could at best be only part of the response from a long-run perspective. The real problem lies in the fact that the specialization pattern generates a lagging path of productivity. In this sense, long-run competitiveness means the ability to gain market share through productivity enhancement rather than by 'artificially' lowering domestic costs. For example, if the authorities attempted to gain competitiveness by setting real wages below the level of real wages in countries with similar productivity levels, the outcome would probably not be long-lasting. In the long run, market forces would likely force a rise in real wages given the consistency that tends to exist between productivity and wages. In this way, gaining competitiveness via productivity rather than via low real wages is much more credible.

As we have already noticed, judging a country's ability to pay is difficult when there is uncertainty. We argued that one way of signaling an ability to pay is to strengthen liquidity in the short run. But, obviously, the country must also be able to honor its debt services in the long run. And for this, it is solvency rather than liquidity that matters. One critical indicator of solvency is the country's growth prospects and, since there is a strong linkage between long-run competitiveness and growth, the former becomes a determinant of the investor's perception of growth sustainability. This creates a linkage between long-run competitiveness and creditworthiness. In such a context, an economic policy oriented at increasing the country's market share in global exports makes sense. The enhancement of competitiveness in the long run ensures sustainability and reduces the probability of being rationed out. In sum, this means that trade specialization patterns, productivity growth and current account sustainability are not independent phenomena. In a sense, sustainability is the name for long-run competitiveness.

CONCLUDING REMARKS

The previous arguments suggest that short-run competitiveness has strong linkages with liquidity and long-run competitiveness has to do with solvency. In practice, nonetheless, it is very difficult to disentangle in which sense competitiveness is being used. Sometimes it refers to a short-run misalignment of relative prices creating balance-of-payment difficulties and at other times it refers to a tendency for the country to show a lagging growth in productivity compared to the rest of the world and, hence, to experience sustainability problems.

We have argued that the origin of this confusion is the fact that 'competitiveness' is a complex issue which has price and non-price dimensions and which embraces micro and macro elements which interact with each other. I will conclude establishing the linkages with the discussion on micro–macro interactions in the previous section.

Let us first examine the effects which run from macro to micro and which may induce long-lasting changes. On the basis of our discussion, we can imagine several channels through which macroeconomic variables may contribute to shaping the morphology of the microeconomic structure. I would like to stress how macroeconomic variables can affect productivity and the systemic determinants of non-price competitiveness.

Assume an unstable macroeconomic setting in which macroeconomic disequilibria of considerable size are recurrent and, hence, the evolution of prices, quantities and financial variables is rather volatile. This will be very harmful to the relative prices' ability to transmit information and to provide agents with the correct incentives for investment and innovation. When prices are too noisy, the market structure weakens. Some markets disappear while others become too thin. For example, high inflation and uncertainty are primary causes of low financial deepening. They also explain the tendency for the length of contracts to shorten and the investors' propensity to fly to quality. Likewise, an environment of uncertainty is not the best for the development of a strong institutional network. An uncertain environment is one characterized by unfulfilled expectations and contracts which are thereby difficult to meet *ex post*. Neither is it a suitable environment for the strengthening of fiscal institutions. Recurrent fiscal crises are inimical to investment in human capital and the consolidation of the national system of innovation.

This kind of setting may create a severe anti-risk-taking bias in the selection of investment projects with its consequences on the non-price micro determinants of competitiveness and productivity, such as the level of financial deepening, the ability to learn and innovate, and the capacity to develop institutions. For example, suppose that trade liberalization eliminates an anti-export bias in the structure of relative prices. In the new scenario one would expect that firms will be restructured to take advantage of the trade opportunities offered. But assume, additionally, that the transition period toward the new equilibrium is characterized by a certain degree of macroeconomic instability and financial fragility. In such an environment, the firms will face difficulties in obtaining the necessary funds for restructuring. In a segmented market, it is highly probable that only multinationals and larger national firms will be able to finance their projects. Many potential entrepreneurs will suffer from the scarcity of funds generated by the flight to quality and will be rationed out of the market. If larger firms can undertake their projects, there will be distribution effects, but social profitability will not suffer that much. If, on the other hand, larger firms do not undertake the project because they do not know how to do it, have problems of scale, or for any other reason, there will be a net loss for society. The ability to compete will be permanently affected. These kinds of micro–macro interactions may, perhaps, explain why many developing countries experience serious difficulties in developing an entrepreneurial class and a more complete market structure. These conjectures are in line with the hypothesis that finance matters and, specifically, matters to comparative advantage. In fact, combining Rajan and Zingales' (1998) assumptions about external dependency ratios with the analyses of trade specialization pattern and firms' capital structure, we have found additional support for the hypothesis that the level of financial deepening impacts competitiveness and trade patterns (Fanelli and Medhora, 2001).

Finally, the forces which run from micro to macro are intimately related to the kinds of market failures and institutional weaknesses we have identified in this chapter. It must be taken into account that market incompleteness creates coordination failures at the aggregate level and that the market structure is much more incomplete in developing than in developed countries. This gives rise to economic settings in which attaining the aggregate consistency of decentralized plans is more difficult and, hence, coordination failures are more frequent while macroeconomic disequilibria tend to be deeper. Developed countries have sophisticated non-market institutions and fiscal and monetary tools which proved to be appropriate and powerful at preventing disequilibria or, at least, at limiting their magnitude and duration. The low quality of its institutions has frequently impeded developing countries from successfully using non-market stabilizing instruments.[7]

The final outcome of weak markets and institutions is higher volatility of stochastic processes. From our discussion it follows that, on the financial side, international market failures and lack of domestic financial deepening play a critical role. They feed volatility to the extent that they create liquidity constraints and make it very difficult to manage risks and intertemporal allocation. On the real side, we must highlight the lack of price flexibility and short-term contracts. We have also seen that duality and a frequently rudimentary specialization pattern are microeconomic elements that may have a permanent bearing on coordination failures and volatility.

NOTES

1. I gratefully acknowledge the comments by Jaime Ros, J.J. Pradelli, and an anonymous referee.
2. For a typical presentation of the WC's reform program see World Bank (1993) and for a criticism, Fanelli *et al.* (1992).
3. These stylized facts are based on the empirical evidence that can be found in Fanelli (2000), Fanelli and Medhora (2001) and Fanelli and Gonzalez Rozada (1998).
4. The notion that trend and cycle should not be sharply separated, nonetheless, has a long tradition. This is particularly so regarding the structuralist approach and the use of three-gap models to account for the lack of growth in the 1980s in LA, during the debt crisis. On this issue, see Taylor (1979) and Taylor (1983).
5. On these issues and the problem of the exchange rate regime choice, see Frankel (1999).
6. On the issue of the velocity of adjustment of the real exchange rate toward equilibrium and the PPP, see Froot and Rogoff (1995) and Edwards and Savastano (1999).
7. This does not imply denying the fact that some of the market failures mentioned in the chapter are also valid for industrialized countries.

REFERENCES

Aghion, P. And P.W. Howitt (1997), *Endogenous Growth Theory*, Cambridge, Mass.: MIT Press.

Benassy, J.P. (1993), 'Non-clearing markets: microeconomic concepts and macroeconomic applications', *Journal of Economic Literature*, **31**(2), June.

Edwards, S. and M.A. Savastano (1999), 'Exchange rates in emerging economies: what do we need to know?', NBER Working Paper 7228, NBER Working Paper Series, Cambridge, MA, July.

Fanelli, J.M. (2000), 'Macroeconomic regimes, growth, and the international agenda in Latin America', Latin American Trade Network Working Papers No 9.

Fanelli, J.M. and R. Frenkel (1995), 'Micro–macro interaction in economic development', *Unctad Review*, New York: United Nations.

Fanelli, J.M. and M. Gonzalez Rozada (1998), 'Convertibilidad, volatilidad y estabilidad macroeconómica en Argentina', *Estudios de Política Económica y Finanzas*, **1**(2) October.

Fanelli, J.M. and R. Medhora (2001), 'On competitiveness, trade and finance in developing countries', in Fanelli, J.M. and R. Medhora, *Trade, Competitiveness and Finance. The Developing Countries' Experience*, New York: Routledge.

Fanelli, J.M., R. Frenkel and L. Taylor (1992), 'The World Development Report 1991: a critical assessment', *International Monetary and Financial Issues for the 1990s*, UNCTAD, New York: United Nations.

Fazzari, S., Glenn Hubbard and B. Petersen (1988), 'Financing constraints and corporate investment', *Brookings Papers on Economic Activity*, N°1.

Frankel, J. (1999), 'No single currency regime is right for all countries or at all times', NBER Working Paper 7338, NBER Working Paper Series.

Froot, K.A. and K. Rogoff (1995), 'Perspectives on PPP and long-run real exchange rate', in G. Grossman and K. Rogoff (eds), *Handbook of International Economics*, vol. III, Ch. 32, pp. 1647–88.

Haque, Irfan ul (1995), *Trade, Technology, and International Competitiveness*, Washington: The World Bank.

Krugman, Paul R. (1996), *Pop Internationalism*, Cambridge, Mass.: MIT Press.
Leijonhufvud, A. (1981), *Information and Coordination*, New York: Oxford University Press.
Levine, Ross (1997), 'Financial development and economic growth: views and agenda', *Journal of Economic Literature*, Vol. XXXV, June.
Obstfeld, M. and K. Rogoff (1996), *Foundations of International Macroeconomics*, Cambridge, Mass.: The MIT Press.
Petersen, Mitchell A. and Raghuram G. Rajan (1996), 'Trade credit: theories and evidence', *NBER Working Paper No. 5602*, June.
Rajan, Raghuram and L. Zingales (1998), 'Financial dependence and growth,' *American Economic Review*, **88**(3), June.
Ros, J. (2000), *Development Theory and the Economics of Growth*, Ann Arbor, MI: University of Michigan Press.
Sachs, Jeffrey and Andrew Warner (1997), 'Fundamental sources of long-run growth', *American Economic Review*, **87**(2), May.
Taylor, Lance (1979), *Macroeconomic Models for Developing Countries*, New York: McGraw Hill.
Taylor, Lance (1983), *Structuralist Macroeconomics*, New York: Basic Books.
Williamson, J. (1990), 'What Washington means by policy reform', in John Williamson (ed.), *Latin American Adjustment: How Much has Happened?*, Washington: Institute for International Economics, pp. 5–20.
World Bank (1993), *The East Asian Miracle, Economic Growth and Public Policy*, Washington: Oxford University Press.

PART VI

The North, the South and Globalization

16. Income elasticities of imports, North–South trade and uneven development*

Amitava Krishna Dutt**

1 INTRODUCTION

The gap in per capita income levels between the rich and poor countries of the world is enormous. In 1998, the average per capita GNP of the countries the World Bank classifies as high-income countries was almost 50 times that of low-income countries, and 67 times that of these countries leaving out China and India. In terms of purchasing power adjusted per capita figures, the gap narrows somewhat, but these multiples remain high, at 11 and 17.

The question naturally arises whether this gap will close over time or widen. Evidence about past trends yields a dismal picture. The standard deviation of the log of PPP adjusted per capita GDP has gone up between 1960 and 1990, implying what is called σ-divergence (Sala-i-Martin, 1996). The Lorenz curve showing income distribution between countries has moved up over the same period, and the Theil index has increased as well (Stocker, 1994). The equation regressing the growth rate of per capita GDP on initial per capita income has a positive slope, implying what is called β-divergence, although the fit is loose (Sala-i-Martin, 1996). Quadratic regressions imply an inverse-U shape for the relation, implying a positive relation between starting income and growth for most of the sample, and a negative relation for a small group of rich countries (Baumol, Blackman and Wolff, 1989; Ros, 2000). Quah (1993) estimates a 5×5 Markov chain transition matrix in which each country's per capita income relative to the world average is the basic data, to show that it implies distributions which show a thinning middle and an accumulation at both low and high tails. This twin-peakedness implies convergence for countries already at high income levels, but not between rich and poor countries. Average real per capita income growth figures for groups of countries tell a similar story: figures from the *World Development Report* show that the growth rate of the richest one-third of countries rose by an annual rate of 1.9 per cent between 1970 and 1995, whereas the middle third went up by only 0.7 per cent and the bottom third show hardly any increase at all (Scott, 2001, pp. 162–3).[1] Pritchett (1997) shows that there has been 'divergence, big time' between the rich and poor countries of the world over the long time span of the last 150 years. In sum, inequality between rich and poor countries has been growing, with convergence among members of a high-income country club.

Despite this evidence on divergence, some argue that this trend is likely to be reversed in the future. Jones (1997), using Quah's method, finds that the estimated probabilities in the transitional matrix imply convergence in the future. Lucas (2000) develops a simulation model in which countries take off (in a probabilistic sense) from a constant level of per capita income in sequence to show that with 'plausible' parameter values, inequality across countries rises initially in a manner consistent with actual trends, but then falls. His result that 'sooner or later everyone will join the industrial revolution, that economies will grow at the rate common to the wealthiest economies, and that percent differences in income levels will disappear' (Lucas, 2000, p. 166) is driven by the assumptions in his model that the probability of takeoff for countries increases with the world average level of per capita income, and that later starters necessarily grow faster than income leaders.

The question of whether rich and poor countries will converge cannot be answered by simply extrapolating from past trends or from simple simulation models. The answer depends on a large number of factors, some relating to the internal dynamics of countries (the neoclassical growth literature stressing the role of diminishing returns to capital for convergence), and others to the interaction between rich and poor countries. The consequences of the interaction between rich and poor countries – often dubbed the North and the South – for convergence have justifiably attracted much attention. This analysis has drawn attention to a large number of mechanisms, some of which tend to produce convergence through what Myrdal (1957) has called 'spread effects', while others lead to divergence or uneven development through 'backwash effects'. These mechanisms include those which rely on patterns of specialization in trade and the role of increasing returns (Singer, 1950; Krugman, 1981; Dutt, 1990), the effects of changes in technology and demand composition on the North–South terms of trade and growth (Prebisch, 1950; Singer, 1950; Dutt, 1988, 1990, 1996), the role of international capital flows (Singer, 1950; Burgstaller and Saavedra-Rivano, 1984), labor migration (Wong and Yip, 1999) and international technology transfers which are emphasized in the work of Lucas (2000) mentioned earlier. Given the large number of different mechanisms and the complexity of each one, it is instructive to isolate individual mechanisms and examine their implications for the question of convergence and uneven development.

This chapter examines one such mechanism: the consequences of North–South trade when the income elasticity of demand for imports of the South from the North is higher than the reciprocal elasticity for the North (owing to the inability of the South to produce technologically-sophisticated income-elastic goods). In his synthesis of a number of contributions – including those of Harrod (1933), Prebisch (1950), Seers (1962), Kaldor (1970) and Dixon and Thirlwall (1975) – Thirlwall (1983) argues that their core proposition is a simple rule which states that one country's growth rate relative to other countries can be approximated by the ratio of the income elasticity of demand for its exports to its income elasticity of demand for imports. For two groups of countries – the North and the South – the relative rate of growth of the South to the North is then given by the ratio of the income elasticity of imports of the North from the South to the income elasticity of imports of the South from the North, implying faster growth for the North, or divergence.

The rest of this chapter proceeds as follows. Section 2 briefly presents the elasticity argument made by Thirlwall and critically examines the conditions under which it is valid. Section 3 uses a simple North–South model of trade following Taylor (1981, 1983) to examine the implications of the elasticity argument in a more general setting. Section 4 examines the implications of introducing trade imbalances and debt accumulation by the South. Section 5 discusses old evidence and presents some new facts about the empirical validity of the income elasticity of imports hypothesis, and section 6 concludes.

2 INCOME ELASTICITIES AND UNEVEN DEVELOPMENT

If we divide the world into two regions called the North and the South, Thirlwall's relation can be written as

$$y_S/y_N = \varepsilon_N/\varepsilon_S, \tag{16.1}$$

where y_i is the rate of growth of output, Y_i, of region i, and ε_i is the income elasticity of demand for imports in region i, with N and S denoting North and South. If, as assumed by Thirlwall and the others, ε_N is low – that is, the North's demand for Southern products is income-inelastic – while ε_S is high – that is, the South's demand for Northern products is income-elastic, we have $\varepsilon_N < \varepsilon_S$, which implies that $y_S < y_N$, so that we have uneven development in the sense that the region with a lower level of income experiences slower growth.

Thirlwall (1983) explains that equation (16.1) holds only under very stringent assumptions, namely: balanced trade between the North and South and constancy of the real terms of trade. This can be verified as follows. Assume that the export function for the North, or equivalently the import function for the South, is given by

$$X_N = \Theta_N (1/P)^{-\mu_S} Y_S^{\varepsilon_S}, \tag{16.2}$$

where $\Theta_i > 0$ is a constant, $\mu_i > 0$ is the absolute value of the price elasticity of demand for the imported good in region i, and $P = P_S / EP_N$, where P_i is the price of the good produced in region i in terms of its own currency, and E is the price of the Northern currency in terms of the Southern currency. For simplicity, we set E equal to unity. We assume, following Thirlwall (1983), that the elasticities are constant. The function shows that the South's level of imports from the North increases with Southern production and income, and falls with the relative price of the Northern good, $1/P$. Similarly, we assume that the export function of the South or the import function of the North is

$$X_S = \Theta_S P^{-\mu_N} Y_N^{\varepsilon_N}, \tag{16.3}$$

which shows that Northern imports of the Southern good increase with Northern production and income and fall with the relative price of the Southern good, P. The balance of payments can be written as

$$P_S X_S + P_N F = P_N X_N, \tag{16.4}$$

where F is the net outflow of capital from the North to South in terms of the Northern good. This implies

$$P X_S + F = X_N. \tag{16.4'}$$

Equation (16.4′), expressed in growth rate form, is given by

$$[1 - (F/X_N)]\,[p + x_S] + (F/X_N) f = x_N, \tag{16.5}$$

where lower case symbols denote the rates of growth of the variable denoted by the upper case symbol, for instance, $f = (\mathrm{d}F/\mathrm{d}t)/F$. Log-differentiating equations (16.2) and (16.3) and substituting into (16.5) we get

$$y_S = (1/\varepsilon_S)\ \{(1-\mu_N-\mu_S)\,p + [1-(F/X_N)]\ \varepsilon_N\, y_N + (F/X_N)\ [f-(1-\mu_N)p]\}. \tag{16.6}$$

In the special case in which trade is balanced and we have $F=0$ and $f=0$, this reduces to

$$y_S = (1/\varepsilon_S)\ \{(1-\mu_N-\mu_S)\,p + \varepsilon_N\, y_N\}. \tag{16.6$'$}$$

and in the special case in which the terms of trade do not change, so that $p=0$, but trade is not necessarily balanced, we get

$$y_S = (1/\varepsilon_S)\ \{\ [1-(F/X_N)]\ \varepsilon_N\, y_N + (F/X_N)\, f\}. \tag{16.6$''$}$$

If we assume that both trade is balanced and $p=0$, we obtain equation (16.1).

Equation (16.1) shows that with balanced trade and constant terms of trade, the imports of the two regions must grow at the same rate. Since the imports of region i grow at the rate $\varepsilon_i\, y_i$, which is the product of the income elasticity of import demand and the growth rate of output, if one region has a higher income elasticity of imports, it will have to grow at a slower rate than the other region to satisfy trade balance.

If the balanced trade and constant terms of trade assumptions are not satisfied, this result will not necessarily hold. If the terms of trade change, equation (16.6′) shows that y_S can deviate from $(\varepsilon_N/\varepsilon_S)y_N$. If the Marshall–Lerner condition is satisfied, so that $\mu_N+\mu_S>1$, which as we shall see below is the condition required for the stability of price adjustment, then it follows from equation (16.6′) that y_S can exceed $(\varepsilon_N/\varepsilon_S)y_N$ if and only if $p<0$, that is, if the Southern terms of trade deteriorates (with balanced trade). The deterioration of the Southern terms of trade will make the North increase its imports from the South and the South reduce its imports from the North, so that the South can grow faster than it could with a constant terms of trade. If we hold P constant, but allow trade imbalances, equation (16.6″) shows that equation (16.1) need not constrain Southern growth, given the Northern growth rate. Assume that the South is the capital importer, so that we have $F>0$. If the amount of foreign capital (in terms of the Northern good) does not change, we have $f=0$. Then, we have $y_S=(1/\varepsilon_S)\ [1-(F/X_N)]\ \varepsilon_N\, y_N<(\varepsilon_N/\varepsilon_S)y_N$, so that Southern growth is actually *lower* than that under no capital flows because total foreign exchange receipts from both exports and capital flows – which is what finances imports and hence growth – grows less than the growth rate of exports. However, if $f>0$, then the growth rate of the Southern economy may be higher than $(\varepsilon_N/\varepsilon_S)y_N$. Increasing capital flows can therefore finance higher Southern growth.

How good a theory of uneven development is this? The answer to this question depends on two further questions. First, are the assumptions of the model realistic enough to make equation (16.1) provide us with an accurate theory of the relative growth rates of the South and the North? Second, is it empirically true that $\varepsilon_N < \varepsilon_S$?

Concerning the first question we can proceed both theoretically and empirically. Thirlwall himself has explored the empirical dimension by using data on export growth and income elasticities of demand for imports for individual countries to find how well the product of the two explains the actual rate of growth of countries. Thirlwall (1979) uses data for a number of developed countries over the post-war period to find that the growth rate of most countries approximates this simple rule. However, when Thirlwall and Hussain (1982) perform the same exercise with developing countries for which income elasticities of import are available, their predictions are not too accurate. They find that terms of trade variations and capital inflows do explain some of the variation in growth rates, and that the mean absolute error of the actual growth rate, y_i, from the predicted growth rate given by x_i/ε_i, is 2.01, which they admit may be regarded as high. A number of others have followed Thirlwall's lead and compared this growth estimate with actual growth rates for other countries and time periods, using more sophisticated econometric techniques to estimate import elasticities. A review of this empirical literature is available in McCombie (1997) and very briefly in Dutt (2002). The results support Thirlwall's predictions based on equation (16.1) in many cases, but do not do so for many other cases, especially for less-developed countries (LDCs). That this is the case should not come as a major surprise, since the equation has been derived under a number of unrealistic assumptions.

In terms of theory, we have already seen that the validity of equation (16.1) requires some stringent assumptions, that is, that trade is balanced, and that the terms of trade are constant. Moreover, we have implicitly made other assumptions in deriving this equation, including: the world can be meaningfully divided into two regions; that the two regions are completely specialized in the production of one traded good each; and that price and income elasticities of import demand for both regions are constant. Abstracting from the appropriateness of these implicit assumptions for now, let us consider the constant terms of trade and balanced trade assumptions.

Two comments are in order about the terms of trade assumption. First, on theoretical grounds it can be argued that changes in the terms of trade should preferably be treated as being explained by a general equilibrium model of the global economy which fully specifies the determinants of Northern and Southern growth. Such specifications are made in

North–South models developed by Findlay (1980) and Taylor (1981, 1983), among others, but not in the formulation described above, since it involves no assumptions about the structures of the two regions which allow us to determine their growth rates. Instead, we have merely 'explained' gaps in growth rates given the artificial assumption of a constant terms of trade. Second, the assumption implies that we are neglecting any consideration of a major concern of several development economists regarding the deterioration of the terms of trade for the South (see especially Prebisch, 1950; Singer, 1950; Spraos, 1983).

On the balanced trade condition, LDCs frequently resort to foreign borrowing and receive other kinds of capital inflows. The development economics literature on the problems of international capital flows for LDCs is immense. It stresses a number of issues such as: the balance of payments effects of profit repatriation and interest payments; effects on the terms of trade due to changes in production; and the effects of the operations of transnational corporations on technology, industrial organization and income distribution. Some of these issues have also been incorporated into North–South models to examine the effects of capital flows for North–South development patterns (see Burgstaller and Saavedra-Rivano, 1984; Dutt, 1989). These important issues, however, are being ignored in the above analysis as a result of the assumption of balanced trade. However, it can be argued that these issues are analytically distinct from that of different import elasticities, and it is therefore not only justifiable, but also preferable, to separate the analysis of the effects on North–South development patterns of import elasticities from the effects of international capital flows. However, it remains true that it is necessary to see to what extent allowing for North–South capital flows affects the analysis of the effects of import elasticities. Moreno-Brid (1998–99) has in fact extended Thirlwall's model of balance of payments constrained growth for a single economy to argue that Thirlwall's theoretical analysis is altered by the introduction of international borrowing, even under simple assumptions.

On the issue of the income elasticities of imports and exports, a cottage industry has developed which estimates these trade elasticities for individual countries. However, there appears to be no systematic empirical evidence which compares the elasticity of Northern imports from the South with respect to Northern income with the elasticity of Southern imports from the North with respect to Southern income.

The next three sections in turn address the three issues just discussed, namely: of developing a general equilibrium North–South model which explicitly analyses the dynamics of global development patterns; examining the implications of North–South capital flows; and the empirical issue of differences in import elasticities.

3 A MODEL OF NORTH–SOUTH TRADE

A model which simultaneousy determines Northern and Southern growth rates and the evolution of the South–North terms of trade can be developed using the structuralist assumptions made by Taylor (1981, 1983) in his pioneering model of North–South trade in which each region produces one traded good (see also Sarkar, 1998). Following Taylor, we assume that the North grows with excess capacity with firms practicing mark-up pricing and with output determined by demand; in other words we assume a Kalecki–Keynes North. While the Northern good is produced under oligopolistic conditions, the market for the Southern good is perfectly competitive, so that the price of the good is flexible and Southern producers fully utilize their capacity. However, the South has a fixed real wage and unemployed labor, so that it has a Marx–Lewis structure. For both regions we assume that output is produced with fixed coefficients of production using labor and capital. In the North firms set the product price according to the mark-up equation

$$P_N = (1+z)\ W_N b_N, \tag{16.7}$$

where z is the exogenously given mark-up which represents the degree of monopoly in the market for the Northern good, W_N the fixed money wage in the North, and b_N is the fixed unit labor requirement for the Northern good. Northern producers determine output according to demand. In the South, firms produce at full capacity, so that we have

$$Y_S = K_S / a_S, \tag{16.8}$$

where a_S is the fixed capital–output ratio and K_S the Southern stock of capital.

There are two income groups in each region; workers who receive wage income and capitalists who receive profit income. In the North, equation (16.7) implies that capitalists receive a share $z/(1+z)$ of the value of Northern output, and workers receive $1/(1+z)$. In the South, workers receive a wage which is fixed in terms of the price of the Southern good (which, as we will assume below, is the only good they consume), so that

$$W_S / P_S = V_S, \tag{16.9}$$

where V_S, the Southern real wage, is exogenously fixed. Consequently, capitalists receive $(1-b_S V_S)P_S Y_S$ in terms of the Southern good as their income, where b_S is the fixed unit labor requirement in the South.

In the North capitalists save a fraction s_N of their income while workers consume all their income. Northern capitalists and workers spend a fraction α of their consumption expenditure on the Southern good and the rest on the Northern good. This fraction is determined according to

$$\alpha = \alpha_0 \, Y_N^{\varepsilon_N - 1} \, P^{1-\mu_N}, \tag{16.10}$$

a formulation which is compatible with a variety of assumptions of price and income elasticities of the demands for the two goods. If $\varepsilon_N = \mu_N = 1$, the shares of consumption expenditure spent on the two goods are constant. If $\varepsilon_N < 1$, increases in Northern income will result in a lower proportion of consumption expenditure being spent on the Southern good, implying that the Southern good is income inelastic. If $\mu_N < 1$, the share of Northern consumption expenditure on the Southern good rises when P rises despite the increase in P, implying price inelastic demand for the Southern good, and conversely if $\mu_N > 1$. In the South workers spend their entire income consuming the Southern good, while capitalists save a fraction s_S and consume the rest, devoting a fraction β to the Northern good and the rest to the Southern good. Analogously with Northern consumers, we assume that

$$\beta = \beta_0 \, (\sigma_S Y_S)^{\varepsilon_S - 1} \, P^{1-\mu_S} \tag{16.11}$$

where, instead of total income as in the North, we use the profit share of income, $\sigma_S Y_S$, where $\sigma_S = (1 - b_S V_S)$, since the income of workers, who spend their entire income on the Southern good, is not available for allocation between the two goods.

Northern firms have an investment function given by

$$I_N / K_N = \gamma_0 + \gamma_1 \, (Y_N / K_N), \tag{16.12}$$

where K_N is the capital stock in the North, and γ_i are positive constants, which shows that the Northern investment rate depends on the rate of capacity utilization measured by Y_N / K_N, because higher capacity utilization implies more buoyant markets and higher profits. Only the Northern good is used as an investment good in the North. In the South, capitalist firms invest their entire saving. We assume that both the Northern and Southern good can be an investment good in the South, and for simplicity assume that a fraction β of total investment is spent on the Northern good and the rest on the Southern good. The stock of capital in neither region depreciates.

Our assumptions imply that the value of Northern imports from the South, that is, of Southern exports, is given by

$$P_S X_S = \alpha\ \{[1+(1-s_N)z]/(1+z)\} P_N\ Y_N,$$

which, using equation (16.10) can be written as equation (16.3), where $\Theta_S = \alpha_0\ [1+(1-s_N)z]/(1+z)$. The value of Southern imports from the North, that is, of Northern exports – noting that the same fraction of consumption and investment demand is spent by Southern capitalists on the Northern good – is given by

$$P_N X_N = \beta\ \sigma_S\ P_S Y_S.$$

This equation, using equation (16.11), can be written as equation (16.2), where $\Theta_N = \beta_0 \sigma_S{}^{\varepsilon}{}_S$. Thus, our assumptions imply that our North–South model has embedded in it the export functions from the previous section.

To analyse the model, we distinguish between the short run and the long run. In the short run we assume that the stocks of capital in the two regions, K_i, are given, and that the markets for the two goods clear through fluctuations in Northern output and Southern (relative) price. In the long run we assume that the short-run equilibrium conditions always hold, and that the stocks of capital change due to investment.

In the short run, we assume that a positive excess demand for the Southern good results in an increase in the relative price of the Southern good, P. The excess demand for the good is given by

$$ED_S = C_{SS} + I_{SS} + X_S - Y_S, \qquad (16.13)$$

where C_{ij} denotes the consumption demand for good i in region j and I_{ij} denotes the investment demand for good i in region j, measured in units of good i with subscripts N and S denoting North and South, as before. Since Southern income can be spent on buying domestic goods or imports (since all Southern saving is invested) so that $Y_S = C_{SS} + I_{SS} + M_S$, where M_i is imports of region i in units of good i, and since $M_S = X_N / P$, we can rewrite equation (16.13) as

$$ED_S = X_S - (1/P)\ X_N. \qquad (16.13')$$

We also assume that a positive excess demand for the Northern good results in an increase in $u = Y_N / K_N$, the rate of capacity utilization in the North. The excess demand for the Northern good is given by

$$ED_N = C_{NN} + I_N + X_N - Y_N. \qquad (16.14)$$

Since Northern income can be used for consuming the Northern good, on imports, and on saving, we have $Y_N = C_{NN} + M_N + S_N$, where S_N is

Northern saving in terms of the Northern good, and since $M_N = PX_S$, we can rewrite equation (16.14) as

$$ED_N = I_N - S_N + X_N - PX_S. \tag{16.14'}$$

Short-run equilibrium, in which u and P do not change, given K_i, requires $ED_i = 0$. Imposing this condition into equations (16.13′) and (16.14′), and using equations (16.2), (16.3), and (16.8), and the savings assumptions for the North, which implies that $S_N = s_N \sigma_N Y_N$, we can solve for the short-run equilibrium values of the terms of trade and the Northern rate of capacity utilizations, which are

$$P = [(\Theta_S/\Theta_N)(uK_N)^{\varepsilon_S}/(K_S/a_S)^{\varepsilon_N}]^{1/(\mu_N+\mu_S-1)}. \tag{16.15}$$

and

$$u = \gamma_0/[s_N \sigma_N - \gamma_1], \tag{16.16}$$

where $\sigma_N = z/(1+z)$, the profit share in the North and where the equilibrium value of the terms of trade can be solved by substituting equation (16.16) in equation (16.15).

Equation (16.16) shows that to obtain an economically meaningful equilibrium value of u we require $s_N \sigma_N > \gamma_1$, which is the standard condition of quantity adjustment models requiring that the responsiveness of saving to changes in output exceeds the responsiveness of investment for stability of output adjustment. The (local) stability of short-run equilibrium also requires that $\partial(ED_S)/\partial P < 0$ in the neighborhood of the short-run equilibrium which, differentiating equation (16.13′) with respect to P and using equations (16.2), (16.3) and (16.8) requires that $\mu_N + \mu_S > 1$, which is the well-known Marshall–Lerner condition.

In the long run, capital stocks grow according to the rates of capital accumulation in the two regions, given by $g_i = I_i/K_i$. Northern accumulation is given, from equations (16.12) and (16.16), by

$$g_N = \gamma_0 + \gamma_0\gamma_1/[s_N \sigma_N - \gamma_1]. \tag{16.17}$$

For the South, we have

$$S_S = s_S \sigma_S K_S/a_S.$$

where S_S is Southern saving in terms of the Southern good. Since investment is made in the form of both Northern and Southern goods, we assume that investment is given by the equation

$$I_S = P^{\xi} S_S,$$

where $\xi < 1$. Combining these two equations implies that

$$g_S = s_S\, P^{\xi} \sigma_S / a_S \,. \tag{16.18}$$

The long-run dynamics of growth and the terms of trade are shown in Figure 16.1. The g_N curve depicts equation (16.17), which shows that g_N is independent of p, and the g_S depicts equation (16.18), which shows that g_S increases with p. Equation (16.15) implies, noting that u and a_S are independent of K_i,

$$p = [1/(\mu_N + \mu_S - 1)]\, (\varepsilon_N\, g_N - \varepsilon_S g_S), \tag{16.19}$$

which shows that the rate of change of P depends on the gap between $\varepsilon_N g_N$ and $\varepsilon_S g_S$. Although our results will be valid whenever $\varepsilon_S > \varepsilon_N$, to fix ideas we assume $\varepsilon_S > 1 > \varepsilon_N$, so that the curve for $\varepsilon_S g_S$ will lie above the curve g_S and the curve $\varepsilon_N g_N$ will lie below the curve g_N, as shown in the figure. Given initial values of K_i, equation (16.15) shows how the equilibrium terms of trade are determined in the short run. The curves $\varepsilon_S g_S$ and $\varepsilon_N g_N$ in the figure, with equation (16.19), then show how P moves over time. For any $P > P^*$, we have $\varepsilon_S g_S > \varepsilon_N g_N$, so that P falls over time according to equation (16.19), while for $P < P^*$, P rises over time.

Now suppose that the initial K_i are such that we start with P satisfying

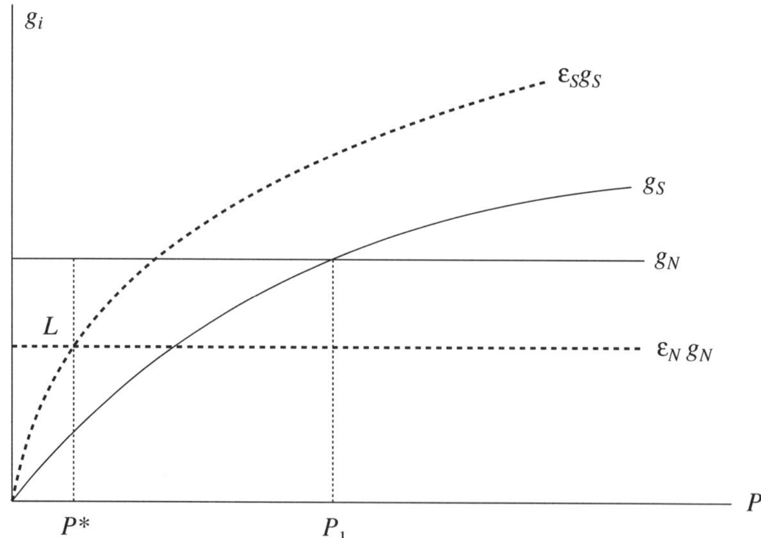

Figure 16.1 Long-run dynamics

$P_1 > P > P^*$, where P_1 is the level of P at which $g_N = g_S$. It follows, then, that we must have $g_N > g_S$, and that $p < 0$. Thus, the global economy will experience declining P and declining g_S, but have a constant g_N, till it reaches the point L, with the terms of trade P^*, at which $p = 0$. This is a long-run equilibrium for the system in the sense that P, g_N and g_S become stationary, as do y_N and y_S. However, we have $g_S < g_N$ at this equilibrium, so that we have continuous uneven development in the sense that $y_N > y_S$.[2] Note that if initially $P > P_1$, we will initially have a phase in which $g_S > g_N$, but the deterioration of the Southern terms of trade will reduce g_S over time until we have uneven development and enter the region in which $P_1 > P > P^*$. If we initially have $P < P^*$, the terms of trade for the South will improve over time until we achieve long-run equilibrium at P^*.

The mechanism by which the world economy arrives at the equilibrium with unequal rates of growth can be intuitively explained as follows. Suppose, initially, that the two regions grow at the same rate. Given the differences in the income elasticities, the demand for the Northern good will increase faster than that of the Southern good. This will imply that the terms of trade will turn against the South. As it does so, Northern growth is not affected (given the special assumptions of our model), but the Southern rate of investment is reduced as the price of the imported portion of its investment goods increases. Eventually, when the terms of trade stabilizes, the South has to grow more slowly than the North.

Thus, our model implies that in long-run equilibrium, when the South–North terms of trade becomes constant, we have uneven development in the sense that Northern capital and output grow at a faster rate than Southern capital and output.

Regarding the terms of trade, we note that there is some association between a deterioration of the terms of trade and uneven development. For the range of terms of trade given by (P^*, P_1) we have both the processes of uneven development and deteriorating terms of trade occurring. However, for the intervals $[P^*, +\infty)$ and $(0, P_1]$, one of the two does not occur. At P^* we have balanced growth of the North and the South but terms of trade deterioration, and for $P > P_1$ we have even development with terms of trade deterioration.[3] At P^* we have a constant terms of trade and uneven development, while below P^* we have uneven development with terms of trade improvement.

4 TRADE AND DEBT

We have so far assumed that for the South, investment is identically equal to domestic saving, so that trade between the North and the South is balanced. We now modify the analysis to allow the South to borrow from the North. If the South can borrow from the North, its rate of accumulation, g_S, is no longer restricted by its savings; as shown by equation (16.6), y_S can therefore be raised by the South by borrowing.

A complete analysis of the dynamics of a North–South model with borrowing requires some assumptions about the determinants of the Southern rate of accumulation, either in terms of the determinants of the investment rate, or in terms of the limits to Southern borrowing, and an analysis of the dynamics of the debt position of the South, measured, for instance, by the foreign debt to output ratio for the South. A model of North–South trade with Southern borrowing has been developed by Taylor (1986), but the focus of that model is on short-term speculative crises. A model which draws on Taylor's (1981, 1983) analysis to address long-run issues is developed in Dutt (1989), where it is assumed that the Southern rate of capital accumulation is exogenously given and foreign borrowing at a given interest rate bridges the gap between Southern domestic saving and this given rate of investment. The model developed there takes Northern and Southern stocks of capital, and the amount of Southern debt (in terms of the Northern good), to be given in the short run, to determine the short-run equilibrium, market-clearing, values of the terms of trade and Northern capacity utilization, much like the analysis of the preceding section, but taking into account capital flows and interest payments. The model then analyses the dynamics of the ratio of Northern to Southern capital stock, and the ratio of Southern debt to the Southern capital stock, for a given interest rate. This model, however, assumes unit income elasticities of demand for the two goods in the regions, which implies that increases in income in the two regions increases imports proportionately for both regions, given the terms of trade.

Here we wish to examine the implications of income elasticities of imports being different for the two regions. Rather than analysing the full dynamics of a model of the sort described above with this assumption, we pursue two simpler routes. First, we analyse conditions which the evolution of Southern debt must satisfy to generate even development at long-run equilibrium at which – following the analysis of the previous section – we assume that the terms of trade are constant, and explore whether these conditions are likely to be satisfied in reality. Second, we introduce some plausible assumptions for determining the evolution of Southern debt or foreign borrowing, and examine the implications for development patterns at long-run equilibrium, again under the assumption that the terms of trade do not change.

Following the first route we note that, with constant terms of trade, equation (16.6″) implies

$$\varepsilon_S y_S = [1-(F/X_N)]\, \varepsilon_N y_N + (F/X_N) f.$$

If $1<F/X_N<0$,[4] this in turn implies that $\varepsilon_S y_S$ is a weighted average of $\varepsilon_N y_N$ and f and must lie between them. Since $\varepsilon_S>\varepsilon_N$, and even development implies $y_S>y_N$, we must have $\varepsilon_S y_S>\varepsilon_N y_N$, which establishes that $f>\varepsilon_S y_S >\varepsilon_N y_N$. Since, with constant terms of trade, equations (16.2) and (16.3) imply $x_S=\varepsilon_N y_N$, and $x_N=\varepsilon_S y_S$, this implies that $f>x_N>x_S$. This implies that Southern net borrowing must increase faster than Southern exports, and moreover, that F/X_N must increase over time. As F/X_N approaches unity, we will have $\varepsilon_S y_S$ approaching f, so that y_S will grow more slowly than f if $\varepsilon_S>1$. The evolution of Southern debt, D, in terms of the Northern good, is given by

$$\mathrm{d}D/\mathrm{d}t = F + i\,D,$$

where i is the rate of interest at which the South borrows. This implies that

$$d=(F/D)+i, \tag{16.20}$$

where d is the rate of growth of Southern debt. Assuming that the interest rate is constant (at least in long-run equilibrium), and assuming that Southern debt grows at a constant rate (also in long-run equilibrium), F/D will become constant, implying that Southern debt and borrowing will grow at the same rate. It follows that if, by borrowing from the North, the South tries to grow faster than the North, and $\varepsilon_S>\varepsilon_N$, its debt will grow faster than its exports, and (with $\varepsilon_S>1$) its debt will also grow faster than its level of output. It is implausible to suppose that, given Southern credit constraints, the option of this kind of foreign debt accumulation is available to the South.

We now turn to the second route, that of imposing some conditions on the evolution of Southern debt or borrowing, to take into account the reality of Southern credit constraints. Accordingly, we use our export equations (16.2) and (16.3), and the balance of payments condition (16.4), to obtain equation (16.6), and impose additional conditions on it. One condition is that the terms of trade become constant. Another condition we use takes into account that Southern debt, or alternatively, Southern borrowing, is limited by some indicator of Southern creditworthiness.[5]

We consider several alternative assumptions to formalize Southern credit constraints. Three impose upper bounds on the ratio of borrowing and debt indicators to Southern output, which we assume to be binding. One assumes that the Southern trade deficit as a ratio of Southern output is constant,[6] so that

$$F/PY_S=\lambda_1, \tag{16.21}$$

another that net Southern capital inflows as a ratio of Southern output is constant, so that

$$(F+iD)/PY_S=\lambda_2, \tag{16.22}$$

and yet another assumes that the stock of Southern debt as a ratio of Southern output is constant, so that

$$D/PY_S=\lambda_3. \tag{16.23}$$

Three alternatives to these assumptions make the trade deficit, net Southern capital inflows, and Southern debt, with respect to the value of Southern exports, rather than Southern output, to be constant,[7] so that we have

$$F/PX_S=\lambda_4, \tag{16.24}$$

$$(F+iD)/PX_S=\lambda_5, \tag{16.25}$$

or

$$D/PX_S=\lambda_6. \tag{16.26}$$

Equation (16.21) implies

$$f=y_S+p \tag{16.27}$$

Equation (16.22) implies, using equation (16.20), that

$$f[(F/D)/((F/D)+i)]+i\,d\,[i/((F/D)+i)]=y_S+p.$$

At long-run equilibrium with F/D constant, and hence $f=d$, equation (16.27) must again be satisfied. Equation (16.23) implies that

$$d=y_S+p.$$

Hence, with $f=d$, equation (16.27) must again be satisfied.

It is straightforward to show, in the same way, that equations (16.24) to (16.26) imply

$$f=x_S+p. \tag{16.28}$$

If we substitute condition (16.27) and $p=0$ in equation (16.6) we get

$$y_S=[1-(F/X_N)]\varepsilon_N\, y_N/[\varepsilon_S-(F/X_N)].$$

If $\varepsilon_S<1$, this implies that the Southern rate of growth will be higher than that given by $(\varepsilon_N/\varepsilon_S)\, y_N$. But in this case, F/X_N must rise continuously over time, which means that so must y_S. Thus, it is possible for y_S to rise indefinitely with the South obeying its credit constraint and without facing a deteriorating terms of trade. However, if $\varepsilon_S>1$, this growth rate must be lower than $(\varepsilon_N/\varepsilon_S)\, y_N$. Moreover, F/X_N must fall continuously over time, which means that so must y_S if it is to obey the above equation. Thus if $\varepsilon_S>1$, the South cannot grow faster than the North by borrowing.

If we now substitute the condition (16.28) and $p=0$ in equation (16.6) we get

$$y_S=(1/\varepsilon_S)\,\{[1-(F/X_N)]\varepsilon_N\, y_N+(F/X_N)\, x_S\},$$

which, using equation (16.3), implies

$$y_S=(\varepsilon_N/\varepsilon_S)\, y_N,$$

which is the same as equation (16.1). Thus, the condition for unequal growth is again the same as it was for the case of balanced trade.

In sum, even if the South can experience foreign capital inflows and temporarily increase its rate of growth above that of the North, given the realities of international credit constraints, with a higher income elasticity for the South than the North, this is unlikely to happen over the long run. If $\varepsilon_N<\varepsilon_S$, and if the South cannot borrow, or allow its foreign debt to grow, at a rate faster than its exports, uneven development occurs just as in the model with balanced trade. If the South cannot borrow or allow its foreign debt to grow faster than its GDP, then uneven development can be avoided, but this is not possible if $\varepsilon_S>1$.

5 THE EMPIRICS OF INCOME ELASTICITIES OF IMPORTS

We now turn to the comparison of income elasticities of imports for the South and the North. It is often argued that poorer countries in general have higher income elasticities of import demand than richer countries because they produce relatively income inelastic goods such as primary products and basic manufactured goods. Thus, as their income increases and they demand more income-elastic goods, their imports increase more than proportionately than their incomes. Rich countries, however, do not have this characteristic because they are able to produce relatively sophisticated income-elastic goods. There are two kinds of studies which can be used to evaluate this argument empirically.

Indirect evidence is available on elasticities from estimates of the income elasticity of the consumption and imports of different types of goods. For instance, Houthakker and Magee (1969) use quarterly data for the US for the period 1947 to 1966 to find that income elasticities of imports are higher for finished manufactures and manufactured foods compared to crude materials, crude foods and semi-manufactures. As is well known, elasticities for manufactured goods are higher than for semi-manufactures and for primary products. Given the classic characterization of poor countries as specializing in primary products and rich countries specializing in manufactured goods, we may be tempted to accept the income elasticity story. But, as extensively documented, there have been significant changes in the composition of LDC exports, with primary products increasingly playing a smaller role, and with manufactures increasing their share, a trend which has been striking for a number of semi-industrialized LDCs (see Reidel, 1984, for instance).

Turning to the direct evidence on income elasticities for imports, Houthakker and Magee (1969) computed income and price elasticities of exports and imports of a number of countries using the following equations with annual data for the years 1951–66:

$$\log M_t = A_0 + A_1 \log Y_t + A_2 \log (P_{Mt}/P_{Dt}) + u_t$$

$$\log X_t = B_0 + B_1 \log Y_{Wt} + B_2 \log (P_{Xt}/P_{WXt}) + v_t$$

where Y_W refers to weighted average of real income of trading partners with constant export shares as weights, P_{WX} is a price index of competing export countries, and P_D is a domestic price index, the wholesale price index. However, almost all the countries for which they estimated export and import functions are developed countries. For most of these countries they find that export and import activity elasticities are not significantly different, although they are for the US and Japan, but in opposite directions. The only developing country for which they compute both export and import elasticities is India, for which the export elasticity is 0.54 and the import elasticity is 1.43. Portugal, among the least developed of the European nations, is roughly the same. Many Latin American countries have foreign income elsaticities which are less than 1.

A large literature has developed which has estimated export and import functions for individual countries, and which therefore provide estimates of income elasticities of imports and world-income elasticities of exports (see Magee, 1975, and Goldstein and Khan, 1985, for surveys). While most of the available evidence is for developed countries, there are numerous studies which include estimates for LDCs as well, including Khan (1974), Bahmani-Oskooee (1986), and Faini *et al.* (1992). However, this large literature does not allow us to draw definitive conclusions about income elasticities of demand for imports and exports for rich and poor countries, since the estimates do not appear to follow a consistent pattern. Bairam (1997) uses the available import and export elasticities to argue that for most developed countries, the elasticity of imports with respect to income exceeds the foreign-income elasticity of exports, while the opposite is true for developing countries, and his Box and Cox general specification equations suggest that export elasticities fall with per capita income while import elasticities do not change over levels of development. He notes that this observation does not square with the Prebisch hypothesis, and it certainly is not consistent with the uneven development hypothesis of this chapter. Thirlwall (1997), however, criticizes Bairam for drawing these inferences from a small and selective group of developing countries which contain mainly newly industrializing countries and few extremely poor countries.

Moreover, it is well known that many of these estimates suffer from a number of problems. First, there are aggregation problems resulting from aggregation over commodities and countries. As we have already noted, the elasticities of exports and imports can be expected to be very different according to commodity groups, so that the structure of trade can be expected to affect the estimated elasticities. Since they aggregate over countries, the imports and exports of particular countries are examined in relation to the rest of the world, not usually disaggregating over trade partners. Second, there are simultaneity problems. This is especially true for export equations, for which it is reasonable to expect that supply and demand factors influence exports, whereas the estimated equations only examine the demand side. Goldstein and Khan (1978) have attempted to overcome this problem using a simultaneous equations approach in which export supply is taken to depend on the price of exports relative to domestic prices and an index of domestic capacity. However, they estimate functions only for developed countries, and although price elasticities of demand are found to be higher than in the single equation models, the income elasticities which concern us here, are similar. Third, there is the issue of omitted variables, the most important arguably being trade restrictions, especially for LDCs. Faini *et al.* (1992) attempt to overcome the problem by using foreign exchange availability (as measured by foreign exchange receipts and lagged reserve levels) to proxy import controls, or by using a direct measure of non-tariff barriers which assumes that the ratio of the marginal propensity to import rationed goods to the overall marginal propensity to import can be approximated by the ratio of restricted imports to total imports. As the authors admit, the former method has many problems, including the problem of the endogeneity of foreign exchange availability, and the latter is extremely data intensive, which allows them to estimate the import equation for only one LDC, namely Morocco.

Arguably the most important problem with these estimates for our purposes is that they attempt to estimate elasticities of exports and imports for individual countries, while our concern is with trade elasticities between the North and the South. We can use country-specific elasticities for this purpose if bilateral elasticities are available, or elasticity estimates are available for rich and poor countries separately. A few bilateral elasticity estimates are indeed available. For instance, Marquez and McNeilly (1988) estimate income elasticities of exports of non-OPEC LDCs to selected developed countries by examining the import functions of the latter countries, disaggregated according to commodity groups using quarterly data for the period 1974–84. Marquez (1990) estimates bilateral elasticities for trade between eight groups, including larger developed countries such as USA, Japan and Germany, other developed economies, OPEC, and non-OPEC developing countries using quarterly data from 1973 to 1985. Both studies find that there are significant dispersions of elasticities to warrant disaggregated studies. Moreover, they find relatively low income elasticities of imports for LDCs, and relatively high import elasticities from LDCs for several rich countries, apparently going against our hypothesis. A major research effort is needed to extend this work to a broader range of rich and poor countries and to take into account more recent data.

Here we pursue the less ambitious route of estimating aggregated data for the North and the South to calculate export and import elasticities for the two groups of countries, equating the North with OECD countries and the South with non-OECD countries.[8] This analysis arguably compounds some of the aggregation problems, and does not deal with the simultaneity and misspecification problems, but at least addresses the North–South dimension of the estimation. The results must, in any case, be considered preliminary ones.

We estimate the import and export functions of the South using the Houthakker–Magee formulation, with the following equations:

$$\log M_t = A_0 + A_1 \log Y_{St} + A_2 \log (P_{Mt}/P_{St}) + u_t$$

$$\log X_t = B_0 + B_1 \log Y_{Nt} + B_2 \log (P_{Xt}/P_{Nt}) + v_t$$

In the import equation, M_t refers to the quantity of the Southern imports, Y_{St} to real income of the South, P_{Mt} the unit price of Southern imports in terms of dollars, and P_{St} the Southern price level in terms of dollars. In the export function X_t refers to the quantity of Southern exports, Y_{Nt} to real income in the North, P_{Xt} the price of Southern exports in terms of dollars, and P_{Nt} the Northern price level, in terms of dollars. Our purpose, of course, is to compare the magnitudes of A_1 and B_1, with the uneven development hypothesis claiming that $A_1 > B_1$. We estimate the functions for the South rather than the North because of the following consideration. Import and export price indexes are available for the North and the South, but not for bilateral North–South trade. Since a much larger share of Northern exports and imports occurs within the North than the share of Southern exports and imports within the South, Southern export and import prices are a better indicator of North–South prices than are Northern export and import prices.

The data used in our estimates, which cover the period 1968–90, were obtained as follows. We took the total value of exports of the South to the North and the value of imports of the South from the North from OECD data. We took the price indexes of Southern exports and imports, and of Northern exports, from the IMF's IFS data. We calculated real incomes of the North and the South using Penn World Table (PWT) data, aggregating GDP over the relevant countries. To calculate export and import quantities for the South we divided the value of exports and imports by the import and export price indexes. To calculate price levels for the North and the South we calculate GDP deflators by dividing nominal GDP aggregates by the real GDP from the PWT. All relevant variables are measured in logarithms.

The results of our estimates of the export and import equations are shown in Table 16.1, using a number of different specifications. A simple ordinary least squares specification yields correct signs for all variables, although the price elasticities are not statistically different from zero. The income elasticities, however, are significantly different from zero, and the export elasticity, at 1.02, is smaller than the import elasticity, 1.16, confirming the uneven development hypothesis. Since the import elasticity exceeds unity, we also find that uneven development also occurs with capital inflows. An instrumental variables formulation using two-stage least squares with lagged values of the independent variable yields similar results, with the export elasticity at 1.07 and the import elasticity at 1.24. Since several of the variables were found to be non-stationary, we also estimated the equations using cointegration analysis. Though the income elasticity measures are higher, and perhaps unreasonably so, the export elasticity at 3.5 is found to be lower than the import elasticity, 6.2.

Table 16.1 Export and import equations

Specification	Equation	Income elasticity	Price elasticity	Adjusted R^2
OLS	Export	1.020280431 (8.29560003)	−0.147225119 (−1.95440066)	0.809294055
	Import	1.164753752 (8.549832029)	−0.232240622 (−0.761356626)	0.922681552
IV	Export	1.066962694 (8.293111313)	−0.254305974 (−3.015219355)	0.754631188
	Import	1.243297688 (8.035004769)	−0.455542074 (−1.199321141)	0.898996711
Co-integration	Export	3.505697637	−0.963417719	
	Import	6.268934386	−1.93204377	

Note: t-values in parentheses.

To examine the robustness of the results in terms of the data we have used, we used an alternative data set, from the World Bank's World Tables for the years 1964 to 1995, and used the World Bank's classification of industrial and developing countries (leaving out countries in other groups) to define the North and the South. The OLS estimate was qualitatively similar to the earlier estimates, with the coefficients of all the equations having the expected signs. The sum of the price elasticities exceeded one in absolute value. Moreover, the Northern income elasticity of Southern exports was found to be 1.27632, and the Southern import elasticity of Southern imports was estimated at 1.67035.

The empirical analysis presented here suffers from a number of problems which we have already noted. Two particularly serious problems are the high level of aggregation involved, and the fact that our analysis ignores restrictive trade policies. While it is beyond the scope of our analysis to examine the full implications of these problems, let alone to correct for them, we can consider two issues regarding these problems which have an important bearing on the question at hand. Regarding the aggregation issue, our equations have aggregated, among other things, over a wide range of commodities, which have arguably different elasticities of exports and imports. Hence, as the commodity composition of North–South changes, one would expect that the elasticities would change, violating the constancy assumption that has been made in our estimation. In particular, it can be argued that because of the steady shift on Southern exports away from primary goods with low income elasticities of exports to manufactured goods with higher elasticities, the Northern income-elasticity of Southern exports has increased over time. This argument tends to weaken the force of our empirical results noted above. Regarding the issue of trade restrictions, it can be argued that the degree of trade restriction will affect the estimated income elasticity of imports. With strong trade restrictions, an increase in income may not result in a large rise in imports due to trade controls, as noted by Thirlwall (1997). With import liberalization which many Southern economies seem to be engaged in, however, the income elasticity will increase over time, thereby exacerbating the problem of uneven development and strengthening the force of our empirical results.

A simple way of examining these issues is to allow the income elasticities of exports and imports to be time dependent. We have experimented by adding a term which is the product of the logarithm of the relevant income variable and a time variable into our export and import equations. Since we did not wish our equation with this product term to pick up a general time trend, which is possible given the non-stationarity of our dependent variables, we also added a time variable to our equations. The results are shown in Table 16.2, which suggests that not only is the income elasticity of exports lower than the income elasticity of imports, but that the gap between the two elasticities tends to grow over time. There is no statistically significant time trend in the export elasticity (although the coefficient is positive), suggesting that over time, despite the change in the structure of Southern exports, the Northern-income elasticity of exports has not increased significantly. Moreover, there seems to be a statistically significant upward trend in the income elasticity of Southern imports, consistent with the view that import liberalization may have exacerbated the forces of uneven development. It appears, therefore, that changes in the commodity composition of Southern exports have not increased the export elasticity, whereas trade liberalization is likely to have increased the import elasticity, thereby exacerbating the problem of uneven development.

6 CONCLUSION

This chapter has focused on one mechanism of uneven development which argues that rich countries, collectively called the North, will grow faster than poor countries, collectively called the South, because of differences in the income elasticities of imports between them. This mechanism has been widely discussed in the literature on international development, among others, by Prebisch, Seers, Kaldor and Thirlwall.

Table 16.2 Time-dependent income elasticities

Equation	Y	t Y	p	t	Adjusted R^2
Export	4.188545612	0.02554346	−0.015173372	−0.682004525	0.939987109
	(8.838552755)	(1.584247488)	(−0.217692804)	(−1.809838132)	
Import	4.720178203	0.118380209	0.131400315	−2.73780722	0.971764518
	(7.739028098)	(4.418895018)	(0.584268501)	(−4.496707054)	

Note: t-values in parentheses.

This chapter has attempted to make three contributions to the discussion of this mechanism. First, it has embedded the assumption of differential income elasticities of imports into a model of North–South trade which draws on the work of Taylor, assuming that trade is balanced, to show that uneven development occurs at long-run equilibrium. Second, it has examined the consequences of Southern borrowing to show that even with capital flows, and under plausible conditions, differential income elasticities of imports imply uneven development. Third, it has presented some preliminary empirical results to suggest that the income elasticity of imports of the South is indeed greater than that of the North, and furthermore, that the elasticity condition under which uneven development occurs even with the capital flows is likely to be empirically satisfied.

It can be argued that the theory of uneven development discussed here takes a very static view of the world economy. Even if poor countries have a higher income elasticity of imports from rich countries than rich countries have from poor countries, this situation is likely to change as the commodity composition of Southern exports continues to change. The analysis of this chapter, however, does not ignore this possibility, but finds that changes in the composition of exports have so far been unable to increase the Northern income elasticity of Southern exports. The changes that can be discerned so far seem to suggest, on the contrary, that increasing globalization due to trade liberalization may have strengthened the force of this uneven development mechanism by increasing the South's income elasticity of imports from the North.

This chapter has therefore shown that North–South trade may have had the effect of resulting in uneven development and that the North–South divergence that appears to be occurring in the world today may be because of differences in the income elasticities of imports for the North and the South.

Before concluding it should be stressed that while this chapter argues that the difference in income elasticities for imports between North and South contributes towards uneven development, it does not imply that such differences inevitably lead to uneven development or to the stagnation of all poor countries. Our theoretical model has tried to isolate the effects of differences in import elasticities by abstracting from other mechanisms that may have a bearing on the question of uneven development. For instance, it is possible that greater integration in the world economy will bring about more rapid technology transfers which will increase Southern productivity growth which can stem the forces of uneven development if the capital–output ratio of the South begins to fall. Moreover, greater integration can also allow the credit constraints faced by the South to become less binding, thereby allowing the South to borrow more, grow faster, and experience greater technological change, thereby catching up with the North. If these other mechanisms are thought to be empirically plausible, we could model their effects using North–South models of the type developed here. What our analysis does imply is that differences in import elasticities will play an inequalizing role even in such models which the mechanisms of catching up will need to overcome in order to result in convergence. Our empirical results are highly aggregative, and it is quite possible that there are several poor countries for which the elasticity condition is empirically violated. Thus, there may well be some poor countries which may be able to catch up with the North. What our analysis does point to is the problem that most Southern countries have in achieving that result.

NOTES

* It is with great pleasure and gratitude that I am contributing this paper to this volume of essays in honor of Lance Taylor. Throughout his distinguished career as one of the world's leading development economists, Lance has always been deeply concerned with the problem of the wide and growing gap between Northern and Southern development, and has written extensively on North–South issues. He wrote a seminal paper modeling North–South interaction, on which this paper draws heavily. Lance's interest in the subject of the paper largely explains my own interest in it, as is the case with many other areas of economics, beginning with the time when he was my dissertation advisor.

** I am grateful to Kajal Mukhopadhyay, in collaboration with whom the empirical research reported in section 5 was done, and to Seok-Hyeon Kim, for excellent research assistance. I am also grateful to seminar participants at the University of Notre Dame, University of Innsbruck and New School University, and especially to Paul Davidson, Duncan Foley, Richard Hule, Kali Rath, Jaime Ros, Herbert Stocker, Lance Taylor, and to Matias Vernengo, for comments and suggestions.

1. There has been much fanfare recently about the implications of the recent, relatively rapid growth rates of China and India, which are among the low-income countries (Dollar and Kraay, 2002). Although the large size of these countries dominates some recent growth figures, it is unclear to what extent the experiences of these relatively controlled and closed (though slowly opening) economies can be replicated in other LDCs, and to what extent these growth rates can be sustained, especially for India.
2. The model and the uneven development result have some similarity with a model developed earlier in Dutt (1988, 1990) which also attempted to explore the consequences of inelastic Northern demand for Southern goods. Both models draw on Taylor's model of North–South trade. However, while the earlier model showed income elasticity in terms of reductions in the share of Northern and Southern expenditure spent on the Southern good as the ratio of Northern to Southern capital stock increased over time, the model here follows Thirlwall in assuming given trade elasticities. A major difference between the two models is that the earlier one characterized uneven development in terms of the instability of long-run equilibrium, whereas the present one shows that uneven development occurs at long-run equilibrium.
3. It should be noted that, as shown by equation (16.19), high (but finite) values of the price elasticities will reduce the speed at which the terms of trade change, but will not affect these results in any other way.
4. If both Southern and Northern exports are positive, equation (16.4′) implies that $F/X_N < 1$. If the South experiences capital inflows, as we assume, $F/X_N > 0$.
5. We use the term 'creditworthiness' to include constraints on portfolio investment and foreign direct investment as well, not just actual borrowing.

6. Moreno-Brid (1998–99) makes a similar assumption, although he neglects to take interest payments into account.
7. Thirlwall and Hussain (1982) assume a constant ratio of foreign capital flows to exports.
8. The results reported here draw on ongoing joint work with Kajal Mukhopadhyay, with the assistance of Seok-Hyeon Kim.

REFERENCES

Bahmani-Oskooee, Mohsen (1986), 'Determinants of international trade flows: the case of developing countries', *Journal of Development Economics*, **20**(1), January–February, 107–23.

Bairam, Erkin I. (1997), 'Levels of economic development and appropriate specification of the Harrod foreign-trade multiplier', *Journal of Post Keynesian Economics*, **19**(3), Spring, 337–44.

Baumol, William J., Sue Anne Batey Blackman and Edward N. Wolff (1989), *Productivity and American Leadership: The Long View*, Cambridge, MA: MIT Press.

Burgstaller, Andre and Neantro Saavedra-Rivano (1984), 'Capital mobility and growth in a North–South model', *Journal of Development Economics*, **15**(1,2,3), May–June–August, 213–37.

Dixon, R.J. and Anthony P. Thirlwall (1975). 'A model of regional growth differences on Kaldorian lines', *Oxford Economic Papers*, July, 201–14.

Dollar, David and Aart Kraay (2002), 'Spreading the wealth', *Foreign Affairs*, January–February, pp. 120–33.

Dutt, Amitava Krishna (1988), 'Income inelasticity of demand for Southern goods, international demonstration effects and uneven development', *Journal of Development Economics*, **29**(1), July, 111–122.

Dutt, Amitava Krishna (1989), 'Trade, debt, and uneven development in a North–South model', *Metroeconomica*, **40**(3), October, 211–33.

Dutt, Amitava Krishna (1990), *Growth, distribution and uneven development*, Cambridge: Cambridge University Press.

Dutt, Amitava Krishna (1996), 'Southern primary exports, technological change and uneven development', *Cambridge Journal of Economics*, **20**(1), January, 73–89.

Dutt, Amitava Krishna (2002), 'Thirlwall's law and uneven development', *Journal of Post Keynesian Economics*, **23**(3), Spring.

Faini, Riccardo, Lant Pritchett and Fernando Clavijo (1992), 'Import demand in developing countries', in M.G. Dagenais and P.-A. Muet (eds), *International Trade Modelling*, London: Chapman and Hall.

Findlay, Ronald (1980), 'The terms of trade and equilibrium growth in the world economy', *American Economic Review*, **70**(3), June, 291–9.

Goldstein, Morris and Mohsin Khan (1978), 'The supply and demand for exports: a simultaneous approach', *Review of Economics and Statistics*, **60**, 275–86.

Goldstein, Morris and Mohsin Khan (1985), 'Income and price elasticities in foreign trade', in R. Jones and P. Kenen (eds), *Handbook of International Economics, Vol. II*, Amsterdam: North Holland.

Harrod, Roy (1933), *International Economics*, Cambridge: Cambridge University Press.

Houthakker, H.S. and Stephen P. Magee (1969), 'Income and price elasticities in world trade', *Review of Economics and Statistics*, May, **51**(2), 111–25.

Jones, Charles I. (1997), 'On the evolution of the world income distribution', *Journal of Economic Perspectives*, **11**(3), Summer, 19–36.

Kaldor, Nicholas (1970), 'The case for regional policies', *Scottish Journal of Political Economy*, November.

Khan, Mohsin S. (1974), 'Import and export demand in developing countries', *IMF Staff Papers*, Vol. 21, 678–93.

Krugman, Paul (1981), 'Trade, accumulation, and uneven development', *Journal of Development Economics*, **8**, 149–61.

Lucas, Robert E. (2000), 'Some macroeconomics for the 21st century', *Journal of Economic Perspectives*, **14**(1), Winter, 159–68.

Magee, Stephen P. (1975), 'Prices, income and foreign trade: a survey of recent economic studies', in P.B. Kenen (ed.), *International Trade and Finance: Frontiers for Research*, Cambridge: Cambridge University Press.

Marquez, Jaime (1990), 'Bilateral trade elasticities', *Review of Economics and Statistics*, **72**, 70–77.

Marquez, Jaime and Carlyl McNeilly (1988), 'Income and price elasticities for exports of developing countries', *Review of Economics and Statistics*, **70**(2), May, 306–14.

McCombie, J.S.L. (1997), 'On the empirics of balance of payments-constrained growth', *Journal of Post Keynesian Economics*, **19**(3), Spring, 345–75.

Moreno-Brid, Juan Carlos (1998–99), 'On capital flows and the balance-of-payments-constrained growth model', *Journal of Post Keynesian Economics*, Winter, **21**(2), 283–98.

Myrdal, Gunnar (1957), *Rich Lands and Poor*, New York: Harper & Brothers (also published as *Economic Theory and Under-developed Regions*, London: Duckworth).

Prebisch, Raul (1950), *The Economic Development of Latin America and its Principal Problems*, Lake Success, New York: United Nations.

Pritchett, Lant (1997), 'Divergence, Big Time', *Journal of Economic Perspectives*, **11**(3), 3–17.

Quah, Danny T. (1993), 'Empirical cross-section dynamics in economic growth', *European Economic Review*, **37**(2–3), April, 426–34.

Reidel, James (1984), 'Trade as the engine of growth in developing countries, revisited', *Economic Journal*, **94**, March, 56–73.

Ros, Jaime (2000), *Development Theory and the Economics of Growth*, Ann Arbor: University of Michigan Press.

Sala-i-Martin, Xavier (1996), 'The classical approach to convergence analysis', *Economic Journal*, **106**, 1019–36.

Sarkar, Prabirjit (1998), 'Endogenous technical progress and North–South terms of trade: Modelling the ideas of Prebisch and Singer on the line of Kalecki–Kaldor', in David Sapsford and John-ren Chen (eds), *Development Economics and Policy*, London: Macmillan and New York: St Martin's Press, pp. 249–57.

Scott, Bruce R. (2001), 'The great divide in the global village', *Foreign Affairs*, January–February, 160–77.

Seers, Dudley (1962), 'A model of comparative rates of growth of the world economy', *Economic Journal*, **72**(285), March, 45–78.

Singer, Hans (1950), 'The distribution of gains between investing and borrowing countries', *American Economic Review*, **40**, May, 473–85.

Spraos, John (1983), *Inequalizing Trade?*, Oxford: Oxford University Press.

Stocker, Herbert (1994), 'A world falling apart? Trends in the international distribution of income', Department of Economics, University of Innsbruck, unpublished.

Taylor, Lance (1981), 'South–North trade and southern growth: bleak prospects from a structuralist point of view', *Journal of International Economics*, **11**: 589–602.

Taylor, Lance (1983), *Structuralist macroeconomics*, New York: Basic Books.

Taylor, Lance (1986), 'Debt crisis. North–South, North–North and in between', in M.P. Claudon (ed.), *World Debt Crisis: International Lending on Trial*, Cambridge, MA: Ballinger.

Thirlwall, Anthony P. (1979), 'The balance of payments constraint as an explanation of international growth rate differences', *Banca Nazionale del Lavoro Quarterly Review*, March, No. 128.

Thirlwall, Anthony P. (1983), 'Foreign trade elasticities in centre-periphery models of growth and development', *Banca Nazionale del Lavoro Quarterly Review*, September, No. 146, 249–61.

Thirlwall, Anthony P. (1997), 'Reflections on the concept of balance-of-payments constrained growth', *Journal of Post Keynesian Economics*, **19**(3), Spring, 377–85.

Thirlwall, Anthony P. and M. Nureldin Hussain (1982), 'The balance of payments constraint, capital flows and growth rate differences between developing countries', *Oxford Economic Papers*, **34**(3), November, 498–510.

Wong, Kar-yiu and Chong-Kee Yip (1999), 'Education, economic growth and the brain drain', *Journal of Economic Dynamics and Control*, **23**(5–6), April, 699–726.

17. Towards balance in aid relationships: donor performance monitoring in low-income developing countries

Gerry Helleiner*

I INTRODUCTION

There is a new paradigm, emphasizing the need for 'partnership' and 'local ownership', in the current mainstream literature on official development assistance to poor countries. It is manifest in much of the writing and rhetoric emanating from the international financial institutions (the International Monetary Fund and the World Bank) and bilateral aid agencies, most notably in connection with the so-called Comprehensive Development Framework (pushed by the World Bank) and the Poverty Reduction Strategy Papers (required for the Highly-Indebted Poor Countries to qualify for further debt relief and official assistance). Is it all just rhetoric? Or can and should aid relationships actually be changed? This chapter argues, in the constructive spirit characteristic of Lance Taylor's many assaults on comfortable orthodoxy, that while current realities still belie the new aid rhetoric, one can easily think of reforms that could begin significantly to narrow the rhetoric–reality gap. In particular, independent monitoring of aid donor performance, in respect of key elements of their stated objectives and promises, at the level of individual aid recipient countries, could begin to balance the inevitable asymmetries in the aid relationship and provide real meaning to the concept of 'partnership'.

The chapter is organized as follows. Section II introduces the new rhetoric of aid partnership and some of its problems. Section III briefly recounts developments in the monitoring of low-income country performance. In section IV, attention shifts to the current (inadequate) systems of aid performance monitoring. Sections V and VI, which constitute the heart of the chapter, describe the principal elements of a truly useful and effective system for the monitoring of aid donor performance at the recipient country level. Section VII offers brief conclusions.

II THE NEW AID PARTNERSHIP: RHETORIC AND REALITY

'Partnership' between the rich countries and the poor, as the latter struggle for development and poverty reduction, has been part of approved rhetoric in the 'development community' for a very long time – at least since 1969 when the Pearson Commission published its report and titled it 'Partners in Development' (Pearson *et al.*, 1969). It has rarely been effectively practised. Some practitioners have long doubted whether it was possible. In a critique of the Pearson Report, when it was released, I. G. Patel accurately anticipated the problems that would inevitably bedevil the aid relationship for (at least) the next 30 years.

> Unfortunately, the concept of a genuine partnership in development . . . lacks credibility. There has never been any real sense of equality between donors and recipients even when they attend the same consortium meetings and sit around the same table in many other forums. For the recipient to be frank about the policies or attitudes of donors in a forum where aid is to be distributed is about as difficult as the proverbial passage of the camel through the eye of a needle. Criticism of donor policies, even when it comes from non-recipients, is seldom answered in the manner in which recipients are obliged to answer the most far-reaching criticism of their own policies. There are obviously two sets of rules . . . A mere equality of opportunity in engaging in dialogue cannot establish parity in decision-making . . . The doctrine of mutuality in monitorship or genuine partnership in development is impractical . . . (Patel, 1971: 305)

By the mid-1990s, the donor-driven character of aid programmes and the limited local 'ownership' that inevitably accompanied them had brought many analysts and policymakers, at last, to the realization that a new kind of 'partnership' between rich nations and poor was required in aid relationships (though not, it must hastily be added, in global economic governance (Helleiner, 2000c)).

As the chairman of the OECD's Development Assistance Committee (DAC) put it:

> If donors believe in local ownership and participation, then they must seek to use channels and methods of co-operation that do not undermine those values. External support must avoid stifling or attempting to substitute for local initiative . . . The principles of self reliance, local ownership and participation which underlie the partnership approach are inconsistent with the idea of conditions imposed by donors to coerce poor countries to do things they don't want to do in order to obtain resources they need. That view of conditionality was always of dubious value. Treating development co-operation as a partnership makes clear that it is obsolete. (OECD, 1996a: 7; see also 1996b)

To make such new partnerships work and to achieve real developing country 'ownership', there has to be a shift away from the previous relatively passive mind-set, common among aid recipients, towards active leadership in the development of 'home-grown' development programmes. Developing countries, particularly their governments, have to develop clearer views as to precisely what forms of external support they require. In one of the relatively few recent statements of Africans' views on these matters, this point is made explicitly and clearly.

> . . . African countries . . . need to more precisely define what external assistance they require, based on clearly defined national goals and an exhaustive mobilization of national capacities and resources. For most countries to move forward it is imperative that both the donors and the recipients seriously rethink the purpose and nature of aid to Africa. No doubt, some aid plays some positive role, but policymakers should initiate a major debate about the potential for channelling aid in a manner that enhances the building and use of African human resources, mobilizes domestic resources, and weans African economies away from an aid dependence that simply does nobody any good. (Mkandawire and Soludo, 1999: 121)

Of course, aid donors must mean what they say about rethinking and reforming current aid modalities. There is still a curious 'disconnect' between donors' general rhetoric on these issues and actual practice on the ground (Helleiner, 2000a; Sweden, 1999).

The current donor consensus that 'aid works' when domestic policies are of the character that the Bank perceives as 'right', and when these policies are truly domestically 'owned', is based on World Bank analysis (Burnside and Dollar, 1997; World Bank, 1998) that has been subject to such serious methodological challenge (Hansen and Tarp, 2000; Lensink and White, 2000) that it cannot be sustained. Yet there is intuitive and obvious sense to the proposition that if overall policies are grotesquely inappropriate, aid is unlikely to have much effect; and that unless sound policies are domestically supported they are unlikely to be sustainable. Argument as to the details of appropriate policy, sequencing, threshold effects, and the role of initial conditions is bound to continue. Now that domestic ownership is so much emphasized one would expect that, when push comes to shove, such argument between donors and recipients would now more frequently grant the benefit of the doubt to recipients. But it is still difficult to find hard supporting evidence of any such change in donor behaviour (as opposed to donor rhetoric). Both the international financial institutions and the bilateral donors continue to seek detailed policy influence, even if it is now ostensibly within a recipient-led 'comprehensive development framework'. In any case, the actual role of ODA is only likely to be comprehensible, and analysis of its effects of use for policymaking purposes, at the level of specific individual countries.

III MEASUREMENT OF PERFORMANCE IN LOW-INCOME COUNTRIES

In the extensive experience and literature of structural adjustment and development in low-income countries there has been no shortage of policy prescriptions and performance indicators for the adjusting countries. From early emphasis on macroeconomic policies and indicators, to later more microeconomic measures, for example privatization and liberalization, to still later emphasis on governance and institutions, and now to poverty reduction, the international financial community has kept the pressure on for policy change and quantifiable measures of their extent. At the same time, concern has grown over the effects of aid dependence, for which appropriate measures also had to be devised. (For a succinct recent summary, see Lensink and White, 1999.) As the emphasis has changed, measurement of aid recipients' 'performance' has frequently become more difficult. Measures of 'good governance' have been devised – incorporating such elements as the extent of the rule of law, assessments of governmental effectiveness, and the frequency of corrupt and illegitimate payments to officials (Kaufman *et al.*, 1999a and 1999b). So have measures of local 'ownership' (Johnson and Wasty, 1993). But how to weight and aggregate the disparate components of concepts like these remains subject to argument; in the end it is a matter of arbitrary judgement.

As concepts of poverty expand to incorporate dimensions other than sheer income, together with education, health and the like, and/or anthropometric measures, for example weight and height for age, similar problems arise. Vulnerability, powerlessness and voicelessness (emphasized, for example, in the *World Development Report, 2000* on poverty) are not easy to quantify; power and voice also raise issues of the distribution of income and assets, which has its own huge literature on alternative measurement approaches. Yet poverty reduction is now proclaimed to be the principal objective of IMF/World Bank programmes and international development assistance. Evidently performance, of the currently approved sort, will be more difficult to measure than it was in the 'old days' of IMF credit ceilings, inflation and growth rates. Of one thing, however, one can be sure: as quickly as new concepts of appropriate policies and performance appear, legions of (primarily Northern) research professionals will embark upon fresh efforts to clarify and quantify them.

One can perhaps understand, and even rationalize, all of this continuing effort to measure policy change and 'performance' in the low-income countries which are, after all, the object of global development effort. But there can be no doubt that the effort has been essentially driven by the 'needs' of the aid donor community, rather than those of the developing countries themselves. One cannot help wondering whether equivalent expenditure on the research priorities of policymakers and researchers based within developing countries would not have been a far more effective use of 'development' funding. I do not propose to enter here into a debate as to what these local research priorities might be; they are bound to be highly area- and country-specific. Rather, I want to call attention to the enormous imbalance in measurement and monitoring effort within the so-called 'aid relationship'.

IV AID PERFORMANCE MONITORING: CURRENT SYSTEMS

What is most striking in the widely-shared aspiration towards a new form of aid partnership is the failure to follow it up with a more balanced approach to performance monitoring. Although the details have changed, nothing essential has changed in the degree of reporting required of the aid-receiving countries or the intensity of monitoring of their performance by the IMF, World Bank and individual bilateral donors. Indeed, with the introduction of the Poverty Reduction Strategy Paper (PRSP), external demands upon already overstretched authorities in the low-income countries have probably risen. Nothing has been done, however, to increase the (extremely limited) transparency or accountability of any of the bilateral aid donors or international institutions as they interact with the low-income countries in a purportedly 'new' form of aid partnership.

What information, and in what form, would be most useful to the low-income partners in the aid relationship? What performance indicators should be measured and reported on the side of individual aid donors?

At present, the only major official source of aid performance data and performance evaluation is the Development Assistance Committee (DAC) of the OECD. Its published data are the product of information supplied by donors themselves. It uses its own (highly arbitrary) definition of official development assistance (ODA), and what it reports (and evaluates) is only at a highly aggregated level, the level of total performance by each individual donor country. Donor performance evaluations are undertaken via 'peer review' by other DAC members. Aid recipients have not been involved in any DAC decision-making – as to the definition of development assistance, the determination of which data to request and report, the nature of its reports and evaluations, and so on. Nor have they been involved in performance evaluations. The DAC is very much a donor organization and it is designed to serve the needs of its members. Recipients are not members and have no voice. If its data reporting systems and performance evaluations are of limited usefulness to aid recipients, this should therefore not occasion much surprise.

Here follows the main elements of what the DAC reports on individual donor ODA performance:

- total (net) ODA flows (disbursements and commitments) and flows to principal recipients (top 15 for each donor),
- total gross ODA disbursements and commitments, and their grant equivalent, as percentage of donor GNP,
- ODA (net disbursements and commitments) and their grant element to low-income countries (LICs) and least developed countries (LLDCs), as percentage of donor GNP,
- ODA (net disbursements) per capita of donor country,
- tying status of total commitments, excluding technical cooperation,
- aggregate technical cooperation commitments,
- aggregate composition of commitments, by major uses and purposes.

Price deflators are presented for each donor, permitting the calculation of constant-price flow data over time. At the level of individual recipient countries, total net ODA receipts – in absolute terms and as a percentage of recipient GNP – are reported.

Unfortunately, there is a significant (typically two-year) lag in the availability even of these data. Valuable as all of these data may be for general and *ex post* analysis, they are of no use to developing country policymakers who require current, country-specific and detailed information for budget preparation and planning. Nor are the performance indicators and peer evaluations usable in the building of partnerships between the donor community and individual recipient countries.

Northern NGOs have made valiant efforts to provide more independent assessments of aid efforts (notably in their *Reality of Aid* reports, for example Randel *et al.*, 2000) and even to publish valuable information on developing country debt to OECD official agencies, but they, like everyone else, are seriously hampered by the lack of transparency in aid and official lending.

V AID PERFORMANCE MONITORING: WHAT IS NEEDED

It is worth asking what the recipients would really like to have reported and evaluated, if they were in charge of the monitoring and evaluation systems. Above all, aid recipient governments require timely and relevant facts relating to donor activities within their countries; they require donor cooperation, in every possible way, in support of their 'own' poverty reduction and development programmes; and they require promises to be kept. The following list of possible indicators of aid donor performance is merely an indicative one. Further elements can easily be added. The relative importance of such indicators will no doubt vary as among individual aid recipients in accordance with country-specific circumstances. In at least one country (Tanzania) the list that follows (with no particular significance to the order in which items appear) has recently been accepted, in principle, as the basis for further effort at (independent) donor performance monitoring.

(i) Recipient Country Specificity of Data

Obviously the most important consideration for aid recipients is that data and evaluation systems relate to their own budgeting and planning needs – and their own country-specific statistical categories and decision-making timetables. To be useful to them, donor performance monitoring and evaluation must take place at the level of activities within their own countries, the activities over which they, at least in principle, have jurisdiction and can exercise their sovereignty. Strange as it would seem to any visiting Martian seeking to understand how 'aid partnerships' work, such recipient-country-level systems, those most likely to be useful to recipients, do not exist.

(ii) Compliance with Recipient Requests for Information

Aid donors evidently feel no compunction to report to the governments of the countries in which they conduct their activities as to what *exactly* they are doing there, what they have done in the past or what they intend to do in the future, let alone to do so in harmonized categories or according to timetables (or, in some cases, even in a language) that might be most useful to the local authorities. In the relatively infrequent instances when national governments have asked donors to supply such information, they have typically pleaded inability to do so or have complained of the inordinate cost of attempting it. In consequence the economic decision-making in the more aid-dependent of the low-income countries is severely constrained in

*Table 17.1 ODA as percentage of GNP**

	1991–92	1996–97
Mozambique	108.7	41.1
Tanzania	49.4	13.4
Uganda	24.8	12.1
Ethiopia	14.1	12.1
Rwanda	20.3	39.2
Zambia	33.6	17.5
Madagascar	14.9	16.5
Mali	17.0	19.0
Malawi	28.6	18.6
Burkina Faso	15.4	15.9
Niger	16.0	15.8
Eritrea	—	17.8
Nicaragua	46.0	39.0

Note: *These figures depend heavily upon the exchange rate used to convert foreign currency expenditures to local currency.

Source: OECD, 1999, p. A62.

terms of critical data. According to DAC data, official development assistance (ODA) amounts to significant proportions of many recipient countries' GNP (see Table 17.1).

The degree of donor compliance with recipient governmental requests for standardized and timely aid data should therefore be an important performance indicator for donors. Such compliance may depend upon the nature of the data request, but donor–recipient dialogue should be able to engender agreement as to what is most useful and feasible to supply. The performance indicator may have to be fairly crude, for example a dichotomous (yes/no) measure for each donor.

(iii) Degree to which ODA Expenditures fall within Recipient Budgetary System

A common popular misconception about ODA is that it is all passed through a recipient government system, even through its budget. For better or for worse, however, this is typically *not* the case. High proportions of ODA expenditures are made *directly* to the suppliers of goods and services to aid agencies – private firms, NGOs, individuals. Some of these direct expenditures are made to nationals (firms, NGOs, individuals, sometimes even local rather than national governments) of the recipient country; traditionally, more have gone to foreigners, notably from the donor country. In the latter case, these funds do not register in either the donor or recipient country's balance of payments statistics, except indirectly when/if their recipients spend some of them in the recipient country. Needless to say, decisions as to the uses and recipients of such 'direct funds' are made exclusively by the donors. In Tanzania, where strenuous efforts have purportedly been made to transfer 'ownership' of development programmes from aid donors to the government, only 30 per cent of ODA was estimated to flow through the government budget in fiscal year 1999 (Government of Tanzania/World Bank, 1999). (Unpublished sources report the same number for fiscal year 2000.) The proportion of each donor's ODA expenditures that finds its way into the national budget system is therefore another reasonable performance indicator for donors; this should be inclusive of debt forgiveness and contributions to debt servicing funds.

(iv) Integration and Coordination within National Plans and Priorities

A related issue is the degree to which donor projects and expenditures are coordinated and integrated into national and sectoral plans and/or recognize the declared priorities of recipient governments. The clearest and simplest manifestation of donor willingness to coordinate their support and follow national leadership is through contributions to sectoral or cross-sector 'basket funds', administered by recipient governments in accordance with objectives and priorities agreed with the contributing donors. Donor support of this kind should be reflected in the data on the share of ODA making its way through the recipients' budgetary systems. But donors may also consciously tailor their activities and projects to recipient priorities, whether national or sectoral, and/or attempt to coordinate their support, standardize their accounting and reporting systems, reduce transactions costs for recipients, and so on without going all the way to 'basket fund' contributions (which some donors are constrained, by their own national legislation, from making). On the other hand, they may continue, as they have so often done in the past, to set their own agendas and to 'push' projects that are not high in the recipients' order of priorities.

Some attempt should be made to assess donor coordination and willingness to accept local priorities in a systematic way. To some degree, what transpires in this respect is the product of the recipient government's determination to take leadership. In this respect, the assessment might be considered as among the most important indicators of the success of the aspired-for partnership, transfer of leadership and achievement of local 'ownership'. Perhaps a quantitative (negative) indicator of this, if it is feasible, is the percentage of ODA commitments or expenditures which appear to 'stand alone', *outside* of agreed priorities or coordination systems.

(v) Shortfalls from ODA Promises

Aid donor announcements and even formal commitments often bear little relationship to subsequent actual disbursements. There are many reasons for this: administrative delays; recipient failure to meet pre-stipulated donor conditions, for example on local cost co-financing; changed political or economic circumstances in either donor or recipient countries, and so on. By no means does all the fault for donor shortfalls (*over*spending does not often occur) rest with the donors. For effective policymaking, however, one must have reasonably accurate resource projections, on a year-by-year basis, and preferably for longer periods such as are covered by a medium-term expenditure framework (MTEF). It may be more important to have *predictable and reliable* resource inflows than to have large flows that are highly erratic and uncertain. There must be a presumption that, where general macroeconomic management remains sound, and particularly in the case of general or sectoral budget support, the primary responsibility for exceptionally large shortfalls rests with the relevant donors. Their actual disbursements should therefore be monitored in the context of their own prior commitments. Their shortfalls, individual and collective, should constitute another performance indicator. It would also be useful to calculate shortfalls in different kinds of ODA, not least those identified as especially valuable in (iii) and (iv) above.

(vi) Compensatory and Contingency Financing

It is important to recognize the exceptional need for liquidity and contingency finance in the poorest and least developed countries. Their structures and size make them peculiarly vulnerable to 'shocks' from weather, terms of trade and even (though this is less widely recognized) private capital flows (Helleiner, 2000b). At the same time, their access to commercial bank finance is limited (and/or costly) and the opportunity cost of the holding of foreign exchange reserves is always high in poor countries. IMF funding availability falls far short of the amounts required fully to offset these countries' shocks. It is, in any case, even in the case of its so-called 'Compensatory and Contingency Finance Facility (CCFF)', not available without new conditions, and hence delays and heavy transactions costs at a time of already increased pressures on policymakers' time and energies;

the IMF thus can no longer be described as a source of increased 'liquidity', even with respect to the limited funds it can provide.

Bilateral donors, who routinely disburse (collectively) far greater amounts in support of poor countries than the IMF or World Bank, could – if they chose – purposefully alter the time profile of their disbursements for budget or balance of payments support in response to individual recipient countries' shock-generated needs for liquidity. Such 'compensatory' variability of donor flows would help to impart greater predictability to entire country programmes rather than merely to donor flows; and this could be extremely helpful to recipient countries. Donors might well devote greater attention to this potential stabilization role. Those able to perform such a role should obviously be favourably recognized for doing so rather than recorded as offering unstable and unpredictable finance.

(vii) Tying of Procurement

The tying of aid has long been recognized as costly to recipients, particularly when it relates both to its use and to its procurement source. It is particularly costly to the poorest countries who are least likely to be able to respond to its potential costs by taking maximum advantage of fungibility. Despite years of effort, OECD DAC members have still not been able collectively to agree to untie all aid to the least developed countries.

Another obvious donor performance indicator, then, is the percentage of ODA which is provided, whether in project or programme form, on an untied basis with respect to country of procurement. Since some donors have been willing to permit local sourcing or sourcing in other poor countries, while retaining the tying requirement on any 'external' expenditures, it would probably be best also to record the percentage of ODA for which such partial sourcing freedom exists. Technical assistance/cooperation raises so many further issues (see below) that these measures of aid donor tying should be calculated exclusive of technical assistance/cooperation expenditures as well as in total.

(viii) Role of Technical Assistance/Cooperation

Technical assistance/cooperation expenditures have played a major role in overall aid to the poorest countries. That role has been controversial and is highly politically sensitive. The emerging consensus among aid analysts is that, great as the need for technical expertise may be in most of the poorest countries, traditional technical assistance/cooperation activities have been signally ineffective in sheer cost–benefit terms (for example Berg, 1993). Expatriate expertise is frequently ill-informed and/or insensitive to local realities; typically generates little domestic learning, memory or capacity-building; sometimes serves donor rather than development interests (including donor monitoring and control objectives); and is always extremely costly. As both developing countries and donors have shifted their emphasis (at least at the level of their rhetoric) to long-term capacity-building, the limitations of the traditional model of expatriate technical assistance have been increasingly recognized. The latest World Bank research report on African prospects states:

> . . . on balance, it is likely that [these] aid programs have weakened rather than strengthened capacity in Africa. Technical assistance has served to displace local expertise and even substitute for civil servants pulled away to administer aid-funded programs – precisely the opposite of the capacity building intentions of both donors and recipients (World Bank, 2000a, chapter 8).

Technical cooperation expenditures in Sub-Saharan Africa still amount to about $4 billion per year and about one-quarter of all bilateral assistance to the region. In some countries these expenditures account for 40 per cent of total ODA (World Bank, 2000a, chapter 8). Under the traditional modalities, these numbers are simply too high, and recipients resent their perceived opportunity costs.

Another suitable (negative) donor performance indicator could be the percentage of its aid which is spent upon donor-country tied technical assistance/cooperation. Although there are plenty of 'useful' expatriates working in poor countries, the presumption must be that this is not generally now a wise use of limited aid funds, particularly when it has not been requested, and that recipient freedom from procurement tying increases overall cost-effectiveness. Hence good donor performance means a low percentage devoted to tied technical assistance. One could imagine some positive indicator of contributions to long-term capacity-building as a complement to this somewhat 'negative' indicator; but this would have to be somewhat subjective and hence more difficult to devise.

(ix) Qualitative Assessments of Ownership, etc.

On other dimensions of the aid relationship there might also have to be resort to more qualitative assessments, undertaken by independent evaluators, of individual and collective donor performance. In one recent such exercise, in Tanzania, an independent assessor assigned letter grades to the collective performance of donors with respect to a variety of promises they had made regarding the transfer of 'ownership' of development programmes (along with relevant commentary) (Helleiner, 1999).

(x) Time Horizon for ODA Commitments

Some attempt should be made to record systematically the degree to which donors have been able to make longer-term commitments, for example within the framework of a Medium-Term Expenditure Framework (MTEF).

(xi) Humanitarian versus Development Assistance

Although the distinction between humanitarian aid and development assistance is sometimes difficult to make, it is critical to efforts to assess the developmental impact of ODA in the poorest countries. Analyses of the growth or investment effects of ODA, of which there have been so many, and about which there has been so much controversy, must make this distinction if they are to carry any credibility; and most do not. DAC publications already draw this distinction in their aggregate data for individual donors. It should therefore be quite feasible to extract these useful specifics at the level of individual recipient countries. There should be no presumption as to which form of ODA is 'better' in this effort to assemble information relevant to analysis of aid's impact.

(xii) Individual and Collective Donor Performance Indicators

All of these indicators should be recorded at the recipient-country level both for individual donors, at least the more significant ones in that particular country, and for the donor community as a whole.

VI OTHER DIMENSIONS OF EFFECTIVE AID PERFORMANCE MONITORING

(i) Independence of Monitoring Authority

Fundamental to the credibility and effectiveness of any such performance monitoring is the independence of the evaluator(s). Neither the DAC (OECD) nor the Bretton Woods institutions can be trusted to be neutral and apolitical in their assessments of donor performance. (There is room for doubt as to their record of neutrality regarding the performance of recipients as well.) Political influences may also bedevil the potential UN role in such activities. Although the UNDP has not as yet shown much interest in issues as potentially sensitive to its own major contributors, it (or possibly UNCTAD) could nevertheless serve as an appropriate financier and organizer of independent donor performance assessments via contracting with private individuals, teams of individuals ('panels'?), or consulting firms to provide these services. The production of the UNDP's annual *Human Development Report* is handled in this manner. So are many of the other research and technical cooperation activities of both UNDP and UNCTAD. Alternatively, the work could be funded and contracted by groups of 'like-minded' donors. In the Tanzanian case, alluded to above, donor funding for the purpose was provided to an established and independent Tanzanian research institution, with the understanding that the detailed terms of reference and the composition of the monitoring group would be mutually agreed in advance between the donors and the Government of Tanzania. Whoever the financiers/organizers, it must be clear to all that the assessors retain absolute independence and that the contractors/donors carry zero responsibility for their conclusions.

(ii) Frequency of Performance Assessments

Since change in aid relationships is likely to take some time and since, in any case, every effort should be made by donors to reduce recipient transactions costs and take a longer view, the current one-year cycle for donor consultations and Consultative Group (CG) meetings is too short. The more balanced assessments of donor and recipient performance here recommended, and probably CG meetings themselves, need not take place so frequently. A two-year cycle might be most appropriate for a start.

VII CONCLUSIONS

Aid relationships have been difficult to change in low-income countries. Despite much donor rhetoric on the need for recipient ownership of development programmes and the building of new forms of donor–recipient partnership, aid-supported programmes are still basically donor-driven. The continuing imbalance in aid relationships is manifest in many ways. An important and previously neglected dimension of the problem is the imbalance in performance monitoring as between donors and recipients. Whereas the behaviour and performance of low-income developing countries is measured and assessed in ever-increasing detail within the international community, the behaviour and performance of their donor 'partners' receives only cursory attention, except at an aggregate level which is of little operational usefulness to individual recipients. When it comes to performance monitoring, as in so many other spheres, the powerful (the donors and the international financial institutions) still call all the shots.

Genuine partnership in development requires the monitoring, by independent assessors, of individual and collective donor performance at the level of individual aid-recipient developing countries. Do donors live up to their rhetoric and their promises? In what measurable ways? It is not difficult to devise measures of donor performance at the recipient country level; and some have been suggested above. Instituting systems of donor performance monitoring at the recipient country level can assist in improving understanding of aid effectiveness; promote the new forms of partnership of which there is so much talk; and, most important, assist policymakers in low-income countries in their difficult task of promoting poverty reduction and development. It is long overdue. It is time for it to be done.

NOTE

* I am grateful for comments on an earlier draft to Albert Berry, Sue Horton and an anonymous referee, none of whom bear any responsibility for the contents of this paper. The paper appeared in *Cooperation South* (UNDP), 2000, No. 2. It was originally prepared for this Festschrift in honour of Lance Taylor, edited by A. Dutt and J. Ros.

REFERENCES

Berg, Elliot (1993), *Rethinking Technical Cooperation: Reforms for Capacity-Building in Africa*, New York: UNDP.

Burnside, C. and D. Dollar (1997), 'Aid, policies and growth', World Bank Policy Research Working Paper 1777, Washington, DC: World Bank.

Government of Tanzania/World Bank (1999), *Public Expenditure Review, FY 1999*, Dar es Salaam.

Hansen, H. and F. Tarp (2000), 'Aid effectiveness disputed', in F. Tarp, *Foreign Aid and Development*, London: Routledge.

Helleiner, G.K. (1999), 'Changing aid relationships in Tanzania (December 1997 through March 1999)', Government of Tanzania, for the Tanzania Consultative Group Meeting, May 3–4; Dar es Salaam, mimeo.

Helleiner, G.K. (2000a), 'External conditionality, local ownership and development', in J. Freedman (ed.), *Transforming Development*, Toronto: University of Toronto Press.

Helleiner, G.K. (2000b), 'Financial markets, crises and contagion: issues for smaller countries in the FTAA and Post-Lomé IV Negotiations', *Capitulos*, Caracas: SELA.

Helleiner, G.K. (2000c), 'Developing countries in global economic governance and negotiation processes', mimeo, Toronto, forthcoming in D. Nayyar (ed.), WIDER volume on global governance.

Johnson, J. and S. Wasty (1993), 'Borrower ownership of adjustment programs and the political economy of reform', World Bank Discussion Paper 199 Washington, DC.

Kaufman, D., A. Kraay and P. Zoibo-Lobatón (1999a), 'Aggregating governance indicators', World Bank Policy Research Working Paper 2195, October.
Kaufman, D., A. Kraay and P. Zoibo-Lobatón (1999b), 'Governance matters', World Bank Policy Research Working Paper 2196, October.
Lensink, R. and H. White (1999), 'Aid dependence: issues and indicators', *Expert Group on Development Issues*, 1999:2, Stockholm: Almquist and Wiksall International.
Lensink, R. and H. White (2000), 'Assessing aid: a manifesto for aid in the 21st century?', *Oxford Development Studies*, **28**(1), February.
Mkandawire, T. and C. Soludo (1999), *Our Continent, Our Future: African Perspectives on Structural Adjustment*, Asmara and Trenton, NJ: CODESRIA and IDRC, African World Press.
OECD (1996a), *Development Cooperation, Efforts and Policies of the Members of the Development Assistance Committee, 1995 Report*, Paris.
OECD (1996b), *Shaping the Twenty-First Century: The Contribution of Development Cooperation*, Paris.
OECD (1999), *Development Cooperation, Efforts and Policies of the Members of the Development Assistance Committee, 1998 Report*, Paris.
Patel, I.G. (1971), 'Aid relationships for the seventies', in Barbara Ward, Lenore D'Anjou and J.D. Runnalls (eds), *The Widening Gap, Development in the 1970s*, Columbia University Press, 295–311.
Pearson, Lester B. *et al.* (1969), *Partners in Development, Report of the Commission on International Development*, New York, Washington and London: Praeger.
Randel, J., T. German and D. Ewing (eds) (2000), *The Reality of Aid 2000, An Independent Review of Poverty Reduction and Development Assistance*, London: Earthscan.
Sweden, Ministry for Foreign Affairs (1999), *Making Partnerships Work on the Ground: Workshop Report*.
Tarp, Finn (2000), *Foreign Aid and Development, Lessons Learned and Directions for the Future*, London: Routledge.
World Bank (1998), *Assessing Aid*, Washington, DC.
World Bank (2000a), *Can Africa Claim the Twenty-First Century?*, Washington, DC.
World Bank (2000b), *World Development Report, 1999–2000*, Oxford and New York: Oxford University Press.

18. The challenges facing international financial regulation

John Eatwell

The financial crisis in the Autumn of 1998 was the first post-World War II crisis in which events in emerging market economies seriously threatened the financial stability of the West, and where the origins of the crisis were clearly to be found in the workings of liberalized markets and private sector institutions. The spark was the financial crisis that overwhelmed many of the Asian economies in 1997, and spread to Russia in 1998, but the centre of the conflagration was the near failure of the hedge fund Long Term Capital Management. More than any of the other problems in the Autumn of 1998, the threats that LTCM's difficulties posed to financial stability throughout the world illustrated beyond all reasonable doubt that the international financial system had entered a new era.[1] This was not a problem of sovereign debt, or macroeconomic imbalance, or a foreign exchange crisis. Instead it was the manifestation of the systemic risk created by the market driven decisions of a private firm, and of the behaviour of free financial markets. The potential economy-wide inefficiency of liberalized financial markets was indisputable.

In August 1998, in one of those remarkable coincidences that in retrospect look like good judgement, Lance Taylor and I had delivered a Report to the Ford Foundation that dealt directly with the problem of systemic risk in liberal international financial markets. We had been drawn to this particular topic because of a shared irritation with the overblown claims for the efficiency of financial liberalization – claims that do not stand up to empirical scrutiny. For example, liberalization of international financial markets has coincided not only with increased financial instability, but also with a worldwide slowdown in the rate of growth. Whether there is a causal link between liberalization and that slowdown is, of course, a complex question. But the argument that liberalization has resulted in a higher growth rate than might otherwise be the case is very difficult to sustain (see Eatwell, 1996).

In our 1998 Report we recommended the establishment of a World Financial Authority (Eatwell and Taylor, 1998). We argued that for efficient regulation the domain of the regulator should be the same as the domain of the market that is regulated. None of the standard tasks of a financial regulator – authorization, the provision of information, surveillance, enforcement, and the development of policy – are currently performed in a coherent manner in international markets. Indeed, in many cases they are not performed at all. In the absence of a World Financial Authority (WFA) the liberalization of international markets has resulted in a significant increase in systemic risk, that is it has been inefficient.

Our prime objective in proposing the creation of a WFA was to test the regulatory needs of today's liberal financial markets. Whether a single regulator is created or not, the tasks that the model WFA should perform must be performed by someone if international financial markets are to operate efficiently.

The goal of this chapter is to take the argument further by identifying the challenges facing international financial regulation today, using the template of a model WFA to identify exactly what the key regulatory tasks might be and thereby to develop proposals as to how they might best be performed. In moving from our initial proposal to this more concrete analysis, consideration must be given not only to the practical developments that have taken place up to now, but also to the international legal and institutional implications of our initial proposals. It is particularly striking that much of the criticism of the idea of a WFA has suggested that the required international cooperation will be impossible to achieve – even when a number of the necessary cooperative mechanisms are already in place! In fact there already exists a body of international legal practice, and a cohort of institutions that would support the further development of the regime of international financial regulation.[2] But that body of legal and institutional practice needs to be assembled and codified in a manner appropriate to today's regulatory needs.

Whilst the emphasis in this chapter will be on the development of policy, a not insubstantial part of the argument will be devoted to analysis. This is because the theoretical framework within which a new structure of international financial regulation might be formulated is lacking. Without such a framework, policy has inevitably been ad hoc, essentially responsive to pressing need, and deprived of overall coherence. In *Global Finance at Risk* Lance Taylor and I set out the skeleton of the requisite theoretical framework. In what follows I hope to put more flesh on the bones.

A COMMON THEORETICAL FRAMEWORK

Over the past three decades the most difficult task of the financial regulator has been to keep up with the changing marketplace that he or she is supposed to be regulating. The speed of change has, if anything, accelerated, with the continuous development of new trading strategies and new 'products', linking assets, markets and currencies in new ways, and creating new risks. In this febrile environment the regulator needs the guidance of a coherent theoretical understanding of the propagation and management of systemic risk, as well as the pragmatic understanding of market institutions and the concrete tools to manage the risk.

Unfortunately, there is no commonly accepted set of theoretical principles defining what financial regulators are supposed to do, and guiding their actions. It is agreed that systemic risk is an externality, but externalities are peculiarly difficult to define in other than the most abstract terms. Where exactly do external costs and benefits fall? What is their scale relative to the economy as a whole? What is the relationship between particular policies to manage the externality and the performance of the economy as a whole? In the world of finance these difficulties are compounded by the fact that the externality of systemic risk is in large part manifest through a beauty contest – through market participants' belief about what average opinion believes average opinion believes (Keynes, 1936, chapter 12; Eatwell and Taylor, 2000, chapters 1 and 3) – and through the impact of changes in beliefs on macroeconomic variables. Assessing the impact of regulation on average opinion is bound to be an art rather than a science, and an imperfect guide to policy.

A further problem in building a coherent theory of regulatory practice is the potential scale of the losses associated with extreme events. Average opinion is typically stable for long periods, dominated by convention. In these circumstances it may be comparatively easy to identify the behavioural relationships that characterize such periods of tranquillity, to believe that they are stable and enduring, and to use them to assess values at risk. Yet these seemingly 'true models' of the marketplace can be completely overwhelmed by a sharp shift in average opinion, driving markets in previously unimaginable directions, and producing potentially catastrophic disruption in the operation of the real economy.[3] These factors pose enormous problems for the policymaker. Are regulations to be constructed on the basis of the models of tranquillity, or are they to take account of potentially catastrophic 'rare' events when the logic of those models is overthrown? How often do 'rare' events actually occur, and what is the relationship between their frequency and the regulation of systemic risk in more tranquil circumstances? Does the cost of defensive regulation against rare events exceed the benefits? Are financial crises simply transitory events, oscillations around the long-run equilibrium of the real economy? Or do crises, and their reverberating impacts on average opinion and on expectations of asset price movements, play a role in determining the long-run performance of the economy, with consequent huge welfare implications?

These questions have both theoretical and empirical dimensions. Lacking generally agreed answers, international financial regulation has proceeded by trial and error, regulatory innovations typically following financial shocks. The device of a hypothetical World Financial Authority is designed, in part, to overcome this piecemeal approach. Starting from the perspective of a single regulator of international markets given the objective of maintaining financial stability by limiting systemic risk, the WFA should assess the costs and benefits of particular measures against that goal. It will obviously encounter the problem of evaluating the distribution of costs and benefits. For example, measures to limit short-term capital flows to emerging markets may enhance the stability of financial markets at little cost to recipient economies, but at significant loss of income to banks in the G10. In these circumstances the WFA (or whatever institution performs its functions) must have the means to develop a coherent analysis of the overall impact on systemic risk, to persuade the participants of the values of the analysis and policies, and to mediate disputes.

MACROECONOMIC AND MICROECONOMIC ASPECTS OF INTERNATIONAL REGULATION

The fact that the externality associated with the risks taken by individual firms is, in many cases, transmitted macroeconomically, requires that regulation be conceived in conjunction with macroeconomic policy. Too often today, regulation is seen as an activity that involves the behaviour and interaction of firms, with little or no macroeconomic dimension. By the very nature of financial risk this is a serious error, and is likely to lead to serious policy mistakes. This is particularly true in an international setting, where a major focus of systemic risk is the exchange rate, a macroeconomic variable, changes in which can lead to rapid redistributions of the values of assets and liabilities.

Financial markets are markets for stocks of assets, the value of which today is dependent on the expectation of their future value. Any factor that leads to a shift in expected future values will have an immediate impact on financial markets, and on the major macro-financial variables, the interest rate and the exchange rate. So the failure of a single firm can, by influencing expectations, have an influence not only on its immediate counterparties, or even firms dealing in similar products, but also, through its impact on expectations, on financial markets as a whole, and, via macro variables, on the real economy at home and abroad.

As noted above, a peculiarity of market expectations is that they seem to be remarkably stable (or tranquil) for substantial periods of time, even when underlying real circumstances might be decidedly unpropitious. In consequence, the financial markets can resemble the cartoon character who, having run off the edge of the cliff remains suspended for some time in mid-air, with no visible (or rational) means of support, before suddenly plunging into the abyss. Periods of tranquillity defined by stable expectations and stable market confidence produce the illusion that financial markets are truly reflecting the real economy. The shattering of the illusion can be catastrophic. Keynes referred to this stability of expectations as 'the state of long-term expectations' which is determined by 'convention' (Keynes, 1936, chapters 5 and 15; Eatwell, 1983). Stable expectations are not necessarily a good thing, since stable pessimism can result in prolonged recession, as, following the burst of the 'bubble economy', the performance of the Japanese economy over the past decade has amply confirmed.

The analytical link between microeconomic risk-taking and the associated macroeconomic externalities has its counterpart in regulatory practice. Microeconomic regulation may be a means of reducing systemic risk, but macroeconomic action may be more efficient. An excellent example of the role of macro-linkages in the formation of regulatory policy has followed the Asian financial crisis of 1997–98. It is clear that an important component of the crisis was the excess foreign-exchange exposure of financial and other institutions in emerging markets. In consequence, the international financial institutions have been urging the authorities in those economies to tighten regulation of short-term forex exposure. The tightening is supposed to take place microeconomically by means of regulations that impact on the actions of individual firms. This is a complex task, and requires a significant input of a scarce resource – trained regulators. Moreover, the quantitative measures proposed are likely to have an uneven effect, limiting the exposure of financial institutions, but missing many holdings outside the financial sector.

The same goal could be attained macroeconomically. Measures that raise the cost of short-term borrowing abroad, such as 'Chilean-style' short-term capital controls, would encourage a reduction in the exposure of all firms, financial and otherwise (Agosin, 1998). The higher cost of short-term foreign borrowing 'prices in' the risk externality and hence increases economic efficiency. This macro approach would also have the advantage of economizing on scarce talent. Yet although capital controls do not today suffer the same level of opprobrium as they did before the Asian crisis, the link between micro and macro means of attaining the same objective is not often made. The neglect of macro-measures is particularly puzzling given that micro-regulation tends to be quantitative and to some degree discriminatory, whilst Chilean-style macro controls are price based and non-discriminatory – characteristics which might be expected to appeal to economic policymakers.

The difficulty of analysing the macroeconomic transmission of the systemic risk generated by the actions of individual firms, is illustrated by a proposal emanating from within the IMF to construct 'macroprudential indicators' (MPIs) to assess the 'health and stability of the financial system'. As currently constructed, MPIs 'comprise both aggregated microprudential indicators of the health of individual financial institutions and macroeconomic variables associated with financial system soundness' (Hilbers *et al.*, 2000; see also Evans *et al.,* 2000).

The attempt to link micro risk to the performance of the macro economy is laudable, and is exactly where the debate on effective international regulation should be conducted. However, there are two flaws in MPIs as currently conceived. *First*, the *aggregation* of the characteristics of individual firms will not result in an indicator that accurately represents the risk to which the economy is exposed. For example, the *aggregate* capital adequacy ratio of the financial sector, one of the indicators collected, could easily conceal major risks – a few prudent institutions with high ratios disguising the presence of the less prudent. Including data on the frequency distribution of such variables does not fully confront this problem, as the distribution does not capture the nature of the risks taken by individual institutions.[4] *Second*, as yet there has been no attempt to link macroeconomic performance and policy to the incentives surrounding microeconomic risk-taking. Not only is the value of capital, and hence the capital adequacy ratio, directly affected by the revaluation of assets consequent upon a change in the interest rate, but also declines in the level of activity can readily transform prudent investments into bad loans. Taking these two points together, it becomes clear that in the analysis of systemic risk micro and macro factors should not be treated separately. The whole is not just greater, but behaves very differently from the sum of the parts.

Effective international regulation requires a new approach to the theory of financial regulation. This new approach must confront the macro-manifestation of systemic risk within the analysis of the impact of firm behaviour. Building on this theoretical approach it must be recognized that the regulator may be able to operate more efficiently in macroeconomic terms than by means of more traditional initiatives at the level of the firm.

PRO-CYCLICAL AND PRO-CONTAGION RISK MANAGEMENT

A further manifestation of the relationship between microeconomic risk and macroeconomic performance derives from the apparently paradoxical links between risk management, the trade cycle and financial contagion. Strict regulatory requirements will result in firms reducing lending as a result of a downturn in the economy, so exacerbating the downturn. In an upturn, the perceived diminution of risk and the availability of regulatory capital will tend to increase the ability to lend, stoking up the boom (see Jackson, 1999).

This pro-cyclicality of regulation is further amplified by the contagion-inducing techniques of risk management. During the Asian crisis, financial institutions reduced their exposure to emerging markets throughout the world. These cutbacks helped spread the crisis, as reduced lending and reduced confidence fed the financial downturn. The key to the problem is, once again, the link between microeconomic actions and macroeconomic consequences. Rational risk-management by individual firms precipitates a macroeconomic reaction that, in a downturn, can place those firms and other firms in jeopardy, indeed could overwhelm the firms' defences entirely. Yet because the links between regulation and macroeconomic policy are so little understood, there is no coherent policy response to this perverse consequence. Under pressure, regulators have adopted pragmatic solutions. At the onset of the Latin American debt crisis in the early 1980s many major US banks were technically bankrupt, since Latin American assets held on their books had lost their entire market value. Nonetheless, US regulators allowed those worthless assets to be evaluated in the banks' balance sheets at their value at maturity, hence boosting the banks' notional capital and preventing a sudden collapse in lending and liquidity.[5] In the Autumn of 1998, many assets held on the balance sheets of financial institutions in London and New York were, if marked to market, worth nothing. Again, the regulators did not insist on an immediate (potentially catastrophic) write-down.

Philip Turner (2000) has argued for a 'microeconomic solution' to the procyclicality of regulation:

> The ideal response to procyclicality is for provisions to be made for possible loan losses (that is, subtracted from equity capital in the books of the bank) to cover normal cyclical risks. If done correctly, provisions built up in good times can be used in bad times without necessarily affecting reported capital.

But he notes that even this sensible provision for 'normal cyclical risks' can run foul of current regulatory procedures:

> The first stumbling block is that tax laws often severely limit the tax deductibility of precautionary provisioning and may insist on evidence that losses have actually occurred. This is important because loan loss provisions increase internal funding for the bank only to the extent that they reduce taxes.
>
> A second possible stumbling block may be the securities laws. For example the SEC in the United States has argued that precautionary provisioning distorts financial reports and may mislead investors. There may then be a trade-off between very transparent, well-documented accounting practices, on the one hand, and the need for banks to build up reserves during good times, on the other.
>
> A third possible stumbling block is that the management of banks may be too eager to report strong improvements in earnings during booms (and so too reluctant during good times to make adequate provision for losses). The present wave of takeovers in the banking industry may accentuate this eagerness: good reported earnings and high share prices serve to fend off takeovers.

But even if these stumbling blocks were overcome, as surely they could be, Turner's proposal of extra provisioning would only serve to alleviate the problems created by the procyclicality of regulation in 'normal' circumstances. It does not address the issue of the tendency of regulatory standards to deepen and widen major downturns, and to fuel booms. This tendency will become increasingly severe in developing countries as they are further integrated into international capital markets, and adopt the required risk management regulatory procedures. For all countries, there is the further difficulty that even if some sort of macroeconomic response were available to offset the pro-cyclicality of regulation, macroeconomic policy is essentially national, whilst the problem may well be international in origin and scope. The very least that a WFA could do is assist in the coordination of macroeconomic responses. At a more general level the presence of a WFA would facilitate the international development of policies that link regulatory risk-management procedures and the needs of macroeconomic balance.

THE CHALLENGES FACING INTERNATIONAL FINANCIAL REGULATION

If the challenges facing international financial regulation today may be best identified through the device of a hypothetical WFA, then: what tasks should be performed by such an Authority? What should be the legal foundation of WFA action? How are the tasks to be performed?

What Tasks should be Performed by a WFA?

A national financial regulator performs five main tasks: authorization of market participants; the provision of information to enhance market transparency; surveillance to ensure that the regulatory code is obeyed; enforcement of the code and disciplining of transgressors; and the development of policy that keeps the regulatory code up to date (or at least not more than 10 metres behind the market in a 100 metre race). These are the tasks that now need to be performed at international level, ideally *as if* performed by a unitary WFA.

For example, it is clear that criteria for authorization should be at the same high level throughout the international market: ensuring that a business is financially viable, that it has suitable regulatory compliance procedures in place, and that the staff of the firm are fit and proper persons to conduct a financial services business. If, in a liberal international financial environment, high standards are not uniformly maintained, then firms authorized in a less demanding jurisdiction can impose unwarranted risks on others, undermining high standards of authorization elsewhere.

Similarly, as far as the information function is concerned, the failure to attain not only transparency but also common standards of information undermines the efficient operation of international financial markets, and creates risk. The persistent inability to agree international accounting standards is a prime example of just such a failure.

Surveillance and enforcement are the operational heart of any effective regulatory system. Without effective, thorough policing of regulatory codes, and uniform enforcement of standards by appropriate disciplinary measures (including exclusion from the marketplace) the international financial system is persistently exposed to unwarranted risks.

Finally, the policy function is the essential driving force of effective regulation. Regulatory codes must be adapted to a continuously changing marketplace. An important component of that change is international. As national financial boundaries dissolve, and as new products are developed that transcend international boundaries by firms with a worldwide perspective, the policy function must ensure that the regulator is alert to the new structure of the marketplace, the new systemic risks created, and to the new possibilities of contagion.[6] This requires a unified policy function, capable of taking a view as to the risks encountered by particular markets and by the international marketplace as a whole.

What should be the Legal Foundation of WFA Action?

All these activities are necessary for the efficient operation of the new international financial order. All point to the need for a single authority determining common rules and exercising common procedures. But there are clear, in some cases overwhelming difficulties in attaining that goal, of which the problem of achieving common accounting standards is but a foretaste. All five core activities involve the exercise of authority, and hence trespass into very sensitive political areas. Nation states are naturally reluctant to cede powers to an international body, even if this might mean the acquisition of (collective) sovereignty over activities otherwise beyond their control. When powers are ceded, this is done typically by treaty, confirming collective rights and responsibilities, and, at least in principle, accountability. But it can also be done by the consensus and by the mutual recognition of self-interest that produces 'soft law'.

Article IV of the Articles of Association of the IMF empowers the organization to 'oversee the international monetary system in order to ensure its effective operation'. To this end the provision that 'the Fund shall exercise firm surveillance over the exchange rate policies of members' has been interpreted as covering general macroeconomic surveillance, and, in the new Financial Sector Appraisal Programme (FSAP), *microeconomic* surveillance of the operations of the financial sectors of member states.[7] The new FSAP surveillance concentrates on the adherence of national regulation and practices to core principles developed by the Basle committees of the G10, the International Organisation of Securities Commissions (IOSCO) and the International Association of Insurance Supervisors (IAIS).[8] It is an activity of considerable sensitivity. Not only will comprehensive surveillance require large resources, but also the IMF could easily be drawn into the position of 'grading' national financial systems, with any downward revision of grades having the potential to produce dramatic financial consequences (IMF, 2000b). Nonetheless, the IMF, as an accountable body the powers of which are defined by treaty, can legitimately perform a surveillance function. Moreover, in due course the IMF will require countries seeking its assistance to conform to international regulatory codes and standards. In other words, it will be able to *enforce* conformity to those standards, with severe financial penalties (withdrawal of offers of assistance) for those who do not comply. It is to be doubted, however, whether it could, other than by persuasion, effectively enforce regulatory codes when they are infringed by the more powerful countries that do not require the Fund's assistance (Eatwell and Taylor, 2000, chapter 7).

But the IMF is using a treaty-sanctioned surveillance function to examine adherence to codes and principles that are not themselves developed by accountable treaty bodies. The rules that the IMF is seeking (experimentally) to embody in its surveillance programme are predominantly formulated within non-treaty, 'soft-law' environments.

As Alexander (2000a) explains:

> Soft law may be defined as an international rule created by a group of specially affected states which had a common intent to voluntarily observe the content of such rule with a view of potentially adopting it into the national law or administrative code.
>
> International soft law refers to legal norms, principles, codes of conduct and transactional rules of state practice that are recognized in either formal or informal multilateral agreements. Soft law generally presumes consent to basic standards and norms of state practice, but without the *opinio juris* necessary to form binding obligations under customary international law.

Soft law evades some of the political difficulty of the assignment of sovereignty implicit in international regulation because it does not impose an obligation, even though there is an expectation that states will take agreed codes seriously. In financial matters the most powerful means of enforcing soft law has been the competitive market. A major example of this process was the rapidity with which OECD and other economies subscribed to the 1987 bilateral agreement between the UK and the US to adopt capital adequacy standards for banks. A failure to subscribe would undermine market confidence in a country's financial sector – too high a price to pay. In 1993 the US reinforced the powers of the marketplace by legislation to exclude from US markets banks that failed to attain the capital adequacy standards.

The adoption by the IMF of soft law as a criterion of surveillance suggests a process of transition from soft law to mandatory regulation, at least for those countries that are beholden to the IMF. Observation of Basle and other codes will become an IMF-imposed obligation. If this happens, new questions will be raised about the accountability of the Basle rule-makers and their counterparts at IOSCO and the IAIS.

Even with this potential 'legalization' of international policymaking and of surveillance (which includes some standardization of the information function in the drive for 'transparency'), authorization and, for the richer countries, enforcement remain national activities – though even here agreements on home–host division of responsibilities inject an international dimension.

There is, in effect, a creeping internationalization of the regulatory function in international financial markets. That internationalization is essentially *confederalist* in character, with national jurisdictions being the predominant legal actors guided by international soft law. So some of the functions of a WFA are being performed. But they are being performed imperfectly. Authorization is still essentially national, the information function is highly imperfect, surveillance (by the IMF) is as yet 'experimental', enforcement is national, and the policy function is predominantly driven by an exclusively G10 consensus. As measured against the template of a proper WFA there is a long way to go.

However, the difficulty of creating an effective framework of international regulation does not derive solely from international legal practice and from politics. An important element of disjuncture derives from history – from differences in national legal systems, in financial custom and practice and in structures of corporate governance. Even within the European Union, for example, there are major differences in national legal systems and in corporate governance that make the introduction of a common regulatory code not only difficult, but potentially damaging (see ECOFIN 2000 for an analysis of these difficulties within the European Union). Regulatory codes that enhance efficiency in one jurisdiction may have exactly the opposite effect in another.

A central theme of Eatwell and Taylor (2000) is that efficient regulation requires that the domain of the regulator should be the same as the domain of the market that is regulated. However, whilst financial markets are 'seamless', they are not homogeneous. In consequence uniform financial regulations often have quite different practical effects. The result is that uniform codes will expose the financial system to different systemic risks in the light of their differential impact in different jurisdictions (Alexander and Dhumale, 2000).

This is the central weakness of the fixed regulatory requirements and ratios emanating from the Basle committees, and, the strength of the Basle system of codes. What is ideally required is that there should be an assessment of the relationship between the financial structure of national jurisdictions and the systemic risk emanating from each jurisdiction. That ideal is probably unattainable, since it would require detailed consideration and negotiation of each hypothetical national case – an overwhelming task. A more pragmatic approach would involve:

a. the construction of specific rules in those cases which refer to basic institutional tenets that are universal, and are necessary for the success of any regulatory environment;
b. in those circumstances where national legal and governance structures predominate, the development of national codes derived from common internationally agreed general principles.

In case (b) regulation is developed at two levels: *first*, a set of general principles, *second*, from these principles should be derived codes that are both flexible as circumstances change and reflect the peculiar legal and governance structures of individual countries. This is, of course, the defining characteristic of the current soft law regime. But at present many of the principles are 'ideal types', to be desired rather than enforced. If principles are to be the foundation of an effective regulatory system they must be expressed through clearly articulated codes, which are regularly tested against the principles they are supposed to embody, and against the systemic risks they are supposed to manage. There will undoubtedly be differences of opinion as to whether a particular set of national codes accurately reflects shared principles, and it will be necessary to put in place powerful procedures for adjudicating disputes (another role for a WFA).

The cause of uniform adherence to principles will be reinforced by market competition, in rather the same manner as competition has led to the widespread adoption of Basle capital adequacy standards. Moreover, increasingly open markets are likely to produce competitive convergence in standards and procedures of corporate governance that will in turn permit a movement toward uniform regulatory codes, that is an increasing role for the universal rules referred to in (a) above.

How are these Tasks to be Performed?

Whilst the template of a WFA clarifies the tasks that must be performed if international financial markets are to be regulated efficiently, it does not provide much guidance as to how the tasks are actually to be performed in the more likely absence of a unitary authority. In practical terms many tasks can and must be delegated to national authorities. But it is important that national authorities should operate within common guidelines. That is the importance of the WFA – not to tell national authorities what to do, but to ensure that in a single world financial market they behave in a coherent and complementary manner to manage the systemic risk to which, in a seamless market, they are all exposed. Effective international regulation will necessarily be confederal, with different responsibilities at appropriate levels of the system. But there must be a coherent confederation with common principles and common values, resulting in (converging) national codes enforced by national authorities to attain common goals.

DEVISING AN INSTITUTIONAL STRUCTURE: THE LEGACY OF POST-WAR INTERNATIONAL FINANCIAL REGULATION

The development of international financial regulation since 1974 has been essentially reactive.

The first major reaction was to the fact of liberalization itself. The three decades following the end of World War II had seen the refinement of the tools for managing systemic risk in *domestic* monetary and financial systems. Allied with the international commitment to the management of financial flows that was a key component of the Bretton Woods system, these domestic arrangements had resulted in 25 years of reasonable financial stability in most OECD countries. This is not to say that there were not financial crises, there were. But they were predominantly of macroeconomic origin, disrupting the microeconomy: high inflation rates undermining confidence in monetary policy, or persistent current account deficits undermining confidence in the exchange rate. The bad old days of microeconomic instability spreading as contagion through the financial sector and destabilizing the macroeconomy belonged to the pre-war era of economic disaster, from which important lessons had been learned.[9] Those lessons were now embodied in appropriate policies and institutions. Important amongst these institutions were powerful regulatory structures and interventionist central banks dedicated to the management of (indeed the minimization of) systemic risk.

There had, of course, been a partial relaxation of wartime and immediate post-war regulation through the 1950s and 1960s. But even at the end of the 1960s the regulatory regime was powerful and national. In the United States domestic money markets were particularly tightly regulated, and President Johnson's interest equalization tax was used to manage international capital flows. Throughout the OECD the public authorities' international role was dedicated to the maintenance of the fixed exchange rate system. The collapse of the Bretton Woods system of fixed exchange rates in 1971 resulted in the privatization of foreign exchange risk. If the private sector was to carry this risk it needed to be able to diversify its financial assets amongst a variety of monetary instruments and currencies. So it was necessary to dismantle much of the post-war international and domestic financial regulation that would have prevented that diversification. But dismantling controls threatened to recreate the unstable pre-war environment (see Eatwell and Taylor, 2000, chapter 1).

As international barriers to financial flows disappeared, national regulators and national central banks were trapped in increasingly irrelevant national boundaries. The domain of banks, investment houses, insurance companies and pension funds became international. In a rapid return to the pre-war norm, it was a microeconomic failure (of the Herstatt Bank in 1974) that threatened severe disruption of the US clearing system and hence of the US macroeconomy. In recent years the Asian crisis also stemmed primarily from failures in the private sector reverberating through the macroeconomy.

An important response to the new environment was the establishment in 1975 of Basle committees at the BIS. These committees reported to the grouping of central bankers of the major economies, the Group of Ten (G10). The task of the committees amounted to an attempt, via consensual decision making, to formulate on an international scale some of the powers that had earlier been deemed necessary to stabilize national financial systems. The scope of those committees has steadily increased since 1975, usually in response to crises (Eatwell and Taylor, 2000, chapter 6). A crucial development came in 1988, with the adoption of capital adequacy criteria. International financial regulation was not just about cooperation, but about the coordination of standards – standards agreed in Basle.

A further important development came in response to the Mexican bond crisis of 1994. The G7 governments, responding to what was perceived to be the excessive instability of financial markets, agreed at their Halifax summit in 1995 that the regulation of international financial markets should not be left to the G10, but should be on the agenda of intergovernmental discussions. At first not much was achieved in concrete terms. Then the Russian bond crisis of 1998, coming as it did at the end of a period of extreme instability emanating from Asia, brought home to G7 governments that their economies are not immune from the contagion of third world financial turbulence. The response was the creation of the Financial Stability Forum (FSF), and establishment of the World Bank–IMF Financial Sector Assessment Program (FSAP) under the direction of the joint Bank–Fund Financial Sector Liaison Committee (FSLC).

The FSF has brought together, on the one hand, the political and the supervisory authorities, and, on the other hand, the regulatory authorities and the macroeconomic policymakers. So, on the operational side, the supervisors are meeting with the politicians and treasury staff who can get things done. On the economic side the FSF brings together regulation and macroeconomic policy, a vital, and up to now missing, component of effective international regulation. At the moment, whilst it has produced some excellent reports, the FSF is a think tank with nowhere to go. It is not at all clear what action will follow the reports, or, indeed, who will act. Having suffered a fright in 1998, the policymakers in national treasuries are retreating from the sort of collaborative view of the world that the establishment of the FSF seemed to foreshadow.

The FSAP involves the Bank and IMF in detailed microeconomic appraisal of the financial markets and regulatory institutions of selected nations. This level of detailed appraisal of private sector structures is a significant change in the involvement of the IMF in a nation's economic affairs, and probably marks a turning point in the surveillance activities of the Fund. The pressure for a new international regulatory regime is leading to a significant reinvention of the IMF.

It is not as yet clear what will prove to be the respective roles of the Basle committees, the Financial Stability Forum and the new Bank–Fund structures in the future management of international regulation. What is clear is that the issues identified in the WFA project have proved to be the fundamental issues that must be addressed if that future management is to be accountable, legitimate and successful.

DEVISING AN INSTITUTIONAL STRUCTURE: THE ROLE OF THE TEMPLATE WFA

In a liberal international financial system each nation faces risks that may emanate from behaviour entirely outside its jurisdiction. As was demonstrated in the Autumn of 1998, even very strong states face risks that may derive from financial crises in poor countries. The desire to manage risks may lead to two polar reactions: *first* the attempt by the rich and strong to manage the poor and weak, to protect the rich from external threat; *second*, cooperation between all countries to manage risk internationally. All procedures for international regulation will fall somewhere on a scale between these two extremes. Other than in the polar first case, international regulation will involve some pooling of sovereignty, even if only at the level of initiating proposals.

Treaties designed to establish international authority and procedures, such as the treaty agreeing the Articles of Association of the IMF, are a pooling of sovereignty in the pursuit of negotiated ends. They also typically contain procedures to ensure some accountability by the international institutions to the national signatories. As Alexander (2000a) has pointed out, the pursuit of international goals by means of treaties has high transactions costs, and may be restrained by uncertainty:

> One set of problems falls under the heading of *transaction costs*. Complexity of the issues, difficulties in negotiating and drafting, the number of participants and similar factors make it difficult for governments to agree on precise, binding and highly institutionalised commitments . . .
>
> Another set of contracting problems concerns the pervasive uncertainty in which states and other international actors must operate. Many international agreements can affect national wealth, power and autonomy. Yet governments can never foresee all the contingencies that may arise under any agreement. They are never certain that they will be able to detect cheating or other threats. They cannot even be sure how they will react to particular contingencies, let alone how others will. These problems are exacerbated by the relative weakness of the international legal system that cannot fill gaps and respond to new situations as easily as domestic legal systems can.
>
> One way to deal with uncertainty is through soft delegation: not to courts, but to political institutions, subject to continuing oversight and control, that can produce information, monitor behaviour, assist in further negotiations, mediate disputes and produce interstitial or technical rules. Another is through imprecise norms that provide general guidelines for expected behaviour while allowing

> states to work out more detailed rules over time. A third way involves crafting relatively precise, but nonbinding, rules that allow actors to experiment by applying the rules under different conditions while limiting unpleasant surprises. All these approaches have costs, including their limited ability to regularise behaviour. Yet on balance they are frequently seen as beneficial, permitting states to achieve some immediate gains from cooperation while structuring ongoing learning: this is a political process that can take states further along the path of the institutionalisation of obligations.

Because treaties must overcome these difficulties they are typically a compromise, and inevitably inflexible. Moreover, because they necessarily embody some degree of accountability to their signatories, they tend to be slow-moving. These are rather unattractive characteristics in the field of international financial regulation. It is therefore not surprising that developments have taken a different route, with the major role being played by the non-treaty committees housed at the BIS, together with IOSCO and the IAIS:

> The process of devising international norms and rules to regulate international banking activity involves a form of international soft law that has precise, non-binding norms that are generated through consultations and negotiations amongst the major state regulators. This particular form of international soft law provides the necessary political flexibility for states to adopt international rules and standards into their national legal systems in a manner that accommodates the sovereign authority of the nation state. States could then move forward through the process of legalisation by building on the collective intent of the major economic powers to develop binding international rules for banking supervision. States could potentially delegate the adjudication of violations to an international financial authority, but states would retain ultimate enforcement authority, including sanctions (Alexander, 2000a).

The problem here is, of course, the predominant role of the major states. An effective soft-law regime works by consensus, and a grudging consensus imposed by the major states upon others is likely to be less effective than a consensus in which all participate. Whilst the existence of a legal structure does offer some protection to weaker countries, whose sovereignty is compromised by the very fact of being economically (and perhaps politically) dominated by the developed countries,[10] the fact that that structure is determined by the G10 raises the obvious question of whose interests are being protected.

The 'obvious' solution of increasing the representation on the Basle committees runs the risk of overloading the decision-making mechanisms, and losing their flexibility. The partial solution adopted at the FSF, of involving a wider range of countries on policymaking committees is attractive, but it may not prove to be widely acceptable if the proposals contained in the reports produced by the FSF harden into concrete policy measures.

Ultimately the choice between a soft law and a formal treaty regime may come to the conclusion: 'both'. The treaty will lay down a method for developing general principles that should guide the regulators, and a mechanism for developing codes derived from those principles. The task of developing the codes can then be entrusted to a less formal body, akin to the current Basle committees.

Today an institutional structure of international financial supervision is emerging which embodies, albeit imperfectly, a few of the features of an idealized WFA. The authorization function is the responsibility of national regulators, with access to markets being determined by the presence or absence of agreements specifying the terms of mutual recognition. The information function is performed partly by the international financial institutions, particularly the BIS, partly by the International Accounting Standards Committee, and partly by national regulators, stock market rules, and so on. The surveillance function is performed by the World Bank–IMF financial sector programme, and by national regulators.[11] The enforcement function is being developed as an implicit outcome of the World Bank–IMF financial sector programme, and is otherwise the responsibility of national authorities. The policy function is in the hands of the BIS committees, IOSCO and the IAIS, the Financial Stability Forum, the IMF, and national authorities.

This list of international regulatory activities has four major features:

1. If the same list were compiled 10 years ago most of the regulatory functions, with the exception of the policy function, would lack any international dimension. Today in all areas other than authorization, international bodies are taking up some of the regulatory tasks.
2. There is an eclectic mix of national institutions, international agreements (soft and hard) and international institutions (with varying degrees of legitimacy). Some powers are developing almost accidentally, such as the emergence of an enforcement power at the IMF via the FSAP programme. Others are developing by design, such as the work of the International Accounting Standards Committee. All are developing under the pressures for effective policy exerted by the process of financial market liberalization, particularly at times of crisis.
3. The list deals only with major international regulatory developments, and omits the growth of *regional* regulation, notably in the European Union. The case of the European Union is particularly interesting since it involves the attempt to develop a fully liberalized, single financial market, characterized by a wide range of different legal practices and structures of corporate governance amongst member states.

4. Measured against the template of a WFA the list displays an international regulatory structure that is limited, even incoherent. It portrays a patchwork response to crises rather than a rational response to the international development of systemic risk.

This patchy, often incoherent structure embodies significant threats to financial stability. On the one hand the growth of international institutions, such as the FSF, induces the feeling that 'something has been done' to tackle systemic risk. On the other hand, the very limited powers of any of the international structures listed above suggest that such complacency is a delusion.

The developments of the past 30 years, and more especially, the innovations of the last three years point to the recognition by states and by market participants of the need for coherent international regulation. But the present conjuncture, in which the predominant rule-making bodies are the Basle committees, IOSCO and the IAIS, whilst the predominant international surveillance body (in so far as there is any international surveillance at all) is the IMF, is an awkward hybrid. Moreover, it embodies the unfortunate impression that rules are made by the rich nations and enforced on the rest.

What is needed is recognition of the power of the WFA template, and the design of international institutions that can meet the demands identified by the template in an accountable, coherent and flexible manner. A number of challenges must be met if this goal is to be attained: (1) the development and acceptance of a common theoretical framework within which to confront the tasks of international regulation; (2) the integration of macroeconomic and microeconomic aspects of international regulation; (3) the development of procedures that (at least) alleviate the tendency for risk management to be pro-cyclical and pro-contagion; (4) the harmonization of risk management in differing corporate governance structures to obtain a common international regulatory outcome: (5) solving the political challenge of accountability in a soft law regime; (6) devising an institutional structure that performs the tasks of the template WFA.

As practical politics, these are rather grandiose objectives. But in pragmatic terms this framework can be used to generate practical proposals for dealing with specific problems (the use of short-term capital controls as the macro component of a regulatory regime was discussed above). These specific proposals are more likely to be agreed upon internationally – if at all – than 'common theoretical frameworks'. But if they derive from the coherent framework of a WFA they are likely to be more effective and ultimately more acceptable, even within a neo-liberal political and economic environment.

SUMMING UP

Two themes dominate this appraisal of the challenges facing the development of an efficient system of international financial regulation: *First*, the need for theory and policy that link microeconomic risk-taking to the macroeconomic propagation of systemic risk. *Second*, the need to develop a coherent and accountable set of institutions through which international policy may be developed and implemented. These two needs were met by the authorities in the immediate post-war era. They reacted to the instability of inadequately regulated markets in the 1930s by producing new procedures and institutions based on what were then new models of macroeconomic management. Internationally, the response at Bretton Woods was to put in place a set of international arrangements that permitted the pursuit of national macroeconomic policies, free from the fear of international financial disruption. The problem of accountability did not arise. Tackling the same problems in the context of today's liberal financial markets requires a reinterpretation of what both macroeconomic policy and market regulation mean, and a reassessment of the institutions required to conduct such policies. The device of a World Financial Authority provides the means of exposing both analytical and institutional questions.

NOTES

1. Alan Greenspan commented that he had never seen anything in his lifetime that compared with the panic of August–September 1998.
2. For example, Will Hutton (1999) in a preview of Eatwell and Taylor (2000) argued that the authors' '. . . logic is impeccable, but it faces one insuperable obstacle. The United States at present has no intention of ceding any regulatory sovereignty to such an authority'. Hutton does not take into account the degree of authority already vested in the consensual decision-making processes of the Basle G10 committees. The capital adequacy requirements of banks in Iowa are determined by a committee sitting in Basle that is not accountable to the US Congress. This approach has not so much involved 'ceding regulatory authority' as the recognition of the advantages of collaborative decision-making. However, Will Hutton's point may become more important as the demands for accountability in international regulation become more strident (particularly from developing countries who have, up to now, had only minor roles in development of regulatory rules and practices).
3. John Meriwether, former CEO of Long Term Capital Management, commented two years after the activities of his hedge fund had led the financial system of the West to the edge of catastrophe, that 'I am not so sure we would have said this earlier – there are times when markets can be much more chaotic than one would ever predict' (quoted in *The Financial Times*, 21 August 2000). But it was not chaos that was the problem, but the design of LTCM's trading strategy. A fundamental error stemmed from the belief that all markets would not move in the same direction at the same time.
4. A further difficulty with the use of capital adequacy ratios as MPIs arises from the

ambiguity surrounding the regulatory role of the ratio: is it a buffer, or is it a charge 'pricing in' the externality of systemic risk? If ratios must be maintained in all circumstances, capital cannot be a buffer to cover losses; it is needed to fulfil regulatory needs. So the size of the capital ratio merely indicates the size of the charge levied on risk-taking. If the ratio is fixed, the charge will not vary significantly as between booms and depressions, yet the risk may undergo large variations.

5. This does not mean that regulatory standards were abandoned entirely: '. . . money centre banks whose loans to heavily indebted countries exceeded their capital in the early 1980s were allowed several years to adjust – but there was no doubt that they would have to adjust' (Turner, 2000).
6. An important recent example was the use of credit derivatives in Indonesia that ultimately spread financial losses to South Korea.
7. Many characteristics of domestic financial systems may be only indirectly connected to 'the exchange rate' as such. Nonetheless, it is not unreasonable to link *domestic* regulation to *international* financial stability.
8. For example, the June 2000 IMF 'experimental' *Report on the Observation of Standards and Codes* (ROSC) for Canada, prepared by a staff team from the International Monetary Fund in the context of a Financial Sector Assessment Programme (FSAP), on the basis of information provided by the Canadian authorities, produced 'an assessment of Canada's observance of and consistency with relevant international standards and core principles in the financial sector, as part of a broader assessment of the stability of the financial system. . . . The assessment covered (i) the Basle Core Principles for Effective Banking Supervision; (ii) the International Organization of Securities Commissions' (IOSCO) Objectives and Principles of Securities Regulation; (iii) the International Association of Insurance Supervisors' (IAIS) Supervisory Principles; (iv) the Committee on Payment and Settlement Systems' (CPSS) Core Principles for Systemically Important Payment Systems; and (v) the IMF's Code of Good Practices on Transparency in Monetary and Financial Policies. Such a comprehensive coverage of standards was needed as part of the financial system stability assessment for Canada in view of the increasing convergence in the activities of banking, insurance, and securities firms, and the integrated nature of the markets in which they operate.' (IMF, 2000a).
9. The distinction between crises emanating from the microeconomy and those that are macroeconomically induced is worth further consideration. Though the second phase of the Great Depression was marked by failure at the micro level, that of the Austrian bank, Credit Anstalt, much of the responsibility for the depression rests at the door of inappropriate macroeconomic policy – particularly adherence to the Gold Standard and domestic monetary policies associated with the Gold Standard (Temin, 1989). Similarly, the recent Korean crisis derived substantially from the decision of the Korean government to join the OECD, and to accept the required liberalization of financial markets. This led to private sector firms increasing their foreign exchange exposure to excessive levels (Chang *et al.*, 1998). In both the 1930s and the 1990s, an inappropriate macroeconomic environment resulted in excessive risk-taking by firms. In the 1950s and 1960s macroeconomic crises were not associated with excessive private sector risk-taking (which was constrained by strict regulation) but with major macroeconomic imbalances.
10. 'Small states . . . may have negative sovereignty costs, since legal arrangements offer them protection from powerful neighbours. Large states, by contrast, would appear to be in less need of legalisation, though in fact they might seek it as an efficient way to structure governance where they can dictate the rules and exert political control over their implementation. Soft legalisation can bridge the gap between weak and strong states. This is especially true of the type of legalisation . . . where norms and rules are binding and relatively precise but authority for compliance is delegated to national political institutions. In this situation weak states are protected by legal rules that fix expectations of behaviour, while strong states maintain influence in political bodies where they can shape future developments' (Alexander, 2000a).
11. In addition, the international surveillance of financial crime, particularly money laundering, is conducted by the Financial Action Task Force (see Alexander, 2000b).

REFERENCES

Agosin, M. (1998), 'Capital inflows and investment performance: Chile in the 1990s', in R. Ffrench-Davis and H. Reisen (eds), *Capital Flows and Investment Performance: Lessons from Latin America*, Paris: OECD.

Alexander, K. (2000a), 'The role of soft law in the legalization of international banking supervision', Working Paper 161, Centre of Business Research, University of Cambridge: forthcoming in *Oxford Journal of International Economic Law.*

Alexander, K. (2000b), 'The legalization of the international anti-money laundering regime: the role of the Financial Action Task Force', *Financial Crime Review*, **1**(1).

Alexander, K. and R. Dhumale (2000), *Enhancing corporate governance for banking institutions*, a paper prepared for the Ford Foundation project on 'A World Financial Authority', Centre for Business Research, Judge Institute of Management Studies, Cambridge.

Chang, H.-J., H.-J. Park and C.G. Yoo (1998), 'Interpreting the Korean crisis: financial liberalization, industrial policy and corporate governance', *Cambridge Journal of Economics*, November.

Eatwell, J. (1983), 'The long-period theory of employment', *Cambridge Journal of Economics*, September–December.

Eatwell, J. (1996), 'International financial liberalisation: the impact on world development', *ODS Discussion Paper Series*, no. 12, New York: UNDP.

Eatwell, J. and L. Taylor (1998), 'International capital markets and the future of economic policy', a paper prepared for the Ford Foundation project *International Capital Markets and the Future of Economic Policy*, New York: Center for Economic Policy Analysis; London: IPPR.

Eatwell, J. and L. Taylor (2000), *Global Finance at Risk: the Case for International Regulation*, New York: The New Press.

ECOFIN (European Union Economic and Finance Ministers) (2000), *Initial Report of the Committee of Wise Men on the Regulation of European Securities Markets*, (Lamfalussy Committee), Brussels, 9 November.

Evans, O., A. Leone, M. Gill and P. Hilbers (2000), 'Macroprudential indicators of financial system soundness', *IMF Occasional Paper 00/192*, Washington: IMF.

Hilbers, P., R. Krueger and M. Moretti (2000), 'New tools for assessing financial system soundness', *Finance and Development*, September.

Hutton, W. (1999), 'America's Global Hand', *The American Prospect*, December.

IMF (International Monetary Fund) (2000a), *Report on the Observance of Standards and Codes: Canada*, Washington, DC: IMF.

IMF (International Monetary Fund), (2000b), *Experimental Reports on Observance of Standards and Codes (ROSCs)*, Washington, DC: IMF.

Jackson, P. (1999), Capital requirements and bank behaviour: the impact of the Basle accord, *Basle Committee on Banking Supervision Working Paper No.1.*

Keynes, J.M. (1936), *The General Theory of Employment, Interest and Money*, London: Macmillan.

Temin, P. (1989), *Lessons from the Great Depression*, Cambridge, Mass.: MIT Press.

Turner, P. (2000), *Procyclicality of regulatory ratios?*, a paper presented at Queens' College, Cambridge, January 2000; prepared for the Ford Foundation project on 'A World Financial Authority', Centre for Business Research, Judge Institute of Management Studies, Cambridge.

19. Developing countries' anti-cyclical policies in a globalized world

José Antonio Ocampo*

The volatility and contagion characteristic of international financial markets, which dominated emerging economies during the 1990s, have deep historical roots.[1] Indeed, from the mid-1970s to the end of the 1980s, Latin America and many other regions in the developing world experienced a long boom–bust cycle, the most severe of its kind since that of the 1920s and 1930s. The shortening but also the intensity of boom–bust cycles have been distinctive features of the 1990s. The latter is reflected, in the words of the Chairman of the Federal Reserve Board, in the fact that the 'size of the breakdowns and required official finance to counter them is of a different order of magnitude than in the past' (Greenspan, 1998).

Viewed from the perspective of developing countries, the essential feature of instability is the succession of periods of intense capital inflows, in which financial risks significantly increase, facilitated and sometimes enhanced by pro-cyclical domestic macroeconomic policies, and the latter phases of adjustment, in which these risks are exposed and the pro-cyclical character of the measures adopted to 'restore confidence' amplify the flow (economic activity) and stock (portfolio) effects of adjustment processes. An essential part of the solution to these problems lies in strengthening the institutional framework to prevent and manage financial crises at the global level.[2] This chapter, however, looks at the role of developing countries' domestic policies in managing externally generated boom–bust cycles. It draws upon extensive recent literature on the subject[3] and upon the experience of Latin America in the 1990s.[4] The discussion is divided into seven sections. The first looks at the macroeconomics of boom–bust cycles in the developing world. The following sections look at the exchange rate regime, liability policies, prudential regulation and supervision, and fiscal stabilization. The final section draws some conclusions.

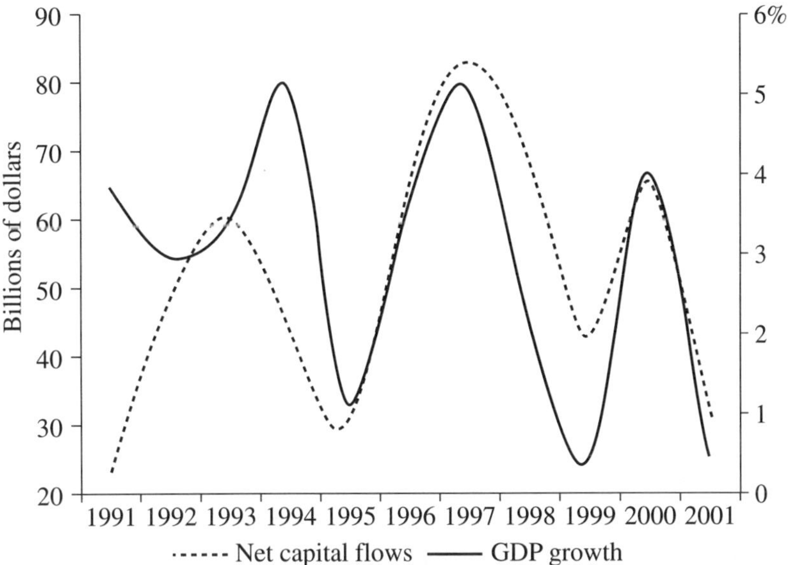

Figure 19.1 Latin America: net capital flows and GDP growth

I THE MACROECONOMICS OF BOOM–BUST CYCLES

The association between capital flows – and, more particularly, net resource transfers – and economic activity has been a strong feature of Latin America over the 1990s (and, for that matter, the past quarter century), as Figure 19.1 indicates. This fact highlights the central role played by the mechanisms through which externally-generated boom–bust cycles are transmitted.

These mechanisms are well known. The boom encourages an increase in public and private spending, which will inevitably lead to an adjustment whose severity will bear a direct relationship to how excessive spending levels were, as reflected in accumulated liabilities. Thus, transitory public-sector revenues and readily accessible external credit during booms generate an expansion of public-sector spending, which will be followed by a severe adjustment later on, when those conditions are no longer present. A private lending cycle is generated by shifts in the availability of external financing and the cyclical patterns of international interest rates and spreads; availability and spreads are associated, in turn, with significant asymmetries in risk evaluation during booms and crises. Private-sector debt overhangs that have accumulated during the boom will subsequently trigger a sharp contraction in lending, usually accompanied by a deterioration in bank portfolios.

Poor prudential regulation and supervision of financial systems, and inadequate experience on the part of financial agents in risk evaluation, will lead to a significant underestimation of risks, further reinforcing credit expansion during booms. Both conditions are characteristic of periods of rapid financial liberalization. Nevertheless, even well-regulated systems are subject to periodic episodes of euphoria, when risks are underestimated. Private-sector borrowing and spending sprees spur sharp upswings in the prices of certain assets, particularly equities and real estate. This generates wealth effects that accentuate the boom in spending, but the reverse will hold true when spending, borrowing and, consequently, asset and real estate prices fall. This process is reinforced by the greater liquidity that characterizes fixed assets during periods of financial euphoria – that is, when buyers are more readily available and financial decisions can be more easily reversed without incurring substantial losses – and by their reduced liquidity during crises. The use of assets as collateral will facilitate booms in private spending and borrowing, but it will then increase the vulnerability of the financial system during subsequent downswings, when it becomes clear that the loans did not have adequate backing. Asset prices will then plunge even further as debtors strive to cover their financial obligations and creditors seek to liquidate the assets received in payment for outstanding debts.

Capital-account booms – as well as high export prices – will also induce an appreciation of the exchange rate and exert adverse pressures on exchange and interest rates during the ensuing busts. Exchange rate fluctuations have significant wealth effects in countries with large net external liabilities. The capital gains generated by appreciation during booms further fuel spending booms, whereas wealth losses generated by depreciation have the opposite effect and may weaken domestic financial intermediaries. This is true even if prudential regulations forbid such agents from holding currency mismatches in their portfolio, as the capital losses incurred by non-financial firms with mixed external and domestic liabilities transform their currency risks into domestic financial risks. Thus, the wealth effects of exchange rate variations are pro-cyclical in debtor countries. The income effects may be so as well, at least in the short run, if the more traditional contractionary effects of devaluation prevail (Krugman and Taylor, 1978).

The associated macroeconomic volatility is costly in both economic and social terms. In economic terms, it increases uncertainty, reduces the efficiency of fixed capital investment and leads economic agents to prefer 'defensive' microeconomic strategies that avoid committing fixed capital to the production process. For all of these reasons, it discourages investment. The higher risk levels faced by the domestic financial system bias lending toward shorter maturities. If severe enough, domestic financial crises will generate losses that amount to the equivalent of large proportions of GDP. In social terms, there is growing evidence in Latin America of ratchet effects of employment, poverty and income distribution through the business cycle.[5] This is associated with permanent losses in human capital during crises: workers who lose labor experience and connections and thus face permanent income losses; children who leave school and never return, and so on. There may also be ratchet effects in the quality of public-sector services as the result of sharp cuts in spending.

The most important policy implication of this is that developing-country authorities need to focus their attention on crisis prevention, that is, on managing booms, since in most cases crises are the inevitable result of poorly managed booms. Concentration on crisis prevention recognizes, moreover, an obvious fact: that the degrees of freedom of the authorities may be greater during booms than during crises. The way crises are managed is not irrelevant, however. In particular, different policy mixes may have quite different effects on economic activity and employment, on the one hand, and on the domestic financial system, on the other.

The following sections of this chapter argue for a mix based on four different sets of policies: (a) managed exchange rate flexibility *cum* capital account regulations to provide room for counter-cyclical monetary and financial policies; (b) strong 'liability policies' to improve countries' debt profiles (which include but go beyond capital account regulations); (c) counter-cyclical management of prudential regulation and supervision of domestic financial systems; and (d) fiscal stabilization. Given the reduced degrees of freedom that authorities have and the reduced effectiveness of some instruments in globalized markets, all policies have limited effects. Thus, pragmatic policy mixes in which these different elements support each other in their counter-cyclical task are called for. The specific emphasis will vary depending on the macroeconomic constraints and traditions of each particular country.

II THE EXCHANGE RATE REGIME

In today's open developing economies, the exchange rate regime is subject to two conflicting demands which are not easily reconcilable. These conflicts are exacerbated by the strong aggregate demand and supply effects that exchange rates have in developing countries and by the reduced degrees of freedom that authorities have in a world of limited policy instruments and reduced policy effectiveness.

The first is a demand for stability. This comes from trade, but also from the capital account and domestic price stability. A classic defense of exchange rate stability is that it reduces the costs of international trade, whereas exchange rate flexibility may be seen as a tax on international specialization. On the other hand, with the dismantling of traditional trade policies, the real exchange rate has become a key determinant of international competitiveness.[6] Given the central role that exports play in the growth process, stable and competitive real exchange rates are essential for sustained economic growth. Alternatively, the combination of exchange rate appreciation and trade liberalization may lead to a structural deterioration in the growth/trade balance trade-off, such as that experienced by Latin America in the 1990s (ECLAC, 2000, chapter 1).[7]

From the point of view of the capital account, a 'hard' peg is seen as a useful instrument to avoid the pro-cyclical wealth effects of exchange rate fluctuations in countries having significant liabilities denominated in foreign currencies.[8] From the point of view of anti-inflationary programs, it is associated with the need to anchor the price level as part of a shock therapy administered after a period of runaway inflation or, more generally, to guarantee macroeconomic discipline and price stability in small open economies. It should be emphasized that these two demands for stability may be inconsistent with the demand deriving from trade. Thus, hard pegs and exchange rate anchors have frequently led to overvalued exchange rates that run counter to the objective of international competitiveness.

The second is a demand for macroeconomic flexibility in the face of trade and capital account shocks. On the trade side, exchange rate flexibility has traditionally been seen as a useful instrument to accelerate relative price adjustments in the face of significant changes in the terms of trade and external demand conditions, or to maintain competitiveness in the face of changes in the exchange rates of major currencies or those of major trading partners. Similarly, significant changes in the availability of external financing generate a demand for flexible macroeconomic variables to absorb the positive and negative shocks that they generate. This demand for flexibility explains the fairly broad trends toward greater exchange rate flexibility that have characterized the world economy since the breakdown of the dollar standard in the early 1970s.

A simple way to present these conflicting demands is to express them as an explicit trade-off between two conflicting policy objectives: nominal price stability and relative price flexibility. The authorities will choose a combination based on their preferences but also on the relative benefits ('price') of flexibility vs. stability, which are determined by both external and internal macroeconomic conditions. Increased international instability (for example, the breakdown of the dollar standard, a period of turmoil in world finance for 'emerging' markets or a world recession) will increase the relative benefits of flexibility, whereas a period of tranquillity (for example, the Bretton Woods system, or a period of stable world economic growth) will increase the 'relative price' of stability. Alternatively, the benefits of flexibility will be higher for larger, less specialized economies, whereas the relative benefits of nominal stability will be greater for smaller, more specialized economies.

The relevance of these conflicting demands is not captured in the call to adopt exchange rate regimes located at either of the two extremes of the spectrum, that is, either a totally flexible exchange rate or a currency board (or outright dollarization). Indeed, the case for regimes at either of the two polar extremes is based on the call to recognize that policy autonomy is quite limited in today's world and, thus, that any attempt to manage the conflicting demands on exchange rate policy should be given up. The 'revealed preference' of authorities in the developing world has been, on the contrary, to choose intermediate regimes in an attempt to reconcile these conflicting demands. Such intermediate regimes either take the form of managed exchange rates (such as crawling pegs and bands) or are characterized by a mix of exchange rate flexibility and central bank intervention in the foreign exchange market (that is, dirty flotation).[9]

Currency boards certainly introduce built-in institutional arrangements that provide for fiscal and monetary discipline, but they reduce and may even eliminate the room for stabilizing monetary and credit policies. They thus tend to generate stronger swings in economic activity and asset prices. Probably as a result of this, these arrangements are not speculation-proof, as the experience of Argentina in 1994–1995 and 1998–2001, Hong Kong in 1997 and, for that matter, of the gold standard in the periphery indicate. More generally, they are not free from pro-cyclical, externally-induced pressure on interest rates. In this type of regime, adjustment to overvaluation (if the economy gets 'locked' in an overvalued exchange rate during the transition, or as a result of effective devaluation by major trade partners or of the appreciation of the currency to which the exchange rate is tied) is painful, as it relies on open deflation to operate. This process is very slow, as the experience of Argentina in 1998–2001 illustrates. Overvaluation in a currency board regime may thus lead to low structural rates of growth mixed with strong business cycles.[10]

On the other hand, the volatility characteristic of freely floating exchange rate regimes increases the costs of trade transactions, thus reducing the benefits of international specialization. As developing countries are large net importers of capital goods, exchange rate uncertainty also affects investment decisions. Learning effects may generate real ratchet effects in the form of 'Dutch disease',[11] whereas ratchet price dynamics increases the risk of rising inertial inflation during crises.

Moreover, the pro-cyclical wealth and (possibly) income effects of exchange rate variations are particularly severe in capital-importing countries. Flexibility certainly deters some short-term flows – particularly portfolio flows and short-term domestic currency-denominated debt – but it is unlikely to smooth out medium-term capital account cycles. Rather, it could enhance them, as the significant capital gains and losses associated with real exchange rate cycles may further encourage 'self-fulfilling' booms and busts. Regulations on currency mismatches of domestic financial institutions and widespread use of exchange rate coverage may limit these endogenous amplifications of financial cycles and are thus essential complements to exchange rate flexibility. However, the coverage provided by private financial agents is likely to be limited or may generate counterpart operations that anticipate the effects of expected exchange rate fluctuations on capital flows.[12]

The ability of a flexible exchange rate regime to smooth out the effects of externally-generated boom–bust cycles thus depends on the capacity to manage a counter-cyclical monetary and credit policy effectively without accentuating pro-cyclical exchange rate patterns. As is well known, this can be achieved through two alternative mechanisms. The first is sterilized intervention in the foreign exchange market, which involves an active counter-cyclical management of international reserves. The basic problem with this option is that higher (lower) domestic interest rates induce short-term capital inflows (outflows) which partly defeats the policy objectives, generating, in turn, additional pressures on exchange rates (Montiel and Reinhart, 2001). The parallel accumulation of international reserves and domestic liabilities by the central bank during booms generates quasi-fiscal losses, which may not be offset by the profits generated by selling the accumulated reserves during ensuing crises (plus the interest earned by the management of reserves in the interim). Mixing managed exchange rate flexibility and sterilized intervention with capital account regulations can help to overcome these problems; the effectiveness of such regulations will be explored in the following section of this chapter. It is thus only under managed exchange rate regimes *cum* capital account regulations that we can speak of effective, though certainly limited, 'monetary autonomy'.

Other features support the choice of intermediate regimes, particularly in very small developing countries. First of all, the 'law of one price' does not hold true even in fairly small economies, as reflected in the fact that real exchange rate variability is only weakly dependent on the size of an economy (ECLAC, 2000, chapter 11). Therefore, although the benefits of exchange rate stability are higher for smaller economies, flexibility still plays a useful role. Secondly, the strong dependence of these economies on foreign trade makes profitability in a broader range of economic activities dependent on the real exchange rate. Finally, the thinness of exchange rate markets makes them subject to stronger volatility under free floating regimes, and the thinness of domestic capital markets limits the chances for sterilized monetary operations. Thus, some exchange rate flexibility is useful (first feature) and may be a necessary counter-cyclical instrument (second feature), and the thinness of markets eliminates the usefulness of free floats (third feature).

One of the advantages of intermediate regimes is that flexibility *can be graduated*, depending on external conditions. This implies that any specific intermediate regime has an embedded 'exit option'. The fact that most flexible regimes are accompanied by some intervention in foreign exchange markets, and that the demand for international reserves has not declined with the more widespread use of some exchange rate flexibility, implies that authorities rarely (if ever) choose a totally flexible regime but instead prefer to use the embedded graduation of flexibility that intermediate regimes provide. This is, in fact, an essential feature which differentiates these regimes from any fixed exchange rate regime, hard or soft, since the latter lacks such an option and thus generates exit costs.

The usefulness of the approach we have outlined here obviously depends on effective incentives for the authorities to behave in a counter-cyclical fashion. In this regard, the exclusive focus of independent central banks on inflation targeting, or the incentives that governments face in post-inflationary environments, tend to generate strong 'exchange rate appreciation biases' that lead to asymmetric interventions. In particular, given the expected effects of the exchange rate on price levels, devaluation during crises is resisted more than appreciation during booms, as was characteristic of Latin America during the 1990s.

Available Latin American evidence is difficult to evaluate in the light of incomplete histories on certain regimes (particularly, the absence of sustained clean floats – the closest example being Mexico since the Tequila crisis), frequent regime changes and the aforementioned policy biases. Figures 19.2 and 19.3 provide some evidence. Figure 19.2 indicates that a low degree of real exchange rate volatility has been characteristic of quite different exchange rate regimes, including Argentina's currency board but also Costa Rica's crawling peg (cum state-controlled domestic financial system), several small countries with 'soft' pegs, and Peru's highly managed float (cum highly dollarized domestic financial system). The highest volatility has been seen in Brazil, which tried, unsuccessfully, to defend an overvalued exchange rate inherited from the Real Plan, and in the two countries

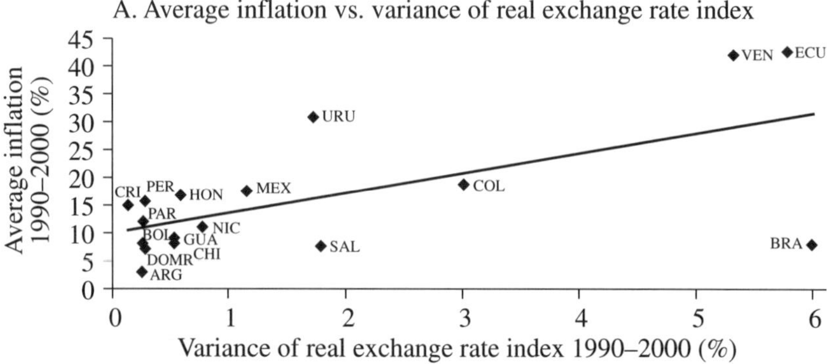

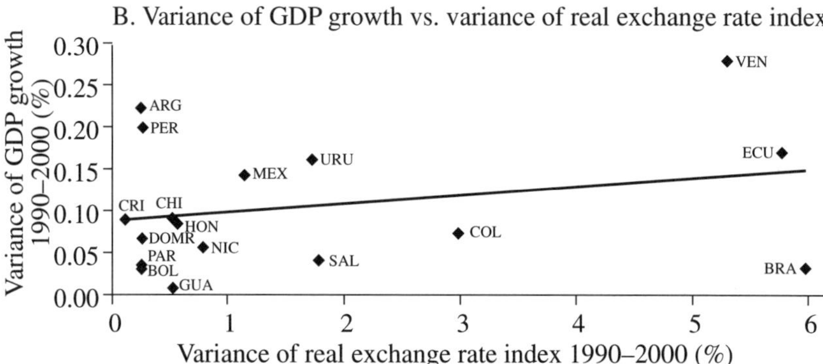

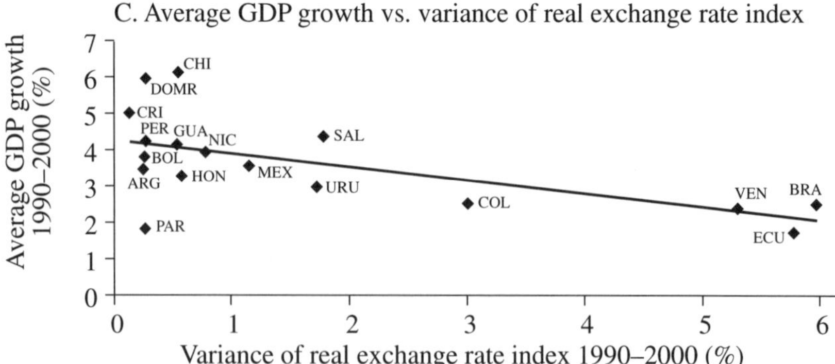

Source: ECLAC.

Figure 19.2 Macroeconomic stability, 1990–2000

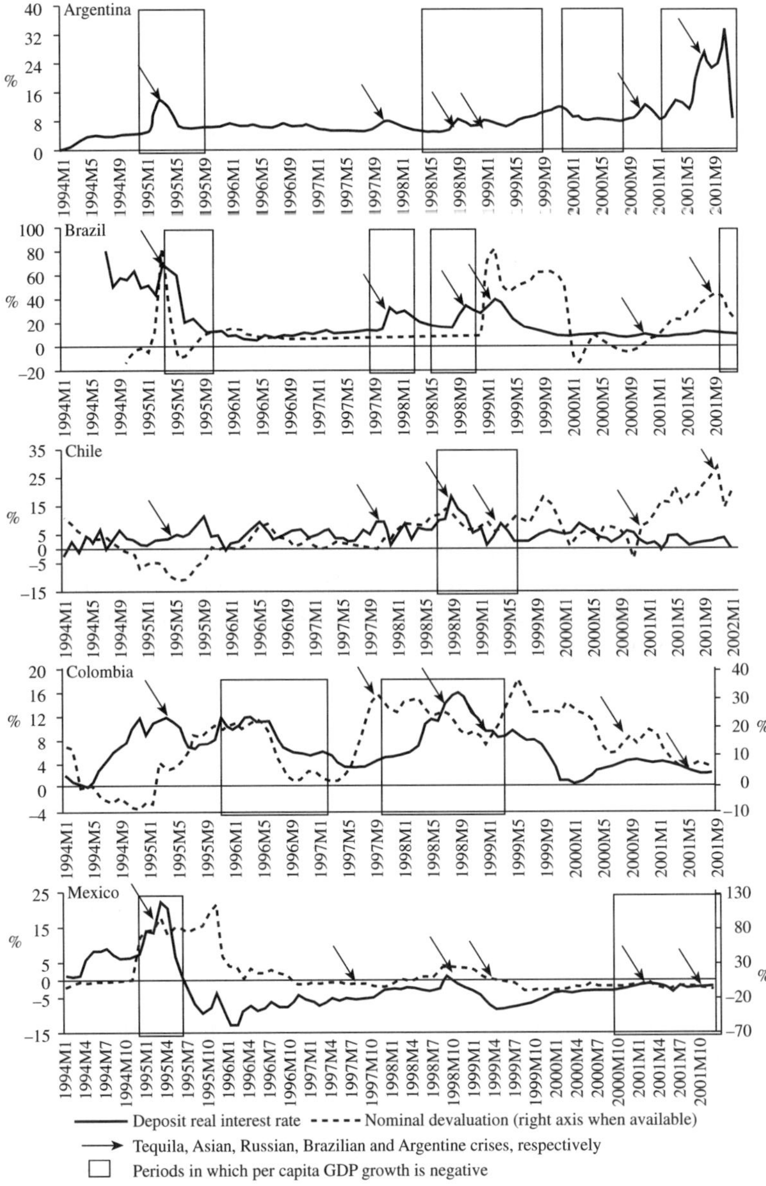

Note: Nominal devaluation: a positive sign denotes a devaluation.

Source: ECLAC and IMF.

Figure 19.3 Devaluation and real deposit interest rates

that experienced the most severe macroeconomic instability throughout the decade (Ecuador and Venezuela). Colombia, which for most of the decade had a system of exchange rate bands, but also El Salvador, with a virtual peg, experienced intermediate levels of real exchange rate volatility.

On the other hand, there is no statistically significant association between real exchange rate volatility and GDP volatility, and only a weak negative correlation between the first of these variables and GDP growth. Argentina, under the currency board regime, may be viewed as an example of a lack of exchange rate flexibility generating high GDP volatility (the highest in the region after Venezuela). A recent analysis of several emerging economies during the Asian crisis indicates that more flexible regimes have done best in terms of reducing GDP volatility, followed by countries with exchange rate bands, while those with hard pegs and, particularly, soft pegs did the worst. This reflects the fact that real interest rate volatility, which tends to be most intense in pegged regimes, has a more adverse effect on GDP volatility than either foreign reserve or nominal exchange rate volatility (Ffrench-Davis and Larraín, 2001).

Generally speaking, authorities have found it difficult to undertake anticyclical policies under *all* regimes. Figure 19.3 illustrates the experiences of five large and medium-sized countries in greater detail: Argentina, with a currency board; Brazil and Mexico, which moved from very narrow exchange rate bands to floating regimes under crisis conditions; and Chile and Colombia, which moved from wide exchange rate bands to floating regimes after the Asian and Russian crises. It must be emphasized that, in all four relevant cases, floats have been 'dirty' when the exchange rate has come under strong (particularly devaluation) pressures.

Interest-rate shocks have been common to all five countries and have been associated with major international events, as indicated by arrows in Figure 19.3. In three of these episodes, a country from the region has been at the center. Most reductions in per capita GDP (identified with rectangles in the graph) have been associated with such shocks, reflecting both the contractionary effects of higher interest rates, but also more direct effects of the external shock (for example, reduced availability of finance, trade contraction in industrial or other Latin American economies) and fiscal adjustment packages. Indeed, the only exception to this rule is the 1996 domestically induced slowdown in Colombia. However, the degree of international contagion has varied from crisis to crisis: the Russian crisis is the only one that affected the five countries simultaneously but, even then, its effects on Mexico were weaker (the boom that the US economy was undergoing was obviously crucial to Mexican performance at the time); if we allow for lagged effects, the Asian crisis is a close second.

Within this pattern, three features stand out. Firstly, after an initial period of turbulence in which high rates of devaluation were accompanied by high interest rates, the move from fixed exchange rates to more flexible exchange rate regimes has allowed a sustained reduction in real interest rates. This means that the 'anomalies' in the evolution of interest rates that are stressed by Hausmann (2000) in his criticism of the move toward freer exchange rates in developing countries are only a feature of transition periods. It should be added that the transition from exchange rate bands to greater flexibility in Chile and Colombia after the Asian and Russian crises also had costs, which have nonetheless been criticized as a result of delayed policy action ('fear to float') rather than as inherent in the graduation of a regime to allow for more flexibility.

Secondly, exchange rate flexibility has indeed allowed countries to face external shocks while avoiding interest rate hikes. This is clearly the case of Chile during the 2001 Argentine crisis and, to a lesser extent, of Brazil during 2001 and Mexico during the Russian crisis. Moreover, in all these cases, the inflationary effects of devaluation have been very moderate. Nonetheless, the countries have not been able to avoid the real effects of external shocks. The exchange rate response may have generated additional short-term contractionary wealth and possibly income effects, at least in those cases where the response was strong.

Thirdly, the adoption of 'autonomous' policy packages during periods of external capital abundance has been rare. The clearest cases are the 1994 and 1997 packages of Colombia, both of which involved strong price-based capital account regulations: the first was aimed at cooling excessive aggregate demand growth while trying to avoid the expected exchange rate appreciation induced by contractionary monetary policy;[13] the second was aimed at avoiding the appreciation pressures generated by booming capital inflows at a time when it was essential to maintain low interest rates to facilitate economic recovery after the 1996 slowdown. The gradual strengthening of capital account regulations in Chile in 1991–1994 (that is, prior, for the most part, to the period included in Figure 19.3) was also aimed at sustaining low interest rates but avoiding the appreciation pressures of booming capital inflows. Such regulations were not, however, strengthened to face appreciation pressures in 1996–1997.[14] The contractionary policy adopted by Mexico since late 2000 may also be seen as an autonomous attempt to cool down the economy. In the absence of capital account regulations, it has induced additional capital inflows and an exchange rate appreciation.

Overall, when exchange rate flexibility is available *before* an external crisis hits, it provides scope for the management of domestic interest rates in a more autonomous way. This is also true when intermediate regimes are graduated to generate more flexibility, though lags in policy decisions to do this may generate costs. On the other hand, when flexibility is adopted as part of a shock treatment that is undertaken when a soft peg (or a narrow exchange rate band) regime breaks down, this result is only achieved after a temporary period of turbulence. However, flexibility does not isolate the economies from real external shocks, and the mix of lower interest rates and adverse wealth effects of devaluation has unclear effects on economic activity. Finally, policy autonomy during periods of abundant capital flows has only been achieved when supported by capital account regulations, but the effects have been transitory.

III LIABILITY POLICIES

The accumulation of risks during booms will depend not only on the magnitude of domestic and private liabilities but also on their maturity structure. Capital account regulations thus have a dual role: as a macroeconomic policy tool, which provides some room for anti-cyclical monetary policies, and as a 'liability policy' to improve private-sector external debt profiles. Complementary liability policies should also be adopted to improve public-sector debt profiles. The emphasis on *liability structures* rather than national balance sheets is due to the fact that they play the primary role when countries face liquidity constraints, together with liquid assets (particularly, international reserves); other assets play a secondary role under those conditions. The need to reduce the costs associated with holding foreign exchange reserves underscores the crucial role of appropriate liability structures.

Viewed as a macroeconomic policy tool, capital account regulations are aimed at the direct source of boom–bust cycles: unstable capital flows. If they are successful, they will provide some opportunity to 'lean against the wind' during periods of financial euphoria, through the adoption of a contractionary monetary policy and reduced appreciation pressures. If effective, they will also reduce or eliminate the quasi-fiscal costs of the sterilized accumulation of foreign exchange reserves. During crises, they may also provide 'breathing space' for expansionary monetary policies.

Viewed as a liability policy, capital account regulations recognize the fact that the market generously rewards sound external debt structures (Rodrik and Velasco, 2000). This reflects the fact that, during times of uncertainty, the market responds to *gross*, rather than merely net, financing requirements, which means that the rollover of short-term liabilities is not financially neutral. Under these circumstances, a debt profile that leans toward longer-term obligations will considerably reduce the level of risk. This indicates that an essential component of economic policy management during booms should be measures to improve the external and domestic maturity structures of both the private and the public sectors.

A Innovations in Capital Account Regulations in the 1990s

A great innovation in this sphere during the 1990s was unquestionably the establishment of reserve requirements for foreign-currency liabilities in Chile and Colombia. The advantage of this system was that it created a simple, non-discretionary and *preventive* (prudential) price incentive that penalized short-term foreign-currency liabilities more heavily and had neutral effects on corporate borrowing decisions (see below). The corresponding levy was significantly higher than the level that has been suggested for an international Tobin tax: about 3 per cent in the Chilean system for one-year loans, and an average of 13.6 per cent for one-year loans and 6.4 per cent for three-year loans in Colombia in 1994–1998. As a result of a drastic change in international capital markets, the system was phased out in both countries in 1999–2000. Other (quantitative) capital account regulations complemented reserve requirements, notably one-year minimum stay requirements for portfolio capital in Chile (lifted in May 2000) and direct authorization of such flows in Colombia.

The effectiveness of reserve requirements has been the subject of a great deal of controversy.[15] There is fairly broad agreement on their effectiveness as a liability policy. In this regard, although there are many other variables that influence the indicators shown in Figure 19.4, they tend to confirm the observation that both countries have an above-average external debt profile. On the other hand, there are heated controversies about their effectiveness as a macroeconomic policy tool. Indeed, as indicated in the previous section, neither country has been free from pro-cyclical macroeconomic policy patterns.

However, judging from the solid evidence that exists with respect to the sensitivity of capital flows to interest rate spreads in both countries, reserve requirements do influence the volume of capital flows at given interest rates. Alternatively, if higher reserve requirements induce new flows through their effects on domestic interest rates, then their ability to generate a stable spread between domestic and international interest rates should be seen as an indication that they are a useful macroeconomic policy tool. In Colombia, where these regulations were modified more extensively over the 1990s, there is strong evidence that increases in reserve requirements have reduced flows (Ocampo and Tovar, 1998 and 2001) or, alternatively, have been effective in increasing domestic interest rates (Villar and Rincón, 2000). Similar evidence is available for Chile (see Agosin and Ffrench-Davis, 2001, and LeFort and Lehmann, 2000, on both of these issues).

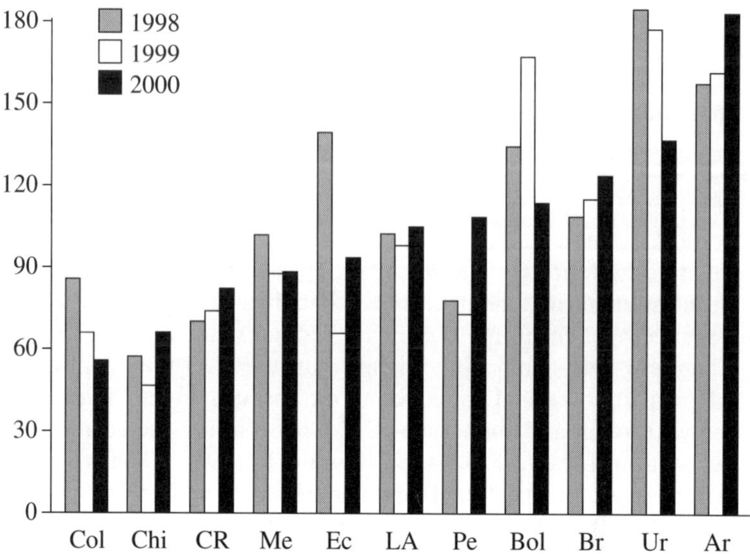

Source: Estimated on the basis of statistics on external debt, BIS-IMF-OECD-World Bank (http://www.oecd.org/dac/debt).

Figure 19.4 Short-term liabilities to banks and debt securities issued abroad as a percentage of international reserves

Moreover, according to the analysis presented in the previous section, there is evidence that the strengthening of capital account regulation improved the exchange rate–interest rate trade-off that authorities faced in the short run under strong pressures from booming capital markets.

Some problems in the management of these regulations were associated with changes in the relevant policy parameters. The difficulties experienced in this connection by the two countries differed. In Chile, the basic problem was the variability of the rules pertaining to the exchange rate, since the limits of the exchange rate band (in pesos per dollar) were changed on numerous occasions until they were ultimately abandoned in 1998. During capital account booms, this gave rise to a safe bet for agents bringing in capital, since when the exchange rate neared the floor of the band, the probability that the floor would be adjusted downward was high. In Colombia, the main problem was the frequency of the changes made in reserve requirements. Changes foreseen by the market sparked speculation, thereby diminishing the effectiveness of such measures for some time following the requirements' modification. It is interesting to note that in both countries reserve requirements were seen as a complement to, rather than as a substitute for, other macroeconomic policies, which were certainly superior in Chile.

Malaysia has also provided major innovations in the area of capital account regulations in the 1990s. In January 1994, this country prohibited non-residents from buying a wide range of short-term securities; these restrictions were lifted later in the year. They proved highly effective, indeed superior, in terms of reducing capital flows and asset prices, to Chilean regulations (Palma, 2002). They also improved the country's debt profile (Rodrik and Velasco, 2000). However, after they were lifted, a new wave of debt accumulation and asset price increases developed, though the debt profile was kept at prudential levels (Kaplan and Rodrik, 2001).

An additional innovation came with the Asian crisis. In September 1998, strong restrictions on capital outflows were established which were basically aimed at eliminating offshore trading of the local currency. It was also determined that ringgit deposits in the domestic financial system held by non-residents were not convertible into foreign currency for a year; in February 1999, this regulation was replaced with an exit tax.

Significant discussions have taken place on the effects of these controls. Kaplan and Rodrik (2001) have provided the strongest argument for the effectiveness of these regulations. Confirming the results of previous studies, they show that they were highly effective in very rapidly reversing financial market pressure, as reflected in the trend of foreign exchange reserves, the exchange rate and offshore interest rates for ringgit deposits. The removal of financial uncertainties, together with the additional scope provided for expansionary monetary and fiscal policies, led to a speedier recovery of economic activity, lower inflation and better employment and real wage performance than comparable IMF-type programs during the Asian crisis. This is true even adjusting for the improved external environment characteristic of the time when Malaysian controls were imposed. Moreover, the country did not receive large injections of capital and, indeed, temporarily cut itself off from external capital markets.

Overall, innovative experiences with capital account regulations in the 1990s indicate that they can serve as useful instruments, both in improving debt profiles (liability policy) and in facilitating the adoption of (possibly temporary) counter-cyclical macroeconomic policies. It has thus been shown that it is possible to design preventive policy instruments that avoid part of the costs of boom–bust cycles in international finance. The basic advantages of Chilean–Colombian price-based instruments are their simplicity, non-discretionary character and neutral effect on corporate borrowing decisions. The more quantitative-type Malaysian systems have proven to have stronger short-term macroeconomic effects.

In any case, all these systems have been designed in countries that chose to integrate into international capital markets. Thus, traditional exchange controls may be superior if one of the objectives of macroeconomic policy is significantly to reduce domestic macroeconomic sensitivity to international capital flows (see Nayyar, 2002, for an analysis of the Indian experience). Simple quantitative restrictions that rule out certain forms of indebtedness (for example, short-term foreign borrowing, except trade credit lines) are also preventive in character.

B Complementary Liability Policies

Direct capital account regulations can be partly substituted by prudential regulation and supervision. In particular, higher liquidity (or reserve) requirements for the financial system's foreign-currency liabilities can be established. Also, the rating of domestic lending to firms with substantial external liabilities can be reduced and the provisions associated with such loans increased. The main problem with these options is that such regulations do not affect the foreign-currency liabilities of *non*-financial agents and indeed may encourage them to borrow more abroad. Accordingly, they need to be supplemented with other disincentives for external borrowing by those firms, such as tax provisions applying to foreign-currency liabilities (for example, allowing no or only partial deductions for interest payments on international loans); public disclosure of the short-term external liabilities of firms; restrictions on the types of firms that can borrow abroad, including prudential ratios that they must meet; and restrictions on the terms of corporate debts that can be contracted abroad (minimum maturities and maximum spreads).[16]

Price-based capital account regulations may thus be more neutral and simpler than an equivalent system based on prudential regulations plus additional policies aimed at non-financial firms. Among their virtues, *vis-à-vis* prudential regulation and supervision, we should include the fact that they are price-based (some prudential regulations, such as prohibitions on certain types of operations, are not), non-discretionary (prudential supervision, on the contrary, is discretionary in its operation), and neutral in terms of corporate borrowing decisions. Indeed, equivalent practices are used by private agents, such as the selling fees that are imposed by mutual funds on investments held for a short period in order to discourage short-term holdings (J.P. Morgan, 1998, p. 23).

In the case of the public sector, direct control by the Ministry of Finance (and the central bank) is the most important liability policy and should encompass borrowing by all public-sector agencies and autonomous subnational governments.[17] Public-sector debt profiles that lean too far toward short-term obligations may be manageable during booms but may become a major destabilizing factor during crises. This observation is equally valid for external and domestic public-sector liabilities, as residents holding short-term public-sector securities have other options besides rolling over the public-sector debt, including capital flight. This is even clearer if foreigners are allowed to purchase domestic public-sector securities.

Thus, when gross borrowing requirements are high, the interest rate will have to increase to make rollovers attractive. Higher interest rates immediately generate an endogenous fiscal deterioration, thereby rapidly changing the trend in the public-sector debt, as happened in Brazil prior to the 1999 crisis (see Figure 19.5). In addition, rollovers may be viable only if risks of devaluation or future interest rate hikes can be passed on to the government, which will generate additional sources of destabilization. Mexico's widely publicized move to replace peso-denominated securities (Treasury Certificates or Cetes) with dollar-denominated bonds (Tesobonos) in 1994, which was one of the crucial factors in the crisis that hit the country late in that year, was no doubt facilitated by the short-term profile of Cetes.[18] The short-term structure of Brazil's debt is also the reason why, since late 1997, fixed-interest bonds were swiftly replaced by variable-rate and dollar-denominated securities, which has canceled out the improvements that had been made in the public debt structure since the launching of the Real Plan. It is important to emphasize that, despite its fiscal deterioration, no substitution of similar magnitude was observed in Colombia during the 1998–1999 crisis; this country's tradition of issuing public-sector securities with a minimum maturity of one year is a significant part of the explanation.

The extent to which it will prove possible to issue longer-term domestic debt securities will depend on the depth of the local capital market, particularly the secondary markets that provide liquidity to those securities. For this reason, measures designed to deepen the countries' credit and capital markets play a crucial role in improving domestic debt profiles. This statement is also valid with regard to the adequate development of long-term private capital markets. However, due to the lower risk levels and the greater homogeneity of the securities it issues, the central government has a vital function to perform in the development of longer-term primary and secondary markets for securities, including the provision of benchmarks for private-sector securities.

The development of such markets will not eliminate, however, the need for an active external liability policy, as deeper capital markets are also more attractive to volatile portfolio flows. Unfortunately, the trade-offs are not simple in this regard, as the participation of international mutual funds may help to deepen domestic capital markets. Thus, the authorities must choose between reduced volatility of capital flows and the development of deeper, liquid domestic markets. The Chilean decision to eliminate the one-year minimum maturity for portfolio flows in May 2000, as well as the

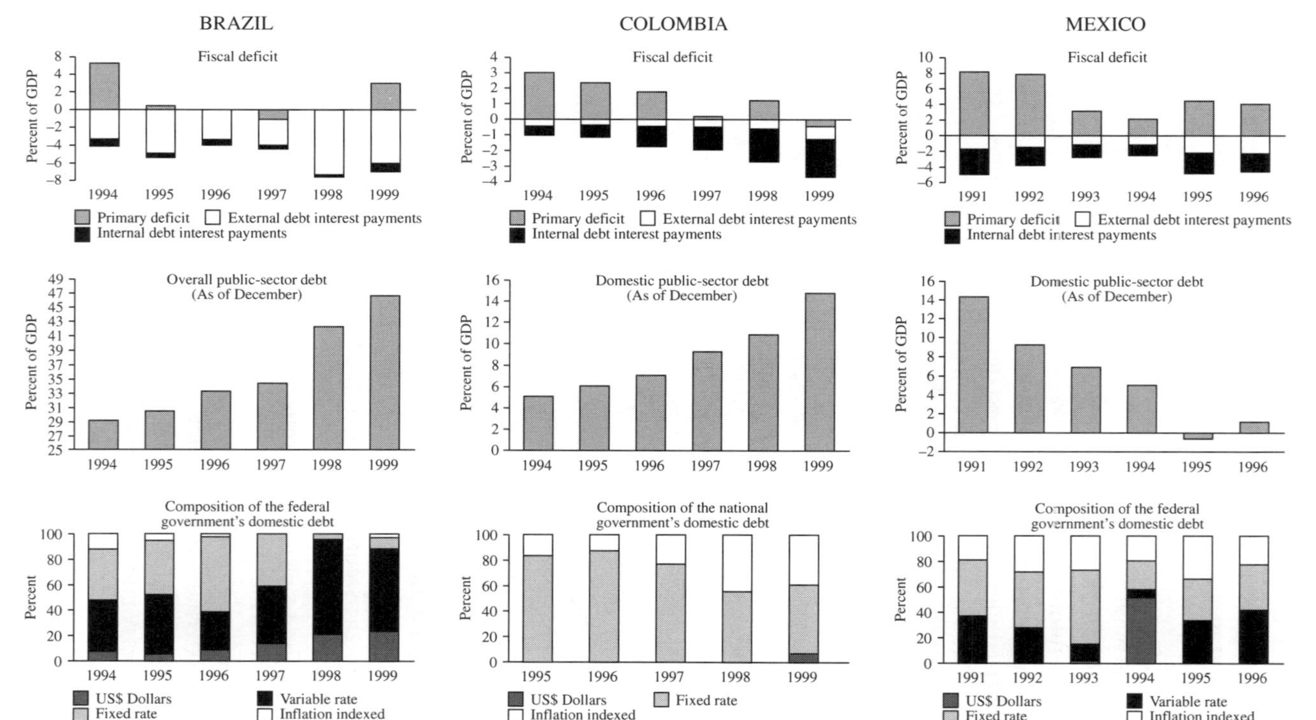

Source: Central Bank of Brazil, IDEA and Ministry of Finance of Colombia, Secretary of Finance and Public Credit of Mexico, Bank of Mexico.

Figure 19.5 Fiscal deficit and public debt

Colombian decision in 1996 to allow foreign investment funds to participate in the domestic market for public-sector securities, may be understood as a choice for the second of these options at the cost of additional capital account volatility. This is, in fact, what happened with portfolio flows in Colombia during the 1998–1999 crisis.

IV COUNTER-CYCLICAL PRUDENTIAL REGULATION AND SUPERVISION

One of the painful lessons that has been learned during recent decades in Latin America, as in the rest of the world, is just how costly financial crises are in terms of duration and cumulative loss of GDP.[19] Some of the greatest costs have to do with the sharp reduction in the time horizon of firms experiencing difficulties, which is also associated with the fact that property rights become largely indeterminate during crises (that is, the proportion of assets which will ultimately be owned by stockholders vs. lenders is subject to significant uncertainties). The losses are not only of a short-term character, since they involve physical assets of firms as well as intangibles (including human and social capital and firms' business reputation, along with the consequent loss of business contacts) that have taken years to build up. Moreover, these losses are incurred even if the firm manages to restructure and survive. Also, the credit system is paralyzed for long periods, thereby impeding the economic recovery.

The fiscal and quasi-fiscal costs of bank rescues are also very high: 4 per cent to 5 per cent of GDP in relatively small crises, such as those of Colombia in the early 1980s and late 1990s; some 15 per cent of GDP in severe ones, such as those that hit Mexico and Venezuela in the mid-1990s or South Korea in the late 1990s; and 35 per cent of GDP or more in full-blown crises, such as those that engulfed Argentina and Chile in the early 1980s or Indonesia in the late 1990s. Thus, one of the best *fiscal* investments that a country can make is to avoid a financial crisis. This means that private risks accumulated by financial intermediaries during booms incorporate a substantial component of public-sector risk. This fact constitutes a powerful argument for state intervention.

The origins of problems that erupt during financial crises are well known. Generally, they are the result of a rapid increase in lending and weak prudential regulation and supervision, a combination that becomes explosive under conditions of financial liberalization in the midst of an external capital-market boom. The underestimation of risks characteristic of environments of economic optimism is then mixed with inadequate practices for evaluating risks, both by private agents and by supervisory agencies.

This underscores just how important the sequencing of financial liberalization processes is and, in particular, how necessary it is to make eventual capital account liberalization contingent upon the prior establishment of appropriate prudential regulation and supervision and the design of satisfactory information systems to guarantee a proper microeconomic operation of markets. Since the learning process – by financial intermediaries, depositors and the authorities – is not instantaneous, the liberalization process needs to be gradual in order to provide enough time for financial intermediaries to learn how to manage higher risks, for depositors to learn how to use the new information channels, and for the authorities to learn how to supervise the system and how to modify prudential regulations and reporting requirements on the basis of accumulated experience.

Prudential regulation should ensure, first of all, the solvency of financial institutions by establishing appropriate capital adequacy ratios relative to the risk assumed by lending institutions, strict write-offs of questionable portfolios and adequate standards of risk diversification. In developing countries, the corresponding regulations should take into account not only the microeconomic but especially the *macroeconomic* risks they face. In particular, due attention needs to be paid to the links between domestic financial risks and variations in interest and exchange rates. In view of the greater financial volatility that characterizes these countries, capital standards should probably be higher than those proposed by the Basle Committee on Banking Supervision of the Bank for International Settlements. On the other hand, strict regulations should be established to prevent currency mismatches (including those associated with off-balance-sheet operations), to reduce imbalances in the maturities of assets and liabilities of financial intermediaries and to ensure the timely write-off of past-due loans. Prudential regulation should be particularly strict with respect to the intermediation of short-term external credits.

In addition, prudential regulation needs to ensure adequate levels of liquidity for financial intermediaries so that they can handle the mismatch between average maturities of assets and liabilities associated with the financial system's essential function of transforming maturities, which generates risks associated with volatility in deposits and/or interest rates. The most important innovation in this area is undoubtedly the Argentine system created in 1995, which sets liquidity requirements based on the residual maturity of financial institutions' liabilities (that is, the number of days remaining before reaching maturity).[20] These liquidity requirements – or a system of reserve requirements with similar characteristics – have the additional advantage that they offer a direct incentive to the financial system to maintain a better liability structure. The quality of assets in which liquidity requirements are kept is obviously essential. In this regard, it must be pointed out that allowing them to be invested in public-sector bonds has increased the vulnerability of the Argentine financial system to public-sector debt restructuring.

Properly regulated and supervised financial systems are structurally superior in terms of risk management. Nonetheless, they are incapable of internalizing all the collective risks assumed during booms, which are essentially of a macroeconomic character and entail, therefore, coordination problems that exceed the capacity of any one intermediary. Moreover, they have a pro-cyclical bias in the way they operate. In fact, it is during crises that, albeit with some delay, the excess of risk assumed during economic booms becomes evident. This ultimately makes it necessary to write off loan portfolios, thereby reducing financial institutions' capital and, hence, their lending capacity. This, in conjunction with the greater subjectively perceived level of risk, is what triggers the 'credit squeeze' that characterizes such periods.[21]

This is why instruments need to be designed that will introduce a counter-cyclical element into prudential regulation and supervision. To guarantee this, provisions should be estimated when loans are disbursed on the basis of *expected* losses, taking into account the full business cycle, rather than on the basis of loan delinquency or short-term expectations of future loan losses, which are highly pro-cyclical. This means, in fact, that provisioning should approach the criteria traditionally followed by the insurance rather than the banking industry.

The major innovation in this regard has been the forward-looking provision scheme introduced by Spain in December 1999 (Banco de España, 2000; Poveda, 2000). Under this scheme, actuarial provisions for 'latent' risks are estimated for homogenous categories of credit according to the possible loss that a typical asset (loans, guarantees, interbank or fixed-income portfolio investments) in this category is expected to have, estimated on the basis of a full business cycle.

The system is, strictly speaking, 'cycle-neutral' rather than counter-cyclical, but it is certainly superior to the traditional pro-cyclical provisioning for loan losses. So, if necessary, a system such as this can be complemented by strictly anti-cyclical 'prudential provisions' applied by the regulatory authority to the financial system as a whole, or by the supervisory authority to certain financial institutions on the basis of objective criteria (for example, the rate of credit growth or the growth of credit for specific high-risk activities). Such counter-cyclical prudential provisions, together with liquidity requirements, are superior to the possible use of capital adequacy ratios for this purpose. This means that capital adequacy requirements should focus on long-term solvency criteria rather than on cyclical performance. Voluntary prudential provisions can also be encouraged. In all cases, it is essential that adequate tax deductibility be granted for provisions. This would, indeed, make provisions a preferable instrument for banks to manage the effects of the business cycle.

Other instruments should also be strengthened during periods of financial euphoria to take into account the increasing risks that financial intermediaries are incurring. Within the realm of monetary and credit policy, higher reserve requirements or restrictions on credit growth during boom periods can perform this function.[22] If assets generate considerable differences in risks, credit ceilings could be established for certain sectors (for example, consumer loans, for non-residential construction, and so on). Within the sphere of regulatory policy, this function can be performed by higher liquidity requirements during booms, especially for short-term liabilities. Ceilings on the reference price for stocks and real estate assets used as collateral (for example, a provision under which no more than a specified, decreasing proportion of an asset's commercial value may be used for this purpose) or stricter loan-to-value ratios could also be imposed. Deposit insurance may also be raised, and stricter standards for debt classification and write-offs could be adopted. Supervision can also be made stricter during booms, particularly for intermediaries experiencing rapid credit growth, which can be required to undertake stress or other special risk tests.

During financial crises, although authorities must adopt clearly defined rules to restore confidence, the application of stronger standards should be gradual in order to avoid a credit squeeze. Of course, in order to avoid moral hazard problems, authorities must never bail out the owners of financial institutions, guaranteeing that their net worth is written off if the institutions are intervened.

It must be emphasized that prudential regulation and supervision have limits and costs that cannot be overlooked. Stricter standards in developing countries to manage macroeconomic risks increase the costs of financial intermediation, reducing international competitiveness and creating arbitrage incentives to use international financial intermediation as an alternative. Some classic objectives of prudential regulation, such as risk diversification, may be difficult to guarantee when macroeconomic issues are at the root of the difficulties. Moreover, prudential regulation involves some non-price signals, and prudential supervision is rife with information problems and is a discretionary activity susceptible to abuse, so the powers of the authorities must be subject to strict limits and controls.

V COUNTER-CYCLICAL FISCAL POLICY

Regardless of what exchange-rate and capital-account regime countries choose, fiscal policy always provides a useful anti-cyclical device. The importance of countering excess fiscal spending during booms became quite clear in Latin America during the debt crisis of the 1980s, since the over-expansion of public expenditure during the preceding credit boom generated fiscal imbalances that ultimately proved to be untenable. The subsequent spending cuts greatly reduced the benefits of public expenditures: investment projects were left unfinished or took much longer to execute than planned, thereby raising their effective cost; the existing structure for the provision of public and social services became disjointed; reductions in real wages led to the loss of valuable staff; and the entire civil service was disrupted. Two lessons were thus painfully learned: that the lack of fiscal discipline during booms is extremely costly, and that 'go–stop' cycles significantly reduce the efficiency of public-sector spending.

The return to a more orthodox policy stance in the 1990s has, nonetheless, maintained unmistakably pro-cyclical fiscal practices (ECLAC, 1998b; Martner, 2000, chapter 5). This is attributable to the pro-cyclical performance of public revenues in the context of high GDP volatility. Under these conditions, setting fiscal targets independently of the business cycle implies that public-sector spending during booms is partly financed by transitory revenues. Moreover, the tendency of debt service to increase during crises as a result of variations of interest and exchange rates in the face of external shocks, implies that primary fiscal (particularly investment) spending must adjust pro-cyclically to meet short-term fiscal targets. This tends to maintain the inefficiencies in public-sector spending characteristic of 'go–stop' cycles. Moreover, through this mechanism, fiscal performance enhances the already excessive volatility of economic activity.

At the same time, other pro-cyclical patterns have become more important than in the past, particularly those associated with the granting of explicit or implicit guarantees to the private sector. Cases in point include explicit and implicit financial guarantees, which are reflected during crises in rescue packages for both domestic financial intermediaries and private firms with large external liabilities. A second, more novel case, is that of public-sector guarantees for private-sector investments in infrastructure (such as minimum revenue or profit guarantees, or explicit coverage of interest or exchange rate risks). Both types of guarantees have three elements in common: (a) they are not always transparent; (b) they encourage *private* spending during booms (it is, thus, during periods of euphoria that implicit public-sector spending in the form of an equivalent 'insurance premium' is actually incurred, indicating that accrued public-sector spending is underestimated); and (c) disbursements (cash spending) are incurred during crises, increasing borrowing requirements and crowding out other public-sector spending. Thus, such guarantees encourage pro-cyclical private-sector spending in non-transparent ways.

This means that fiscal reforms must both firmly establish the principle of fiscal sustainability and adopt targets that avoid pro-cyclical biases in fiscal policy. The first objective has been reflected in the adoption of fiscal responsibility laws in several Latin American countries in recent years. The second implies that fiscal targets should be based on a definition of the desired structural fiscal surplus or deficit or, alternatively, of a medium-term public-sector debt-to-GDP target. The short-term surplus or deficit would then be determined on the basis of that structural stance and current deviations from potential GDP.

An important complement to this new way of determining fiscal policy would be to design mechanisms to temporarily sterilize public-sector revenues. The experience gained from the use of stabilization funds for commodities having a significant fiscal impact – the National Coffee Fund in Colombia, the copper and petroleum stabilization funds in Chile and, more recently, the petroleum stabilization funds of Colombia and Venezuela – must be extended to develop broader fiscal stabilization funds (ECLAC, 1998b).

The magnitude of resources accumulated in a fiscal stabilization fund would depend on the income elasticity of public-sector revenues. However, the tax structures of Latin America generally lack a high degree of elasticity, basically due to the low share of corporate income tax revenues, the item with the highest income elasticity in industrialized countries (Martner, 2000, chapter 5). For this reason, flexible tax rates could be used as a complementary instrument, particularly in the face of sharp private spending cycles. The best candidate is obviously a tax on the source of the spending booms. This is the traditional argument for taxing exports subject to temporary price bonanzas, which has served as the basis for the design of traditional commodity stabilization funds. A similar argument can be used to justify a tax on capital inflows, as this is the major source of the private-sector spending boom today (Marfán, 2001). It is interesting to note that this argument is *additional* to those associated with the greater monetary autonomy that such an instrument can provide (see section III). Indeed, it holds true even if such an instrument is totally ineffective in reducing capital inflows. Moreover, under those conditions, revenues are actually maximized; if saved,[23] they will thus facilitate the adoption of an anti-cyclical *fiscal* policy. A second-best argument will lead to temporary hikes of VAT rates under such conditions (Budnevich and Le Fort, 1997).

The alternative of using counter-cyclical public-sector spending policies to offset private-sector spending cycles is more controversial. A well-designed social safety net to protect vulnerable groups during crises is the best alternative in this regard. Indeed, an essential advantage of social safety nets is that the associated spending is intrinsically counter-cyclical. In other cases, offsetting mechanisms are more controversial. Go–stop public-sector spending policies are inefficient, as we have seen. Moreover, an excessive reliance on counter-cyclical public-sector spending policies – rather than a more balanced mix which also relies on fiscal revenues and stabilization funds – may generate disequilibria between supplies of public and private goods that can have substantial distributive effects, as the recipients of goods and services provided by the public sector are not the same agents as those that benefit from private spending. For these reasons, it is certainly preferable to determine the growth of public-sector spending (aside from that associated with social safety nets) on the basis of long-term criteria.

These tax and spending policies must be complemented by adequate mechanisms to manage public-sector guarantees. With respect to financial risks, the liability and anti-cyclical regulatory policies analysed in previous sections of this chapter are the proper answer. In relation to other guarantees, it is necessary for the 'insurance premium equivalent' of such guarantees to be regularly estimated and budgeted for and for the corresponding resources to be transferred to special funds created to serve as a back-up in the event that the corresponding contingencies become effective.

Finally, it should be emphasized that an anti-cyclical fiscal policy greatly facilitates a broad-based prudential regulation of booms. In particular, the counterpart of the resources accumulated in fiscal stabilization funds during booms would be increased foreign exchange reserves and reduced currency appreciation. Such reserves also provide 'self-insurance' against sharp cuts in foreign exchange availability and are the necessary counterpart to smoother fiscal adjustment during crises.

VI CONCLUSIONS

The volatility of capital flows generates a strong pro-cyclical performance in developing countries. An essential part of the solution to this problem lies in strengthening the institutional framework for the prevention and management of financial crises at the global level. This chapter focuses, however, on the role of domestic anti-cyclical policies in the developing world, which are a necessary counterpart of such an international architecture.

The basic argument made in this chapter is that adequate counter-cyclical policy packages can be adopted based on a mix that involves: (a) managed exchange rate flexibility cum capital account regulations; (b) strong 'liability policies' aimed at improving private- and public-sector debt profiles; (c) strong prudential regulation and supervision of domestic financial systems, with anti-cyclical components; and (d) a counter-cyclical fiscal policy based on general fiscal stabilization funds.

Given the more reduced degrees of freedom that developing-country authorities possess in today's globalized world, all policies have, nonetheless, limited effects. Thus, pragmatic strategies in which these different elements support each other in their anti-cyclical task are called for. The specific emphasis will vary depending on the macroeconomic constraints and traditions of each particular country.

NOTES

* I am grateful to Yilmaz Akyüz, Amar Bhattacharya, Ricardo Ffrench-Davis, Gerry Helleiner, Daniel Heyman, Manuel Marfán, Carlos Massad, Liliana Rojas-Suárez, Jaime Ros, Lance Taylor and Leonardo Villar for their comments on previous drafts of this paper. I am also grateful to María Angela Parra for assistance.

1. See, for example, in relation to Latin America, Bacha and Díaz-Alejandro (1982).
2. There is an extensive literature on these issues. See, for example, Eatwell and Taylor (2000), Eichengreen (1999) and Ocampo (1999, 2001, 2002).
3. Among the many recent contributions to the analysis of this issue, see ECLAC (1998a, Part Three; 2000, chapter 8), Ffrench-Davis (1999), Furman and Stiglitz (1998), Helleiner (1997), Ocampo (1999, chapter 5), Stiglitz and Bhattacharya (2000) and World Bank (1998, chapter 3).
4. See ECLAC (2000, 2001a and 2002).
5. See, for example, ECLAC (2000, chapter 8; 2001b, chapter 3) and Lustig (2000).
6. We will not deal here, however, with the literature on the long-run determinants of the real exchange rate. It suffices, for our purposes, to note that nominal exchange rates influence real exchange rates through the business cycle. One way of posing these issues is to say that access to external financing is one of the determinants of the real exchange rate, alongside others (the terms of trade, the fiscal stance, relative productivity trends in tradables vs. non-tradables, and so on), and that the magnitude of the external financing–real exchange rate link is not independent of the exchange rate regime.
7. This deterioration of the growth–trade balance trade-off seems to be a feature of most of the developing world. See UNCTAD (1999, Part Two, chapter IV).
8. Hausmann (2000) and Calvo (2001).
9. For recent defenses of intermediate regimes, see ECLAC (2000), chapter 8, and Williamson (2000). For interesting reviews of recent controversies on exchange rate regimes, see Frankel (1999), Velasco (2000) and Braga de Macedo, Cohen and Reisen (2001).
10. More price flexibility will help in this regard, but may generate other problems. Thus, in the gold standard era, price flexibility tended to generate additional domestic financial risks during crises (due to the rapid increase in real debts generated by deflation, which may be thought of as equivalent to very high *real* short-term interest rates). It also generated a strong short-term bias in domestic lending which was associated with the need to rapidly reduce nominal portfolios during periods of monetary contraction.
11. Krugman (1990, chapter 7) and van Wijnbergen (1984).
12. Thus, private institutions with open positions in domestic currency may cover them with domestic-currency-denominated debts. In this case, the counterpart of the net coverage

provided in the futures market is a current capital outflow (Dodd, 2001). Foreign investors can cover themselves directly with larger domestic currency liabilities, with a similar effect.

13. Devaluation came in this case with a lag, in the early months of 1995, due to the speculation generated prior to the August 1994 strengthening of regulations. Although it coincided with the Tequila crisis, it was unrelated to it. Appreciation pressures resurfaced when capital regulations were relaxed in early 1996. See Ocampo and Tovar (1998 and 2001) and Villar and Rincón (2000).
14. Agosin and Ffrench-Davis (2001); Ffrench-Davis and Larraín (2001).
15. For documents which support the effectiveness of these regulations, see Agosin (1998), Agosin and Ffrench-Davis (2001), Cárdenas and Barrera (1997), Le Fort and Budnevich (1997), Le Fort and Lehmann (2000), Ocampo and Tovar (1998 and 2001), Palma (2002), Rodrik and Velasco (2000) and Villar and Rincón (2000). For an opposite view, see de Gregorio *et al.* (2000) and Valdés-Prieto and Soto (1998). There have also been explicit taxes on foreign-currency borrowing in other countries, notably Brazil.
16. For an analysis of these issues, see World Bank (1998, p. 151), and Stiglitz and Bhattacharya (2000).
17. ECLAC (1998b, chapter VIII).
18. See Sachs *et al.* (1996) and Ros (2001).
19. See IMF (1998, chapter 4). On the situation in Latin America, see also Rojas-Suárez and Weisbrod (1996) and ECLAC (2002).
20. Banco Central de la República Argentina (1995, pp. 11–12).
21. For a recent analysis of these issues and policy alternatives for managing them, see Bank for International Settlements (2001, chapter VII); and Borio *et al.* (2000).
22. For an analysis of some of these alternatives, see the sources quoted in note 21 and Stiglitz and Bhattacharya (2000).
23. This includes cases in which the revenues are reflected in a quasi-fiscal surplus of the central bank that is not transferred to the government.

REFERENCES

Agosin, Manuel (1998), 'Capital inflow and investment performance: Chile in the 1990s', *Capital Inflows and Investment Performance: Lessons from Latin America*, in Ricardo Ffrench-Davis and Helmut Reisen (eds), Paris and Santiago: OECD Development Centre/ECLAC.

Agosin, Manuel and Ricardo Ffrench-Davis (2001), 'Managing capital inflows in Chile', *Short-term Capital Flows and Economic Crises*, in Stephany Griffith-Jones, Manuel F. Montes and Anwar Nasution (eds), New York: Oxford University Press/United Nations University (UNU)/World Institute for Development Economics Research (WIDER).

Bacha, Edmar and Carlos F. Díaz-Alejandro (1982), 'International financial intermediation: a long and tropical view', *Essays in International Finance*, No. 147, Princeton, NJ: Princeton University, Department of Economics, International Finance Section, May.

Banco Central de la República Argentina (1995), *Informe anual*, Buenos Aires, October.

Banco de España (2000), *Boletín Económico*, January.

Bank for International Settlements (2001), *71*st *Annual Report*, Basle, 11 June.

Borio, Claudio, Craig Furfine and Philip Lowe (2000), 'Procyclicality of the financial system and financial stability: issues and policy options', paper presented at BIS Annual Meeting of Central Bank Economists on *Marrying the*

Macro- and Microprudential Dimensions of Financial Stability, 9–10 October, 2000.

Braga de Macedo, Jorge, Daniel Cohen and Helmut Reisen (eds) (2001), 'Monetary integration for sustained convergence: earning rather than importing credibility', in Jorge Braga de Macedo *et al.* (eds), *Don't Fix, Don't Float*, Paris: OECD Development Centre Studies.

Budnevich, Carlos and Guillermo Le Fort (1997), 'Fiscal policy and the economic cycle in Chile', *CEPAL Review*, No. 61, April.

Calvo, Guillermo (2001), 'The case for hard pegs in the brave new world of global finance', in Jorge Braga de Macedo *et al.* (eds), *Don't Fix, Don't Float*, Paris: OECD Development Centre Studies.

Cárdenas, Mauricio and Felipe Barrera (1997), 'On the effectiveness of capital controls: the experience of Colombia during the 1990s', *Journal of Development Economics*, **54**(1), special edition, October.

De Gregorio, José, Sebastián Edwards and Rodrigo Valdés (2000), 'Controls on capital inflows: do they work?', *Journal of Development Economics*, **63**(1), October.

Dodd, Randall (2001), 'Derivatives and international capital flows', paper presented at the UNU/WIDER-ECLAC Seminar, *Capital Flows to Emerging Markets Since the Asian Crisis*, Helsinki, October.

Eatwell, John and Lance Taylor (2000), *Global Finance at Risk: The Case for International Regulation*, New York: The New Press.

Eatwell, John and Lance Taylor (eds) (2002), *International Capital Markets – Systems in Transition*, New York: Oxford University Press.

ECLAC (Economic Commission for Latin America and the Caribbean) (1998a), *América Latina y el Caribe: políticas para mejorar la inserción en la economía mundial*, Santiago: CEPAL/Fondo de Cultura Económica.

ECLAC (Economic Commission for Latin America and the Caribbean) (1998b), *The Fiscal Covenant. Strengths, weaknesses, challenges*, Santiago.

ECLAC (Economic Commission for Latin America and the Caribbean) (2000), *Equity, Development and Citizenship*, Santiago.

ECLAC (Economic Commission for Latin America and the Caribbean) (2001a), *Una década de luces y sombras: América Latina y el Caribe en los años noventa*, Bogotá: CEPAL/Alfaomega.

ECLAC (Economic Commission for Latin America and the Caribbean) (2001b), *Social Panorama of Latin America, 2000–2001*, Santiago.

ECLAC (Economic Commission for Latin America and the Caribbean) (2002), *Growth with Stability: Financing for Development in the New International Context*, Libros de la CEPAL, No. 67, March.

Eichengreen, Barry (1999), *Toward a New International Financial Architecture: A Practical Post-Asia Agenda*, Washington DC: Institute for International Economics (IIE).

Ffrench-Davis, Ricardo (1999), *Reforming the Reforms in Latin America: Macroeconomics, Trade, Finance*, London: Macmillan.

Ffrench-Davis, Ricardo and Guillermo Larraín (2001), 'How optimal are the extremes? Latin American exchange rate policies during the Asian Crisis', paper presented at the UNU/WIDER-ECLAC Seminar, *Capital Flows to Emerging Markets Since the Asian Crisis*, Helsinki, October.

Frankel, Jeffrey (1999), *No Single Currency Regime Is Right for All Countries or at All Times*, Essays in International Finance No. 215, International Finance Section, Department of Economy, University of Princeton.

Furman, Jason and Joseph Stiglitz (1998), 'Economic crises: evidence and insights from East Asia', *Brookings Papers on Economic Activity*, No. 2.

Greenspan, Alan (1998), 'The structure of the international financial system', Remarks at the Annual Meeting of the Securities Industry Association, Boca Raton, Florida, November.

Hausmann, Ricardo (2000), 'Exchange rate arrangements for the new architecture', *Global Finance from a Latin American Viewpoint*, Paris, Development Centre Seminars, Inter-American Development Bank (IDB), Organization for Economic Co-operation and Development (OECD).

Helleiner, Gerald K. (1997), 'Capital account regimes and the developing countries', *International Monetary and Financial Issues for the 1990s*, vol. 8, New York: United Nations Conference on Trade and Development (UNCTAD).

IMF (International Monetary Fund) (1998), *World Economic Outlook*, Washington, DC, May.

J.P. Morgan (1998), *World Financial Markets*, New York, 7 October.

Kaplan, Ethan and Dani Rodrik (2001), 'Did the Malaysian capital controls work?', *NBER Working Paper Series*, No. 8142, Cambridge, MA, February.

Krugman, Paul (1990), *Rethinking International Trade*, Cambridge: MIT Press.

Krugman, Paul and Lance Taylor (1978), 'Contractionary effects of devaluations', *Journal of International Economics*, No. 8.

LeFort, Guillermo and Carlos Budnevich (1997), 'Capital-account regulations and macroeconomic policy: two Latin American experiences', *International Monetary and Financial Issues for the 1990s*, vol. 8, New York: United Nations Conference on Trade and Development (UNCTAD).

LeFort, Guillermo and Sergio Lehmann (2000), 'El encaje, los flujos de capitales y el gasto: una evaluación empírica', *Documento de Trabajo*, No. 64, Central Bank of Chile, February.

Lustig, Nora (2000), 'Crises and the poor: socially responsible macroeconomics', *Economia, A Journal of the Latin American and Caribbean Economic Association (LACEA),* No. 1, Brookings Institution, Washington, DC, December.

Marfán, Manuel (2001), 'Rol macroeconómico de la política fiscal', paper presented at the Seminar 'Development theory at the threshold of the twenty-first Century', ECLAC, Santiago, 28–29 August.

Martner, Ricardo (2000), 'Estrategias de política económica en un mundo incierto', *Cuadernos del ILPES*, 45, Santiago.

Montiel, Peter and Carmen M. Reinhart (2001), 'The dynamics of capital movements to emerging economies during the 1990s', in Stephany Griffith-Jones, Manuel F. Montes and Anwar Nasution (eds), *Short-Term Capital Flows and Economic Crises*, UNU/WIDER Studies in Development Economics, Oxford University Press.

Nayyar, Deepak (2002), 'Capital controls and the world financial authority – what can we learn from the Indian experience?', in John Eatwell and Lance Taylor (eds), *International Capital Markets – Systems in Transition*, New York: Oxford University Press.

Ocampo, José Antonio (1999), *La reforma del sistema financiero internacional: un debate en marcha*, Santiago: CEPAL/Fondo de Cultura Económica.

Ocampo, José Antonio (2001), 'International asymmetries and the design of the international financial system', *Serie Temas de Coyuntura*, No. 15, March, Santiago: CEPAL.

Ocampo, José Antonio (2002), 'Recasting the international financial agenda', in

John Eatwell and Lance Taylor (eds), *International Capital Markets – Systems in Transition*, New York: Oxford University Press.

Ocampo, José Antonio and Camilo Tovar (1998), 'Capital flows, savings and investment in Colombia, 1990–96', in Ricardo Ffrench-Davis and Helmut Reisen (eds), *Capital Flows and Investment Performance: Lessons from Latin America*, Paris and Santiago: OECD Development Centre/ECLAC.

Ocampo, José Antonio and Camilo Tovar (2001), 'An empirical evaluation of the effectiveness of price-based controls on capital inflows', *Mimeo*, ECLAC, September.

Palma, Gabriel (2002), 'The three routes to financial crises: the need for capital controls', in John Eatwell and Lance Taylor (eds), *International Capital Markets – Systems in Transition*, New York: Oxford University Press.

Poveda, Raimundo (2000), 'La reforma del sistema de provisiones de insolvencia', Paper presented at the APD Conference, Madrid, 18 January.

Rodrik, Dani and Andrés Velasco (2000), 'Short-term capital flows', *Annual World Bank Conference on Development Economics 1999*, Washington, DC: The World Bank.

Rojas-Suárez, Liliana and Steven R. Weisbrod (1996), 'Banking crises in Latin America: experiences and issues', in Ricardo Hausmann and Liliana Rojas-Suárez (eds), *Banking Crises in Latin America*, Washington, DC: Inter-American Development Bank (IDB).

Ros, Jaime (2001), 'From the capital surge to the financial crisis and beyond: Mexico in the 1990s', in Ricardo Ffrench-Davis (ed.), *Financial Crises in 'Successful' Emerging Economies*, ECLAC/Ford Foundation, Washington, DC: Brookings Institution Press, forthcoming.

Sachs, Jeffrey, Aaron Tornell and Andrés Velasco (1996), 'The Mexican peso crisis: sudden death or death foretold?', *NBER Working Paper Series*, No. 5563, Cambridge, May.

Stiglitz, Joseph E. and Amar Bhattacharya (2000), 'The underpinnings of a stable and equitable global financial system: from old debates to a new paradigm', *Annual World Bank Conference on Development Economics 1999*, Washington, DC: The World Bank.

UNCTAD (United Nations Conference on Trade and Development) (1999), *Trade and Development Report, 1999* (UNCTAD/TDR/1999), Geneva.

Valdés-Prieto, Salvador and Marcelo Soto (1998), 'The effectiveness of capital controls: theory and evidence from Chile', *Empirica*, No. 25, the Netherlands: Kluwer Academic Publishers.

Van Wijnbergen, Sweder (1984), 'The Dutch disease: a disease after all?', *Economic Journal*, No. 94.

Velasco, Andrés (2000), *Exchange-Rate Policies for Developing Countries: What Have We Learned? What Do We Still Not Know?*, New York: United Nations Conference on Trade and Development (UNCTAD)/University of Harvard, Center for International Development.

Villar, Leonardo and Hernán Rincón (2000), 'The Colombian economy in the nineties: capital flows and foreign exchange regimes', paper presented at the Conference on *Critical Issues in Financial Reform: Latin American/Caribbean and Canadian Perspectives*, organized by The Munk Centre for International Studies Programme on Latin America and the Caribbean, University of Toronto, Toronto, June.

Williamson, John (2000), 'Exchange rate regimes for emerging markets: reviving the

intermediate option', *Policy Analyses in International Economics*, Washington, DC: Institute for International Economics, September.
World Bank (1998), *Global Economic Prospects and the Developing Countries, 1998–99*, Washington, DC, December.

20. Institutional challenges of globalization and the developing countries

Andrés Solimano

INTRODUCTION

Globalization has become both a household term and an important historical phenomenon. The geopolitics of globalization has several precedents: the end of the cold war, the collapse of communism and a reconfiguration in the balance of power towards Western countries and capitalism. The economics of globalization suggests that increased global economic interdependence can be a powerful engine for wealth creation and prosperity. On the other side however, globalization also tends to be associated with frequent financial crisis and volatility and its benefits are unevenly distributed across countries and regions. In view of these elements, globalization poses an important challenge to the existing institutional matrix, created in the mid-1940s, composed of the United Nations, the Bretton Woods Institutions (BWIs) and the World Trade Organization (successor of GATT) and other institutions. In turn, at national level globalization tends to reduce the degree of effective autonomy for national governments to pursue their own development goals of growth, stability and social equity. A main challenge of public policy in the era of globalization is the seizing of the opportunities it opens while at the same time managing the tensions and problems it poses, particularly for developing countries. This requires, among other things, addressing the adequacy of the institutional framework (or governance structure), accompanying globalization, a main subject of this chapter.

The chapter is organized around several sections. First, it provides an historical background on early and late twentieth century globalization episodes and other main developments of the last 120 years, or so, to put the current wave of globalization in historical perspective. Then the chapter reviews, briefly, main analytical views, both orthodox and heterodox, on globalization and development and examines the opportunities, tensions and dilemmas posed by globalization. Then it turns to the institutional challenge of making globalization more compatible with global financial stability and national development.

The chapter highlights both the need for re-examining the mix (and overlapping) between global and regional financial institutions and the consistency between reform of global and regional institutions and changes in national policies and institutions. The relative roles and allocation of responsibilities of global and regional institutions need to be analysed and evaluated in terms of the following criteria: value of regional versus global knowledge, patterns of interaction with borrowing countries, capacity of response to crisis, particularly in intermediate and small countries, voice and representation for developing countries and transition economies. In addition, the chapter argues the need for refocusing national policies towards reducing volatility and equalizing opportunities among members of society in the framework of pro-growth policies.

HISTORICAL BACKGROUND AND RECENT EVENTS

The last decades of the nineteenth century (say from the 1870s) to the early twentieth century (up to 1914) was a period of rapid growth of the global economy based on the expansion of international trade and free capital mobility under the gold standard along with massive international migration from Europe (the 'Old World') to the US, Canada, Argentina, Australia, New Zealand (the 'New World').[1] This liberal international economic order came to an end with the disarray brought about by World War I, which in turn was followed by a period of high inflation and macroeconomic turbulence of the 1920s in several major European economies, and thereafter, by the Great Depression of the 1930s.

These events during the inter-war period radically reshaped prevailing ideas on how to stabilize global and national economies, and the role of international trade and capital movements as engines of growth and prosperity. Global capitalism was seen as an inherently unstable system; prone both to periods of volatility and inflation, as in the 1920s, or to recessionary trends without self correcting mechanisms that assure full employment, as was patently demonstrated in the 1930s.

A new set of global financial institutions emerged in the mid-1940s, known as the Bretton Woods Institutions. The International Monetary Fund was given the mandate of assuring a normal payments system under a system of fixed exchange rates, and providing external financing to countries running balance of payments deficits. The role of the World Bank was to provide long-term financing for economic reconstruction and development.

A period of considerable stability, rapid growth and reduced inequalities took place from the late 1940s to the early 1970s;[2] this period, called the 'golden age of capitalism', was based on a (globally and nationally) regulated market economy. This regulated market economy could be defined by a myriad of global, and later regional institutions.

During the 1990s, there were important policy reform processes in Latin America, the former Soviet Union and Eastern Europe. Large macro imbalances were corrected in Latin America, inflation declined and economic growth resumed, coinciding with the return of capital flows to the region and the deepening of market-oriented reforms. Nevertheless, annual GDP growth averaged only 3.3 per cent in the decade. This was a moderate pace of output expansion (punctuated by recessionary cycles in 1995 and 1999 and more recently in 2001), still insufficient to reduce poverty and improve living standards in the region. On the structural front economic openness has brought about a more competitive environment for previously protected national economies. The former socialist economies of the Soviet bloc started a process of transition to capitalism with varying degrees of success. Particularly complex has been the reform process in Russia, in former Soviet Republics and in the Balkans. The general point to be made here, is that of a significant shift to a market economy in both Latin America and the former socialist bloc which marks a radical departure in these two regions from the policies followed in the 40 years preceding the 1990s.

The globalization process of the 1990s was punctuated by recurrent episodes of financial instability such as the Mexican crisis of 1994, the Asian crisis of 1997, the Russian crisis of 1998 and the Brazilian crisis of early 1999. In the early twenty-first century, the crises of Turkey and Argentina must be noted. In view of these experiences, we can say that the current process of globalization is being accompanied by a greater frequency of currency and financial crisis than in the 'golden age phase' (from the 1950s to the early 1970s) and the first wave of globalization of the late nineteenth century. The frequency of financial and currency crisis is rivaled only by the crisis-ridden period of the 1920s and 1930s.[3]

To finish, it is worth highlighting several differences between pre-1914 and late twentieth century globalization. First, the degree of capital mobility of late twentieth century globalization in both currency markets and in bonds, equity, short-term credit and other financial instruments is unprecedented in history. The dominance of 'financial globalization' in the current globalization period is a crucial feature of this historical phase. Second, in pre-1914 globalization, there were no global financial institutions aimed at stabilizing the world economy, financing development and economic bodies, setting global rules for international trade in goods and services such as the GATT and then the World Trade Organization. At the political and diplomatic levels, there was no such global forum as the United Nations. Third, there was a change in the leadership (that is, the 'hegemon') in the two waves of globalization. The first globalization wave was led by England as the dominant 'superpower' in the late nineteenth century. The international monetary system was anchored around the British pound and the gold standard.[4] In contrast, in the second globalization wave of the late twentieth century, the process is being led by the United States and the US dollar under a flexible exchange rate regime. Fourth, pre-1914 globalization came across with mass migrations (to the US and other countries). Instead, late twentieth century globalization is coming along with lower migration flows and movement of people across countries and continents relative to the total population of sending and receiving countries.

THINKING ON GLOBALIZATION: ORTHODOX AND HETERODOX VIEWS

Globalization involves increased trade in goods and services, enhanced financial integration and greater mobility of people across national boundaries. In addition, globalization implies particular patterns of insertion of developing countries in the world economy, its institutional architecture and other forms of global power relations.

Neoclassical theory supports free trade on the grounds that economic integration bolsters a more efficient structure of production and expanded consumption opportunities that, in turn, must lead to higher national (and world) income and welfare.

The case for free capital mobility is more contentious, even in the framework of neoclassical theory. On the one hand, it is recognized that removing barriers for capital to go from areas with lower rates of return to countries with higher rates of return must increase global real income, and contribute to the saving pool of recipient countries which are often capital-scarce economies. However, speculative short-term capital mobility can be also destabilizing, and the promotion of free capital mobility is not a guarantee of stable, speedier, growth for recipient countries.

In fact, neoclassical trade theorists such as Jagdish Bhagwati (2000) make a distinction between free trade and free capital mobility, noting that both forms of economic integration are not equivalent in terms of their economic rewards because of the speculative nature of short-term capital inflows. This belief is also shared by Nobel prize winner James Tobin, who has proposed a tax on international financial transactions to reduce excessive capital mobility across countries. In general, this literature is favorable to globalization understood as trade integration but more skeptical when dealing with capital flows, particularly of a short-term nature. In turn, free labor mobility constitutes an interesting case. The advocacy for free trade and free capital mobility rarely extends to the free mobility of people, in spite of the fact that freer international migration should increase real income by allowing labor to migrate from areas with lower labor productivity to areas with higher labor productivity. It is apparent that we live in a world with significant differences in the 'freedom to become global' between human-made objects (goods and money) and actual people (see Solimano, 2001a).

Heterodox theories of international economic relations such as center-periphery, dependency theory and unequal exchange were developed in the 1940s and 1950s by authors like Prebisch (1950), Emmanuel (1972) and were formalized by Bacha (1978) and Taylor (1983). Although these theories were developed well before the current process of globalization, which started in the 1980s and 1990s, they still can help to identify issues related to the current globalization wave, particularly in terms of the distribution of gains of globalization for developing countries and the limited degrees of freedom of developing countries to affect global outcomes.

In general, these approaches emphasize that international trade takes place under 'unequal conditions' between the 'North' (center, developed countries) and the 'South' (periphery, underdeveloped economies). In general the 'North' is where technical change mostly originates and where physical, human and institutional infrastructure is superior.

A main conclusion of this heterodox literature is an asymmetrical distribution of the benefits of international trade between center and periphery. In addition, it is proposed that there are not enough degrees of freedom in the international system to allow the South (periphery) to choose its own rate of economic growth or terms of trade, which are determined by macroeconomic equilibrium complemented by certain institutions in the North. In turn, the South (periphery) carries a disproportionate share of worldwide economic adjustment costs to global shocks like deterioration in terms of trade, fall in world demand and slowdowns in capital flows (see Lance Taylor, 1983, chapter 10, for a formal exposition of these theories). Heterodox theories propose that main global economic decisions are made by the governments of the North, who hold the main decision-making power in the global, and to less extent regional institutions that 'govern' the global economy. These theories stress an asymmetric decision- and power-capacity in the institutional matrix of globalization between developing and developed countries.

EVALUATION

The economic order of the early twenty-first century offers both opportunities and risks to developing countries and other actors in the global economy. The drastic reductions in barriers to international trade have opened the door for export-led growth. In fact, for small- and medium-sized economies with limited internal markets,[5] the possibilities for rapid economic growth lie, to a large extent, in production oriented towards international markets. The historical experience of the last three decades of the century shows that countries that have managed to grow at very rapid rates, say 7 per cent, 8 per cent or more per year, have all relied on strong export growth, with exports expanding at a faster rate than GDP. This has been the case of East Asia since the 1960s (up to their current crisis), China, since the mid-1970s, Chile since the mid-1980s and others.

Another argument in favor of globalization is that it expands freedom (Micklethwait and Wooldridge, 2000). The idea is that, by increasing opportunities, globalization also encourages freedom to be exercised. Interestingly a similar argument is put forward, regarding development rather than globalization, in Amartya Sen's 1999 book, entitled precisely, *Development as Freedom*.

Globalization also increases the potential access to a wide variety of consumption goods, new technologies, knowledge, ideas and international best practices in different fields and realms. These can include a new product design, a new investment project, a new production technology, a new managerial practice, or even a certain set of institutions that has proved successful in other places, and, eventually, a model of society.

Of course the mere acquisition or imitation of foreign products, technologies or foreign social models to local conditions with all their specificities and idiosyncratic features is not a guarantee of success. It is just a potential benefit (or cost if misused) derived from broadening the set of choices open to the participants of the global economy.

Every coin has two sides; thus it is also important to recognize that globalization poses tensions and dilemmas to countries integrated in the world economy.[6] It is clear that globalization has spread unevenly across the developing world. Private capital inflows are largely concentrated in a group of large developing countries. Sub-Saharan Africa and other poor countries in other continents receive fewer benefits from trade, capital mobility and technological improvements developed in the North. Another tension of globalization is associated with the fact that in a more interdependent and interlinked world economy any adverse global or regional shock, for example the Asian and Russian crisis of 1997–98, rapidly propagates to other economies which often have little economic contact with crisis-countries. One propagation (contagion) mechanism at work can be a decline in the import volumes and/or changes in the real price of commodities (oil, copper, timber, and so on). Economies that depend heavily on a few main commodities as their main source of export earnings and fiscal revenues can be hit hard by these shocks. Another transmission mechanism is asset markets. Highly integrated financial markets tend to transmit global, regional or local shocks much more rapidly than in past decades when financial markets were less integrated. Portfolio shifts affect exchange rates, interest rates and economic activity. As the volumes of financial intermediation and currency transactions are enormous nowadays, shocks can be greatly amplified in a more or less synchronized fashion with destabilizing effects on many economies. This source of financial volatility was largely absent in the world of the 1950s, 1960s and early 1970s when multilateral lending, public financing, aid and foreign direct investment dominated global capital movements.

There is ample empirical evidence showing that uncertainty and volatility penalize capital formation (and productivity growth) with adverse effects on economic growth.[7] Thus instability and volatility can ultimately be viewed as a tax on growth and prosperity.

In many instances, this instability originates from abroad. However, the quality of the domestic policy response in the face of adverse external shocks matters. The nature and timing of the domestic policy response can soften or increase the impact of these shocks.

Another tension of globalization lies in its social effects. As globalization is often associated with increased instability of output and employment, this affects, among other things, job security. As labor income is the main source of earnings for the majority of the population under capitalism, job insecurity is socially disruptive and brings tensions to the fabric of society. In addition, flexibility in labor markets required to compete, successfully, in international markets, tends to erode long-term work and personal relationships between firms and employees, workers and managers, which traditionally give a sense of security to people. Another open discussion is whether foreign trade and globalization narrow or widen income disparities. Traditional trade theory suggesting factor price equalization across countries seems of little relevance in a world of large per capita income differentials (between, say, Sub-Saharan Africa and the OECD); moreover, convergence in income levels (per person) is, at least, very weak across regions and nations.

In addition, globalization gives a premium to people with sophisticated skills, high levels of education, and entrepreneurial traits. These are people better equipped to survive and succeed in the more competitive world brought about by globalization. The mirror image of this is that unskilled labor, uneducated workers and a marginalized population are likely to benefit less in a more competitive world economy. Thus income and wealth inequality can be amplified, underscoring the need for public policy to correct these inegalitarian trends. Globalization can induce both divergence and convergence of per capita incomes across countries and regions. In late twentieth century globalization, divergence is particularly serious in Sub-Saharan Africa, Russia and several former socialist countries and other lagging Asian and Latin American low-income countries.

Another criticism of globalization is that it tends to transmit the cultural patterns of large countries to the rest of the world through imitation of consumption patterns, global mass media and other means of influence. This trend could, eventually, lead to homogenization of values, thereby reducing cultural diversity and national identities. On the other hand, globalization allows, at the same time, to broaden the set of ideas, knowledge and other cultural practices available to people and regions that were previously detached from better knowledge of other realities in the world.

INSTITUTIONAL CHALLENGES OF GLOBALIZATION

A main geopolitical challenge of the era of globalization has been the emergence of a uni-polar world around the United States as 'hegemon' following the end of the Soviet Union in the early 1990s. The end of the cold war has brought about the end of armed conflicts in certain areas (for example Asia, Central America) but brought new conflicts in Central Europe, for example in the former Yugoslavia and in some former Soviet republics. According to the historian Eric Hobsbawm (1999), the process of nation-building in what was the soviet bloc is still an unfolding process, nearly a decade after the dissolution of the Soviet Union. There are complex new challenges like international terrorism, the spread of HIV-AIDS, and the persistency of ethnic conflict that tend to strain the capacity of global political institutions, such as the UN and others. Dealing appropriately with these issues is non-trivial and requires considerable political will, financial support and consensus from the member countries.

Returning to economic and financial dimensions of globalization, the financial architecture of the early twenty-first century is facing several important challenges:

Maintenance of global and domestic financial stability. This is becoming a very complex task. Capital flows move very fast across national boundaries responding to changes in relative asset returns, information about investment opportunities and changes in national economic policies. As the

Mexican, Asian and Russian crises of the 1990s show, the external imbalances to be financed (and the outstanding financial liabilities to be served) in crisis situations are of a huge magnitude. This strains (or even exceeds) the existing resources available to the IMF and other multinational lending institutions which have to prepare, in a short time, emergency loans of an unprecedented size. Rescue packages of 10, 20 or 30 billion dollars (or more) towards countries, before or after suffering speculative attacks on their currencies, were not uncommon in the second half of the 1990s.

Anticipation of crisis. International financial institutions (IFIs) and markets alike have serious problems anticipating and then responding to macro and financial crises, particularly in countries with serious governance problems. Moreover, when the crisis takes place and the IFIs come with rescue packages, they create a moral hazard problem by giving, implicitly, incentives to market participants for excessive risk-taking in the anticipation of future bailouts. Nevertheless, it is fair to note also that market participants and international private risk-grading agencies often fail to anticipate crises (the latter even tend to aggravate shocks in confidence when they downgrade countries in the midst of a crisis).

Balance of payments and development lending. The exact dividing lines between balance of payments financing (the realm of the IMF) and development lending (the scope of multilateral developments banks) have become less clear. This was already the case in the 1980s when both Bretton Woods institutions started to lend in tandem for balance of payments support as private financing dried up as a consequence of the debt crisis. Again meeting the large external financial needs associated with the crises of the 1990s required a combination of balance of payments support from the Bretton Woods Institutions and the Regional Development Banks. Several observers point out that crisis management is more the realm of the IMF than of development banks.

National and global banking systems regulation. In order to strengthen the banking system at the national level, and therefore strengthen the foundations of global financial stability, it is necessary to enforce the Basle Capital accord of 1998, signed by over 100 countries, which recommends core principles of bank lending, reserves, transparency and others. This should be complemented with appropriate mechanisms of banks' surveillance, and reporting of relevant information for both banks and corporations. Also, it is important to recognize an asymmetry of the system in which national banking systems are much more regulated than the global banking system.[8]

Global civil society's criticism of the IFIs. The 1990s have seen the eruption of an active global civil society/NGO movement with national counterparts, composed of environmentalist groups, social activists and labor unions, which has started to challenge the policies and practices of the IFIs and is prompting the quest for reform. The summits of the IFIs and G-7 are becoming showcases of protests by a plethora of civil society organizations, against global institutions and the club of richer nations. At a more substantive level, the practice of conditionality attached to policy-based lending by the International Financial Institutions is becoming more controversial in consideration of issues such as ownership of programs, overloading of conditions and the internal political impact of externally-imposed policies.

National Macroeconomic Management. As mentioned before, globalization poses several economic challenges for national governments and its institutions of macroeconomic management. On the one hand, globalization is seen as a disciplinary force for national governments that undertake unsustainable economic policies (high fiscal deficits, unsound financial policies, and so on) as these policies are penalized by international investors and global capital markets. However, the other side of this is that fiscal policy tends to lose its capacity to act as a counter-cyclical instrument oriented to maintain full employment and pursue redistributive and social goals. The fact is that international financial markets are very sensitive on the stance of fiscal policy of a country and use it as an indicator of the degree of 'macroeconomic responsibility' of governments. Governments are encouraged to follow persistently austere fiscal policies in order to satisfy financial markets and to gain credentials of serious fiscal behavior.

PROPOSALS OF REFORM OF INTERNATIONAL FINANCIAL INSTITUTIONS

The current wave of globalization is a classic example of rapid economic change in need of an institutional infrastructure that could guarantee stability and social integration at global, regional and national levels. In a way, we face nowadays a similar situation to that described in Karl Polanyi (1994)[9] when he analysed the social disruption and conflicts of the early twentieth century following the first wave of globalization and marketization, and highlighted the need for 'mediating institutions' to regulate rapid change.

Several proposals of reform have been put forward in the last few years regarding the governance structure of the global economy and the global polity. These proposals have focused on the mission of the UN system and the Bretton Woods institutions and other operative aspects of these institutions.

Here it is important to remember that global and regional institutions, either the UN or the Bretton Woods institutions, are 'owed' by national governments and therefore their reform will reflect the priorities of their member countries, particularly of those who make the largest financial contributions to these institutions. In general, developing countries have a limited voice in the decision-making process that affects the world economy and its global institutions.

Let's focus on reform proposals for the International Financial Institutions.

The IMF and the World Bank

Regarding the IMF, proposals range from abolition (Milton Friedman among the academics, George Schultz among former policymakers) to reform, the latter including the proposals of the Meltzer report, which included academics such as Jeffrey Sachs, Allan Meltzer and others. Other proposals, particularly from financier George Soros (Soros, 1998), include to convert the IMF into a global Central Bank complemented by an international credit-insurance corporation which would guarantee international loans (up to a limit), charging a fee.[10]

The main thrust of most reform proposals is to focus the IMF around two main functions: i) maintenance of global financial stability, including crisis-prevention and crisis-management; ii) lender of last resort. Regarding these functions, Fischer (1999) makes a distinction between crisis management and lender of last resort, noting that they do not always coincide. For example, historically, in the US, it was the Treasury, clearing-houses and even the financier J.P. Morgan in the early twentieth century that performed the role of lenders of last resort, crisis managers or both. Regarding the IMF, Fischer (1999) asserts that, in practice, the Fund has played the role of crisis manager during the 1980s and 1990s; in addition, the function of lender of last resort can also be carried out by the Fund and he notes that this would be facilitated if the Fund could 'create money'. However, the IMF is able, subject to the approval of its board of directors, to issue Special Drawings Rights (SDRs). This amounts to creating liquidity to supplement existing reserve assets. Another important discussion relates to the implications of the 'Bagehot Principle' (1873) which states that the lender of last resort should lend freely to clients, at a penalty rate, on the basis of a marketable collateral in the ordinary course of business when there is no panic. One issue is to what extent unlimited lending by the Fund is feasible in crisis situations. Another issue is the connection of this principle with conditionality. Some observers have argued that charging penalty interest rates in crisis situations should be a substitute for policy conditionality.

Coming back to the Soros proposal, a global Central Bank would require a mandate to print global money, a feature unlikely to be given to the IMF or any other international institution. Nevertheless, as our previous discussion suggests, the lender of last resort does not necessarily need to have the ability to create money, so the need of having a global Central Bank is less clear.

Other schemes supplementing the crisis-prevention and crisis-management functions, call for a sort of global bankruptcy court, which would seek a more balanced distribution of the costs of financial crisis by engaging foreign lenders to share part of the costs of the financial crisis.

Another area of financial governance is the regulation of banking systems and the enforcement of capital standards and other practices of prudent banking behavior. A new, ambitious proposal for creating a World Financial Authority (WFA) is developed by Eatwell and Taylor (2000; see also the chapter by Eatwell in this volume). The WFA, according to the authors, would be a global financial regulator performing the tasks of authorization, provision of information, surveillance, enforcement and development of policy.

A recent report on reform of the World Bank and the IMF is the Meltzer Report, commissioned by the US Congress. The recommendations of that report center around some of the following issues:

- Focus the IMF in preserving global financial stability.
- Reduction of World Bank financing to middle-income developing countries and increase of funding to poorer economies via grant-making.
- Representation of member countries in the decision-making and governance structure of the Bretton Woods Institutions.
- Nature of policy conditionality.
- Effectiveness of counter-cyclical lending by the IFIs during crisis situations.

The issue of crowding-in and crowding-out of private capital inflows associated with lending by the BWIs is relevant. While private financing of infrastructure projects is generally available, the availability of private external financing for projects in the social sectors (education, health, social security) including support for institutional reform is much more limited. This makes for complementarities between international public and private lending to developing countries.

The role of the Bretton Woods Institutions is relevant in crisis situations, particularly when private capital flows withdraw from countries experiencing crisis. It is important to secure an effective counter-cyclical role for the Bretton Woods institutions in putting together external financing packages to all countries that need it. Also, the concentration in the distribution of lending between middle-income/large economies *vis-à-vis* lower-income/small economies is another issue of relevance. In this connection, the Meltzer report argues in favor of the World Bank shifting its lending from middle-income developing countries with access to international capital inflows (for example, Argentina, Brazil and Mexico) towards assisting poor economies through grant-making. This recommendation raises important distributional questions regarding the allocation of international lending. However, it needs further critical analysis since middle-income developing countries do not always have uninterrupted access to global capital markets (for example during financial crisis); in addition, some middle-income developing countries (for example, Brazil, India) have large contingents of poor and marginalized people living within their frontiers and therefore fall within the mandate of the Bank as a poverty-reducing institution. Moreover, the financial implications for donor countries of going from a Bank to a grant-making agency are significant, and the convenience and feasibility of this move need to be clarified.

The topic of developing countries' representation in the IFIs is very relevant as the capital structure of these institutions, established long ago, does not represent current economic realities of emerging and developing economies. In addition, developing countries' representation and influence in the governance structure or the BWIs depends on their share of the capital structure of these institutions. In addition, there is not an equivalent to the G-7 or G-10 at the level of developing countries and transition economies. Mechanisms of information sharing and collective action for poor, middle-income countries and transition economies are lacking.

During the 1980s and 1990s, domestic policy reform in borrowing countries was encouraged through conditionality by the Bretton Woods institutions in exchange for loans. Recent empirical evidence tends to show that unless borrowing countries are convinced of the need to adopt economic and institutional reforms that in turn have legislative and social acceptance at home, conditionality can be ineffective or even counter-productive.[11] A fresh look at the concepts and practice of conditionality, and the scope for partnership and participation is required.

In addition there is a need for a renewed look at the content of program design that fits the era of globalization. This includes a careful consideration of the degree of fiscal austerity in adjustment programs, avoiding the design and implementation of unnecessary recessionary programs that can be socially destabilizing if they lead to increasing unemployment and poverty for a protracted period of time. Also, the IFIs are now including in program design, issues of transparency and governance practices that are of a complex nature, politically sensitive and not always easy to implement.

GLOBAL AND REGIONAL FINANCIAL INSTITUTIONS: THE MIX

Let's turn now to the mix and balance between global financial institutions (IMF, World Bank) and regional financial institutions (for example, regional and sub-regional development banks) in managing the challenges and financial needs of globalization. Is the current allocation of responsibilities and balance of influence between global and regional institutions adequate? What should a workable division of labor be between global and regional institutions, that avoids overlapping of lending and inter-agency competition? These are complex questions that require further reflection and analysis. In recent years, we have seen the emergence as relevant actors, in terms of volume of financing and policy advice, of regional development banks, (for example IADB, EBRD, ADB, AFDB)[12] and other sub-regional financial institutions, including reserve funds to face (limited) balance of payments needs. Some examples of these sub-regional institutions in Latin America are: CAF (Andean Development Corporation) and FLAR (Latin American Reserve Fund). An adequate balance between global and regional institutions requires an understanding of the comparative advantages and corporate capabilities of each type of institution.

Regional financial institutions often have certain informational advantages about economic, political and cultural realities of member countries, over global institutions which, by design, accommodate a larger set of countries from different continents. As we have seen, knowledge and local ownership of programs are essential to ensure a good development impact of projects and the political feasibility of the policy advice given by lending institutions. In addition, there is a greater degree of country representation for developing countries in the most important decision-making bodies (Board of Governors and Board of Directors) of the regional institutions than in the executive boards of global institutions that tend to be influenced by G-7 countries. In contrast, regional development institutions are less exposed to global best practices and knowledge of a broad range of country experiences across continents than the global institutions like the IMF and the World Bank. In turn, conditionality is often more strict in global institutions, whereas regional development banks tend to develop a pattern of interaction with client-countries closer, perhaps, to partnership.

It is important to reiterate, as mentioned before that, ultimately, regional and global institutions are 'agents' that implement the mandates of the 'principal' (the national governments). However, these mandates are filtered by: a) the bureaucratic structures of the regional and global IFIs, and b) the respective voting power of individual countries; in turn, a direct function of their economic importance in the world (or regional) economy.

These two 'filters' are very important in shaping the actual operation of global versus regional financial institutions and account for some differences in patterns of operational behavior, organizational cultures and representation of member countries between global and regional institutions.

Regarding division of labor between global and regional financial institutions (more relevant for development banks) it is clear that co-financing of operations and more coordination in lending priorities and technical assistance is needed.

NATIONAL POLICIES

A well functioning institutional system on a world scale requires that reforms in global and regional institutions are complemented by reforms in national institutions and policies. In that sense, there must be a basic consistency between the global economic regime promoted by the global institutions and the policy regimes at national level. For example, if global institutions promote free trade, then the trade regime of member nations must be consistent with an open trade system. In turn, global priorities and global rules of the game must ultimately be consistent with the national priorities of developed, developing and transition economies. This exercise in harmonization of priorities and policies at the different levels is not simple, again the voice and representation of the developing country matters here.

Turning to the content of national policies in the era of globalization, it is often argued that globalization, besides its potential for enhancing global growth, tends to reduce the influence of domestic economic and social policies on development outcomes. Thus, an important question is to what extent it is possible to design national policy packages that regain a greater degree of national autonomy in pursuing policy objectives of full employment, stable growth and a more equitable income distribution. A focus on vulnerability–mitigation policies and social equity is appropriate. At the level of macroeconomic policy, the issue is how to define exchange rate, fiscal policies and capital account regimes (for example, including a discussion of taxes on short-term capital flows) that reduce the vulnerability of the national economy to external shocks and global business-cycles. In the field of macroeconomic management, there is a need to explore the room for counter-cyclical fiscal policy. Regarding the exchange rate regime, flexible exchange rates, dollarization, currency boards and monetary unions are being considered now as better alternatives than fixed exchange rates and exchange rates bands. However, it is a useful reminder that exchange rate regimes need to be discussed along with other policy fundamentals.

Social policy in the era of globalization is a very important topic *per se*.[13]

The experience of the 1990s shows that excessive volatility needs to be counteracted by appropriate social institutions that offer social insurance and economic security to people. Another lesson that can be extracted from the 1990s is that targeting in the delivery of social services tends to leave out the middle class. A fresh look at issues of universality versus targeting in the access to social services is needed. In addition, the device of adequate institutions of conflict management is very important in societies afflicted with significant inequality of income and wealth because of regional fragmentation or ethnic diversity.

CONCLUDING REMARKS

Globalization, the main economic trend of the early twenty-first century, offers a significant potential for expanded trade, international investment and technological advance from which developing countries can benefit. However, so far these benefits of globalization and the gains of increased global integration are unevenly distributed across and within nations. In addition, global interdependence has come along with significant macroeconomic volatility, and several serious financial crises have developed in the second half of the 1990s. We are living in a world of more possibilities, but also of increased risks.

These features of globalization require an adequate institutional response that ensures stability, steady prosperity and a more equitable distribution of the rewards of globalization. The existing global institutional matrix was formed in the mid 1940s, around the UN system and the Bretton Woods institutions under a different balance of power across nations, and in a world of fixed exchange rates and very limited private capital mobility. Later, after the 1960s, regional financial institutions emerged on account of greater autonomy of different regions and the expanded financial needs of the development process. This chapter has reviewed different proposals of reform of the international financial institutions and roles of the IMF and World Bank, highlighting implications for developing countries regarding policy conditionality, the counter-cyclical role of lending by multilaterals, the concentration of financing to middle-income versus low-income developing countries, access to liquidity at times of crisis and the voice and representation mechanisms of developing nations in the decision-making process of these institutions.

The chapter also stresses the need to reassess the allocation of responsibilities, coordination mechanisms and overlapping between Bretton Woods institutions and of regional financial institutions. The design of reforms of the IFIs must incorporate important considerations of corporate capabilities of each type of institution. Institutional cultures differ between global and regional institutions, as does the nature of knowledge (global vs. regional) generated and disseminated by each type of institution. Furthermore, differences arise in the patterns of interaction with client-countries and in the representation-mechanisms in both global and regional IFIs. Finally, the chapter also calls attention to the need for global, regional and national policy harmonization, structured around growth-oriented policies that reduce volatility and promote social equity.

NOTES

1. See Solimano (2001a), O'Rourke and Williamson (2000).
2. See Solimano (2001b).
3. See Bordo *et al.* (2001).
4. For an interesting discussion of the effects of the international monetary system on the main political events of the twentieth century, see Mundell (2000).
5. This is also valid for large economies; in fact, China started to grow at a faster pace after 1977–78, when it stimulated export-oriented growth and foreign direct investment.
6. See Rodrik (1997), Sachs (1999) and Solimano *et al.* (2000).
7. See Pyndick and Solimano (1993).
8. See Eatwell and Taylor (2000) on this topic.
9. See K. McRobbie, K. Polanyi-Levitt (2000) for a re-examination of Polanyi's view in light of contemporary globalization.
10. See Micklethwait and Wooldridge (2000).
11. See Collier (2000).
12. Inter American Development Bank (IADB), European Bank for Reconstruction and Development (EBRD), Asian Development Bank (ADB), African Development Bank (AFDB).
13. See Solimano (1998, 1999a) and Solimano *et al.* (2000) for a discussion of these issues.

REFERENCES

Bacha, E. (1978), 'An interpretation of unequal exchange from Prebisch–Singer to Emmanuel', *Journal of Development Economic*, **5**, 319–330, North Holland.

Bagehot, W. (1873), *Lombard Street: A Description of the Money Market*, London: William Dowes and Sons.

Bhagwati, J. (2000), 'Globalization in your face', *Foreign Affairs*, July/August, pp. 134–9.

Bordo, M., B. Eichengreen, D. Klingebiel and M.S. Martinez-Peria (2001), 'Financial crises. Lessons from the last 120 years', *Economic Policy*, April.

Collier, P. (2000), 'Consensus-building, knowledge and conditionality', Paper presented at the Annual Bank Conference on Development Economics, The World Bank.

Eatwell, J. (2000), 'The challenges facing international financial regulation', mimeo. Queens College, Cambridge, UK.

Eatwell, J. and L. Taylor (2000), *Global Finance at Risk: The Case for International Regulation*, New York: The New Press.

Emmanuel, A. (1972), *Unequal Exchange: A Study of Imperialism*, New York: Monthly Review.
Fischer, S. (1999), 'On the need for an international lender of last resort', *The Journal of Economic Perspectives*, **13**(14), Fall, pp. 85–94.
Hobsbawm, E. (1999), *On the Edge of a New Century*, New York: Free Press.
Kaul, I., I. Grunberg and M. Stern (1999), *Global Public Goods. International Cooperation in the 21st century*, New York: Oxford University Press.
McRobbie, K. and K. Polanyi-Levitt (eds) (2000), *Karl Polanyi in Vienna. The Contemporary Significance of The Great Transformation*, Montreal, New York, London: Black Rose Books.
Micklethwait, J. and A. Wooldridge (2000), *A Future Perfect. The Challenge and Hidden Promise of Globalization*, Crown Business.
Mundell, R. (2000), 'A reconsideration of the twentieth century', *The American Economic Review*, June.
O'Rourke, D. and J.G. Williamson (2000), *Globalization and History. The Evolution of a Nineteenth-century Atlantic Economy*, Cambridge, MA: MIT Press.
Polanyi, K. (1994), *The Great Transformation. The Political and Economic Origins of Our Time*, Boston: Beacon Press.
Prebisch, R. (1950), *Economic Development of Latin America and its Principal Problems*, New York: United Nations.
Pyndick, R and A. Solimano (1993), 'Irreversibility and aggregate investment', Macroeconomics Annual, National Bureau of Economic Research, Cambridge, MA.
Rodrik, D. (1997), *Has Globalization Gone too Far?*, Washington, DC: Institute of International Economics.
Sachs, J. (1999), 'Making Globalization Work?', *The Economist*.
Sen, A. (1999), *Development as Freedom*, New York: Alfred A. Knop.
Singer, H. (1950), 'The distribution of gains between investing and developing countries', *American Economic Review*, **40**, 473–85.
Solimano, A. (ed.) (1998), *Social Inequality. Values, Growth and the State*, Ann Arbor, MI: The University of Michigan Press.
Solimano, A. (1999a) 'Globalization and national development at the end of the 20th century', *World Bank Policy Research Working Paper*, 2137.
Solimano, A. (1999b) 'Beyond unequal development: an overview', *World Bank Policy Research Working Paper*, 2091.
Solimano, A. (2001a), 'International migration and the global economic order: an overview', *World Bank Policy Research Working Paper*.
Solimano, A. (2001b) 'The evolution of world income inequality: assessing the impact of globalization', *mimeo*, ECLAC, UN.
Solimano, A., E. Aninat and N. Birdsall (eds) (2000), *Distributive Justice and Economic Development*, Ann Arbor, MI: The University of Michigan Press.
Soros, G. (1998), *The Crisis of Global Capitalism. Open Society Endangered*, New York: Public Affairs.
Taylor, L. (1983), *Structuralist Macroeconomics*, New York: Basic Books.

Lance Taylor: list of publications

1968

1. 'Development Patterns: Among Countries and Over Time' (with Hollis B. Chenery), *Review of Economics and Statistics*, November, **50**: 391–416.

1969

2. 'Development Patterns: A Simulation Study', *Quarterly Journal of Economics*, May, **83**: 220–41.
3. 'Intertemporal and Intercountry Patterns of Industrial Growth' (with Hollis B. Chenery), in *Sectoral Aspects of Projections of the World Economy: First Interregional Seminar on Long-term Economic Projections, Elsinore, Denmark, 14–27 August, 1966. Vol. II, Discussion Papers*, New York: United Nations.
4. 'A Dynamic Nonlinear Planning Model for Korea' (with David Kendrick), in Irma Adelman (ed.), *Practical Approaches to Development Planning: Korea's Second Five-Year Plan*, Baltimore: Johns Hopkins Press.

1970

5. 'The Existence of Optimal Distributed Lags', *Review of Economic Studies*, January, **37**: 95–106.
6. 'Numerical Solution of Non-Linear Planning Models' (with David Kendrick), *Econometrica*, May, **38**: 453–67.
7. *Notes and Problems in Microeconomic Theory* (with Samuel Bowles, David Kendrick, and Mark Roberts), Chicago: Markham Publishing Co.

1971

8. 'On Investment Timing in Two-Gap Models', in Hollis Chenery (ed.), *Studies in Development Planning*, Cambridge, MA: Harvard University Press.
9. 'Numerical Methods and Nonlinear Optimizing Models for Economic Planning' (with David Kendrick), in Hollis Chenery (ed.), *Studies in Development Planning*, Cambridge, MA: Harvard University Press.
10. 'Foreign Exchange Shadow Prices: A Critical Evaluation of Current Theories' (with Edmar Bacha), *Quarterly Journal of Economics*, May, **85**: 197–224. Reprinted in A. Harberger *et al.* (eds), *Benefit Cost Analysis: 1971*, Chicago: Aldine-Atherton, 1972, in R.S. Eckaus and P.N. Rosenstein-Rodan (eds), *Analysis of Development Problems: Studies of the Chilean Economy*, Amsterdam: North-Holland, 1973.
11. 'Dynamic Input–Output Planning with Optimal End Conditions: The Case of Chile' (with Peter Bentley Clark), *Economics of Planning*, **11**(1–2): 10–30.

1973

12. 'Welfare Gains from Optimization in Dynamic Planning Models' (with Hans G. Bergendorff and Peter Bentley Clark), *Economics of Planning*, **13**(1–2): 75–90.
13. 'Two Generalizations of Discounting', in R.S. Eckaus and P.N. Rosenstein-Rodan (eds), *Analysis of Development Problems: Studies of the Chilean Economy*, Amsterdam: North-Holland.
14. 'Growth and Trade Distortions in Chile, and their Implications in Calculating the Shadow Price of Foreign Exchange' (with Edmar Bacha), in R.S. Eckaus and P.M. Rosenstein-Rodan (eds), *Analysis of Development Problems: Studies of the Chilean Economy*, Amsterdam, North-Holland.
15. 'Investment Project Analysis in a Model of Optimal Growth: The Case of Chile', presented at the IEEE Conference on Automatic Control, Miami Beach, December 1971, in R.S. Eckaus and P.N. Rosenstein-Rodan (ed.), *Analysis of Development Problems: Studies of the Chilean Economy*, Amsterdam: North-Holland.
16. 'Neoclassical Projections of Foreign Exchange Needs in Chile', in R.S. Eckaus and P.N. Rosenstein-Rodan (eds), *Analysis of Development Problems: Studies of the Chilean Economy*, Amsterdam: North-Holland.
17. 'The Economics of Malnourished Children: An Example of Dis-

investment in Human Capital' (with Marcelo Selowsky), *Economic Development and Cultural Change*, October, **22**: 17–30.

1974

18. 'Practical General Equilibrium Estimation of Resource Pulls under Trade Liberalization' (with Stephen L. Black), *Journal of International Economics*, February, **4**: 37–58.
19. 'Short-Term Policy in Open Semi-Industrialized Economics: The Narrow Limits of the Possible', *Journal of Development Economics*, June, **1**: 85–104.

1975

20. 'Theoretical Foundations and Technical Implications', in Charles R. Blitzer, Peter B. Clark, and Lance Taylor (eds), *Economy-Wide Models and Development Planning*, London: Oxford University Press.
21. 'The Misconstrued Crisis: Lester Brown and World Food', *World Development*, **3**: 827–37.

1976

22. 'The Unequalizing Spiral: A First Growth Model for Belindia' (with Edmar L. Bacha), *Quarterly Journal of Economics*, **90**: 197–218.
23. 'Cereal Stocks, Food Aid and Food Security for the Poor' (with Alexander H. Sarris), *World Development*, **4**: 967–76. Reprinted in J.N. Bhagwati (ed.), *The New International Order: The North–South Debate*, Cambridge, MA: MIT Press, 1977.

1977

24. 'Research Directions in Income Distribution and the Economics of Food', *Food Research Institute Studies*, **16**(2): 29–45.
25. 'Sraffa and Classical Economics: Fundamental Equilibrium Relationships' (with Edmar Bacha and Dionisio Carneiro), *Metroeconomica*, **29**: 39–53.

1978

26. 'Buffer Stock Analysis for Agricultural Products: Theoretical Murk or Empirical Resolution' (with Alexander H. Sarris), in F.G. Adams and S.A. Klein, *Stabilizing World Commodity Markets*, Lexington, MA: D.C. Heath.
27. 'Contractionary Effects of Devaluation' (with Paul Krugman), *Journal of International Economics*, **8**: 445–56.
28. 'Brazilian Income Distribution in the 1960s: "Facts", Model Results and the Controversy' (with Edmar L. Bacha), *Journal of Development Studies*, **14**: 271–97.
29. 'The Political Economy of Egypt: An Opening to What?', *Middle East Review*, **10**(4): 10–15.
30. 'Food Security for the World's Poor' (with Alexander Sarris and Phillip C. Abbott), *Technology Review*, **80**(4): 44–54.

1979

31. 'Identity-Based Planning of Prices and Quantities: Cambridge Neoclassical Models for Brazil' (with Eliana A. Cardoso), *Journal of Policy Modelling*, **1**: 83–111.
32. 'Grain Reserves, Emergency Relief and Food Aid' (with Alexander H. Sarris and Philip C. Abbott), in William R. Cline (ed.), *Policy Alternatives for a New International Economic Order: An Economic Analysis*, New York: Praeger Publishers for the Overseas Development Council.
33. 'Vanishing Income Redistributions: Keynesian Clues about Model Surprises in the Short Run' (with Frank J. Lysy), *Journal of Development Economics*, **6**: 11–29.
34. *Macro Models for Developing Countries*, New York: McGraw Hill.
35. 'Analysis and Projections of Macroeconomic Conditions in Portugal' (with Rudiger Dornbusch and Richard S. Eckaus), in L.S. Graham and H.M. Makler (eds), *Contemporary Portugal: The Revolution and its Antecedents*, Austin and London: University of Texas Press.

1980

36. 'Macro Food Policy Planning: A General Equilibrium Model for Pakistan' (with F. Desmond McCarthy), *Review of Economics and Statistics*, **62**: 107–21.

37. 'Agriculture and the Rest of the Economy: Macro Connections and Policy Restraints' (with Graciela Chichilnisky), *American Journal of Agricultural Economics*, **62**: 303–9.
38. *Models of Growth and Distribution for Brazil* (with Edmar L. Bacha, Eliana A. Cardoso, and Frank J. Lysy), New York and London: Oxford University Press.
39. 'Food' (with Nevin S. Scrimshaw), *Scientific American*, **243**(3): 78–88.
40. 'Basic Needs Macroeconomics: Is it Manageable in the Case of Egypt?' (with Youssef Boutros-Ghali), *Journal of Policy Modelling*, **2**: 409–36.
41. *Egypt: Economic Management in a Period of Transition* (with Khalid Ikram and others), Baltimore and London: Johns Hopkins Press for the World Bank.

1981

42. 'IS/LM in the Tropics: Diagramatics of the New Structuralist Macro Critique', in William R. Cline and Sidney Weintraub (eds), *Economic Stabilization in Developing Countries*, Washington, DC: Brookings Institution.
43. 'South–North Trade and Southern Growth: Bleak Prospects from a Structuralist Point of View', *Journal of International Economics*, **11**: 589–602.

1982

44. 'Back to Basics: Theory for the Rhetoric in the North–South Round', *World Development:* **10**: 327–35.
45. 'Food Subsidies in Egypt', in Nevin Scrimshaw and Mitchel B. Wallerstein (eds), *Nutrition Policy Implementation*, New York and London: Plenum.
46. 'Food Price Inflation, Terms of Trade, and Growth', in Mark Gersovitz, Carlos F. Diaz-Alejandro, Gustav Ranis, and Mark R. Rosenzweig (eds), *The Theory and Experience of Economic Development: Essays in Honor of Sir W. Arthur Lewis*, London: George Allen and Unwin.

1983

47. *Structuralist Macroeconomics: Applicable Models for the Third World*, New York: Basic Books.

48. 'Macroeconomic Policy in the Third World: A Structuralist Perspective', in Kenneth C. Nobe and Rajan K. Sampath (eds), *Issues in Third World Development*, Boulder, CO: Westview Press.

1984

49. 'Defense Spending, Economic Structure, and Growth' (with Riccardo Faini and Patricia Annez), *Economic Development and Cultural Change*, **32**: 487–98.
50. 'Mexico's Adjustment in the 1980s: Look Back Before Leaping Ahead', in Richard E. Feinberg and Valeriana Kallab (eds), *Adjustment Crisis in the Third World*, Washington, DC: Overseas Development Council.
51. 'Social Choice Theory and the World in Which We Live' (reviewing Amartya Sen, *Choice, Welfare and Measurement*), *Cambridge Journal of Economics*, **8**: 189–96.
52. 'Macroeconomic Adjustment in a Computable General Equilibrium Model for India' (with Hiren Sarkar and Jørn Rattsø), in Moshe Syrquin, Lance Taylor, and Larry Westphal (eds), *Economic Structure and Performance: Essays in Honor of Hollis B. Chenery*, New York: Academic Press.

1985

53. 'A Minsky Crisis' (with Stephen A. O'Connell), *Quarterly Journal of Economics*, **100**: 871–85.
54. 'A Stagnationist Model of Economic Growth', *Cambridge Journal of Economics*, **9**: 383–403.
55. 'The Theory and Practice of Developing Country Debt: An Informal Guide for the Perplexed', *Journal of Development Planning*, **16**: 195–227.
56. 'The Crisis and Thereafter: Macroeconomic Policy Problems in Mexico', in Peggy B. Musgrave (ed.), *Mexico and the United States: Studies in Economic Integration*, Boulder, CO: Westview Press.

1986

57. 'Debt Crisis: North–South, North–North, and in Between', in Michael P. Claudon (ed.), *World Debt Crisis: International Lending on Trial*, Cambridge, MA: Ballinger Publishing Company.

58. 'Developing Country Finance and Debt' (with Jonathan Eaton), *Journal of Development Economics*, **22**: 209–65.
59. 'Trade and Growth' (First W. Arthur Lewis Lecture, National Economic Association), *Review of Black Political Economy*, **14**(4): 17–36.
60. 'A Macro Model of an Oil Exporter: Nigeria' (with Kadir T. Yurukogulu and Shahid A. Chaudhry), in J. Peter Neary and Sweder van Wijnbergen (eds), *Natural Resources and the Macroeconomy*, Oxford: Basil Blackwell.
61. 'Terms of Trade and Class Conflict in a Computable General Equilibrium Model for Mexico' (with Bill Gibson and Nora Lustig), *Journal of Development Studies*, **23**: 40–59.

1987

62. 'SAM's Impact on Income Distribution' (with Bill Gibson and Nora Lustig), in James E. Austin and Gustavo Esteva (eds), *Food Policy in Mexico*, Ithaca, NY: Cornell University Press.
63. 'IMF Conditionality: Incomplete Theory, Policy Malpractice', in Robert J. Myers (ed.), *The Political Morality of the International Monetary Fund*, New Brunswick, NJ: Transaction Books for the Carnegie Council on Ethics and International Affairs.
64. 'Trade Patterns in Developing Countries: 1964–1982' (with F. Desmond McCarthy and Cyrus Talati), *Journal of Development Economics*, **27**: 5–39.
65. 'El Plan Austral (y Otros Choques Heterodoxos): Fase II', *El Trimestre Economico (Numero Especial)*, **54**: 155–75.
66. 'Macro Policy in the Tropics: How Sensible People Stand', *World Development*, **15**: 1407–35.

1988

67. 'La Apertura Economica. Problemas hasta Fines del Siglo', *El Trimestre Economico*, **55**(1): 67–174.
68. 'Macro Constraints on India's Economic Growth' (V.K. Ramaswami Lecture), *Indian Economic Review*, **23**: 145–65.
69. *Varieties of Stabilization Experience*, Oxford: Clarendon Press.
70. 'Macro Effects of Myriad Shocks: Developing Countries in the World Economy', in David Bell and Michael Reich (eds), *Health, Nutrition, and Economic Crises*, Dover, MA: Auburn House.

71. 'Planner's Progress' (a review of *Development Planning: The Indian Experience*, by Sukhamoy Chakravarty), *Economic and Political Weekly*, **23**(42).
72. 'Long-Run Income Distribution and Growth' (with Persio Arida), in Hollis Chenery and T.N. Srinivasan (eds), *Handbook of Development Economics, Volume I*, Amsterdam: North-Holland.

1989

73. 'Demand Composition, Income Distribution, and Growth', in George R. Feiwel (ed.), *Joan Robinson and Modern Economic Theory*, London: Macmillan.
74. *Stabilization and Growth in Developing Countries: A Structuralist Approach*, New York: Harwood Academic Publishers.
75. 'Resource Transfers from Agriculture' (with M. Agnes R. Quisumbing), in Sukhamoy Chakravarty (ed.), *The Balance between Industry and Agriculture in Economic Development III: Manpower and Transfers (Proceedings of the Eighth World Conference of the International Economic Association)*, London: Macmillan.
76. 'Short-Run Macroeconomics' (with Persio Arida), in Hollis Chenery and T.N. Srinivasan (eds), *Handbook of Development Economics, Volume II*, Amsterdam: North-Holland.
77. *Nicaragua: The Transition from Economic Chaos toward Sustainable Growth* (with José Antonio Ocampo and others), Stockholm: Swedish International Development Authority.

1990

78. 'The State and Industrial Strategy' (with Helen Shapiro), *World Development*, **18**: 861–78.
79. 'Structuralist CGE Models', in Lance Taylor (ed.), *Socially Relevant Policy Analysis: Structuralist Computable General Equilibrium Models for the Developing World*, Cambridge, MA: The MIT Press.
80. 'Mexican Food Consumption Policies in a Structuralist CGE Model' (with Nora Lustig), in Lance Taylor (ed.), *Socially Relevant Policy Analysis: Structuralist Computable General Equilibrium Models for the Developing World*, Cambridge, MA: The MIT Press.
81. 'Devaluation, Capital Flows, and Crowding-Out: A CGE Model with Portfolio Choice for Thailand' (with Jeffrey A. Rosensweig), in Lance Taylor (ed.), *Socially Relevant Policy Analysis: Structuralist*

Computable General Equilibrium Models for the Developing World, Cambridge, MA: The MIT Press.

82. 'Real and Money Wages, Output and Inflation in the Semi-Industrialized World', *Economica*, **57**: 329–53.
83. 'Turkish Experience: Summary and Comparative Notes', in Tosun Aricanli and Dani Rodrik (eds), *The Political Economy of Turkey: Debt, Adjustment, and Sustainability*, London: Macmillan.
84. 'Fiscal Issues in Macroeconomic Stabilization: A Structuralist Perspective', *Ricerche Economiche*, **44**: 197–213.

1991

85. *Income Distribution, Inflation, and Growth: Lectures on Structuralist Macroeconomic Theory*, Cambridge, MA: MIT Press.
86. 'Foreign Resource Flows and Developing Country Growth', Helsinki: World Institute for Development Economics Research.
87. 'Economic Openness: Problems to Century's End', in Tariq Banuri (ed.), *Economic Liberalization: No Panacea*, Oxford: Clarendon Press.
88. 'Stabilization and Adjustment', in *Stabilization and Adjustment, Perspectives on Adjustment and Economic Reform in Africa*, United Nations Development Programme/Structural Adjustment Advisory Teams for Africa, New York: United Nations Publications.
89. 'Foreign Resources and Developing Country Growth: A Three-Gap Analysis', in Anthony B. Atkinson and Renato Brunetta (eds), *Economics for the New Europe*, International Economic Association Conference Volume No. 104, London: Macmillan.

1992

90. 'Lance Taylor (born 1940)', in P. Arestis and M. Sawyer (eds), *A Biographical Dictionary of Dissenting Economists*, Hants, UK: Edward Elgar Publishing Ltd.
91. 'Structuralist and Competing Approaches to Development Economics', in A.K. Dutt and K. Jameson (eds), *New Directions in Development Economics*, Hants, UK: Edward Elgar Publishing Ltd.
92. 'Growth and Adjustment in Developing Countries: A Gap Model Approach', in Kumaraswamy Velupillai (ed.), *Nonlinearities, Disequilibria, and Simulation: Essays in Honour of Björn Thalberg*, London: Macmillan.

93. 'Polonius Lectures Again: The World Development Report, the Washington Consensus, and How Neoliberal Sermons Won't Solve the Economic Problems of the Developing World', *Bangladesh Development Studies*, **20**: 23–53.
94. 'Agriculture-Led Growth', *The Indian Economic Review*, **27** (special number in memory of Sukhamoy Chakravarty): 101–12.
95. 'The *World Development Report 1991*: A Critical Assessment' (with José María Fanelli and Roberto Frenkel), in United Nations Conference on Trade and Development, *International Monetary and Financial Issues for the 1990s (Vol. I)*, New York: United Nations.

1993

96. 'The Rocky Road to Reform: Trade, Industrial, Financial, and Agricultural Strategies', *World Development*, **21**: 577–90.
97. 'Income Distribution, Trade, and Growth', in Robert E. Blecker (ed.), *Trade Policy and Global Growth*, Armonk, NY: M.E. Sharpe for the Economic Policy Institute.
98. 'The Rocky Road to Reform', in Lance Taylor (ed.), *The Rocky Road to Reform: Adjustment, Income Distribution, and Growth in the Developing World*, Cambridge, MA: MIT Press.
99. 'A Three-Gap Analysis of Foreign Resource Flows and Developing Country Growth', in Lance Taylor (ed.), *The Rocky Road to Reform: Adjustment, Income Distribution, and Growth in the Developing World*, Cambridge, MA: MIT Press.
100. 'Stabilization, Adjustment, and Reform', in Lance Taylor (ed.), *The Rocky Road to Reform: Adjustment, Income Distribution, and Growth in the Developing World*, Cambridge, MA: MIT Press.
101. 'The World Bank and the Environment: *The World Development Report 1992*', *World Development*, **21**: 869–81.

1994

102. 'Financial Fragility: Is an Etiology at Hand?', in Gary Dymski and Robert Pollin (eds), *New Perspectives in Monetary Economics: Explorations in the Tradition of Hyman P. Minsky*, Ann Arbor, MI: University of Michigan Press.
103. 'The Postsocialist Transition from a Development Economics Point of View', in Andrés Solimano, Osvaldo Sunkel, and Mario Blejer

(eds), *Rebuilding Capitalism: Alternative Paths after Socialism and Dirigisme*, Ann Arbor, MI: University of Michigan Press.

104. 'Roundtable Presentation', in Andrés Solimano, Osvaldo Sunkel, and Mario Blejer (eds), *Rebuilding Capitalism: Alternative Paths after Socialism and Dirigisme*, Ann Arbor, MI: University of Michigan Press.
105. 'Public Enterprises, Private Enterprises, and the State', in Amitava Dutt, Kwan Kim, and Ajit Singh (eds), *The State, Markets, and Development: Beyond the Neoclassical Dichotomy*, Brookfield, VT: Edward Elgar.
106. 'The Market Met its Match: Lessons for the Future from the Transition's Initial Years', *Journal of Comparative Economics*, **19**: 64–87.
107. *The Market Meets its Match: Restructuring the Economies of Eastern Europe* (with Alice Amsden and Jacek Kochanowicz), Cambridge, MA: Harvard University Press.
108. 'Is the Market Friendly Approach Friendly to Development? A Critical Assessment' (with José María Fanelli and Roberto Frenkel), in Graham Bird and Ann Helwege (eds), *Latin America's Economic Future*, London: Academic Press.
109. 'Economic Reform: India and Elsewhere', *Economic and Political Weekly*, **29**: 2209–11.
110. 'Hirschman's Strategy at Thirty-Five', in Lloyd Rodwin and Donald Schon (eds), *Rethinking the Development Experience*, Washington, DC: The Brookings Institution.
111. 'Gap Models', *Journal of Development Economics*, **45**: 17–34.

1995

112. 'Pasinetti's Processes' (reviewing Luigi L. Pasinetti, *Structural Economic Dynamics: A Theory of the Economic Consequences of Human Learning*, and Mauro Baranzini and G.C. Harcourt (eds), *The Dynamics of the Wealth of Nations: Growth, Distribution and Structural Change*), *Cambridge Journal of Economics*, **19**: 697–713.
113. 'Comment on Little, *Economic Models in Development Economics*', in Daniel Little (ed.), *On the Reliability of Economic Models: Essays in the Philosophy of Economics*, Boston: Kluwer Academic Publishers.
114. 'Environmental and Gender Feedbacks in Macroeconomics', *World Development*, **23**: 1953–61.

1996

115. 'Sustainable Development: An Introduction', *World Development*, **24**: 215–25.
116. 'Stimulating Global Employment Growth', in John Eatwell (ed.), *Global Unemployment: Loss of Jobs in the '90s*, Armonk, NY: M.E. Sharpe.
117. 'Growth, the State, and Development Theory', in Andrés Solimano (ed.), *Road-Maps to Prosperity: Essays on Growth and Development*, Ann Arbor, MI: University of Michigan Press.
118. 'Environmental Feedbacks in Macroeconomics', in C.W.M. Naastepad and Servaas Storm (eds), *The State and the Econonomic Process*, Cheltenham, UK: Edward Elgar.
119. 'Finis to Laissez-Faire', in Abu Abdullah and Azizur Rahman Khan (eds), *State, Market, and Development: Essays in Honor of Rehman Sobhan*, Dhaka: University Press.

1997

120. 'The Links between Economic Growth, Poverty Reduction, and Social Development: Theory and Policy' (with Santosh Mehrotra and Enrique Delamonica), in Santosh Mehrotra and Richard Jolly (eds), *Development with a Human Face*, New York: Oxford University Press.
121. 'Editorial: The Revival of the Liberal Creed – The IMF and the World Bank in a Globalized Economy', *World Development*, **26**: 145–52.

1998

122. Trade Liberalization in Developing Economies: Modest Benefits but Problems with Productivity Growth, Macro Prices, and Income Distribution' (with José Antonio Ocampo), *Economic Journal*, **108**: 1523–46. Reprinted in Huw David Dixon (ed.), *Controversies in Macroeconomics*, Oxford: Blackwell Publishers, 2000.
123. 'The Revival of the Liberal Creed: The IMF, the World Bank, and Inequality in a Globalized Economy' (with Ute Pieper), in Dean Baker, Gerald Epstein, and Robert Pollin (eds), *Globalization and Progressive Economic Policy: What are the Real Constraints and Options?*, New York: Cambridge University Press.
124. 'Politica Macroeconomica, Pobreza, y Equidad en America Latina y el

Caribe' (with Enrique Ganuza), in Enrique Ganuza, Samuel Morley, and Lance Taylor (eds), *Politicas Macroeconomicas y Pobreza en America Latina y el Caribe*, Mexico DF: Fondo de Cultura Economica.

125. 'Capital Market Crises: Liberalization, Fixed Exchange Rates, and Market-Driven Destabilization', *Cambridge Journal of Economics*, **22**: 663–76.
126. 'A Cure for the Woes' (with John Eatwell), *The World Today*, **54**: 275–6.
127. 'Growth and Development Theories', in Fabrizio Coricelli, Massimo diMatteo, and Frank Hahn (eds), *New Theories in Growth and Development*, New York: St. Martin's Press.

1999

128. 'Lax Public Sector, Destabilizing Private Sector: Origins of Capital Market Crises', in United Nations Conference on Trade and Development, *International Monetary and Financial Issues for the 1990s*, vol. 10.
129. 'Introduction', in Lance Taylor (ed.), *After Neoliberalism: What Next for Latin America?*, Ann Arbor, MI: University of Michigan Press.
130. 'Globalization, Liberalization, Distribution, and Growth: Developing and Transition Economies', *Proceedings of the American Philosophical Society*, **143**: 187–93.
131. 'The American Stock-Flow Trap' (with John Eatwell), *Challenge*, **42**(5): 34–49.

2000

132. *Global Finance at Risk: The Case for International Regulation* (with John Eatwell), New York: The New Press.
133. 'Capital Market Crises: Liberalization, Fixed Exchange Rates, and Market-Driven Liberalization', in Jim Stanford, Lance Taylor, and Ellen Houston (eds), *Power, Employment, and Accumulation: Social Structures in Economic Theory and Practice*, Armonk, NY: M.E. Sharpe.
134. 'Introduction: Structural Adjustment, Labour Markets, and Employment – Some Considerations for Sensible People' (with Rolph van der Hoeven), *Journal of Development Studies*, **36**(4): 57–65.
135. 'The Consequences of Capital Liberalization', *Challenge*, **43**(6): 38–57.

2001

136. 'Outcomes of External Liberalization and Policy Implications', in Lance Taylor (ed.), *External Liberalization, Economic Performance, and Social Policy*, New York: Oxford University Press.
137. 'External Liberalization, Economic Performance, and Social Policy' (with Janine Berg), in Lance Taylor (ed.), *External Liberalization, Economic Performance, and Social Policy*, New York: Oxford University Press.
138. 'Argentina: A Poster Child for the Failure of Liberalized Policies?', *Challenge*, **44**(6): 28–44.
139. 'Liberalizacion de la Balanza de Pagos en America Latina: Efectos sobre el Crecimiento, la Distribucion, y la Pobreza', in Enrique Ganuza, Ricardo Paes de Barros, Lance Taylor, and Rob Vos (eds), *Liberalizacion, Desigualdad y Pobreza: America Latina y el Caribe en los 90*, Buenos Aires: Eudeba.

2002

140. 'Introduction' and 'A World Financial Authority' (with John Eatwell), in John Eatwell and Lance Taylor (eds), *International Capital Markets: Systems in Transition*, New York: Oxford University Press.
141. 'Global Macroeconomic Management', in Deepak Nayyar (ed.), *Governing Globalization: Issues and Institutions*, New York: Oxford University Press.

2003

142. 'Exchange Rate *In*determinacy in Portfolio Balance, Mundell–Fleming, and Uncovered Interest Rate Parity Models', *Cambridge Journal of Economics*, forthcoming.
143. *Reconstructing Macroeconomics: Structuralist Proposals and Critiques of the Mainstream*, Cambridge, MA: Harvard University Press, forthcoming.

Index